Remembering the War Dead:

British Commonwealth and International War Graves in Ireland since 1914

Fergus A. D'Arcy

ISBN: 0-7557-7589-9

Baile Átha Cliath
Arna fhoilsiú ag Oifig an tSoláthair
Le ceannach díreach ón
Oifig Dhíolta Foilseachán Rialtais,
Teach Sun Alliance, Sráid Theach Laighean, Baile Átha
Cliath 2,
nó tríd an bpost ó
Foilseacháin Rialtais, An Rannóg Post-Tráchta,
51 Faiche Stiabhna, Baile Átha Cliath 2,
(Teil: 01 - 6476834/35/36/37; Fax 01 - 6476843)
nó trí aon díoltóir leabhar.

―――――――

Dublin
Published by the Stationery Office
to be purchased directly from the
Government Publications Sale Office
Sun Alliance House, Molesworth Street, Dublin 2,
or by mail order from
Government Publications, Postal Trade Section,
51 St. Stephen's Green, Dublin 2,
(tel: 01 - 6476834/35/36/37; fax: 01 - 6476843)
or through any bookseller.

Design and layout: Ciaran Murphy
Typesetting: True Focus Design
Editorial: Elizabeth Mayes
Printed by: Brunswick Press Ltd. Dublin

Price: €22.00

The Office of Public Works
Oifig na nOibreacha Poiblí

To my wife Ann

and children Ann, Caitriona, Caroline and Andrew

*In memory of all who gave their lives
for peace and freedom*

Contents

Abbreviations

AA	Assistant Architect	IWGC	Imperial War Graves Commission
ATS	Auxiliary Territorial Service	NA	National Archives, Kew
CO	Colonial Office		
CSO	Chief Secretary's Office	NAI	National Archives of Ireland
CWGC	Commonwealth War Graves Commission	NLI	National Library of Ireland
CRO	Commonwealth Relations Office	OPW	Office of Public Works
DCC	Dublin Cemeteries Committee	OPWSTSG	Office of Public Works, St. Stephen's Green, Dublin
DEA	Department of External Affairs	RAMC	Royal Army Medical Corps
DFA	Department of Foreign Affairs	RCIC	Royal Canadian Infantry Corps
DO	Dominions Office	RHK	Royal Hospital Kilmainham
DT	Department of An Taoiseach	TCD	Trinity College Dublin
FIN	Department of Finance	UCDA	University College Dublin Archives
GA	Glasnevin Archives		
INWM	Irish National War Memorial	WO	War Office

Acknowledgements

Two years ago the question arose if there might be sufficient archival sources available to recreate the history of how the Office of Public Works came to be responsible for the maintenance of war graves in this country. I could not be certain at the time but surmised that a few months spent surveying the likely archives and sites might yield an answer. Those few months revealed a far greater wealth of documentary material than anticipated, the mining of which has resulted in this publication. In that excavation process many debts were incurred to archivists, librarians, historians and relatives of those who are today commemorated on the headstones of these war graves.

The acknowledgement of these debts should begin with the Office of Public Works itself. Here, Ken Moore, Valerie Ingram, Patricia Doherty, Aiden Murphy, George Moir, Aaron Gracey, the staff of its Library and Registry, together with Desmond McCabe and the OPW's Regional Officers were a never-failing source of help; so too were the editor for this volume, Elizabeth Mayes, and Evelyn Keating. I might add that while the Commissioners of the OPW invited me to undertake this history, they gave me a completely free hand in the process: the results, opinions, and errors, hopefully few, are entirely my own.

Historically, their partners in the work of identification, care and maintenance, have been the Commonwealth War Graves Commission, whose headquarters in Maidenhead and regional office in Leamington contain an extraordinary wealth of material. As an extremely busy organisation which is not a public archive in the normal sense, it was generous to a fault in the access it afforded me to its Irish files. The Director, Mr David Parker, in the best spirit of the Irish Regimental motto, Faugh-a-Ballagh, cleared the way and provided invaluable signposts. I owe a special thanks to him, to his tireless and ever-patient archivist, Maria Choules, and her head office colleagues Peter Holton, Derek Butler, as equally to the Leamington team of David Symons, Alohke Ghosh, Val Sargeson, and their man in the field, Antony Rose. Equally valuable for the diplomatic, or occasionally undiplomatic, aspects of the story is the National Archives at Kew whose staff helped greatly in identifying rich veins of relevant material. Thanks are due also to Eleanor Gawne, archivist at the British Architectural Library, Victoria & Albert Museum, for permission to consult the Lutyens letters, and to the Imperial War Museum, the National Maritime Museum and the National Portrait Gallery for permission to reproduce illustrations from their collections.

For their generous support in regard to the history of German war graves in Ireland I wish to thank Wolfgang Weithoff, Cultural Attaché of the German Embassy, Dublin, Elke von Boeselager of the Auswärtiges Amt, Berlin and Peter Paessler of the Library and Archives of the Volksbund Deutsche Kriegsgräberfürsorge, Kassel.

Back in Dublin, the National Archives of Ireland proved a treasure trove: one's delight in discovering its holdings only augmented by that of its staff in aiding the discoveries. A special thanks to the ever-resourceful Ken Hannigan and his colleagues, Caitriona Crowe, Brian Donnelly, Aideen Ireland, Mary Mackey, Gregory O'Connor, Elizabeth McEvoy and Tom Quinlan, who all went to endless trouble in exhuming files, especially the cemetery ones probably never used since the OPW first deposited them some years ago. Michael Kennedy of the Royal Irish Academy, with his unrivalled knowledge of Irish Foreign Affairs and his expertise in matters coastal, was generosity itself, with material, advice and anecdotes.

A special thanks is also due to the staff of the Dublin City and Dun Laoghaire public library service, in particular those in the local branch library at Stillorgan, all of whom went to great trouble in assisting with various sources, as did Seamus Helferty and the staff of the Archives Department, University College Dublin, James Quinn of the Dictionary of Irish Biography, their colleagues in the James Joyce Library, UCD, those of the Library of Trinity College Dublin, Lar Joye and his colleagues in the National Museum, the Irish Architectural Archive, The Military Archive and the National Library of Ireland. A debt no less is due to the staff of the archives and public library services of Carlow, Clare, Cork, Kildare, Longford, Meath, Westmeath, Wexford, Mayo, Sligo and Donegal: in particular to Dermot Mulligan, Roisín Berry, Kieran Burke, Noel Comber, Mario Corrigan, Theresa O'Kelly, Margaret Carolan, Lorna Farrell and Martin Morris. The many cemetery custodians were also a generous source of help, in particular, OPW 's John McCullen of the Phoenix Park, George McCullough and colleagues in Glasnevin, Rosaline Dunphy of Dun Laoghaire Rathdown Council and her colleagues in Dean's Grange, John Goodbody and colleagues of the Religious Society of Friends, and Jenny Tapping and Mark Waldron at Sutton and Morden Council in London. To all of their institutions, archives and libraries, thanks are expressed for access and permission to quote from their collections.

A large number of individual persons helped practically and with advice: Nicholas Furlong who gave permission to use and actually supplied photographs from the splendid volumes of *Wexford in the Rare Oul' Times;* Bill Roche, Pam Alexander and David O'Morchoe of the Royal British Legion; Vivien Igoe in Dublin for advice and information concerning the Royal Hospital Kilmainham burial grounds; Tadhg Moloney in Limerick for invaluable advice and information; Ernest Armitage of Wesley College; Tony Roche of the Photographic Unit, Department of the Environment; Ciarán Murphy, designer; Conall O'Brien in Wexford and Mide Gerrard in Nenagh; Ann D'Arcy and Seamus Brady in Dublin; Anne Donaldson and Billy Good in County Cork; Gus O'Halloran in Clare; Nancy Murphy in Nenagh and Mrs Teresa Kelly in Crinkill National School, Offaly; Keith Jeffery in Belfast and Richard Doherty; Mrs Phyllis Clarke in Sligo; Susan Easby and her mother, Maureen, in Cleveland, England; Art Cockerill in Canada, and Linda and Carl White at Memorial University, Newfoundland. A word of appreciation to Padraic and Mary O'Reilly of Shannon Images is not out of place: photographers extraordinaires, they travelled far and at times, I suspect, risked life and limb, like myself, in trying to get access to or escape from some of the wilder burial places.

To my wife Ann, for constant encouragement and support, my best thanks; so too, for their frequent enquiries on progress, to our daughters Ann, Caitriona, Caroline, and our son, Andrew; and not forgetting Sophie, Aaron, Amy and Ben who shortened long days and brightened dull ones.

Fergus A D'Arcy
Dublin, November 2006

Foreword by Minister

As Minister of State with special responsibility for the Office of Public Works (OPW), it gives me great pleasure to introduce this unique book which traces the history of all those men and women whose lives were ended prematurely in the two great conflicts of the last century, World Wars I and II. Unlike other historical research that has looked solely at the Irish men and women who died in these conflicts, this book reflects on all those nations involved in both wars and their countrymen and women who were laid to rest on this island. It is the broad scope of this research that makes this book unique in modern Irish historiography.

The issue of those who served in both world wars in the Commonwealth and Allied forces has in recent years received considerable public attention. We have also witnessed an increased willingness on the part of many Irish families to acknowledge a part of their family history that may have remained 'secret' for many years. The graves of the war dead from both WW1 and WWII, totaling in excess of 3,000 in the Republic, had been a subject for many that was rarely spoken about and thankfully this change in national attitude has been marked with the construction of the Peace Park and War Memorial at Messines and last year, 2006, saw the 90th Anniversary

Commemoration of the Battle of the Somme in our own National War Memorial Gardens in Islandbridge, Dublin.

This original work, drawing on hitherto unused archive sources, serves to highlight and document the circumstances in which the Irish Government accepted responsibility for the 3,000 plus graves of serving men, women and boys from over twenty different nations in all continents and shows how the OPW have discharged their duties over the last ninety years. It is also very opportune that the timing of this publication coincides with the ninetieth anniversary of the foundation of the former Imperial, now Commonwealth War Graves Commission.

I wish to thank the author Professor Fergus D'Arcy and the many others who have helped in the production of this volume, and I do hope that you find this not only a great source of information, but also a real pleasure to read and enjoy.

Noel Ahern, T.D.
Minister of State at the
Department of Finance
(with special responsibility
for the Office of Public Works)

Introduction

It is often said and it was for long true that the Irish contribution to the waging of the First and Second World Wars was a story woefully neglected and wilfully forgotten. Two hundred and fifty thousand, perhaps, made that contribution to the First World War with their service; thirty-five thousand, perhaps, with their lives. A further one hundred and twenty thousand from the whole island served in the Second World War, some seven thousand, perhaps, paying the ultimate price.[1] Victims in world conflicts as they were, their very remembrance seemed to fall victim to a collective amnesia.

Today it is no longer the case that the history of their contribution is ignored. In respect of the First World War, in particular, important general studies over the last twenty years have included work by Tom Johnstone (1992), Myles Dungan (1997), and Keith Jeffery (2000).[2] While the Second World War has not been as well-served, there are, nevertheless, significant studies, best exemplified by Richard Doherty (1999) and (2002), Girvin and Roberts (2000) and Robert Fisk (1983).[3]

Likewise, although the impact of the First World War on Ireland itself had long been a neglected field, it has been well-opened up by the work of David Fitzpatrick and his students since the late 1980s. Such work was followed by newer and important local studies, by, among others, Niall MacFhionnghaile (1987), James Durney (1999), Paul Maguire (2002), Donal Hall (2005), and P.J. Clarke & Michael Feeney (2006).[4]

The study of war remembrance in general owes a large debt to Jay Winter (1995). Since then, the understanding of war remembrance in its Irish context has been enhanced by Jane Leonard (1996), Judith Hill (1998), Anne Dolan (2003) and Nuala Johnson (2003).[5]

There is one aspect, however, that has not received attention: the story of the remembering or forgetting of the more than 5,700 soldiers, seamen and air force personnel of the two World Wars, from over twenty nations, who died and were buried, remembered or forgotten, in this country itself. In Ireland, north and south, lie the graves of at least 3,800 dead of the 1914-1918 and of over 1,900 of the war of 1939-45.[6] Men and women, old and young in death, they were Irish and British, Commonwealth and international. They and their last resting places might have been long forgotten and, perhaps, forever lost to sight, had it not been for the efforts of the Commonwealth War Graves Commission and the Office of Public Works in identifying, registering and marking these graves in the Irish Free State and Republic: temporarily at first, with wooden crosses, permanently thereafter with standard headstones or memorial walls of alternative commemoration. It was a task which took a long time to complete: indeed, a long time even to begin. The First World War was already three years old before the Imperial War Graves Commission was founded to commemorate its dead. It was well over a decade after this again before the Office of Public Works in Dublin was brought formally and fully into the humanly delicate, politically sensitive and administratively demanding business of identifying, registering, commemorating and caring for these war graves.

By the time the First World War was over and the Imperial War Graves Commission had commenced its mission, the Office of Public Works already had a long history behind it. Founded in 1831, and therefore marking its 175th anniversary in 2006, its range of responsibilities had grown to a remarkable extent in the course of that time. From government offices to public gardens, housing to harbours, dispensaries and drainage, prisons and

penitentiaries, memorials and ancient monuments, its remit seemed ever to expand. The war graves of the conflict of 1914-1918 became, in time, an additional responsibility it did not seek, as did those resulting from the conflict of 1939-1945. They added another dimension to its many-sided history. That general history of the OPW is shortly to be published. This present study is a separate undertaking.

As for the Imperial, or since 1960, Commonwealth War Graves Commission, it has had three formal histories: the first, *Immortal Heritage*, was written by its founder, Sir Fabian Ware, in 1937; a second, *The Unending Vigil*, by Philip Longworth, was first published in 1967; the third, *Courage Remembered*, by Edwin Gibson and Kingsley Ward, appeared in 1989. Excellent in themselves, they have virtually nothing to say on the history of war graves and war grave administration in the Irish Free State and Republic. Indeed, in Irish historical writing in general, apart from the occasional sentence, here and there, in two or three of the various Irish war histories already mentioned, the matter of war graves in Ireland has never been the subject of any single book.[7] There is, therefore, within the context of Irish history itself, the history of Anglo-Irish relations, and the history of the Commonwealth War Graves Commission in its dealings with Ireland, a considerable gap which this present work hopes to bridge.

This study does not pretend to be, in any sense, a military history; nor is it even a history of the Irish war dead of 1914-1918 and 1939-1945; rather, it aims to be a history of the World Wars' dead in the Ireland of the Free State and Republic. Essentially, it is a study with three strands. Firstly, it is a diplomatic history of the British and Irish Governments' relations on the issue of what was to be done with the graves of the World War dead. Secondly, it is an administrative history of how the Commonwealth War Graves Commission and the Office of Public Works managed their related and respective responsibilities for the graves of these dead. Thirdly, and finally, it is a history of more than three thousand individuals who came to die or be buried in this jurisdiction, forgotten or remembered, as a result of these wars. These people were Irish and British; German, Austrian and Italian; Belgian, Norwegian and Dutch; Japanese, Chinese and Russian; Australian, Canadian, American and New Zealand, and from other nations besides: hence the title, *Remembering the War Dead: British Commonwealth and International War Graves in Ireland since 1914.*

They lie here today, men and women, old and young in death, in every county, commemorated in large urban or military cemeteries, in secluded country churchyards and isolated coastal burial grounds – their headstones silent witnesses to their own tragedies and sacrifice.

One hopes that this history, whether as act of piety to the past or as record for the future, may not be without interest or some value: this, for its own sake, but also for whatever fresh light it may shed, in particular, on the relations between Ireland and Great Britain. In this study, that light is reflected in, or more truly, perhaps, refracted through the prisms of the Commonwealth War Graves Commission, the Office of Public Works, the Dominions and Commonwealth Relations Office and the Department of External, now Foreign, Affairs. Refracted though that light may be, one also hopes that it may illuminate a particular past which, for all its troubles, has not been without some honour on all sides.

At the Going Down of the Sun
And in the Morning
We Will Remember Them

Fredrick Daniel Parslow, V.C., Master,
H.M.T. "Anglo-Californian"
4 July 1915

Cobh Old Church Cemetery
Co. Cork

Chapter 1

Wages Of War: Ireland, 1914-21

At 8.30 am on the morning of 4 July 1915 the *S.S. Anglo-Californian* was ninety miles south west of Cobh, en route from Montreal to Avonmouth, when an alert look-out spotted a submarine breaking surface a mile distant. The ship's master, fifty-nine year old Frederick Parslow, ordered evasive action and all speed. The unarmed vessel sent out SOS messages which were picked up by two destroyers, *Mentor* and *Miranda*, and the anti-submarine decoy ship, *Princess Ena*. The German submarine U-39, under Kapitänleutnant Walther Forstmann, closed on the unarmed vessel and began firing with deck-gun. For an hour and a half, as huge damage was inflicted, Parslow kept up the zig-zag attempt to evade, but his bridge was blown apart, and two of his four boats were destroyed. He himself was killed, while his son, who was second mate, eventually brought the vessel safely into Cobh, with captain and eight crew dead, seven wounded and eight missing. On 24 May 1919 Parslow senior was posthumously awarded the Victoria Cross, the first Merchant Navy man ever to receive one. His son, Frederick, who was awarded the DSC for his role in this encounter, was lost in March 1938 when the *Anglo-Australian*, of which he was master, vanished without trace beyond the Azores.[1]

Parslow and his dead crewmen were buried in Cobh Old Church Cemetery, County Cork, their graves eventually marked by standard Commonwealth War Grave Commission headstones. Parslow's is therefore the first such mariner's headstone in this state to carry the initials VC. Although Parslow's heroism and the posthumous award of the Victoria Cross for the first time ever to a Merchant Navy man are of intrinsic interest, there are other aspects of the story which are of relevance to the specific history of Commonwealth and international war graves in Ireland: that relevance is a result of the *Anglo-Californian's* cargo and mission. It was, in fact, carrying from Canada a cargo of over 900 horses, destined for use on the Western Front. A strange cargo, it might seem, until it is considered that in the course of the First World War, Canada shipped some 30,000 and the United States some 600,000 horses to the European battlefields.[2] As for the men on board, those who died with their ship's master exemplified the international dimensions of the First World War, even as it came to present itself in Ireland. Among those interred near him in Cobh Old Cemetery were Able Seaman Thomas Adams, 53, of Kent; Horseman David McGregor, 25, of Anfield, and Isaac Voss, 54, born in Leicester but domiciled in Canada; from Canada also, Horsemen M. Burke, 52,

NEAR RIGHT
*Frderick Parslow, Master
of the Anglo-Californian.*

FAR RIGHT
*Capt. Parslow's son, also
Frederick.*

from Montreal and Archibald Ronald, 33, also from Montreal; from Ireland, Horseman David O'Neill, 45, of Belfast; and two horsemen from Russia, F. Licho, 41, and F. Pugnag, age unknown. At the time of their deaths and burials, the Imperial War Graves Commission had not yet come into existence, and when it did, in 1917, these men would not have qualified for war grave status. However, by the time the Commission had reached the point of being able to do anything at all in Ireland – to identify, register and mark the war graves with temporary crosses and finally with permanent standard war grave headstones – this situation had changed: in March 1921, members of the Merchant Navy who died as a result of enemy action were rendered eligible for war grave status – some 12,000 British Merchant Navy in over 3,300 vessels, lost without trace in the First World War, thereby qualified.[3] It was in this way that Cobh Old Church Cemetery eventually came to have its standard war grave headstones to these men.

Lusitania:

By the time of the attack and losses on the *Anglo-Californian*, Cobh town and Cobh cemeteries had already been visited with the fatal consequences of the First World War. It was almost exactly two months before this that the

liner *Lusitania* secured its tragic place in history. Not the luckiest of names for a ship, *Lusitania* was the name of an earlier ship wrecked off Newfoundland in June 1901; a Portuguese vessel of the same name, with 800 on board, was wrecked off the Cape of Good Hope in April 1911. Now, on 7 May 1915, this third *Lusitania*, en route from New York to Liverpool, fell victim to naval warfare. At 2.15 p.m. on that afternoon the German submarine U-20, under Kapitänleutnant Schwieger, got her in his sights, ten miles off the Old Head of Kinsale. According to him, a single torpedo – according to *Lusitania* witnesses, two torpedoes – struck the vessel. Whatever the case, the results constituted an event of calamitous proportions. Of 1,959 people on board – 1,257 passengers and 702 crew – no fewer than 1,198 were drowned, including over 290 women and over 90 children. The vessel reportedly went under within fifteen minutes and it was little short of miraculous that over 760 were saved by the ship's boats and the trawler, *Bluebell*, which had come to the rescue. In those fifteen minutes many more perished than did on the British or Irish side during the entire Anglo-Irish conflict of 1916-1921. Such a scale of losses was almost unprecedented at the time, exceeded only by the *Titanic's* dead of over 1,500.

For diverse reasons, the sinking of the *Lusitania* acquired legendary status – as war crime, diplomatic disaster, contested mystery and appalling human tragedy. It has, consequently, generated an extensive and critical literature.[4] For the people of Cobh it had an enduring impact, leaving its legacy on the landscape by monument and memorials.

Of its thousand and more dead, none were soldiers on active service and the claims to the contrary by hostile sources at the time have been discounted. Nevertheless, under the extension of the Imperial War Graves Commission Charter in 1921, at least thirty-seven of those buried in Ireland were accorded war grave status. Of these, some twenty-nine were British crew, the vast majority of whom came from Liverpool, Birkenhead and Bootle. Of sixty-six Irish-born crew lost, as listed by Molony,[5] seven were later commemorated with war grave markings, four from what was to become the Free State and three from the North. There was one Norwegian, forty-year old matron, Anna Enderson, laid to rest in Cobh along with five other females, four of whom were stewardesses: the fifth was Ballymena-born typist, Sadie Hale, who is commemorated in Belfast City Cemetery. The oldest of those with war grave status was one of the watch, George Cranston of Dumfries and Bootle, aged sixty-three,

and who is remembered with another of the watch, Richard Chamberlain of Edge Hill, Liverpool. They were interred in St. Multose's Church of Ireland Churchyard in Kinsale. All the rest, bar Sadie Hale, are interred in Cobh Old Church burial ground. The youngest victim whose burial plot is commemorated as a war grave, was fifteen-year old Ordinary Seaman John Thomson, born in Dumfries but resident at Birkenhead. Among the seven war graves of Irish-born were those of Fireman John Toale from Co Louth, Fireman Isaac Linton from Co Down, and Surgeon James McDermott, 38, born and reared in Douglas Road, Cork. His father, Captain McDermott, had been Board of Trade Superintendent in Cork, before moving to Britain where James was resident in Wallasey, Cheshire. Charming and well-liked, he had served for seven years as physician on several Cunard liners before this ill-fated trip: he had not been due to sail but went as replacement for the ship's usual doctor who was laid up with rheumatism. His sister waited in vain for his safe arrival in Cork, and like the others, he was buried and later commemorated by standard war grave headstone in Cobh Old Church Cemetery.[6]

Forgetting remembering:

As for collective commemoration by public monument in Cobh, as will be seen in other major instances later in this study, it became the subject of protracted delays and neglect. The sculptor Jerome Connor began work on his commission in 1930 but local objections to his design and other delays meant that only the base had been prepared before the Second World War broke out. The sculptor died and his monument lay unfinished for twenty years more. The looming prospect of the fiftieth anniversary of the *Lusitania's* loss rekindled some urgency, thanks to the efforts of sculptor Donal Murphy and the intervention of a concerned American, Thomas Fox, who pressed Taoiseach Seán Lemass on the matter. The anniversary came and went before the efforts of the Arts Council finally resulted in its completion over 1968-1970.[7]

In the aftermath of the *Lusitania* disaster, as the war proceeded, Cobh Old Church Cemetery was to accommodate the graves of many other war dead of this conflict: some 127 of them registered by the War Graves Commission in the years that followed. The very diversity of these later victims set a pattern that was to follow in the history of the war graves, in Ireland, of the two World Wars: Army, Navy, mercantile marine; from Ireland, England, Newfoundland, Belgium; from regiments as diverse as The Royal Munster Fusiliers, the Worcestershire Regiment, the Canadian Infantry and the Newfoundland Royal Naval Reserve; from Royal Navy vessels, such as H.M.S. *Colleen*, H.M.S. *President* or *Tiger*, to merchant vessels like *Cavina*, *Hyndford* and *Feltria*. The last-named was another Cunard ship, out of London, and was attacked and sunk by German submarine eight miles southeast of Mine Head, Waterford, on 5 May 1917. The captain and forty-four crew were lost: only three were found, buried and commemorated in Ireland, all in Cobh Old Cemetery: Fireman Henry Hooper of Bristol, eighteen-year old Seaman Henry Jones of Lavender Hill, Battersea, and eighteen-year old Wireless Operator Stanley Linnett of Sheffield.

Laurentic:

It was in 1917 also that a lesser-known casualty of the war at sea deposited its dead in even larger numbers. The 15,000-ton White Star liner R.M.S. *Laurentic* was taken over by the Admiralty, at first as a troop-carrier; as such she was commissioned as a Canadian Expeditionary Force vessel, capable of carrying up to 1,800 soldiers. She was, therefore, one of the major vessels in the transport of the many Canadian troops for battle in Europe. Later she was fitted

LEFT
*Lusitania
memorial stone in Cobh Old
Church Ccemetery*

out as an armed merchant cruiser – an idea intended also for the *Lusitania* but not carried out. *Laurentic* was en route for North America with 350 passengers and a cargo of gold bullion: some thirty-five ingots of gold, then valued at £5 million sterling, today worth £250 million, was sent to pay for munitions of war. Off Malin Head, on the night of 25 January 1917, she struck two mines, laid only days before by German submarine U-80, and sank with the loss of over 350 from a complement of around 750.

Of the lost, some sixty-six were found, identified and buried in Ireland: sixty-two in Upper Fahan, St. Mura's Church of Ireland Churchyard, two in Cockhill Catholic Cemetery, County Donegal and two in County Down – Lieutenant Thomas Steele at Tullylish (All Saints), and Engineer Lieutenant R. R. Mitchell in Hollywood Cemetery. One of the two interred in Cockhill also came from County Down, Steward Thomas Craig, 32, from Killough, where he left a widow, Lily, of the Bangor Arms Hotel. Among the youngest of those to be commemorated at Upper Fahan was nineteen-year-old Able Seaman Frederick Sheedy of the Australian Navy, who was born in Adamstown, New South Wales. Another Australian victim whose remains lie in St. Mura's was Francis L. Royle, 25, from Essendon, Victoria. Two members of the

Newfoundland Navy also perished in the tragedy: Seaman Samuel Mayo Hooper, 20, from Montier Bay, and Seaman Arthur White, 27, from St. George's, Newfoundland. Three Irish crew members who perished with them were Seaman John Fleming, 25, of Dunmore East, Waterford, Michael Lynch, 28, of Youghal and Colman O'Donnell, 25, of Galway City. At least twenty-one of the sixty-two were crew members, but the majority of those identified and who came, in time, to be commemorated in Upper Fahan were Royal Marines or other British Navy personnel, most of them from England. As with *Lusitania*, so with *Laurentic*: it was to have another namesake of equal ill-fortune which also fell victim to German attack, off Donegal's coast, in the Second World War.[8] The tragedy of the first *Laurentic* was to concentrate in County Donegal the largest number of war graves caused by a single event in Ireland during the First World War for almost a year – until, that is, October 1918, a month before that war's end.

Leinster:

It was on 10 October 1918 that the next major marine tragedy off Ireland's shores occurred, when the R.M.S. *Leinster* was torpedoed by U-123, under Oberleutnant Robert Ramm, and sent to the bottom, little more than one hour out

from Dun Laoghaire, or Kingstown as it was then called. At the time, she was carrying about 180 civilian passengers of whom 115 perished; approximately 490 military personnel, of whom some 326 to 340 were killed; 76 crew, including captain, of whom 37 died, and 22 postal sorters, of whom all but one were lost. In all, of the total of over 770 who travelled, over 530 lost their lives.[9]

Of the 320 to 340 military personnel who were killed it is not possible to say how many remains were recovered. This single greatest disaster in the modern history of the Irish Sea, however, also created the largest concentration of war graves in any Irish cemetery arising from a single event. Grangegorman Military Cemetery became the final resting place for some 145 of those military personnel who died in the *Leinster* sinking.[10] These thereby constituted the largest single cluster of graves and memorials in Grangegorman out of its total Commonwealth war grave registration of 613 First World War and 11 Second World War souls. Over 20 were interred there on 13 October, close on 60 on 14 October, and over 50 on 15 October.[11] Mostly they were British, going on leave; to a lesser extent, Irish members of the British Forces, returning to war from leave. They also included, however, military personnel from the United States, Australia, Canada and

New Zealand. So suddenly did this crisis occur that some of the Colonial and American dead were buried in hastily prepared ground in the cemetery which was only consecrated for burial purposes three weeks later.[12]

Having entered the war on 6 April 1917, by war's end the Americans had over one hundred navy vessels using Irish ports. In addition, the United States Naval Aviation Forces had established five naval air bases in Ireland, in addition to sixteen in France and two each in England and Italy. Those in Ireland were located in Berehaven, Cobh and Whiddy Island, Cork; Aught Point in Donegal; and Ferrybank in Wexford.[13] From their headquarters in Paris their operations were directed by Captain Hutch Cone. In October 1918 he had completed inspecting the naval air installations in Ireland when he travelled to return to Paris. Although badly injured, he was one of the fortunate survivors among the fifteen or so Americans, as estimated by the American Consul in Dublin as having been on board the *Leinster*. Not so fortunate were at least four US Navy and two US Army personnel who perished in the sinking.[14] Unlike their British and Colonial allies, the Americans normally did not leave their dead at rest in foreign soil, and those buried in Grangegorman were exhumed and repatriated on various dates between 1920 aand 1922.[15]

Over 330,000 Australians had volunteered for service in this war, and by its end some 59,000 had perished[16]. Among Australian military personnel on board the *Leinster,* presumably returning from leave, it is not certain how many died. Lieutenant Francis Laracy, a Gallipoli survivor, three times wounded in battle since enlisting in October 1914, was visiting relatives in Ireland when he boarded the *Leinster* to return to base. His body was never found. Likewise, Australian nurse, Winifred Stirling, was visiting Ireland when she was drowned. Some seven Australian soldiers are thought to have been lost. Three were buried in Grangegorman: Private Joseph Barnes, 28, of the 48th Battalion Australian Infantry, from Henley Beach, South Australia; Private Edwin Carter, 33, of the 29th Battalion Australian Infantry from Victoria; Private M. E. Smith, of the 19th, from Coolabah, New South Wales.

Among New Zealanders of whom 112,000 saw overseas service, 17,000 lost their lives in this conflict. There were seven New Zealand military known to be aboard the vessel, including Army Medical doctors Duggan and Bassett, who both died in the disaster. Also killed were Lieutenant Henry Doyle, 28, of Auckland, an officer of the Wellington Regiment, and an Australian-born Lance Corporal, Peter Freitas of the New Zealand Army Service Corps: they were both laid to rest in Grangegorman, where they are remembered to this day.

Over 458,000 members of the Canadian Forces served abroad, and some 57,000 perished in the course of the First War. How many Irish-born were among their number is not possible to say. As to the *Leinster* victims, there were fourteen Canadian soldiers and one Canadian nurse on board, ten of them being lost. Thirty-nine year old Nursing Sister Henrietta Mellett of the Canadian Army Medical Corps, from Co Mayo, was on leave to visit her mother; she did not survive the tragedy and was interred in Mount Jerome Cemetery, Dublin – one of thirty-five Commonwealth war graves memorialised there to this day. Private James Finleon of the 4th Battalion Canadian Infantry, from Auburn, Ontario, was laid to rest in Grangegorman. So too was Lieutenant Donald Gwyn, 22, from Quebec, a soldier of the Royal Canadian Dragoons, a recipient of the Military Cross. Other Canadian victims included Private Michael Biggane from Waterford, whose story features in a later chapter,[17] and Captain Edward Milne, 30, a Scot with a colourful history in Ireland before service in the war and death on the *Leinster.* He grew up in Galway and became a reporter on the *Galway Express* before emigrating to Canada in 1909,

before emigrating to Canada in 1909, where he joined his brothers, farming in British Columbia. Wounded in action, and on his way to England for further medical attention, he was in no condition to save himself when the *Leinster* went down.[18] He is commemorated today on a memorial erected by his widow in Bohermore Cemetery, Galway: here he is one of at least seventeen war dead of the First War and three of the Second, in the same burial ground as Lady Gregory, Padraig O'Conaire and William Joyce, Lord Haw-Haw.

As is clear from this, not all *Leinster* war graves are, therefore, in Grangegorman. Lieutenant Christopher Domegan, 22, an RAF officer from North King Street, Dublin, was buried in Ardcath, County Meath; Captain Matthew Murphy of the Royal Army Medical Corps in Cloyne Cathedral Churchyard, County Cork and Lieutenant Robert Bassett, also of the RAMC, in St. Finbarr's, Cork. Finally, there was Lieutenant Colonel Charles H. Blackburne of the 5th Battalion Dragoon Guards, with a distinguished military career before and during the war, and who was posted to the Curragh in Easter Week 1916. His entire family was with him on the *Leinster*: wife Emily, seven-year old son Charles, eleven-year old daughter Beatrice, and governess. Only the widow survived; the daughter Beatrice was lost without trace.

Father and son were buried together in the officers' burial ground of the Royal Hospital Kilmainham Cemetery, the only *Leinster* war graves in this place: the other seven Royal Hospital war graves, located in the 'Other Ranks' Plot, are those of seven soldiers killed in the 1916 Insurrection. Among other British war dead of *Leinster*, Private Joseph Barraclough, 33, of Shipley, Yorkshire, had already given service in the West Yorkshire Regiment before being posted to the Royal Defence Corps. He was returning there, on leave, when he perished, along with twenty-six other identified members of the Corps. He was buried in Grangegorman and, over twenty years later, his circumstances were to feature as an issue when it came to perpetuating his memory.[19]

Inevitably, too, there were losses from members of Irish regiments returning from leave: four from the Royal Munster Fusiliers, five from the Royal Irish Regiment, one from the Royal Irish Fusiliers, three from the South Irish Horse, four from the Royal Dublin Fusiliers, three from the Leinster Regiment, six from the Irish Guards, one from the Connaught Rangers, as well as Irish members of British regiments, Royal Navy and RAF. Finally, one of the ship's two Quartermasters, Arklow-man Henry Tyrrell, 57, of Tivoli Road, Dun Laoghaire, became one of

LEFT
At centre of image, a row
of Leinster war grave
headstones in
Grangegorman.

many Merchant Navy war dead to be commemorated among the seventy-five Commonwealth war graves of the First World War in Dean's Grange Cemetery, Dublin.

Geography of the war dead:

The many deaths from these major shipping casualties of the war at sea, apart from the many other fatal sea-war tragedies, such as those of the *Nicator, Bayano*, and *Haverford*, are of note in this context: they are substantially responsible for the concentrations of war graves in certain counties like Cork, Dublin and Donegal, and in certain burial grounds such as those at Cobh, Grangegorman and Upper Fahan.

However, the most salient feature of the war graves of this period is their sheer diversity. Every year from 1914 to 1921 saw its war grave burials.

For classification as a war grave and for the purposes of subsequent commemoration by the Imperial War Graves Commission – as will be explained more fully in the next chapter – those dying of wounds, disease or illness resulting from the War, and expiring before 31 December 1921, were deemed eligible for such recognition. The numbers of such burials in cemeteries in the counties that were soon to constitute the Irish Free State and Northern Ireland, respectively, were approximately – at a minimum – as in Table 1:

Table 1:
CWGC War Graves of 1914-1921, registered in Ireland[20]

Year	Irish Free State	Northern Ireland	Total
1914	94	19	113
1915	341	161	502
1916	404	184	588
1917	369	168	537
1918	799	343	1,142
1919	329	219	548
1920	202	93	295
1921	52	16	68
Subtotal	2,590	1,203	3,793
Unidentified	12	24	36
Total	2,602	1,227	3,829

There were, therefore, at least 3,800 such burials as registered by the IWGC by the time it had largely completed its registration process in the mid- 1930s. The figures do not include war dead who might have been overlooked, or, more likely, not registered for recognition due to opposition, indifference or untraceability of next of kin: allowing, say, ten percent for these, the figure could have been as high as 4,500. The figures include provision for those known to be war dead but whose identity was not known – a problem much greater in the war-death burials in Ireland for the Second World War than for the First. The figures in Table 1 also include British military personnel killed in the course of the Anglo-Irish conflict during the years 1916 to 1921.

That category, when it came to war grave status, however, was problematic for the IWGC and the British authorities, as will be seen in the next chapter. The figures for 1914 are understandably lower than for the other war years, since they comprised only five months of conflict. Those for 1918 are disproportionately much larger than for any other war year, perhaps reflecting a much larger number of cases of seriously stricken being invalided back to Ireland, the return of units from the front, or the effects of the influenza epidemic then raging. [21]

As to the distribution of these burials, no county in the whole island was without its graves of war in this period, no more than in the case of the Second World War. The situation, county by county, for the area that was to become the Irish Free State is as illustrated in Table 2:

Table 2:
CWGC War Graves of 1914-1921, registered in the Irish Free State

County					
Carlow	19	Kilkenny	44	Offaly	30
Cavan	14	Laois	23	Roscommon	12
Clare	37	Leitrim	10	Sligo	10
Cork	522	Limerick	97	Tipperary	110
Donegal	168	Longford	20	Waterford	49
Dublin	946	Louth	41	Westmeath	55
Galway	45	Mayo	23	Wexford	43
Kerry	41	Meath	32	Wicklow	35
Kildare	160	Monaghan	16		

Total: 2,602

FAR LEFT
New Zealand headstones of
World War One,
Grangegorman Military
Cemetery

NEAR LEFT
Memorial to Henry Tyrrell
of Arklow, Quartermaster
of Leinster, Dean's Grange
Cemetery, Co. Dublin

For the counties that came to constitute Northern Ireland, the numbers of burials are as presented in Table 3:

Table 3:
CWGC War Graves of 1914-1921, registered in Northern Ireland

County	Total
Antrim	621
Armagh	85
Down	264
Londonderry	156
Fermanagh	39
Tyrone	62

Total: 1,227

Clearly, the larger concentrations in the cities and counties of Dublin, Cork and Belfast, straddling Antrim and Down, represent a combination of their population size and strategic significance: they had the largest number of public and church cemeteries in the country and the greatest number of barracks, as well as of military hospitals and personnel. Dublin and Cork also had large military cemeteries: in Cork's case, Ballincollig, Cork City, Fort Carlisle and Fermoy – while Cobh was a special case in itself; in Dublin's case, Grangegorman Military Cemetery, and in Limerick where King's Island Military Cemetery and Mount St. Lawrence's held the remains of many soldiers. The presence of military cemeteries combined with barracks and hospitals also explains the relatively high number in Co Kildare. Tipperary County, likewise, had its share of military barracks, and military plots in local cemeteries, in Tipperary Town, Templemore, Cahir and Clonmel, as did Westmeath, with its major barracks at Athlone.[22] The same can be said of Offaly, where there was the headquarters of the Leinster Regiment at Birr, Crinkill Barracks and Birr Military Cemetery at Crinkill. Similarly Donegal, with the major naval base at Lough Swilly, another nearby in Lough Foyle, and a small military encampment at Finner, fits into this category. In addition, however, Donegal, notoriously, was the graveyard of many a victim of naval conflict in this and in the Second World War.

Bearing in mind that, as a matter of policy, the dead of British Empire and Commonwealth Forces were buried and commemorated where they fell, or as close to it as practicable, and that repatriation was prohibited – with a few notable exceptions to be seen later[23] – it would be unwise to read too much into these tables: otherwise it might seem reasonable that there be a positive relationship between a county's incidence of recruitment and its numbers of war graves, as in the obvious cases of Dublin, Cork, Antrim and Down. However, the situation is

BELOW
Recruiting for war:
Ireland and Australia

Irish War of 1916-1921: British military personnel, of whatever origin, who died in this were also, eventually, deemed to have war grave status. This clearly would help augment the Dublin and Cork numbers where casualty rates in the Anglo-Irish War were highest: likewise, the presence of military hospitals in Belfast, Dublin and Cork would naturally have added to the totals in these areas. Nonetheless, for counties such as Clare and Kerry, at around forty each, to have twice the number as, say, Sligo and Carlow, is intriguing. In Clare's case there was, for example, a tradition in Kilrush of enlistment in the Royal Navy,[24] and in North Clare – as for example, in Ennistymon – there were family traditions of British military service, as witness the Connoles and Hallorans.[25] Nevertheless, as has been pointed out, Clare and Kerry were the two counties with the lowest rate of World War casualties in the whole country, and it has also been indicated that Clare contributed far less than its share of recruits, especially during the years 1914-1916.[26]

Conjecture or interpretation, of course, is seriously complicated by the fact that the war graves were not just Irish, but those of British, Irish and Commonwealth military forces (and merchant navy personnel), whether born and enlisting in their 'home' regiments, or born in Britain or Ireland and later enlisting in a Dominions regiment. The opposite even occurred: there is one case of a South African enlisting in the RAF, dying in Ireland and buried in Grangegorman: Lieutenant Gordon Midgley, 22, was born in Cape Province where his parents ran the Ocean View Hotel in Humewood, Port Elizabeth.

It is not really possible to hazard a safe estimate of the ratio between British and Irish who came to be commemorated in such war graves. As will be seen in later chapters, much may depend on a particular cemetery or location: special cases in Cobh, Grangegorman or Upper Fahan with a majority of British; special cases like Tralee, with a majority of Irish. The diverse nature of this war's impact, however, is clearly seen in the war graves of personnel from the Dominions and Dominion regiments: at least sixty-eight Commission-registered Dominion graves of the First World War are in the Irish Free State and at least forty-one in Northern Ireland, for which see Table 4:

FAR LEFT
A South African
remembered in
Grangegorman:
Lt. Gordon Midgley, RAF

NEAR LEFT
James McDermott,
Surgeon of the Lusitania.

Table 4:
Dominion war graves in Ireland,
1914-1921

Country	IF State	N Ireland
Canada	31	30
Australia	22	6
New Zealand	8	3
Newfoundland	4	1
South Africa	3	1
Total	68	41
Total: 109		

Of the three South Africans commemorated in the Free State, two were members of South African regiments, the third a member of the RAF.

Overall, the First World War left a legacy of at least 3,800 known war graves on this island. They were dispersed in over 740 separate burial grounds: over 500 in the Free State; over 240 in Northern Ireland. Out of more than 2,600 war graves in the former, some 900 were concentrated in twelve military cemeteries.

Grief on your graves her tribute lays
And Gratitude her homage pays
And Love, with proud yet wistful eye
Keeps vigil while ye sleeping lie

James Ferres
To Those who Sleep in Flanders Fields

Chapter 2

The Military Cemeteries, 1914-28

In the context of the war graves of 1914-1921, there were, in what became the Irish Free State, twelve burial grounds or plots that had been used exclusively for the interment of British military personnel and their next of kin. Arbour Hill is not among them, as it had ceased to be used for this purpose when it was replaced by Grangegorman Military Cemetery, on Blackhorse Avenue, Dublin, from 1876. Of the twelve, nine bore the formal title of Military Cemetery, regardless of size: Ballincollig, Birr, Cork, Curragh, Fermoy, Fort Carlisle, Grangegorman, Limerick (King's Island) and Tralee.

Three were otherwise titled, though exclusively used for the military or their kin: the Royal Hibernian Military School Churchyard, Phoenix Park; the Royal Hospital Cemetery, Kilmainham, and the Cahir Military Plot in the Church of Ireland Churchyard at Clogheen. The number of 1914-1921 war graves in each military cemetery, as recorded by the Commonwealth War Graves Commission, is as in Table 5.

There was no formal handing over of the military cemeteries, en bloc, in 1922, when the British evacuated. In some cases, because of complex legal wrangles over War Office property, Ballincollig, Cork and Limerick King's Island were not handed over, legally, until 1928. Fort Carlisle, on the other hand, at the mouth of Cork Harbour, was maintained by the British until the cession of the Treaty Ports in 1938: it was subsequently renamed Fort Davis.[1]

Table 5:
CWGC registered war graves in Military Cemeteries in Ireland

Cemetery	War Graves	Cemetery	War Graves
Grangegorman	613	Tralee	10
Curragh	103	Royal Hospital Kilmainham	8
Cork	83	Fort Carlisle	5
Limerick King's Island	39	Cahir	4
Fermoy	22	Birr	3
Ballincollig	10	Royal Hibernian Military School	1

Grangegorman:

Opened in 1876, Grangegorman Military Cemetery was already the last resting place for over 3,000 soldiers, even before it became the principal site for war grave burials arising from the years of conflict 1914-1921.[2] Here were buried military casualties of the 1916 Insurrection: some immediately, others soon after, as in the case of forty-six reburials from the grounds of Dublin Castle, thirteen of them on 19 May 1916, a further thirty-three on 20 May 1916.[3] Others were exhumed and reburied in Grangegorman on 21 October 1920: nine from King George V Hospital, (now St. Bricin's), five from the grounds of Dublin Castle, four from Portobello Barracks and two from Trinity College grounds; others followed later, indeed, some forty years later.[4] As already seen, it was also the burial ground for the vast majority of the military casualties of the *Leinster* disaster, as well as for those soldiers of the First World War who died while in hospital or at home in the Dublin region. Like all the military cemeteries so styled, it was the property of the War Office; however, in its physical position as an annex to the Phoenix Park, its grounds were actually maintained for the War Office by the OPW from the outset. This fact, especially in the 1920s, may well have saved it from the fate of most of the others, as will emerge in due

course. Together with the small ones at the Royal Hibernian Military School and the Royal Hospital, Kilmainham, it was the only military cemetery for whose grounds the OPW accepted unbroken responsibility in the transition from British to Irish governance, into the early and middle 1920s.[5]

According to a War Office directive of March 1898, 'Military Cemeteries should be strictly reserved for soldiers who die in the service and for members of their families who may die during the soldier's service'.[6] This instruction in due course was to be ignored, so that Grangegorman came to accept the interment of ex-soldiers long out of service. One example was the Crimean veteran, James Fitzpatrick, Rifle Brigade, who died in the North Dublin Union aged seventy-six and was buried in the cemetery on 11 February 1913. Similar was the case of Sergeant William Parkinson of Bayview House, Sutton, Co Dublin: a veteran of the Indian Mutiny, he died aged eighty and was interred in Grangegorman on 17 May 1913. The practice continued even when the First World War broke out: two other Crimean veterans, seventy-two-year old James Murphy and eighty-six-year old T. Harpar were laid to rest in Grangegorman Military Cemetery in January and June 1917, respectively.[7] With the passage of time, what began

as a practice appeared to acquire the status of a right. Even after the British departure, the OPW admitted that their ex-soldiers resident in the State might still have rights of burial, as, by custom and practice, might one near relative of ex-soldiers interred there.[8] It did not take long for this to be tested. In February 1924, a Mrs Brady, on behalf of her mother, Mrs Gregory, whose son, Gunner James Gregory, had died of wounds and had been buried there in February 1918, asked that the mother be allowed burial in the same grave in due course. Having consulted their Minister, Finance authorised the OPW to allow this burial, but added that it was 'advisable not to give a general permission for the interment of relatives in the graves of ex-soldiers'. She duly passed away in March 1928 and was interred beside her son.[9]

In November 1924, Mrs Elizabeth D'Arcy of Mountjoy Street, Dublin, applied to the War Office for a similar permission. She wished to be laid to rest, in due course, in the grave of her son, Sergeant Michael D'Arcy of the Royal Irish Rifles. He died in Newport, Isle of Wight, in January 1921, after a career in which he had been awarded the Distinguished Conduct Medal, the highest award for valour after the Victoria Cross.[10] As his mother put it herself:

I am in a very bad state of health at present, and would like to have some information as to what is to be done in case of developments.

Her request, sent on to the OPW, was granted. The 'developments' took a little while but she duly passed away in June 1943 and was interred beside her son.[11] One month after her request in 1924, Finance gave a general permission for other relatives with similar requests, on condition that convincing cases were made.[12] By 1931, the IWGC could confirm to the British Legion that twelve such burials of ex-soldiers' relatives had been allowed: in fact, apart from over sixty burials of ex-soldiers, close on thirty relatives were buried there between 1924 and the end of 1930.[13]

Grangegorman was unique among the Irish military cemeteries in that it was the only one which also provided war graves for British Commonwealth Forces' personnel of the Second World War. Furthermore, as to the privilege of a near relative being allowed burial there, as late as 1967 Gertrude Gilmore, a Dublin-based widow, made such a request to the CWGC. Her husband, a Flight Lieutenant of the RAF, had died in Aden in 1926 and she had lived in Rathmines since 1929. Her father, a member of the Royal Engineers, and her soldier-brother had been buried there; the family had been stationed in Ireland

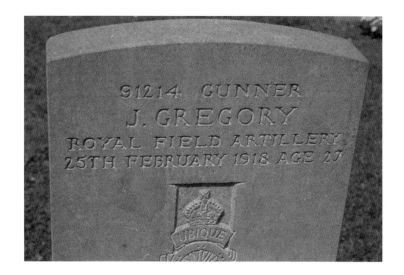

from 1906 to 1922. As she remarked, in pleading her case:

Now an elderly widow – alone – [I] wish to settle my affairs… I will be grateful if you will kindly grant this request – to be buried in the Military Cemetery, Blackhorse Avenue – this little cemetery is beautifully kept.[14]

Such burials of relatives still took place there as recently as the year 2000.[15]

The Curragh:

The military camp at the Curragh was the largest in the country: a huge encampment during the Napoleonic Wars, capable of temporarily housing 10,000 infantry, it became a permanent military establishment from 1855. Its impact at that stage, especially on the racing fraternity and the sheep-grazing interests, was such as to precipitate legislation in the form of the Curragh of Kildare Act, 1868. It was through this legislation that a specific area was walled around for a designated military burial ground – a vital need, now that so many troops were stationed there at any one stage.[16] At the time of the British evacuation in 1922, no specific arrangements were made in relation to responsibility for the cemetery and the actual deeds to this property were not transferred from the War Office to the Irish Government until 1927.[17]

By that time, the Department of Defence and its military on the Curragh were wondering about their rights or responsibilities there: the Quit Rent Office left them in no doubt that they were responsible for the upkeep of the cemetery; furthermore, it got the distinct impression that the Department of Defence 'were anxious to treat this area as not within their control and to which, therefore, they have no duty'.[18]

In 1922 General HQ in the Phoenix Park reckoned that the Curragh Military Cemetery contained over 1,930 graves of which, it claimed, some 152 were those of soldiers who died in the period 1914-1921. This is at odds with the Curragh Command's own listing, in November 1921, of 106 graves of the First World War and of 8 graves of soldiers who died between 30 April 1920 and 31 August 1921.[19] For the years 1914-1918, the Commonwealth War Graves Commission lists 103 war graves of personnel who died in the Curragh Camp or in its nearby Military Hospital. Given the constant coming and going of different military units, especially in a time of war, there was an unusually large extent of regiments represented by the memorials in remembrance of those who lie there. They range from the 21st Empress of India's Lancers to the Royal Highlanders or Black Watch. No single regiment, not even Irish, predominated:

the largest clusters were the war graves of ten Royal Dublin Fusiliers, five Leinsters and three Connaught Rangers. The oldest of old soldiers recorded there was Private John Lilley, 62, of the 9th Reserve Cavalry Regiment and formerly a sergeant of the 10th Hussars; the last recorded as buried there was Private John Ramsay, 19, of the 6th Dragoon Guards, who died in an accident on 9 July 1921.

The Smaller Military Cemeteries:
The Royal Hibernian Military School in the Phoenix Park had a small war grave cemetery on which the new Free State Government directly sought the advice of the War Office, in anticipation of requests for burials there. This secluded graveyard in the School grounds had been opened in April 1851 to receive the remains of boys and staff of this unique military establishment.[20] There was only a single IWGC-registered war grave of 1914-21: that of twenty-two year old Lance Corporal Bernard L. Martin of the 1st Battalion Leinster Regiment, who died of influenza in March 1919, and whose parents lived in Chapelizod.[21] The War Office hoped that the new government would allow the burials of persons closely associated with the School, either as old boys, former staff or next of kin of persons already interred there; otherwise, they advised

strongly against any further burials, as the area was so small and the danger of disturbing existing graves so great. In October 1924 the Cabinet decided in favour of this, and the Department of Defence subsequently instructed the OPW to follow this policy. It was then left to the OPW's discretion whether to permit or prohibit. There were occasional burials there over the decades which followed, one as late as October 1997.[22]

Almost directly across the River Liffey, the Royal Hospital Kilmainham had one plot for officers and a second for 'Other Ranks'. After the burials of the *Leinster* victims, Colonel Blackburne and his son, in October 1918, neither plot was much used again. There was a small number of burials of former Royal Hospital pensioners and staff, the final one, that of Etienne Walter Bishop, former Infirmary Sergeant, taking place on 5 June 1954.[23] The Military Plot at Cahir, Kilcommon, Co. Tipperary, was given to the War Office in perpetuity, in September 1885, by the Diocesan Trustees of the Church of Ireland, out of their own secluded graveyard there. Of its known total of forty military graves, the four war graves of 1914-1921 were all of British soldiers of the Royal Field Artillery: three from 1915 and the final one, of Lance Bombardier B.C. Shreeve, from February 1920.[24]

The Military Cemetery at Crinkill, Birr, Co. Offaly, was connected with the major barracks there – headquarters of the Leinster Regiment – which was established in 1809 to accommodate up to 1,000 infantry. The cemetery originally was within the site of this barracks from 1855, but relocated to Crinkill Military Cemetery in 1875. By the time of the British evacuation, the known 188 military graves included only four war graves. One was of a Leinster Regiment soldier, Sergeant Whyte, who died nine days after the War's commencement; the second died very late, Private James Goldring, on 2 November 1918, nine days before its end; the third died after the War's end but within the eligibility period for war grave status – Thomas Allen of Hastings. A Quartermaster Sergeant of the Middlesex Yeomanry, in March 1919 he was one of the earliest aviation fatalities in this country. Piloted by Flight Lieutenant Taylor, the plane took off from Crinkill Airfield on 28 March 1919; during a nose-dive stunt it struck a tree; it then crashed into the roof of nearby Crinkill House where Justice of the Peace Henry Friend and his wife had risen from bed, minutes before the aircraft came through their bedroom ceiling. The pilot escaped with minor injuries, but Thomas Allen died of his injuries the next day. The war grave of Co. Offaly's most distinguished casualty of the First World War, however, is not in the military cemetery here but in Birr Old Graveyard: Irish Guards Major William Edward Parsons, 5th Earl of Rosse, died of his wounds and was buried there in June 1918.[25]

The Cork Military Cemeteries:

Of the four Military Cemeteries in Cork County, the largest was the old garrison cemetery in Cork City, associated with Victoria Barracks. The latter, originally called New Barracks, was established over 1801-1806, and renamed Victoria Barracks in 1901. The Cemetery first came into use in 1849; according to a report of 1931, the earliest headstone found there was dated 1849, which coincides with a tenure agreement of April of the same year.[26] Victoria Barracks was renamed Collins Barracks after the departure of the British. In response to a War Office enquiry of March 1922, British Army Headquarters in Dublin estimated that there were 975 soldiers' graves there; of these, they reckoned 141 had been opened over the period 4 August 1914 to 31 August 1921, a figure that far exceeded the number which the Imperial War Graves Commission could find for registering: they identified 83 war graves there, around the year 1930. Either the War Office had got the number wrong or the cemetery register was lost and the

temporary grave markings obliterated over the intervening eight years.[27] The latter is possible: this Military Cemetery was not handed over by the War Office to the OPW until 1928, and there is a 1931 IWGC report that the Royal Engineers were trying to fix the wooden crosses into concrete bases there, as late as 1926.[28]

Although there was a very diverse range of regiments represented in the eighty-three known war graves of 1914-1921, there were some significant clusters, especially among the Irish Regiments: twelve men of the Leinster Regiment, ten of the Royal Dublin Fusiliers, nine of the Connaught Rangers, as against only two of the Royal Munster Fusiliers. Their dates of death and indeed, the dates of death in general among the eighty-three, showed no significant clustering in any one of these years. One of the very earliest to die was also one of the youngest: Michael Maloney of Limerick, a private in the Munsters, was only eighteen years old, and the War only nine days on, when he died on 13 August 1914. There were two women soldiers, both Queen Mary's Army Auxiliary Corps: M. Wright who died on 12 November 1918, the day after the War ended, and M. K. Harrick of Cork, who died on 4 September 1919. All eighty-three were either Irish or British, with one exception: Robert Matthews,

35, of Alberta, who drowned on 7 May 1915 – presumably a victim of the *Lusitania* disaster – had been a lieutenant of the 60th Battalion Canadian Infantry.

The Military Cemetery at Ballincollig was older than that in Cork City. Judging from its earliest headstone, it was first used in 1813, although the land of which it was a part was first leased to the military in 1804-1805.[29] In 1922, so far as the British Army authorities could glean, it held ninety-four graves of which, they believed, twelve had come into use over the years 1914-1921. The IWGC recorded a figure of ten, all on different dates: four in 1916, one in 1917 and one in 1920. All British, they were Royal Field Artillery personnel – naturally enough, since Ballincollig had been, for over a century, a major ammunitions manufacturing centre and the principal Munster depot for the Artillery. There was only one exception among these ten: seventeen-year old Londoner E. C. J. Stratton, who died in June 1920, was a member of the 17th Lancers. None of the ten died in war: five passed away from illness, two from accidents, two as a result of suicide and one from causes not specified.[30] Ballincollig was closed to burials in 1922.

Fermoy Military Cemetery, also closed in 1922, had been in use since 1860, in association with the large military

Near Right
Memorial to Old Boys,
Royal Hibernian Military
School, who died in World
War One.

Far Right
The headstone of Lance
Corporal Martin of
Chapelizod, Royal
Hibernian Military School.

barracks there. After 1922 it fell into such neglect that, within a decade, none of its twenty-two war graves of 1914-1922 could be identified with certainty, and, as described later, recourse had to be had to a free-standing, collective memorial.[31] Fermoy's twenty-two identified war dead of 1914-1921 comprised soldiers from a wide range of British and Irish regiments, including the Royal Munster Fusiliers and Connaught Rangers, but there was no significant clustering either in terms of regiments or dates of death. The last burial appears to have been that of Private W. H. Exley of the York and Lancaster Regiment, who passed away on 13 July 1921.

By contrast, four of the five war graves in Fort Carlisle were of men of the Munster Fusiliers who died on separate dates in 1916 and 1917. The final recorded burial there was of Major Geoffrey Lee Compton-Smith, 2nd Battalion Royal Welch Fusiliers. While travelling by train through Blarney on 16 April 1921, he was captured and held hostage by the IRA, as a bargaining counter for four IRA men captured in the previous February. Sir Peter Strickland, General Officer Commanding, the British 6th Division, and Military Governor of the Martial Law Area, had been told that if these four were executed, Compton-Smith would meet the same fate. The four, Maurice Moore, Patrick O'Sullivan,

Thomas Mulcahy and Patrick Ronayne, were duly executed on 28 April, and the Major was, in consequence, shot.[32] He was buried secretly on a hillside at Donoughmore, having penned a farewell letter to his wife Gladys and daughter Annie.[33] News of his fate became public following the British capture of documents in a raid on IRA premises in Dublin on 26 May 1921. Despite the offer of a substantial reward, no information as to the whereabouts of his remains emerged.[34] Enquiries from former Welsh MP, George Lloyd Davies, to Minister for External Affairs, Desmond FitzGerald, as late as 1925, brought no news. FitzGerald was told by the Department of Defence that, despite exhaustive inquiries, it had not been able to elicit information. FitzGerald explained that, due to the Civil War and the fact that the Cork No.1 Brigade who had carried out the execution were anti-Treaty, it had not been possible to find out where the remains were located. In hope, he concluded: 'I have no doubt that as the Civil War recedes further into the background…we will be able to get more information'.[35] In the circumstances, his hope was realised sooner than might have been expected: in March 1926 the local Gardaí were informed of the location and on the evening of Tuesday 2 March they found his body buried in Barracharing Bog, between Donoughmore and

Blarney.[36] It was removed to what had by then become Collins Barracks, for repatriation. However, instead of being sent home to England, it was handed over, with full military honours, to the British Adjutant at Spike Island for interment in Fort Carlisle.[37] The cemetery was not used after 1922; it was renamed Fort Davis in 1938, after the return of the Treaty Ports.

Limerick and Tralee:

Of the other two Military Cemeteries in Munster, that in Limerick, at King's Island, was conveyed to the War Department by the Commissioners of Woods and Forests in July 1856, in a transfer of eighty acres, one of which was 'for the interment only of such of Her Majesty's Troops or others belonging to Her Majesty's service as shall die at Limerick'.[38] It was on 4 August 1928 that a British representative, S. P. Skinner, from Spike Island, handed over 'the Buildings, Register of Graves, Inventories and Tools' to Joseph O'Donoghue, the local officer of the OPW in Limerick. Six years later, the Minister for Finance, in whom the eighty acres were legally vested, conveyed by lease the seventy-nine acres of this former military property to the City of Limerick, which wanted to use the land surrounding the one-acre cemetery for housing.[39]

The Cemetery's thirty-nine war graves of 1914-1921 represented some diversity as to regiment but the Welch Fusiliers comprised nineteen of them, fourteen dying in 1918, between July and November, the remaining five in 1919. Unusually, however, there were neither members of Irish regiments nor any soldier with an Irish address, listed among the thirty-nine; there was only one Commonwealth soldier, John Anderson of Melbourne, a Corporal of the 3rd Field Company, Australian Engineers, who died on 17 December 1915. There were no burials after June 1921.

As to the last of the twelve Military Cemeteries, that in Tralee was associated with the major depot for the Royal Munster Fusiliers. This cemetery was bought by the War Office in December 1899.[40] Six of its ten war graves were those of Irishmen, five of them members of the Royal Munster Fusiliers, of whom two had addresses in Kerry, and one each in Limerick and Cork and Waterford. The sixth of these Irish, Private Daniel O'Brien of Glencar, had served twenty-five years in the Royal Dragoons, Boer War experience included, but actually died a member of the 15th Battalion Canadian Infantry (Ontario Regiment), in January 1918 at the age of fifty-four. There were three British soldiers interred here, and, finally,

one New Zealand Forces member, John Walsh from Dunedin, a driver with the New Zealand Field Artillery when he died in February 1919.

A New Zealand soldier dying and buried in County Kerry might appear bizarre but such was the diverse nature of the First World War's impact. Even in Ireland, strange though Walsh's case may have been, it was far from unique: as seen earlier, there were sixty-eight Dominion war graves in the Free State and forty-one in Northern Ireland. Little enough of their solitary stories is known. Consider, however, in conclusion, the case of Private R.E. Kinchington of the 3rd Battalion Australian Infantry. Born in Queensland and domiciled in Sydney, the twenty-five year old Robert Emmett Kinchington was on leave in Killarney when he died from illness arising from his war wounds, on 6 February 1919. He was awaiting transportation home to Australia when he passed away, and was buried, instead, in Killarney New Cemetery.

For many years his grave was a source of anxiety for his mother, Ellen. In the early 1930s she was contacted by the IWGC to see if she wanted her son to be remembered by a Commonwealth War Grave headstone. She accepted the offer and duly paid her seventeen shillings to have it engraved with a personal inscription. In August 1934 the stone was inscribed and erected: she was notified in 1935. Thirteen years later, in January 1948, in her eighty-third year, she wrote again to complain that visiting Australians claimed the grave was neglected and the inscription barely visible.[41] Whatever the truth of the charge, this war grave, as others in Killarney Town and Kerry County, became the innocent casualty of a political dispute, to be described later.[42] It was not resolved until almost thirty years after Private Kinchington's death. Of such haplessness is the story of the World War graves in Ireland composed, as the chapters which follow will seek to recount.

*The tumult and the shouting dies -
The captains and the kings depart -*

*Rudyard Kipling
Recessional*

Chapter 3

The Imperial War Graves Commission, 1917-1923

As the British Army prepared for the withdrawal of its troops in the course of 1922 from what was to become the Irish Free State, the General Officer Commanding in Ireland, Sir Nevil Macready, was greatly concerned with those they were leaving behind, both the very old and the very young. There were, for example, the old soldiers of the Royal Hospital Kilmainham. In January 1922 it still had in residence 126 military pensioners, of whom 115 were Irish and the remainder English, Scots and Welsh.

In a letter to the War Office on 7 January 1922, Macready made it clear that there was

a general feeling, certainly among the Military men, and I believe among many others in this country, that this building should be preserved under its ancient Charter and not be handed over to the tender mercies of a Government whose interest might not be sufficient to maintain and care for this landmark of history.[1]

Indeed, he went so far as to suggest, in a note of considerable prematurity if not of total naiveté, that *should there be any idea that members of the Royal Family would from time to time visit the Irish Free State, an event that would, in my opinion, not only be popular in this country but would go far to assist in restoring good feeling between Great Britain and Ireland, no more suitable residence could be found than the Royal Hospital.*

In the event, his worst fears were realised, as the premises experienced an uncertain and deteriorating future over the succeeding decades until rescued and restored in more recent times. Uncertain, too, was to be the fate of its surviving residents. Remaining in residence there until 1929, then promised or threatened with transfer to Dr Steevens' Hospital, they were finally shipped out to the Royal Hospital, Chelsea. The seventeen willing to go, varying in age from fifty-five to eighty-five, departed on Saturday 25 May 1929. The remaining six, unwilling or too infirm to make the journey, simply became out-pensioners.[2] One of the last of these to be buried in the Royal Hospital grounds was Royal Irish Fusilier Laurence Ennis. He had elected to go on out-pension rather than end up a Chelsea pensioner, died in the South Dublin Union on 1 March 1930 and was laid to rest in Kilmainham two days later. The last of those who transferred to Chelsea passed away on 17 September 1952.[3] The Charters were revoked and the Governors finally dissolved with effect from 31 December 1955.[4]

Of concern, also, to the departing General, would be the fate of the young boys of the Royal Hibernian Military School. This remarkable institution, occupying over thirty-three acres in the Phoenix Park, was founded originally as

NEAR RIGHT
*Sir Gordon Nevil Macready,
General Officer
Commanding in Ireland*

FAR RIGHT
*British evacuation of the
Curragh*

the Hibernian Society in 1764, initially to help children made orphans by the deaths of their soldier fathers in the Seven Years War. In 1767 it opened a home in the Phoenix Park with 140 such children. By the mid-1780s, in Dublin alone, it was estimated that some 1,400 children of dead soldiers or soldiers overseas were begging in the city's streets. Early in the nineteenth century responsibility for the institution was taken over by War Office and it was renamed the Royal Hibernian Military School.[5] By 1922 it had some 410 boys aged between eight and fifteen years in training for a life in the British Army. In a separate despatch to the War Office Secretary on the same date as his letter concerning the Royal Hospital, Macready expressed concern about their future and remarked

It would be a thousand pities if this School was abolished and handed over to any authority other than to whom the Forces of the Crown look for support and encouragement.[6]

In the event, the School was abandoned and the boys marched out of the Phoenix Park, transferring first to Shorncliffe Barracks, Kent, and then in 1924 to the Duke of York's Royal Military School at Dover. Indeed, the last surviving boy trainee soldier of the School, Michael Kilduff, is still hale and hearty at ninety-three.[7] As for the

premises, with its simple but beautiful church and surrounding cemetery, it is, today, St. Mary's Hospital.

Of equal concern for Macready was the fact that they were leaving behind over 620 comrades killed in the conflict in Ireland from 1916 to 1921.[8] In addition to these were the British, Irish and Commonwealth soldiers, sailors, airmen and female services personnel killed in or dying in Ireland of wounds or illness contracted while on active service in the World War. To these 2,600 plus, in the Free State, in turn, were added the garrison dead of Britain's imperial wars of the previous two centuries – some 8,000 soldiers buried in military cemeteries, public cemeteries or private burial grounds throughout Ireland. It was, however, the war dead and pre-war dead in the twelve military cemeteries that most concerned him.

On 28 February 1922, writing from General HQ in Parkgate Street, Macready addressed this concern to the Secretary of the Imperial War Graves Commission and recommended that 'if at all possible, all Military Cemeteries in Southern Ireland be taken over by the Imperial War Graves Commission after the evacuation of British troops'. Such a move would ensure their being treated in a manner similar to those in France or Flanders, would ensure their being

kept in good order and 'facilitate visits by relatives'. He recommended further, however, that 'if relatives should wish to remove a body for burial in England, at their own expense, arrangements should be made with the Provisional Government to afford them every assistance'.[9] He concluded that 'unless definite arrangements can be made to ensure that these Cemeteries are in the care of British representatives, much feeling will be created amongst the Units and relatives interested'.

Macready's letters and despatches of January-February 1922 proved to be the prelude to the history of international war graves administration in Ireland. Thus began the politics of the British and Irish governments and their respective agencies, the Imperial War Graves Commission and the Office of Public Works, when it came to the care, maintenance and marking of the war graves of British and Irish, Commonwealth and international soldiers and civilians buried in this country as a consequence of the two World Wars.

The Imperial War Graves Commission:

The British Government at its highest level took up Macready's concerns when, on 10 February 1922, its Provisional Government of Ireland Cabinet Committee considered a 'memorandum regarding Military Cemeteries' and instructed their Secretary, Lionel Curtis, to sound out the War Graves Commission.[10]

That the initiative to involve the Imperial War Graves Commission should almost certainly have first come from Macready is not surprising. The Commission originated in a British Red Cross unit sent to France in 1914, led by Fabian Ware, former journalist, schoolmaster and then imperial administrator under Milner in South Africa. Ware dedicated his services to the Red Cross from September 1914. By the spring of 1915 his unit had become preoccupied with the work of marking and recording the graves of those killed in battle. Already, in October 1914, he had persuaded Macready, who was then Adjutant-General to the British Expeditionary Force, of the need to register and mark the graves of the fallen.[11] Macready in turn persuaded the Commander-in-Chief, Sir John French, to secure War Office sanction for the creation of a graves' registration organisation as an integral part of the army in the field.

The result was the establishment of the Directorate of Graves Registration and Enquiries in 1916.[12]

It was Macready who saw to it that Fabian Ware's unit became that Directorate, thereby launching Ware on a mission that for him never ended until his death in 1949, a few weeks short of his eightieth birthday. Ware's concern for the care of the war graves in France and Belgium, whenever the war would end, convinced him of the need for a new, permanent body with executive powers to manage not just British, but also imperial graves from Britain, Belgium and France, to Turkey, Egypt and beyond. His memorandum proposing 'an Imperial Commission for the Care of Soldiers' Graves', drafted in early 1917, won the support of the Prince of Wales who put to government the case for an imperial war graves organisation under Royal Charter; it was proposed that it would have a permanent secretariat and an executive comprising representatives of all the Dominions. On 13 April 1917 the Imperial Conference approved the idea and recommended the establishment by Royal Charter of the Imperial War Graves Commission[13], with Ware as its vice-chairman and effective leader until his death.

By the time of its actual coming into existence as a legal entity, on 21 May 1917, Ware's organisation had already accomplished a huge amount of work, recording the deaths and places of burial of the legions slaughtered in Europe and beyond. Through the Anglo-French-Belgian Agreement of August 1917 the Belgian Government generously agreed to acquire, at its own cost, the lands needed for the burial and commemoration of the British Empire war dead and to hand these lands to the Imperial War Graves Commission for cemetery construction, commemoration and perpetual care.[14] The governments of France, Italy, Serbia, Greece and Egypt followed in affording similar privileges and provision.

The principles underlying the IWGC's work were formally approved by the Imperial Conference in 1918. The principle of equal treatment of all war dead was central. Memorials to the fallen were to be permanent, uniform and display no distinction in shape or size on account of rank or station. More significant still was the principle that no exhumation for repatriation would be permitted. The fallen were to be interred and commemorated in a cemetery close to where they had fallen, and those whose relatives might have afforded the cost of repatriation were to be denied it in the interests of all.

As Adjutant General in 1915, Macready secured an order forbidding exhumation on the grounds of hygiene, but also 'on account of the difficulties of treating impartially the claims advanced by persons of different social standing'. After the end of the war the IWGC took the decision to adhere to the ban on exhumation and repatriation:

A higher ideal than that of private burial at home is embodied in these war cemeteries in foreign lands, where those who fought and fell together, officers and men, lie together in their last resting-place, facing the line they gave their lives to maintain.[15]

This was a policy decision steadfastly upheld in the face of bitter opposition.

The costs of running the Commission, of erecting temporary wooden crosses and later of permanent, standard memorial headstones, and of maintaining the graves in perpetuity were to be shared by all the participating governments of the Empire, on the ratios of the recorded dead of each participant state. By the war's end the Commission's work extended from Britain, through Europe to Egypt, and even further afield. Within twenty years of its establishment, the IWGC had commemorated by memorials over 580,000 identified and over 180,000 unidentified British Commonwealth dead of the First World

War. Of these, some 35,000 plus were the graves of Irish soldiers, sailors, air force and medical services personnel.

The Commission and Ireland, 1917-1922:

If Macready thought that the issue of the disposal of military cemeteries in Ireland was only a matter of passing over the responsibility to the IWGC, he seriously oversimplified a complex situation. It did not seem to occur to him that the government of independent Ireland might entertain a different view from his, as to who looked after what on Irish Free State territory.

Quite separately from this consideration, the IWGC itself had such a monumental task on its hands, in the war and immediate postwar years, that Ireland might well have been a footnote or afterthought even if graves in Ireland should come within its remit. Indeed, how far and precisely in what way the care and commemoration of the dead of war fell within the Commission's brief was by no means clear as conflict on the Continent petered out and conflict in Ireland flared up.

Historically, before the First World War, the Office of Works in London looked after British war graves and cemeteries from Athens and the Crimea

FAR RIGHT
A memorial to the dead
of H.M.S. Wasp. 1884,
Bunbeg Church of Ireland
Churchyard, Co. Donegal.

NEAR RIGHT
H.M.S. Mars

to China and Japan, yet who looked after what in Ireland was not certain. For the graves of Royal Navy men killed in naval disasters such as that of the *Mars* in Cork or the *Wasp* in Donegal, the Admiralty looked after them itself or paid others to do so.[16] For soldiers who died while on service in Ireland, their local garrison regiments tended to appoint one of their own or locally resident, retired soldiers to undertake the caretaking. Much depended on what cemetery it was and who was the cemetery authority. It was all uncoordinated and haphazard. So, when it came to Ireland in the years 1917 to 1922, while Fabian Ware was always zealous, the Commission itself was coy. Admittedly, as early as July 1921, the Commission was making enquiries about some names of those interred in the Curragh Military Cemetery where, as has been noted earlier, there had been eight burials of British Army personnel between April 1920 and July 1921. However, it is likely that this interest arose from members of the British public requesting information and not from any active policy from the IWGC at the time.[17]

The original initiative for action appears to have come from the Army Council, via the War Office. This, in turn, was most likely in response to queries and concerns sent from specific localities in Ireland where problems of maintenance were being experienced first hand. With the departure

of British troops in 1922 the military cemeteries faced serious neglect. Writing to the War Office that November, the retired Major Cheeseman wanted to know what steps were being taken for the upkeep of Fermoy Military Cemetery, as he was led to believe that 'at present no attention is being given to the grounds'.[18] At Tralee, the old caretaker O'Connor, appointed in 1903, was discharged in April 1920. No successor was appointed, with predictable results.[19] Similarly, an ex-warrant officer of the Leinster Regiment, R. Nixon, who had been stationed in Birr until his discharge in 1922, and who continued to live on there after discharge, wrote directly to the IWGC in the summer of 1923. He complained about

the ruinous condition into which the Military Cemetery at Birr [has fallen], the walls being knocked down…the headstones and crosses are all damaged and glass wreaths broken, the place on several occasions has been a grazing ground for donkeys and goats.[20]

He felt

ashamed as an Ex-Service man to see the resting place of several of my old comrades in such a dilapidated condition.

The Army intervenes:

From the beginning of 1922 the Army Council and the War Office began pressing the Colonial Office to bring the question of the disposal of the military cemeteries in Ireland to their own government, for action.[21] Lionel Curtis, on behalf of the Colonial Office, wrote on 3 March 1922 to enquire what exactly was involved, how many graves in how many cemeteries. The War Office in turn sought this information from GHQ in the Phoenix Park. It is interesting that the supplied information sent from Dublin to the War Office in response was deficient. It listed 7,530 graves of military personnel interred in the eight military cemeteries of Ballincollig, Birr, Cork, Curragh, Fermoy, Grangegorman, Limerick and Tralee: some 1,034 of these had been interred between August 1914 and August 1921, but the list omitted the other military cemeteries of Arbour Hill, Cahir (Kilcommon), Fort Carlisle and the Royal Hibernian Military School, Dublin.[22]

Under pressure, the Colonial Office had approached the IWGC to request that the latter consider the matter. M.E. Antrobus, who was to have a long association with the Irish Government and the IWGC stretching into the 1940s when he was posted to Dublin, wrote to the IWGC's Principal Assistant Secretary, Lord Arthur Browne, on 28

April 1922; he enclosed the information supplied from GHQ in Dublin and asked when the Commission might reach a decision on its attitude to the military cemeteries in Ireland. Browne replied on 2 May 1922 that the Commission hoped to decide its position at its next meeting.[23]

Several months passed before an impatient Winston Churchill, then chairing the Cabinet Subcommittee on Irish Affairs, indicated that he would be 'glad to receive any observations which the Commission may now have on the subject'.[24] For all its undoubted energy and address, the IWGC was in a dilemma when it came to the Irish Free State and its military graves. That dilemma was created by three distinct elements: the first was the issue of defining what constituted a war grave; the second was the matter of practicality; and the third was the question of jurisdiction.

Definitions, dates and impracticalities:

In determining whose grave was to be accorded war grave status, to be commemorated by standard Commission headstone and looked after in perpetuity, the original Charter of 1917 confined the Commission's responsibilities to those members of the Imperial Forces who died in the Great War 'from wounds

Right
Boys of the
Royal Hibernian Military
School on parade,
Phoenix Park.

inflicted, accident occurring or disease contracted while on active service'.[25] This original 1917 definition did not rest at that minimal statement and, for reasons that are not entirely clear, had to be revisited. The timing of this revisitation is interesting, commencing as it did in February 1922, at the very point when the Army Council and War Office began to press for action. It was at its 42nd meeting, on 21 February 1922, that the Commission again took up the matter. Fabian Ware, as vice-chairman, pointed out that the issue of definition was a difficult one which they had frequently addressed in the past.

One problem was that the original definition of 1917 would allow the graves of many who had never actually taken part in any fighting to be treated as war graves, once they had died in service through accident or illness. Related to this was the matter of dating. The *Termination of the Present War (Definition) Act* of 1918, and an Order in Council following it, fixed the end of the Great War as 31 August 1921. Under this, an opposite difficulty arose: men who had seen fighting and had experienced wounds inflicted or disease contracted in the course of the war but who had died as a consequence after 31 August 1921 would be buried in graves that would not be classed as war graves. Furthermore, with the Anglo-Irish conflict ending

in truce in July 1921, Ware himself pointed out to his colleagues 'the graves of British soldiers killed in the recent disturbances in Ireland would become war graves', and he thought that some of the Dominions would not agree to this, although, technically, they were war graves.

Indeed, as it emerged at a meeting of the Commission two months later, the New Zealanders took a very strict line on what constituted 'active service'. Sir James Allen, their representative on the Commission, reported the New Zealand position that active service did not commence until their military personnel had actually departed from that country for the theatres of war in Europe.[26] In face of the difficulties of definition and date, Ware had moved that these matters be referred to a subcommittee comprising the Adjutant-General, Sir James Allen, and Sir Henry Maddocks, Coalition Conservative MP for Nuneaton. In a discussion with Lionel Curtis that same month on the question of military cemeteries in Ireland, Ware told him of this and, in early March, while that Committee was still deliberating, and with a long way to go, Curtis was already pressing Ware for a copy of the subcommittee's report as soon as it would be available. In late March it was reported that, although the subcommittee had been meeting, it was unable to reach any agreed conclusion, but would meet again to see if it could.[27] By April they still had not reached an agreement and the delay in deciding the matter 'had caused the greatest possible embarrassment to the staff of the Commission'. Matters came to a head in late May 1922 when a resolution defining a war grave was finally carried.

It read:

1. The Commission should accept as a war grave the place of burial of any officer or man of His Majesty's Military and Naval Forces raised in any part of the Empire, who had died during the period 4th August 1914-31st August 1921, inclusive, from wounds inflicted, accident occurring or disease contracted while on active service.

2. The expression 'Active Service' shall mean any whole time military or naval service during the period 4th August 1914-31st August 1921, or any part time military or naval service whilst in action during the same period.

3. Provided that any participating Government may indicate that in its view certain graves are not war graves and may decline to accept responsibility for their treatment.[28]

The compromising third clause enabled Allen to accept the formulation for New Zealand. Nevertheless, this new formula had the effect of rendering eligible for war grave classification the grave of any soldier, of whatever nationality, serving for the British and dying on active service in Ireland during the Anglo-Irish conflict. This, however, was far from making it possible for the Commission to meet the clamant expectations of the Army Council, War Office and Colonial Office. For them, the immediately pressing issue was that of military cemeteries – not of individual war graves in the over 500 separate cemeteries that held the remains of British military personnel in the Irish Free State.

Typical of the kind of practical problem reaching their desks was the quite reasonable representation made by Lieutenant Colonel S. G. Faber, the Officer Commanding the Royal Engineers on Spike Island. He understood, incorrectly at the time, that it was proposed that the IWGC would take charge of military cemeteries in Ireland, and he wanted to know when the Commission would take over responsibility for Cork Military Cemetery. The caretaker, G. Soames, who had been managing the place since 1899, wanted to give up the position and return to England. Faber was proposing to appoint a substitute and pay him

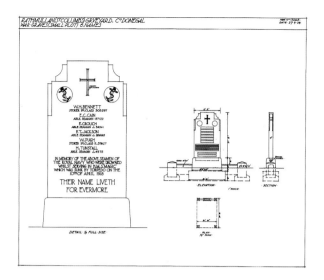

from the local funds of the Army. He contacted the IWGC on 25 May 1922 only to be informed by Arthur Browne, two days later, that the Commission had 'no present intention of assuming charge of Military Cemeteries in Ireland'.[29] As far as the Commission was concerned, although it was constructing and managing major war cemeteries in Belgium and France, it had no responsibility for military cemeteries elsewhere. Not until it was granted a Supplemental Charter in 1923 was it empowered to take over responsibility for the ancient cemeteries of distant wars such as those of the Peninsular Campaign and the Crimea.

Although the Commission had reached a new definition on 23 May, it appears to have been slow in communicating it to government. It was not until 8 June that they sent a copy of their minutes to the Colonial Office. Here the Colonial Secretary now wondered if this would enable the Commission 'to come to a decision on the question raised by the Army Council regarding these cemeteries', and, on 15 July 1922, told the IWGC that Churchill wished to hear from them on the matter. The reply, which now came quickly, was not one the Army wanted to hear: Arthur Browne, replying for the IWGC on 22 July, stated bluntly, as he had already done to Faber in Cork, that while the IWGC

recognise the responsibility for the graves of serving soldiers who died and were buried in Ireland between 4 August 1914 and 31 August 1921, they were unable to accept responsibility for the care and maintenance of military cemeteries generally.

Explaining that they had 'gone seriously into the matter', 'in the present condition of Ireland they cannot take any steps towards the erection of memorials over graves in that country'. They concluded by passing the problem back to the Secretary of the Cabinet Committee on Ireland, remarking that the Commission 'would be very grateful for any suggestion you might make in that connection'.[30] He, in turn, passed the problem back to the War Office, and asked if the Army Council had any suggestions to make, given the state of affairs in Ireland, where civil war erupted with the seizure of the Four Courts on 13 April 1922.

In all of this correspondence during the first half of 1922 there appeared to be an assumption that there was no problem of jurisdiction. It did not seem to occur that the Provisional Government of the Irish Free State might well have a view in the matter. Understandably, the latter had enough on its plate to cope with the living without worrying too much about the dead, whosoever or wheresoever they might be. Yet it was not until May 1923

that the British Government, having drawn a blank, temporarily, with the Commission, now approached the Free State Government.

In the meantime the problem of its war dead in Ireland became more complicated for the Army Council. Apart from not being able to get any movement or action to mark and maintain the graves of its dead in Ireland up to the cut-off date of 31 August 1921, it lost a further thirteen soldiers, dead and buried in the Free State after that cut-off date. The Army Council was insistent that these be marked with headstones and cared for.

In February 1922 Macready had written to the IWGC asking that his men dying and buried in Ireland after the cut-off date be accorded war grave status. Browne for the IWGC had responded on 25 March in a remarkably blunt manner:

The Commission will under no circumstances treat as War Graves the graves of men who died after 31 August 1921, and he was not even in a position to say how the graves of those who died [in Ireland] before that date would be treated.[31]

Despite this rebuff, Macready persisted, this time by appealing to the War Office to have the cost of commemorating the recent military deaths borne at public expense by a charge on the Army Votes. At the War Office, Sir Herbert Creedy took up Macready's cause and shared the Army view that it would be unfair that the cost should fall on individual regimental funds. In late July he approached the Treasury with these exceptional cases, 'for whom no authority exists to provide gravestones etc. at public expense'.[32] He requested that they be a charge on the Army Estimates and that the Treasury likewise authorise a similar expenditure 'for following this course in the case of any other soldiers who may have to be buried in Ireland under similar circumstances'. Before the Treasury Lords would agree to this they insisted on securing the views of the IWGC as regards the graves of those killed or dying 'during the recent period of unrest' in Ireland, up to 31 August 1922 [sic].[33]

Ware replied that, as far as the IWGC was concerned, they could not designate as war graves those of service personnel dying after 31 August 1921. This response notwithstanding, the Treasury, surprisingly, agreed to meet the costs of taking care of these additional thirteen, even if it took a long time to do so. On the last day of November 1922, four months after Creedy's plea, the Treasury informed the War Office that this cost would be met out of public funds, 'provided that the death circumstances were such that the IWGC would have treated them as war graves had it not been for the limiting date'.[34] Furthermore, in a rather odd rider, the Treasury official, Barstow, added that the Treasury Lords 'think that it will be convenient if arrangements can be made for the Commission to erect headstones over the graves in question, as agents for the Army Council, at the same time as the Commission's work is put in hand [in Ireland].' This was despite the fact that the Irish Free State had not been consulted in the matter and that the Commission itself, as recently as July 1922, had declined to get involved in Ireland.

There matters appeared to have rested until the end of the year, when Major Cheeseman's concerns about the future of Fermoy Military Cemetery precipitated a series of exchanges between the War Office and the Imperial War Graves Commission. The former, on receipt of Cheeseman's inquiries, wondered if the Commission was maintaining this cemetery, and guessed 'probably not'. But, since the Fermoy Military Cemetery was in a part of Ireland that had been evacuated, 'it seemed to us that you would be the proper authority to carry on the maintenance', and asked the Commission to respond.[35]

It was a curt enough response that issued from Arthur Browne in December: 'we

have made no arrangements for the maintenance of this or any other military cemetery in Ireland'. He added that, of the 127 graves in Fermoy Military Cemetery, in any case, only 24 fell within the category of war graves with which the Commission has the power to deal. He wondered if the War Office had 'yet' made any arrangements 'for the maintenance of Military Cemeteries generally in Free State Ireland?' To this, next day, a weary War Office official remarked: 'If the IWGC cannot undertake the work, we suppose there is nothing for it but to employ caretakers', in which case the matter of supervising them would become problematic. The question then arose whether there had been any contact with the Free State Provisional Government. Edward Coles of the War Office reported, on 16 January 1923, that they could not find any correspondence on the matter, nor was he aware of the question having been raised before with them. Coles then referred to the example of South Africa as a precedent, where 'the Union government agreed to maintain the military cemeteries as part of the general arrangement under which military lands were transferred to them'. He went on to suggest that 'perhaps the Free State Government will agree that the Office of Works should maintain the cemeteries either free of charge, as in the case of South Africa, or on a repayment basis'. In further exchanges down to 24 January 1923, the Commission and the War Office agreed that the latter would now press to have the whole issue taken up by the Cabinet Committee 'with a view to making arrangements with the Irish Free State.'[36]

If the War Office and the IWGC now wanted the matter to go to Cabinet, they had nonetheless to go through the Treasury, where a different view prevailed. On 2 March 1923, Cubitt of the War Office finally wrote formally to the Treasury, who were considering the general question of the transfer of War Department property to the Free State. He did so fully along the lines laid out in Coles's memorandum of 16 January, citing the South African precedent. However, within the Imperial War Graves Commission there were still doubts and hesitations. In the same week in which Cubitt wrote to the Treasury, Arthur Browne expressed misgivings to his superior, Fabian Ware. Remarking how 'delicate' the whole matter was, he observed that 'the cemeteries will have in them the graves of many who were killed in fighting Irish Free State Forces and I doubt if the Free State Government would be prepared to maintain them, either on a repayment basis or on any other basis – in any case loyalist opinion would be outraged by this suggestion, I think – and the protests from relatives

would be many and bitter and difficult to answer'.[37] Two days later he reiterated these misgivings to Major Lord Stopford, asking his opinion of the War Office proposal, and suggesting 'we could get the memorials and graves looked after by local representatives, but if it is to be done by the Free State Government it will only lead to trouble'.[38]

Ironically, even as he expressed these misgivings, the Works Department of the Imperial War Graves Commission was already contacting a few local firms of monument masons and cemetery authorities in the Free State to make preliminary enquiries. By 9 March such firms and cemetery caretakers in four localities in Carlow, Wicklow and Waterford had been contacted concerning arrangements for maintenance. Furthermore, in early April the Commission's Director of Works urged Browne to consider the appointment of two Area Inspectors, one for Northern Ireland and one for the Free State so that 'the Commission's work in Ireland may be proceeded with'.[39]

Meanwhile, having considered Cubitt's letter of 2 March, the Treasury's Otto Niemeyer formally contacted the Undersecretary of State at the Colonial Office (Irish Branch) on 23 May 1923. He enclosed, for the Secretary of State's

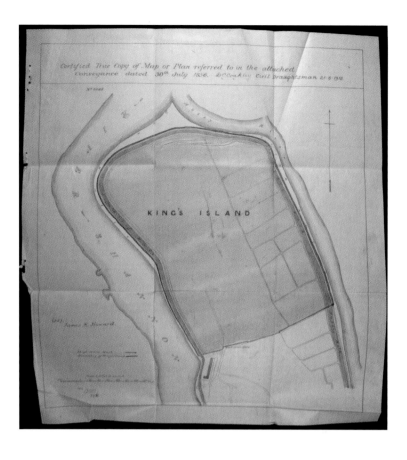

information, the correspondence which had developed with the War Office and the IWGC on the maintenance of war graves and the erection of headstones 'at public expense'. He confided that the Treasury Lords agreed with the War Office proposal that the Free State Government 'should be asked to allow the Board of Works to maintain military cemeteries either without cost to the Imperial Government or on a repayment basis' and the Treasury wanted the Colonial Office's views on this proposal. He added, however, that while the war graves were 'a liability of the IWGC, it may be convenient that the Free State should at some date undertake this service, or alternatively, that the [Free State] Government should contribute to the cost of the IWGC'.

Niemeyer concluded that, while it would be reasonable that the Free State should maintain the British military pre-war graves at their own expense, the Treasury doubted whether the time was ripe for proposing to the Free State that it should pay to maintain the war graves or to contribute to the costs of the IWGC.[40] Before the reaction of the Colonial Office to this was communicated, the whole matter became sidelined by a quite different development.

The boast of heraldry, the pomp of pow'r
And all that beauty, all that wealth e'er gave,
Awaits alike th'inevitable hour,
The paths of glory lead but to the grave.

Thomas Gray
Elegy in a Country Churchyard

Chapter 4

Execution - Repatriation, 1920-1924

On Saturday 9 July 1921 a truce in the Anglo-Irish conflict was agreed between Nevil Macready, General Officer Commanding in Ireland, and Eamon deValera, President of Dáil Éireann. It came into effect two days later.

The Lost:

A month before this, on 5 June 1921, three young bandsmen of the 1st Battalion, Manchester Regiment, attached to Ballincollig Barracks, dressed in military uniform, were spotted on the road at Srelane Cross, near Ovens. Arrested there by the IRA, they were moved three miles across country southwest to Aherlea. They were held in custody in a disused house, one mile south of Aherlea village. The commanding officer of the IRA column who took the three assumed they had been sent out on an observation mission by the British military authorities. In consequence, they were tried, executed and hurriedly buried in a yard attached to the house.[1] For the next two years the whereabouts of their bodies remained unknown to their military superiors, the local authorities or their next of kin. Of these three youths, Matthew Carson of Manchester was eighteen, C. A. Chapman of Oldham was seventeen, and John Cooper, also of Oldham, was sixteen.

These were three of at least eighteen British military personnel who disappeared, presumed dead, most of whose identities were known but the whereabouts of whose remains were not. In addition there were at least two who were killed and buried whose identities, as well as whereabouts, were not known when the Truce ended formal hostilities on 11 July.[2] Sometime between the middle of April and the end of May 1921, two British soldiers of the Machine Gun Corps disappeared. They apparently either deserted or, by instruction, went to join a travelling circus then touring Cork. The two had been quartered in the RIC Barracks in Charleville Main Street and had become friendly with some local girls and their families. On returning from visiting these one night, they were shot and buried two miles away, in an undisclosed location. For almost thirty years they lay there undiscovered. At the beginning of the 1950s the local Garda Sergeant met with an official representing the Imperial War Graves Commission and Office of Public Works: he told the official of his understanding that the British military authorities assumed they had gone absent without leave by joining the circus which had been in the town a few days before. In June 1951 it was reported to the IWGC that the remains had been accidentally discovered by a local farmer. Soon after this they were buried in

the grounds of Charleville Holy Cross Cemetery Extension where a headstone was erected for them in 1953. They remain without names to this day.[3]

As for the other missing British military personnel, one was Cadet Cecil Guthrie, from Kirkcaldy, a former RAF officer who was a member of the Auxiliaries stationed in Macroom Castle. On 1 November 1920, in Ballyvourney, he ordered local man Jim Lehane from his house and shot him dead.[4] Four weeks later Guthrie was involved in the Kilmichael Ambush of 28 November in West Cork. Here eighteen Auxiliaries were ambushed by Commandant Tom Barry's Flying Column of thirty-six IRA Volunteers.[5] Sixteen Auxiliaries were killed, one cadet, H. F. Forde, survived, having at first been thought dead, and Guthrie escaped. He fled but was captured near the bog of Anahala where he was shot and buried in an unmarked grave.[6]

Another of the lost, Lieutenant H. M. Genocchio, was arrested in Cork City by Republican Police, and charged with involvement in several local robberies. On his person at the time of his arrest were, among other items, gold watches and chains, a lady's handbag, £15 in cash, as well as a revolver. He was lodged in a Republican 'jail' in the city for eight days. On attempting to escape he was

shot dead. His body was brought to the morgue, and later on the evening of its deposit there, it was apparently taken by the British military to Victoria Barracks for conveying back to England for burial. What happened after its deposit in the morgue is not clear, but Genocchio's name was on a list of the disappeared dead, supplied to General Richard Mulcahy, Chief of Staff and Defence Minister, for information as to whereabouts.[7]

An eighth Briton whose body's whereabouts remained unknown was Private R. W. Williams of the 2nd Battalion, Royal Welch Fusiliers, who met his death dramatically at Bunratty Bridge. On the night of 9-10 July 1921 the local IRA set about the bridge, causing a breach in it as it curved on the Ennis side. At 2 p.m. on Sunday 10 July two British Army motorcycle despatch riders crossed the bridge from Limerick and, despite some local people trying to warn them of the breach, both plunged into the river below. One rider saved himself but Williams was seen by local publican, Mrs Ryan, and her daughter, to go under. His body was swept down the river and found by a local farmer two or three weeks later, caught up in bulrushes on the east side, two hundred yards north from Bunratty Bridge. The local farmer who found him had also witnessed the fatality. He dragged the

body from the river and buried him nearby.[8] Williams died the day after the Truce had been agreed, the day before it came into effect.

If the Truce terminated formal hostilities it did not end military fatalities. On Wednesday 26 April 1922, three British intelligence officers and their driver were captured by Irregular Forces. Ironically detained in Macroom Castle, from which the Auxiliaries had ventured to their deaths in Kilmichael, they were executed as spies and buried in a 'lonely and wild part of the county', about five miles northwest of Macroom, in an unidentified location.[9] They were Lieutenants R. A. Hendy of the 1st Royal Warwickshire, K. R. Henderson of the 2nd Green Howards and G. R. A. Dove of the 2nd Hampshire Regiment. Over a year before that, Dove had been one of the Hampshires who led the assault on an IRA house at Clonmult in East Cork. Here, on 20 February 1921, some thirteen Volunteers were killed, and, of eight captured, two were subsequently executed at the Hampshires' Cork headquarters, Victoria Barracks. Dove was later named in a captured British intelligence document as one of those who had gathered up the IRA dead.[10]According to the Dublin correspondent of the London *Times*, Dove and his colleagues were now forced to assist in the digging of their own

grave pit, and the first victim was a small white dog, the pet of Lieutenant Dove, followed by the three officers and the driver, Private J. Brooks. In presenting the story in December 1923, the *Times* correspondent at first reported that the four men had been on a fishing expedition. The correspondent, however, quickly sent a correction which the paper printed in the same issue. He now wrote that

The statement was inaccurate and I wish to correct it from a fuller examination of the evidence than was possible from the moment when it was written. The Secretary for War said last July in the House of Commons that the three officers were on active duty when they were kidnapped. It is also known that when they left Ballincollig Barracks on their last journey they carried no fishing tackle with them'.[11]

Some months later it was agreed between the British and Irish authorities that the deaths of Genocchio and the Macroom Four would not be the subject of any official investigation but that their cases would be submitted to the Compensation (Ireland) Commission. As the President of the Executive Council of the Irish Free State, W.T. Cosgrave, explained to Mulcahy: they were 'unable to discover anything concerning them which would be satisfactory to the relatives', and both sides agreed that if

the relatives were to press for an inquest, he would explain that:

an inquest would be of no use, that we much regretted the murders and have no hesitation in condemning them and that we are prepared to submit the cases for compensation…that we suggest this method so that the relatives might be spared the anguish of having the cases argued in the Courts.[12]

The Manchester Band Boys:

As for the three Manchester Regiment band boys: distraught at being unable to get any firm information from any official body as to where they had been buried, Matthew Carson's father, an ex-Army man himself and now a clerk in a Lancashire factory, travelled to Ireland when the factory closed for annual holidays in mid-August 1921, to try to discover his son's grave. He made inquiries in the Bandon district, with the sympathetic and active assistance of the Civic Guards there. On Saturday 18 August 1921, 'in a very lonely place at the end of a long lane leading to a ruined farmhouse', he had 'a spot dug up and there found the remains of the three poor boys. They were practically only the bones, the six Army boots, parts of shreds of the uniforms'.[13] He had the remains placed in one large coffin and conveyed to Bandon, six or seven miles away, where they were buried in Bandon Workhouse Cemetery. His son was a Catholic and the father was promised that Matthew could be buried in the Catholic Cemetery, 'only about a mile and a half from where they had been lying', if he could identify him.

The account, in his own words, verbatim, follows:

I could not, of course, identify my boy, but if I could, I on no account would have separated him from the other two poor boys with whom he died and slept for the past two years. This was they [sic] reason why we had to put them in the paupers' ground.

Carson then returned to his home in Manchester and told John Cooper's parents what he had managed to do in Ireland. He also told the boy Chapman's parents but found that the latter's father 'is indifferent'. Cooper's parents, from Oldham, helped him with some of the expenses he incurred to prevent 'the poor boys' remains lying in a field like dogs'.

Despite these efforts, Carson senior remained deeply troubled that they should have now ended in a pauper's grave in a workhouse cemetery. Indeed, long before he had even travelled to find the grave, he had petitioned the British Compensation (Ireland) Commission to have the boys buried elsewhere in

Ireland or to be brought home.[14] As a consequence, the Army Council on 29 May 1923 called on the Colonial Office to request the Irish Free State authorities to consent to the removal of their bodies and those of certain other British officers and men, including the Macroom Four, to a better place, as the relatives might wish. In making this request, the Army Council confessed that it had no official information as to the boys' burial place, but understood '*they are buried in a field near Kilcrea*'.[15] H. J. Creedy of the War Office earnestly urged the Duke of Devonshire, as Colonial Secretary, to get the Free State's consent to the removal of these remains

either to a cemetery in Ireland or to this country, according as the relatives may desire.[16]

Some weeks later, the Colonial Office contacted the Governor-General in Dublin with a view to ascertaining the whereabouts of the remains. His secretary, N. G. Loughnane, was furnished by them with a list of eighteen officers and men killed between October 1920 and April 1922, the whereabouts of whose remains were unknown or uncertain, and whose relatives were pressing for information. Loughnane spoke with Richard Mulcahy, asking if he would institute enquiries with a view to identifying burial locations,

to afford the relatives of the deceased the consolation of knowing that Christian burial was accorded to the dead and that the graves can be visited by them…

He invited Mulcahy to communicate directly with these relatives if he so wished, and wanted to know if Mulcahy and the Government would facilitate removal to Britain if the relatives so desired.[17]

Mulcahy duly instituted enquiries. In the case of Private Williams at Bunratty, a search was conducted by troops of the National Army. They spent several days excavating the muddy bank of the Bunratty River, in what proved to be a futile attempt to locate the Chester man's remains. Although the likely spot was pointed out by the local man who had buried him, the Army officers and medical doctor who attended the scene concluded that the remains had simply sunk too deep for recovery from the marshy ground.[18] When the War Office had received news of the likely location of his remains, it contacted the IWGC in August 1925: it wished to ascertain if, in view of the fact that he had been killed before 31 August 1921, the IWGC would be prepared 'to undertake the expense and the necessary arrangements for the exhumation and reburial, should the relatives desire this to be done'. Sadly for his relatives, the IWGC replied that

in ordinary circumstances the Commission would be prepared to undertake the expense concerning arrangements for exhumation and reburial in a suitable cemetery; as, however, the question of war graves is under discussion between the Undersecretary of State, Dominions Office, and the Free State Government, and pending a decision, the IWGC has no power to take any action or to incur any expenditure.[19]

Over twelve years later, the IWGC, through the OPW, commemorated Williams by way of a memorial in Bunratty Old Graveyard. It is one of the very few Kipling Memorials in the country, commemorating those whose grave location is not known, and so-called after Kipling's suggestion that the stones for such graves bear the inscription, from Ecclesiasticus 44.13, 'Their Glory Shall Not Be Blotted Out'.

While Mulcahy's enquiries were progressing, the hapless Carson wrote to the War Office in some distress, in August 1923, two years after he had himself discovered his son's body near Bandon:

Now, Sir, if I, a poor working man, was able to have this done, surely the great British Government could have arranged [it]. I wish to point out that only for the great sympathy and assistance the Civic Guards at Bandon gave me I would have failed badly… What I wrote to you now is to ask, now that you know definitely where they [sic] poor remains are, are you going to leave them in practically in a pauper cemetery [sic]. These poor boys were murdered simply because they were serving in the British Forces.

Now, Sir, are you going to do anything in the matter. Please don't write to tell the poor boy's mother and myself that the matter will receive attention and then forget about it as is often the official manner, I have served twenty three and a half years, all colour service in the British Army, with nearly half of it foreign. Another son has served through the whole War in the British Royal Navy. Another son through the War and is still serving in the same service.
Yours respectfully,
R. Carson

[P.S.] *PLEASE WHAT WILL YOU DO. REMEMBER THE DIED SOLDIERS.*

Carson's plea was not ignored. On 10 September 1923 the Colonial Office formally requested the Free State to exhume the bodies of the Manchester Band Boys and to move them to a more suitable cemetery.[20] Around the same time, G. G. Whiskard of the Colonial Office and Rowlands of the War Office met to discuss the whole issue of 'the disposal of the remains of murdered soldiers' further. They agreed that the

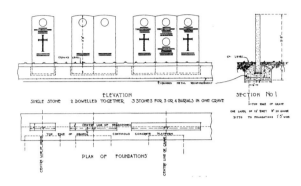

HEADSTONES, 1 INCH DETAILS OF FOUNDATIONS

SINGLE STONE   2 DOWELLED TOGETHER   3 STONES FOR 3 OR 4 BURIALS IN ONE GRAVE

ELEVATION

SECTION No.1

PLAN OF FOUNDATIONS

War Office would now formally request that the Band Boys' remains be again exhumed and be brought to Dublin, under Civic Guard supervision, for interment in Grangegorman Military Cemetery. Here, it was proposed, a service would be conducted for them by the chaplain attached to the Royal Hospital, Kilmainham, all expenses to be met by the War Office.[21]

Meanwhile, on 12 October 1923, Mulcahy reported back to Loughnane the results of his enquiries into the burial locations and their attendant circumstances. He was unable to shed any light on whether or not Christian burials had been effected, except in the case of the Manchester Regiment Band Boys. He made clear that 'every facility will be afforded any relatives of the deceased who wish to visit the burial places', and that should any relatives wish to have any of the buried removed to England or re-interred 'in existing military cemeteries in Ireland', every possible facility would be provided for transport to cemetery or port of embarkation. In addition, unless the relatives indicated to the contrary, 'full military honours will be tendered...by Free State National Forces'.[22] He was still unable to locate the exact burial places of the three intelligence officers and their driver killed at Macroom, nor that of Cecil Guthrie killed near Kilmichael,

nor that of Private Williams, nor of eight other officers and men.

In reporting this to the Colonial Office, Loughnane referred to the Guthrie case: Guthrie's father had been pressing him, and simultaneously the Colonial Office, for over a year, and he was anxious to assure the dead officer's father that the Irish Free State military authorities

have in fact done their best to find his son's grave. Unless he [Guthrie] gets some assurance, he may perhaps think that they have not made a serious effort, and, as I have been in correspondence with him nearly a year, I feel a personal obligation to assure him that everything possible has been done.[23]

Loughnane's proposal to write personally to Guthrie's father was especially welcome to the Colonial Office whose official, Freeston, believed that 'no doubt a further letter from yourself will do much to turn the edge of his wrath'.[24] In the event, three years later, on 26 November 1926, Guthrie's remains were unearthed and removed for reinterment to Inchageela old graveyard.[25]

As for the remains of the Macroom officers and private whose whereabouts in October 1923 still eluded Mulcahy, within two months they had been located, on the land of a small farmer. He claimed, or so it was reported,

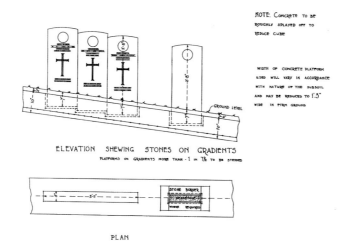

NOTE: Concrete to be roughly splayed off to reduce cube

WIDTH OF CONCRETE PLATFORM USED WILL VARY IN ACCORDANCE WITH NATURE OF THE SUBSOIL AND MAY BE REDUCED TO 1'.3" WIDE IN FIRM GROUND

GROUND LEVEL

ELEVATION SHEWING STONES ON GRADIENTS

PLATFORMS ON GRADIENTS MORE THAN 1 IN 7½ TO BE STEPPED

STONE BORDER

PLAN

that he had been forced, by local anti-Treatyites, to accommodate the remains there, because he had taken the pro-Treaty side in the ensuing Civil War.[26] They were exhumed on 11 December 1923, the physician father of Lieutenant Dove being the only relative of the four men present. He recognised his son from a tobacco pipe found in one of his pockets. The recovered bodies were taken to Cork, escorted by Free State troops, accompanied by Dr and Mrs Dove. As the men were casualties who lost their lives while the Truce was in force, the entire expense of the operation was borne by the Free State; they were buried at Aldershot on 14 December 1923.[27] A large detachment of troops, with military band, awaited their arrival and embarkation, to the sound of the Last Post, on board the *Moorfowl,* taking them on their last journey to Aldershot via Fishguard.

In regard to the willingness of the Free State authorities to accommodate the wishes of the Band Boys' relatives, Mark Sturgis, who had served in the last days of the Dublin Castle administration, was able to convey the Free State's assurance to the War Office 'that the wishes of the parents will be scrupulously observed', and Sturgis wanted to know if General Mulcahy's offer 'to accord full military honours by the Free State National Forces' should be accepted.[28]

At the same time, the War Office now wanted to involve the Imperial War Graves Commission. On 19 October 1923 Cubitt wrote to Browne about 'giving a decent burial to the three band boys of the Manchester Regiment who were killed by Sinn Féiners in June 1921'. As they perished before 31 August 1921, cut-off date for the World War, he suggested that 'the question of their graves was technically one for your Commission'. He insisted that the War Office had 'no desire to trespass on your territory', but, 'as you have not yet got going in Southern Ireland, it was best that we should carry through this particular case'. The War Graves Commission had no objection and, indeed, were 'very glad you are doing so'.[29]

It seems that the War Office had decided that they were to be buried in Grangegorman Military Cemetery, as, on 20 October 1923, it requested the Colonial Office to make such arrangements with the Free State Government.[30] It would appear, however, that the relatives wanted the remains repatriated, and their wish in this regard prevailed, after further delays. On Thursday 4 September 1924, almost one year later, the Band Boys' bodies were again exhumed. They were taken in covered trucks to Cork the next day. Here, as the local press recorded, 'an impressive military funeral was witnessed in the city', as an escort of Free State troops handed over the remains to Colonel Heywood, the British Officer Commanding the South Irish Coast Defences. [31]As they were brought aboard the *Moorfowl,* a detachment of Irish soldiers, lined up opposite Penrose Quay, presented arms and the coffins were brought on board to the sound of the Last Post.[32] On arrival in England, they were brought to Ashton-under-Lyne (Hurst) Cemetery where they are commemorated by standard war grave headstones to this day.[33]

All of this was in contrast to family requests for the exhumation and reburial of Irish Volunteers executed by British Forces. Of thirty-nine Volunteers executed by the British between 1916 and July 1921, thirteen had been put to death in Cork Military Detention Barracks and then transferred to Cork Jail where they were buried, uncoffined, over the period February to May 1921.[34] The jail governor had not been told who they were at the time of these executions and burials and he had gathered the information together from daily newspaper reports. He had no objection to the exhumation and reburials, but when the relatives' request came to the Department of Justice, the Minister, Kevin O'Higgins, advised his Cabinet colleagues that, in view of the

lapse of time and the impossibility of distinguishing some of the remains from others, he felt it would be 'unseemly to disturb the remains' and that Government should advise the relatives accordingly.[35] There they remain to this day, commemorated by a memorial unveiled by deValera in July 1948.[36]

Ambiguities:
When it came to death and burial in the First World War, central to British Army practice and to the principles of the Imperial War Graves Commission was the prohibition of exhumation and repatriation of remains. Nevertheless, when it came to the conflict in Ireland, from Easter 1916 to the Truce in July 1921 and beyond, significant exceptions appear to have been made, at least to the outsider at this remove. This exceptionalism embodies the conflicting views and understanding of that conflict as entertained by the opposing sides. Whereas for the militant nationalists, the Anglo-Irish conflict was a war of self-determination and a war against Empire, for the British political and military establishments it was in effect a civil war, a murder campaign by terrorists and a war against traitors.

While such polarities existed, they were not just between these opposing persuasions, but within the British camp

itself, between the War Office and the IWGC, and within the IWGC itself. Was the Anglo-Irish conflict a part of, an extension of, the First World War? If so, the IWGC could deem the British Forces' fallen in Ireland, at least up to 31 August 1921, to have merited commemoration by standard war grave cross and headstone. If it were a different kind of conflict, parallel to, but separate from the First World War, why should the dead of this conflict be remembered with war grave headstones? As seen in the previous chapter, and as shall emerge more clearly in the next, the issue caused perplexity and hesitation within the IWGC itself.

This was hardly surprising: as is clear from several quite recent historical accounts, notably from those by Charles Townshend and Peter Cottrell,[37] there was a reluctance to admit that it was a war at all. In the end, when it came to the conflict in Ireland, the IWGC had to defy its own rules by accepting repatriation: at the same time, for those of them who had died before 31 August 1921, it provided standard war grave headstones.

RIGHT
The Leinster Regiment Memorial, Birr Military Cemetery, Crinkill, Co. Offaly

We boast our splendid heritage
in the old fighting race
Yet, have we marked the cry the comes
from each dead soldier's place

Stephen Gwynn
The Irish Brigade
1914

Chapter 5

Approaching The Free State, 1923-1924

In the bitter aftermath of the Anglo-Irish conflict and Civil War there was reluctance on the part of elements of the British establishment to press the general question of the future of its war graves in Ireland. Unfolding events were to disclose divisions within that establishment, and even divisions within the divisions. Chief among the interested parties were the Colonial Office, soon to become the Dominions Office, the War Office, the Treasury and the Imperial War Graves Commission. At its simplest, the War Office and Colonial Office wanted immediate action, while the Treasury and the Commission were more circumspect. Even within the Commission itself, as will further emerge, there were hesitations and divided opinions.

Even as the Civil War spluttered to an end in May 1923, the Treasury thought it untimely to approach the Free State about the care of the graves of the recent British dead. Nevertheless, in a fairly direct response, Devonshire, in early June, proposed to invite the Free State Government to consider a proposal that they should accept responsibility for the old pre-war military cemeteries, to be maintained by the Board of Works in Dublin. However, of the alternatives whether the Free State should pay or be paid for the maintenance costs of the 1914-1921 graves, he was firmly

of the view that 'an arrangement for repayment by His Majesty's Government of the expenses incurred need alone be considered'.[1] Waterfield replied for the Treasury three days later. He wanted to press the Colonial Office further 'on the question of asking the Free State to undertake this work free of charge… before we concur with your view that this alternative should be ruled out from the start in favour of a repayment arrangement.'[2] What they had in mind were the graves of 1914-1921; as far as pre-war graves were concerned, they held the view that the Free State should maintain these at its own expense.[3] As far as the Treasury was concerned, since the Free State Government has claimed that 'the whole of the military property in lands and buildings in the Free State has passed into their possession under Article 11 of the Constitution', no concession should be made on the cost of war graves maintenance, at least until the ultimate financial settlement between the two states has been concluded.[4]

This was in June 1923. In the meantime, impatient for action, the War Office pressed the IWGC to appoint representatives to a conference on the subject.[5] However, even before this was mooted, the IWGC approached the Colonial Secretary directly, on 15 June 1923, concerning 'the graves of officers and men in Southern Ireland who died during the war and which may come within the powers of the IWGC'. On behalf of the Commission, Browne explained that

up to the present the Commission have not even considered that they could usefully take any steps to arrange for the proper registration and marking of these graves, but in view of the somewhat improved conditions now existing in that country I am to enquire if, in the opinion of the Duke of Devonshire, the Free State Government might be approached with a view to assisting in the matter.[6]

If the Colonial Secretary agreed, Browne suggested, as a first, tentative step, that the Free State be asked 'whether they would be prepared to correct and complete lists of graves which would be furnished to them' by the Commission and to add any others which the Free State might discover.

At the conference between the War Office and the IWGC held on 9 July 1923, it was agreed that the Commission should be asked to take 'complete control' of the whole issue, on an agency basis, until 'the Free State was prepared to decide whether or not it would accept the transfer' of responsibility'.[7] It was at this stage that the Colonial Office made a semi-official approach to the Free State Government. On 23 July 1923 Lionel Curtis wrote personally to Loughnane,

the senior official in the office of the Governor-General, with a radical suggestion that the Free State itself might institute a permanent commission to manage all military graves in Ireland.[8] In light of the subsequent chequered history of all war graves and memorials in this State, Irish, British Commonwealth and international, it might have proved an inspired proposal: given its origin and timing, fate destined otherwise.

Uncertainties, confusions:
What Loughnane's response was is not evident but, ironically, the matter was now becoming one of practical concern within the Free State Government itself. In March 1923 the Commissioners of Public Works entered the arena with a practical problem. Included in the property they took over from the War Office in 1922 was Grangegorman Military Cemetery, and, while they had taken it over, the OPW was unclear if 'it has been definitely decided that the responsibility for its management and control rests with the Irish Government'. The resident caretaker needed to be paid and a further two labourers were required to help maintain the grounds in place of the six soldiers whom the British War Office had assigned originally for its upkeep. Were it the case that 'the maintenance of the cemetery is a British

liability', the OPW Commissioners 'would be glad to know whether there is any objection to our communicating with the British War Department with a view to our undertaking the care of the Ground as an agency service'.[9] The reply they received was eminently unhelpful: responding on 21 March, C. N. Ryan of Finance confessed

I am not quite clear as to the present position… this Cemetery would appear to be in the same position as, say, a British Cemetery in France or Gallipoli, and, if so, your proposal to act as Agents for the War Office would, I think, meet with no objection from here.[10]

None the wiser, the OPW, in May 1923, again asked for clarification. Having consulted Defence and Local Government, each of whom separately thought it must be a charge on Free State funds, Finance then approached the British Treasury for a view.[11] On the Treasury's behalf, Waterfield's reply, though polite, did not advance the matter:

The question of the future maintenance and use of Military Cemeteries in the Free State area is now being considered on our side in general terms, and I suggest that the application of any general principles that may be agreed upon, to this particular cemetery, be deferred for the present.[12]

This was no consolation whatever to ex-British serviceman James Boyd of Boyle, Co Roscommon. On 18 June 1923 he contacted the Dominions Office to express his concern for the care of Asylinn Cemetery and begged to be appointed its caretaker since he was already looking after a few of the war graves there for people of the town. There were, at the time, at least five Great War dead buried in Asylinn, at least four of them from Boyle itself. Three of them were Connaught Rangers and all of them were young, being between seventeen and thirty-one years of age at the time of their deaths. Six years later, Boyd was still writing to deplore the 'very bad condition' of the graves there.[13]

The matter now went into a very long period of inaction. In late August 1923 Waterfield of the Treasury contacted Whiskard at the Colonial Office in some exasperation, commenting that

As you know, we have not even succeeded in getting a reply from the Free State to our proposal that they should assume all liability for current expenses in respect of War Department property transferred to them as of 1 October 1922.

Rather optimistically, however, he added that 'there seems no reason to suppose that they will object to giving such an undertaking', and, if so, he wanted to

BELOW
OPW 1930's drawing,
template for Queen Mary's
Army Auxiliary Corps.
Cap Badge

know if the Colonial Office still held the view that the Free State 'should not be asked to undertake the work of maintenance of cemeteries free of charge to the Imperial Government'. He insisted that the Treasury's opposing view that the Free State should pay

is only a reasonable suggestion and it seems quite unnecessary to rule it out from the start by inviting them to act only as our Agents on payment terms.[14]

Two weeks later, the Colonial Office followed up Curtis's overtures of late July, when Whiskard contacted Loughnane on 12 September 1923. Explaining that there had been 'considerable correspondence' with the Treasury, War Office and IWGC about the graves of British soldiers 'who died in Ireland before and during the Anglo-Irish struggle of recent years', matters had at last reached a point when, on the British side, 'we are ready with concrete proposals…to put before the Free State Government', but, on lines quite different from those suggested by Curtis. The Colonial Office wanted to know if Curtis's idea of a permanent Free State commission had been 'definitely ruled out of court' so that they could bring forward their own proposals.[15] Loughnane responded a week later. He explained that, on receiving Curtis's July letter, he contacted the Minister for

Defence, General Mulcahy, and followed it up with several conversations on the matter with the Minister. The latter promised to give the Curtis proposal very careful consideration, asked for a list of all the military cemeteries, and for information as to how they had been maintained in the past. Once this information would have been supplied, Loughnane promised 'to press for an early decision, which I do not doubt will be favourable'.[16]

Even as Curtis had been privately in touch with Loughnane, so likewise Cubitt of the War Office had been in private correspondence with Sir Philip Hanson, Chairman of the Commissioners of Public Works in Dublin. Informally, Hanson had advised Cubitt of the OPW's readiness to assume responsibility for keeping the cemeteries in good order,

the cost to be refunded from British funds and the arrangement [to be] regarded as merely temporary pending the settlement of a definite scheme.

It is not clear if Hanson consulted his fellow Commissioners or the Government in making this offer.[17] If this indicated some movement on the Irish side, however informal, there was also development in London. At the Colonial Office, Freeston was able to advise that

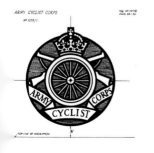

the IWGC were now willing 'to accept custody of all British Military Graves in the Free State, irrespective of date' so long as the Dominion Governments consented to the appropriate legal extension to the IWGC's terms of reference. There was no reference to the likely reaction or position of the Irish Free State in this regard. Freeston now optimistically assured Whiskard that 'the War Graves Commission… is moving in the matter, and it is hoped that in the course of a few months they will be ready and able to take over the Irish Cemeteries'. Time and events would tell a different tale.

In spite of Freeston's September optimism that the Imperial War Graves Commission were now 'willing to accept custody of all British Military Graves in the Free State, irrespective of date', the Army Council in October entertained a different view. It drafted a letter to the Treasury saying that they had

now been informed by the IWGC that they were at present unable to assume responsibility for the non-war graves, even on a repayment basis, and that, while the Commission are seeking an extension of powers, a decision on that point is not possible for a considerable time.[18]

Consequently, it was extremely important that the military cemeteries (which, they incorrectly informed the Treasury, came to eight in number) should not be allowed in the meantime to 'fall into a state of neglect and disrepair'. The Army Council understood that the attitude of the Free State Government was 'sympathetic', and the Council, therefore, now reverted to their original suggestion of 2 March 1923 that 'the Irish Free State should be asked to allow their Office of Public Works to carry out the service of caring for and maintaining these graves'. In support of this request they commented that the IWGC 'have indicated their concurrence on the proposal', and added that, if repayment became the basis of an arrangement with the Free State, then the cost would be shared between the War Office and the IWGC 'in proportion that the number of war graves in each cemetery bears to the number of other military graves'. They wanted the Treasury to approve these proposals so that the Army Council could now ask the Colonial Secretary 'to approach the Irish Free State Government with a definite proposal'.

Extending the Charter - empowering the Commission:

Sooner perhaps than the War Office or Army Council could have hoped, the IWGC secured, on 6 November, a Supplemental Charter, as a result of a resolution by the Imperial Conference

then meeting in London. By Order in Council it came into operation on 19 December 1923. Significantly, it permitted the IWGC to take responsibility for military graves outside of the official dates of the Great War, if requested to do so by any government in the Empire. In advance of this development, on 13 December 1923, Whiskard attended a conference with the leading personnel of the IWGC, its vice chairman, Fabian Ware, its principal assistant secretary, Arthur Browne, and its head of finance, Sir Herbert Ellissen. Reporting on this conference, and on the implications of the Supplemental Charter, Whiskard now concluded:

It is open to us, therefore, to ask the Commission to undertake the care and maintenance of all military graves in Ireland, some of which date back more than 100 years; and, so far as Sir Fabian Ware is concerned, he would be very glad to accept such a request.[19]

Fabian Ware anticipated, however, that some members of the Commission who 'have strong Irish prejudices' might raise objections. The New Zealand member of the IWGC, Sir James Allen, would cause difficulties. He held strong opinions on Irish matters and, in Ware's view, would 'certainly oppose the undertaking by the Commission of any work in Ireland'. Allen, an arch-imperialist and conscriptionist who lost his youngest son at Gallipoli in August 1915,[20] could not see why the Empire, as a whole, should pay for matters arising from a conflict in which the Empire, as such, was not concerned. Furthermore, carrying matters to an extreme, and in the light of the powers conferred by the Supplemental Charter, Allen was afraid that the Commission might be requested by the Free State Government to undertake 'the care and maintenance of IRA graves in exactly the same way as it is part of its duty to look after German graves in this country and in the Dominions'.

Whiskard regarded Ware's fear of Dominion members' objection as exaggerated and thought the antidote to such a fear lay in Britain, not the Empire, paying for the maintenance of war graves in the Irish Free State. With this assurance Ware then suggested that the Colonial Office write to the IWGC

in as strong terms as possible, simply asking them to take over the construction and maintenance of all soldiers' graves in Ireland and stating that… the British Government would be prepared to bear the cost of maintaining all such graves.

Entertaining an option – Free State membership:

Whiskard had to restrain Ware's enthusiasm, pointing out that the concurrence of the Government of the Irish Free State had first to be secured. They agreed immediately, however, to preparation of a draft text to be despatched to Dublin once approved by the various interests in Britain. Their discussion then turned to their belief, ill-founded as it transpired, that on receipt of such a despatch, the Irish Government would request representation on the War Graves Commission. They entertained this belief on the basis of a debate in Dáil Éireann in November 1923. Whether this debate had been engineered by Major Bryan Cooper in association with certain interests in Britain such as the British Legion, or in Ireland, such as General Sir William Hickie, is not clear, but Cooper put down a question in Dáil Éireann on 21 November 1923: he asked, 'in view of the fact that nearly 50,000 Irishmen were killed in the European War', if the Minister for External Affairs would make representations to the British Government for Irish Free State membership of the Imperial War Graves Commission. FitzGerald, as Minister, replied that the matter was under consideration 'and it is hoped that a final decision will soon be reached'.[21]

Indeed, even as Whiskard was conferring with the IWGC in the latter's London offices, Hynes, a representative of the Irish High Commission in London, actually called in to solicit information on the structure and finances of IWGC membership. He was met by Arthur Browne and, according to the latter, actually gave Browne to understand that in his, Hynes's, opinion, the Irish Free State would join the IWGC and that Mr McNeill, the High Commissioner 'would himself sit'.[22]

Ware and Whiskard were agreed that if the Free State sought membership 'it was neither desirable nor possible to do otherwise than agree', so long as the Free State accepted the 'properly ascertained share of the expenses', which was based on the number of dead belonging to the various Dominions. On the figures mentioned by Cooper in the Oireachtas, the 50,000 would constitute an annual charge of £70,000 out of the IWGC's total annual expenses of £1,000,000 plus. On the basis of the IWGC expenses for the year 1921-1922, amounting to £1,258,139, this would have placed the Irish Free State fourth in a list of nine contributing states, behind the United Kingdom at £1,000,000, Canada at £90,000 and Australia at £80,000, and way ahead of New Zealand which was next at £25,000.[23]

RIGHT
Asylinn Cemetery,
Co. Roscommon.

Whiskard duly had the despatch drafted and copied it to the IWGC, War Office and Treasury for comments.[24] In his letter to the Treasury, he repeated the Colonial Office fears, as against the Treasury's hopes, of the Irish Government's paying up:

I feel sure and I think you will agree that the time has not yet come, and probably will not come for some years, when we can ask the Irish Government themselves to undertake the care and maintenance of British military graves in Ireland.

But, revealingly, his fear was not based on Irish feelings about the British, but rather, the other way round:

I do not doubt that the Irish Government would accept this proposal, but it would, I think, in present circumstances, seriously affront opinion in this country.

He therefore hoped that the Treasury 'will not raise any objection to the proposal which we now desire to make' and requested a speedy response. In a similar letter to the War Office, he concluded:

I think you will probably agree that the time has now come when this matter might be dealt with directly between the War Graves Commission, ourselves and the Free State.[25]

Drafting divisions:
The draft despatch, returned by Ware to the Colonial Office on 19 December 1923 with minor amendments, was a model of brevity and a monument of insensitivity. It informed the Free State that the British Government had been considering the future care and maintenance of the graves of British Naval, Military and Air Force personnel in the Free State. It confessed to being unclear as to the exact numbers: it estimated the number of burials, between the start of the Great War in 1914 and the British evacuation of the Free State in 1922, as exceeding 2,000 and that the number dating from before 4 August 1914 might be in the region of 7,000 to 8,000. It explained how the IWGC had now received an extension to its Charter,

permitting it, if it so desires, and not otherwise, to provide for the construction and maintenance of British military graves other than those of men killed in the European War, and His Majesty's Government proposes therefore to approach the Commission with a view to the taking over the custody and maintenance of all such Graves within the area of the Free State.[26]

Ware got them to drop the word 'custody' since it could be taken to imply that the Commission would be responsible 'for the protection and policing of cemeteries'. The draft continued:

Should your Ministers concur in this proposal and should the Commission accept the invitation addressed to them… they would send over an inspector or inspectors who would be introduced to… the Ministry of Defence of the Irish Free State in the hope that the Ministry would be able to offer them assistance, and, if necessary, protection in the carrying out of their duties.

The draft concluded by hoping for an early reply as the next meeting of the IWGC was scheduled for January 1924. In the last days of December 1923 Whiskard thanked Ware for his amendments, which the Colonial Office adopted, and told him he was still awaiting the reactions of the War Office and the Treasury. In addition, however, he was now having to consult the Admiralty and bring them into the circle as the Admiralty had gone on a solo run: it had entered into an agreement of its own with the Cobh (Queenstown) Urban District Council for the maintenance of naval graves there, at a cost of £7 per annum.[27]

When the Treasury first drafted its own response to the Colonial Office, on the last day of 1923, it proved very unhelpful to the Colonial Office's position. The Treasury Lords were unable to accept the Colonial Secretary's view that it was not practicable 'to consider any arrangement by which the financial responsibility for the cost of maintenance of these graves should be thrown upon the Free State Government'. The Treasury went on to distinguish the three categories of i) pre-war graves, ii) war graves, and iii) post-war graves. As to the pre-war graves, in accordance with the general principle of the transfer of War Department property in 'Southern Ireland' to the Government of the Free State, and likewise in accordance with the practice in the other Dominions, the responsibility lay with the Free State Government, at the expense of Irish funds, even if that Government preferred the IWGC to do the work.

In regard to post-war graves, the Treasury agreed that it would be 'undesirable' that the Irish Government should be asked to take up the care and maintenance of the graves of men who died 'in Southern Ireland during the recent disorders': in these circumstances the Treasury thought it best that the British Government should invite the IWGC to undertake this part of the work 'at the expense of Imperial Funds'.

As for the war graves proper, the Treasury agreed with the Colonial Office that these should be entrusted to the IWGC, 'subject, however, to the appropriate contribution to the

BELOW
Enlisting the Irish:
1914 War Recruitment
Poster

expenses of the Commission being made by the Irish Free State as by every Dominion', and that the Free State, 'if they wish', should be represented on the Commission. Such membership, it added, however, would probably necessitate yet another Supplemental Charter.[28]

While this draft was in preparation by the Treasury, Whiskard on 14 January pressed Waterfield for a response to the Colonial Office Draft Despatch, as 'we have not even approached the Free State Government on the subject, pending an intimation from you that the Treasury see no objection to the scheme'.[29] It must have been with some dismay, therefore,

when the Treasury's draft reply was sent out, unchanged, to Whiskard by Otto Niemeyer on 21 January 1924. It certainly infuriated Arthur Browne of the Commission. In a letter of the same day, to the IWGC's legal advisor, he commented:

I think we should have protested against the Treasury attitude… the only thing we can ask the Free State Government to pay for is 'German-killed' officers and men. The Treasury apparently contemplates the Free State helping to pay for British soldiers killed, for instance, in the 1916 Rebellion. The Free State will no doubt agree to this if we will put up Headstones to those members of the Free State Forces who fought against us in that Rebellion.[30]

RIGHT
Entrance Arch,
Curragh Military Cemetery,
Co. Kildare.

If ye break faith with us who die
We shall not sleep, though poppies grow
in Flanders fields.

John McCrae, MD, Canadian Army Medical Corps
28 January 1918

In Flanders Fields, Punch, December 1915.

Chapter 6

Offer And Counter-Offer, 1924-1926

January 1924 saw a new Government, the Labour Party's first, in power in Britain, and a new Colonial Secretary in office in the person of J. H. Thomas. On 26 January, doubtless in preparation for a despatch on war graves whenever it would be agreed in London, he sent to the Governor- General a copy of the IWGC's Supplemental Charter of 19 December 1923, its earlier Supplemental Charter of 10 August 1921, and the original Charter of 10 May 1917, in addition to the IWGC annual reports from 1919 to 1921[1]. He followed this on 21 February by sending the final version of the Colonial Office text, as Despatch No 115, to the Free State. It substantially replicated the original draft, with one departure: that, in the case of 'post-war' graves, the cost would be met, not as the Treasury wanted, out of imperial funds, but rather as the Colonial Office proposed, out of British funds. He looked forward to hearing 'at the earliest convenient date an expression of your Minister's attitude to the above proposals'.

That earliest convenient date took a long time in coming. The Department of External Affairs had plenty of advance warning as to the contents of this Despatch. As early as the day before Thomas had sent the IWGC Charters to Dublin in January, it had already sent an advisory memorandum to the

Secretary of the Executive Council for the latter's consideration. The central point of this memorandum was whether the Free State should or should not nominate a representative to the IWGC. In putting that point it advised that the Irish Government's share 'would be at least equal to Canada's, at £75,000 in 1920-1921'[2]. External Affairs' request that the subject of this memo be brought to Cabinet 'at an early date' was partly realised: it appeared on the Agenda of the Cabinet meetings of 9 February and 26 February 1924, but, on each occasion, its consideration was postponed.[3] As if to prompt the Free State, on 10 March Thomas, in reference to his Despatch No 115, sent the Governor-General, Tim Healy, copies of the *Fourth Annual Report of the Imperial War Graves Commission, 1922-23.*[4]

Time passed: on 24 April 1924 External Affairs reminded the Government Secretary of the need for a response, only to be curtly told that 'it rests with your Minister to have the matter brought up again and to ensure that a decision is duly given'.[5] Ten days later, External Affairs again inquired as to the status of the memorandum, and reminded the Government that the Colonial Office proposal to entrust the care of the war graves to the IWGC implied Free State participation in the general expenses of the Commission and not just in the

expenditure involved in war graves in Free State territory.

A Free State offering:

External Affairs now made a very radical and simple suggestion which, ironically, embraced the unthinkable first mooted sarcastically by the Commission's exasperated Arthur Browne:

As a compromise it is suggested that we should reply that while it would not be possible for the Saorstát to accept the financial responsibility of membership of the Commission, the Government would take over the entire charge of all British Graves whatsoever in the Saorstát.[6]

The Cabinet considered the External Affairs proposal, as an alternative to that of the Colonial Office, on 8 May 1924 and decided to refer it to the Minister for Finance, Ernest Blythe, for a report.[7] It was a report which took a long time in coming.

The delay on the Irish side was understandable: the Government, for one thing, was caught up in the 'Army Mutiny' over the months from March to October 1924; for another, during that same period, its relations with Britain were more concerned with the living than the dead, insofar as the Government was preoccupied with the Boundary Question. Such considerations notwithstanding, Cosgrave was exercised in general about the absence of address: he berated the Government's legal officer, Kennedy, at this time, over important despatches 'lying unanswered in your office for over a year', noting to him that, in one case, seventeen reminders had been sent, and ended his reprimand by attaching a schedule of despatches from the Colonial Office which had been 'unduly delayed'.[8] The various delays on both sides did not help the situation. On the very day, 5 May 1924, that External Affairs reminded McDunphy, Secretary of the Executive Council, of the need for a response to the Colonial Office, the secretary of the Fermoy Branch of the Legion of Irish Ex-Servicemen, L. J. Phelan, wrote to the Secretary of State for War to complain about the 'very shocking condition' of Fermoy Military Cemetery, and since

there is no one looking after same, the Legion would appoint the ex-caretaker, Michael Quin, to look after the place if the [British] Government would allow a small remuneration.

Cubitt of the War Office deflected Phelan's query on 20 May by saying the matter was receiving attention but that it was involved 'in the general question of the future maintenance and upkeep of all military cemeteries in Southern Ireland which is now under discussion'[9].

Nevertheless, the Colonial Secretary who, on 14 May, had requested a reply to his Despatch of 21 February, was able to use Phelan's letter, a week later, to exert further pressure on the Irish Government: he requested the Governor-General to place the Legion's Fermoy correspondence before the Irish Ministers[10].

By late June Finance had considered the External Affairs' advice, and on 24 June advised the Cabinet that full membership of the IWGC would involve unacceptable expenses. It therefore recommended the adoption of External Affairs' radical alternative. Four days later, on 28 June, the Cabinet accepted this proposal[11]. A week after this, Healy finally responded to Thomas's Despatches, expressing his Ministers' regrets that they could not accept 'the financial responsibility which membership of the Commission involves', but that 'they were willing to take over the entire care and maintenance of all British graves whatsoever in the Irish Free State', and looked forward to the British Government's reception of this proposal.[12] It is profoundly ironic that even as the Government decided to take upon itself the entire care and maintenance of all British Forces' war graves in the State, the very next item on its agenda at that Cabinet meeting was to consider a request from the widow of Arthur Griffith to have his grave removed from the Army Plot and reburied in the family plot, in her exasperation at the perceived Government neglect of his grave.[13]

Compounding confusions:
The immediate reaction on the British side is not evident. Strangely, the entire matter appears to have disappeared from the agenda of the Colonial Office, War Office and War Graves Commission for over three months.

At the beginning of September, the Colonial Office revisited the matter, writing directly to Ware concerning Healy's Despatch and inviting Ware to offer his personal views on the Irish Government's offer before Whiskard would formally refer it to the Service Departments[14]. What may have been Ware's response is not clear but, in October 1924, Whiskard met him in conference with Browne and Ellissen of the Commission, on the subject of Healy's despatch of 7 July. The detailed record of these conversations reveals a considerable extent of complexity and confusion between the British and Irish Governments on the one hand, and, within the British side, between the Colonial Office and the Commission on the other. Such was the complexity that

Ware, at one point, 'only wished that some clause had been inserted in the Treaty so that the question of war graves in Ireland could have been dealt with under that Treaty'.[15]

Central to that confusion were issues of definition. What were Irish war graves? Were they the graves of Irishmen who fought for the British and died and were buried outside and inside Ireland, before, during and after the 1914-1918 War? Alternatively, were they war graves of British and British Commonwealth soldiers in Irish Free State territory? What was involved in care and maintenance? Did it mean the mere cleaning of what was already in situ, or did it also involve the construction of a grave and/or the erection of headstones as well as the cleaning of existing ones?

Referring to the original Treasury letter to the Irish Free State which had caused his assistant, Arthur Browne, such agitation, Ware wondered if Dublin may have misunderstood it:

that the Free State may have thought that they were being asked to participate in the expenses of the Commission in respect of Irish war graves, which might be taken as referring to the graves of the Irish regiments. If the Free State Government were agreeing to bear the costs of the graves of the Irish regiments in Ireland, why should they not bear the costs of Irish graves all over the world?

He added, later, that

If the Irish Government came in and were asked what their contribution would be in proportion to the number of dead of their Dominion in the war, the answer would be 'none'.

He then asked:

whether they were part of the Empire in the Commission or a friendly country outside, such as France and Belgium? The Commission had declined the offer of these countries to look after British graves.

In response, Whiskard referred to his own Colonial Secretary's Despatch and said that there were two possibilities they had meant to express: 'he was not sure whether they had been expressed clearly'; they were either a) that the Free State should become a full member of the IWGC and 'should pay its proper share for the maintenance of graves all over the world', or b) matters should remain as they are but that the Free State should pay the costs of simply maintaining existing war graves in the Free State, 'whether these graves were Irish or not'. Ware, thinking out loud, then wondered:

Could it possibly be said that the graves of Irish regiments in Belgium were the graves of the dead of the Free State?

Partly answering his own question, he remarked that 'Canadian regiments contained many British soldiers but that they were included for the purposes of the Commission contribution as Canadians'. He then suggested that they should get back to the Irish authorities and put it to them that the Colonial Office would be prepared to recommend that the Irish should be admitted 'on a totally different basis'; that the British Government should continue to regard the graves of Irishmen [outside Ireland]as those of her soldiers and should continue to pay for them, and that the only financial expenditure likely to them was for graves in Ireland.

Cutting through all the complexity, Whiskard thought they should 'accept the Free State offer, even with the complication that it placed them in the position of foreign countries'. At this point Ellissen interjected that, although political difficulties prevented the IWGC carrying out their duties in respect of the graves in Ireland, 'they were obliged to look after them when it was possible and that was an obligation which could not be delegated'. In the end they all agreed that no progress could be made without discussion with the High Commissioner. With his characteristic zeal, Ware wanted to send an inspector to the Free State immediately, to look after the graves while these discussions were being arranged, but Whiskard ruled this out.[16]

Searching for clarity:

The day after this conference, Whiskard contacted Waterfield at the Treasury to inform him of his intention to seek discussions and clarifications with the Free State's High Commissioner, on three points.

Firstly, that while the IWGC was legally obliged to mark by headstone and to maintain the war graves 'unless the Free State wished to do so', but it was not clear from its 7 July Despatch whether the Free State was willing to erect headstones as well as to maintain the graves.

Secondly, the Colonial Office thought the Free State misunderstood what full membership of the IWGC would cost, namely, that the total number of the graves of Irish dead would cost it £80,000 to £90,000 a year to mark and maintain. Whiskard was confident that the British Government 'would not think it reasonable for the Irish Free State to be expected to take on such a charge': on the contrary, that if the Free State joined the Commission, 'it would cost only for the number of war graves in the Irish Free State – which would be about £6,000 to £7,000 a year'.

Thirdly, as yet another option, Britain would propose 'to accept with gratitude' the Free State offer to take over care and maintenance within its area, but would mark them and erect headstones at British expense, and thereafter maintain them at Irish expense. He wanted an early reply from the Treasury as the War Graves Commission 'is being much pressed by relatives of soldiers buried in the Free State'.[17]

While the Treasury's response was not immediately clear, by mid-November the Minister for Finance in Dublin was wondering what had happened in regard to any reply from London to Dublin's July Despatch. External Affairs advised him on 14 November that no reply had been received from the Colonial Office.[18] In the event, it was over a month before Waterfield replied to the Colonial Office and, when he did, the Treasury had abandoned its hard line and had fallen in completely with the Colonial Office view: if the Free State joined the Commission, it would be expected to pay only for war graves in Ireland. At that stage Waterfield was advised that the number of such graves stood at 2,047, and that the cost of erecting headstones where none existed would only be £5,000, and only about £800 per year for maintenance thereafter. He added that, since the Free State was apparently unaware of these figures,

they might now assist in persuading the Free State to become a member. He understood that Fabian Ware 'decidedly favoured this course'. He therefore asked Whiskard to push this line rather than the course the Irish had offered in July: 'the latter proposal should be kept in the background and only brought forward if the first is completely rejected'.[19]

Requesting reconsideration:
This, subsequently, formed the basis of the British Government's formal reply which came on 9 February 1925 from the new Conservative Colonial Secretary, Leopold Amery. He expressed his Government's appreciation of the July 1924 offer but, 'before deciding whether to avail themselves of it', he wanted to present the Irish Government with some clarifying details concerning the financial aspects of the whole business, and wanted to know if erecting headstones as well as maintaining grave sites was included in the Free State's offer. He considered it possible that the Irish may have rejected the suggestion of Commission membership, 'by an imperfect acquaintance with the financial liabilities involved'. Far from expecting the Free State to pay for the upkeep of 'the number of war graves of Irishmen throughout the world', it proposed rather that it cover the expense of war graves only within Free State territory. They

did not think the initial cost of providing headstones would exceed £5,000 a year during construction, and that, once completed, the annual maintenance cost thereafter 'should be a comparatively modest sum'. In light of these figures he asked the Government in Dublin to reconsider its decision not to join the Imperial War Graves Commission.[20] It took a very long time indeed for the Government in Dublin to reply. Further despatches from Amery on 7 May and 4 July 1925 went unanswered, as he pointed out in yet another despatch of 21 September 1925.[21]

Within the IWGC and the War Office, exasperation was growing. In July 1925 Arthur Browne remarked:

Negotiations with the Irish Government are not progressing and I have no inkling of what will happen. It may end in our not looking after the graves but entrusting them to the Free State Government.

He added that they demurred at writing letters to next of kin asking for particulars, as this only

arouses expectations of some action on our part, will lead to correspondence in the press and cause embarrassment to the Commission and possibly also to the Free State...Records points out that settlement of the question is overdue and would welcome anything which precipitated a decision.

However, if the Records Section of the IWGC was champing at the bit, Browne was fearful that, if the Commission opened up the issue to public gaze, the result would be 'an acrimonious correspondence unless we can say we propose to do something. If we say we cannot, the question will probably be ventilated in Parliament'. He wondered if Fabian Ware 'should now decide whether we should or should not write to the relatives regarding graves in Southern Ireland'.[22] It would appear that Ware decided to do nothing for the time being since, three days later, Browne wrote formally to the Colonial Office about the difficulty of answering letters of enquiry from next of kin, and wondered 'if it is anticipated that an early decision on this matter may be expected by the Government of the Irish Free State'.[23]

Meanwhile in Dublin, during May and June 1925 there were exchanges between External Affairs and Finance over the precise financial commitment of the differing proposals. On 26 May External Affairs put it to Codling of Finance that it was now up to his Minister 'to decide which proposal would be the more economical'.[24] No reply was forthcoming and, as late as the first week of February 1926, External Affairs was asking again, as it had done already on 26 May, 9 October and 4 December 1925, 'whether

a decision has been reached. The matter has been under consideration since 21 February 1924 and the Dominions Office continues to press for a reply'.[25] This inordinately long delay is difficult to explain and raises the question whether it was the result of foot-dragging by the Minister for Finance, consequent upon the difficult atmosphere created by the Boundary Commission dispute which was coming to a head over the same period.[26] Despite its under-resourcing and its still relatively subordinate position as a Department of Government at that time[27], External Affairs could not be blamed for the delays.

The unsettled dead:

Almost five years had passed since the Truce and still no resolution of the war graves question was in sight. In that time, the process of deterioration advanced, even as, in different quarters, the sense of frustration grew. Relatives and friends of these dead in Britain and Ireland continually pressed the IWGC and the War Office for information as to the graves of their lost ones. Local Church of Ireland clergymen from time to time expressed concern about grave-site neglect. Typical was the complaint of the Rev. Ralph Meredith, Rector at Buncrana. Explaining to the IWGC in July 1925 how, during the war, Buncrana was 'an important naval base as well as a military camp', soldiers and sailors were buried in the parish graveyards, their graves marked by British Government-supplied temporary wooden crosses. These crosses had decayed or fallen and his parish did not possess the funds to replace them. Approaches to the Admiralty produced no solution and he wondered therefore what the IWGC might do.[28] All they could do was pass his complaint on to the Colonial Secretary 'as the Minister concerned in the negotiations with the Free State'.

With as much impatience wrote the Rev. Mr Howard of Donagh Rectory, Glasslough, Co Monaghan, in the same month:

Will you please kindly let me know if anything has been decided re Soldiers' Graves in the Irish Free State? About five years ago an officer came to this parish and took measurements of the grave of No. 45288, Private Robert Steenson of the 16th Battalion Cameronians who was killed on 16 May 1918, age 24. He was the fourth son to make the supreme sacrifice. The family would have replaced the little cross with something more worthy but they have been waiting to see if the War Graves Commission would make a move in the matter. I should be grateful for any information.[29]

Untypical, but equally telling, perhaps, was the letter from the Rev. J. C. Lord of Kilbrogan Rectory, near Bandon. It concerned the grave of Henry Grattan Beamish of the Royal Army Medical Corps. Poisoned by gas on the Western Front, he died in England in August 1916 and was buried in Kilbrogan. His brother, George, a police superintendent in Bath, would have pressed the IWGC to do something for his brother, had he himself not passed away in November 1920. As local rector, Lord took up the case for care and maintenance with the IWGC in September 1926, only to get the by-now standard reply that they could do nothing pending a decision between the British and Free State governments and suggesting that he might approach the latter. In response, he wrote on 30 September, baldly stating

We do not require the Free State Government to care and maintain Henry Grattan Beamish's grave…we will do the looking after ourselves. I am sure his father would have erected a memorial but he died shortly after his son and left his family badly off.[30]

During the same period, smarting from their demobilisation and felt neglect and abandonment, the very large numbers of Irish ex-servicemen of the British Forces now living in the Free State remained determined to remember their fallen comrades and became angry at the neglect of their burial places. Their complaints came from various parts of the Free State. By the mid-1920s these

individuals had coalesced into the Legion of Ex-Servicemen and shortly after that they became the Southern Ireland Area of the British Legion. As individuals, or collectively, they repeatedly made representations to the authorities in Britain and in Ireland regarding the state of the cemeteries and the war graves.

Most active among these was J. J. Tynan, organising secretary for the League and the Legion, who prominently represented their views to listening and deaf ears alike for the next twenty years and more. Early in August 1925 he addressed the IWGC secretary to ask what action it proposed to take, especially in regard to the military cemeteries, which 'in some places…are going to ruin'. He wished to know if the IWGC had any scheme for the erection of tombstones in Ireland over the graves of the men who served during the Great War. All he could be told in reply was that the Commission 'have no power to take any action', pending a decision arising from ongoing discussions between the two governments.[31]

One month later, M. Scanlon, secretary of the Tralee branch of the Legion, contacted Tynan to complain of the appalling state of the British military cemetery at Ballymullan, Tralee. He and an associate found it in a 'deplorable condition':

BELOW
OPW 1930's drawing, template for Connaught Rangers Cap Badge.

The man who is the 'supposed' caretaker has horses and goats grazing over the graves of the immortal dead and the place is full of manure – crosses and wreaths torn up from the graves and a stable erected in the cemetery…a disgrace to humanity.

He hoped it might be possible to have it reclaimed for future burials of 'our own British ex-servicemen'. No one had been buried there 'since the British left the country' and there were in the district many ex-servicemen who had no place to be buried. Tynan sent this letter to the Commission, who, repeating their plea of powerlessness to act until the outcome of governmental discussions, nonetheless sent the correspondence on to the Dominions Office.[32]

One month later, another broadside came, from a retired Indian Army officer, Colonel T. G. Peacocke, then living in Lumville House on the Curragh. An old associate of his, General Sir Alexander Cobbe, at the India Office, to whom he wrote in October 1925, received Peacocke's complaints about 'the neglected condition of the Curragh's Military Cemetery, 'overgrown with grass and weeds', the 'derelict condition of the chapel….the roof…completely burnt over a year ago'. As far as Peacocke was concerned, 'it is scandalous that the place should be allowed to get into its present condition'. In a letter marked

confidential, Browne replied to General Cobbe on 17 October, to say that the issue was 'one of the reserved matters still awaiting settlement between the two Governments'. His additional remarks are interesting in highlighting the psychological as well as the political sensitivities of the whole matter. Explaining how, when the Free State had been invited 'some time ago' to join the Commission, it had offered instead 'to be responsible for all British military graves in the Free State', this offer had placed the Commission and the British authorities in something of a fix: 'we were not quite sure at the time if such a course would be acceptable to the majority of people whose kin are buried in Ireland'. He proceeded to explain that they were still awaiting the Free State's reply to the Dominions Office request that they reconsider their unwillingness to take up IWGC membership. He concluded:

I have had a large number of letters from all parts of the Free State protesting against the neglected condition of the graves but I have been obliged to reply that proper maintenance of war graves in Southern Ireland is involved in the general question of the future maintenance of cemeteries in Southern Ireland, whether war or prewar, which is under discussion between the two Governments.[33]

LEFT
Colonial Secretary
Leopold Amery.

Repeating reminders:

If the entire question appears to have been forgotten in the depths of the Department of Finance, it was hardly so across the water. Lord Cross, at the Treasury, raised it with Ware in November 1925, saying that he had sent out reminders to the Free State, and that, if Ware had heard nothing, he had better get the Dominions Office to prod the Free State once more.[34] Three months later, Browne told the IWGC's Director of Records that Ware was going to see the Irish High Commissioner. A month later again, Cross wondered if he himself should now 'incite the Dominions Office to administer to the Irish Free State a further prod on the subject of participation in the work of the Commission'.[35] Even as Cross wondered, Ware, in some anxiety, now tried an indirect approach, soliciting the good offices of that elder statesman and voice of the Irish in Britain, T. P. O'Connor, a Privy Councillor since 1924. He wanted O'Connor to make 'discreet enquiries and advising me if there is anything possible we could do'. O'Connor contacted Joe Devlin, leader of the Nationalist Party at Westminster. O'Connor described Devlin to Ware as 'one of your best recruiting officers in Ireland…[who] has always had the deepest interest in the soldiers who fought on our side'. Nothing, however, appears to have come of this initiative.[36]

A further despatch issued from Amery on 4 June 1926, calling for a reply to those of 9 February, 7 May, 4 July and 21 September 1925. External Affairs sent this latest missive on to Finance. In tandem with Amery's letter, Whiskard addressed O'Hegarty, Secretary to the Executive Council, on the same date. He, too, requested a reply as 'the prolonged delay is putting us in a very awkward position'.[37] O'Hegarty sent this forward to Seán Lester in External Affairs on 10 June, adding his own note of urgency: 'Mr Lester, please give me matter for reply'. Joseph Walshe, Secretary of External Affairs, replied to this next day and pointed out tartly:

I am to state that the matter has been before the Department of Finance for over a year and that dozens of reminders have been sent to them, including letters urging that the matter should receive attention, without result. WE cannot move until Finance gives a decision as to which of the alternative proposals they are prepared to accept.[38]

Two more months went by, with Finance still silent. As for the Imperial War Graves Commission, in some desperation, late in July 1926, Browne again approached the Dominions Office with a provocative proposal – that the Commission leave aside the whole matter of the pre-war military cemeteries, to be settled some day

by the two governments, and that it move immediately itself to make local arrangements for the marking and maintenance of war graves in individual cemeteries. If Dominions Secretary Amery could be persuaded to agree to this, perhaps he would ask the Free State Government if it had any objections to the Commission's 'making their own arrangements'.[39]

Browne was doubtless driven to this by the latest adverse reports from Ireland. One of these related to the graves of seventeen sailors of H.M.S. *Racoon*, sunk on 9 January 1918 on its way to Lough Swilly. They were buried in St. Columb's Church of Ireland Churchyard, Rathmullan, County Donegal, which was, a visitor reported, 'in a disgraceful state, with cattle grazing over the graves and absolutely no attempt made to keep the place in order'.[40] Another report, of the same month, but from the far end of the country, related again to Tralee Military Cemetery where another visitor was 'surprised and shocked at the condition it was in'.[41]

In response to Browne's proposal, Whiskard explained that the Dominions Office had been 'making every effort both by official and personal communications to obtain a reply from the Irish Free State Government on the main question'. Being hopeful that a reply would be soon forthcoming, he did not think it 'advisable to take action in the sense you suggest'.[42] On the very day that Browne had written, his superior, Ware, received a rather interesting communication from Colonel E. C. Heath, General Secretary of the British Legion in Britain. He had toured British Legion branches in Ireland and in Dublin had had 'a most cordial' interview with President Cosgrave. He raised with the Taoiseach the apprehension at times expressed in Britain that, in the Free State, headstones, Crosses of Sacrifice and Stones of Remembrance could not be put up 'for fear of desecration'. Heath wanted Cosgrave's assurance that he could report back to Britain that such fears were without foundation. The Taoiseach told Heath that 'the spirit of the people was now quite all right but that damage might be done by one or two ill-disposed people, or that some 'village idiot' might do something which the Government and the people would greatly regret'. Cosgrave mentioned three recent cases of damage to public monuments and went on to advise 'not [to] press the case for War Graves at the moment', but added that he felt that 'he would be able in the quite near future to advise you to proceed'. Heath himself was 'delighted' to find War Memorials in several places, and added:

There is no cause to fear that these will ever be maliciously damaged or violated in any way, and, if it is possible for them to stand in conspicuous places in small towns, I feel certain that the time is not far distant when you will be able to carry on your normal and important work throughout the whole of Ireland.[43]

Nevertheless, two more months went by without a response from Finance. In mid-August 1926 Whiskard again contacted O'Hegarty, to say that 'the continued absence of any reply to our despatches on this subject is placing us in a most embarrassing position'.[44] As if one department of government did not know what another was doing, or not doing, O'Hegarty acted on this by reminding External Affairs that 'this matter has now been outstanding for eighteen months and it would be very desirable that an early reply be forthcoming'. External Affairs' immediate response to this is not extant, perhaps fortunately.[45]

Finally deciding:

At long last, however, in April 1926, Finance did the figures, and they were hardly higher mathematics when done. Under 'Scheme A', in which the Free State would make a contribution to the IWGC, Finance estimated an annual cost during a three to four year period of construction in the region of £5,000, totalling £17,500 approximately, and

an annual maintenance contribution to the IWGC thereafter at £800. Under 'Scheme B', in which the Irish Government would simply take full charge of all British war graves, it was estimated to cost £10 per headstone for 1,800 graves, totalling £18,000, and again an annual maintenance cost thereafter of £800. The cost difference and the calculations hardly warranted an eighteen-month gestation period. On receiving this from Finance, External Affairs forwarded it to the Cabinet with a recommendation in favour of the slightly more expensive scheme of total Free State responsibility.[46]

Despite this, matters did not move apace, and, on 7 October 1926, Amery wrote directly to the Taoiseach, Cosgrave, summarily rehearsing the whole history of the exchanges, expressing appreciation for the generosity of the Irish proposal of 7 July 1924, but still adverting to the British request for reconsideration of IWGC membership, made in February 1925. Noting that there had been no effective communication on the matter, he asked Cosgrave before he came over for the Imperial Conference, if he could look into the business. He ended:

Meanwhile we have reason to believe that in many parts of the Free State these graves have fallen into, or are falling into a condition of

extreme dilapidation, and I am sure that you will recognise how anxious we are that the outstanding questions should be settled... May I ask you to take such steps as will ensure that we may receive an early reply to my despatch of February 9th, 1925.[47]

Exactly one week later Cosgrave explained that the question

was held up for some time pending consideration of certain financial aspects of the matter. I am glad to say that this has now been satisfactorily adjusted and a despatch will be shortly issued on the lines that we will take charge of all the British graves here, including the cost of placing headstones over the War Graves, the number of which, I understand, is estimated to be approximately 1,800.[48]

On the day after this, External Affairs was informed of Cabinet approval of their recommendation, and on 1 November 1926 Governor-General Healy conveyed the decision, in Despatch No 240, to the Dominions Office.

Healy expressed regrets at the delay in replying to London's Despatch of February 1925, stated that his Ministers were still unable to accept membership of the Imperial War Graves Commission, offered to maintain all British war graves in the Free State, and undertook to meet the cost of providing

and erecting headstones over those of the Great War.[49]

Whether the final phrase was a case of careless wording or a deliberate attempt at obfuscation is not clear. Immediately, however, it raised questions in the Dominions Office and the War Graves Commission: did the phrase include or exclude the graves of British soldiers killed in the Free State, or dying there, up to 31 August 1921, and, were pre-war graves included? When Cosgrave and his delegation attended the Imperial Conference in London, later that month, O'Hegarty was quizzed on this by a Dominions Office official.[50]

Unfortunately, when Finance had done its figures they did not include the post-war graves of those killed between November 1918 and 31 August 1921. These were estimated at around 200 and Lester in External Affairs had to get Finance to sanction their inclusion.[51] On 24 December 1926, Codling of Finance confirmed that their estimate of 1,800 referred only to those dying in the Great War, and not to those killed in 1916 or dying in the Anglo-Irish conflict. The question of meeting the costs of headstones for these, he believed, should be submitted to the Executive Council. In further exchanges, however, Finance came to accept the External Affairs view that since the principle of responsibility

LEFT
H.M.S. Racoon Memorial, St. Columb's, Rathmullan, Co. Donegal.

RIGHT
A page from Ireland's Memorial Records 1914-1918 (artwork by Harry Clarke).

had been accepted by the Cabinet, there was no need to seek further approval for the inclusion of the additional two hundred of 1916 and 1919-1921.[52] The fact that these figures were widely at variance with the now generally accepted numbers of British Forces killed – 132 in 1916 and 642 in 1919-1921, totalling 774 – went unremarked at the time by either government.[53]

In the meantime, still not sure what, if anything, was happening, the British Legion General Secretary, Colonel Heath, renewed his inquiries to Cosgrave on 14 December 1926. The reply which came from Cosgrave's office in late January, while not definitive, was positive:

Considerable progress has been made in the matter since your interview with the President and…a final settlement between the British and the Irish Free State Governments may be anticipated in the immediate future. For your personal information I may say that the arrangement will probably be that the Irish Government will undertake the full care and maintenance of the War Graves and the provision and erection of headstones. President Cosgrave desires me to state that he appreciates your interest in this matter which is receiving the attention of the Government.[54]

In Britain, when told of the renewed Free State proposals, the Service Departments welcomed them. For the War Office, A. E. Widdows told the Dominions Office that the Army Council noted the proposals 'with satisfaction', especially the clarification that war graves of the Anglo-Irish conflict would be included. In similar spirit, Charles Walker of the Admiralty had no objections and, in the event of these proposals becoming an actual agreement, he was anxious that particular attention be given to naval graves in Cobh Cemetery, especially to those who died in the *Mars* disaster of 1902 and those who perished in Submarine *A5* in 1905.[55] The formal clarification came from O'Hegarty to Stephenson of the Dominions Office on 9 February 1927, stating that instructions had now been issued to the Office of Public Works to arrange for the care and maintenance of British war graves, for the placing of headstones on the graves of those soldiers, sailors and airmen of the Great War, the Insurrection of 1916 and of the later Anglo-Irish conflict, who died from wounds, accidents or diseases contracted while on active service. Such, at last, was the end of the beginning.[56]

BELOW
Recruitment poster, 1914.

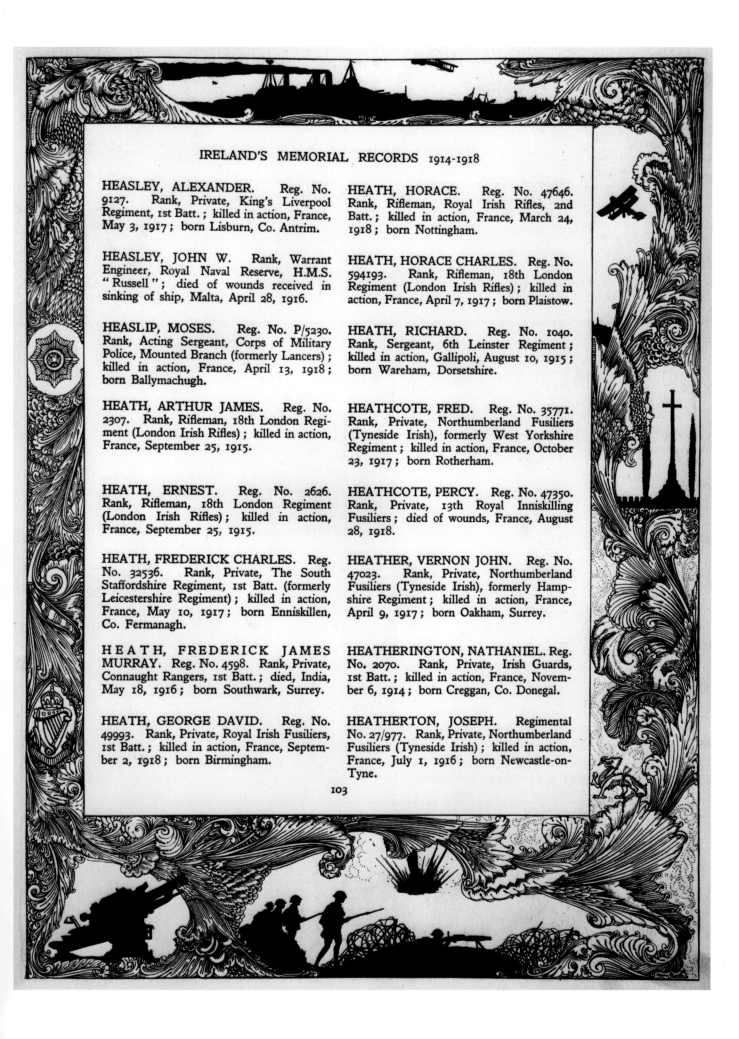

HEASLEY, ALEXANDER.   Reg. No. 9127.   Rank, Private, King's Liverpool Regiment, 1st Batt.; killed in action, France, May 3, 1917; born Lisburn, Co. Antrim.

HEASLEY, JOHN W.   Rank, Warrant Engineer, Royal Naval Reserve, H.M.S. "Russell"; died of wounds received in sinking of ship, Malta, April 28, 1916.

HEASLIP, MOSES.   Reg. No. P/5230. Rank, Acting Sergeant, Corps of Military Police, Mounted Branch (formerly Lancers); killed in action, France, April 13, 1918; born Ballymachugh.

HEATH, ARTHUR JAMES.   Reg. No. 2307. Rank, Rifleman, 18th London Regiment (London Irish Rifles); killed in action, France, September 25, 1915.

HEATH, ERNEST.   Reg. No. 2626. Rank, Rifleman, 18th London Regiment (London Irish Rifles); killed in action, France, September 25, 1915.

HEATH, FREDERICK CHARLES.   Reg. No. 32536.   Rank, Private, The South Staffordshire Regiment, 1st Batt. (formerly Leicestershire Regiment); killed in action, France, May 10, 1917; born Enniskillen, Co. Fermanagh.

HEATH, FREDERICK JAMES MURRAY. Reg. No. 4598. Rank, Private, Connaught Rangers, 1st Batt.; died, India, May 18, 1916; born Southwark, Surrey.

HEATH, GEORGE DAVID.   Reg. No. 49993. Rank, Private, Royal Irish Fusiliers, 1st Batt.; killed in action, France, September 2, 1918; born Birmingham.

HEATH, HORACE.   Reg. No. 47646. Rank, Rifleman, Royal Irish Rifles, 2nd Batt.; killed in action, France, March 24, 1918; born Nottingham.

HEATH, HORACE CHARLES. Reg. No. 594193.   Rank, Rifleman, 18th London Regiment (London Irish Rifles); killed in action, France, April 7, 1917; born Plaistow.

HEATH, RICHARD.   Reg. No. 1040. Rank, Sergeant, 6th Leinster Regiment; killed in action, Gallipoli, August 10, 1915; born Wareham, Dorsetshire.

HEATHCOTE, FRED.   Reg. No. 35771. Rank, Private, Northumberland Fusiliers (Tyneside Irish), formerly West Yorkshire Regiment; killed in action, France, October 23, 1917; born Rotherham.

HEATHCOTE, PERCY.   Reg. No. 47350. Rank, Private, 13th Royal Inniskilling Fusiliers; died of wounds, France, August 28, 1918.

HEATHER, VERNON JOHN.   Reg. No. 47023.   Rank, Private, Northumberland Fusiliers (Tyneside Irish), formerly Hampshire Regiment; killed in action, France, April 9, 1917; born Oakham, Surrey.

HEATHERINGTON, NATHANIEL. Reg. No. 2070.   Rank, Private, Irish Guards, 1st Batt.; killed in action, France, November 6, 1914; born Creggan, Co. Donegal.

HEATHERTON, JOSEPH.   Regimental No. 27/977. Rank, Private, Northumberland Fusiliers (Tyneside Irish); killed in action, France, July 1, 1916; born Newcastle-on-Tyne.

103

Their glory shall not be blotted out

R. W. Williams, Private
Royal Welch Fusiliers
10 July 1921

Bunratty Old Graveyard
Co. Clare

Chapter 7

Clearing The Decks, 1926-1928

If the news at last from Dublin disarmed the Admiralty and Army Council, it left Arthur Browne of the IWGC happy, but still cautious. He asked the Dominions Office if there was now any objection to the IWGC's getting into direct contact with the Free State authorities to begin the process of enabling them 'to carry out their generous offer'. The IWGC wanted to clarify certain points of important detail 'before we finally accept their offer or renounce our own undoubted responsibilities'. He and his vice-chairman, Ware, agreed, from their past experience, that otherwise there could be 'very great trouble, particularly with the relatives'.[1] Within the British establishment it seemed that the last word lay, as in the past, with the Imperial War Graves Commission. On 22 February 1927, Lord Cross of the Treasury contacted Ware to confirm that the War Office and the Admiralty 'have given their blessing to the proposed arrangements' and that 'the Treasury is prepared to add its own, but, as we always do our best to cooperate with your Commission, I think I had better send this note in case you have any observations to make before we act'.

The IWGC concern to have direct contact with Dublin and to clarify certain points of detail was taken up by Whiskard and conveyed to Dublin in the last week of February 1927.[2] The response was positive, with Cosgrave's Office and External Affairs agreeing that the IWGC might indeed communicate directly with the Office of Public Works on matters of detail. This permission was formally conveyed to the Dominions Office on 3 March 1927; they, in turn, sent it on to Browne.[3]

Surprisingly, after the delays on the Irish side, Ware did not respond, apparently being away from his desk. Cross had to contact him again in early April, complaining that, in Ware's absence, it was impossible 'to obtain any expression of Graves Commission opinion'. He stressed:

We can hardly delay longer in giving formal approval of what seems to me, so far as it goes, a satisfactory proposal. I send this last line to give you an opportunity of putting in an objection.[4]

Ware now telephoned Cross to explain that there were 'certain outstanding difficulties' which he wanted to get settled before 'any final decision was come to in the matter'.[5] It was not stated what these difficulties were, and, in the absence of evidence in the files, one surmises from what had passed and from what was yet to come in the years ahead, that the central concern of the IWGC was one which the Irish authorities actually shared: the issue of communications: what were to be the protocols of communication between the Commission and Ireland, and what were to be the procedures for communicating with next of kin of the war dead?

Establishing direct contact:
Eventually, on 13 April, Fabian Ware contacted Thomas Cassedy, the OPW Secretary, to confirm he had heard from the Dominions Office, and to state that Captain T. W. Newham of the Commission's Works Department, as their senior official responsible for war graves in Britain, would be sent to Dublin to discuss details such as the special kind of headstone that all the Dominions used to mark permanently the graves of the fallen. By coincidence, it was on the same date that Cassedy wrote to the IWGC, stating baldly that the OPW had been entrusted with the duty of providing and erecting headstones over the graves of the 1914-1918 war dead, and requesting information as to the number and location of these graves.[6] Over time, the number of graves and of cemeteries was changing. In briefing Newham for his Dublin visit, the IWGC Director of Records, Colonel Harry Chettle, reported the number of burials as 2,034, in 329 cemeteries, but he had heard of an additional 476 other burials in an additional 180 cemeteries as reported to the Commission by next of kin, as well as by Army inspectors before 1921, and which had yet to be verified.[7] Even at this point, however, Browne was indicating to the Dominions Office that the IWGC was awaiting more information and clarification – which he was confident the OPW would deliver to them – 'before the Commission can definitely agree that they are justified in foregoing their responsibilities under their Charter to the relatives of the dead'.[8]

Captain Newham arrived in Dublin, to a cordial welcome, in late April 1927, and met with William J. Veale of the OPW. Here he was informed that the official design for IWGC headstones would be adopted and that the OPW would wish to use IWGC expertise. He was further assured that the OPW Commissioners were 'anxious to get to work early', and thought that the most reliable records would be those relating to the eleven military cemeteries now under OPW control and with which they hoped they could 'do something at once'.[9]

The Commissioners proposed to write formally to Sir Fabian Ware, with a view to commencing the work.[10] Newham left Dublin on 22 April and reported back to a very pleased Sir Fabian. The latter wrote to Cassedy, on 4 May, stating that the IWGC would immediately complete and transmit a list of war graves in these eleven cemeteries as suggested, to be followed later by draft lists of war graves for every county in the Free State.[11]

Even in this early overture to the OPW, Ware's enthusiasm was close to transgressing the boundaries of caution. In the draft version of the letter, he explained that, before a standard headstone could be prepared, its details had to be referred to the relatives, for correction of particulars and for the text of personal inscription, if desired. He suggested very reasonably that

if it would be any convenience for your Government, they [the IWGC] are prepared to do this…in that event we would issue to the relatives a letter of which the accompanying draft is forwarded for your concurrence or amendment:

Dear Sir or Madam,
The Government of ~~Southern Ireland~~ *the Irish Free State [sic] propose to erect on war graves in* ~~Southern Ireland~~ *the Irish Free State [sic] memorials of a pattern similar to those which have been erected throughout the world and in order that this may be done correctly I should be glad if you would be good enough to complete the enclosed forms as explained therein.*

What seemed very reasonable and intended, perhaps, as a courtesy, may well have owed more, however, to the very real apprehension within the Commission that British next of kin in Britain might well be upset, if not outraged, if the Irish Free State Government were to write to them requesting details of lost ones, especially if they had been killed in Ireland itself. At the same time, from Dublin's perspective, Ware's suggestion could be taken as a trespass on Irish jurisdiction.

Within nine days Ware was able to send the OPW a draft list of war graves in the military cemeteries, and indeed in ordinary cemeteries. In sending these schedules, he still needed to know the OPW response to his offer that the IWGC would contact all the next of kin. In answer to Ware's original offer of 4 May, Cassedy replied that the OPW wanted to wait until receiving the full schedules and 'until the full extent of the problem is known'.[12]

A Commission non-consenting:

As late as May, therefore, the Free State offer of 11 February 1927 had still not been formally accepted by Britain: while the Dominions Office, Treasury and Service Departments were all happy to accept, the IWGC had still not formally signalled acceptance. On 21 May Cross inquired of Ware if his negotiations with the OPW, following on Newham's visit to Dublin, had 'now reached a stage that will justify the

RIGHT
Form of consent to be
signed by next of kin for
erection of permanent
IWGC war grave
headstone.

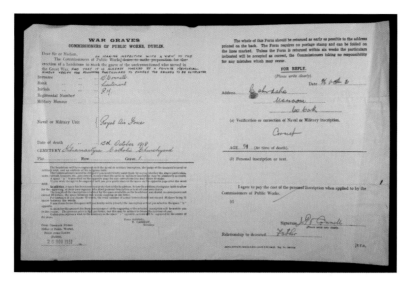

Treasury in informing the Dominions Office that no objection is seen to the Governor-General's proposals'. One month later again, Whiskard of the Dominions Office commented to Browne that 'he would be glad to know how things stand'.[13]

As it happened, the Commission's recent caution owed as much to a concern for political developments in the Free State as it did to the sensitive issue of communication with relatives. The relative political stability of the two years following the end of the Civil War drew to a close over 1926-1927; deValera founded the Fianna Fáil Party in 1926 and contested the June 1927 General Election, winning forty-four seats against the governing Cumann na nGael's forty-seven. The new party entered the Dáil in August 1927; Cosgrave's Government was saved from defeat in a no confidence motion by the casting vote of the Speaker, Michael Hayes, on 16 August. In the soon-ensuing second general election, deValera's Fianna Fáil increased its tally of seats to fifty-seven; Cosgrave's Cumann na nGael secured sixty-two seats, however, and their return to power brought another five years of relative stability.

The IWGC took a close interest in these developments, keeping press cuttings of political commentary on the Free State parties and of the political complexion of the Cosgrave Government, once reconstituted. Browne explained as much to Whiskard at the end of June 1927, stating that the Commission was waiting till the new Dublin administration had settled down 'and the new Office of Works reorganised before troubling them again'. But, when Whiskard asked Browne if the Dominions Office might answer enquiries by stating that 'the Irish Government had definitely taken over [the handling of the war graves]', he received from Ware a remarkable negative:

No, we did not regard the matter as settled until we had a reply to our questions and know that the thing was going to be done satisfactorily and [that] the Commission had never yet agreed to the proposals for handing over.

He told Whiskard that the IWGC had sent to the OPW 'all the information in our power' but that the Commission

would very much like an answer to our question about our approaching relatives on their behalf and a statement that they concur in our suggestion. [14]

Against the background of these delays, the dead of Rathmullan came back to haunt the Commission. At the end of July, the new Rector of St. Columb's Church of Ireland parish, Rev. Andrew

Noblett, complained to the IWGC of the absence of proper war grave headstones, and added:

As it seems unlikely that the Free State will ever erect Headstones over British Sailors, may I suggest that the Rector, Churchwardens and Select Vestry of the Parish should be given a fixed sum for the erection of a memorial with names inscribed thereon as well [as an] annual sum for keeping the graves in order. I expect the War Graves Commission could do this and save time and negotiations with the Free State Department.

In response, the Commission regretted that they could not see their way to consider the suggestion, but hoped 'very shortly to conclude an agreement' with the Free State for erecting permanent headstones'.[15]

It can have been no consolation to the Rev. Mr Noblett or to others that, over the entire course of that summer, matters stood still. In mid-September 1927, another Treasury official, J. H. Pinsent, contacted Ware concerning arrangements with the Free State for war graves 'in its territory'. He referred to Cross's letters of 22 February and 4 April to Ware and asked 'how matters stand?', since a formal Treasury reply to the Dominions Office letter of 5 November 1926 'can hardly be delayed

much longer'. In a reprimanding tone he concluded:

You are, no doubt, aware that we, for our part, have naturally no objection to the proposals of the Irish Free State and have only postponed informing the Dominions Office to this effect in order to leave you time to settle up some of the details.[16]

Ware's very prompt reply was frank:

The point is this. We never felt justified in altogether abandoning our obligation to the relatives with regard to these war graves in Ireland until we had some reasonable assurance that the Irish Government were going to carry out the work as much to the relatives' satisfaction as we have been able to perform it in the past. We therefore entered into direct negotiations with the Irish Government office concerned and on the whole things appeared to be coming to a satisfactory conclusion when the first of the recent political crises in Ireland arose.

He went on to explain further:

There is no reason to think that Mr Cosgrave's Government were not going to meet us in every way we desired but there was, evidently, some hesitation on their part to commit themselves just before the election and we therefore had to wait until these crises were over. The moment the new Government is established we shall approach the Irish office concerned again, and, if we handle the matter carefully, as we are doing, I have

NEAR RIGHT
Simon Fraser, Lord Lovat,
Dominions Office

FAR RIGHT
The grave of
John James Donohoe,
Irish Guards,
Arklow Cemetery,
Co. Wicklow.

10741 GUARDSMAN
JOHN JAMES DONOHOE
IRISH GUARDS
22ND NOVEMBER 1917 AGE 22

little doubt of success. I think that you will find that the Dominions Office fully appreciated the situation…The Irish people were actually at the polls when you were writing to me.[17]

Six weeks later, in a follow-up to his letter of 4 May which had suggested the services of the IWGC in contacting relatives, 'for the convenience of your Government', Ware contacted Cassedy of the OPW to ask 'whether your Government has now come to any decision in the suggestion'.[18]

Curiously, Finance and the OPW had anticipated this when, on 27 October 1927, Codling informed the OPW Commissioners that his Minister thought they should seek the loan of an officer from the IWGC 'on a repayment basis', and that letters of inquiry to relatives should be issued from the offices of the OPW Commissioners.[19]

Cassedy replied to Ware on 18 November 1927, expressing regret at the delay in answering Ware's of 4 May. His reply, however, was as frank and direct to Ware as had been Ware's to the Treasury: the OPW had carefully considered Ware's offer of assistance in identifying graves and in dealing with relatives:

While we should be very glad to avail ourselves to the full of the assistance described in your letter, we are instructed that the letter of enquiry to relatives should issue from this Office and we would therefore limit our application to the Imperial War Graves Commission to a request for aid in the work of identifying the graves and carrying out the necessary investigations.

If the Commission could afford us the loan of an officer experienced in this work on a repayment basis, we would be glad to be informed of the conditions on which the services of such an officer could be procured.[20]

It was as if to bring new pressure on Dublin that, between Ware's letter of 31 October and Cassedy's reply of 18 November, a rather specific intervention in a particular case came to the Minister for External Affairs from Downing Street. Lord Lovat of the Dominions Office, on 10 November, sought information regarding the grave in Arklow of an Irish Guard, John James Donohoe. At the age of twenty-two, Donohoe had died at the War Hospital in Epsom in November 1917, and been brought to Arklow for burial. His father, Andrew Donohoe of Kabul House, contacted the IWGC in late October 1927, to inform them that the memorial cross 'erected by the Military then stationed here', had fallen down, rotten, and required to be renewed. Transmitted by the IWGC to the Dominions Office, the enquiry was raised with External Affairs by Lord Lovat, Dominions

Under Sectreary of State, explicitly in the context of the Irish Free State offer as conveyed on 9 February 1927. He enclosed Andrew Donohoe's letter 'for such action as His Majesty's Government in the Irish Free State may consider desirable'. It was the first time that the Dominions Office, as distinct from the IWGC, had ever transmitted a specific letter of precisely this kind to an Irish Government.[21]

Divisions and misgivings:

The OPW's wish to have the loan of an experienced war graves officer was very welcome news to the IWGC, as its Records Director, Harry Chettle, confided to Arthur Browne.[22] Fabian Ware, however, remained distinctly uneasy. His unease revealed deep rifts in the British approach to the whole question. At the Dominions Office, Harry Batterbee[23] asked Ware to provide him with 'a confidential letter as to our present difficulty with the Irish Free State'. Doubtless, Batterbee sought this in advance of a visit to London by FitzGerald, now Defence Minister, to see Lord Lovat.[24] In a reply marked 'personal and confidential' on 25 November, Ware complained that 'the arrangement which has been made is one for which Whiskard and the Treasury (in particular Lord Cross) are personally responsible'. He elaborated:

We have always felt here that the financial aspect of the question influenced the decision perhaps a little too much. For instance, under the Versailles Treaty we had the right to claim from Germany the permanent marking and maintenance of all our graves here, but the feeling of relations was so strong that this work should be done by British hands, that we undertook the whole expense of that work.

He confessed that

While I do not for one moment consider that the analogy is a happy one – some people might consider it ~~strange~~ [sic] strained, we have at the same time to realise that many of the relatives of the men killed in Ireland still harbour at least unfriendly feelings towards the Irish, some of them a very bitter feeling. It was for these reasons that we suggested to the Free State Government that we should undertake all that personal communication with the relatives of the dead….

Ware went on:

…the arrangement with the Free State Government is not one which we have made ourselves. I even think that if we had undertaken it we might have persuaded the Free State to become full members of the Commission.

Explaining to Batterbee that they had sent 'one of our best men' to see the OPW officials and that the negotiations 'have been carried out in the best

spirit, and all other points have been satisfactorily arranged except this one, he concluded:

What we have to face is this:
i) *There is no way of avoiding direct communications with the relatives;*
ii) *If a Department of the Free State, as they desire, undertakes this, they are certain to receive some painful, even abusive replies. I speak with great experience of these relatives, many of whom in their grief, have not spared us although they had no real grievance or shortcomings to complain of… I think we shall have an extremely difficult task to persuade the relatives in many cases to allow the Irish to put up these headstones.*

As far as Ware was concerned, in all of these circumstances, the only practicable solution was that the IWGC should be allowed to send an official to do the work – 'and this we have done in Northern Ireland' – and, if necessary, he could be attached to one of the Irish Departments 'but should communicate with the relatives in our name'.[25]

If Ware had been frank and forthright, Lord Lovat was more circumspect and understated when he raised the issue with a visiting Irish delegation at the end of November. He mentioned

A slight difficulty which might arise…In all other parts of the world the British graves

were being looked after by the War Graves Commission. He feared that some English people might not wish to correspond direct with the Board of Works in Dublin about the graves of their relatives, and he wondered whether, in that case, there would be any objection to correspondence going through the War Graves Commission in London. Mr FitzGerald assured him that his Government would not make any difficulty.[26]

Whatever FitzGerald, Minister for Defence since June, had allegedly assured Lovat, as reported by Walshe of External Affairs to his Minister, McGilligan, was subsequently contested by Seán Lester, in April 1928, but at the time the British were clearly of the view that FitzGerald was not the source of difficulty. In a telephone conversation with Ware in February 1928, Sir Edward Harding, then Assistant Undersecretary of State at the Dominions Office, remarked that 'he had seen Mr FitzGerald who was all right but that the Office of Works, Dublin, were a little troublesome'.[27] If the OPW were 'troublesome', it was hardly by their own initiative. As the evidence has already indicated and as they themselves admitted, they took their instructions in the matter from the Minister for Finance, Blythe, who, presumably, was taking a more stringent line than FitzGerald.

Problems of communication:

Whatever negotiations were happening towards the end of November on this question of communicating with relatives of the dead, Ware followed up his letter of 25 November to Batterbee with another one a week later. Arguing that since the Dominions Office did not want to pursue the IWGC line that the Free State might yet take up full Commission membership, all Ware could now suggest was 'some sort of working compromise', along lines which Batterbee duly replicated in a direct communication to Walshe of External Affairs on 20 December 1927: they sincerely appreciated the Free State Government's offer and had 'no desire to alter in any way that arrangement'; nevertheless,

For the reasons which Lord Lovat explained to Mr FitzGerald and the force of which, I think, the Minister appreciated, it seems to us that it would be preferable from several points of view that the work of communicating with relatives, where such communication is necessary, should be performed through the Imperial War Graves Commission.

In this very lengthy letter he went into considerable detail, explaining the Commission's chartered obligations, the specialised nature of the work, and mentioned the practice in Canada where an IWGC officer, paid from IWGC funds, corresponded directly with the relatives. He 'understood Mr FitzGerald to agree that it would be desirable to conform to the Canadian procedure so far as conditions permit'. Batterbee then formally proposed i) that for next of kin resident in Great Britain and Northern Ireland, the necessary forms be sent out by the IWGC officer to be loaned to the OPW, with a covering letter from the Irish Free State Government, requesting that the completed forms be returned to the IWGC in London; and ii) that for next of kin resident in the Irish Free State the completed forms be returned to the IWGC officer attached to the OPW, who would then forward the forms to the IWGC in London. There the Commission would collate the forms and complete all the particulars, so that the full schedules could then be sent back to the OPW for implementation. Batterbee proposed that if this were acceptable, then Fabian Ware should visit Dublin to discuss the details directly with the Free State Minister of Public Works. [28]

On the same date, by separate mail, Batterbee again wrote to Walshe to enclose a strong letter of complaint from Tynan of the British Legion in Ireland. Tynan's Irish Area Council wanted to know 'if any decision had been arrived at' by the governments, and complained of the absence of headstones generally and about the neglected condition

RIGHT
IWGC war grave
headstones,
The Military Plot,
Cahir Church of Ireland
Cemetery, Co. Tipperary.

of Tralee military cemetery in particular. He reminded the reader that correspondence on the subject 'has been passing since 1924....My Council is of the opinion that the time has now arrived when something should be done to have this matter finally settled'.[29]

On Walshe's receipt of Batterbee's first letter of 20 December – one which Ware had only reluctantly endorsed – Lester prepared a forthright minute, on 24 December 1927. It immediately pointed out that Batterbee's communication asked for more than Walshe's record of the conversations in London suggested, that is, that communications with all relatives, whether in the Free State or elsewhere, was to be done through the IWGC:

Relatives in Great Britain and Northern Ireland will write direct to London; those in the Free State will write to an officer of the Commission who will have a Dublin Office. We shall merely do the work and pay for it.

Incisively he continued:

This Department's object in making the agreement was principally to keep out the IWGC but the present suggestion would nullify that intention. We refused to accept membership of the IWGC and by agreement with Britain undertook full responsibility for the graves.

Batterbee now says the Commission are 'formally charged under their Charter with the care of the graves', and must be associated with the work.

Lester insisted that the agreement between the Governments involved 'the suspension, in fact if not in law, of the authority of the Commission and placed responsibility on the Irish Free State Government'. He remarked, baldly, that the IWGC 'was never invited by either Government to undertake the care of graves here', and that, 'if we agreed to the proposal we would lose both politically and financially'. He suggested instead that the Free State might permit:

(1) *Residents in Great Britain and Northern Ireland to communicate with London; all Saorstát residents with the Board of Works;*

(2) *Invite periodical inspection of work – on behalf of relatives in Great Britain, not on behalf of Irish Free State residents;*

(3) *Accept assistance of an officer on loan to the Board of Works for a specified period;*

(4) *Undertake to supply information to the Commission for the compilation of printed Registers.*[30]

BELOW
OPW 1930's drawing,
template for Royal Defence
Corps. Cap Badge.

Confoundings:

Matters were now to get a lot more complicated. Firstly, Cassedy of the OPW contacted Ware on 7 January 1928, requesting a reply to his query of 18 November as to the terms on which they might secure the loan of an expert officer. A week later, Ware reported this to Batterbee, remarking:

I am getting rather into difficulties in Ireland… you will remember that it was because of Mr Cassedy's suggestion that they should communicate directly with the relatives, using such an officer loaned by us, in any way they pleased, that I approached you in the matter and you raised the question with Mr Walshe. The question is whether I can tell Mr. Cassedy that his Minister is in communication with you?[31]

In the end, on 17 January 1928, Batterbee informed Murphy of External Affairs that any reply to the OPW's request for information as to conditions for the loan of an officer depended on answers to his, Batterbee's, letter of 20 December: this had proposed that the IWGC conduct the communications with relatives, and that proposal was made 'after a discussion here between Lord Lovat and Mr FitzGerald on the occasion of the latter's visit to London at the end of November'.[32] Three weeks later, Harding of the Dominions Office telephoned Ware, requesting him 'not to send our men to Dublin

until the principle was settled between the two governments'. With his usual frankness, Ware replied that he would have 'handled matters differently' by sending the IWGC representative over, 'as this might have the effect of the Office of Works being only too pleased to get behind the Commission'.[33]

Nothing on the matter was settled between London and Dublin by late March 1928, when Cassedy gave an account of the situation to Codling at Finance. As requested by Finance back in October 1927, he had contacted the IWGC for information and had received no definitive reply, despite a reminder, and, as the OPW understood that External Affairs was in correspondence on the subject, 'we have refrained from pursuing the matter'. The information supplied by the IWGC in the summer of 1927 did not contain the addresses of relatives, so the OPW could not contact the latter as instructed by Finance on 27 October. Cassedy suggested that the OPW could conduct a trial exercise, choosing a small cemetery like Arklow with seven war graves, and endeavouring to verify the details by neighbourhood enquiries; using the local OPW Assistant Architect, they could invite tenders for headstones 'in order to get a sense of the costs involved'. He concluded, however, that the Minister

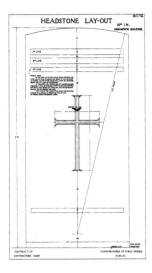

for Finance might consider this proposal 'undesirable' until the External Affairs' exchanges with London had reached a conclusion.

In an endeavour to bring matters to a conclusion, on 30 March 1928 Murphy prepared a draft External Affairs letter of reply to Batterbee. It rehearsed the 'misapprehension as to what Mr FitzGerald said would be acceptable' in his late November discussions in London. It claimed that FitzGerald had understood 'your point to be that in cases where relatives objected to communicating with any authority other than the IWGC there should be no objection on our part to the correspondence in those cases being carried on by the Commission'. It strongly asserted that the Irish side could not agree that all communications with relatives whether in the Free State or elsewhere should be done by the IWGC, but to meet the difficulties between them, Dublin was prepared to agree:

i) *that in the case of next of kin resident in Great Britain and Northern Ireland, such forms as may be agreed upon, should be sent out by the IWGC and all correspondence with such relatives be done by the IWGC who will then supply the appropriate information to the Commissioners of Public Works.*

ii) *that in the case of next of kin resident in the Irish Free State or elsewhere, other than in Great Britain or Northern Ireland, forms should be sent out by the Commissioners of Public Works and to be returnable to them.*

The draft added that 'we should like to have for a period the loan from the Commission of a competent officer' and there would be no objection 'as far as the Government is concerned, to the periodical inspection on behalf of relatives in Great Britain and Northern Ireland of the work being done by the Commissioners of Public Works'.

The draft concluded by extending an invitation to Fabian Ware to visit Dublin to discuss details. Following consultations with Cassedy, FitzGerald and McGilligan, this draft went out, unchanged, to the Dominions Office on 3 April 1928, almost four years after the original Irish Free State offer.[34]

Compromising conclusions:

This final overture constituted a reasonable compromise, even if not exactly the kind of one that Ware and the IWGC had wanted. Firstly, the Free State accepted that certain relatives who could not bring themselves to deal with Dublin could go through the Commission. Secondly, whereas, originally, the Irish side would not object

LEFT
*International War Graves
Commissions group:
Col. Harry Chettle is
2nd row from back,
3rd from left.*

to relatives from Britain or Northern Ireland coming to inspect the work, now it went further by not objecting to periodical inspection by persons acting on behalf of such relatives: inevitably, such agents could be and would be an inspector or inspectors of the IWGC.

At the same time, there was introduced an element that, strangely, had not been mentioned at any time before: that it would be the OPW and not the IWGC that would handle and control correspondence with all areas other than Great Britain and Northern Ireland. Given that there were Australian, Canadian and other Commonwealth war graves in the Free State, and given that their governments were all members of the Commission in their own right, this represented a more extensive assertion of jurisdiction by the Irish Free State than was implied in the OPW's simply controlling dealings with Irish Free State-resident next of kin.

It was not until 25 April 1928 that the Dominions Office sent Ware a copy of this letter from Dublin. It invited Ware's comments and hoped that the IWGC 'may be able to comply with the External Affairs' invitation to visit Dublin 'as soon as conveniently possible'.[35] Another month passed before Ware replied, on 22 May 1928, confessing that he would not be free to travel to Ireland until July at the earliest, but he would write to Lester to ask if his Director of Records, Colonel H. F. Chettle, might be accepted in his place. Finally, seven years after the first overtures, Ware, the last element in the British complex, accepted:

We quite agree to the conditions in Mr Lester's letter and think they provide a satisfactory solution.[36]

*Memory is the only thing
That grief can call its own*

J. Kelly, Corporal, Royal Army Medical Corps
18 June 1920

Grangegorman Military Cemetery
Dublin

Chapter 8

Commencing The Work, 1928-1935

'We shall be very pleased to see Colonel Chettle on 6th June', wrote Seán Lester to Fabian Ware, on 26 May.[1] So began the formal working relationship between the IWGC and the Irish Government in 1928. Harry Chettle duly arrived in Dublin on 5 June, returning to London on the 9th. His first meeting with Lester proved 'very friendly' and the External Affairs man took him directly to the Office of Public Works. Here he was introduced to Sir Philip Hanson, chairman of the Commissioners, to its secretary, Cassedy, and to William J. Veale, the senior official who would be responsible for war graves.

Cassedy told Chettle that they were so overworked in the OPW that, effectively, the whole of the IWGC work would have to be done by the yet-to-be-appointed IWGC expert who, no doubt to Chettle's and Ware's relief, 'would have a free hand'. Cassedy further suggested that they begin with a visit to some of the former military cemeteries which, together, held over 900 of the 2,000 war graves thought to exist at that stage. He was taken that same day by 'an energetic and capable OPW official' to visit the Curragh Military Cemetery, and was met there by Army Captain Keenan whose attitude 'was all that could be desired'. On the following day he was shown around Grangegorman Military Cemetery by Pearson and Joyce of the

OPW, both 'very cordial and helpful'.

In his three working days in the Dublin region he was shown around twelve cemeteries, finding mixed conditions. Of the Curragh, which he found in 'fairly good order', he remarked that 'although entirely left to nature, it is respected and presents a very peaceful and attractive appearance'.

By contrast, in nearby Naas Catholic Cemetery, where eventually some fifteen soldiers of the Great War, mostly from the town and surrounding district, were to be commemorated,[2] the grass was long, the caretaker, it seemed to Chettle, never cutting it, the temporary wooden crosses not always legible and some of the war graves not marked at all. Grangegorman was well planted with trees and the Royal Hibernian Military School Cemetery he found 'extremely well kept'. Likewise, he was impressed with the Royal Hospital Kilmainham Burial Ground, just then in the process of transfer from War Office to OPW and containing the graves of five British soldiers 'who fell in Easter Week 1916'. He visited the Dublin Friends Burial Ground, opened in 1860 at Temple Hill, Blackrock. It contained the war grave of a Quaker RAF man, 2nd Lieutenant A.O. Coghill, who died aged twenty-six in September 1918. His widow, Jesse Coghill, lived in Rathgar and, eleven years after

NEAR RIGHT
Royal Hibernian
Military School

FAR RIGHT
Grangegorman Military
Cemetery

Chettle's visit, gave permission for the erection of a standard IWGC headstone.[3] The standard headstone was never erected, as the Quakers had, and still have, a strict protocol in respect of headstones where only the person's name and dates, without title, letters or any other description, are permitted. Yet, in Coghill's case, they departed from their own norms in allowing his RAF affiliation, though not his rank, to appear – a combatant Quaker being a rarity if not a contradiction – and allowed the word 'killed' rather than 'died'. The grave and cemetery were maintained 'to the highest standards of the Commission' – and of the Friends – by a caretaker who was an ex-soldier of the Irish Guards.

Dean's Grange, too, was' well kept', but the varying expansiveness of the plots surprised him. His final visit was to the old church and burial ground at Kilgobbin, Stepaside, 'small and well kept', and where there was commemorated an officer of the Army Veterinary Medical Corps, Major Hubert M. Lenox-Conyngham, a veteran of the Somaliland campaign as well as the Great War – not far from the grave of the famous, or notorious Richard 'Boss Croker' of Tammany Hall and racing fame.[4]

After his Dublin visit Chettle reported with what seems surprise and relief:

With one insignificant exception, every official or private person whom I saw was willing or anxious to give me any information for which I asked, though the keenness of their interest in the subject varied considerably. I could find no trace whatever of practical antipathy to the British or ex-British soldier or to the idea of honouring his grave. The irreconcilable attitude is apparently confined to the purely political sphere. I found no reluctance to discuss either the Great War or 'Our Wars' and no tone of bitterness in the discussion.[5]

A fly in the ointment:

For all Colonel Chettle's relief, there was one mishap or misapprehension on his part which caused confusion and precipitated a flurry for some months afterwards. In discussing the loan of an experienced IWGC officer, Chettle had assumed that the Irish Government would pay this officer's salary, and when he mentioned this to them, '*both Mr Cassedy and Sir Philip Hanson took this for granted*'.[6] A delegation of Lord Lovat and Sir Edward Harding was to visit Dublin over 12-13 July, and in a request for an advance briefing as to how Chettle had got on, Ware advised them that the IWGC were having some problem in finding the ideal officer; but, he stressed that the IWGC had agreed to lend a man and added, with emphasis, 'they [the Free State] are going to pay his salary'.[7] A week later

Batterbee was back to Ware, following Lovat's meeting with P. J. McGilligan, Minister for External Affairs in Dublin. Lovat and Harding were happy to tell McGilligan that 'everything was in train' and noted that the Free State had agreed to pay the salary of the officer to be seconded. This was news to McGilligan. He referred them to Batterbee's own letter of 20 December 1927, which the Dominions Office had copied to Ware on 21 December: in this it was clearly stated that the officer would remain on the IWGC payroll. This left Lovat and Harding perplexed, and Batterbee now invited Ware's comments on the matter.[8]

On Ware's behalf, Browne quizzed Chettle as to how it was that up to his Dublin visit the correspondence files showed that the IWGC was to pay the salary, 'but after your interview it was taken that the Free State wished the man to be paid by their Department'. Chettle replied;

I cannot imagine why I overlooked the agreement that the attached officer should remain on our pay list. I went to Dublin with the idea that the Free State would pay him.[9]

Although this matter was concluded to Dublin's satisfaction, it created subsequent difficulties in the recruitment of the expert officer.

The search for a suitable man:

In what followed, it was as if the fates conspired to ensure that the IWGC's mission to Ireland would be constantly thwarted. In the course of the 1920s one of the internal tensions within the IWGC was the issue of security and permanence of tenure for its employees. The Commission was run on a fairly tight budget and it was wary of increasing its permanent establishment. The Commission's search for a suitable officer commenced with an offer by Chettle to an inspector named Thorn, working for them in Belgium. In July 1928 Chettle told Thorn that the job in the Irish Free State would guarantee him employment up to September 1929 and that the experience would enhance his chances of employment outside of the Commission thereafter.[10] Thorn turned the offer down and, a week later, Ware confided to Hanson in the OPW that they were experiencing difficulties in getting 'a good person', as they all 'want permanence'. He asked Hanson if there were any possibility that the Free State might keep the officer on as an inspector once the construction phase of the project had been completed, as such a prospect would make the Irish job more attractive. Hanson offered to consult Finance 'without delay', but apparently with predictable results.[11]

While awaiting a response to this and on Thorn's declining the offer, Chettle then offered it to a colleague of Thorn's, Major Kinnear, then working in Ypres. Apparently he gave Kinnear to understand that the Irish were going to pay for it and he had 'no good reason to suppose…that the Irish Treasury will refuse to give effect to it'.[12] On Ware's instructions, at the end of July Browne wrote formally to Kinnear to offer him the position in Dublin with the title of Registration Officer. It was offered without permanency, on the very optimistic basis that 'the Irish graves would be cleared up in a year' : seven years later the project was still not 'cleared up'.

Kinnear initially felt it would not pay him to take it without permanency, but on 24 July he wired Browne to say he would accept it. Embarrassingly, an IWGC official, Oswald, then wrote to tell the Major that the financial details and other conditions of the post had not been settled since they were – mistakenly – awaiting the Dublin Government's confirmation that it was going to foot the bill. A very disgruntled Browne had to write Kinnear to this effect, remarking by the way to Ware, 'the whole thing has placed me in a very awkward position and I hope you will put the matter right'.[13] On 2 August, Ware, on vacation in Scotland, and still thinking

that it was up to the Irish Government to approve the salary and conditions, confided his concern to Browne that he disliked Kinnear's quest for permanence and feared that the post, in any case, 'might fall through altogether as the Irish authorities may change their minds'.

It was early in October before Ware could apologise to Hanson at having misunderstood the salary issue. Even then, with this cleared up and put behind them, he still had to confess to the OPW that he had 'not yet found the right man to recommend for the position'. It was, therefore, in a surprisingly by-the-way manner that he mentioned 'a capable officer, Captain P. E. Vesper, who has been doing similar work in Northern Ireland for the last five years'. He felt that Vesper might fit the bill at least 'in the initial stages of the work', and Vesper, if interested, would be clearly given to understand that it was to be 'a temporary arrangement'. He had not yet spoken to Captain Vesper, in case the Free State thought there might be objections to his acting 'in this dual capacity'.[14]

FAR LEFT
Memorial to Major Hubert M. Lenox-Conyngham, Kilgobbin, Stepaside, Co. Dublin

LEFT
Lt. A.O. Coghill, standard Quarker headstone, Friends' Burial Ground, Temple Hill, Co. Dublin

The Captain arrives:

It was in such an incidental manner that the remarkable relationship between Captain Vesper and the Irish authorities originated. It turned out to be a longer, more enduring and more positive one than either side could ever had anticipated at the outset. Born in 1886, Philip Edgar Vesper, having seen First World War service in the Machine Gun Corps, joined the IWGC and served as its chief clerk in Macedonia from April 1920 to December 1923. He was then appointed Area Inspector for Northern Ireland. There he had carried out his work unobtrusively until the Commission's difficulties in procuring a man for the Free State brought him to attention.[15]

On 8 October 1928, an anxious Whiskard at the Dominions Office, not having heard any news on the subject since mid-July, now asked Ware how matters stood. Browne replied for Ware, two days later, to say that 'the little misunderstanding about the payment of salary has been cleared up and we hope very shortly to arrive at a working agreement'. On the very next day, Hanson wrote from the OPW to say that there was no objection to Vesper's appointment – 'I think it will be an admirable arrangement' – and looked forward to seeing him shortly in Dublin.[16]

Vesper arrived in Dublin at the end of October 1928, following a briefing session with Chettle in London. He settled in at the Ivanhoe Hotel in Harcourt Street, within easy walking distance of the Office of Public Works. With some initial delays in securing secretarial assistance, he immediately set about the work, commencing with cemeteries in Dublin City and County. From the outset he encountered unorthodox situations arising from the chaos and pressures of the Easter Rising. In the grounds of Dr Steevens' Hospital he found war graves in what was actually the Hospital garden and surmised these would need some special kind of treatment. It proved to be one of those instances where appropriate action took a long time to come: as late as 1951 the British Legion was complaining of their neglect.[17] Likewise, in the grounds of Dublin Castle he came upon the graves of five officers which would require some kind of special treatment. Here again, the deed was a long journey from the wish. On 17 May 1963, thirty-five years later, in a quiet ceremony attended by the British Military Attaché and Catholic and Church of Ireland chaplains, they were exhumed and reinterred in Grangegorman Military Cemetery.[18]

Before October was out, Vesper had started on Grangegorman Military Cemetery with its 600 plus war graves.

His early experience convinced him that it was 'extremely unlikely we shall want to start erecting headstones before next summer', as there would be insufficient completions to justify awarding a contract, but he estimated for 1,000 headstones to be completed before the end of 1929. He was happy to report that 'all is progressing in an entirely satisfactory manner'.[19]

Soon he and the OPW would be supplied from the IWGC in London with lists of Irish war graves, remarkable in their diversity as to location and nationality. A single list which reached them in mid-November, containing over fifty names, related to records originating in Ottawa, Melbourne, St. John's, Newfoundland, and Wellington, New Zealand, all despatched to the IWGC in London back in 1920-1921. They involved the graves of Newfoundland naval personnel buried in Donegal, Australian infantrymen in Tipperary and Kerry, Canadians in Cork and Dublin, New Zealanders in Cork and Kerry.[20] Behind this and every other list which followed down the years, as has been seen and will be seen again, were stories of tragic loss and untold personal grief.

The Press complains:

News of the commencement of the work soon reached the national and international press. With a circumspection that marked his entire career in Ireland, where he almost never put a foot wrong, Vesper wisely declined to be interviewed and referred journalists to his superiors in the OPW.[21] Nonetheless, his arrival and the commencement of the task secured extensive press notice from the *Irish Times* and *Derry Weekly* to the *Daily Mail* in London, the *Daily Mail* in Brisbane and the *Gaelic American* in New York. In common, they reported Dáil Éireann's vote in the 1927-1928 Estimates of £5,000 for this work, which later had to be re-voted due to the delays in completing arrangements over 1926-1928. There were predictable varieties of view. The *Irish Times*, in January 1929, complained of the 'lack of satisfactory arrangements' and deplored the failure of the Government to join the Imperial War Graves Commission in full membership, even as the *Derry Journal*, not unfairly, deplored the neglect of the 'Patriot Graves', while the *Gaelic American* asked 'Why Honour British Soldiers?'.[22]

Inevitably, the decision of the Government to fund the work would excite opposition hostility. In a debate on the Estimates for Public Works in May 1929, the Parliamentary Secretary, Bourke, gave a clear and detailed exposition of the nature of the Government commitment on

British war graves. They estimated a total of 10,000 pre-war graves, 3,000 graves of the Great War, Easter Rising and Anglo-Irish War, and a possible additional 200 graves yet to be found, verified and registered. These 3,200 would require headstone construction at a cost of £5,000 a year for a possible five years and a further £900 a year for maintenance. Some weeks later, in an intervention during a Senate debate in July on the 1929 Appropriation Bill, Senator Kathleen Clarke, widow of executed 1916 leader, Tom Clarke, raised the whole question of what an Irish Government was doing spending money on caring for British war graves. She thought it

an extraordinary position that here in this country £25,000 can be voted for such purposes while the patriot dead are left uncared for....I have every objection to any money being spent on British military graves in Ireland, but when it comes to voting money away for such a purpose while our own graves lie derelict, I have a violent objection to such a course.[23]

Nevertheless, despite the problem of the comparative neglect of the war graves and memorials to the national heroes, what most surprises is that Kathleen Clarke's was the only voice raised in opposition in the Free State Dáil and Seanad at the time. Certainly, Chettle's observations during his short visit to

Dublin were borne out by Captain Vesper's early experience of his years of secondment – all the more surprising given the tensions that could arise suddenly, even during this period, well before de Valera's election to office was followed by a change of atmosphere.[24]

Singing the wrong song:

On the occasion of the annual Sports Day at Trinity College, Dublin, in 1929, an invitation was sent to James McNeill, Healy's successor as Governor-General. He duly attended, during the playing of 'The Soldier's Song' as national anthem. The Dublin press stridently reported this, not sparing in detail or comment. As the *Irish Independent* headline put it: '*Students Clash: Anthem Blunder in Trinity Leads to Trouble.... Insult to Injury*'.[25]

On 10 June 1929, King George V was rather surprised to learn of the incident from the Dublin correspondent of *The Times*. His private secretary, Lord Stamfordham, asked the Dominions Office to find out
what is really happening. The King can hardly imagine that Mr McNeill is in favour of the disuse of 'God Save the King' which throughout the whole of the British Empire is regarded as the National Anthem.[26]
The results of these inquiries confirmed, or even exceeded, the worst suspicions in Windsor Castle. Not only did they learn

RIGHT
Earl Granard

FAR RIGHT
Sidney Webb,
Baron Passfield,
Dominions Secretary

that the Governor-General had acted on the advice of the Saorstát Government, as a statement from President Cosgrave attested, but the Governor-General 'not only asked for 'The Soldier's Song' to be played, but refused to be received with 'God Save the King' in its stead'.[27] High Commissioner Smiddy was summoned to meet Dominions Secretary, Sidney Webb, now Baron Passfield, who deplored the incident and hoped everything that could be done would be done, to prevent it 'engendering bad feeling and intensifying old animosities'.[28]

Two days later, the King, having heard the substance of Passfield's discussion with the Irish High Commissioner, hoped that

without any bitterness of feeling the people of the Irish Free State will gradually come into line with the other Dominions where 'God Save The King' is given priority to their respective National Songs on official occasions where His Majesty's representative is present.[29]

Meanwhile, the Irish Liberal peer, Earl Granard, who had commanded the 5th Battalion Royal Irish Fusiliers during the Great War and whose house at Castle Forbes, Co Longford, was burnt down during the Civil War, entered the lists, with a letter to Cosgrave on 12 June. Cosgrave's reply was a masterly exercise in tightrope-walking, across the precipice

that divided militant nationalist and militant unionist Ireland: 'No nation but has its national anthem', as distinct from 'the National Anthem of England', he politely stated in reply, and continued:

Nor yet again do we take the view that the National Anthem of England is the Anthem of the Commonwealth of Nations...I believe that we have made the relations between Britain and Ireland better than we found them. We hope to make them better still. This, however, can only be accomplished if there is a proper appreciation of the circumstances...of this country... If this State is to be saved for the Commonwealth, we must safeguard the lives of the citizens of this State from extremists on the one side and the life of the nation itself from extremists on the other.[30]

Passfield was not impressed by this and told Smiddy as much in July. The matter eventually petered out, however, but it is a testament to Cosgrave's attempt at even-handedness that, at this very time, as will be seen later, he brought into the realm of the practical the long campaign of the Irish National War Memorial Committee for the creation of a fitting tribute to the Irish dead of the Great War.[31]

Dublin to Donegal:
Meanwhile, not far from the strife of Trinity College Sports Days, Captain

LEFT
St. Anne's, Ballylaneen,
Co. Waterford,
last resting place of the poet
Tadhg Gaelach
Ó Súilleabháin, and
Leinster victim,
Private Michael Biggane

Vesper and his OPW colleagues quietly pursued the business in hand. From its outset, the work of location, identification, verification and registration entailed a large volume of form-filling and correspondence. Early in 1929 he was provided with the support of a clerk, D. O'Keeffe, and a secretary-typist, Olive Kidd, though in the field he had to conduct his own extensive correspondence with the OPW and IWGC, at the end of every day. His work in Northern Ireland continued at this time but, by fortunate coincidence, it was now becoming less demanding as the construction aspect of it neared completion.

During his first five months he concentrated on Dublin, Wicklow, Kildare and Donegal, this last because of its proximity to his Northern Ireland commitments. Here, for example, in February 1929, he had visited the Upper Fahan Cemetery near Buncrana where he reported on its well-maintained, small country churchyard containing the graves of sixty-two sailors of the *Laurentic* who had been buried in one large plot, purchased in war time by the Admiralty. It was marked by a large naval memorial, a twelve-foot granite cross and plinth of four panels containing the names of the officers and men. This plot had been maintained free of charge by the local Select Vestry since its inception. [32]

In Dean's Grange, Dublin, by contrast, in March 1929, he found an extensive suburban cemetery with Protestant and Catholic sections and separate denominational chapels. Here was the diversity typical of large burial places. Of some seventy-four war graves, twenty-two had private memorial stones; a further few were marked by temporary, wooden military crosses still in good condition; but the vast majority were unmarked. Eventually, in February 1936, a maintenance agreement was signed between the Dean's Grange Cemetery authorities and the OPW, embracing almost all of the seventy-four war graves, as only seven of the total were still being maintained by relatives. [33]

In these first few months he investigated and registered 920 war graves in thirty-eight cemeteries and churchyards. In the case of many of the smaller rural burial places, no cemetery register existed, the only record being local memory. In such cases he had to draw plans and sketches showing with precise measurement the exact location for each such grave. He had to rely heavily, therefore, on the expertise and goodwill of the OPW's regional assistant architects, local clergy and Gardaí, and where applicable, cemetery caretakers. Mistakes, though inevitable, were surprisingly rare. When they occurred, very considerable trouble

RIGHT & FAR RIGHT
Memorial to Canadian
soldier and Leinster victim,
Michael Biggane,
Ballylaneeen,
Co. Waterford

was taken by the OPW officials and Vesper in trying to put them right.

Consider the case of Chief Petty Officer and Coastguard, Michael Mahony. He had been a crew member of H.M.S. *President II*, and had died on 23 May 1916. In their original files at headquarters, the IWGC had recorded him as buried in Kildimo Cemetery, and assumed this was in County Limerick. When Vesper visited Limerick to investigate and verify, he could find no trace of the grave. What perplexed him was that the IWGC's records gave section, row and grave numbers for the plot, something which he had thought was very unusual for small rural burial places in Ireland, and certainly did not hold for the two cemeteries he located in the Kildimo district. He told Chettle as much in September 1933 and added that the local OPW official had drawn a blank.[34] He thought therefore that Mahony might have been buried in one of the larger Limerick cemeteries that used grid references. A fortnight later, Chettle responded that the Admiralty had it that he was interred in Section 1, Row 1, Grave No 9, of Kildimo Cemetery in County Clare. Vesper enlisted the help of the OPW's Limerick architect, Joseph O'Donoghue. The latter's enquiries convinced him that 'no one young or old ever heard of a Mahony with coastguard connections in Old Kildimo, but there was a coastguard named Michael O'Shaughnessy buried there in an unmarked grave'. O'Donoghue was able to provide a scaled sketch of its exact location.[35]

Still thinking that O'Shaughnessy was the right name, eight months later Vesper remained perplexed, since 'there is no cemetery in or near Kildimo with official grave numbers', and he found it curious that the Admiralty described Kildimo as being in County Clare. He undertook to pursue the matter further when next in the area. Then, in February 1935, O'Donoghue reported a breakthrough. He had contacted an old coastguard acquaintance, Michael Pryall of Kilrush, and a Garda Sergeant Lynch of Quilty, County Clare. Sergeant Lynch confirmed a Michael Mahony buried in a Kildimo Cemetery near Miltown Malbay. He had located a family friend, a local merchant named Casey, who had actually borne the cost of Mahony's funeral until later reimbursed by the widow. Casey knew the exact location of the grave and the latest address of the widow, Annie Mahony, who lived in Appach Road, Brixton, whom O'Donoghue now contacted. Annie Mahony wrote to him, confirming the details of her late husband's career and final resting place. She had continued to visit the grave occasionally, as her modest finances permitted, and confided:

LEFT
The Dean's Grange
Cemetery war grave of
Lt Cyril J Massy, RAC,
who died on 7 April 1947,
aged 21.

'I am so relieved to hear his grave will be attended to as I am too far away myself to visit it as often as I should like to…thanking you for your efforts to find the grave'. In a later letter, to William Veale at the OPW, she added: 'I know my late husband would wish his grave to bear the national headstone'.[36]

The complexity and not infrequent duplication of Irish place-names occasionally caused Vesper, the IWGC and the OPW some confusion. In a letter to the IWGC Secretary in December 1936, Veale pointed out that, as far as they were concerned, there was no Kildimo in County Clare, that the relevant Ordnance Survey sheet showed a Kildeema townland two miles east of Quilty and six miles south of Miltown Malbay. The OPW and IWGC agreed henceforth to alter their records so as to describe the graveyard in question as Kildeema Burial Ground, County Clare.[37]

Making steady progress:
In addition to locating, identifying, verifying and registering the precise sites of the 2,000 plus war graves, the work involved negotiations with cemetery authorities for permission to erect headstones, and where possible, to acquire the plots for maintenance. In addition there was the correspondence with relatives for permission to erect the

headstones or to procure from them the text of personal inscriptions and the fee for inscribing them. Only then could the masonry contractors be brought on board by a process of public tender. As for dealing with relatives, in the first six months the OPW team had written to over 350 families for verification of details. It was anticipated that delays would arise in securing their return, and it was not uncommon for key relatives to have left for Britain or further afield.

There was, for example, the case of Michael Daniel Biggane of Bunmahon, County Waterford. He had emigrated to Canada and had enlisted as a private in the Canadian Army Service Corps. Shipped, with so many other Canadians, for the war in Europe, he had been on leave, visiting his family, when he was drowned in the sinking of the *Leinster*, on 10 October 1918. His body, with others, was washed up on the Isle of Man, from where it was shipped for burial in Ireland. He was laid to rest in Ballylaneen, County Waterford, in St. Anne's Catholic Churchyard, across the road from the ancient Ballylaneen cemetery that holds the remains of Tadhg Gaelach O'Súilleabháin, the eighteenth-century Irish poet. For some unknown reason, when his name was sent from the IWGC to Vesper at the OPW, in November 1928, on a schedule of Dominion casualties buried in

RIGHT & FAR RIGHT
British war graves of
1916 in the garden of
Dr Steevens' Hospital

Ireland, his date of death was incorrectly recorded as 10 November 1918, an error which is repeated in all official records since then. Vesper located his grave on his visit to Ballylaneen on 26 November 1930. The OPW contacted the family, with the standard request for permission to erect a war grave headstone, only to find that the father had died some years before, and the mother more recently. His brother, Patrick, was soon traced to Fulham. Patrick Biggane had quite firm views on the matter: 'I would like you to definitely understand that you are not to proceed with erection without my consent'. It was not that he was against his soldier-brother being commemorated as such, but that, with the plot already containing the remains of the parents and his sister, as well as his brother Michael, Patrick could not see how a sole Commonwealth war grave headstone could be erected there:

For your information, I would like to tell you that my brother's grave was recently opened for the burial of my mother, R.I.P. The plot which my father bought contains three graves and these had been filled by my father, sister, and my brother; I had to open my brother's grave, he being the longest dead, and of course, wishing to have my mother and father resting as near as it was possible to do so. You will see that you cannot carry out the erection of a headstone because my mother remains there too.

He went on:

Now, may I suggest another alternative which is likely to give satisfaction to all parties, and that is: I have already got details and prices of headstones and will probably select which I intend to have erected to all four now, if you wish to commemorate my brother's loss, you can do so by contributing to my headstone. You will please communicate this to the Canadian authorities for whom your [sic] acting and let me know the outcome at your earliest convenience and please do not forget my earlier remarks.[38]

Veale responded for the OPW, with regret that 'we are unable to entertain your suggested alternative'. Private Michael Biggane is commemorated still by the CWGC in its register and database, but his memorial is the family one that his brother, Patrick, had erected.[39]

In general, Vesper was hopeful that securing the permission to erect headstones would not prove costly. In the majority of small, rural cemeteries it was not customary to charge a permission fee, and, in cases where it was customary, his hope that it would be waived was usually realised. By November 1929, within a year of his arrival, having verified over 1,200 war graves, he had got almost the whole of the 'consents to erect' and acquisition of plots free of charge, and was getting close to the point when the OPW could invite tenders.[40]

Over the next few months rapid progress was made in this preliminary work. By the end of March 1930 some 1,300 war graves in 140 cemeteries and churchyards had been investigated and verified and the OPW had sent out 1,250 final verification forms to next of kin. In addition, the first three headstone contracts had been placed, for the Curragh and Grangegorman Military Cemeteries and for two special memorials for twenty-three naval graves in Rathmullan.[41] In reporting to the OPW Commissioners, Vesper paid a warm tribute to the 'conscientious and efficient services' of his two assistants, and added, 'other members of staff always give me whatever help they possibly can'.[42] In reporting twelve months later again, some 1,770 war graves in 276 cemeteries had been verified, covering the Leinster counties and Tipperary. Permission to erect had been given free of charge in almost every case. Over 1,740 families had been contacted and over 650 stones actually erected. A year later again, the number of verified sites had risen to 2,200 out of an estimated 2,500 in 372 out of an estimated 530 cemeteries. Relatives at 2,130 addresses had been successfully contacted and over 900 graves permanently memorialised. By spring 1933, when they had come upon an additional 30 cemeteries, they had verified 2,430 graves in 478 burial places out of a now estimated 550.[43] At the end of 1933 Ware was able to report to the IWGC that

the arrangements originally made have in general worked out admirably and that there had been no friction between the Commission and the Free State Government or, so far as the Commission is concerned, between the Free State Government and the relatives,

and, despite some possible difficulties which patience and goodwill would overcome, 'Captain Vesper had carried out his duties with steady success'. However, it was not all to be plain sailing, as a later chapter shall disclose.[44]

Getting the record straight:

Vesper was proud of the work that he and his OPW colleagues were managing to accomplish, and indeed, was anxious to see it projected and promoted to best effect. Beginning in 1931, he enclosed some photographs of the work in Kildare, Dublin and Donegal, for possible use by the Commissioners for the OPW's annual report. The Commissioners may have shared his sense of satisfaction at the progress of the work but they preferred to report in a matter of fact, understated way. In July 1931 they decided not to publish illustrations of the work and they repeated that decision in the years that

BELOW
Recruitment poster, 1914.

followed, despite the fact that their annual reports were well-illustrated at the time. Vesper enthusiastically recommended potentially good group sites in Cork and Limerick military cemeteries in 1932, but his OPW superior, Veale, thought it better to postpone publishing such illustrations until the 1933/1934 draft report.[45] Two years later, in the autumn of 1935, Veale advised the Commissioners that it would be 'unwise to give the stones publicity'.[46] In response, Commissioner O'Hegarty put the nail in the coffin of photographic publicity for the project:

In view of the Department of Finance desire that our Annual Reports should be compressed....and the doubtful suitability of such photographs for illustrative purposes, I think the proposal might well be dropped.

Indeed, the annual reports themselves were compressed out of existence by Finance after 1940 and did not reappear until exactly fifty years later.

For all Vesper's enthusiasm, both the IWGC and the OPW were blessed in his tact and sensitivity. On a brief visit to London at the beginning of April 1929, he stressed to Browne the importance of the IWGC making a high-level goodwill visit to Dublin. He repeated this in a confidential letter written from Belfast in mid-April, enclosing a copy of his first report to the OPW, and urging that 'such a visit might be of value in maintaining interest in the Commission's work generally and it would confirm the fact that the Commission were especially interested in the work in the Saorstát'; but, he was clearly anxious that 'there should be no mention that the proposed visit was suggested by me'.[47]

If he was frustrated in his attempts to get illustrations into the OPW annual reports, he was acutely conscious of the need to give the work publicity in the annual reports of the IWGC itself. However, inseparable from this awareness was his considerable concern as to how this was to be done. He wrote to Arthur Browne in August 1930 suggesting that 'it might be of considerable interest and diplomatically sound to make some special comment in the Commission's next Annual Report respecting the arrangements which have been made with the Saorstát Government', and mentioning the progress to date. He was quick to add, however, that if the IWGC agreed to this

It would be essential to send the OPW a draft...as it would be necessary for them to communicate with the Minister for the Interior [sic]; such action, however, would be appreciated by the Free State but if the invitation to comment was omitted, it might, in my opinion, be taken as a 'slight', or at least a lack of interest on the part of the Commission in the work being carried out by the Free State.[48]

There subsequently grew up the practice that all IWGC draft annual reports, where they related to Ireland, were transmitted to External Affairs and the OPW for vetting before publication. The same proved true when it came to the important Cemetery Registers for Ireland, which the Commission in 1931 were preparing for publication in three volumes covering Dublin, Munster, and the remainder of the Free State. The IWGC Director of Records informed Cassedy of the OPW that they

desire that the introductory statement, as drafted, should be examined and altered, if necessary, so that the references, which they deem essential, to Military operations and events in Ireland shall be made with due discretion.

He had in mind, in particular, two of the historical events which had brought about the existence of a number of these graves, namely, the sinking of the *Leinster* and the Easter Rising. Cassedy ran this draft past the Department of External Affairs who in turn referred it to the Office of the President, where Cosgrave himself used the red pen to make a number of corrections and amendments. In a handwritten note of 10 November 1931, he pointed out that the Introduction's reference to

3,000 Volunteers and Citizen Army personnel taking part in the Easter Rising in Dublin 'is ludicrous and should not be given in any official publication'. Cosgrave added, in reference to the opinion of his own secretary, O'Hegarty, 'as far as I know your figure of 900 is on the big side'. O'Hegarty actually wanted any reference to the sinking of the *Leinster* and to the Easter Rising removed, thinking that the *Leinster* reference 'has the appearance of propaganda and as such is out of place in a publication which is purely a memorial of the dead', but Cosgrave overrode him, remarking 'I do not see that there is much objection to publication of the description of the confllict'.[49]

These comments were passed back to Walshe in External Affairs, who duly transmitted them to the OPW. Apart from requesting the deletion of the *Leinster* passage, and the correction of the 3,000 to 900 in the passage entitled 'The Conflict of Easter 1916', he had no other objection to the IWGC's text or to its proposal to inform relatives of its impending publication. Indeed, he himself had discussed it with Cosgrave's secretary and, although the latter remained uneasy, he 'agrees that we cannot object to some description of Easter Week appearing in the introduction provided the facts are accurate'.[50] These Irish Cemetery

Registers were a very small part of the IWGC's large project to produce them for its war graves all over the world, and, unsurprisingly therefore, it was almost four years before the proofs for the Irish volumes were sent to the OPW for final comment. A relieved Cassedy was able to enclose copies of the proofs to External Affairs showing that Dublin's editorial suggestions had been fully taken on board.[51]

Peace, perfect peace
Until the day break

George Geddes, father and son,
Skipper & Trimmer,
H.M. Drifter "Speedwell V"
28 October 1916

Kilscoran Churchyard
Co. Wexford

Chapter 9

Construction, 1929-1935

The construction part of the war graves project, which involved producing, inscribing and erecting the headstones, began in Dublin with Contract No 1, of 304 memorials for Grangegorman Military Cemetery, awarded to Messrs C. W. Harrison of Pearse Street, on 23 January 1930. It was followed immediately by a second contract to Harrison's for 305 memorials in the same cemetery. By 1932 Harrison's were extensively engaged in Dublin City and County, north and south. [1] Investigations into Waterford, Cork and Limerick began in the course of 1930-1931[2] and the major contract for Munster went to Thomas McCarthy and Sons of Copley Street, Cork, who began their work in 1930. This included the erection of a special memorial screen wall in Fermoy Military Cemetery in memory of twenty-two soldiers whose graves could not precisely be located.[3] In South Leinster and the West, the work was assigned to Robins Bros of Portarlington.[4] The contract for the Northwest and border counties went to Monaghan of Mountcharles. The great bulk of this construction was completed by the summer of 1935, with only minor works taking the OPW into 1937-1938.[5]

This large undertaking was conducted with a minimum of fuss and, with the exception of a few robust disputes between the OPW and three local authorities as described later[6], met with relatively little trouble at a national, political level, as distinct from a personal or familial one. As regards the latter, it was not all plain sailing.

With the coming to power of deValera and Fianna Fáil in March 1932, Vesper certainly felt a change of atmosphere, and reported as much to his London superior, Fabian Ware, in August 1933. He was careful to preface his report with positive comments and insisted that

my relations with all Authorities and Officials in general and the Staff of the Office of Public Works in particular, have been and continue to be excellent. No attached officer could have been more kindly treated or more readily assisted.

Nonetheless, he had to face the fact that what he called 'some minor difficulties which always exist have been increasingly conspicuous since the change of Government early last year'. He found that the very great majority of relatives of the war dead in the Free State were 'very keen to get the standard headstones erected', but

the increasing feeling of resentment against England on the part of many people and the extreme views (of different sections) of such a large portion of the population are more prominently evident.

RIGHT
War grave contractor
CW Harrison of Dublin

FAR RIGHT
War grave contractor
Thomas McCarthy of Cork

Thus far he had encountered no instances of malicious damage to the IWGC headstones already erected, even when 'Pilgrimages to the graves of Irish Patriots bring them close to war graves. It would only need one bad case to be a precedent for others'.[7]

The Cross of Sacrifice – The Stone of Remembrance:

Vesper, despite his own bonhomie and the cordial climate he found within the OPW, was always skating on thin ice and knew it, even before deValera's advent to office. In Dublin, in September 1931, he had had a visit from Chettle who reported back on Vesper's virtues, but also on his difficulties. In Chettle's report to Ware, he praised Vesper as

doing the work energetically, thoroughly, economically, in the spirit of which we ask and with an absence of friction which is really his greatest service to us.

In case the IWGC vice-chairman, however, was not au fait, 'there are special problems in the Free State which it is difficult to put on paper'. Not least among them, apart from 'the large area and scatteredness', were

the lingering feelings of resentment which are illustrated in the IRA plots of so many cemeteries and the difference in outlook which

tends to make an Englishman impatient or hopeless.

He confessed that Vesper faced many challenges and, not least among them, he had 'the whole question of Crosses of Sacrifice to deal with'.[8]

The Cross of Sacrifice, and the Stone of Remembrance, were, from the early 1920s, standard monuments in IWGC cemeteries in Britain and its battlefield burial grounds across the world. The Cross, designed by Reginald Blomfield, and the Stone of Remembrance, designed by Sir Edwin Lutyens, while elegant and evocative, were large and expensive memorials. Lutyens' Stone was a standard twelve feet high, on three raised steps, bearing the inscription 'Their Name Liveth for Evermore'. Blomfield's Cross of Sacrifice, faced with a symbolic bronze sword, stood eighteen feet high in its smallest version and thirty-two feet high at its largest. Both were expensive to make, transport and install. This notwithstanding, 400 Stones of Remembrance and 1,000 Crosses of Sacrifice had been erected, the world over, by 1927.[9] Ware was determined to have them for the Irish Free State: Northern Ireland in due course would have six Crosses of Sacrifice, but no Stones of Remembrance, in its larger cemeteries.[10]

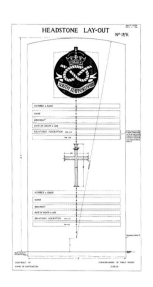

RIGHT
OPW drawing 1930,
Headstone layout with
Regimental badge.

In July 1929 he supplied the Assistant Finance Officer of the IWGC with a list of eight cemeteries in the Free State, each containing forty or more war graves which he supposed 'will normally for their size, have a Cross of Sacrifice erected in them'. He tabulated these eight as follows:

Cemetery	Approx. No. of Burials
Cork Military	76
Curragh	104
Dean's Grange	71
Glasnevin	140

and added: '*There may be other cases of the same category. What are we going to do about this?*'[11] Two years later, despite Chettle's intimations to him concerning the delicacy of the Irish situation, Ware contacted the OPW to express the hope that Hanson and he might soon be able to meet:

amongst other things I should like to discuss with you in due course is the desirability of erecting our large Cross of Sacrifice in some of the Free State cemeteries. This marks our War Cemeteries everywhere else.[12]

This was in spite of quite explicit advice given to him by Chettle following a visit

to Dublin by the latter. In October 1931, Chettle advised him that Vesper felt this question 'should be left to be dealt with last', and Chettle himself added:

until the present unrest in Ireland had died down, I don't think it advisable to ask the Irish Government to emphasise its work for the Commission by putting up Crosses of Sacrifice.[13]

Cemetery	Approx. No. of Burials
Grangegorman	614
Limerick St. Lawrence	44
Queenstown	74
Upper Fahan Donegal	66

Exactly three years later, following upon his third visit to the OPW in Dublin, Chettle advised Ware directly and bluntly:

it would be useless and dangerous to raise the question of putting up War Stones or War Crosses in the present state of public feeling.[14]

There the matter rested and there it rests still to the present day: no Cross of Sacrifice or Stone of Remembrance marks any cemetery in the Irish Republic, the only ones anywhere being those in the Irish National War Memorial Garden in Islandbridge, Dublin.[15]

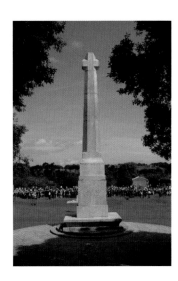

Fighting to remember:

However inclement the political climate may have been, there was no gainsaying the IWGC's claim that the majority of the next of kin wished to see the standard IWGC headstones erected over the graves of their war dead. The marching to cemeteries and ceremonies of remembrance by all sides, whether Republicans or British Legionaries, in the fraught Free State of the 1920s and 1930s, never resulted in collective acts of desecration or malicious damage in cemeteries, and never became a serious impediment to the marking of the war graves. Vesper's sound judgement and common sense saved the IWGC from political blunders in this raw-edged Ireland. Nevertheless, it was not a trouble-free progress, as Vesper, the OPW, and their contractors were to find.

Misunderstanding and disappointment arose over issues of eligibility. The question of the cut-off date, 31 August 1921, caused grief in Ireland as it did in Great Britain and the Commonwealth at large. Typical were the cases of Margaret Byrne and Daniel Mulcahy. A war widow of Francis Street, Limerick, Margaret wrote to the OPW in February 1933 to apply for a standard headstone over her dead husband's grave. Edward Byrne had been a private in the Royal Munster Fusiliers. Suffering disabilities, he was discharged in 1925 and passed

away on 18 April 1932. It was hard for her to accept that his date of death rendered him ineligible. Similar was the case of Daniel Mulcahy. He wrote on 3 July 1934 from Evergreen Street, Cork, to request a stone for his son, Michael who had served with the 9th Battalion of the Munsters. He was totally disabled during the Great War, was discharged on 12 January 1917 and died on 20 April 1932. His father's application met with the inevitable and identical negative response. These examples were by no means exceptional. Between 1933 and 1938, similar ineligible applications came from Ballina, Ballinasloe, Moville, Thurles, Tipperary and Waterford.[16] There were also misunderstandings of a more profound nature. On 20 November 1935, the *Irish Press* carried a feature on the just published *Report of the Commissioners of Public Works for the year 1932-1933* which showed that, up to 31 March 1933, some 2,436 British war graves had now been verified in 476 cemeteries, and that 1,232 war grave headstones had been erected.[17] On the same day, doubtless having read the *Irish Press* report, Joseph Purcell of Athy, County Kildare, wrote to the Commissioners to request a war grave headstone for his brother, Daniel William Purcell. Daniel had died on 13 May 1926 and was buried in his native village of Arless, Ballickmoyler, County Carlow. According to Joseph, his brother had

been a member of the 5th Battalion, Carlow Brigade of the IRA, from 1917 to the Civil War ceasefire in 1923. He had been interned in the Curragh and later at Gormanston, where he went on hunger strike during the Civil War. He died from heart trouble and his mother and brother, lacking funds, now approached the OPW, as 'my mother and I would like to have a small tombstone with a scroll, to have his name inscribed on it'. Whether with embarrassment or without, the OPW Secretary wrote to Joseph Purcell, in December 1935, to express regret that the OPW has 'no provision in our Vote which will enable us to undertake this work'.[18]

Feuding to forget:

In July 1932 at Paulstown, County Kilkenny, the monument sculptors Robins Bros, began to erect a standard war grave headstone over the burial plot of Private Michael O'Neill of the 4th Battalion, Royal Irish Regiment. He was killed on 19 March 1916, aged twenty one. They were confronted by relatives who refused to allow Robins to proceed. The contractor contacted Vesper for instructions and an investigation was initiated by Veale. On 10 August 1932 Veale wrote to the dead man's mother, Kate O'Neill of Talbot's Hill, Clifden, County Kilkenny. The previous

December they had sent her a form of consent, which she duly signed, verifying the particulars and granting permission for the standard IWGC headstone. They then understood, from Robins, that she now objected and they wanted to know from her, directly, if the contractor 'is correct in stating that you object to the erection of the headstone at our expense'.[19] Mrs O'Neill responded immediately:

I did not raise any objection to your erecting the Headstone at your own expense nor knew nothing about any objecting been [sic] made… didn't even know the Headstone had arrived, nobody has any authority to raise any objection. I am verry [sic] thankful to you for erecting it.[20]

Veale, accordingly, wanted to know from the contractor whether any other relative or caretaker had raised the objection, and, at the same time, assured Mrs O'Neill that they noted her wish to have the stone erected and would arrange for same when the contractor was again back in the area.[21]

It did not come to pass. Six years later, a memorandum from William Brandon of OPW head office to district assistant architect, J. H. Williams, revealed that the unnamed relatives, who, apparently, were the actual grave owners, had refused permission. Robins subsequently used the stone for his

contract in Roscommon, having stored it at his Portarlington works for three years after 1932.[22] In the resultant dispute as to what Robins, therefore, owed the OPW who had paid him for the job, and as to what they owed him for his having stored the stone for three years, Brandon suggested that Robins be simply asked to agree, in principle, to carve a new stone for Private O'Neill and to erect it free of charge, 'if called upon to do so by the Board at any future date'. In July 1941, the district assistant architect reported that 'the grave is still unmarked and there has been no private memorial erected since last inspection'.[23] Nor was one ever erected in Paulstown Cemetery thereafter. Instead, the War Graves Commission made arrangements with the OPW to provide alternative commemoration: today Private O'Neill's name can be found inscribed on Panel 5 of the Grangegorman Memorial Screen Wall.[24]

Another Kilkenny case arose from the death of Private James Conway of the Royal Army Service Corps, who passed away on 1 September 1916 and came to be buried in Ferrybank Catholic Churchyard, County Kilkenny. When Vesper visited the site in July 1930 he found that in this old churchyard the graves were never bought out nor was any record of their exact location kept. The local people, in the course of time,

had acquired 'recognised rights of burial' in particular plots where their next of kin were laid. The effective cemetery authority was the local parish priest, Fr Edward Brennan. When he gave his permission for the erection of a standard stone he added, in a letter to Vesper,

The friends of the deceased don't seem eager to avail of your kind offer. They say other members of the family are buried in the same plot of graves and they wouldn't wish for a stone omitting their names.

However, he concluded, 'I believe the stone, if erected, would not be interfered with'.[25]

Reassured by this, perhaps, the appropriate headstone was made but, as the district assistant architect reported three years later, when the contractor proceeded to install it, the relatives objected and the stone was returned to the contractor's works in Dublin.[26] Six years later, in June 1939, another site visit still found no stone erected, and, sadly,

the site of the grave and ground in its vicinity are covered with grass and blackberry bushes four feet high. There is nothing to show that any grave has been made here.[27]

As Vesper made his way around the country, his investigations were doubtless

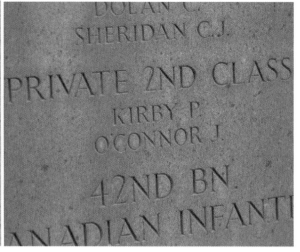

raising expectations among local next of kin. Thus, similar cases arose in County Cork in 1932. One concerned the grave of Able Seaman John Hayes, who died on 6 January 1916 and was buried in the old graveyard of Rosscarbery, where his plot was just twelve yards from the ruins of the ancient abbey. His grave was covered with an unmarked slab. This burial ground was in the charge of the West Cork Board of Health and Public Assistance and, in March 1932, they gave the OPW permission to erect a standard headstone. His brother, as next of kin, may well have wished to have had the headstone placed there but, on 6 May 1932, he wrote, simply, to the OPW, as follows:

*Dear Sir,
I have informed some of my friends who have a right to the burying plot, about the Erection of a Headstone. They said they would not allow it. So that ends the matter.*

*I remain, Yours sincerely
D.J. Hayes.*

He had fully completed the Verification Form, save for his signature of consent, and returned it to them in this manner.[28]

Almost identical circumstances attended the treatment of the grave of Private Patrick Kirby, buried in Kilshannig Church of Ireland Churchyard, County Cork. He died serving in the RAF

in October 1918, leaving a widow at Broom Lane, Mallow. Vesper conducted his usual local investigations and found Kirby was actually buried in a grave plot whose sole control lay with his cousin, J. Byrne, of Main Street, Mallow. Whatever Mrs Kirby may have wanted, the cousin had a private headstone already in place at the plot. Vesper reported, following his site visit in November 1932:

It is marked by a private permanent memorial upon which the soldier's name is not inscribed, and Mr. Byrne has definitely stated that he would not permit any inscription to be added nor will he allow any further memorial to be erected, and has definitely stated that he will, under no circumstances, permit a standard or any other memorial to be erected.

Half a century later, Patrick Kirby was commemorated on the Grangegorman Memorial.[29]

Not far from here there was another case, but involving a much longer time of travail. It concerned the last resting place, at Skibbereen Chapelyard Graveyard, of Lieutenant Patrick John Herlihy of the RAF, who died on 5 December 1918. In November 1919 his cousin, Denis Herlihy, wrote from Shreelane, Leap, County Cork, to the Directorate of Graves Registration and Enquiries in London to point out that

no cross or memorial had been erected
to mark the dead lieutenant's grave.
They replied, in December 1919, to say
they could arrange to have a temporary,
military wooden cross erected at the
site if he so desired. However, early in
January 1920, cousin Denis replied,
this time from Ranelagh, Dublin, now
stating:

*I think it would be more appropriate if the
relatives of the deceased erected a suitable
memorial when conditions are more favourable
than at present. While thanking you for
suggested erection of temporary wooden cross by
the Military, I will not, in the circumstances,
trouble them in the matter.*[30]

Twelve years had passed when Vesper
visited the graveyard, during his Munster
tour of investigation. Following on
that site visit, and though armed with
the registration details of 1919-1920,
he was unable to locate the unmarked
grave. The OPW nonetheless managed
to contact Denis Herlihy again, with a
postal address still in Ranelagh. They
told Herlihy that they proposed to erect
a headstone if he would kindly mark
the exact spot on a sketch they sent him.
Three years passed without result. Still
in pursuit of the matter, in June 1935
the OPW asked Vesper's advice as to
whether, in the circumstances, they
should erect a memorial somewhere
in the chapel grounds, simply inscribed

'Buried in this Graveyard'. Vesper
advised against: 'No: the next of kin's
letter of January 1920 goes to show
the Relatives don't particularly desire a
headstone'.

However, later in 1935, the district OPW
officer, J. Parnell Martin, managed to
locate Denis Herlihy again, now living
at Thorn Hill, Skibbereen, and, in
October the latter took the OPW officer
to the exact location. The lieutenant
had been buried in his father's grave,
topped by an uninscribed covering slab.
Veale of the OPW sent Herlihy a final
Verification Form in November 1935
but, on its not being returned, he now
informed Herlihy that 'it is assumed that
you do not desire to have a standard
headstone erected over the grave of Lt.
P. J. Herlihy'. Five years later again, in
April 1940, the district OPW officer
visited the site and confirmed that
all that marked Lieutenant Herlihy's
plot was 'an undressed slab over it'.
Lieutenant Herlihy, however, was not
entirely forgotten, his name coming to
be alternatively commemorated over
forty years later, on Panel 10 of the
Grangegorman Memorial.[31]

Not far away, in the parish of Inishcarra,
another such case unfolded around the
same time. Here, in South Kilmurry
Graveyard, lay the remains of Thomas
Kerr of Bandon, a boatman in the
Royal Navy Coastguard Service. He

died on 17 November 1918 and would have been eligible for a standard war grave headstone. Vesper visited the site in November 1931 and located the grave in the plot of the Bradfield family, who were in-laws. The Bradfields were themselves no strangers to the Great War: Elizabeth Bradfield married local farmer James Good of Callatrim, outside Bandon, and they had four sons who fought in the conflict. They were not strangers to the War of Independence, either: Tom Bradfield identified himself as one of the few Protestants in West Cork who were self-confessedly loyalist, and open about it. It cost him his life.[32] The four Bradfield sons today, with others, are commemorated by the Bandon War Memorial. The Kilmurry plot was marked by an old Bradfield family headstone. This notwithstanding, Vesper was told by a family member that there would be no objection to an IWGC headstone being erected for Kerr. Yet, when in September 1932 the OPW sent the Verification Form to the widow, Mrs Kerr replied, in pencil:

My husband is buried in Kilmurry but there is a Headstone there and it was only an obliged grave [sic] given me in my trouble its not my own place so I have no authority to do anything about it and it's sad for me to be reminded of his death again so often.

Over fifty years later, Thomas Kerr received alternative commemoration on the Grangegorman Memorial. [33]

Poverty and pride:

While the work of construction generally made steady progress in the 1930s, family circumstance could create hard cases when it came to the matter of personal inscriptions on the stones. There was the case of Sergeant Pobjoy, Royal Field Artillery, buried in St. George's Burial Ground, Whitworth Road, Drumcondra, Dublin. He died on 23 July 1920. In January 1929 the cemetery authorities gave permission for his commemoration and that of two other war dead, by standard headstone. However, it was one of the exceptionally few authorities who held out for a permission fee: out of 550 with over 2,500 war graves, a fee was demanded by cemetery authorities only in respect of eight cemeteries for permission to erect headstones, and in only one case in the whole country, in Sligo, was a fee exacted for title to the grave.[34] The St. George's Select Vestry pointed out that the cemetery expenses exceeded its income. They eventually relented, to the extent of accepting a fee of fifteen instead of thirty shillings per permission.[35]

Pobjoy's widow, Elizabeth, ordered a personal inscription for his stone: the

simple words 'Thy Will Be Done' cost four shillings and four pence to engrave. Then, in December 1930, she had to request more time to pay:

I was in a position to pay it when I first ordered it a long time ago – but since then the firm that employed me went out of business and I lost my position....I trust you will be able to hold the matter over for a little longer as I am anxious that these words should appear on the headstone.[36]

Two years went by when Veale wrote to tell her they could now only hold off until the end of January 1933: on 31 January she remitted the amount in full and thanked them for waiting. The cemetery, with its three war graves of 1914-1918 and its single one of 1939-1945, remained in excellent order thereafter, during caretaker Henderson's time from the early 1930s to1956, when he resigned in ill-health, and after that, during the caretaking years of his successor, Luke Doran.

Conscious of the problem of inability to pay, Ware had sought Hanson's support for a policy of flexibility and discretion when it came to hard cases. As he observed to the OPW chairman in May 1929:

We felt that in the great majority of cases this inability was genuine and was deeply regretted and we decided that, as a matter of grace, we would, wherever inability to pay was established, add the cost of the personal inscription to the Commission's account.

Pointing out that this difficulty had arisen in about ten per cent of cases, he wondered if the Free State Government would be willing to follow suit. Hanson's response appeared surprisingly unyielding:

...personally I cannot see why there should be any difficulties. The relatives know beforehand that they must pay for the personal inscriptions and they are given the alternative of accepting or rejecting on the score of cost, the opportunity.

Under these circumstances what we propose to do is to make all arrangements for the erection of the headstones, and to ask the relatives to forward to us the cost of the proposed personal inscriptions. If, after sending them a second application, the cost is not forthcoming, then we shall be obliged to omit the personal inscription.

In a concluding remark, however, he appeared to relent, observing that *if any case occurs in which a relative...is unable to pay for it but asks that it be added to the headstone at our expense, we will, of course, consider such an application on its merits.*[37]

Such a special case arose sooner, perhaps, than he anticipated, and Ware lost little time in bringing it to the OPW's

attention. It concerned the war grave in Grangegorman of Joseph Barraclough of Shipley, Yorkshire. A private of the Royal Defence Corps, and previously of the West Yorkshire Regiment, he was drowned in the sinking of the *Leinster* on 10 October 1918, aged thirty-three. He was one of twenty-nine RDC men aboard, and was probably going home on leave.[38]

On receiving the usual IWGC forms, his only son, George, wrote from Bradford in March 1929:

Dear Sirs,
As son of my father, Joseph Barraclough, I feel grateful to know that a stone will be put on my dad's grave. I never remember my dad and now I am left an orphan as my mother died on Armistice Day two years ago, and since, I have been unable to work due to sickness. I am only sixteen years old and not having had an opportunity to work I cannot pay for a personal inscription but would very much like one on the stone. Do you think it is possible to help me? I would like the following:

HE DIED THAT WE SHOULD LIVE.

I am now dependent on my relatives for my existence. I have no pension and as there is a lot of unemployment in Bradford I cannot get any situation. Could you oblige me by advising me if I could obtain any assistance from a source that may exist for the purpose of helping boys which are in a position similar to myself.[39]

As Ware said, in reporting this to Hanson, 'there are exceedingly few cases of this kind', and he hoped for a sympathetic Saorstát response.[40] Barraclough got his memorial stone.

Completions:

Despite family disagreements over the matter of memorials, what is striking is that they appear to have been a tiny minority of the recorded installations, and the evidence suggests that relatives generally were keen to have the standard headstone, whenever possible. Notable in this regard is the case of the Slatterys of Darragh, near Ennis County Clare. Captain Francis Slattery, the 8th Field Company, Royal Engineers, died on 9 January 1919, at the age of twenty-six. His remains were interred in an unmarked grave in Ballynacally (Kilchreest) Old Cemetery, nine miles southwest of Ennis.

Vesper first visited the cemetery in January 1933, but could find no one, neither caretaker nor older residents, who knew where the grave was located. He therefore wondered if there might have been a registration confusion with Kilchreest, County Galway, a few miles southwest of Loughrea. In the IWGC Records Division, however, Chettle was adamant that there was no such mistake: the father, Thomas Slattery, had insisted

1914 – 1918   1939 – 1945
THOSE HONOURED
ON THESE PANELS
GAVE THEIR LIVES
IN TWO WORLD WARS
AND ARE BURIED
ELSEWHERE IN IRELAND

THE FACING MEMORIALS
COMMEMORATE THOSE OF
THEIR COMRADES IN ARMS
WHOSE GRAVES ARE IN
CORK MILITARY CEMETERY

that there was a family headstone but without his son's name inscribed. Eventually, Vesper wrote to Thomas, a retired national school teacher, who undertook to point out its exact location to caretaker Michael O'Toole. Thomas Slattery managed to meet O'Toole at the cemetery in June 1933 and they drew a sketch of the exact location and sent it on to the OPW. Thomas signed the consent form on 21 August 1933, adding the text of a substantial personal inscription, but failed to post it. The dead Captain Slattery's brother, Michael, then living in Clapham, London, contacted the OPW, in February 1934, to tell them of his father's death and of his discovery of the unposted consent form, which he now sent them with the text of personal inscription.[41] He was deeply anxious to know how matters stood. Three years later, the OPW district officer, T. J. McCarthy, visited the cemetery in November 1937 and reported the grave and memorial thus:

could not be much better – neat, new, cut-stone plinth encloses grave – cross neatly inscribed, [the stone] in perfect condition, recently erected.[42]

By the time of McCarthy's report on the grave and memorial of Captain Slattery, the work of construction had been largely completed. Some 2,545 war graves had been verified, and some 2,128 standard headstones in 545

cemeteries erected.[43] Indeed, in July 1935, the OPW Secretary was able to write to the IWGC to say that the work had so far progressed that they found it possible 'to release Captain Vesper on the 4th instant, to take up duty with you'. The OPW stressed, however, that they so valued his knowledge and judgement that they hoped the IWGC would not object if Dublin continued, through correspondence, to seek his advice and expertise even after his departure, as indeed Dublin did.[44]

As for Vesper himself, with the end of his formal secondment in sight, he prepared a detailed 'handing-over' report to the OPW, on 2 July 1935, with ninety per cent of the work completed. By the end of his six years of secondment, he and the OPW had had to deal with approximately 2,550 war graves in 550 cemeteries. He had personally visited and verified all of them, with the exception of four war graves, in four isolated cemeteries, of which they had only recently been apprised. He was able, therefore, to hand over all 550 individual cemetery files to his OPW colleague, Brandon. His report commented on the precise status of every contract and there remained only three substantial matters to be dealt with – the arrangement of war grave maintenance contracts, the provision of a special memorial in Glasnevin, and the

LEFT & RIGHT
Drogheda WWI
Memorial including the
name of the poet
Francis Ledwidge (detail)

resolution of certain issues of principle regarding headstones for County Sligo and County Clare. All three are the subject of the chapters which follow. He concluded with a warm tribute to William Veale:

I could not have worked under a more just and considerate supervising officer, while my staff have on all occasions been most conscientious, energetic and efficient. [45]

Right
A sailor of the 1939-1945 War: Known unto God. Dugort, Achill Island, Co. Mayo

I have fought the good fight
I finished my course
I kept the faith

G. Grey, Gunner
Royal Field Artillery
11 October 1919

Grangegorman Military Cemetery

A SAILOR
OF THE
1939-1945
WAR
ROYAL NAVY
FOUND 17TH DECEMBER 1940

KNOWN UNTO GOD

Fondest Memories of
Maisie Spratt
Late of Dromore Co.Down
18-9-1940 – 9-11-2000.

Obstruction, 1931-1937

One of the most peaceful and untroubled examples of the full process of war graves administration related to the remains of Lieutenant Colonel Roger Casement, Royal Field Artillery, who passed away on 21 December 1917, aged fifty- seven. He was buried in Killiskey Church of Ireland Churchyard, an arcadian retreat one mile from Ashford, Co Wicklow. When Vesper visited, in June 1931, he found 'an attractive country churchyard...[with] large private burial plots belonging to prominent local residents and Estates. The whole is well looked after and has a most pleasant and restful appearance'.[1] Casement's was, and remains, the sole war grave there. At the end of August 1931 Canon Moore, the local rector, informed the OPW that his cemetery authorities and the widow, Catherine Isabel Tottenham Casement, of Cronroe, gave 'full approval' to the erection of the standard headstone.[2] Six years later, the OPW applied successfully to Canon Moore's successor, Rev. W. E. Vandaleur, to secure a maintenance agreement.[3] Seven years later again, Catherine having passed away, Vandaleur sought and secured permission to have her name added to the headstone. Every year, from then till the present, all was reported 'in perfect order'.[4]

Remains and refusals:
Not so peaceful and orderly were the circumstances arising from the remains of another Roger Casement, first cousin of the Lieutenant Colonel's father, Julius, and himself a childhood visitor to their Cronroe home.[5] As the OPW concluded the construction phase of its work and began entering the second phase of establishing agreements for the maintenance of the war graves, it ran into unexpected trouble in County Kerry. Here, the civil and military cemeteries at Tralee, so frequently the subject of complaints of neglect in the 1920s, continued so into the 1930s. In May 1936, Tynan of the British Legion wrote to the OPW to recommend an ex-soldier, Barrett, of Haig's Terrace, Tralee, as a suitable person to be caretaker of Tralee's war graves and offered, in addition, to find suitable caretakers for the remaining war graves in other Kerry cemeteries. The OPW declined the offer as they were in communication with the Kerry Board of Health on the matter.[6] In April 1936 they had sent a standard letter to the Board to seek a maintenance agreement for three war graves in Killarney New Cemetery: one was that of Private Robert Emmett Kinchington of the 3rd Battalion, Australian Infantry, who died in Killarney in 1919 while awaiting transportation home. As briefly described earlier, his mother, Ellen, in 1934 had paid for the personal

RIGHT
The headstone to
Lt Roger Casement and
his wife, Catherine,
Killiskey, Co. Wicklow

inscription to go on his Commonwealth headstone. The Secretary replied in May, enclosing an extract from the minutes of the Kerry Board of Health meeting of 28 April:

Order – inform Board of Works that the Board [of Health] will consider the maintenance of these graves when the remains of the late Roger Casement have been returned to Ireland by the British Government.[7]

The response, if it took the OPW by surprise, did not come out of the blue. While requests for the repatriation of Sir Roger Casement's remains had first been made during 1929-1931, concern over the issue increased in Irish Government circles when deValera came to power in 1932. Public pressure intensified in the course of 1935 and questions were posed in both the Irish and British parliaments.[8] With rumours circulating that Pentonville Prison, which housed his remains, was to be demolished, deValera was questioned in the Dáil by Deputy Norton, who referred to the 'widespread desire on the part of the public that steps would be taken officially' to secure repatriation, especially in the light of the opportunity 'that may not arise again'. DeValera replied that he had made enquiries, and, privately, he had appealed to Prime Minister Stanley Baldwin, but to no avail.[9] As to public agitation in the matter, deValera himself urged

that it would be counter-productive. Norton and other deputies reopened the question in March and April 1936. With some point, Norton remarked that when the British Government had requested the repatriation of dead British soldiers, that request had been granted: he asked deValera if the British had been reminded of this when the Irish Government had requested the repatriation of Casement's remains. The response was in the negative:

The Government does not consider that any additional reason was required to support the application or that any reference to the transfer to England of the remains of British soldiers was necessary or would have been appropriate.[10]

Repeated attempts were made from the 1930s through to the 1950s, equally in vain, and it was not until January 1965 that Prime Minister Harold Wilson relented and finally agreed, leading to the Irish State Funeral for Casement on 1 March 1965.[11] In the meantime, if the deValera Government was placed on the horns of a dilemma by rejection in 1936, the OPW was similarly impaled by the Kerry Board of Health's refusal to maintain its British war graves. Officials of the OPW drafted and redrafted possible replies to the Kerry authorities, phrased and rephrased so as not to ignite controversy or inflame opinion. Eventually, on 12 June 1936,

with Commissioner Diarmuid Ó hÉigeartaigh's blessing, the OPW formally replied. It explained that it was obliged to secure the maintenance of the war graves and trusted that

the Co. Kerry Board of Health will co-operate with us in securing that the twelve war graves in the Cemeteries under their control shall be kept clear of weeds and loose soil and generally in a condition befitting the Cemeteries [and those interred therein][sic].

It concluded by hoping that, if the Kerry Board

do not see their way to make a contract with us like other Cemetery Authorities…they will offer no objection to our making a contract for maintenance by some other party and will afford the Contractor, so employed, the facilities for execution of the work.[12]

Having considered this letter at its meeting on 23 June 1936, the Kerry Board resolved:

We ask the OPW to draw the attention of the British Government to the fact that the Board are undertaking the maintenance of war graves and asking that they would be good enough to take up the representations of the entire Irish nation and demand the return of the remains of Roger Casement to Ireland in accordance with their rights.[13]

On receipt of this, Ó hÉigeartaigh suggested to his fellow Commissioners that they respond by taking this resolution as actually an undertaking by Kerry to take up maintenance and that the OPW would refer their resolution to External Affairs, which they duly did on 11 July 1936.[14]

Incredibly, there the matter rested, untouched and unsettled, for over ten years. In the summer of 1946, the district assistant architect of the OPW, G. P. O'Shea, reported on the overgrown state of the war graves in the five Kerry cemeteries of Cahersiveen, Killarney, Killorglin, Keel and Tralee which were under the Board of Health's control. In response, Brandon at Head Office suggested that, given that the functions of the Board of Health were now exercised by the County Manager, perhaps a personal approach by O'Shea might bear fruit. The latter duly approached the County Secretary who, encouragingly, 'seemed to think their wishes could now be met'. O'Shea consequently advised his superiors that a formal request should go to the County Secretary, and 'the letter, I think, should issue from Head Office'.[15] But, OPW Head Office demurred:

It is thought the wiser course would be to deal indirectly in the matter. We merely require to be

permitted to make arrangements with individual cemetery caretakers.

Brandon therefore instructed O'Shea to get the County Secretary to sign, or have the caretakers sign, the individual maintenance agreements.[16] In January 1947 the Kerry County Manager informed O'Shea that there would be no problem if the OPW did a separate deal with each caretaker, as long as these caretakers were remunerated separately for this work.[17]

The five caretakers duly signed, on various dates in January and February 1947, and in this protracted way the siege over Casement's remains and British war graves in Kerry public cemeteries was finally lifted. It was a pity for one aged and distraught mother in distant New South Wales, that the OPW Secretary, P.S. Carney, did not append his signature until May 1948. In her eighty-third year, in January 1948, Ellen Kinchington, as described in Chapter Two, wrote from there to complain that the grave of her son, Robert Emmett Kinchington, was neglected and its inscription barely visible: as she herself concluded: 'I feel very incensed about the affair as I had five sons in that War and lost three'.[18]

It would have been no consolation to her had she known that so deplorable was the state of cemeteries generally in Ireland at the time, and so gross their neglect by local authorities, that the Government considered projects for their clean-up as a suitable object of public employment schemes.[19]

Regimental badges:

If Kerry was unique in making difficulty over maintenance agreements[20], a much more serious difficulty from the early 1930s had already arisen elsewhere. In late October 1932 a special meeting of Sligo Corporation was convened to consider a request from the OPW to erect standard IWGC headstones over war graves in Sligo Town Cemetery. The graves at issue at the time were four: Private A.E. Thomas of the Suffolk Yeomanry, who died in May 1918; Private Robert Burnside of Holborn Street, Sligo, a member of the 5th Battalion Connaught Rangers, who died of wounds in 1915; Private Peter Meehan of West Gardens, Sligo, a soldier of the 2nd Battalion Royal Irish Regiment, who died in August 1916; and Private E. Sherlock of Mail Coach Road, Sligo, a member of the Machine Gun Corps, who died in January 1920. Following a debate, a motion was put:

That the Council take exception to any British emblem been [sic] erected in Sligo Cemetery over those who died in the great war [sic] and if

FAR LEFT
Connaught Rangers Cap
Badge.

MIDDLE LEFT
South Irish Horse
Regimental Cap Badge.

NEAR LEFT
Royal Dublin Fusiliers
Cap Badge.

(These images are with the
kind permission of the National Museum of Ireland)

*such emblems are withdrawn from the private
memorial we will give the matter our due
consideration.*

Alderman Michael Nevin who proposed
this motion argued that 'while this
Council and the people of Sligo always
honour and respect the dead', 'we have
quite enough Imperial signs throughout
this country without bringing them into
our cemeteries'.

A rather oddly worded alternative was
proposed by none other than Alderman
John Jinks:

Resolved,
That we grant the request of the Imperial War
Graves Commission to erect 4 Headstones in
Sligo to the Memory of the 4 mentioned names
who lost their lives in the late European War
but we cannot give any guarantee as to injury to
Head Stones but all care will be taken to have
same seen to as is to other Headstones in
Cemetery.

In supporting his stance, Jinks observed:

I don't agree at all with what Alderman Nevin
says about Imperial signs. These four young men
went out in the Great War and lost their lives.
They are belonging to Sligo; and I think it is in
very bad taste and very narrow-minded for any
man here to stand up and not respect the dead.[21]

On a more famous, or notorious,
national occasion, Jinks was associated
with political misfortune when, in
August 1927, his unexpected absence
from a crucial vote of no confidence
saved the Cosgrave Government from
defeat: this time his motion was defeated
and the original carried, by seven votes
to five, with one abstention.[22] The
Council simply could not accommodate
headstones that bore the regimental
badges of the units of the dead soldiers,
surmounted, as these badges were,
with the Crown. Nine months later, the
OPW applied to County Clare Board of
Health Secretary, John Quin, for similar
permission in respect of twenty British
Commonwealth war graves in ten of its
cemeteries.[23] The Clare Board discussed
the matter in August 1933 and, like
Sligo, objected to the regimental badges
being engraved. The OPW let matters
rest for almost two years.

The IWGC was made aware of these
problems following a visit to Dublin by
Harry Chettle in October 1934. That
November, the Commission agreed that
if the objections persisted and the OPW
thought that only some compromise
could break the impasse, they would be
glad of an opportunity to consider the
same, 'though they would naturally be
reluctant to agree to a serious departure
from the normal design'.[24]

At this point, in late 1934, with the IWGC prepared to wait and see, it is not clear if the British Legion had been pressing the issue behind the scenes, as would be evidently the case a few months later. However, under whatever compulsion, in March 1935 Captain Vesper was authorised by the OPW to go down to Clare to meet with the Board of Health, to see if the obstruction could be removed. He was none too hopeful. To Chettle, on Friday 29 March, the eve of his journey, he confided: 'I fear I have a difficult task but I hope to be able to let you know I have succeeded, but please don't be too optimistic'.[25] The Board of Health met, ironically, on April Fool's Day, and by post of the same date, Vesper confessed to Chettle:

I am very sorry to say that I completely failed today and I know how I dislike to admit defeat. Believe me – it simply couldn't be helped. From the early stages I saw it was rather hopeless and then, when I realized all was against me, I tried hard for an adjourned consideration rather than an adverse decision, which was unanimous.

Never during his time in Ireland had Vesper to admit to so definitive a defeat. In his presentation he made it clear that he had attended on behalf of the OPW, on the invitation of the Clare authorities, and emphasised that it was Free State Government work, paid for by the Free State. He referred to the fact that the Clare Board had kindly consented to the headstones and objected only to their featuring regimental badges. He explained that the headstones were of standard design the world over and that they had been approved by the various Christian churches. He pleaded that their objection was depriving the relatives and the dead of that to which they were entitled, and hoped that the Board of Health members would favourably reconsider the matter. But, as the national press proclaimed, to the consternation of the OPW, the decision against concession was unanimous.[26] Vesper was dismayed but determined to avoid controversy, for, if the Clare and Sligo examples were followed more widely, the consequences could have been calamitous.

Adding to Vesper's misery at this stage was the restless British Legion in Ireland. He was compelled to meet with them soon after the Ennis debacle, and told Chettle he hoped that, in this at least, he had 'succeeded in preventing any intervention on their part'.[27] Publicly he may have succeeded, but, behind the scenes it would appear otherwise. It is almost certain that the Legion contacted the British Army authorities in England: when the War Graves Commission executive met in May 1935, it had before

it a letter from the Adjutant-General urging that the OPW

should be asked to bring pressure to bear on the local authorities to secure the erection of headstones with the badges….he could not in any circumstances agree to the erection of the stones without the badges.

However, the IWGC saw eye-to-eye with the OPW and not with the Adjutant-General or the Legion. After a 'considerable discussion' it was agreed

it would be unwise to take any action for the present and that the matter should be allowed to stand and be re-opened when there seemed to be any likelihood of a favourable settlement.[28]

Over a year later, in relation to the situation in Clare, Veale asked assistant architect McCarthy to make 'discreet inquiries to ascertain if there is any likelihood of permission being now granted'. McCarthy responded to the effect that the same objections would be raised: 'I might add that the very same members still hold seats on the Board'.[29] Consequently, with the concurrence of the Department of Finance and, indeed, of the IWGC, the OPW decided to delay further action, 'in the hope that circumstances would ultimately permit the erection of the headstones in Sligo and Co Clare to the standard design'.

Enter The Legion:
The setback at Ennis in April 1935 came just as Vesper was concluding his work in Dublin. In July 1935 he returned to his duties in Northern Ireland where he was hospitalised following a serious accident while completing his work there. In the meantime, the British Legion in Ireland continued to strain at the leash, impatient of action as regards Sligo and Clare. At the beginning of May 1936, Tynan wrote to the OPW to request the names and addresses of next of kin of those buried in the war graves of both counties.[30] On 30 May Veale replied, for the OPW, by asking why Tynan needed this information. By coincidence, on the day before this, Brandon, in a private letter to Vesper, intimated that Sligo Corporation was about to relent on its opposition to regimental badges. Brandon clearly had sound information as to this prospect since the crucial meeting that removed the obstruction was not to take place until 3 June 1936. Brandon added that this development was 'entirely independent of any action on our part'.[31] This would appear a rather strange observation in view of the fact that a personal approach by the local OPW official to the Sligo Town Clerk, followed by a formal request from Veale of the OPW to the Sligo authorities led to a reconsideration and a reversal of the Corporation's original opposition.[32] Finally, on 19 August 1936,

RIGHT
The grave of
Robert Emmett
Kinchington,
Australian Infantry,
Killarney, Co. Kerry

the OPW Secretary, Cassedy, was able to convey formally to the IWGC the news of Sligo's change of heart. In the course of this communication he told the IWGC of the OPW's reluctance to meet Tynan's request for names and addresses: he suspected that Tynan and the Legion would use them to intervene in the Sligo and Clare business, 'an intervention that might not be advantageous'.[33]

Upon receiving no acceptable help from the OPW, on 14 August Tynan sought the information directly from the IWGC. By this stage Vesper had been seconded to Salonika – home of his first work for the Commission – and it was here that he received, in private letters from Brandon and Olive Kidd, his former OPW secretary, news of the Sligo breakthrough. At the same time, while there, he was consulted by Chettle as to how to handle Tynan's pressing for the names and addresses. His advice and comments to Chettle were revealing:

There surely can be little doubt that the Office of Works were correct in their apprehension that the application they received was for the purpose of some intervention in Sligo and Clare.....
You will agree this only confirms that which I have always contended about this interference of the British Legion – viz., The Commission and the Office of Works must remain united (I mean, be of one opinion – as I think we are). I believe I have conveyed to you before that there is

real prejudice and definite animosity between the British Legion and the Office of Works. I really believe the former rather delights in this state of affairs and take it as a matter of course, and this makes our problem all the more delicate.

Referring to the good news from Sligo, he advised that the IWGC or the OPW should communicate it to the Legion, 'so as to hold their hand in this connection'. He then added:

Now, as regards Clare, any intervention is more dangerous there than it would have been in the case of Sligo. You will remember I have repeatedly expressed myself very clearly and very strongly to the British Legion on this subject. I can only repeat my old warning that if (contrary to the advice of the Commission and Office of Works) they insist on interfering they will not only make the Board of Health more obdurate but they might cause incalculable trouble. I would again remind you that the British Legion are not so much anxious about getting the headstones erected as they are to show their own members and supporters that the 'Area Council' are 'taking' a strong part in the matter. Can you conceive anything so futile, dangerous and stupid?

He concluded:

I was at the meeting in Clare and I know the 'atmosphere'; I say there may be a chance by friendly negotiation but we or the Office of Works will never 'force' them and certainly

*the British Legion will not. If I may tender my
advice: it is that the Commission leave the matter
as far as possible to the Office of Works and
we (the Commission) might convey to the Office
of Works that we are in accord and in full
sympathy with them.*[34]

Vesper's advice was accepted and, wise
though it clearly was, it was a strategy
for the long haul. Clare Council was
proud of its republican credentials
and demonstrated as much, to itself
anyway, when in the following year, in an
entirely different context, it called on the
Government in Dublin to give

*every assistance, financial and otherwise, in
having removed from Nelson's Pillar, Dublin,
the figure of a British Admiral, and replacing it
with the figure of the father of Republicanism –*
      Theobald Wolfe Tone.

Adopted unanimously.[35]

This too, as it transpired, was something
else for the long haul.

Abandoning the badges:

The OPW, however, did not let
the matter drop. Early in 1937,
Commissioner Ó hÉigeartaigh took up
a suggestion from the Clare assistant
architect that they simply erect the
stones without the regimental badges.
He put this to OPW chairman Joseph

Connolly and fellow Commissioner
Pierce Kent, and remarked that 'adding
the regimental badges could wait until
the objection to them was waived',
and that the IWGC might be prepared
to accept this as a way forward.[36] In
early June the OPW proposed this to
the IWGC in respect of sixteen of the
then twenty war graves in the ten Clare
public cemeteries, so constructed as to
leave a slightly proud area blank, which
might be inscribed with a badge later.
As for the remaining four graves, almost
in a single plot in Kilrush (Shanakyle)
Cemetery, it was proposed to erect a
special 'central' memorial, designed by
their architect, Harold Leask, and on
which the regimental badges would not,
in any case, need to appear. Chettle, on
behalf of the IWGC, replied positively,
but somewhat astringently:

*the intentions of the Board [of Works] in respect
of the War Graves at Shanakyle and elsewhere
in Co. Clare are noted. I am to express the
IWGC's appreciation of the desire of the
Board to complete the work of marking these
graves.*[37]

Anxious to conclude its construction
work, in September 1937 the OPW
now wrote again to the Clare Board
of Health, stating that since it was the
sole authority whose war graves had
not yet been memorialised by standard
headstones, the OPW,

rather than leave them unmarked, proposed to erect them without badges, but, with name, rank and regiment of the soldier, date of death, and the words

'HE SERVED AND DIED IN THE GREAT WAR. HIS NAME LIVETH FOR EVERMORE'

inscribed.[38]

Meeting on 27 September 1937, the Clare Board of Health debated the matter. One member, Seán Hayes, claimed that the Board of Health did not object to anybody honouring the soldiers who died in what they considered a righteous cause. Such men had the courage of their convictions and, personally, he honoured brave men who had the courage to fight and die, if necessary, for their convictions, but that the regimental badges on tombstones would be 'a perpetuation of British propaganda'. The meeting concluded with the Board making an order granting the application of the OPW.[39]

BELOW
OPW 1930's drawing,
template for Royal Army
Service Corps. Cap Badge.

If this was some consolation to the OPW, it was a matter of irritation and anxiety for Vesper, now back from Greece and once again in the North. From Cookstown, at the end of September, he sent Chettle cuttings of the press reports on the proceedings in Clare.[40] Privately he believed the OPW was

unwise in asking the permission of the Clare Board to erect headstones without badges, when it had already been given this concession at the unhappy Ennis meeting of April Fool's Day, 1936. The Clare Board had now been given the opportunity of 'confirming a reverse decision', and the press reporting 'is very unfortunate; it may make other authorities and individuals wonder whether this Board is not right, and tend to make a few of the stones already erected a little unpopular'.[41] Chettle agreed but 'do not think we had better comment on the situation at this stage'. In the end, tenders for what now came to a total of twenty-four unmarked war graves in County Clare's public cemeteries were invited. If these stones without badges were more than the IWGC would wish to stomach, no better alternative was available. Clare did not then, nor for long after, change its mind: the problem would return in the years and decades ahead to haunt the relations of the IWGC and the British and Irish governments.[42]

Love's last gift - Remembrance

William Bennison, Private
1st Reserve Regiment of Cavalry
10 October 1918

Grangegorman Military Cemetery
Dublin

Chapter 11

Glasnevin: A Special Case, 1922-1937

When Vesper visited Glasnevin Cemetery in October 1931 he encountered what was, even then, a veritable city of the dead, the largest and most diverse burial ground in Ireland. Originally occupying nine acres, it had expanded to the extent of one hundred and twenty.[1] Founded as Prospect Cemetery in 1832, it was the burial place of Daniel O'Connell, the leading figure in its foundation, who also became its most famously memorialised presence. It is typical of O'Connell's liberalism that he founded it as a non-denominational burial ground. Although owned by a charitable trust, it became, in more ways than one, the national cemetery. This was most obviously so since it came to hold the remains of many notable national figures, from O'Connell through Parnell, Collins and Griffith to de Valera and Sir Roger Casement. More than that, it came to provide the last resting places of over 200 Irish and British men and women who served in the two World Wars. It came to hold the remains of those who fought against, as well as those who fought for Irish independence, of those who fought against the Treaty, as well as those who fought for it.

Indeed, the Cemetery administration itself, known as the Dublin Cemeteries Committee (DCC), became caught up in the troubles of those times. The DCC had its headquarters at the time in Rutland (now Parnell) Square. During the Civil War its premises came under fire, from the opposing forces, over the week from 30 June to 8 July 1922. As the DCC Secretary reported on 12 July:

The town office staff remained on duty at Head Office during the recent disturbance until 1pm on Friday 30th ultimo when it was found impossible to remain any longer without imminent danger as considerable damage had been done to the upper portions of the premises by rifle fire. Your secretary and staff were then obliged to vacate the Office. It is the intention to lodge a claim with the Provisional Government for the damage when the extent of same is estimated.[2]

On the same day, and quite separately, Cemetery Superintendent, J. W. Geary reported the unexpected and unorthodox arrivals of separate funeral parties on 5 July. First came two commercial delivery trucks, commandeered from Thom's and Eason's of Abbey Street, one of them bearing the remains of William Clarke, killed in Hill Street, on 29 June. A Commandant Sean Harling, with three boys and a girl, all armed with revolvers, demanded Clarke's immediate burial, Harling claiming he would be accountable for the cost. Clarke was promptly buried in a new grave in St. Paul's section.

Later that day, Captain Toomey delivered the bodies of three officers

and soldiers of the 'Government Army', producing an order from General O'Duffy at Portobello Barracks, to have a plot selected for the burial of troops 'killed during the recent action'.[3] The plot he chose became 'The Army Plot' and here commenced the troubled history of relations between the DCC and the new Irish Government, its Army and leaders. By the end of July 1922 some sixteen Free State soldiers had been buried in this plot and neither the cost of their burial or that of their plot had been remitted. Army chief accountant, Gearóid O'Sullivan, requested the details of the cost at this time, in response to a letter from the cemetery authorities, but it was a very long time before any settlement was reached, with much haggling in-between.[4] The process of negotiation and settlement was to become greatly complicated by the separate, but related, exchanges over the grave plots of Arthur Griffith, and Michael Collins.

A place fit for heroes?

Arthur Griffith died of a brain haemorrhage on 12 August 1922 and was interred in Glasnevin four days later, the first Irish leader to be buried as Head of State. Michael Collins was killed six days later and was buried there on 22 August. The question of how best to mark the graves and to commemorate these men soon became one of trouble and confusion. Joe McGrath, at that time Minister with responsibility for Labour, Industry & Commerce, and Economic Affairs, was deputed by President Cosgrave to inspect the site of Griffith's burial. On 13 October 1922, accompanied by M. J. Heavey of the Commission on Agriculture, McGrath inspected the site and was told by the Superintendent Nowlan that the forty by twenty-six foot plot would cost £2,300. They immediately concluded that this plot was 'altogether inadequate for the purpose'.[5] McGrath requested the DCC not to dispose of any ground in the vicinity, for the present, as the Government might wish to avail of all the ground there available.[6] It was unacceptable to McGrath and Heavey that the existing site, if turned into a 'Griffith Circle', would only turn out to be twenty-six feet in diameter, in contrast to Parnell's Circle at eighty feet and O'Connell's even larger. As Heavey put it:

Without in any way disparaging the greatness of Parnell, I think it would be generally conceded that if National Monuments are to be taken as a reflection of national esteem, and they are, then a 'Griffith Circle' should never be inscribed or constructed that will be dwarfed for all time by the 'Parnell Circle'.

He reported that an eighty-foot Griffith Circle would cost from £9,000 to £10,000 to purchase, and he was of the opinion, unwisely, that

if the Cemetery Authorities were approached in a diplomatic manner a generous gesture on their part would be forthcoming, especially having regard to the fact that the site of the 'Parnell Circle' was given for the purpose without any compensation.[7]

On 20 October 1922, the Accountant General and later Comptroller and Auditor General, George McGrath, brother of Joe, shared this opinion and conveyed it, with a copy of Heavey's memorandum, to the Cathaoirleach of An Dáil, Michael Hayes, who undertook to place them before President Cosgrave, with particular reference as to 'how the Cemeteries Committee should be approached'.[8] On the same day, John O'Connell, Secretary of the DCC, wrote to Joe McGrath to ask the exact extent of ground the Government required for Griffith's plot, adding 'I shall then be in a position to let you know the price of same'.[9]

Whatever about generous gestures, when George McGrath and Heavey met the DCC on 6 November, the former told them that the Government wanted an eighty-foot circular plot for Griffith and that

If the Cemetery Committee dealt with the matter in the proper spirit...the Government would be responsible for the additional cost of the ground required to give an eighty-foot diameter:

and, as he reported to Cosgrave,

Mr Heavey and myself had in mind a sum of £5,000 or £6,000 for an area which would give an eighty-foot circle and I believe that it is quite probable that the Cemetery Committee will make an offer to accept this sum or something less...it would appear that the Cemeteries Committee will not view the transaction from the point of view of £.s.d[10]

The DCC duly staked out an eighty-foot circle and, in November, invited the Government representatives to view it.[11] Heavey went out to Glasnevin again and suggested an alteration that would remove any need to relocate Griffith's remains: Coyle, Chief Clerk of the DCC, told him they would have to consult the widow, Maud Griffith. In the course of his report to his DCC superiors, he also mentioned the Collins/ Army Plot, the cost of which would be £3,714, in addition to the £603 outstanding on soldiers' burial fees to date.[12]

Early in 1923, Heavey wrote to Coyle concerning the Griffith and Collins Plots, with Coyle noting that their cost would be £10,425. In reporting Heavey's letter,

RIGHT
Generals Collins &
Mulcahy in procession at
the funeral of
Arthur Griffith

Coyle mentioned the Government's hope that the DCC would offer a reduction, and, when Coyle asked Heavey to put this in writing, Heavey replied that 'he would prefer the concession coming from the Committee without his writing'.[13]

The price of remembering:

Whatever about Government expectations on price, what now developed was a protracted period of inglorious haggling. George McGrath complained on 18 January that they still 'have not yet succeeded in getting a quotation for the proposed Griffith Circle' : then, on the very next day, Glasnevin was asked to meet 'two members of the Free State Government' to move forward the business of Griffith's Plot.[14] Within seven days of this, McGrath and Heavey again met DCC representatives, only to be told that the going price for the area they were requesting for Griffith would be £10,430, but that the full DCC General Committee would meet shortly to decide its final price.[15] At that meeting, on 7 February 1923, the DCC decided to grant the plot requested for £5,000 and considered this a major concession, since 'it was the most valuable site in the Cemetery'. This grant came with the condition that 'the Government accept this offer in writing within six months'.[16] Unhappy with this substantial reduction,

George McGrath complained to Dáil chairman, Michael Hayes, a few days later:

The price seems rather high, particularly when it is taken into consideration that under the proposal they would receive £5,000 cash down, against receiving £10,000 at the end of eighty or one hundred years by selling the plots individually.

Heavey took up the substance of McGrath's complaint directly with the DCC later in February, and asked them to reconsider the price in the light of McGrath's argument.[17] A forthright reply issued from O'Connell one month later:

This ground was acquired…many years ago at a considerable expense; in addition to annual payment of county rates and income tax, a very considerable sum was expended in laying out and draining the ground which has had to be maintained at a heavy yearly outlay. My Committee...could dispose of the whole of this ground within two years at more than £5,000 to other parties. Having regard to all these facts you will no doubt agree that the reduction made in the price (on account of the late President Griffith having been interred therein), is very substantial.[18]

Heavey retorted immediately to complain that 'the price you mention represents a rate of no less than £43,000

per English acre'. At this point, in March 1923, an impasse had been reached and, with no further reduction prospectively in sight, matters were now to become somewhat more complicated, arising from the issue of the nearby Collins and Army Plots.

Enter the Irish-Americans:

In 1922 a group of Irish-Americans, led by the New York stockbroker, former intelligence officer and judge, Edward Francis Kinkead, made it known to T. A. Smiddy, the Free State representative in Washington, that they wished to pay for the purchase and upkeep of the grave of Michael Collins, 'as they wanted to do honour to his memory, jointly with that of the late President Griffith'.[19] Since Collins's grave lay within the Army Plot, George McGrath's response to Smiddy's communication was to say that they would probably have to take the whole plot and that 'in these disturbed times' no arrangements had been made with the cemetery authorities regarding its purchase. He got Cosgrave to take the matter up with the Army authorities: in a note of 9 January, he pointed out that 'we haven't yet succeeded in getting terms for a Griffith Circle' and that 'the Army people' had not yet made any arrangements with the cemetery authorities either: 'I have merely been informed that they took over the plot themselves'.[20] To avoid having to move Collins's remains, he hoped the Army might be able to arrange with the DCC to have another eighty-foot circle for the Army Plot, with Collins's grave in the middle.

Cosgrave contacted Mulcahy as Commander-in-Chief, on 18 February, saying they now had a quotation for the Griffith Circle and asking Mulcahy to get one for the Collins/Army Plot as soon as possible, so that the two quotations could be sent to Kinkead and his associates. Mulcahy's reply on 3 March was not helpful. He felt it undesirable to do anything about a monument to Collins until 'the present situation comes to an end'.[21] Mulcahy was acting on a determination of the previous day when the Army Council decided that 'it is very undesirable that any monument be erected over the soldiers' plot until it is definitely closed'.[22] Nevertheless, within a month, Mulcahy submitted a proposal for the Army Plot which Glasnevin told him would cost £4,012. He made it absolutely clear that 'An Army Graves Committee would control the Plot'. He asked Cosgrave's blessing for his scheme before submitting it to Glasnevin for a final quotation.[23] Indeed, so determined was the Army Council to retain control that they decided in June that

the Army would take up the purchase of this plot by voluntary subscription. Arrangements to be made that a slip will be issued through

each pay book on the pay day before the Collins anniversary, announcing a collection on the pay day following that anniversary –

a scheme that appears to have run into the sands.[24]

The Glasnevin authorities, unfortunately, were not too impressed. In March they had had a visit from the Army's Captain McNamara, who sought a costing for additional Army burial space. Then, in May, they were notified by the Adjutant-General that the Army intended to erect a map board to publicly identify the precise burial places of individual soldiers interred in the Army Plot. They replied, testily, that the Committee hitherto never permitted any erection to be placed in a plot in which the exclusive right of burial in perpetuity had not been previously secured. They added that the Army had still not paid them the £3,696 for the original plot. Furthermore, the Cemetery Authority was still owed £903 for the burial fees of the soldiers already interred. They concluded by stating that they would secure the additional ground and permit the map board 'when Plot No 1 has been purchased and the burial fees due, paid'. As for the additional plot now sought, this would cost £4,012.[25]

In the meantime, early in May, with the agreement of the Cabinet, Cosgrave wrote formally to Kinkead concerning the offer to pay for the Griffith and Collins sites: the Griffith Plot, eighty feet in diameter, would cost £5,000, and the Army Plot, incorporating Collins's grave, £7,700: 'your kind offer to present these sites to the Nation will be most gratefully accepted'.[26] Kinkead replied from New York on 7 June 1923 to say they had organised a Griffith Grave Committee, with oil tycoon Edward L. Doheny as chairman. He indicated that this Committee wanted to fund the Griffith Plot first, leaving the Collins and Army Plot for future consideration. They intended to ask one hundred friends to subscribe $250 each, and Kinkead expected 'the required amount will be raised within a short time'.[27] On this basis Cosgrave ordered the completion of the negotiations with Glasnevin.

A long time passed before they heard from Kinkead again. Meanwhile the negotiations with Glasnevin over the Army Plot continued. McNamara met the DCC again in late June 1923. The DCC stood by the £7,700 for the Army and Collins Plot and the Captain felt that if they would reduce this to £6,000 'the Military Authorities would pay that amount'.[28] Glasnevin reconsidered and, on 5 July, informed the Adjutant-General that they would settle on £6,000 for the whole Army and Collins Plot.[29] Just as the Army had concluded this deal with the DCC, Heavey of the Land Commission, on the very next day, telephoned Glasnevin to see if he could get them to lower again the price of the Griffith Plot from its £5,000 asking price. He was told by the Acting Secretary that they had already made a substantial reduction and there was little prospect of altering this, but he could if he wished make another application to the General Committee of the DCC.[30]

At this stage, almost a year after the burials of Griffith and Collins, nothing had been settled, and neither burial fees nor plot fees discharged. Nothing more happened in the matter until well into the autumn of 1923. Whereas Cosgrave had been pressing for a conclusion six months before, now, in October 1923 the Army wanted a clear Government go-ahead for the purchase of the Army and Collins Plot.[31] On 10 October the Cabinet gave the permission for the Army to complete the purchase at £6,000. However, when Army Finance Officer, Thomas Gorman, on 19 October, pressed the Ministry of Finance to execute the purchase on behalf of Defence, he ran into unexpected trouble. Despite the Cabinet decision, Finance questioned Gorman as to who decided, or how it was decided, that a sum of £6,000 should be paid. Finance mentioned that there had been talk of the DCC giving the land as a free gift to the nation but that whoever had negotiated the £6,000 had now stymied this possibility. All the perplexed Gorman could reply was that the initiative had come from the Army leadership and that the Cabinet had twice approved a deal, on 2 May and again on 11 October 1923.[32]

Exit the Irish-Americans:

With these delays continuing, now came embarrassing news from America. On 31 January 1924 Kinkead informed Smiddy in Washington that they had sent out one hundred and twenty letters to prominent Irish-Americans, soliciting $250 each and, in reply, had received only eighteen answers. The Griffith Commemoration Committee in New York resolved therefore to return these eighteen cheques, as it was decided 'to await a more favourable opportunity and possibly devise a new plan to handle the matter'.[33] It was over a month later that George McGrath informed Cosgrave of this debacle, adding 'it appears we shall have to do the needful at home'. He remarked separately to Heavey on the same day that 'it seems the matter has not been taken very seriously on the other side'.[34] Ruefully, on the following day he remarked to Smiddy concerning Kinkead's letter:

I am sorry that he did not communicate the failure of his appeal before this, as it places people here in a rather awkward predicament. I

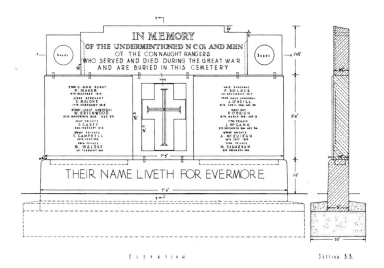

IN MEMORY
OF THE UNDERMENTIONED N COs AND MEN
OF THE CONNAUGHT RANGERS
WHO SERVED AND DIED DURING THE GREAT WAR
AND ARE BURIED IN THIS CEMETERY

THEIR NAME LIVETH FOR EVERMORE

ELEVATION   Section b.b.

*do not think the President would have allowed
such an appeal to be mentioned if there were the
slightest doubt of its success.*[35]

Smiddy's response was that the Minister
for Finance would now have to be
approached for the required funds,
as an appeal for private funds was
'inadvisable'. George McGrath also
sought out Michael Hayes whose advice,
on 29 April, was that it would be best
to settle up the whole business with
the DCC and obtain the title deeds of
the Griffith Plot and give them to the
widow. Hayes did not think it advisable,
however, for McGrath or Heavey to
see Mrs Griffith as 'he fears that she is
inclined to act unreasonably'.[36]

An overdue urgency to the business
now owed everything to Maud Griffith's
growing impatience. She had contacted
Glasnevin 'to have a monument erected
on the grave immediately'.[37] Finance had
continued fiddling while Maud Griffith
fumed. In March, one of Finance's
officials actually contacted the DCC
secretary and asked that the charge
for military interments, then standing
at £1,007 15s. be reduced.[38] In late
June they were asking McGrath and
Heavey for the Griffith Plot files as the
proposed purchase of the Plot was 'being
considered by this Ministry'.[39] While
the burials bill was being negotiated,
Griffith's widow erupted and poured

forth her wrath on the Government. On
19 June 1924 she wrote to the DCC to
request the removal of her husband's
remains from the Griffith Plot, for re-
interment in a family grave:

*The condition made with Messrs Cosgrave, J. J.
Walsh, M. Hayes, E. Duggan, etc., in August
1922 that the grave was to be bought and
given to me, has not been fulfilled: that was the
promise for which I put aside my own wishes
that the grave was to be my property, having
[been] divided in life, (although no fault of our
own), I want to be with my husband in the
grave.*[40]

The DCC sent a copy to Heavey and
on 12 July 1924 Cosgrave's secretary
told the Army Finance Office that
'the President wanted the question of
purchase and maintenance of the Army
Plot settled at once', as 'a question of
the greatest urgency', and the Army was
told to sort it out quickly with Finance.[41]

Such was the new-found sense of
urgency that Cosgrave himself arranged
a meeting with the Cemetery Committee
at Government Buildings on Saturday
19 July to discuss the Griffith, Collins
and Army Plots.[42] As a result, the DCC
conveyed to Gorman its decision to
revise its charges downwards, from
£6,000 to £3,000 for the Collins and
Army Plot, and from £5,000 to £360
7s. 6d. for the Griffith Plot.[43] Further

haggling between Army and Cemetery brought the cost of the Collins and Army Plot down by £300 to £2,700.[44] With 188 deceased soldiers now in the Army Plot, it was formally conveyed to the Minister for Finance by the DCC on 22 August 1924. On that same date the DCC finally received a cheque from the Army Finance Office to cover the costs of the original Griffith and Collins Plots and for all the unpaid burial bills to date. The Army requested the DCC to vest the Collins and Army Plot in the Minister for Finance and the Griffith Plot in Mrs Griffith's name.[45] Even after this, in December 1925, Finance wondered if it might be possible to recover the £2,700 from Glasnevin.[46]

Maintaining the graves of the Patriot Dead:

The original Army and Government ambitions for great eighty-foot circles disappeared as the Griffith Plot shrunk to a twenty-four by twelve-foot rectangle, the Army Plot to a seventy-two by twenty-eight-foot rectangle, and Collins's plot to eight by four foot.[47] No memorials followed from Government or Army. Mrs Griffith had to erect and pay for her own, as did the Collins family, in 1939. As to maintaining the plots with minimal decency, it appears that the very least was done. No one seems to have thought it either an honour or a duty to care for the graves.

At the very time, in 1931, when Captain Vesper was setting out on behalf of the IWGC and the OPW to commemorate the war graves of British and Commonwealth troops in Glasnevin, an internal Department of Finance memorandum of that April noted that the Army Plot:

is not marked in any way to identify it as the Army Plot and there is nothing on the spot to show where the remains of any particular soldier (even of the late Commander-in-Chief) are buried.

Remarkably, in a deleted passage of the memorandum, the writer continued:

Compare this with what is being done in the case of British military graves mentioned below. The condition of things in this regard is amazing and shows neglect of the feelings of the relatives of the deceased soldiers buried in the Plot. Unless remedied, there will be an outcry one of these days.

The writer added:

Markings on the Plot: absolutely none. Even the inscriptions on the glass cases on General Collins' grave are obliterated.[48]

So much for the Army's Map Board proposal of 1923. McElligott of Finance told General McMahon, on 21 May

1931, that the President wanted to know who was in the Army Plot, and went on:

We understand that, at the moment, the Army Plot is not marked in any way and there is nothing on the spot to show where the remains of any particular soldier are buried.[49]

Passing the buck:

In April 1923, over a year before they had purchased their burial area, Mulcahy had insisted that 'an Army Graves Committee would control the Plot'. Two years later, in May 1925, the Minister for Defence, P. Hughes, complained that 'the present appearance of the Plot is such as to reflect some discredit on the Army'. His secretary, writing to the Minister for Finance, remarked:

It seems the responsibility for the maintenance has not yet been assigned. The Minister desires that the care and control of the decoration of the Plot should be undertaken by this Department.[50]

On the same date, Defence sent an official out to Glasnevin with an identical message, that the Department wanted to maintain the Army Plot. Glasnevin had no problem with the proposal provided that the Minister for Finance, 'in whom the plot is vested', issued the requisite authorisation.[51] Anxious that the care and maintenance be undertaken at once,

Defence pointed out that 'this can be carried out by existing personnel serving under this Department and, practically speaking, would cost nothing'.[52] Noting that Defence was pressing for an answer, Finance decided it 'should stave them off', until it was decided what kind of kerbs and monument were to be erected around the plots.[53] Officially nothing was done: it was not until 1957 that the Plot got its kerb; not until 1967 did it get its monument.[54] Unofficially, a Commandant Ennis, probably in desperation, had been sending out two Army gardeners to tend the plots and these incurred the displeasure of the Glasnevin authorities by tending to and taking in more ground than had been assigned to the Army.[55]

One year later, in 1926, the Department of Defence secretary, O'Connor, told Finance that his Minister felt 'the undertaking of this work by this Department should not be postponed until a definite decision is come to as to what kind of monument is to be erected on the Plot'. He complained that all the Glasnevin authorities would do was to cut the grass, and Defence was receiving representations about 'the neglected state' of the Army and Collins Plot. The Griffith Plot was little better. In August 1925 the DCC received a complaint from Maud Griffith about a row of trees obscuring her husband's plot and there

was no sign indicating which plot it was. They responded by felling and pruning and affixing a tablet bearing Griffith's name in the ground near to his grave.[56] Defence now repeated its request of 1 May 1925 that the Minister for Finance authorise the Army to undertake the job. On 14 April 1926 Houlihan of Finance conveyed to Glasnevin and Defence his Minister's authorisation to have the Army officially assume responsibility for care and maintenance.[57]

Whatever happened over the next few years, in August 1928 the Minister for Defence changed his mind and

now feels that the work might be more satisfactorily and conveniently undertaken by the Commissioners of Public Works who, perhaps, carry out similar work in cemeteries in Grangegorman and the Hibernian School.

He hoped Finance might concur and requested them to make arrangements for the future, with the OPW to take responsibility, while Defence would retain the right or power to grant permissions for burials.[58] Dagg of Finance consulted the OPW and, on the latter's behalf, P. J. Raftery replied by pointing out that their care of Grangegorman and the Hibernian School was practicable because they were within or beside the Phoenix Park whose staff saw to their maintenance. In

a classic piece of shifting responsibility, Raftery suggested that Department of Agriculture staff in the nearby Botanic Gardens might be deputed to maintain the Army Plot if Defence felt it no longer wished to do so. As an alternative, he suggested that the Glasnevin authorities be asked to provide full-scale care on the basis of an annual charge or by way of a lump sum payment for perpetual maintenance. Raftery pointed out that this was what had been done with the 1916 Memorial in Glasnevin, by means of the Dora Sigerson Shorter Bequest. Finance thereupon kicked the problem back to Defence, suggesting O'Connor find out what Glasnevin might charge for an annual maintenance contract. [59]

The situation soon approached farce. A new Secretary to Defence, Lieutenant-General Peadar McMahon, wrote on 27 February 1929, to the DCC to ask if Glasnevin would take up full maintenance, only to receive the coy reply from its secretary:

I am directed to say that the Committee are of opinion the above-named Plot has been nicely kept and to respectfully state they are not prepared to undertake the care of the Plot.[60]

As far as the DCC was concerned, the care of these plots 'involved a big responsibility which they would prefer not to undertake', and they 'could not do the work with the present staff'. Glasnevin's position was that 'the care of such a national plot should rest with the Government'. In this dilemma the OPW, at Finance's suggestion, offered, as an emergency measure, to lend the services of an OPW gardener on the strict understanding that he would work under Army directions and that the Army would continue to accept full responsibility for the care and upkeep of the Army graves. With no other acceptable alternative available, McMahon accepted this arrangement temporarily, but determined to reopen the issue with the DCC in the following year. [61]

Eighteen months later, Defence repeated its request to the DCC. On this occasion the DCC paused, seeking advice from their Superintendent who estimated that year-round maintenance and dressing would cost between £31 and £58. Finally, in August 1930, the DCC decided to accept full care of the Collins and Army Plot for one year on receipt of payment of £50 from the Department of Defence. [62] In the following year, 1931, Defence promptly paid its £50 for a further twelve months. Then, in December 1931, while wishing to renew arrangements for 1932, asked if the DCC could reduce the charge for full-year care and dressing. They were told that the £50 was already a special rate

and did not even include an overhead charge.

They concluded that if he so desired, the Minister could return to the older arrangement whereby his own Army staff managed the graves of Griffith, Collins and the national soldiers. [63] Defence decided to stick with the annual fee for DCC maintenance, year after year until 1949, when Glasnevin wanted an increase from £50 to £75. In sanctioning the increase, D. Warren of Finance added the wry comment:

It is pretty clear, I think, that Defence don't want the work back, that the Office of Public Works are reluctant to take it and that the Dublin Cemeteries Committee seem none too keen on it. [64]

So much for the patriot dead.

Glasnevin – the Commonwealth War Graves:
In the midst of these procrastinations, Captain Vesper quietly pursued the tenor of his way. Not that his way was untroubled either. Glasnevin presented a challenge more complex than anything he had so far encountered in Ireland. As he reported to Harry Chettle in October 1931 when he had completed identifying and registering the war graves there, they were very scattered over its then extent of 110 acres. It was not just the question

of their dispersal but also their diversity that posed a challenge. He found some 149 war dead there up to February 1932. Some were in privately owned, maintained and memorialised graves; some were in unsecured plots; others were in pauper ground. Furthermore, in a cemetery that was well laid out, with pathways in good condition and its maintenance 'generally entirely satisfactory', he also found a cemetery that was tightly run.[65] The extensive code of bye-laws was strictly enforced and any proposals by anyone for memorials were to be submitted in detail for vetting by the authorities. Thus, when a Mrs Fitzpatrick of Temple Street, Dublin, at the time of Vesper's first visit, sought to erect a temporary memorial, she was told that none could be erected unless the plot was purchased. Even then, as the maximum height allowed for a temporary memorial was two foot six inches, she would have to reduce her proposed memorial by one foot in order to comply with regulations.[66] The written consent of each grave owner had to be obtained before anyone, including next of kin, could erect any memorial.[67]

Of the 149 war graves Vesper identified up to February 1932, half were privately owned and the other half unsecured, that is, those where relatives had failed to exercise an option to purchase, up to the end of three years. He observed

that 'we can hardly expect the Cemetery Authorities to make them over to us, while the cost of acquiring them would be very great, even if possible'.
It is important to stress, at this point, that the DCC had no objection in principle to the erection of the standard headstones of the Imperial War Graves Commission. In October 1931 they were first contacted by the OPW who requested facilities for Vesper, as its inspecting officer. The DCC ordered that 'all facilities be provided' and that the inspecting officer should

consult with the Superintendent in regard to all details connected with erections and their foundations etc., the particulars of arrangements arrived at after consultation to be submitted by the Office of Works, in advance, to the Committee for approval.[68]

Vesper met with Superintendent Nowlan on 12 October 1931 and personally encountered the difficulties he later reported to Chettle. Nowlan was anxious to assist him in 'any possible way', and they entered into detailed discussions over the months which followed. By February 1932 Vesper had to report to his superiors that 'in all the circumstances, the erection of standard headstones over these unsecured graves would appear to be quite impossible'. He and Nowlan then discussed the possibility of a central

memorial which, Vesper remarked, would have 'an additional advantage as there are a number of war graves in the Poor Ground (St. Paul's Plot) which in any case cannot be marked'. He added that the cost of a central memorial would be 'less than that of 150 separate headstones'. He was assured by Nowlan, who felt that the DCC would not object. Vesper therefore asked the OPW architect, Harold Leask, who had been involved in the construction of the ill-fated Cenotaph on Leinster Lawn, to prepare a rough plan of such a memorial.[69] In early April, Vesper reported in similar terms to the IWGC, telling Chettle that

As we dealt with the various problems we should have to contend with in this Cemetery, even in respect of 'secured graves', we came upon difficulties which I think it would be probably impossible to overcome...this is a particularly complicated case.

He added that he and Nowlan had identified a possible site for a central memorial, which site 'we should probably have to purchase from the Cemetery Committee'. However, before making any formal proposal to the OPW, Vesper needed to get clearance from the IWGC. Chettle promptly provided him with this, assuring Vesper 'unofficially but definitely that the Commission would probably adopt the course that

you suggest'.[70] The site which Nowlan and Vesper had identified was a modest eight by eight foot plot and when the Glasnevin authorities viewed it, they settled on an equally modest selling price of £25.[71]

When Chettle next visited, in October 1934, he reported enthusiastically to Ware on the 'excellent position' provisionally chosen by Vesper for this central screen wall memorial, in the south-east end of the cemetery, close by the old entrance next to the gardener's house.[72] Even better was to follow in the next year. When the OPW formally submitted plans for the memorial to the DCC, the plans were not only approved, but, in sharp contrast to the situation respecting the National Army graves and Collins Plot, the DCC decided to grant the site free of charge: the OPW had to pay only for the foundation and construction work. In January 1935 Vesper met the DCC Visiting Committee at the site and secured their agreement for a three-foot path from the Broad Walk to the proposed memorial.[73]

It took little time for the OPW to finalise plans and specifications for the memorial: on 1 March 1935 the DCC approved them. They further excelled themselves in March 1936 when they approved the proposed inscription and then waived the normal fee for the Certificate of Approval, for a site which now measured twenty-one feet by ten, instead of eight by eight. [74] The OPW placed the memorial construction contract in the course of 1935 for what, by then, had risen to 162 war graves.[75] The work was completed early in 1937. By that stage, as noted earlier, Vesper had left Dublin, but in April 1937 he made a return official visit and, among other undertakings, inspected the new First World War Memorial, 'recently completed'. He described it as an excellent example of special treatment. Conscious of context, he added:

It will be remembered that in this Historical

Cemetery, containing the graves of so many leaders, who held extreme views, the great difficulty was the question of a suitable site and there can be no doubt that the site finally given by the Cemetery Authorities is nearly ideal in the circumstances….The design is admirable, the construction has been well carried out and the whole forms a dignified and suitable monument.[76]

Its completion went unmarked by any unveiling ceremony. It was one of the memorials that Vesper hoped to see reported photographically, but which the OPW Commissioners declined to do in their annual reports.

BELOW
Enlisting the Irish:
1914 War Recruitment
Poster

Call him not dead, thy fallen soldier son
But say "the warfare waged, the victory won"

William A.N. Dobbyn, Lieutenant
Lancashire Fusiliers
4 January 1917

Memorial Plaque, Christchurch Cathedral
Waterford

Chapter 12

Islandbridge:

The Irish National War Memorial, 1919-1939

At the time of Vesper's arrival in Dublin to take up work in the OPW, T. J. Byrne, its Principal Architect, appeared before the President and his Cabinet on 29 October 1929, at Cosgrave's request. There he made a presentation on the construction of 'a monumental park' on twenty-five acres of the Long Meadows Estate, across the Liffey from the Phoenix Park, at Islandbridge.[1] The purpose was to make provision for an Irish national war memorial to commemorate the Irish dead of the 1914-1918 War. The Cabinet accepted the proposal outlined. They agreed that the Irish National War Memorial Committee's spokesman, Senator Andrew Jameson, should be invited to discuss the proposal in detail with Byrne and his superior, OPW chairman, Sir Philip Hanson.

The Way of Remembrance:

For Andrew Jameson and his colleagues it was the end of a decade of disappointment and the beginning of another of hope – and frustration. The long quest for appropriately perpetuating the memory of the Irish war dead began at a meeting hosted by the Lord Lieutenant, John French, Earl of Ypres, at the Vice-Regal Lodge, Phoenix Park, on 17 July 1919.[2] Upwards of one hundred people, including the Lord Mayor of Belfast, Captain Lombard Murphy and General Sir William Hickie, convened to decide on a permanent memorial to the fallen. Out of this meeting came an executive committee under the chairmanship of the Unionist lawyer, Sir Dunbar Plunket Barton. Among the other eight members were Andrew Jameson, General Hickie, Lady Arnott, Mr Justice Hanna and the Co Wicklow golfer and Red Cross volunteer, Vivian Brew-Mulhallen.

The Irish National War Memorial Committee determined, as the best remembrance, to raise funds for the construction of a Great War Memorial Home for soldiers and sailors passing through Dublin and which would feature a Record Room displaying volumes containing the names of all Irish who had died in the conflict. With Jameson as Treasurer, they set up a War Memorial Fund and, over the next few years, they raised £50,000, from all over Ireland, and lodged it in a public trust until an approved scheme would be in train. Over the same few years, with partition, the departure of British troops from twenty-six counties, independence and civil war, the idea of a Memorial Home became impracticable. Nevertheless, by 1923, the INWM Committee had managed to publish the names of many of the fallen in their lavishly produced eight-volume *Ireland's Memorial Records*.

Having considered several war memorial proposals over the same few years, the INWM Committee, at a general meeting on 28 March 1924, decided on a scheme to purchase the ground in Merrion Square from the Pembroke Estate, to erect a memorial in its centre, and to open it to all as a public park.[3] Before expending time and finance on legal clearance, they sounded out the Government to see if it would be prepared to support this proposal by taking over the perpetual maintenance of the park, once the INWM Trustees had acquired it. The Finance Minister was advised by the OPW that such maintenance would cost the exchequer £1,600 per annum and before further refining this rough estimate, he wanted to know if Cabinet colleagues objected to the proposal on any other ground.[4]

Early Armistice Days:
The Merrion Square proposal came to Government at an inauspicious time. From 1923 the Free State accepted invitations to attend the London Armistice Day ceremonies at the Cenotaph at Whitehall and at Westminster Abbey, though Cosgrave declined to attend in person. He and his Cabinet colleagues invited Lord Glenavy to represent the Government at the Abbey and Sir Bryan Mahon to lay a wreath on their behalf at the Cenotaph.

A similar invitation was extended by Government and accepted by Mahon for Armistice Day 1924.[5] However, when it came to similar ceremonies in Ireland, where, in the 1920s, there may have been up to 150,000 First World War veterans, the Government was uneasy. Admittedly, in 1924 it did not object to the erection of a memorial in the grounds of Dublin Castle to the memory of members of the Irish Bar who fell in the Great War, and indeed, explicitly approved the wording of the plaque.[6] This notwithstanding, when the League of Irish ex-Servicemen in Dublin requested permission in October 1924 to erect temporarily a Celtic Cross on College Green, as a centre point for their Armistice Day celebrations, Justice Minister O'Higgins advised his colleagues that, while this cross 'was really destined for Guillemont...the temporary erection of the cross might be taken as a precedent and might possibly lead to trouble in the future'.[7] Furthermore, when Cosgrave, as Taoiseach, was invited by the League to attend their 1924 College Green ceremonies, he took the position that *on careful consideration he does not think that his presence at the Ceremony would be of advantage and that it would not be proper for him to attend. His personal view is that it would be hypocritical for him, having regard to the fact that he was imprisoned by the British Government during the world war, to accept such an invitation as this.*

As to whether the Governor-General should attend, Cosgrave felt that 'it would be anomalous for the nominal head of the State to be present at the Ceremony when the President had declined to attend'[8].

In the light of this, and knowing that the Government was going to lay a wreath at the London Cenotaph, the League's chairman, W. P. Walker, felt it would help deflect criticism if the Government were to do likewise in respect of the College Green ceremony. He suggested to Desmond FitzGerald, Minister for External Affairs, that Colonel Maurice Moore might be invited to do so for the Government, if the President and Governor- General felt compelled to be absent. This was an inspired choice, since Moore was both a distinguished ex-British officer, formerly in command of the 1st Battalion Connaught Rangers, and a nationalist who went on to train the Volunteers in the War of Independence: one who had privately lacerated Nevil Macready for creating a reign of terror in Ireland.[9] It was a suggestion which the Cabinet accepted and they duly invited Moore to lay the wreath.[10] Such State representation at the Dublin ceremonies continued until November 1933.[11] In permitting the ceremonies at all, the Cabinet had overruled the Garda authorities, whose Commissioner had advised that the permission for the Cenotaph and ceremony on College Green should not be granted.[12]

In the years which followed, the Government continued to be represented at the ceremony in Whitehall; while Cosgrave declined a personal invitation to attend the London ceremonies of 1926, when the Dominion prime ministers were all present for the Imperial Conference, he sent his Vice-President, Kevin O'Higgins, to represent him.[13] In Dublin, however, they now accepted the Commissioner's advice and refused permission for the 1925 ceremony to be held on College Green. With permission, the League of Irish ex-Servicemen, now transformed into the British Legion (Southern Ireland Area), switched the proceedings to St. Stephen's Green.[14] In the following year, 1926, the Legion applied to the OPW and was granted permission to hold their ceremony, with temporary cross erected, at the Wellington Monument in the Phoenix Park. The Park now became established as the venue for their annual Armistice Day ceremony. However, it was an occasion that was not untouched by troubles: the practice of parading to and from the venue gave rise to scuffles and skirmishes between Legionaries and Republicans.

A monument for Merrion Square?

It was against this background that the INWM submitted its Merrion Square proposal to the Government in 1924. The Cabinet considered it on 1 December, only to reject it: that is, they held that 'financial considerations precluded the Government from undertaking the maintenance of any new parks in Dublin'.[15] That, however, was not the end of the matter. The INWM took the proposal to the Dublin City Commissioners: they, in principle, were prepared to accept the gift of the Merrion Square park, subject to the Courts' approving such use of INWM funds, but subject also to a special Act of the Oireachtas to enable the Merrion Square authorities to dispose of it, having regard to certain existing rights in the use of the ground. The City Commissioners' decision, when it became public, occasioned a wrathful reaction from some. Eighty-two year old John Sweetman, now of Kells, County Meath, but for sixty-eight years a resident of Merrion Square, in a letter to Cosgrave, denounced the Commissioners' approval for turning the Square into a 'perpetual memorial park in honour of some deceased Irish soldiers of the English Army'. He wanted to know if Cosgrave and his Government had sanctioned this. He enclosed a copy of a protest letter to the *Irish Times* which the latter had failed

to publish and which then appeared in *The Leader*. He repeated his protest to Cosgrave, nine days later, when he declined the latter's invitation to the annual Griffith-Collins commemoration at the Leinster Lawn Cenotaph. Cosgrave's office was sufficiently concerned at Sweetman's complaint and circulated his correspondence to the Cabinet, 'as it is suggested that the Executive Council were concerned in the decision regarding the proposed War Memorial in Merrion Square'.[16]

By March 1926 the Irish Free State Commissioner, James McNeill, wanted to know the Government's official position on the Merrion Square project as the issue was being discussed in London. Ó hÉigeartaigh advised him that 'the Executive Council was not favourably disposed' and were convinced that the Dáil would refuse to pass the necessary legislation. He added:

There is considerable opposition from two different viewpoints – those interested in ex-soldiers' welfare want the money spent on welfare proposals such as housing, hospital or charitable assistance for ex-soldiers and their families, while a large section of nationalist opinion regards the scheme as part of a political movement of an imperialist nature and view it with the same resentment as they view the exploitation of Poppy Day in Dublin by the most hostile elements of the old Unionist class.[17]

In March 1926 the High Court gave favourable judgement for the use of INWM funds for the project; with this, and the City Commissioners behind them, the INWM Trustees then brought forward a private bill in the Senate a year later.[18] However, as Cosgrave and colleagues predicted, it was doomed almost from the outset. The War Memorial promoters in the Senate were themselves divided. Sir Bryan Mahon, for example, thought the Merrion Square proposal impracticable since the numbers turning up on Armistice Days far exceeded the Square's capacity – 'at least 100,000 people trampling on the ground'– and he strongly preferred a war memorial in the Phoenix Park. Likewise, General Sir William Hickie explained how an almost unanimous vote of the British Legion's twelve districts and one hundred and thirty branches in the Free State had come out against the Merrion Square proposal. As he pointed out, when St. Stephen's Green held the 1925 commemoration, some 120,000 people inevitably caused great disruption and, like General Mahon, he came to oppose the proposal and the Bill. Similarly, Maurice Moore declined to support it. The hapless Andrew Jameson, himself opposed to a Phoenix Park monument, 'costing £45,000, where only few people would see it', was at a loss – 'I hardly know what to ask the House to do'. In the end,

on the casting vote of the chairman, the Bill was sent to the Dáil for consideration by a Joint Committee of both Houses. But in the Dáil debate which followed on 29 March 1927, the Government finally came clean with its true view when O'Higgins formally opposed the Bill on behalf of the Executive Council. His reason, and theirs, as he insisted, came simply to this: 'I do not want to see the little park in front of this State's seat of government dedicated to the memory of those who fell in the Great War.' His view was not based on personal hostility to those who had fought and died in that conflict: he himself had one brother who died serving in the British Army, and another who served in the Navy, but survived the war. He hoped that

there will always be respectful admiration in the minds of Irishmen and Irishwomen for the men who went out to France and fought there and died there, believing that by so doing they were serving the best interests of their country…yet it is not on their sacrifice that this State is based and I have no desire to see it suggested that it is.[19]

In these circumstances, it was no surprise that the Bill was withdrawn when the matter next came before the Senate, in April 1927.[20]

Wandering in the wilderness:

Upon reaching this impasse, the Trustees of the INWM approached the Minister for Finance in March 1928 with a new proposal – that the monument to the war dead might be a memorial arch at the entrance to the Phoenix Park. The OPW could see no practical or aesthetic objection to the new proposal, which might actually enhance pedestrian and vehicular access to the Phoenix Park. While the Finance Minister did not see the Government opposing this, neither could he see them adopting it as a Government measure, thinking the Government would prefer to leave it to a free vote in the Dáil. In June 1928 he had the proposal brought to Cabinet for discussion. When that discussion took place a month later, they decided against a stone archway memorial there[21].

Here the matter rested until a somewhat desperate Jameson contacted Cosgrave in February 1929, in advance of a meeting of the INWM Committee where he feared he would have nothing 'to tell them except the history of our failures'.[22] Arising from this, on 2 March 1929 McDunphy, the Assistant Secretary to the Government, circularised all Departments and Ministers with a resumé of some twelve separate proposals which the INWM subscribers and Committee had considered in the past.

Of these proposals, Cosgrave was reported as being uneasy with any monument or memorial hall, as likely to be open to abuse. He invited his ministers to consider the various ideas to see 'if any solution can be found for the utilisation of the Fund', and asked them to report back. Their responses over the next two months were varied and not very enthusiastic. Justice had no strong view but preferred a housing scheme; Local Government preferred a children's education scheme, as did Lands and Fisheries; Defence preferred the idea for a Hugh Lane gallery.[23]

Time passed, nothing happened, until McDunphy, on 12 June 1929, contacted Paul Banim in the President's office to remark 'I do not know whether the President is still interested in the matter after the delay which has elapsed'.[24] At this point Jameson, still at a loss, contacted Cosgrave to state that the INWM Trustees had tried – in vain – to secure a site on private lands for a war memorial. Changing tack slightly, in view of the Government's aversion to a memorial arch for the Phoenix Park entrance, he now asked the Government if it would grant them a suitable site within the Park itself. On 25 September 1929, Cosgrave, stressing confidentiality, turned to the OPW Commissioners to inquire if they had any lands 'adjacent to the Phoenix Park between Conyngham

British Legion
Letter-heading

Road and the river Liffey' that might satisfy the request for a war memorial site. The OPW Principal Architect, T.J. Byrne, reported back that the strip of land indicated by Cosgrave was unsuitable as it was too low to the river and in too poor a condition, but that they had, indeed, identified a site. It was in these circumstances that Cosgrave, on 28 October, now requested Byrne to see him next day, before the Cabinet meeting commenced.[25]

Here Byrne presented a proposal for a monumental park on the Long Meadows Estate, consisting of twenty-five acres then in use as allotments. It had been purchased over 1904-1906 by the Office of Woods and Forests as a deliberate, pre-emptive measure to safeguard the Phoenix Park and its environs from encroachment and undesirable development. It was now vested in the Minister for Finance and was administered by the Office of Public Works.[26] From this, Byrne presented the prospect of a square, open space of nine acres, with ceremonial approaches, trees, shrubs and flower beds surrounding a suitable monument, and this the Cabinet 'considered satisfactory'.[27] They agreed that Jameson be invited to discuss the proposal with Hanson and Byrne.

On Saturday 9 November 1929 the INWM Committee visited this Islandbridge site. Having waited so long for prospects, the Committee now wanted something tangible in writing from the Government other than 'the existence of an undeveloped site'. They were not ungrateful, and Jameson conveyed his Committee's feeling of generally being in favour of accepting the proposal. Cosgrave assured him on 18 November that the Cabinet would now be asked for authority to proceed, which it duly gave next day. That same day, Byrne at the OPW was asked to start preparing estimates of what it might cost the State over and above the £50,000 which the INWM had at its disposal. Cosgrave went further: in order to help Jameson overcome the scepticism of some of his INWM associates, he sent Jameson a statement on 2 December 1929, regretting 'the many delays', asserting that 'it is in the main a big question of remembrance and honour to the dead', but reminding him and them that 'it is idle, moreover, to ignore the fact that there is a certain hostility to the idea of any form of War Memorial'. Nevertheless, considering that 200,000 Irishmen had served in the War and that up to, or in excess of 100,000 people attended Armistice Day commemorations in Dublin in the 1920s, he commented further that 'it must always be a matter of interest to the head of the Government to see that a project – which is dear to a big section of our citizens – should be a success'. He explained that since the proposal involved a memorial plot which would be within a new public park, the Government would ask the Dáil, not only to approve the grant of the site, but 'the expenditure of a substantial sum of money' for laying out the Park and its subsequent maintenance, thereby augmenting the INWM's own project funds. This letter, as Jameson responded, was 'most welcome intelligence to the Committee who have been wandering in the wilderness for so many years'. [28] Where before there had been silences and delays, there now was a sudden flurry of exchanges and meetings between Cosgrave, Jameson and the OPW Principal Architect. Cosgrave could now tell Byrne that Jameson was getting the distinguished architect Sir Edwin Lutyens over to view the site and that 'personally I am quite satisfied with the whole matter as it stands'. [29]

Conception:

For all his sense of failure to date, Jameson had pulled off a coup in securing the interest of Edwin Lutyens. He was, after all, the artist pre-eminent in the architecture of war remembrance, with a vision for the heroic. His was the design of the Imperial Commonwealth War Graves Commission's Stone of Remembrance. He was already the designer of the Cenotaph in Whitehall, the Tower Hill Memorial for merchant seamen in London, and later of the powerful Somme Memorial at Thiepval. Furthermore, married to an Irishwoman, he had known Ireland well for over twenty years before Jameson approached him, and had worked on Howth Castle, Lambay Island and Heywood Gardens. [30] It was not until July 1930 that Jameson managed to get him to come over to visit the site and meet Cosgrave who was 'quite charming'. He was much taken by Cosgrave's escort of an army colonel and two detectives, followed by a taxicab carrying six armed men. [31] After this visit, Lutyens was commissioned by the INWM Trustees to prepare a design. Given the extent of his practice and commitments, this took time. The Irish correspondent of the English *Sunday Times* commented in August 1930 that 'the question of the war memorial has lapsed once again into a period of deathly silence', and observed sarcastically on the site which the Government had granted, that 'there would be much opposition to placing this shrine in a distant backwater which will mainly serve as a playground for the children of Inchicore'. However, he admitted that 'this is the nearest site that is considered politically expedient, and the protection of which can be reasonably assured', and conceded that

Lutyens considered 'the site has great possibilities'.[32]

In November 1930 the OPW Architect prepared a long and detailed report on Lutyens' design, which Byrne regarded as 'admirable for the purpose and worthy of the strongest recommendation'. He estimated the cost to the INWM fund for the actual Memorial Garden and buildings to be £56,000 and the cost to the Government for the surrounding park, approaches, a three-arched bridge over the Liffey and arched footway over Chapelizod Road, as likely to cost £52,500. With everything else taken into account, Byrne estimated the total project at £169,000, with the Government liable for £109,000 of this, if everything Lutyens had proposed went ahead. Byrne's Report came before Cabinet on 29 November and was approved in principle, as was the proposal to commission a scale model from Lutyens at £400, to be shared between Government and INWM.[33] It was May 1931 before the model had been completed in London and, on 20 June, the OPW advised the Government that it had arrived and was ready for inspection. Cosgrave and four other ministers duly inspected the model on Saturday 11 July 1931, finding it to their satisfaction. [34] Another six months passed before Byrne was instructed to meet Lutyens in London, to prepare plans

and an accurate estimate. Interestingly, when the INWM Executive Committee met on 14 December to hear Byrne's report on the Lutyens plans, it did so at the OPW Offices where, under Dunbar Plunket Barton, they gave their approval for the Lutyens scheme. However, since each of the two parties had limited their respective contributions to £50,000, the more exotic ancillary aspects of the design, such as the triple-arched bridge over the Liffey, had, in the end, to be jettisoned, as beyond the limits of the available finance – the Government's £50,000 being taken from a Dáil Vote of £250,000 for national relief works under the Unemployment Relief Act of 1931. In presenting his report, Byrne indicated that, if it were approved, an early start could be made on the parts of the work that would provide jobs for the unemployed.[35]

Commencement:
Work began on clearing the site on 28 December 1931, not without controversy as to who was to be employed. [36] Cosgrave had issued verbal instructions to Byrne to divide the work 'fifty-fifty' between British and Irish ex-Servicemen and by the first week in January 1932 some 164 men were employed on this basis. Hanson of the OPW was being pursued on this issue by a Mr O'Sullivan of Dublin Corporation and requested

clearance to state that this was the case. One source, in fact, claims the majority of those employed had served in both armies.[37]

Even as the work was getting under way, so too was the general election, which saw Cosgrave and Cumann na nGael ousted and deValera and Fianna Fáil installed in office in February 1932. The change of government brought changes in participation in war commemorations. Although the new deValera administration continued to take part in external war ceremonies, within the country this was no longer the case. After November 1933 it withdrew its official presence from Armistice Day proceedings in Dublin. There were new prohibitions on the wearing of uniforms or display of flags, and the sale of poppies was restricted to a single day instead of a week as formerly permitted.[38] Nevertheless, it did not impede the work on the Islandbridge Memorial Park. Indeed, the new Cabinet, in September 1933, authorised the Minister for Finance to conclude the formal agreement between Government and the INWM Committee which inaugurated the Memorial Garden part of the whole project.[39] Eighteen months later the Cabinet approved the text of the inscription:

TO THE MEMORY OF
49,000 IRISHMEN
WHO GAVE THEIR LIVES
IN THE GREAT WAR,
1914 – 1918.[40]

By that stage the work was well advanced and when, in August 1935, Lutyens, then working on Liverpool Cathedral, went with Byrne to Islandbridge, he was well pleased:

Site work is nearly finished … so I sent out for the masons a 16/ -bottle of whiskey – shared with six masons, Byrne, Lyburne, Campbell and myself – 10. We finished the bottle.[41]

Two years later, as the work was nearing delivery, Sir Dunbar Plunket Barton, still Chairman of the Executive Committee of the INWM, reflected on the eighteen years of endeavour since the meeting under French, at the Vice-Regal Lodge on 17 July 1919. He paid a warm tribute to the governments of Cosgrave and deValera, 'both of which were most courteous, considerate and sympathetic'. He noted that the scheme had never become the subject of party controversy. This, while remarkable but true, did not disguise the fact that the whole project had generated tensions elsewhere. This was so, not only within the INWM Committee itself where, for long, the Phoenix Park Memorial option did not enjoy unanimous support, but

between the INWM Committee and the British Legion and its antecedent bodies. Admittedly, both had certain personnel in common, most famously General Sir William Hickie. Similarly, they had some shared ambitions and activities, such as the desire to see war memorials to fallen Irishmen erected in Flanders and Gallipoli. Nonetheless, each body had a different style and approach.

External Affairs – ambivalent remembrance:

In the early 1920s, indeed, this particular objective on the part of each caused considerable irritation to Government in general and to its man in Brussels in particular, Count Gerald O'Kelly de Gallagh. The efforts of the Cork branch of the Legion of ex-Servicemen to erect a memorial at Mons, and those of the INWM Committee to erect memorial crosses in Belgium and Gallipoli, caused him to complain bitterly to his superiors in External Affairs over 1923-1924. When, on 11 November 1923, a memorial was unveiled at Mons in memory of Irish war dead in Flanders, no one from the Irish Free State Government was there, but the British Military Attaché and John French, the Earl of Ypres, together with General Sir Nevil Macready, were present. O'Kelly complained:

this demonstration in the name of Ireland organised with the approval of the British Authorities ... and of undoubted potential publicity value ... completely ignored the new status of Ireland. I would suggest in the elementary interests of our national status that representations be made in the proper quarter to prevent, for the future, the Earl of Ypres or General Macready from being permitted to identify themselves with Ireland in international functions of this kind.[42]

In the following summer, when, under the direction of Albert Jacobs, the Cork Branch of the Legion of ex-Servicemen arranged to visit Ypres, the External Affairs Secretary now complained of the shortness of the notice Jacobs had given in applying for a collective passport for a travelling party of 250, but he wired O'Kelly that 'there are several reasons why we should be particularly anxious to oblige this body' and urged him to seize the initiative with the Belgian authorities.[43] Indeed, Jacobs had requested External Affairs that O'Kelly be involved at the Ypres ceremony and that O'Kelly should invite the King of the Belgians. External Affairs now complained 'if we had known earlier about it, perhaps it would have been possible to capture the ceremony'.[44] By 1 July External Affairs were now praising Jacobs as an 'exceedingly capable organiser' and his travelling party as 'the most important group that has

visited the battlefields from this country'. Consequently, the Minister now asked O'Kelly to 'take a prominent part in the celebrations'.[45] With this event over, however, External Affairs had changed its mind about Jacobs, observing that 'the whole affair was extremely badly organised by Jacobs and Co', but the Minister was gratified at the prominent role played and the speech made by O'Kelly at the occasion.[46]

The satisfaction was not long enjoyed. The INWM Committee's and Legion's activities in Belgian war remembrance had already given rise to further irritation, causing O'Kelly to complain angrily. He wanted to know the Free State's official position towards such memorials raised by Irishmen:

These people apparently always act as the humble servants of the British connexion and, when abroad, carry on under the auspices of the British Military Attaché. It seems quite right that memorials should be erected to Irish soldiers who fell in Belgium in the Great War, but it seems utterly wrong that the glory and kudos thereof should as a matter of routine be associated in the mind of the Belgians with Britain and Britain only.

He was confident that General Hickie would concur that it would be more dignified and more in keeping with the national status in every way if, in future, such functions were carried out entirely independently of the British Embassies abroad.[47] A year later, on reading in his *Irish Times* about a proposed war ceremony in Belgium, O'Kelly wanted plenty of advance notice from his superiors as to what was proposed and what action they wanted him to take, 'so as to avoid anything resembling last year's fiasco'.[48] The proposed occasion was the dedication of the Munster Memorial Cross at Ypres, being organised by Hickie and the INWM Committee.

Further aggravation was to arise in 1926 when Hickie, the Legion and the INWM Committee again incurred the wrath of O'Kelly. Hickie made arrangements in Belgium in regard to the Wyschaete Memorial, without consulting O'Kelly, or, apparently, External Affairs, and allegedly made his Belgian arrangements through the British Embassy. O'Kelly wanted External Affairs to find out if this was the case and, if so, to point out to Hickie that 'this is the kind of action which makes it almost impossible for us to stand on our own feet abroad'.[49] By 30 July 1926, O'Kelly was fulminating at the situation. He understood that Hickie was to ask Cosgrave to appoint a representative to attend the Wyschaete Memorial ceremony: however, if the event were organised by Hickie under the auspices of the British Embassy, then the position of the Saorstát representative would be invidious. Indeed

the situation has been so badly compromised by General Hickie's Committee in the first instance, that I submit that, as matters now stand, we should take no official notice whatever of the proceedings …So far as can be judged, the proceedings will develop into a Union Jack-waving parade with a stressing of the Imperial note.[50]

Consequently, unless instructed explicitly to the contrary, O'Kelly proposed to absent himself from the Wyschaete commemoration. In the event, however, Hickie had already been reprimanded by External Affairs, the Minister requesting him to inform his Committee that it was 'not customary for citizens or organisations in the Saorstát to approach External Governments directly and to inform him that the Department of External Affairs is at their service for such purposes'. Hickie quickly mended fences, apologising for having 'mistaken the method of approach', and stating he would now ask the President to appoint a representative to attend the Ceremony.[51] On receipt of an invitation from General Hickie, O'Kelly was now instructed to attend the unveiling of the memorial to the 16th

Irish Division. Deploring the fact that the occasion was 'essentially a British Army Divisional Celebration', he was consoled that the British Military Attaché was 'exceedingly dissatisfied' with the treatment he himself had received from the organisers. O'Kelly's final assessment of the occasion was that

as much as could be retrieved has been retrieved from a situation which appeared irrevocably lost beforehand. Though in some ways the celebrations seemed undoubtedly to underline the dependence of Ireland on Britain, in the eyes of the Belgian public, it has undoubtedly served to advertise the efforts of Ireland in the Allied cause and of the fraternity in arms of Ireland and Belgium during the war[52].

Although displaying some ambivalence in the early 1920s, the Free State Government came to accept the necessity to be seen willingly and actively to participate in the external war commemorations by other governments or by Irish-based British ex-Servicemen's bodies, be they the INWM Committee or the British Legion. By contrast, at home, their presence was nominal at best, non-existent at worst, at Armistice Day and Remembrance Sunday events.

BELOW
1914 War Recruitment Poster

Internal politics: Legion, Government and War Remembrance:

If the Irish Governments experienced some tension at the activities of the Legion and the INWM Committee abroad, there was equally an edginess between these bodies themselves at home. The zeal of the British Legion in Ireland tried the patience of the INWM Committee, as it did of the IWGC and OPW over war graves. But the INWM Trustees and the Legion needed each other. By its own admission, in 1937, the Legion did not represent the majority of ex-Servicemen in Ireland, who remained outside its ranks.[53] This notwithstanding, from its emergence in 1925 as a coalescence of various individuals and British ex-Servicemen's organisations, the British Legion had become the de facto organisers of the annual Armistice Day Commemorations throughout the State and beyond, and, given that the INWM Committee wanted a war memorial, it had to live with this. As Senator Jameson confessed to Cosgrave in October 1931,

The British Legion have taken so much interest in all our proceedings and are such an important body in the discussion about the War Memorial that I think it is in all our interests to meet their ideas where we can.[54]

The Government's attitude to war commemoration within the State was similarly ambivalent to its attitude abroad. The holding of Armistice Day ceremonies in the capital was allowed every year until the outbreak of the Second World War and the adoption of neutrality. While unruly scenes or disruption led to the refusal of College Green in 1925, where it had been permitted in 1924, the public commemoration was allowed to switch to St. Stephen's Green.[55] Further disruption there led to its transfer to inside the Phoenix Park in 1926 and this was allowed as the annual venue even after deValera came to power in 1932, until in 1940 it was transferred to the new War Memorial Park in Islandbridge.

As regards Government representation at the British Legion's Dublin Armistice ceremonies, at no point did the President, any members of Government or, while his office existed, the Governor-General, personally attend them. This was despite formal, annual invitations from General Hickie on behalf of the Legion. However, the Government did send a representative, beginning with Maurice Moore in 1924 and thereafter, Dáil Deputy, Patrick Shaw of Westmeath, laid a wreath at the ceremony on behalf of the Government, down to 1931.[56] Likewise, while no member of Government attended the annual religious ceremonies in St. Patrick's Cathedral, Dublin, a representative was deputed to attend.[57] However, with the change of administration as of 1932, the deputised representation of Government at the Phoenix Park ceremony ceased. While permission was given to hold the ceremony there, as to the annual invitation to the President to lay a wreath, in October 1932, the Cabinet agreed 'the proposal should not be acceded to'.[58] Again, the attendance at St. Patrick's Cathedral by way of representative ceased as of 1936.

Nevertheless, despite the developing political extremism of the 1930s, the deValera Government, which could have prohibited them, permitted the ceremonies and parades from the city to the Phoenix Park, on strict conditions that Union Jacks were not displayed, nor 'British fascist uniforms worn'.[59] These conditions were not always followed to the letter, as McDunphy complained when he personally noticed Legion flags, with Union Jacks, displayed at Eden Quay in November 1935, or when the Legion was photographed with flags partly displayed, at the Pro-Cathedral in Marlborough Street in November 1936.[60] Despite these transgressions, the permissions continued.

Islandbridge – hope deferred:
This was the background against which the imminent completion of the Islandbridge Park and War Memorial Gardens raised the questions of inauguration and first use. A building trade strike in 1937 had delayed the completion of the project. In anticipation of its completion, Jameson, in March 1937, raised with deValera the question of its handover and formal opening, and 'if it is to be a public one'.[61] Seeking his Cabinet colleagues' views, deValera was told by his Minister for Finance, McEntee, that a formal handing over by the Trustees to the Government would be 'a graceful gesture' and that its avoidance 'would provoke unfavourable comment': he thought it would have a 'reconciling influence' and create 'a good impression beyond the Border and upon British public opinion'.[62] However, a long delay ensued before the Cabinet decided its position. In August 1937 the OPW was approached by the INWM Committee, in association with the Legion, for permission to use the War Memorial Garden instead of the Phoenix Park.[63] The OPW Commissioners, now, as previously with the proposal for War Grave photographs in their annual reports, were uneasy. They were opposed to any 'avoidable publicity' in connection with the memorial, but felt that, if there had to be publicity, it were better that it be tied in with the Annual Armistice Day Commemorations rather than stand alone. Commissioner Ó hÉigeartaigh conveyed these reservations

BELOW
OPW 1930's drawing, template for Royal Dublin Fusiliers Cap Badge.

and misgivings to his superior in the Department of Finance when he copied the INWM Committee's request to Walter Doolin on 2 September 1937.[64] He added that the OPW believed Jameson and INWM Trustees were being pressurised by the Legion – 'rather against their better judgement' – into 'raising the question of a ceremonial opening'.

Rather cannily, Doolin, in reporting this to Maurice Moynihan, the Government Secretary, agreed with the OPW because, if the permission to use Islandbridge 'were granted now, it would ease the pressure on the Trustees for a formal opening ceremony and might help to shelve the question entirely'. On the principle of whether there should be any ceremonial opening of the Memorial Gardens and Park by the President, Doolin would offer no opinion, but, in practical terms, Finance was

gravely concerned that such a ceremony, inevitably attended by a great deal of publicity both before the event and after, might stir persons with the outlook of those who blew up recently the statue of George II into activity which might involve the destruction of the Memorial.

Given the amount of taxpayers' money involved, 'such destruction would be deplorable'. Nonetheless, Finance favoured giving the permission but

thought that the decision in this instance should go to Cabinet.[65] Privately and informally, the OPW's Ó hÉigeartaigh told Doolin that the Legion was trying to force the hands of the Trustees to secure a formal opening of the Memorial Park, in a separate ceremony, before 11 November.

Ó hÉigeartaigh advised Jameson that 'the safety of the monument might be endangered if there were undue publicity', a view which, apparently, Jameson accepted. Doolin at Finance was well aware of this danger, having already discussed it with the Secretary of the Government back in April.[66] Even before Ó hÉigeartaigh had told Jameson this, the Cabinet had already agreed, on 3 September 1937, to leave the decision on a formal opening to de Valera. [67]

In the meantime, with these hesitations ongoing, de Valera promised Jameson to have the request for use of Islandbridge 'dealt with immediately', and, having informally consulted Cabinet colleagues, agreed on 9 September to grant the INWM Committee's and Legion's request.[68] Vigorous behind the scenes negotiations must have transpired between the INWM Committee and the Legion in the weeks that followed. Hermione Wilson, INWM Secretary, a month later told Jameson that the Legion had reconsidered their own request:

LEFT
Fountain and pavilion,
National War Memorial
Gardens, Islandbridge

having regard to the recent planting of young trees and shrubs, they had decided that a large assembly might damage the gardens in their infancy. Consequently, they had now asked the OPW for permission to revert to their old venue, in the Phoenix Park proper, for their November 1937 commemorations.[69] On the very next day, a clearly relieved Jameson informed deValera of this about-turn on the use of the Islandbridge venue 'which you had kindly arranged for me after our last conversation on the subject'.[70] The return to the Phoenix Park was permitted and, furthermore, despite the reservations of the Garda Commissioner, the Department of Justice and the Government instructed him to allow the processions and related activities to proceed as in former years.[71] Nevertheless, growing impatience at the delay in inaugurating the Memorial was manifest in the ranks of the Legion. Early in 1938, on the occasion of a visit to Dublin by Major General Sir Frederick Maurice, head of the Legion in Britain, the Taoiseach agreed to receive him on the understanding it was purely a courtesy call. However, when Maurice addressed the Legion itself in February, there was a strong protest from them at the delay in opening, as the *Irish Press* reported.[72]

Then, in August 1938, doubtless in anticipation of being able to use the completed War Memorial Garden for their annual commemoration, Major Tynan inquired of Government as to plans for an opening ceremony. He was told the Taoiseach would consider the matter on his return from the League of Nations Assembly at Geneva – a year after the Cabinet had left the decision to him.[73] Apparently receiving no further response, Tynan and Captain A. P. Connolly, the Legion's Chairman, called to the Taoiseach's Department on 25 September, seeking some clue as to the Government's intentions, with Connolly obviously not too hopeful since he indicated that he was going to apply to the OPW for permission to use the Phoenix Park 'as usual, he hoped, for the last time'.[74] By mid-October 1938 they had reconciled themselves to the summer of 1939 as the earliest practicable time for an opening ceremony, even as deValera was seeking an urgent meeting with Jameson to clarify the INWM Committee's position on the matter vis-à-vis the British Legion.[75] When they met, deValera indicated his agreement in principle to holding a formal opening ceremony in the summer of 1939 and was prepared to be there himself. Jameson wanted a quiet, all-ticket affair and was against any elaborate demonstrations 'which Connolly of the Legion and others of like mind had in mind'.[76] Further emphasising his intention to be present at a formal opening in July or August 1939, deValera asked Moynihan to meet the Legion's leaders in mid- December 1938 and they were given this assurance, 'conditional on the absence from the ceremony of any display which might tend to create ill-will or resentment or to embarrass the Government'. Asked by Moynihan if it was intended to involve guests from Northern Ireland, Connolly indicated that 'it would be virtually impossible to exclude Northern Ireland in view of the fact that the Memorial is an all-Ireland one and that a considerable sum had been contributed in the North towards its erection'. Connolly suggested that, were the Taoiseach willing, the Governor-General and Prime Minister of Northern Ireland might be invited. It was agreed that, subject to Government scrutiny, the guest list was a matter for the INWM Trustees, but, it had yet to be resolved whether the scope of that list would be ' (a) all-Ireland only, (b) all-Ireland plus Great Britain and the Dominions, or (c) the two foregoing plus the former allies'.[77] By mid-January, Walshe of External Affairs and Moynihan had agreed that the (a) option was to be the preferred.[78] After much coming and going between Wilson of the INWM Committee and the Government, by the beginning of April 1939 it was settled: Sunday 30 July would be the inaugural date, a date for which the Legion had indicated a strong preference.[79]

Hope destroyed:
Before the month was out, all this was set aside by the deteriorating international situation. On 5 April 1939 Britain announced plans for the evacuation of two and a half million children in the event of war and began preparing the details of the Military Training Bill which was to introduce conscription. On 26 April deValera called in Connolly and Tynan and told them a postponement was now inevitable 'in view of the altered circumstances'.[80] DeValera explained to them that when on 15 December 1938 they had been informed of his intention to authorise and to attend an opening, at that time he felt 'it would have a good effect by signifying that Irishmen who took different views in regard to the War of 1914-1918 appreciated and respected each other's views'. But the international situation and the 'ferment it had generated here had altered the situation', not least because of Britain's announced intention to introduce conscription, 'and the possibility that an effort might be made to apply it to our fellow countrymen in the Six Counties'. Although Tynan insisted that the Legion would be anxious to proceed, Connolly felt it preferable to postpone rather than have a restricted ceremony.[81] Unaware of this, two INWM representatives, Brew-Mulhallen and C. W. Robertson, called next day to Government Buildings to discuss

LEFT
Somme Commemoration,
Islandbridge, July 2006

inaugural arrangements and were seen by Kennedy, the Assistant Secretary. On being told of the Taoiseach's advice to Connolly and Tynan, the INWM delegates offered no comment, but asked what Connolly's reaction had been. Kennedy formed the impression that the INWM men 'were not displeased' and gathered 'they were under the impression for a long time that there would be no formal opening ceremony' and that de Valera and Jameson had agreed on this. In concluding comments to the Government Secretary, Kennedy remarked:

It is quite clear that the proposal to have an opening ceremony has been sponsored all along by the British Legion and that they have brought a good deal of pressure to bear on the Trustees to fall in with their views.[82]

In these circumstances, a report in the *Irish Times* on 16 May 1939, announcing the 'Irish War Memorial Opening on July 30th: Earl of Cavan to perform the Ceremony', caused some consternation and hasty denials. On the same day, the irrepressible Tynan wrote to Moynihan to resurrect plans for the opening, given that 'the difficulty in the matter of conscription has, happily, now been removed'. This may have been a little premature, as it was not until 26 May that Churchill 'yielded to a formidable campaign' advising against

conscription.[83] Tynan, however, went on into details such as who was the person actually to unveil the monument, proceeded to ask the Government for finance to cover the cost of the grand opening, and concluded by regretting the incorrect announcement in the *Irish Times* which must have come to that newspaper through Belfast.[84] An apologetic Connolly saw Kennedy at Government Buildings the next day to try to explain how the premature and erroneous report might have appeared in the press, but, like Tynan, he assumed that now that the conscription issue was out of the way, he thought that 'the status quo' had been restored and that the Legion 'were free to go ahead and make arrangements' for the opening. Kennedy assured him that he was under 'a complete misapprehension' that conscription alone was the cause of the Taoiseach's change of mind.[85] Connolly quickly prepared a draft statement contradicting the *Irish Times'* report, brought it back to the Taoiseach's Department where de Valera himself approved it, and it was then released, with the addendum that the 30 July date had been 'purely provisional', and 'in the present hourly changing state of international affairs, may prove to be quite optimistic'.[86] Connolly followed this up with a further and final statement, published in the press on 21 June 1939, effectively announcing the

BELOW
Enlisting the Irish:
1914 War Recruitment Poster

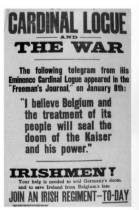

end of any opening by 1939 and hoping to have it in the summer of 1940.[87]

As for the Trustees of the Irish National War Memorial, in Kennedy's view as expressed to Moynihan, they

have at all times adopted a very reasonable attitude in regard to the completion of the Memorial and the opening ceremony. In fact, were it not for them, it is improbable that the British Legion would have so quietly acquiesced in the postponement of the opening ceremony.[88]

In the end, that opening was never to happen.

The annual Armistice Day commemoration was indeed held at the War Memorial Garden from 1940, without parades or undue displays – until November 1945, when the ban on the parade was revoked. On the occasion of first use, in November 1940, the Gardaí on duty were all armed, but from 1941 the Garda authorities decided to dispense with this, as fears over security diminished.[89]

As seen in an earlier chapter, when Colonel Harry Chettle visited Islandbridge in 1941, he was greatly impressed by the splendid Memorial, with its working fountains and its gardens. Yet, it was a solitary kind of splendour and the Memorial's history thereafter was to remain a chequered, and for long, unhappy one: the project had not been fully completed as it had been originally envisaged; the fear of malicious damage or destruction was never entirely dissipated, and over the following decades, deterioration set in.[90]

***Until the day break
And the shadows fade away***

*George Dixon Morrow, Royal Canadian Artillery
30 April 1941*

*Ballinakill (St. Thomas) Churchyard
Co. Galway*

Chapter 13

The Onset Of The Second World War, 1937-1941

Over the years 1935 to 1937 an end was in sight to the task of placing official headstones over the graves of the war dead buried in Ireland. If the OPW, in this regard at least, could at last heave a sigh of relief, the Imperial War Graves Commission still had a niggling worry. What troubled it were the issues of communication and periodic visitation into the future. Because, uniquely, the Irish Free State had taken a sovereign control of the whole business, the presence of the Commission was on sufferance, whereas elsewhere, their inspectors could visit and investigate at will.

In April 1928, Seán Lester of External Affairs had assured Harry Batterbee at the Dominions Office that this would not be a problem.

....there would be no objection, as far as the Government is concerned, to the periodical inspection on behalf of relatives in Great Britain and Northern Ireland of the work being done by the Commissioners of Public Works.[1]

However, in November 1934, when the IWGC wrote formally to the OPW Secretary suggesting an annual visit of inspection by one of their officers, the OPW replied in a non-committal manner, in April 1935, simply outlining the steps being taken to maintain the graves into the future.[2] Subsequently, when Vesper was back in Belfast in 1936, completing his work in the North, he raised the issue with Chettle, remarking that Lester's 'sanction' 'was, as you know, shelved by the Free State'. He thought there was little point in raising the matter with Dublin again, especially while the work of establishing war graves' maintenance agreements was still in progress. Once all this would be completed, he surmised, the Free State might write informing them of the completion, and this might offer the IWGC the opportunity to open the matter of visitation and inspection again. He concluded, however, that if the IWGC were going to 'try and insist on this, then the matter had not better be left too long'.[3] He repeated this advice in a detailed memorandum on 31 July 1936, which was prompted by a friendly, personal letter from Brandon seeking advice. Vesper stressed the unsatisfactory and hazardous nature of current personal or semi-official correspondence between Brandon of the OPW and himself: if Brandon mentioned officially to his OPW superiors any advice Vesper had given him, 'the Free State Government would strongly object. The communications issue and the issue of visitation should be put on a formal basis'.[4] Vesper's superiors in London let the issue lie until his impending courtesy visit to Dublin in the last week of April 1937. On the assumption that he was

allowed to visit some cemeteries during the visit, he was advised that he should take up the issue of periodic visitation.[5]

Periodic visitation:

Vesper considered his visit over 27-29 April 'highly successful'. At his meeting with Veale, whom the OPW Commissioners formally deputed to see him, he requested that the IWGC might be given an annual statement on the war graves' situation and, when Veale said they could let the IWGC have copies of the OPW's annual reports, Vesper persisted and asked specifically that the OPW might send an annual letter offering greater detail. However, when Vesper moved on to ask permission for periodic visits by 'a responsible officer from the Commission', the OPW had anticipated this, and the Board's Commissioners had advised Veale that they 'hoped that Captain Vesper will not press this matter', as the Board had no power to grant it. Furthermore, as Veale clearly advised Vesper, the OPW Commissioners 'were not anxious to press their Ministry of External Affairs who had previously ignored the question'. Clearly, External Affairs under Joseph Walshe as Secretary and with deValera as Foreign Minister – and simultaneously Taoiseach – was a different place from what it had been under Lester, McGilligan and Cosgrave

in 1928. Ironically, Veale had insisted Vesper visit a few of the cemeteries, affording the latter the opportunity, laughingly, to point out that here he was actually going to do what he was seeking permission to do. Vesper drew attention to Lester's letter of April 1928 of which the OPW, or at least Veale, was unaware. Veale promised to raise the question of visitation with the OPW Board and when Vesper called the following day, Wednesday 28 April 1937, he was informed that the Board was not in a position to give a response: he thereupon arranged to call again on the day following. He used the interval to check out the Glasnevin War Memorial and also the 'all Ireland Garden of Remembrance' at Islandbridge, which he found to be a 'truly magnificent memorial'.

Strangely, as he examined the OPW's method of operation in a discussion with William Brandon, he undermined the IWGC's case for periodic visits of inspection by finding that the OPW's

system of maintenance inspections is, in effect, similar to our own in the United Kingdom and Northern Ireland' [sic]. Indeed, the District Architect for each county visits the war graves in his county before certifying further payment under the maintenance agreement.

Indeed, by the time of this visit of Vesper's, he was able to report that, of the total of 555 Cemeteries, ninety per cent of them were now subject to OPW maintenance agreements.[6]

Despite their preoccupation with a building strike, then at its height in Dublin, the OPW Commissioners considered the IWGC request for an annual statement and permission for periodic official visitations. Through Veale, they said they would consider the former and refer the latter to 'the appropriate authorities' and inform the IWGC of the outcome. Critical exchanges soon took place between the OPW, Finance and External Affairs. On 12 May 1937, the day after Vesper reported his April visit to Chettle, the OPW Secretary, Fagan, wrote to the Secretary of the Department of Finance concerning this visit and Vesper's production of Lester's 1928 letter. Remarking that Lester's letter 'may have been so worded with a view to avoid authorising inspection by the Imperial War Graves Commission as such', he added:

We have refrained from any expression of agreement on periodical inspection by the IWGC Officers without your further instructions as the matter is one of general policy.

When Fagan sought directions as to a reply, Dagg's response, at Finance, was to pass the matter on to Walshe in External Affairs a fortnight later. The latter reported deValera as conceding that the IWGC's understanding was 'reasonable', given Lester's text. Walshe added that the Minister for External Affairs, that is, deValera, saw

no grounds for withholding the concurrence of the Commissioners of Public Works on the principle whereby any of the officials of the IWGC passing through Saorstát Éireann, to or from their inspections in the Six County area, should have liberty to visit war graves in Saorstát Éireann.

Crucially, he added:

if an informal invitation to the IWGC were conveyed in these terms it could hardly be regarded by them as giving them more than an unofficial courtesy position in virtue of their special interest in the war graves in Saorstát Éireann of British citizens who have no relations here.[7]

It was well it were so, because Veale already, at the point of Vesper's departure, had invited him to visit 'at least once a year so that you may pay us an official, or in any case, a semi-official visit'. Vesper was pleasantly taken aback and reported that

knowing Veale as I do, as a strict Civil Servant, it seemed to me that he had either been authorised to say something of the kind, and certainly he meant it in his capacity as Chief Official for the war graves in the Irish Free State, as well as a personal friend.

Vesper had received a reception remarkable in its extent and warmth on the occasion of this visit: he found that the OPW staff

had only the most friendly feeling toward the Commission throughout, and especially now as a Government Department, they appear above all to be anxious to discharge their obligations on behalf of that Government, conscientiously and thoroughly. I have received constant proof of this.[8]

That his visit had been a success became evident in July 1937 when Veale wrote formally on the visitation issue. He could now tell Vesper that the OPW Commissioners saw no objection 'to your officials inspecting War Graves in the Saorstát when passing to or from their inspections in Northern Ireland'.[9]

Intriguingly however, Vesper felt the need to parse and analyse the tone and content of this note, in commenting to Chettle at IWGC headquarters three days later. He noted firstly that Veale's communication was written in a personal manner but that this was not surprising

in the circumstances, 'the position being that the OPW were anxious not to refuse our request, while they knew that the Ministry for External Affairs felt unable to accept'. Observing that there was 'a very strict regulation' in the Free State Civil Service that no official might write personal letters dealing with official matters, Vesper concluded that the go-ahead given for inspection visits, in Veale's letter, 'becomes official because Mr Veale has clearly received instructions from both the Ministry for External Affairs and the Commissioners, to write this letter'. Consequently he urged his superiors to ensure that an IWGC official called at the OPW at least once a year, and visited some war grave sites, and that a formal response to Veale's letter should be sent in order to secure the position.[10]

Relations between the IWGC and OPW continued on a businesslike, sensitive basis in the years which followed. The former was careful to send proofs of the Ireland paragraphs in its draft annual reports for scrutiny by the OPW, and Raftery, in return, was quick to reply with helpful comments. Indeed, the text for the 1938 IWGC annual report suggested that the end of a long road was about to be reached: the OPW Commissioners had made 'further progress towards the completion of the permanent marking of War Graves' and maintenance agreements 'have now been made in the majority of cases'.[11]

Furthermore, the arrangements for visitation which Vesper had urged and, indeed, engineered in 1937 bore fruit in 1938 when he was drafted in to pay a visit on his way from Northern Ireland in April. The occasion was historic, in its own modest way, when he officially presented a copy of Fabian Ware's *Immortal Heritage* – the first official history of the IWGC, published in 1937 – to the OPW Library; historic too because in the meantime, the Irish Free State had become Éire on 29 December, necessitating a fresh attention to nomenclature in future IWGC annual reports.[12] Ironically, it was left to the impetuous Ware to remonstrate, in a memorandum to his Director of Records on 18 March:

Are you responsible for the use of the word ÉIRE, on page 33 of the Annual Report just published? If so, why were you not consistent and did not substitute the words Deutschland, La Belgique, La France etc for their English equivalents?[13]

In fairness to Ware, Sir Edward Harding, in an official communiqué and informal note on 29 December 1937, had advised Ware that under the new Irish constitution, effective from that date, the name of the State was 'Éire' or 'Ireland', but another memo from Harding, on 18 May 1938, invited attention to the provision that the former Irish Free State 'shall be styled or known as Éire'.[14] These concernments apart, there was little for the OPW or the IWGC to worry about when Vesper paid the 1938 or, indeed, the April 1939 visit – all very minor matters. There was, however, one odd exception - a piece of past history that became an ominous overture to the future.

Graves of German and Austrian war dead:

A little known fragment of Irish history is one relating to German military personnel and civilians imprisoned in Ireland during the course of the 1914-1918 War. They were a tiny number by any of the horrific yardsticks through which that calamity has been measured or assessed. For themselves, families and friends, this was of little account – their stories were as lamentable as any.

Once the war commenced, German and Austrian civilians living in Ireland fell under as much suspicion as they did in Britain. Typical was an RIC Report of March 1915 on six civilians then living in Mayo; sixty-six year old Arthur Gumbauck and fifty-four year old Englebert Wehrly were Germans in the jewellery trade, living in Ballinasloe and Ballina respectively. Engelbert's wife,

THE ONSET OF THE SECOND WORLD WAR, 1937-1941

Catherine, though British-born, did not escape the stigma of being numbered among 'Alien Enemies at large in County Mayo'. Neither did the forty-one year old governess, Annie Brohn Knight, in Castlebar, nor the forty-year old Austrian, Alieda, widow of a British Colonel Buchanan, of Westport. Finally, fate dealt a harsh hand in life to forty-three year old Fr. Joseph Bruger, born in Alsace in 1872 . Suddenly made a German by very recent historical geography, but 'entirely French in his ideas', he had, thus far, spent his life in the Nigerian missions and came to Westport to recover his health.[15]

Unlucky, too, was the German Louis Yung [sic-Jung?] who had been a band conductor on a Clyde pleasure boat when he secured a new position in the Palace Theatre, Cork, in October 1913, playing the double bass in the orchestra. Briefly returning to Scotland in May 1914, he came back to Cork in search of a new contract in August, but the Palace Theatre manager refused to re-employ him as, with the outbreak of war, he had suddenly become an alien. The manager, although believing Yung, who was destitute, to be 'perfectly harmless', sent him away to Macroom – the marshalling yard for enemy aliens in Cork. From there he ended up interned in the detention camp barracks in Templemore. His distraught wife, living in Cheltenham with their three children under five, was herself penniless by November 1914. Her husband had no money to send her from being 'ordered out of Cork and sent to Macroom with all other aliens from Cork'.[16] Very quickly on the outbreak of hostilities, civilian internment and prisoner of war detention camps were set up in various parts of the island, those at Templemore Barracks, County Tipperary, and at Oldcastle, County Meath, being especially notable, and it was to these in particular that detainees from all over Ireland, north and south, were eventually sent.[17]

12 Clare Place,
Bath Road,
Cheltenham,
Nov. 15, 14.

Dear Sir,

    I shall be very grateful if you can help me in any way as I am in extreme distress through the internment of my husband (a German) at Templemore, Ireland,. I was entirely dependent upon him and now I am quite destitute and have three children under five to provide for.

    My husband was employed at the "Palace" Cork as Bassist in the Orchestra at a salary of 35/- per week, but through his detention I have had no support from him since June last. He was ordered out of Cork and sent to Macroom together with all other aliens from Cork. The wives of the others went with their husbands and were, and still are being, provided for, but they will do nothing for me here. I came here this being my native county, but I find myself excluded from charities on account of my nationality. The Board of Guardians are giving me 6/- weekly for the next 2 weeks, but will grant nothing regularly or adequate.

    I can assure you I have suffered great hardship having sold nearly all of my few belongings and several days last week we had no food at all nor fire. At the present moment I am penniless and at my wits end to provide for the coming week so Sir if you can give me quick relief I shall be thankful. The Police here will verify all my statements if you wish. Sincerely trusting that something can be done for me.

               Yours sincerely,

               (Mrs) N. YUNG.

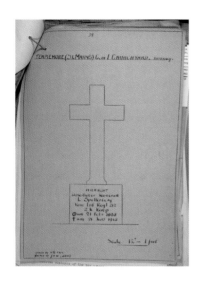

NEAR LEFT
OPW sketch of
memorial to German World
War One internee, Anton
Gierszewski, in Templemore
Catholic New Cemetery,
Co. Tipperary

FAR LEFT
OPW sketch of memo-
rial to Ludwig Spellerberg,
at St. Mary's Church
of Ireland Churchyard,
Templemore

Templemore Barracks held several hundred German prisoners of war in four concentration cages in the two barracks squares, 'complete with barbed wire, searchlights and sentry towers'.[18] Some, including Italians, Bohemians, Austrians, Germans and Luxemburgers, were released following petitions from friends and family, when the Home Secretary was satisfied of their being in the clear – much to the annoyance of Major General Friend, Officer Commanding the Troops in Ireland in 1916.[19] However, not all were so relatively fortunate; their history has hardly been written and breaks the surface only in the occasional source. One such, John Smith's history of Oldcastle, describes the old workhouse there being offered to the War Office, for detention purposes, in 1914. By 1916 it held over 570 civilian internees as enemy aliens.[20]

At the very outset of their working relations, following on the agreement of 1926, the IWGC began sending to the OPW details of cemeteries containing war graves. In the course of this, in May 1927, Chettle mentioned to his superior, Lord Arthur Browne, that they had 'a few ex-enemy graves' in their Irish Free State records. In one instance, however, that of St. Mary's Churchyard, Templemore, they had a unique case – a cemetery containing no British war graves, 'only enemy war graves'. He wondered whether they should send it on to the OPW and was advised affirmatively – his advisor, Browne, commenting that the Irish Free State 'presumably take over the responsibilities of the British Government under the Treaty of Versailles' in respect of enemy graves. Consequently, on 13 May 1927 they sent to the OPW details of the graves of German prisoners of war 'so far as they are known'.[21] At this stage, however, they were certainly not a priority: it was eighteen months later before the Minister for Finance gave approval to the principle of headstones being placed on the graves of prisoners of war, but it was to be a very long time before practice followed endorsement of the principle.[22] The IWGC itself was not absolutely certain of an obligation to erect permanent markings on enemy war graves. In reply to a question on this point from Vesper in Dublin in 1930, Chettle advised him that the IWGC did not consider it was obliged to do so, but admitted that the Germans had interpreted the Versailles Treaty as imposing such an obligation. He concluded, however, by stating that the British Government had decided to mark permanently German war graves in Britain and Northern Ireland, and that a small tablet 'has now been placed on the great majority of German combatants' graves here'.[23]

As for interned German civilians who died in Ireland during internment, Chettle advised the OPW that the British Government was made responsible by the Versailles Treaty to maintain their graves but there was no obligation to erect headstones on them.[24] Meanwhile, the German Legation in London began inquiring about their compatriots' war graves in the Irish Free State; Batterbee at the Dominions Office advised Arthur Browne of the IWGC to 'put them off somehow, as negotiations were still going on between the British and Irish Governments', presumably on the issue of the secondment of a war graves expert.[25] That expert, Vesper, in the course of his investigations of Templemore Catholic Cemetery in County Tipperary in April 1930, came upon the grave of a German soldier, Anton Gierszewski, who had died as a prisoner of war in November 1914. His comrade internees had erected 'a beautiful tombstone with Celtic Cross in white marble on a limestone base', but which, in the course of time, became completely obliterated with weeds and shrubs, according to an OPW minute of January 1937.[26]

Not until September 1936 did the German authorities directly approach the OPW on the subject, and then it was probably in response to a family inquiry rather than as a general issue of policy: the Legation in Dublin inquired about the maintenance, in Oldcastle Catholic Cemetery, of the grave of the civilian, Franz Seemeier.[27] At that point, in September 1936, the OPW queried its responsibility. Acknowledging that the IWGC maintained enemy war graves as an international obligation under Versailles, it supposed there was 'no direct instruction to OPW to have to do the same?'. The IWGC had sent them details of one Austrian and five German internees or prisoners of war who had died and were buried in the Free State. The particulars were verified: three of them had privately-erected, permanent memorials and three had nothing. However, it decided that, as a matter of grace, it would mark and maintain them in the way the IWGC did, until the OPW rediscovered a file of 1928 in which Finance had already given them authority to do so.[28]

In conducting local enquiries on behalf of the German Legation, the OPW's district architect, Raymond Boyd-Barrett, gave a report on the case of Franz Seemeier, a Bavarian born in 1887, who died on 30 January 1917 and was buried in the Catholic ground of Oldcastle Cemetery. His grave was marked by a six-foot high, limestone cross, bearing the inscription, 'The sod of Erin lies lightly over him R.I.P.' His plot was being very well-tended by some

LEFT
Oldcastle Workhouse, as painted by a German internee, who was a prisoner at the camp in 1917.

local person. He tried to locate the grave of another German civilian internee, August Bockmeyer. There was no clue as to its whereabouts, a reported cross being missing and the graveyard being 'overgrown with grass and weeds and the whole now closed for fifteen years'. The unfortunate Bockmeyer, a twenty-six year old civilian of seafaring background, had tried to escape from the Oldcastle detention camp in September 1916. He was shot in the attempt, died from his wounds shortly after and was buried in the nearby workhouse graveyard, known as 'The Potter's Field'. [29]

By now the German Legation had become more concerned and more systematic in its approach: in December 1936 it sent the OPW a request for a report on the state of maintenance of six war graves, citing a note it had had from External Affairs eleven years before, in which the latter had represented to local authorities their responsibility for this maintenance.[30] The Legation now listed the following:

Walter Richter:
Drumcannon Cemetery, Co. Waterford

Erwin Bernhard Schatz:
The Asylum Cemetery,
Mullingar Mental Hospital

Ludwig Spellerberg:
St. Mary's Church of Ireland,
Templemore

Anton Gierszewski:
The Catholic New Cemetery,
Templemore

August Bockmeyer:
Oldcastle Workhouse Cemetery

Franz Seemeier:
Oldcastle Catholic Cemetery.[31]

Of these, Schatz's in Mullingar and Richter's in Waterford were well-maintained; Spellerberg's and Gierszewski's in Templemore were not, though their memorials were in

MEMORANDUM relative to the release of certain aliens from Oldcastle Detention Camp.

Serafino Binelli. This man was interned on the 14th August by order of the Home Secretary, but on representations being made by the Italian Consul at Dublin that Binelli though an Austrian Subject, was of Italian nationality, his release was recommended with the concurrence of the G.O.C. The Home Secretary on the 3rd September sanctioned his discharge.

Jean Emile Marx. This man was interned by the Military Authorities on the 20th February. He subsequently submitted through the American Embassy a memorial praying to be released on the ground that he was a subject of a Neutral State, the Grand Duchy of Luxembourg. The G.O.C. offered no objection to the man's release under conditions, and the Home Secretary sanctioned his discharge under an Order applying him under Article 30(1) of the provisions of the Aliens Restrictions Orders relating to alien enemies.

Rudolph Spacek. Spacek was interned by order of the Home Secretary on the 5th October, but on receipt of further representations the Home Secretary authorised his discharge on certain conditions which were fulfilled. The Military Authorities do not seem to have been consulted in the matter.

Francis Stanicka. This man, an Austrian Subject of Bohemian nationality, was interned on 18th August by order of the Home Secretary, but on submission of a memorial from him supported by testimonials from the London Czech Society, the Home Secretary directed his discharge. The Military Authorities were not consulted.

LEFT
list of Aliens released from Oldcastle Detention camp, 1916

THE ONSET OF THE SECOND WORLD WAR, 1937-194

*RIGHT
IWGC design for German
War Graves as requested by
OPW in 1936*

perfect order; Bockmeyer's, in Oldcastle Workhouse, could not be found. However, between July and December 1937 the delinquent local authorities had cleaned up the Templemore and Oldcastle Cemeteries, as a grateful Herr Hempel noted to de Valera.[32]

By February 1937 the Legation was pressing the OPW directly for news, which it now was promptly sent, and the OPW was pressing the IWGC for information on the design of the memorials they issued for German interned civilians buried in the U.K. Curiously, the IWGC had agreed with the Germans a design for these in 1934, but as late as October 1938 the design for permanent memorials for dead German combatants had still not been agreed between the British and German authorities.[33] Indeed, on 15 May 1939 the IWGC were due to meet their German counterparts to discuss the form of permanent memorial for German war-dead in Britain of 1914-1918,[34] and in an ironic note to Vesper on 17 April Chettle was to remark concerning the one known Austrian war grave in Ireland, 'you might tell them [the OPW] that their one Austrian internee should now be treated as a German' – the Germans having invaded Austria on 11 March 1938. Then, on 25 May 1939, Chettle reported that no progress had been made with the

Germans on the design question and, ominously but unprophetically, confided 'we shall probably have to wait another six months or more'.[35] More it was, as Britain declared war on Germany on 3 September 1939.

The outbreak of war:

The First World War, unprecedented up to that time in the scale of its slaughter and in the losses, too, of some 35,000 Irish lives on active service, had a profound impact on this country. Even though a very small figure by contrast, at 3,500 plus, the number of its military casualties who died in and were buried in this country was five times what it was to be for the Second World War. Nevertheless, in a number of ways the conflict of 1939-1945, in terms of burial, identification, marking and memorialising, posed greater problems for the Irish Government and its local authorities than the War of 1914-1918 had done for the then British Government in Ireland. With a more deadly weaponry and a more ferocious technology, the transport and delivery of death was grievous and intense. While the Irish State was neutral, Ireland was more closely a theatre of casualty and death, whether as a result of aerial or naval conflict. German U-boat and aerial onslaught on shipping around Ireland's coasts brought the horror

of bloated bodies washed ashore like a recurring nightmare. Problems of identification and registration of war deaths posed a serious challenge. The conflict and its consequences became profoundly international, so that even neutral Ireland became a burial ground for Americans and Canadians, Chinese and Dutch, Italians and Norwegians, as well as Irish, British and Germans.

In some ways this war started 'slowly' enough, and it was not until the Battle of the Atlantic, from July 1940 to July 1941, that the fuller results of savagery surfaced on Irish beaches. The story of the War has been told extensively elsewhere and requires no summary repetition here. For the purposes of the study of war graves, it is enough to consider how this second world conflict affected the relations between the Imperial War Graves Commission and the Office of Public Works on the one hand, and those of the British Commonwealth and Irish Governments on the other, in the matter of marking and commemorating the War's dead and buried in Ireland.

The overtures began in early February 1940 when Fabian Ware telephoned Percivale Leisching, Assistant Undersecretary of State at the Dominions Office, to sound out their views regarding 'war graves in Éire

arising from casualties of the present war'. While they had arrangements completed for all parts of the Empire under the IWGC Charter, having regard to Éire's constitutional position and the fact that she was neutral, he felt it would be inappropriate for him to send an IWGC official directly to Dublin. He diplomatically suggested that the Dominions Office should be the channel for overtures.[36]

Stephenson of the Dominions Office advised Ware, in response, that any overtures from Britain to Éire should first go through Sir John Maffey, their representative in Dublin, adding that 'right now was not the time'. Maffey would need to be briefed by Ware and the Dominions Office and then be left to use his own discretion as to the timing and manner of an approach to Dublin. Both the Dominions Office and Ware in the IWGC approached the matter quite gingerly – the normally zealous Ware remarking that, whenever the subject be raised, it were best it be initially confined to cases of bodies washed ashore, and added:

The question of dealing with Irishmen serving in the British Army who had subsequently died as a result of wounds in Éire might present greater difficulties and had better not be raised for the time being.[37]

Nevertheless, as instructed, on 15 May 1940, the day when the Germans occupied the Netherlands, Sir John Maffey called to External Affairs on the matter of British and Commonwealth war-dead. He recalled 'the very satisfactory arrangement in regard to British War Graves' which had been negotiated in the 1920s and was anxious for a similar arrangement in the context of this new conflict. He represented the concern of the Imperial War Graves Commission for appropriate burial and marking of the graves. He was told the matter would be 'looked into'.[38] Oddly enough, Maffey did not report this back to London, as Leisching noted in August 1940, causing J. E. Stephenson to remind Maffey, in September, that the IWGC had been looking for news or feedback since April. Ware's April letter was both circumspect and prophetic:

it is possible that a certain number of British seamen may lose their lives through enemy action near the coasts of Éire or their bodies may be washed ashore (as has already happened in some neutral countries) and buried.

He added that the Commission would welcome any information from the Éire Government and any assistance from them in temporarily marking and caring for such graves.[39]

Further promptings from the IWGC in May and August still brought no news from Maffey in Dublin, leading N. E. Costar at the Dominions Office to remark 'I hardly think the present a suitable moment for stirring this sleeping dog. Unless Sir Fabian writes again, put by'.[40] 'Hardly a suitable moment for stirring this sleeping dog' was a somewhat inappropriate observation on 31 August 1940: a few days before this, Maffey began sending Irish press newspaper cuttings concerning bodies washed ashore on the Donegal coast in the wake of shipping sent to the ocean bottom, most notoriously that of the *Arandora Star*.[41]

In the meantime, following Maffey's visit to them in May, External Affairs decided it was time to open a new file in respect of military and naval men 'buried here during the last eight months'. They added that although

a new arrangement would be necessary…clearly no new arrangement shall be made that would add to public expenditure under this head, and therefore it will be necessary to keep any new scheme entirely distinct from that of 1924 [sic]. There is, indeed, no need to advert to the previous scheme at all, in official correspondence with the British Government, regarding 1939-40 burials. Apart from the danger of appearing to undertake additional financial burdens in regard to British graves, undue reference to the 1924

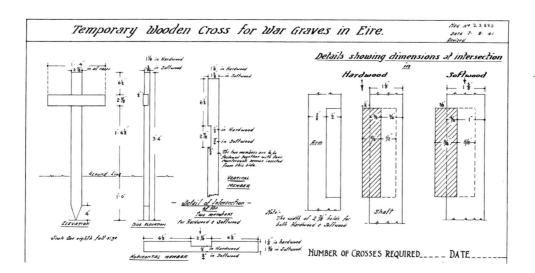

OPW drawing 1941, Temporary Wooden Cross for War Graves in Éire.

LEFT
*OPW drawing 1941,
Temporary Wooden Cross
for War Graves in Éire.*

scheme [sic] might render it more difficult for us to arrive at a satisfactory settlement of the political issues involved.

Putting it more explicitly, External Affairs held that

where we were prevailed upon to consent to the inclusion of British regimental symbols on the headstones supplied for the pre-1922 graves, we might not wish to make a similar concession now.

They decided to consult the OPW informally on the purely technical aspects of Sir John Maffey's concerns, to agree a suitable plan of action 'without prejudice' to the Government's final decision on the principles at issue.[42] External Affairs, however, seemed in no particular hurry despite the fact that, in mid-August, they began sending details to the UK's Office in Dublin of bodies being washed ashore in the north-west. The UK's representative, M. E. Antrobus, on receipt of these reports, commented that 'this of course raises the point dealt with in Stephenson's letter to Maffey of the 25 April. We took this up with the Department of External Affairs at the time but had received no reply'. He went on to say that External Affairs would be 'making an arrangement similar to that made for the last war'.[43] In this he was presuming much.

It was August 1940 before External Affairs took up the matter with the OPW. There, Raftery agreed that the 1920s agreement was inappropriate in this new war situation but, nonetheless, felt it would be useful to involve the IWGC, 'to act as a kind of buffer between British relatives and our people'. Perhaps with a more optimistic view of the likely duration of this war than was warranted, Raftery confessed himself untroubled by the financial aspects of the new war grave business: 'we might carry a relatively light burden vis-à-vis all the foreign governments interested, as part of our international duty to be humane', and he thought that the actual work likely to be involved 'would be negligible'. Fifteen years and five hundred and fifty bodies later, many buried in the most remote and desolate of locations, with huge correspondence on identification, registration, conveyance of personal effects, in some cases exhumation, and in all cases handling the grievances of grief-stricken relatives whether directly or indirectly – he might have entertained a different view. At this point, one year into the war to the very day, Raftery and the OPW did not know the extent of the casualties in Ireland. As a practical matter, he suggested that External Affairs might secure these figures from the Garda Síochána, 'before the matter of a new Anglo-Irish Agreement is brought to Government'.[44]

— *Specification* — | CROSSES TO BE DELIVERED WITHIN..........DAYS FROM DATE OF ACCEPTANCE OF TENDER.

The timber shall be reasonably well seasoned, clean, sound and without shakes of any kind. Hardwood may be native or imported. Soft wood may be native larch or pine, or imported Red deal. Contractors tendering shall quote alternative prices for crosses built with (A) Hardwood or Pitch Pine. (B) Softwood. In each case the variety of wood proposed to be used shall be stated.

The members shall be hand planed all round with surfaces quite smooth, free from spawls and ready for painting, all arrises being "blunted" by two plane strokes. The dimensions indicate the minimum net finished scantling of the members. The screws shall be 1⅝" No 12 steel for softwood and 1¼" No 12 brass for hardwood.

The arm and shaft shall be accurately checked to give a very tight driving fit. The notches shall be well doped with thick white lead paint before the members are assembled, all surplus paint being wiped off the surfaces. Contractors shall quote for the supply of _____Crosses delivered in one consignment free in Dublin as will be directed.

The search for new arrangements:

In the meantime, at the end of August 1940, Fabian Ware and the IWGC, understandably impatient for developments, alerted Vesper that they wanted him to go down to Dublin on his way home from Northern Ireland, 'for an informal and non-committal discussion' with the OPW about the new war graves situation.[45] Chettle, in turn, duly alerted Veale at the OPW that Vesper had been requested to call in October.[46] In advance of this visit, N. G. Nolan in External Affairs at last began to requisition the previous history of war graves, their numbers and costs involved.[47] He was preparing the ground to enable External Affairs to make up its mind what kind of war graves agreement it wanted, to get Finance and the OPW behind it, and then to present it to Government, hopefully for adoption – and that then Maffey would be 'brought into the picture'.[48] Whatever about temporary arrangements, central to Nolan's thinking on the matter was that, as regards permanent memorials to the British Commonwealth war dead, 'the entire cost should be borne by the British Government' – a position, he felt, that the Irish Government could stand over in facing the Germans and Italians in a similar situation.[49]

On his arrival in Dublin, Vesper went to Antrobus and Maffey for briefings, and then on to Veale and T. J. Burke at the OPW. Here he quickly found it

abundantly clear that Mr Veale (or the Office of Public Works as a whole) knew nothing whatever about any negotiations between the Commission and the Ministry of External Affairs. He (Veale) was most candid and said they had received no information or instructions about 'War Graves' since those concerning the 1914/18 War Graves when I [first] went to Éire.

While true perhaps for Veale, it was not completely accurate, to this extent: the OPW Secretary, back in April 1940, had received from External Affairs a copy of the IWGC Supplemental Charter of 5 March 1940 which extended the IWGC's power to the 'present war' but the OPW Commissioners held that they had no function to perform 'unless and until they received instructions from the Department of Finance'.[50]

Veale, however, now suspected that 'something is going on' since he knew 'a man from External Affairs' recently had been questioning his colleague Burke about the cost of war graves. Architect Burke, in his discussion with Vesper, confirmed this: he 'immediately and without prompting told Vesper that a man named Nolan from External Affairs' had wanted to see Vesper. It was a not too comfortable Vesper who, on returning from the OPW to the UK Office in Mount Street, Dublin, found that Antrobus, too, was very anxious for him to meet Nolan. Vesper thought this was beyond his brief from the IWGC, which was simply to talk to the OPW and he was uneasy about getting in beyond his depth. Nevertheless, Antrobus arranged for Vesper 'to see Mr Nolan, sometimes called Dr. Nolan'.[51] Vesper could be forgiven his unease: Dr Nicholas Nolan, then Counsellor at External Affairs, was 'a notorious martinet', a master of rebuke who subsequently went on to become Secretary to the Department and finally Secretary to the Government. Nolan effectively ran the External Affairs, and indeed, the whole Irish Government approach to the war graves issue, from this point in 1940.[52] On the British part, Vesper went to Nolan on the pretext of learning 'what they were already doing – not what they might do' – and raised the practical issue of the importance of identifying new graves in cemeteries where 'no official record of graves was kept or no system of numbering in place'. He was given assurances on this and then Nolan volunteered the information that the general question of Irish Government war graves policy was 'still under consideration' and that no decision had been reached. On reporting back to the UK Office, Vesper and Antrobus 'both felt I could do no

more', and Vesper duly returned to war graves duty in the North. On hearing the details of Vesper's 1940 visit to Dublin, Ware contacted Stephenson at the Dominions Office to suggest now that if Dublin were prepared to take some responsibility for the British graves in Éire of this war, he felt it would be helpful if Chettle could be introduced by Maffey to External Affairs, 'to open discussions for a definite agreement', and, in the event of which, Captain Vesper's services could be offered 'as before'.[53]

All this, however, was highly speculative. Unknown to Vesper, the IWGC or the Dominions Office, External Affairs had already drafted outline proposals which Frederick Boland sent to Finance for consideration in mid-October. By late December the Minister for Finance had agreed that these proposals be put to Government.[54] In that process, whatever they proposed to do for British and Commonwealth war graves, they intended to do for the Germans and their allies. Consequently, unsure of how to handle German war graves, External Affairs inquired of the British how they were handling their enemies' graves. Ware, on being consulted, explained that the British had taken full charge of enemy war graves of 1914-1918 in the UK, and that the Commission had borne the entire cost of erection

and maintenance. As to this new war's enemy graves, there was no question of permanent marking until the conflict would be concluded and that, as regards temporary marking and maintenance, this too was borne by the IWGC.[55] Both Stephenson and Ware were confident of a positive outcome of the present case, Ware in particular being fulsome about the Irish handling of the graves of the previous war.

As I think you know, the way in which the Government of Éire carried out their previous undertaking… fulfilled all our desires – we shall be glad to renew or continue the very friendly relations established in 1928.[56]

In the meantime, based on this information from the British, External Affairs had an informal meeting with the German Legation and indicated that their war graves would be treated exactly as those of British and Commonwealth dead, that the issue of permanent memorials would not be considered until the end of hostilities, but that the Irish Authorities would undertake the maintenance of German war graves and their marking by temporary wooden crosses.[57]

It was on the last day of 1940 that External Affairs had submitted its formal proposal to Government. Essentially it suggested that, as regards permanent

memorials, Government would undertake an arrangement, 'on the same lines as approved in 1926', 'provided that the entire cost of the provision and erection of headstones is borne by the British Government', and that under the new arrangement no regimental badges would appear on the headstones. Furthermore, the standard form of wording for the headstone inscriptions should be settled in agreement with the Irish Authorities. The arrangements were to apply to all belligerents. In presenting these proposals to Government, External Affairs thought the expenditure on maintenance and temporary marking would not be considerable.[58] The Cabinet, not surprisingly, approved the draft proposals at its meeting on 21 January 1941, except for the matter of regimental badges on headstones, 'which it was decided should be left to the Taoiseach for decision'.[59] As events would show, on this matter a decision was made to make no decision.

A month after this, the matter surfaced again, in a decidedly odd manner. Writing for External Affairs to the Department of An Taoiseach, Boland explained that

The Minister of External Affairs sees no reason in principle why objection should be raised to the engraving of regimental badges or other insignia on headstones placed on British war graves in

RIGHT
A page from Ireland's
Memorial Records 1914-
1918
(artwork by Harry Clarke).

this country. Having regard, however, to the fact that, in the past, objections were raised by the County Clare Board of Health and the Sligo Corporation to the erection of headstones bearing British regimental badges in cemeteries under their jurisdiction, the Minister for External Affairs intends to make some further inquiries before arriving at a definite conclusion on the matter.[60]

Given that the Minister for External Affairs was also the Taoiseach, deValera, it might have appeared to be a somewhat bizarre communication. Given, however, that the interested parties felt it was not practical to proceed with permanent headstones while the war was on, and that no one knew how long it would last, deValera's postponement of a decision on this was not unreasonable. What was, perhaps, unreasonable was how long it took in the end. In the meantime, there was a mounting toll of casualties as the Battle of the Atlantic raged, and none more tragic or more pitiable, perhaps, than that arising from the sinking of the *Arandora Star*.

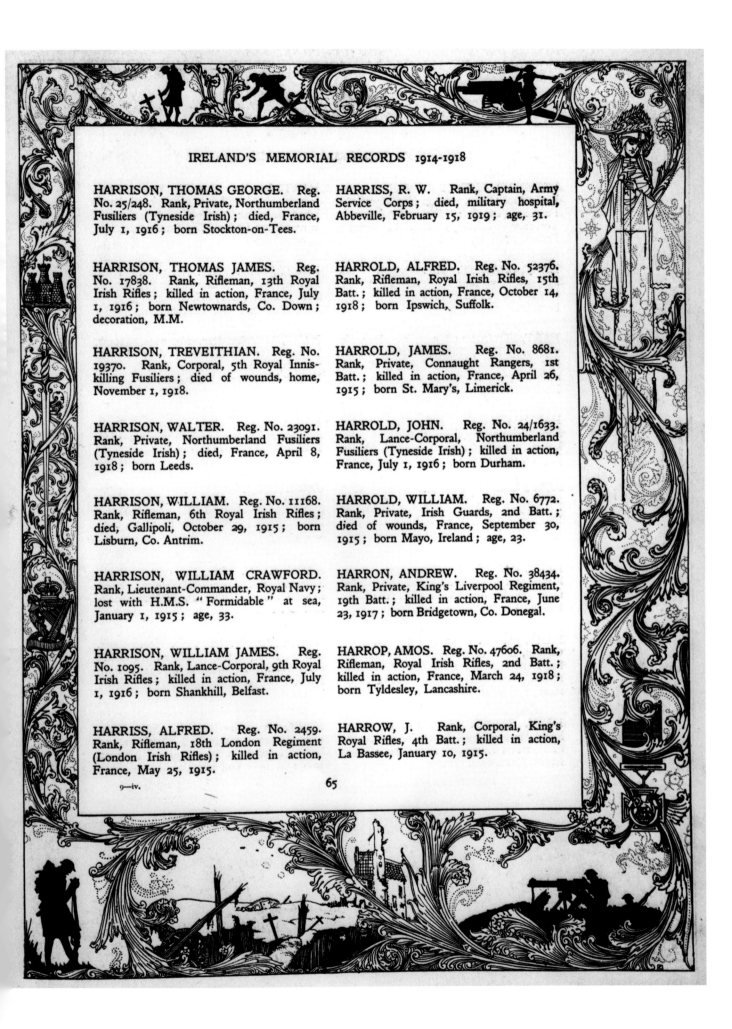

IRELAND'S MEMORIAL RECORDS 1914-1918

HARRISON, THOMAS GEORGE. Reg. No. 25/248. Rank, Private, Northumberland Fusiliers (Tyneside Irish); died, France, July 1, 1916; born Stockton-on-Tees.

HARRISON, THOMAS JAMES. Reg. No. 17838. Rank, Rifleman, 13th Royal Irish Rifles; killed in action, France, July 1, 1916; born Newtownards, Co. Down; decoration, M.M.

HARRISON, TREVEITHIAN. Reg. No. 19370. Rank, Corporal, 5th Royal Inniskilling Fusiliers; died of wounds, home, November 1, 1918.

HARRISON, WALTER. Reg. No. 23091. Rank, Private, Northumberland Fusiliers (Tyneside Irish); died, France, April 8, 1918; born Leeds.

HARRISON, WILLIAM. Reg. No. 11168. Rank, Rifleman, 6th Royal Irish Rifles; died, Gallipoli, October 29, 1915; born Lisburn, Co. Antrim.

HARRISON, WILLIAM CRAWFORD. Rank, Lieutenant-Commander, Royal Navy; lost with H.M.S. "Formidable" at sea, January 1, 1915; age, 33.

HARRISON, WILLIAM JAMES. Reg. No. 1095. Rank, Lance-Corporal, 9th Royal Irish Rifles; killed in action, France, July 1, 1916; born Shankhill, Belfast.

HARRISS, ALFRED. Reg. No. 2459. Rank, Rifleman, 18th London Regiment (London Irish Rifles); killed in action, France, May 25, 1915.

HARRISS, R. W. Rank, Captain, Army Service Corps; died, military hospital, Abbeville, February 15, 1919; age, 31.

HARROLD, ALFRED. Reg. No. 52376. Rank, Rifleman, Royal Irish Rifles, 15th Batt.; killed in action, France, October 14, 1918; born Ipswich, Suffolk.

HARROLD, JAMES. Reg. No. 8681. Rank, Private, Connaught Rangers, 1st Batt.; killed in action, France, April 26, 1915; born St. Mary's, Limerick.

HARROLD, JOHN. Reg. No. 24/1633. Rank, Lance-Corporal, Northumberland Fusiliers (Tyneside Irish); killed in action, France, July 1, 1916; born Durham.

HARROLD, WILLIAM. Reg. No. 6772. Rank, Private, Irish Guards, 2nd Batt.; died of wounds, France, September 30, 1915; born Mayo, Ireland; age, 23.

HARRON, ANDREW. Reg. No. 38434. Rank, Private, King's Liverpool Regiment, 19th Batt.; killed in action, France, June 23, 1917; born Bridgetown, Co. Donegal.

HARROP, AMOS. Reg. No. 47606. Rank, Rifleman, Royal Irish Rifles, 2nd Batt.; killed in action, France, March 24, 1918; born Tyldesley, Lancashire.

HARROW, J. Rank, Corporal, King's Royal Rifles, 4th Batt.; killed in action, La Bassee, January 10, 1915.

9—iv.

65

And bid their angry tumult cease
and give for wild confusion, peace

Clive Darrall, Private
The Welch Regiment
2 July 1940

Culdaff Church of Ireland Churchyard
Co. Donegal

Chapter 14

From *Arandora Star* To *Mashona*:
Atlantic War Dead, 1939-1941

Growing up in Carndonagh, County Donegal, as a boy in the 1940s, Paddy McClure was mystified by a headstone inscription in the local cemetery: it was in memory of an Italian man who had died at sea and been washed up on Donegal's coast. For Paddy, it became a lifelong quest to learn how Cesare Camozzi, originally from Iseo in Italy, but for long settled in Manchester, came to find his last, earthly resting place in Carndonagh Cemetery.[1] The same sense of wonder might have beset anyone who became aware that the quiet, sometimes desolate, and remote graveyards of the entire north-west and west coasts were littered with the remembered and forgotten dead of the Second World War. These dead and buried, far from home, were in many cases the victims of the Battle of the Atlantic. While the struggle between the Allies and Germany for control of the North Atlantic lasted, technically, from September 1939 until May 1945, it reached its most ferocious phase in the western North Atlantic over the period from the summer of 1940 to that of 1941.

On 15 May 1940, the Netherlands fell victim to German invasion, as did Belgium on the 28th. By 4 June the Allied evacuation of Dunkirk had been effected; two days later, that of Narvik spelt the end of Norwegian independence. Six days later again,

German troops were marching in triumph down the Champs Elysées in Paris. By 10 July, British convoys were being attacked in the Channel as, that same month, the Channel Islands fell to the occupying Nazis. With the fall of France and the Channel Islands, the Germans were poised to strangle the sea routes in and out of Britain. By the end of the next twelve months, however, Hitler's attention had turned more intently eastward, with his invasion of the Soviet Union on 22 June 1941. By that date, Operation Sealion, his planned invasion of Britain, was put aside. His marine forces continued to wreak havoc, but they had failed to destroy, utterly, the British Navy and Merchant fleets, or to wrest mastery of the North Atlantic from the British.

Nevertheless, the toll exacted by the German war machine was exceedingly heavy. To the end of December 1939, 158 British merchant ships, grossing 498,000 tons, had been lost. Over the twelve months to the end of December 1940, the number of British ships lost was 728, grossing 2.725 million tons; over the next twelve months, to the end of December 1941, 892 ships grossing 3.047 million tons. Thereafter, there was a decline in the number of ships lost, to 782 grossing 3.695 million tons, to December 1942; then down to 361 vessels grossing 1.678 million tons to the

end of December 1943.[2] During the course of the war, over 30,000 British merchant seamen died in the conflict; over 2,100 ships sunk, 1,315 of them by U-boats.[3] In the six months July to December 1940, more than 540 Allied ships had been sunk.[4] Of crews not rescued from sinking ships, the vast majority were lost, never to surface. Only a tiny minority of these war dead were carried ashore, on the western and northern coasts of Ireland and Scotland. Nevertheless, that tiny minority formed a sepulchral presence on the landscape of littoral Ireland. The history of some of these unfortunates is the subject of the pages which follow.

The Arandora Star:

At 4 a.m. on Tuesday, 2 July 1940, the *Arandora Star* sailed from Liverpool en route for Newfoundland. On board were a crew of 174 officers and ratings, a military guard of 200 men, and, guarded by them, 1,300 Germans and Italians. These comprised 734 male Italian internees, 86 German prisoners of war and 479 German internees. The ship was unescorted. At 6.15 a.m., some seventy-five miles west of Bloody Foreland, Donegal, she was torpedoed by the German submarine *U-47*, commanded by Kapitänleutnant Günther Prien. The torpedo struck the engine room, wrecking the turbines and

the generators. The vessel was plunged into complete darkness and all internal communications destroyed. An SOS was picked up and answered by Malin Head Radio Station. Out of fourteen lifeboats, the crew and military escort managed to launch ten, together with approximately forty out of ninety rafts, all soon full to overcrowding with desperate crew, guards and prisoners. At 7.15 a.m. the ship was listing beyond recovery and, five minutes later, Captain Moulton and his senior officers walked over the side, into the rising waters. At that point, the *Arandora Star* keeled over and sank. For Günther Prien it was yet another triumph in a relatively short, spectacular career of destruction. The *U-47* was his first command, from September 1939, and in the first few months of what was called 'the phoney war', he had already sent 66,000 tons of Allied shipping to the ocean floor. Most daringly, in October 1939, he had slipped through British naval defences at Scapa Flow and dealt them a serious blow by sinking the battleship *Royal Oak*, with the loss of over 800 officers and men: for this he was personally decorated by Hitler, on the steps of the Reich Chancellery.

Now, on this new mission out of Kiel, from 14 June 1940, he had sunk nine ships and, homeward bound for Germany with a single stern torpedo left, he sent the *Arandora Star* to its

---

grave. Within a year, promoted to Korvettenkapitän, he had sunk 245,000 tons of Allied shipping. Then, on 7 March 1941, he and the crew of *U-47*, in turn, met their end when sunk by depth charges from the destroyer, H.M.S. *Wolverine*. As for the *Arandora Star*, it lost 13 officers, 42 crew, 91 out of 200 soldiers, and 713 Italian and German civilian internees and prisoners of war.[5]

As for the survivors, at 9.30 a.m. on Tuesday, 2 July 1940, an RAF Sunderland came over the scene, dropping aid packages. Six hours later, a Canadian destroyer, H.M.C.S. *St. Laurent*, under Commander H.G. de Wolfe, arrived to the rescue. His vessel spent five hours plucking survivors from the oil-covered waters before being joined by the British destroyer H.M.S. *Walker*. By the evening of Wednesday, 3 July, the *St. Laurent* had rescued a remarkable 868 people, who were landed next day at Greenock. The *Arandora Star's* Captain Moulton, twelve of his officers and forty-two of his crew, were not among them. Indeed, an appalling litany of 805 out of the 1,673 did not survive. It was an inglorious end for a ship that had seen happier years.

The *Arandora Star* was a legendary liner of the late 1920s and 1930s. She was built by Cammell Laird at Birkenhead in 1927 for the Blue Star Line, as one of its five luxury cruise ships. From then until September 1939 Captain Edwin Moulton took her, bearing the world's elegance, on voyage after exotic voyage: winter cruises to the Mediterranean and West Indies; summers to the Baltic capitals. Then came war.

She was on passage to New York when war was declared and her return journey took her to Falmouth, where the crew was temporarily paid off. The Admiralty took over: Captain Moulton found himself now commanding a troop carrier. Between early June and 1 July 1940, the *Arandora Star* played an important role in vital evacuations. On 4 June, escorted by the aircraft carrier, H.M.S. *Glorious*, and the anti-aircraft-cruiser, H.M.S. *Coventry*, she entered the fjord at Narvik, which had been retaken from the Germans, and took on board 1,600 RAF officers and men, together with some French and Polish troops out of the 25,000 who were evacuated from northern Norway, in advance of that country's final fall to the Germans in June 1940. Escorted back some of the way by *Glorious* and two destroyers, *Acasta* and *Ardent*, all three of these were engaged and sunk by the *Scharnhorst* and *Gneisenau* on 7 June. The *Arandora Star* safely disembarked her troops at Glasgow, before being ordered to Brest, to effect evacuations from France. Other rescue missions were undertaken to

Quiberon Bay and to Bayonne, and finally, to St. Jean de Luz, where 1,700 troops and refugees were taken on board, including a contingent of Polish staff and soldiers; all were safely landed at Liverpool. It was in Liverpool on 29 June that the officers of the *Arandora Star* were briefed on the next and fateful mission – the transportation of over 1,200 internees and 86 prisoners of war to Newfoundland. In preparation, she had been transformed into a virtual prison ship, bedecked with barbed wire barriers.

Italian internees:

The story of these internees constitutes one of the more lamentable episodes in Britain's war-time history. As in the First, so now in this Second War — but more acutely — the dread of invasion and the fear of fifth columns in their midst caused Government and people to react with hostility and suspicion to 'foreigners', regardless of circumstance. Under the 1939 Defence Regulations, provision was made 'for the custody on security grounds of persons against whom it was not practicable to bring criminal proceedings'.[6] Germans, Austrians and Italians resident in the UK when the war started suddenly acquired the status of enemy aliens. It mattered little, or not at all, whether they had

been living and working there for twenty years and more or that they might have recently fled from Nazi and Fascist persecution in their countries of origin. As far as the authorities were concerned, they were suspect: the object was, in Churchill's phrase, to 'collar the lot!'. The Home Office issued instructions that led to the rounding up of aliens in Britain, in May and June of 1940. Those taken up were whisked away from wives and children, with no explanations and no information as to where they were going, or what their futures might be. By early June 1940, some 12,000 Germans and Austrians had been interned, 2,500 of whom were said to be pro-Nazi. By the same time, of some 18,000 Italians then living in Britain, some 4,100 were interned between 1940 and 1942, sequestered in camps under military supervision, mainly in Scotland, the Isle of Man and south-west of England.[7] Civilian internees aside, by the war's end Britain held over 400,000 prisoners of war in several hundred camps.[8]

The 'lifting' and incarceration of the civilian internees did not go completely uncontested. The matter was raised in Parliament, notably by George Strauss, MP for Lambeth North, and Graham White of Birkenhead East. Robert Boothby, MP for Aberdeen, spoke of the particular case of the Jewish Czech

financier and Anglophile, Richard Weininger, refugee from Prague and anti-Nazi, who wanted to fight for Britain; he found, instead, solitary confinement in Brixton Prison, despite appeals to Churchill.[9] As for the *Arandora Star*, four days after its survivors were landed at Greenock, the questions began in the House of Commons. On being questioned by Strauss and Sorensen of Leyton West, the Minister for Shipping, Ronald Cross, admitted that the *Star* had not been escorted: he explained that such was her speed, none was deemed necessary.[10] As for refugees from the Nazi regime being on board and among the victims, he denied this categorically, quoting Anthony Eden, the Secretary of State for War, to the effect that all the Germans on board were Nazis and that none of them had come to the UK as refugees.

Someone was being economical with the truth. Among the German internees was twenty-five year old Anglophile and Oxford graduate student, Herman Solf, son of Germany's Ambassador to Japan who had been sacked by Hitler in 1939; twenty-five year old factory foreman, Franz Laumen from Krefeld, working in Britain since 1933; among Austrians, the socialists Karl Mayerhoefler and Kurt Regner, refugees on the Nazi's wanted list; among Italians, A. F. Magri, Chairman of the Italian League for the

Rights of Man – established among Italian expatriates to fight Mussolini – and the Jewish Italian, Umberto Lamentani, broadcaster for the Italian Service of the BBC. The ages of the interned Italian civilians who ended up on the *Arandora Star* ranged from sixteen-year old Luigi Gonzaga of Bedonia and London to sixty-eight year old Charles Domenico Marchesi of Codogno and London.

By 16 July, in the Commons, Anthony Eden was still insisting that all the internees on the *Arandora Star* were Italian Fascists and Class A Germans or Austrians, but, under pressure, added 'I am making further inquiries on the point'.[11] Nor was the pressure entirely domestic: that same morning, the Foreign Secretary, Halifax, had protested to the Home Secretary, Anderson, about 'what had been a very bad business'. He himself had been on the receiving end of strong representations from US Ambassador, Joseph Kennedy, about the transportation of internees, and, in particular, concerning the treatment of resident Italians.[12] A subsequent inquiry under the Labour peer, Harry Snell, announced in August and reporting to the War Cabinet in late November 1940, never addressed this assertion at all, despite a telling memorandum from four of the survivors. It emerged that the ultimate decision to transport

interned refugees had been taken by Lord President of the Council, Neville Chamberlain, now in his own last days.[13]

Worse was to follow. In the wake of the disaster, with internment camps bursting at the seams, and the threat of invasion looming larger, further transportations occurred. A reluctant Canada had been prevailed upon to accept some 4,000 civilian internees from the UK and 3,000 prisoners of war. By the end of the war in Europe Canada held close to 34,000 German prisoners.[14] Then, on 3 July, Chamberlain told the War Cabinet that Australia was prepared to take in some 6,000 aliens. He thereupon arranged for another ship to transport some 3,000 of these from England. That ship, the *Dunera*, sailed from Liverpool at midnight on 9-10 July, its internees boarded at the point of fixed bayonets. Incredibly, some 200 of these were survivors of the *Arandora Star* tragedy of seven days before. As the Duke of Devonshire explained to the Lords at the end of July, it was 'desirable both to husband our resources of food and get rid of useless mouths'.[15]

The tragedy of the *Arandora Star* took place seventy-five miles west of Bloody Foreland. It was not too long before the consequences presented themselves on the rocky shores of Donegal, Sligo and Mayo. Of the estimated 446

Italians who perished[16], one of the first of those identified, on being washed ashore, was sixty-one year old Ernesto Moruzzi, a native of Bardi and resident of Aberdare in Wales. On the morning of 30 July 1940 his body was found at Cloughglass, Burtonport, County Donegal. On his person was a wallet containing a membership card for the Neath Constitutional Club. He left behind in Aberdare his widow, Maria. Also perishing with him, but not washed ashore, were his fifty-three year old brother Peter, and a twenty-three year old nephew, Pietro. Ernesto and the young Pietro had been taken into custody on 11 June 1940, never to see their families again. Although Peter and Pietro were never found, the London Metropolitan Police had established that the younger man had indeed been a transported internee of the *Arandora Star*. Ernesto's remains were laid to rest in the windswept, but beautiful, island-cemetery of Cruit, four miles north of Burtonport. So it was reported to an Irish priest, Rev D. H. O'Sullivan at Neath. He made inquiries two years later, on behalf of the widowed Maria; she wanted to know the exact location, as she was determined to visit Ernesto's grave.[17] A week after his remains were discovered, at mid-morning on 6 August 1940, the body of badly decomposed fifty-two year Leonello Corrieri from Wallasey was washed ashore at

Bunaninver, Bunbeg, Donegal. He had been interned at Woodhouse Lea Camp, near Edinburgh. His face was eaten away; a canvas sandal only on the right foot; dressed in grey flannel coat and trousers. Inside his jacket pocket he carried the following letter from his daughter, Yolanda:

*30 Sea View Road
Wallasey, Cheshire
Wed 19 June:*

*Dear Daddy,
I am so happy to get your card this morning, just how happy you will never know. Are you keeping quite well? If there is anything you want at all, just let us know and I'll send off at once. The weather being so nice is of course good for business I am managing quite well so don't worry about me. Mummy is keeping well and will write you a long letter to-morrow. We have not heard anything from Johnnie yet, but I am hoping we shall have news in the morning. I'll let you know as soon as we have heard from him. I want to catch the post so Mummy and I send all our love.*

Yolanda.

Little else was found: a pipe cleaner, pocket knife, gold pocket watch and chain. Corrieri was buried in Magheragallon Graveyard at Bunbeg on 6 August 1940.[18] At 7 a.m. on the day following, further north, on the east coast of Tory Island, was washed ashore the remains of six-foot, fifty-year old Luigi Giovanelli, face unrecognisable and left arm missing. He hailed from Bardi but had been for many years resident in London. He was interred on Tory Island on that same day. On the day after this, the badly decomposed remains of Luigi Tapparo, part-dressed, part-naked, came ashore in Co Mayo at Drumrea, Binghamstown. Aged forty-two, and born in Bollengo, he had worked in the Royal British Hotel, Edinburgh, before being interned and transported, to his death. He was buried next day at Termoncarragh Graveyard, near Belmullet.[19]

On 9 August at Colourt Strand, the remains of forty-nine year old Cesare Camozzi, originally from Iseo, but long living in Manchester, came ashore. Interned in the Woodhouse Lea Camp at Glengorse, Midlothian, he had, with his wife, run the Monogram Café in St. Peter's Square, Manchester. When found, his body was in an advanced state of decomposition, right hand missing. The local authorities telephoned the Café and he was identified through a letter from his wife, Minnie, found in his pocket, and with it, Cesare's unposted reply. The local parish priest said a requiem mass for him, on 10 August, before Camozzi was interred in Carndonagh Catholic Cemetery.[20]

RIGHT
Neville Chamberlain

The people of Carndonagh arranged for local undertaker and mason, Eddie Doherty, to carve and erect a monument in his memory. On the evening of that same day, further down the coast, at Castletown, Easkey, Co Sligo, the badly decomposed remains of Mateo Fossaluzza, a forty-three year old native of Cavasso, and later resident in London, were washed up. He was identified by receipts from Wakefield Building Society and a St. John Bosco medal. He was buried in Easkey Cemetery on 12 August.

German internees:

Among German internee victims of the *Arandora Star* disaster was a native of Bremen, Hans Möller, who lived in Hammersmith, London, until he was arrested on 24 November 1939. On 29 July 1940, his remains were found at Maghery, near Dungloe, in advanced decomposition. He had been dressed in grey check suit, white shirt and wearing a life-belt: on his person, inside a black wallet, was a song-book, within the cover of which was written, 'In memory of many a sing-song whilst making nets in Hut D21, Warner's Camp, Seaton, Devon, 7 April 1940' – one of the principal internment camps in England. He was buried the next day in the remote and desolate graveyard of Termon, near Maghery. His identity was

unknown, but inside his wallet was a slip of paper bearing the name 'Turnbull & Asser, Ltd., 71-72 Jermyn Street, London'. When the Irish authorities made inquiries at this firm, they spoke to the company's secretary, Dora Eileen Lucas. On being given a description of the body and the details of the personal effects found on it, she was able to identify it as that of Hans Möller, her fiancé, of Iffley Road, Hammersmith, and native of Bremen.[21]

Among other Germans whose bodies were washed ashore was that of the tragic Franz Kirste, whose remains drifted to land at Cloonagh, Lissadell, Co Sligo, on 11 August 1940. A British ration book found on his body identified his address as Fawley Road, North London.[22] At External Affairs there were doubts as to how best to deal with his personal belongings. As a German, his death would have been communicated to the German Legation in Dublin. Kirste, however, was no ordinary German. In 1933, he left Germany in a hurry and fled to Prague where he had become involved with a group, the Czech-Slovak Friends of German Refugees. A staunch anti-Nazi, he again fled, this time to Britain, after the German invasion and annexation of Czechoslovakia. Like other Germans in Britain, despite being an opponent of Hitler's regime, he was interned early in 1940. Notebooks

*LEFT
Magheragallon Cemetery,
Co. Donegal*

found on his person suggest that he was in 'failing mental health', the repetitive scribblings suggesting the onset of a breakdown.

At External Affairs, D. R. McDonald, consulting Nolan, thought that, in view of Kirste's anti-Nazi sentiments, 'it would be unnecessary to inform the German Legation of this case', and that, either all his papers be destroyed, or retained in safe-keeping by the Gardaí, with the exception of Kirste's ration book, which should be sent to Antrobus at the Office of the UK Representative in Dublin. Nolan's initial reaction was to divide Kirste's notes into three parts: anti-Nazi documents to be retained in a sealed envelope; the innocuous documents to be sent to the German Legation, the ration book to the British. For reasons unclear, Nolan had second thoughts and, on advice from the Assistant Secretary in External Affairs, decided, in January 1941, to send all Kirste's papers to Antrobus at the UK Dublin Office.[23]

While no one was certain at that time, inquests on Kirste's and those of sixteen other bodies washed up along the Donegal-Sligo shorelines, believed they were all victims of the sinking of the *Arandora Star*.[24]

British soldiers:
Its victims were not only German, Austrian and Italian internees. Troops who were guarding these prisoners were also numbered among the bodies that littered the north-west coast from Mayo to Donegal. One of the main units engaged in escort duty on that fateful day was the 4th Battalion Devonshire Regiment. Its casualties included seventeen-year old Private Peter Clarke from Kentisbeare, Devon, buried in Cruit Island Catholic Cemetery, possibly the youngest victim of the disaster, after the sixteen-year old Italian internee, Luigi Gonzaga. Clarke's comrade, nineteen year old Private William F. G. Chick, a native of Dorset, was washed up over 150 miles away, at Belmullet, and is buried there in Kilcommon Erris Church of Ireland Churchyard. Close by him, there, lies also twenty-one year old Donald E. V. Domican of Cardiff, a private in the 5th Battalion Welch Regiment, twenty-two year old Gunner Wallace Goodwin of Rutland, who served with the Leicestershire Yeomanry, and Trooper Frank S. Carter of the Royal Dragoons. Washed ashore also in Mayo were twenty-one year old Edward Lane, of Kingsteignton, Devon, who served in the 7th Battalion, Devonshires, now remembered in Ballycastle New Cemetery, northwest of Killala, and Stanley Darnell, a private in the RASC, aged twenty-five, from Surrey, whose

FAR RIGHT
The grave of
Owen Mitchell of Torquay,
in Roslea Cemetery, Easkey
Co. Sligo

MIDDLE RIGHT
Pte Donald Domican
Kilcommon, Erris, Belmulet
Co. Mayo

NEAR RIGHT
Pte Peter Clarke of Devon
in Cruit Island Cemetery
Kincasslagh, Co. Donegal

remains lie in Fallmore Graveyard, west of the remote Blacksod Point.

Further up the coast, twenty-three-year old Owen Mitchell from Torquay in Devon, also with the 7th Battalion, Devonshires, is remembered in Easkey (Roslea) Cemetery in Sligo. Another 7th Devonshires' Private, Francis Palmer of Plympton, is commemorated in St. Mura's Church of Ireland Churchyard, at Upper Fahan in Donegal. These soldiers' deaths and burials were not, even then, forgotten. Consider the letter written to External Affairs in August 1940 by Mrs Iseult Cochrane of Stranorlar, County Donegal:

Dear Sir,

I understand that the bodies of some English soldiers from the S.S. Arandora Star have been washed up on the coasts of Donegal. Do you think you could put me in touch with the proper authorities as I would like, if possible, to undertake to look after their graves and to be able to communicate with the relatives of those who were identified. Being English myself, I thought it might bring them some little consolation to know that their graves would be looked after by one of their countrywomen for as long as I would be able to perform this work. I hope it is possible for my offer to be accepted.

Yours truly,
Iseult Cochrane.[25]

Laid to rest also in St. Mura's, along with these soldiers, are eight other named and two unidentified casualties of at least seven other vessels of the naval war in the region: at the same time, at least sixty-six bodies washed ashore from the *Arandora Star* were and remain unknown.[26]

The Mohamed Ali El Kebir:

In the weeks and months which followed, a grim succession of doomed ships added their crews and passengers to the list of the war dead on the north-west coast. Even as the *Arandora Star's* luckless were still being washed ashore, they were joined, among others, by the lost of the S.S. *Mohamed Ali El Kebir*. This 7,500-ton Egyptian steam freighter, carrying around 1,000 troops and supplies, left Avonmouth, Bristol, for Gibraltar. On 7 August 1940, 250 miles due west of Malin Head, she was intercepted by *U-boat 38*, under Korvettenkapitän Heinrich Liebe, and sunk with the loss of at least fourteen officers and crew and about ninety-five soldiers. She was the third British troop transport to be lost since the War's beginning. The remarkable fact was that so many, estimated variously between 740 and over 1,300, survived, having been saved by the arrival of the destroyer H.M.S. *Griffin*.[27] Among the unfortunate was the ship's master, John Pratt Thomson,

LEFT
Roslea Cemetery, Easkey,
Co. Sligo

today remembered in St. Mura's Upper Fahan by a Commonwealth war grave headstone. Thirty-two bodies of *Mohamed Ali El Kebir's* crew were washed up on the beaches of Mayo, Sligo and Donegal, over the period 27 August to 19 September 1940.[28] Among those never found was Arklow man and Quartermaster, William J. Tyrrell.

The Manchester Brigade:

Late in September, the 6,000-ton S.S. *Manchester Brigade*, en route to Montreal from Manchester, with a complement of sixty-two crew, under Captain Fred Clough, was in convoy off the Mayo coast when sunk by *U-boat 137*; Clough and over fifty crew were killed. Among the lost, washed ashore, were Royal Marine Ernest Aspin, buried in Chapel Strand Cemetery on Arranmore Island, Donegal; Chief Engineer Sydney Perry of Scarborough, first laid to rest in Clondahorky (Strangers') Burial Ground, Dunfanaghy; Second Officer Griffith S. Jones, washed up at and buried on Cruit Island, Kincasslagh; washed up and laid to rest there also was First Officer, William E. Todd of Hull. The ship's storekeeper, Takeshi Uyeda, was washed ashore at Carrick, Derrybeg, on 10 October 1940, as reported by the Garda Superintendent at Templecrone, four days later. Uyeda was born in Kumamoto, Kynshu, Japan, on 20 June

1898, and settled at Endbridge Street, Salford, married to a local girl, Florence. The Japanese Consul requested delivery of Uyeda's personal effects to the Consulate, despite the fact that Uyeda was a British subject.[29] Uyeda was buried in Magheragallon Catholic Cemetery, which, while in a remote location by the sea, is kept in manicured condition today: here a permanent CWGC headstone marks Uyeda's grave.[30]

Finally, another victim of the *Manchester Brigade's* destruction was a master mariner with a distinguished past – Vice-Admiral Humphrey Hugh Smith, D.S.O., formerly of H.M.S. *Eaglet*. Aged sixty-four, he had served in the First World War and was the author of two books of seafaring reminiscence, *A Yellow Admiral Remembers* and *An Admiral Never Forgets*.[31] Superintendent Connery reported the remains washed ashore on Tory Island on 12 October. Indeed, over each of the days, 10th, 11th and 12th October, he reported nine bodies washed onto the shores of this region, some so badly decomposed as to be beyond identification.

Among others, desperate enquiries came from Olive Cozens of Leicester for news of her husband Frank, Ordinary Signalman on the ship. Likewise, the parents of R.E. Foster, Petty Officer

Telegraphist, from Mortlake, London, pressed for information. Admiral Smith's widow, Jean, of Radnage, Bucks, advised them that the Gardaí in Donegal might be able to help. Regrettably, the latter could only surmise that Cozens and Foster might have been among the unrecognisable 'unknowns' from the vessel. As for the Vice-Admiral, he was laid to rest in the tiny, secluded Bunbeg Church of Ireland Cemetery. Within two years, a question arose as to whether Smith, Todd and other Merchant Navy war dead were entitled to have their graves marked by temporary wooden crosses. The OPW's query in this matter was answered in the affirmative, Veale reporting to Brandon in February 1942: 'Spoke to Dr Nolan. The Department of External Affairs, on considered grounds, have decided that these graves are within the scope of the scheme'. So it was that the graves of Todd, Smith and others of the *Manchester Brigade* were marked by the distinctive white crosses until the permanent standard headstones took their place in the mid-1950s. However, the Admiral was an exception, remembered instead by a unique, private, permanent memorial, in brilliant white, resting flat on the earth.[32]

The Patroclus and the Laurentic:
Six weeks after the loss of the *Manchester Brigade* off Bloody Foreland, the U-boat commander 'silent Otto' Kretschmer continued to wreak havoc. On the night of Sunday 3 November, commanding *U-99*, he attacked and sank a merchant vessel, the 6,000-ton banana boat, *Casanare*, en route from West Africa. The *Casanare's* distress signals alerted the 18,000-ton, armed merchant cruiser, H.M.S. *Laurentic* (a namesake successor to the *Laurentic* of the First World War, and no less unfortunate): also on patrol in the area was the 12,000-ton H.M.S. *Patroclus*, then homeward bound from convoy duty. Kretschmer torpedoed *Laurentic* twice, but it took a third missile from *U-99* to sink her, with the loss of 76 out of a total complement of 382. The ace U-boat Captain who, by war's end, had sunk more allied tonnage than any other German submarine commander, then turned to the oncoming *Patroclus*, racing too late to *Laurentic's* rescue. Firing three torpedoes at *Patroclus*, two of which struck home, *U-99* then dived for cover from an approaching Sunderland flying boat. When he surfaced next morning he found both *Laurentic* and *Patroclus* still afloat. Further missiles finally sent one after the other to the ocean floor. Over 630 crew were rescued by H.M.S. *Hesperus*, under Captain Donald MacIntyre, as Kretschmer and *U-99* made good their escape. Four months

later, MacIntyre, now in command of another destroyer, H.M.S. *Walker*, finally caught up with and sank *U-99* east of Iceland, taking Kretschmer and forty of his crew as prisoners of war.[33]

As for the Sunday night and Monday morning of 3-4 November 1940, nine crew of the *Casanare*, forty-nine of the *Laurentic* and seventy-nine of the *Patroclus* lost their lives. There are no records to date of any of the *Casanare's* lost nine as coming ashore on the north-west coast, and only one member of the *Laurentic*: thirty-four year old Able Seaman, Roy McLeod, buried close by the lost of the First World War's *Laurentic*, in Upper Fahan, St. Mura's Church of Ireland Churchyard. As to the *Patroclus*, two unidentifiable remains from that vessel came ashore: on 16 September, one at Bunbeg, interred in Magheragallon; on the next day, the other at Bartragh Island, Mayo, and laid to rest in Crosspatrick, Killala. These apart, three identified dead *Patroclus* crew members were found washed up. The remains of the ship's Radio Officer, twenty-three year old Victor Coleman of Birmingham were washed ashore at Rosnowlagh, Donegal, on 10 December, over a month after his death; two half-crowns, two pennies and a gold wrist watch were the only effects on his person, apart from his Radio Officer's certificate, dated London 29

April 1938. He was buried next day at Mullinashee Church of Ireland Burial Ground, Ballyshannon.[34] John Alex McDonald, a twenty-six year old able seaman from Liverpool, was washed ashore at Renvyle, Co Galway, and laid to rest in Renvyle Catholic Cemetery, where a temporary wooden cross marked his grave, from the summer of 1942 until the 1950s, when he was permanently commemorated there.[35] Buried alone, in a far corner of this desolate cemetery, his permanent headstone, facing out to sea, bears the inscription:

Remember Me When Hope Is Dead
I will give you faith to burn, instead. Scottie.

Finally, Seaman Harry Kirkpatrick, of Long Hope, Orkney Islands, was cast up at Cushleka, Mulranny, County Mayo, on 18 December 1940. His body, badly decomposed, bore a 'forget-me-not' scroll tattoo on his right forearm; a wristwatch with his name inscribed, his sole possession when found, was sent to his mother Ellen (née Robertson) of Myra Cottage, Longhope, whose only son he was.[36] He was laid to rest in Holy Trinity Burial Ground at Achill Sound on 18 December 1940, close by Seaman George Walters of the *Upwey Grange* and beside another Scot who had perished three months earlier:

Sapper George Ironside of Cunrine, Aberdeenshire, who had lost his life in the sinking of the *Mohamed Ali El-Kebir*. On 9 November 1940, Harry Kirkpatrick's mother had received official notification that he was lost from the *Patroclus*. Then, in late December, she came upon an item in *The Bulletin* of 22 December 1940, citing service number P/X18380A, which was identical to her only son's; the report also described the tattoo. Upon her contacting the Orkney Constabulary, they took up her case with the Gardaí at Mulranny, who were satisfied with her identifying connection with the dead seaman. She wanted to secure the return of her son's remains to Orkney, but in the event, his remains lay undisturbed in Holy Trinity Graveyard, at Achill Sound.[37] They were soon to be joined by yet another Scot, twenty-six-year old John Murphy of Dalmelly, Argyllshire. He was to die on 2 February 1941, in the bombing of the small Glasgow-registered steamship, *The Sultan*. It says something of the naval conflict of the Second World War that, in this quiet graveyard at Kildavnet, of eleven Commonwealth 1939-1945 War Graves there, seven are of unidentified merchant seamen.

The Nerissa:

Three months after the attack on *The Sultan*, the Glasgow-built S.S. *Nerissa*, en route from Halifax, Nova Scotia, to Liverpool, was discovered north west of Rockall by *U-boat 552* and was sunk on the night of 30 April-1 May 1941, thirty-five miles west of St. Kilda in Scotland. In reverse from the case of the *Arandora Star*, the *Nerissa* was a troopship ferrying soldiers from Canada to the UK, and became the only troopship in the war to lose Canadian troops on route to England. The losses were severe – 82 crew, 124 passengers and its Captain, G. R. Watson. The surviving 51 passengers, 29 crew and 3 stowaways were landed at Derry.[38]

Of the 207 known to be lost, only 12 are known to have drifted ashore, 8 south of the Border, 1 north, and 3 on the west coast of Scotland. Of the 8, 6 were Canadian and American and 2 were British.[39] One of these two was a *Nerissa* steward, thirty-year-old Ernest Winspear of Scarborough. He was in the water one week short of three months when his skeleton was found at Lagg, Malin Head, on 20 July 1940. On what was left of his clothes were found thirty Canadian dollars and the photograph of a girl.[40] He was buried in Carndonagh Old Workhouse Cemetery, his grave marked by a small iron cross. Garland, Secretary to the Canadian High Commission in Dublin, took an interest in him: given the many Canadians on the *Nerissa*, it

LEFT
Canadian troopship, S.S.
Nerissa, Newfoundland.

was understandable that he thought that Winspear was one, but Nolan satisfied him that responsibility for notifications and personal effects would go to the UK Office in Dublin, his nationality having been established.[41] A workhouse graveyard was no ideal burial place and, on Thursday 4 May 1954, his remains were exhumed and re-interred in the more fitting resting place of St. Mura's, Upper Fahan.[42] One who was a Canadian victim of the sinking of the *Nerissa* was twenty-year old Lieutenant Thomas Elvin Mitchell of the Carleton and York Regiment from St. Stephen, New Brunswick: his temporary wooden cross would become the OPW sample for all Canadian crosses in Ireland.

The remains of another *Nerissa* victim, RAF Wing Commander Archibald Graham Weir, came ashore at Corrain Point, in Blacksod Bay, County Mayo, on 4 July 1941. An Oxford graduate who had already served in the First World War, he left behind his widow, Mary Evelyn Oldfield, who also had to bear the loss of her two sons, Major Adrian J. A. Weir, MC, and Flying Officer Archibald N. C. Weir, DFC. On his person, when found, were letters from his daughter, Diana, in Keble College, Oxford, and his wife, Mary, in Shaftesbury, Dorset.[43]

Although he was found on 4 July, the news did not reach his widow until mid-September. To the Rector of Belmullet she then wrote, thanking 'all the authorities who performed the last sad duties and rites'. She continued:

As it is apparently not allowed to send money out of the country, I fear I cannot at present send anything to pay for flowers to be put on the grave, or to send a little thanks offering for your church in return for what you have done – that must all wait till peace comes. But if you would add to your kindness by telling me about the funeral and the grave and whether anything was recovered from the body, I should be so very grateful. I wonder if his signet ring was still there, which is of great sentimental value to us, being made of his parents' wedding and engagement rings – and there might have been something – it is so tragic to know so little... I know nothing at all about his end and very little of his voyagings. Just a few little details pieced together from survivors' stories.[44]

Mary Weir was as good as her wish. When peace came and the issue of grave maintenance arose, an agreement was entered into between the OPW and the Belmullet Church of Ireland Cemetery authorities for the upkeep of eleven British war graves there. None, however, was needed for that of Commander Weir; the local OPW officer reported that his grave 'is well maintained by the relatives and it is expected they will continue to do this'.[45]

BELOW
1914 War Recruitment
Poster

Near Right
*Crewman Jack S. Johnson
of Mashona, in Kilcommon
Erris Churchyard.*

Far Right
*U-boat Commander,
'Silent Otto' Kretschmer*

The Mashona:

The most intense phase of the Battle of
the Atlantic reached its climax with the
sinking of H.M.S. *Hood* by the *Bismarck*,
on 24 May 1941: out of a crew of 1,419,
only three survived as, incredibly, it went
to the bottom in minutes. Three days
later, on Tuesday 27 May, revenge came
when the 45,000-ton *Bismarck* itself was
sunk. In the attacking Home Fleet that
contributed to its destruction was the
British navy destroyer, *Mashona*. On the
day following the sinking of the *Bismarck*,
the *Mashona* was among a number of
British warships that were attacked
by the Luftwaffe. It was sunk off the
west coast of Ireland, with the loss of
one officer and forty-five men, from a
complement of 190.

Among the five identified bodies washed
ashore was that of nineteen-year-old
Ordinary Seaman Ronald Woodward.
Garda Superintendent Tomás de Burca,
of the West Galway Division, reported
the finding of his body near Clifden on
Tuesday 1 July 1941, five weeks later.
His last possessions were a cigarette
case, a woman's earring and a diary of
eighteen-year old Elsie May Blankley
and himself.[46] He is buried in Ballinakill
(St. Thomas) Church of Ireland
Churchyard, at Moyard. When Vesper
visited his grave a decade later, in May
1951, he found it unmarked, beside that
of Canadian Artillery Officer, George

Dixon Morrow, a victim of the *Nerissa's*
fate; Morrow's plot bore the Canadian
white wooden cross.[47]

His other four shipmates were all found
on the Mayo coast: 'Jubilee Jack' Tweed,
forty-four year old Petty Officer from
Southampton, was found washed ashore,
without evidence of identity, at 5.30 on
the evening of Thursday 3 July 1941, at
Clare Island, Louisburgh. Here he was
laid to rest, the sole war grave in a tiny
walled-off, square plot, adjoining the
Clare Island Catholic Burial Ground.
His grave was originally marked by
four rough stones, one at each corner,
the only war grave in the plot. By the
autumn of 1955 he had been given
a permanent, standard war grave
headstone.[48]

Among the youngest to die in service
must have been the seventeen-year old
boy, Peter Clifford McGlade, of Redcar,
serving his time on the *Mashona*. On
27 June 1941 his body came ashore
at Surgeview, on Blacksod Bay, badly
decomposed. He was buried in Fallmore
Graveyard, beside Private Stanley
Darnell, victim of the *Arandora Star*.

Further up the coast, Leading Seaman
Jack Springett Johnson of Dagenham
was found two days after McGlade, at
Iniskea North Island. He was buried
in Kilcommon Erris Church of Ireland

Churchyard in Belmullet, but a veritable saga of mistaken identity surrounded him and his grave for over a decade. The plot was originally marked in the name of another Royal Navy seaman, H. D. Beattie. In June 1950, the IWGC was informed by the Admiralty that Beattie was alive; thereafter, painstaking investigations between the Gardaí, the OPW, External Affairs and the IWGC eventually resolved the matter. The confusion was created in part by the fact that an identity card for Harold D. Beattie was found in Johnson's pockets, as well as papers relating to Johnson. He was buried on 30 June, in Grave 12 in the Belmullet Church of Ireland Churchyard, in the name of Beattie. Adding to the confusion was the fact that the Church of Ireland parish of Kilcommon Erris was a huge one in extent, that there was a very isolated district called Kilcommon Erris, twelve miles from Belmullet and that there, in Pulatomish Graveyard, was buried a J. S. Johnson washed ashore at Barnatra in May 1941, as the Castlebar Gardaí informed the OPW District, in December 1950.

Some confusion also surrounded the last of these casualties, F. G. Wheeler, an electrician aboard the *Mashona*. His body was found by local man Michael O'Donnell, at Cloughmore, Achill Sound, on 27 June 1941. Among his possessions were electric light bulbs, fuses, pliers, two pound notes, and a St. Christopher medal. He was buried in Kildavnet Catholic Graveyard, unmarked. He left behind his widow, Mabel, at Kettering, Northants. For reasons unclear, the IWGC and UK Representative Office were unsure of this man's identity and circumstances. It is possible that the confusion was created by mistakes over the unfortunate man's initials, as reported to them. For five years his widow did not know where he had been laid to rest. In late 1945, the Commodore of the Royal Naval Barracks at Chatham was able to identify the subject as Frederick George Wheeler, a naval rating mechanic at Chatham, who had been reported missing from the *Mashona*, presumed killed. His grave had been marked by a wooden cross in the summer of 1942.[49]

By that stage, as Vesper later recalled to Chettle, 'very few remains were washed ashore after that period'.[50] Although the Battle of the Atlantic continued, and technically did not end until 8 May 1945, as far as relentlessly depositing its dead on Ireland's shores, the peak had passed by mid-1942. This, of course, was no consolation to the families and friends of the many nationalities who perished on Ireland's shores and hills in the years that followed, even as in the years before.

Mein Los war der Tod
Unter irischem Himmel
Und ein Bett
in Irlands gutter Erde

verse by Stan O'Brien
German War Cemetery

Glencree
Co. Wicklow

Chapter 15

German War Dead, 1939-1945

There was no extraordinary pattern, chronology or geography for the dead of the more than twenty nations whose remains came to rest forever, or for a time, in Ireland[1]. Among those in active service, the heaviest concentrations occurred among naval and merchant marine crews and passengers, then airmen. Over time, these fatalities were at their greatest in the years 1940 to 1942; in location, their remains became concentrated in larger urban cemeteries and in the several hundred small burial grounds of the north-west, west and south-west coasts; but no county was without its graves of the Second War, no more than its graves of the First.

Unsurprisingly, British and Irish constituted the greater proportion of these casualties. Thereafter it was the Germans, followed by Commonwealth casualties from Canada, Australia and New Zealand; after that, small numbers of Europeans, including Norwegians, Swedes, Dutch, Belgians and others; even smaller numbers of Asians, including war victims from Aden, China, Ceylon, and Japan; then some few Americans and finally, the unquantified, untraceable 'unknowns'.

The German litany:
The vast majority of the Germans who died and were buried here were airmen; other than these, they were internees and prisoners of war, in particular those from the *Arandora Star*. By the autumn of 1940 German aircraft were almost in daily breaches of Irish territory as they passed over the south and west coasts, on their way from airfields in France, to attack British convoys in the Northern Channel. It was on 20 August 1940 that the first of these crashed spectacularly into Mount Brandon in Kerry. The commanding officer, Oberleutnant Kurt Mollenhauer, and his crew miraculously escaped with minor injuries and became the first German airmen to be interned in the Curragh for the duration of the war.[2]

Not so fortunate were Rudolf Söchtig, Wilhelm Lorenz and Rudi Wachtler, who were killed on 27 September 1940 when their aircraft went down off the Wexford coast. Lorenz and Wachtler were both found on the same day almost a month later, on Sunday 20 October 1941, not far from each other at Ardcavan and Clonelland, Courtown, respectively. The twenty-three year old Gefreiter Lorenz, headless, boots and right sock missing, an empty Mauser revolver in his holster, was found floating, well inside Wexford Harbour, by Edward Nolan of Ardcavan, at 11.30 o'clock that Sunday morning.

NEAR RIGHT
The graves of Rudolf
Söchtig and Erwin Schatz,
German War Dead
Cemetery, Glencree, Co.
Wicklow.

FAR RIGHT
The graves of Wilhelm
Lorenz and Kurt
Tiggemann, German War
Dead Cemetery, Glencree.

From papers found on his person, he was identified as a flight sergeant, born in Angermunde, forty miles from Berlin, in 1917. He was buried that same evening at St. Ibar's Cemetery, Crosstown.[3] His was the first of several burials in what became, in effect, 'the German plot' of St. Ibar's. The body of his comrade, Rudi Wachtler, a twenty-two year old holder of the Iron Cross, floated in to Salleen Strand, three quarters of a mile from Tara Hill, near Gorey, that same Sunday evening, and was spotted by local man, Matt Redmond. An inquest recorded death by asphyxia, and he was buried at Clonattin Old Cemetery, near Gorey.[4] Their comrade, Söchtig, also the recipient of the Iron Cross, was not found until a month later, on 18 November, a good distance north, and in strange circumstances. At Ennerilly, in Brittas Bay, Wicklow, that afternoon, an Arklow man, James Rowe, was drawing gravel from the shore. Four hundred yards north of the Ennerilly River, at the bottom of a high cliff, he came upon the young Brandenburg man's body, embedded in sand in a small cave in the rocks, 'only the feet and left shoulder protruding'. The remains were in a very bad way, both hands missing; only skull and bones for head and feet; the parachute harness entangled in the legs; in his pockets a few German coins and a French-German dictionary. Following the inquest at Keogh's licensed premises

at Jack White's Cross, he was buried in Rathnew Cemetery at noon on 20 November. As reported by the local Gardaí, the German Minister, Edward Hempel, turned up to receive Söchtig's remains, laid a wreath on the plot and, 'raising his right hand in Nazi salute, spoke in German for a short time. Afterwards, he photographed the grave from four angles'; he then left, thanking the Gardaí for all they had done.[5]

Five days after these deaths, on 29 September 1940, another three German airmen were among five crew of a Heinkel shot down off the Wexford coast by an RAF Hurricane. As before, it was almost a month before the remains of these three drifted ashore: Gefreiter Franz Günther, barely twenty-two, was discovered at Morris Castle, two miles from Kilmuckridge, on Saturday evening, 19 October; on his body was a Lourdes medal. He was laid to rest in Kilmuckridge Burial Ground on the following day. On the same evening as Günther's burial, the body of Feldwebel Horst Birkholz, his ID card unreadable and his identity unknown till later, was found at the water's edge in Ballyvaldon, and was interred in Killilla Burial Ground at Blackwater, twelve miles north of Wexford.[6] The third airman, Gefreiter Rudolf Firchau, was washed up at Ingard Point, Fethard, on 23 October 1940. He was buried – close by

the graves of three unidentified British seamen of the First War – in that one-time dwelling place and burial ground of the Knights Templar of seven hundred years before, at Templetown.[7]

As with the victims of ships that were sunk, so too with the crews of aircraft that ditched into the sea: many more were lost than were ever washed up on shore, or scooped up, lifeless, from the water. Typically so were the cases of two identified Germans whose remains appeared out of nowhere in September and October 1940: Dr Johannes Sturm was reported as washed ashore on 27 September 1940, a solitary remains at Kiggale, County Galway – followed a month later by his flight comrade Theophil Schuldt, whose remains came ashore on 22 October 1940 and were interred in the lonely Ballyconneely Protestant Cemetery near Clifden.[8] Four others of the crew of this weather-reconnaissance mission were never found identified: buried in Kiggale, also, was the unidentified body of a German washed ashore on Dynish Island, near Lettermullen, Galway; unidentified also, the remains of a six-foot German who came ashore at Aillebrack on 13 November and interred at Ballyconneely.[9] Eleven days before Schuldt's burial, two Germans came down off the coast near County Louth: Leutnant Horst Felber from Pommern

was found, left boot on, right boot off, two weeks after his death, on Mosney beach at Laytown. Local man, Patrick Coogan, found him at 8 a.m., lying face down in a pool of water, his air-filled life jacket intact, and on his jacket the Iron Cross;[10] he was buried in Mornington Chapel burial ground. His comrade, twenty-year old Gefreiter Walter Hoppmann of Filberg, was discovered at Callystown Strand, miles further north, at Clogherhead, by a local youth collecting driftwood. He was buried in the Louth Board of Health Graveyard, known as Drogheda Calvary Cemetery, on 27 October, his grave marked by a wooden cross.[11] They had been two of a crew of four of a Luftwaffe Dornier shot down by the RAF.

By the start of December 1940, with the conflict in the Atlantic intensifying, Boland was sending the legations gruesome lists of 'unknowns': an 'A' list of twenty-four unidentifiable bodies of five Germans, twelve Italians, two Swedes, two Chinese, a Belgian, a Canadian and a Japanese and a 'B' list of forty unidentifiable bodies, probably British, judging from the remains of documents found on what was left of them. Some of them grim in the extreme, as in a clipped report from External Affairs to the UK Office in Dublin: ' body of man, entirely naked and almost denuded of flesh', came

ashore at Ballyliffin Bay, Clonmany, Donegal, and was laid to rest in Carndonagh.[12]

The first half of 1941 saw further batches of names added to the German litany of the dead in Ireland. On 5 February, a German Condor, 1/KG40, flying off the West Cork coast, got into difficulties. At around 9.30 that morning it was heard in the vicinity near Durrus, flying low in poor weather conditions. Local people in the vicinity of Dunmanus Bay heard its engine's intermittent sound before it came into view, smoke pouring from it. It crashed with terrific force, eight hundred feet up a mountain at Cashelfean, five of the six crew being killed instantly. Commanded by Oberleutnant Paul Gömmer, and based in Bordeaux, it had been harrying shipping in the North Atlantic over the previous months. As recently as 29 December, it had severely disabled the 5,200-ton *S.S. Trevarrack*, close by the entrance of Lough Foyle, and may well have sent her to the bottom.[13]

The inquest into this crash and fatalities was held in Clonakilty Courthouse under Acting Coroner Dr Charles Nyhan on Saturday 8 February. Apart from the difficulties of the times which it revealed, not least for medical staff like Dr Nyhan, who faced acute petrol shortages and the pressure to attend to many war-time emergencies, his investigation revealed a remarkable story of heroism. When Gömmer crashed at Cashelfean, a young local woman, Mary Nugent, with complete disregard for her own safety, entered the wrecked aircraft and dragged the injured Feldwebel Hohaus to safety. She was found tending the wounds of the sole survivor when the local defence force and Garda officers arrived on the scene.[14] The plane had burned itself out, and in the process burned some of the crew beyond recognition: Gömmer, Werner Albrecht, Willi Dose, Walter Clasen and meteorologist Dr Erhard Herrstrom all perished. They were buried, originally, in Bantry Abbey Burial Ground, overlooking Bantry Bay, where today there is a monument to the victims of a peacetime catastrophe, the explosion of the oil tanker *Betelguese*, at Whiddy Island, on 8 January 1979[15].

The Cashelfean deaths were followed a few weeks later by another solitary case, that of Friedrich Schütz, found floating in Kenmare Bay on 2 March. This Luftwaffe sergeant had been stationed at Rennes, and, three weeks before his own reported death, on 23 February, his father, an officer in the German army, had been killed. The son was buried in Kenmare Old Catholic Cemetery.[16] Of the four crew of a Heinkel downed by the RAF, he was the only one to be recovered and laid to rest.

Other casualties followed, in twos and threes through March and April 1941, especially on the Cork coastline.[17] On 5 March 1941, the remains of Leutnant Toni Böhner were washed up near Dingle, where he was buried in Cnoca'chairn Graveyard.[18] On 15 March, Feldwebel Günther Koch of Dusseldorf was killed and, seven weeks later, on 5 May, was found floating in the sea at Ring, Clonakilty; in his pockets were a photograph of a lady, an Iron Cross, one private letter, a diary with final entry on 12 March, and over his flying-suit, a life-jacket. He was laid to rest in the graveyard of St. Joseph's County Home, at Gullanes, Clonakilty[19]. On 1 April, three airmen were killed and, five weeks later, were found within two weeks of each other: Gefreiter Hans Hegemann between Rosscarbery and Clonakilty in Dirk Bay, Galley Head, on 3 May; twenty-two year old Gefreiter Heinz Dahmen of Arnoldsweiler, at Bullen's Bay, near the Old Head of Kinsale, on 7 May, headless and arms broken; and Feldwebel Wilhelm Eckold, on 13 May, floating in the sea off Barry's Head, east of Kinsale. Eckold's remains were covered in oil and were in a gruesome state of disintegration: 'hands and feet practically severed'. He was brought ashore at Nohoval Cove by boat, on 13 May. These three, respectively, were buried in Ringrone Graveyard, Castlefreke Burial Ground and Nohoval

Catholic Cemetery.[20] In the early hours of 6 May, a Heinkel with four crew took flak and crashed into the sea off Wexford, near the Blackwater Lightship. Apparently, the only body to surface in Ireland was that of Oberfeldwebel Erwin Seyfried of Hamburg, wearing an unopened parachute, life-jacket and overalls; in his pockets an Iron Cross, a silver bombing decoration and a silver ring, 'souvenir de Bretagne'. He was washed ashore at Raven Point, Curracloe, on 8 May, and interred shortly after, in the German plot at St. Ibar's, an iron cross recording his name.[21]

Finally, from this litany, on 10 June 1941, five perished together after their bomber aircraft crashed, off the Wexford coast at Carnsore: Unteroffizier Alois Mittermaier, Unteroffizier Josef Niebauer, Oberfeldwebel Rudolf Peschmann, Obergefreiter Hubert Modrzejewski and Dr Herbert Rumpf. All were buried in St. Ibar's, with a single, large wooden cross bearing the bomber's number.[22] A single wooden cross also came to stand between the two war graves of Leutnant Kurt Tiggemann and Gefreiter Ehfried Kolwe, who were killed on 11 October and came to be buried in Rathnure Cemetery, Killane, Co Wexford: a single cross, as the authorities were unable to determine which grave was which.[23] Killed, also on that date, when their plane

crashed in the Blackstairs Mountains, were Oberfeldwebel Wilhelm Böhmer, Obergefreiter Hans Szuflita, Willi Falk and another man, never identified.[24]

The number of named Germans killed in action and washed ashore began to taper off somewhat after this time. On 14 February 1942, the remains of Oberfeldwebel Werner Bonnefeld were washed ashore at Lunnaigh Strand, near Bunbeg, Donegal, fairly intact except for the missing eyes; a holder of the Iron Cross, he was buried in Magheragallon Catholic Cemetery.[25] On 3 March 1942, a group lost their lives in an air crash at Mount Gabriel, Schull, off the coast of West Cork – all unrecognisable: Oberleutnant Walther Thalheim, Unteroffizier Herbert Billa, Oberfeldwebel Edward Kreiss and Inspector Georg Endres were all buried in a single grave in Bantry Abbey, marked by a single cross.[26] They were accorded full military honours, with a military band in attendance, along with Catholic, Church of Ireland and Methodist clergymen.[27]

Bantry Bay was again to feature, in 1943, when on 23 July four crew members of a German aircraft were killed, their aircraft crashing at Ballinacarriga Hill, south of Dursey Head: thirty-three year old Riegerungsrat Bruno Roth, twenty-three year old Unteroffizier Hans Auschner,

twenty-two year old Obergefreiter Johannes Kuschidlo, and nineteen-year old Gefreiter Gerhard Dümmler. In this case all four were buried, side by side, at Ballaughbee Burial Ground, Allihies, Co. Cork.[28] Bodies of individual named and unnamed Germans continued to be washed ashore after this time, but the incidence had peaked as the Battle of the Atlantic moved further west and diversified from 1942.

However, there was one remarkable case of serving German military personnel who, though on active service elsewhere, ended their military careers in Ireland. It involved the Irish merchant vessel, *Kerlogue*. In the Western Channel, on 23 October 1943, she herself had been attacked, mistakenly, by Polish airmen in Mosquito fighter-bombers attached to the RAF; although there were no fatalities, four of the crew were badly wounded. Three months later, after a major naval battle in the Bay of Biscay, *Kerlogue* chanced by; Captain Tom Donohue and his nine crew effected the rescue of 164 German survivors, landing them at Cobh. They became the largest single contingent of German internees, 164 out of a total of 261, to spend the rest of the Second War in the Curragh. Two of their number, however, did not survive: Adolf Braatz and Helmut Weiss died of injuries and were buried, originally, in Cobh Old Cemetery.[29]

A solicitous legation:

The German Legation, more so than
the British or any other, was quick in
pressing for information, punctilious in
providing for wreaths and ceremonies,
and persistent in protesting when the
condition of the graves did not meet
their expectations. As already seen,
they were first to provide verified lists of
their war dead buried in Ireland.[30] They
were the first to press for their marking
by temporary wooden crosses, and the
only ones to insist, as a matter of course
rather than exception, that photographs
of the burial plots be provided. Having
regard to the weather conditions at
a given time of the year, and having
regard, also, to the remoteness of some
of the sites, it was not always possible to
satisfy them with the quality of print or
the speed of despatch they expected.

Already, in January 1941, Dr Henning
Thomsen, Secretary at the German
Legation, was pressing Belton in
External Affairs because the relatives
of Horst Felber and Walter Hoppmann
wanted their bodies exhumed from
their plots in Drogheda and returned
to Germany, after the war. He was
told what might be entailed in this,
but it would appear that, four years
on and with the war over, they never
were repatriated.[31] By August 1941,

the German Minister in Dublin was
complaining to Boland about the state
of the dead airmen's graves, and the
latter got Nolan to press the OPW for
action.[32] By early December 1941,
Boland was sending to the OPW a
message marked 'Urgent', requesting
the position regarding the erection of
temporary crosses on the thirty-three
German war graves known at that
point.[33] Hempel was so impatient that
he was threatening to take the business
under his own control, presumably by
hiring contractors independently of
External Affairs and the OPW. Boland
had to request him to desist 'for the
moment', as the contracts for twenty-
eight of the thirty-three had gone out,
and the making of the crosses had been
delayed while they were waiting for the
timber to season. Hempel's urgency, it
would appear, was to have the crosses
in place before Christmas, 'as that was
a time of the year when Germans liked
to visit and place wreaths on graves': so
William Brandon at the OPW advised
his Assistant Architects – though how
Germans, or anyone else outside of
Ireland, proposed to visit in the middle
of a World War remains interesting[34].
Immediately thereafter, he sent a
Legation staff member to visit all these
graves.

The matter, however, was not as simple
as it may have seemed to the German

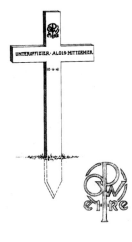

Legation in Dublin. There was, for example, the solitary grave of Gefreiter Willi Krzossa, killed on 30 June 1941, and buried in Dursey Island Cemetery. The OPW told External Affairs that they simply could not guarantee that his cross would be erected in time enough to satisfy the Germans: it was one hundred miles away from the OPW architect's office in Cork, and, petrol shortages and transport problems aside, Dursey was 'often inaccessible at this season of the year'.[35] In urging the OPW to action, Boland pleaded, on the last day of 1941, that 'any delay would involve the risk of independent action by the German Legation, which would be humiliating for us'. In pressing Fagan, Boland also indicated that the Germans wanted a photo of each grave, after its cross had been erected over it, and added ruefully, 'it is better that we should try to get these photographs for the German Minister than that some member of the German Legation staff should go round with a camera, taking the photographs himself'.[36]

The New Year brought no let-up: on 2 January Boland now followed up his New Year's Eve plea to Fagan with a request that the Germans wanted the negatives as well 'in case they should require more than one print'. From Veale in the OPW came the laconic 'Secretary, we can do this – provided we are paid

for the negatives'.[37] They could, but it took time: it was September 1942 before photographs of the four German war graves in Bantry Abbey were taken, only to be found unsatisfactory and they had to be redone.[38]

A constant vigil:
In regard to the upkeep of their graves, the German authorities in Dublin kept a close eye on them. In December 1941 the OPW Head Office alerted all its Assistant Architects: 'we are being pressed by the Department of External Affairs for a general report on the condition of the German War Graves… Please return reports to us without further delay'. All this, no doubt, was in response to complaints that Nolan at External Affairs had received, and to which he alerted the OPW as far back as August.[39] It may have seemed to work: Hempel wrote fulsomely to de Valera, in early April 1942, to express

the thanks of the German Reich and particularly of the Chief of the German Luftwaffe, Reichsmarshall Hermann Göring for the great friendliness which the Irish Government has proved by taking care of the maintenance of the graves of the German war dead in Ireland.[40]

To some extent the fulsome praise was premature: off Hempel went the next

NEAR LEFT
German military funeral,
Co. Wexford.

FAR LEFT
Image from German War
Dead Cemetery.

week, on vacation in the south-west, and took the opportunity to inspect some of the graves of his fallen fellow-countrymen. He reported back to External Affairs, in person, immediately upon his return: the solitary grave of Friedrich Schütz in Kenmare 'was nicely kept', but when it came to Bantry Old Abbey, he did not mince his words: 'the graves are disgraceful'.[41] A flurry of phone calls from OPW Head Office to Cork brought the calm response from the Assistant Architect: he claimed that as recently as 20 March his officials had visited the two German grave plots there, 'but apparently found no cause for complaint'.[42] Nolan was unconvinced and earnestly urged the OPW to pay particular attention to the supervision of the Bantry Abbey caretaker, 'to avoid any further complaints from the German Minister'.[43] Over time it appears to have worked. By the winter of 1943 Hempel was still visiting war graves. In Wicklow and Wexford he found that generally speaking the graves bore signs of being extremely well looked after' and expressed his appreciation, qualified by only a minor complaint about the length of the grass at the German graves at Clonattin in Gorey, and Killilla, near Blackwater.[44]

By the summer of 1942, forty German war graves had been verified, and thirty-six had their crosses and maintenance agreements in place; by the summer of 1944, the number of such graves stood at forty-two, for which forty had secured their temporary crosses and upkeep; by the end of the 1950s the German and Irish Governments had firm verifications on a total of fifty-three such graves of German war dead. As the story later unfolded, however, at least a further possible 116 German war dead were uncovered: behind this unexpected increase lies the story of the origins and creation of the German War Dead Cemetery at Glencree.[45]

BELOW
Template for German
wooden cross.

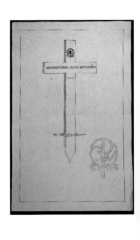

RIGHT
Drawing for temporary
wooden crosses for German
war graves

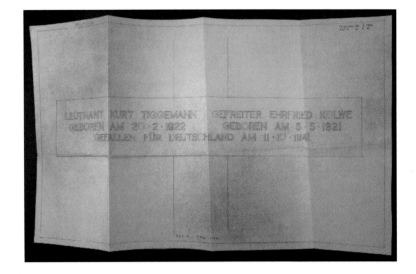

Into the mosaic of victory
Was laid this precious piece

R. 'Mack' Sutherland, Radio Officer
S.S. "Serbino"
21 October 1941

Gweesalia Graveyard
Co. Mayo

Chapter 16

British And Irish War Dead, 1939-1947

When it came to the Second World War and the numbers of its war graves on this island, the relative positions on either side of the Border came to be reversed. As seen at the outset of this study, the First World War and general conflict of 1914 to 1921 were responsible for over 2,600 war graves in the Irish Free State, as against over 1,200 in Northern Ireland. The conflict of 1939-1945, by contrast, resulted in over 500 war graves in what, soon after, became the Republic of Ireland, and over 1,400 in Northern Ireland.

Given that the former was neutral and that the latter was directly involved, with large naval and air bases, there is no surprise in these relative figures. Of course, being burial figures, they have nothing to say on the origins of those buried and remembered: some of those buried in Northern Ireland war graves will have come from Éire; some buried in Éire, will have come from the North; some buried in both jurisdictions will have come from neither. With these qualifications admitted, the relative totals year by year, over the years of war grave status eligibility, are as in Table 6:

Of the 539 known commemorated war graves in the Republic as registered by the CWGC, the totals for each county are as in Table 7:

The comparable figures for Northern Ireland are set out in Table No. 8:

With over 500 Second World War graves of Commonwealth Forces in the Republic, their numbers were five times those of the German war dead buried there. The vast majority of these, naturally, were British and Irish, killed in ships sunk or damaged in attack, or in aircraft crashes; otherwise, they were largely composed of Irish members of the Commonwealth Forces who died at home from wounds, disease or illness. The exact number of these is not yet established. The only reliable countrywide register is that of the Commonwealth War Graves Commission; it is comprehensive but not definitive, listing the graves of those it has registered and has marked. How many are not registered, or not marked at all, it is not possible to say: nevertheless, it is a reasonable presumption that the CWGC register has captured the great majority.

Near Left
S.S. Dunvegan Castle in Capetown Harbour.

Table No. 6:
CWGC War Graves of 1939-1947, registered in Ireland

Year	Republic of Ireland	Northern Ireland
1939	5	11
1940	99	162
1941	63	264
1942	43	222
1943	57	218
1944	71	186
1945	75	162
1946	53	90
1947	37	76
Unidentified	36	32
	539	1,423

Total: 1,962

Table No. 7:
CWGC War Graves of 1939-1947, registered in the Republic of Ireland

Carlow	2	Kilkenny	7	Offaly	7
Cavan	6	Laois	5	Roscommon	4
Clare	8	Leitrim	3	Sligo	22
Cork	62	Limerick	24	Tipperary	12
Donegal	79	Longford	3	Waterford	11
Dublin	140	Louth	7	Westmeath	8
Galway	15	Mayo	56	Wexford	14
Kerry	10	Meath	5	Wicklow	17
Kildare	9	Monaghan	3		

Total: 539

Table No. 8:
CWGC War Graves of 1939-1947 registered in Northern Ireland

Antrim	629	Fermanagh	117
Armagh	67	Londonderry	234
Down	323	Tyrone	53

Total: 1,423

Table No. 9:
British Royal Navy and Merchant Navy War Graves of 1939-1947 in the Republic of Ireland

Year	1939	1940	1941	1942	1943	1944	1945	1946	1947	Total
Royal Navy										
British	0	9	6	0	2	1	0	0	0	18
Irish	0	1	2	3	4	4	10	7	2	33
Subtotal		10	8	3	6	5	10	7	2	51
Merchant Navy										
British	0	15	8	1	0	0	0	0	0	24
Irish	0	2	2	0	1	2	1	3	4	15
Subtotal	0	17	10	1	1	2	1	3	4	39
Total	0	27	18	4	7	7	11	10	6	90

NEAR LEFT
The grave of Thomas
Shannon, DSM, of
H.M.S. Drake, in Sligo
Town Cemetery.

FAR LEFT
Magheragallon Catholic
Cemetery, Co. Donegal.

Royal Navy war dead:

Of the 500 plus, close on 100 are
the graves of Royal Navy and British
Merchant Navy personnel who lost
their lives at sea or were washed ashore.
For these, the CWGC Register for the
Republic of Ireland indicates some
ninety-five named individuals who
were accorded war grave status as Irish,
British and other: ninety Irish and
British, two Canadians, two Norwegians
and one Spaniard. The yearly totals of
these deaths illustrate the point made in
an earlier chapter, that the most intense
phase of fatalities occurred over the
period 1940-1942. Bearing in mind that
for recognition as a Second World War
Grave, the CWGC established the dates
of 3 September 1939 to 31 December
1947 – allowing a two-year post-war
period for those dying from war wounds,
disease or illness, as they had done for
the First World War – the incidence is
indicated in Table No 9.

Among Royal Navy vessels whose war
dead were buried in Ireland, one of
the earliest casualties was the *Dunvegan
Castle*, a Belfast-built steamer of 15,000
tons, launched in 1936, taken over by
the Admiralty in September 1939, and
refitted as an armed merchant cruiser.
On 27 August 1940, off the West of
Ireland, she was torpedoed by *U-46*
under Kapitänleutnant Endrass. She
was hit three times, between 7 and 10

o'clock that night. The vessel, despite
explosions in the engine room, managed
to stay afloat until early next morning
when she sank, with the loss of four
officers and twenty-three crew. Captain
Ardill and 249 survivors were landed
safely in Scotland. The vessel was one of
seven armed merchant cruisers sunk in
the North Atlantic in the second half of
the year 1940, most of them victims of
U-boat attacks.[1]

Of the twenty-seven fatalities, only five
bodies were washed ashore in Ireland,
all five British, although Able Seaman
James Buckley of Sheffield may have
been second-generation Irish. He was
buried in Magheragallon. Of the four
other dead shipmates whose remains
were recovered, Leading Seaman
Thomas Clint Ambrose of Kent and
Sub-Lieutenant Denis Smedley of
Surrey were laid to rest in Chapel
Strand, on Arranmore Island, west of
Burtonport, while in Tullaghobegley
Church of Ireland Churchyard their
shipmates, Sub-Lieutenant Robert
Gourlay Anderson from Kincardineshire
and Seaman Walter Redford, became
the only victims of the naval conflicts
of the Second World War to be
commemorated there. Anderson's
body was washed ashore at Ballyness
Strand, Falcarragh, County Donegal, on
10 September 1940, his grave marked
originally by a small iron cross.[2] After

NEAR RIGHT
*SS Athenia torpedoed off
Rockall on the day World
War Two began.*

the loss of his vessel, Captain Ardill retired. As for Kapitänleutnant Endrass, having been honoured by the Reich with the Knight's Cross shortly after despatching the *Dunvegan Castle*, he perished with all forty-seven crew, on 21 December 1941, when his new charge, the *U-567*, was sent to the bottom, north-east of the Azores, by depth charges from H.M.S. *Deptford*.

Three years later, in January 1943, in very severe weather off the Donegal coast, during an escort convoy to Gibraltar, the minelayer H.M.S. *Corncrake* foundered with the loss of all on board. Only two of the lost were ever found in Ireland, eighteen-year old stoker, Vincent Lavery, who was buried in Killybegs Old Graveyard, and seaman Charles Walmsley of Grimsby, interred in St. Mura's at Upper Fahan, close by sixty-eight victims of the 1914-1918 War and eight others of the 1939-1945 War; the latter included crews lost in *Laurentic, Manchester Brigade, Mohamed Ali El Kebir* and *Nerissa*. Not all whose war-death recognition was in association with the same Royal Navy vessel died at the same time, or even in the same year. Crew of H.M.S. *Caroline* whose war graves are in Ireland included eighteen-year old Wren, Margaret Clarke from Waterford, daughter of Lieutenant Commander Joseph H. Clarke; she passed away on 28 January 1941 and was laid to

rest in Ballynakill Church of Ireland Churchyard, in County Waterford. A temporary cross and a maintenance agreement for the young woman's grave were put in place by the end of 1943, when an OPW site visit found the grave in good order.[3] Another *Caroline* crew-member, Warrant Officer Stanislaus Gaffney, died in February 1945; his grave in Glasnevin was verified by the OPW that April, with a temporary cross being erected in June, and a permanent memorial by his relatives, by the mid 1950s; he is remembered on the Second World War Memorial there.[4] Lastly from *Caroline* was Able Seaman Thomas Flavin of Ballincurra, who died after the war, on 27 September 1946, and was buried in Mogeely Catholic Cemetery, northeast of Midleton.

Likewise, from the crew of H.M.S. *Drake*, Second World War namesake of H.M.S. *Drake* sunk by torpedo off Rathlin Island in October 1916, were Signalman Thomas Shannon, DSM, of Sligo, who died in May 1942 and was interred in Sligo Cemetery; stoker James Perrott from Dublin, who passed away in May 1943, interred in Mount Jerome; stoker Patrick O'Brien of Ballymacoda, Cork, who died in January 1944 and was buried there in The Hill Cemetery; and finally, sixty-one year old John Curry of Aghada, who died in May 1946 and is laid to rest in Upper Aghada Cemetery.

Of the Royal Navy war dead buried in this country, the final victim to die while the war was still being waged was Petty Officer Edward Byrne of H.M.S. *Raleigh*, who died five days before the war ended, on 9 August 1945, and is interred in Mount Jerome.[5]

British Merchant Navy war dead:
The first British Merchant vessel to be sunk by U-boat in the Second War was the S.S. *Athenia*. The war was hardly nine hours old when the 13,000-ton vessel, with 1,100 civilian passengers, was torpedoed at 7.40 p.m. on 3 September, with the loss of 118 lives, 200 miles west of Ireland: 'the first blow in the Battle of the Atlantic'.[6] The first Merchant Navy vessel with victims commemorated in Ireland was the S.S. *Accra*, nine months later. In convoy, en route for West Africa, this 9,000-ton Belfast-built vessel was torpedoed by *U-34* off Ireland's west coast early in the afternoon of 26 July 1940. Of its almost 470 passengers and crew, only eleven passengers and eight crew were lost when their lifeboat capsized. Of these nineteen, only one was identified, when his remains came ashore at Cruit Island: forty-five year old Second Engineer William Caswell is commemorated on the island-cemetery to this day.

Two weeks later, on 8 August 1940, while homeward bound to London from Buenos Aires, the 9,000-ton *Upwey Grange* under Captain W. E. Williams met a similar fate, 200 miles west of Achill, when it was targeted by *U-37* under the command of Kapitänleutnant Viktor Otto Oehrn. She was struck by two torpedoes on her port side, one of them exploding in the engine room. She went down in rough seas, with the loss of thirty-six out of eighty-six, but they managed to get two boats away. That under First Officer Ellis was picked up three days later by the trawler *Naniwa*, 150 miles from the scene of the attack and fifty miles west of Achill Head; however, Captain Williams's boat, with thirty-three crew and three passengers, was never seen again. Known to have been in Williams's boat was Engineer Clifford Mackrow from Ilford, washed up on the Mayo coast and buried in the Belmullet Church of Ireland Cemetery of Kilcommon Erris, where, two years later, his grave was marked by a wooden cross. By 1954 he was permanently remembered there by a CWGC headstone, his grave, and others, tended by the church caretaker, Matilda Farrell.[7] Washed ashore, also on the day of the sinking, were the remains of nineteen-year old apprentice, Geoffrey Butcher of Orpington. He was buried in the historic Rathfran Graveyard, within sight of the ancient ruins of the Franciscan

NEAR RIGHT
*Rathfran Cemetery war
graves of Upwey Grange
crewmen, Geoffrey Butcher,
Orpington and Arnold
Walmsley, Bolton and
unknown, Co. Mayo.*

FAR RIGHT
*The grave of William
Caswell, 2nd Engineer,
Accra, on Cruit Island,
Co. Donegal.*

Priory to one side, and to the other, facing the sea toward Rathfran Bay. He is remembered today beside the grave of an unknown sailor and that of twenty-five year old Private Arnold Walmsley of Bolton, who had lost his life on the previous day. Only three other *Upwey Grange* casualties are known to date to be buried in the Republic: forty-seven year old Able Seaman George Walters, buried in Achill Holy Trinity Church of Ireland Churchyard; the skeleton of an unknown sailor washed up at Islandcroin, Dungloe, on 18 September,[8] buried in Termon Old Graveyard; and the remains of Edward Hugh Mayes, thirty-three year old son of Major Richard Mayes of Northampton, washed up at Annagh Head, Mayo, on 15 September and buried in Termoncarragh.

Two weeks after the finding of Edward Mayes's remains, the Gardaí at Belmullet heard from Nancy Cotton of Northampton. She had been shown a cutting from the *News Chronicle* of 20 September which carried the story of the finding of the remains of a British naval officer, E. K. Mayes of Whately Terrace, Northampton. On inquiring of the Admiralty and the ship's owners, Houlder, she was told that the *Upwey Grange* had been sunk on 8 August and that an Edward H. Mayes was serving as its Second Officer; she added: 'I have been assured that Mr. Mayes, my

fiancé, was the unfortunate victim'. She requested precise details of the burial place and concluded:

If, by any chance, there was a blue and gold enamel badge sewn behind the lapel of his uniform, bearing the inscription 'Ah, quel est bon le bon dieu', could you please let me have this – It is my school badge from the Convent of Notre Dame, Northampton.

One week later, Inspector Ryan of Belmullet was convinced that the man washed ashore at Scotchport, Belmullet, on 15 September, was her fiancé: a blue enamel badge was indeed sewn behind a lapel of his jacket, bearing not the full inscription referred to by Miss Cotton, but the letters 'N.D.H.S.' – which, he presumed, meant Notre Dame High School. The identifying badge was duly sent to her.[9]

In the same general area, not as far from the coast, on 13 November 1940, the 5,000-ton *Cape St. Andrew*, en route for Bombay, was torpedoed by *U-137* and sunk with a loss of fifteen crew out of a complement of sixty-eight. Alone among the identified dead that came ashore in Ireland was forty-year old Royal Marine, Archie Lovegrove of Wantage, Berkshire. A gunner on this armed merchant vessel, he was washed ashore at Ballygorman, Malin Head, on 12 December, and interred originally in Carndonagh Workhouse Cemetery.[10]

*BELOW AND LEFT
Rathfran Abbey &
Rathfran Cemetery,
Co. Mayo.*

Compared with the mortality from the *Upwey Grange*, that from the loss of the M. V. *Glenmoor*, over three months later, was proportionately far greater. In convoy, en route from Cardiff to Alexandria, with 7,000 tons of coal, all but two of her thirty-one crew were lost when she was torpedoed by *U-103* on 27 November 1940, 200 miles west of Ireland. Three weeks later, on 10 December 1940, the remains of eighteen-year old apprentice, Stanley Creed of Eastbourne, were washed up at Brinaleck, south-west of Bloody Foreland. Following the loss of the *Glenmoor* on 27 November, his mother heard nothing further until mid-September 1941, when the Registrar General of Shipping and Seamen informed her that Creed's remains had been buried in Magheragallon Cemetery. She was distressed at the delay in being informed, not least because it made the certainty of identification more difficult, in her eyes. From the Registrar General's description, however, she concluded 'there is little doubt that this is the body of my son, and, failing further evidence, my husband and I are prepared to admit full identity'. They wanted his body exhumed and returned home, but this was not to happen.[11] Two days later the vessel's Second Radio Officer, Leonard Smith of New Malden, Surrey, was washed ashore at Inishfree Island near Burtonport, and he was laid to rest in Termon Old Cemetery directly south across the water.[12]

In the spring of the following year, among the many vessels attacked and sunk was the steam trawler *Aberdeen*, out of Lowestoft, this time off the east coast, on 11 March 1941. The bodies of Skipper John C. Barber of Grimsby and his second mate, William Coe of Milford Haven, were washed ashore on the Louth coast. The skipper's came ashore at Clogherhead on 29 April 1941 and Coe's at Baltray on 1 May 1941; he had been washed overboard from a lifeboat that was launched as the *Aberdeen* went down.[13] They were buried in Calvary Old Cemetery, Drogheda, whence, twenty years later, their graves became the subject of an outcry in Britain[14]. While the litany of ships and seamen lost off the Irish coast was long, the list of identified dead from any single vessel continued to be short. Thus, when the 4,000-ton *Serbino*, en route from Mombasa and Freetown to Liverpool, was torpedoed by *U-82* off the west coast on 21 October 1941, losing fourteen of its sixty-five crew, only one of the dead was found and identified in Ireland: Second Radio Officer Robert 'Mack' Sutherland, from Hampshire, was washed ashore at Gweesalia, Co Mayo, on 13 December.[15] He was buried there, in Gweesalia Graveyard, in almost as lonely and isolated a place as

the sea in which he perished, but with an inscription more memorable than most:

*Into the mosaic of victory
Was laid this precious piece*

For men of the Irish Merchant Navy, during the war and for long afterwards, similar official remembrance was slow in coming, as was any history of their role in keeping neutral Ireland supplied in wartime. Over the period July 1940 to November 1941 there were some forty deaths from attacks on fifty-one Irish vessels.[16] By the war's end some 149 known merchant navy men had lost their lives from attacks on Irish-registered vessels: 128 Irish, 18 British and 3 others. Three Irish merchant vessels were lost without trace during the war, and without any known endeavour on the part of the Irish State to discover what had happened to them and their seamen. The story of their sacrifice, and that of all the Irish Merchant Navy men, was not fully chronicled until the work of Frank Forde and others from the 1980s; their lives and deaths were not publicly memorialised or officially commemorated in Ireland until more recent times.[17]

British and Irish casualties of the air war:
While never as numerous as the casualties of attacks on shipping, the deaths of Air Forces' personnel buried in Ireland were, at most times, no less dramatic, and occasionally as mysterious. At 2 o'clock on the afternoon of 22 October, the firemen on a Great Southern Railway train travelling along the coast, spotted a body protruding from the sand on the Wicklow side of Newcastle. On investigation it proved to be the remains of Flying Officer G. R. B. Peters, No.79 Squadron RAF, whose body came ashore at Grange, Newcastle, on that day. He had been killed on 29 September.[18] Little else was known of him at the time and he was buried next day in Rathnew Cemetery.[19] It was a rare enough occurrence for the year 1940, but in the next year there were multiple losses from aircraft crashes.

On 18 April 1941 four RAF men were killed when their aircraft crashed at Kylebeg, Blessington, Co Wicklow: twenty-three year old Sergeant Stanley Wright of Old Trafford, Sergeant Frederick Erdwin, twenty-three year old Pilot John K. Hill of Croydon, and twenty-year old Sergeant John F. Lamb of Carlisle were laid to rest in St. Mary's Burial Ground in Blessington village. They were the only Commonwealth-commemorated Second World War

graves there, joining local man Sergeant Edward Garland of the British Columbia Regiment, 2nd Canadian Mounted Rifles, as its only First World War casualty.[20]

In the same month, on the far side of the country, a body believed to be that of RAF Sergeant Stanley Goodlet of Edinburgh was washed ashore on the 14th, near Oranmore. Headless, but still with collar and black tie, he wore a watch which had stopped at 2.33. The Gardaí believed he was a crew member of a plane that had crashed in Galway Bay on 19 March; the remains were interred in Oranmore Cemetery on 15 April 1941, and the grave marked by a temporary wooden cross bearing his name, by June 1942.[21] Doubts as to the identity kept External Affairs and the British authorities in exchanges of information down to the early 1950s. In 1953 the British Air Ministry was reviewing the case, observing that another crew member of the same aircraft had been unaccounted for, and the fact that the back of the watch bore the initials 'T.C.K' or 'T.C.R.' did not help. In the end, he was permanently commemorated on a panel of the Air Forces Memorial, Runnymede.[22]

At the other end of 1941, on 3 December, another RAF crash, of a Sunderland flying-boat, *Pluto*, killed at least nine other British airmen, this time at Duckmore Strand, Doonbeg, south of Milltown Malbay, County Clare. Among the dead, twenty-year old Sergeant Maurice Fox of Kent was found washed ashore at Mutton Island, two miles north-east of the crash site at Killard. His well-attended funeral went from the Church of Ireland at Spanish Point to the churchyard at Milltown Malbay. The Irish Army, under Captain Daly representing the Chief of Staff, marched in formation to the graveside, sounded the Last Post and discharged three volleys in tribute. Two survivors, Lieutenant Fleming and Sergeant Masterson, were able to list the dead and to identify two of them from four photographs found near the site: these were Lieutenant Arthur Doncaster, buried in Killard Church of Ireland Churchyard, and Lieutenant Walker, missing, never found.[23] Doncaster had been washed ashore further up the coast at White Strand, Carramore Point, as had nineteen-year old Aircraftsman Albert Bennett of Liverpool, who was buried close by in Killard. So, too, had twenty-one year old Frederick Lea of Norfolk and twenty-five year old Sydney Epps, buried side by side with Maurice Fox in Milltown Malbay.[24] Beside them, too, was the unidentifiable body of another of the five missing from the crew of eleven; it had been washed up on 21 December, even as two others had been

at Tromora Castle fifteen days before. Early 1942 brought further deaths off the east coast, notably on 24 February when an RAF aircraft crashed, during a snowstorm, into the sea off Cahore Point. Despite the poor visibility, at 1 p.m. two fishing vessels saw it flying low, not more than 200 feet above them, heading towards land but never making it. When they reached the scene, fishermen of the two vessels, Peter Dockrell and Christopher Gaffney of Arklow, found only oil slick, little pieces of wreckage, a life-raft and, after a time, two bodies that floated to the surface. Three days later, with full military honours, Sergeant Alexander Sherlock-Beard with addresses in Seaford, Sussex and Hamilton, Ontario, and Sergeant Jack Rostern, of Manchester, were laid to rest, side by side, in Arklow Cemetery. Flying out of RAF Silloth, Cumbria, they had only been three weeks in training at that Coastal Operational Training Unit when their Hudson AM 834, on a routine training mission, with a crew of four, went down: Sergeants A. R. Rylatt, the Pilot, and A. W. McGarva, the Air Gunner, were never found.[25] Over Sherlock-Beard's grave, the headstone inscription reads:

Greater Love Hath No Man Than This,
That A Man Lay Down His Life For His
Friends

while that of Wireless Operator Jack Rostern reads simply

Resting
Where No Shadows Fall

In February 1943 an Irish Sergeant in the RAF, Air Gunner John Kenny, of Crampton Quay, Dublin, was killed during training exercise in Britain. He was brought home and buried in St. Patrick's Plot in Glasnevin Cemetery. At the war's end his brother, William, called to the OPW to inquire why there was no headstone to him, as the War Office, apparently, had promised the family. The OPW informed him that, as they understood it, his was not a war grave and his name had not been on any list supplied to them by the IWGC. In any case, they were still far from the point where any headstones for 1939-1945 war dead were being erected. As far as they were concerned, William's only recourse was directly to the War Graves Commission in England. William Kenny persisted and his dead brother was duly commemorated on Panel 2 of the Glasnevin Second World War Screen Wall Memorial.[26]

Given the considerable care normally taken by External Affairs and the great trouble generally gone to by the OPW to honour their war grave obligations,

an odd case which occurred over a year later was uncharacteristic. It concerned Air Bomber Richard Irvine of the Royal Canadian Air Force. For some reason not clear, the British Red Cross asked their Irish counterparts for information concerning the war grave of this flying officer. The Irish Red Cross in February 1945 contacted Defence who referred the query to External Affairs. The Irish Red Cross understood that one of such name had been interred in Mount Jerome in 1944. Warnock of External Affairs replied, rather briskly, on 28 February 1945 that 'it has not been possible to obtain any information concerning this grave or any other information regarding F.O. Irvine'.[27] Remarkably, Richard Irvine was a local man, his parents living in Monkstown, Co Dublin, and a communication with the Mount Jerome Cemetery authorities, where it was thought he had been buried, would have quickly established that, having died on 6 June 1944, he was indeed buried there five days later.

Quite the worst tragedy of 1943 occurred in Co. Kerry, at 4 o'clock on the morning of 28 July, when a BOAC flying boat, en route from Lisbon with seven crew and eighteen passengers, crashed into Mount Brandon. Patrick Corkery of Slieve Glas, four miles away, heard the explosion as the aircraft disintegrated. In difficult conditions he made his way to the scene, on foot, and then retraced his steps to alert the nearest Gardaí. Although ten lost their lives in the carnage, miraculously fifteen survived. Among the ten killed and buried in a communal grave in Kiliney Churchyard, south of Castlegregory, were Colonel Sydney Pullinger of the Royal Engineers and Group Captain David Stannard of Surrey. In this case, BOAC themselves erected a memorial for all the dead,[28] and further action by the OPW and IWGC at the time was deemed unnecessary. Although individual Irish and British RAF members continued to be casualties who came to be buried and commemorated in Ireland in the war years that followed, nothing as large as the BOAC tragedy recurred for the remainder of the war.

Typical of airforce personnel who died in the years that followed were Irish men and women like Una Evans of the WAAF, dying in England, buried in Doneraile, St. Mary's Churchyard, or, like Nancy Fahey of Ballybride, County Roscommon, coming home to die in Ireland. Nancy, the eldest of four children born in the village in 1920, of her own accord joined the Women's Auxiliary Air Force, not following the immediate example of any neighbours or relatives, although her father, Thomas, had served with the Connaught Rangers during the First

War. She was based in Manchester until, working in a sanatorium in Altringham, she contracted TB, and, with the war still on, was brought home by her mother in March 1945. Her family tried to nurse her back to health but she died in hospital in November, and is remembered today by two memorials in St. Coman's Cemetery, Boyle: a standard CWGC permanent war grave headstone and a very fine family memorial in which her name is inscribed with obvious fond remembrance and respect.[29]

Of some twenty-seven identified female personnel of the British Commonwealth Forces registered with the CWGC as buried and commemorated in Ireland, the majority were not RAF, but Auxiliary Territorial Service, of whom there were at least fourteen. They ranged in age from nineteen-year olds Christina

O'Donoghue in Glandore and Eileen Mills in Sligo, through twenty-four year old Lorna Scott-Martin, née Oulton, of Clontarf Castle, to thirty-seven year old Isabella Mullinger in Cahir. There were eight members of the Women's Auxiliary Air Force, from twenty-year old Rosemary Cox, interred in St. Patrick's, Dundalk, following her death in April 1945, to thirty-six year old Sergeant Bridget Gilbourne, who died on 14 June 1946 and is commemorated in Castletown Conyers Old Graveyard, Co Limerick. Of the remainder, three were nursing sisters: Anna Kearon in Arklow, Mary Power in Stradbally, Waterford, and Mary O'Shea in St. Finbarr's, Cork. The youngest of the females commemorated was the already mentioned eighteen-year old Wren, Margaret Clarke of Waterford; the other member of the Women's Royal Naval Service identified at this time is Gertrude Canning, interred in Ballybogan, Donegal, but commemorated on the Screen Wall Memorial in Grangegorman Military Cemetery. Some of them had come from families with military or naval service, like Margaret Clarke or Anna Marjorie Kearon of Arklow, in whose family there had been a strong seafaring tradition. For the most part, however, at this point, the majority of the influences that shaped their personal histories, and those very histories themselves, remain elusive.[30]

Greater love hath no man than this
That a man lay down
His life for his friends

Edward Alexander McCord, Wireless Operator
Royal New Zealand Air Force
15 October 1942

Ardagh Cemetery,
Co. Longford

Commonwealth and Other War Dead, 1939-1947

In the early summer of 1951 Vesper was investigating war graves in West Cork. In Castletownroche his attention was drawn to a grave in the Catholic Cemetery. There he came upon the last resting place of what he took to be a Czech soldier, Private G. Metzke, who died on 17 December 1942. No memorial marked Metzke's grave and his circumstances were something of a mystery. 'It seemed very strange that this Czech should be in the village', he remarked, as he completed his Graves Registration Report form.

On consulting the Gardaí, Vesper found that the local Sergeant's memory went back nine years, to a day when the 'Czech' turned up in one of the village shops, to purchase food. A colleague of the Sergeant arrested Metzke, 'as a suspicious character', and brought him to the station. Here he confessed to being a deserter from the Czech army and, on being searched, was found to have a loaded revolver on him. Soon after, while eating the food he had bought, he took poison and killed himself. He was buried in unconsecrated ground in the cemetery.[1] His name and nation apart, in all other respects he was, to the locals, essentially, 'an unknown'. For Colonel Dan Bryan of the Irish Defence Forces' intelligence service, as also for the German Legation in Dublin, whose documentation on the subject was in Bryan's possession, Metzke was a Sudeten German, of questionable sanity, engaged in espionage in various countries including Britain; from there he came to Co. Cork via Northern Ireland.[2]

In general, however, for the authorities, whether Irish, British or other, the many dead and unrecognisable 'unknowns', victims of war, constituted a considerable difficulty. Often enough, even where their nationality was known, the problem might be to establish which person they might have been out of two or more crew from a burnt-out aircraft, or a vessel that foundered, leaving victims in charred remains, or in the water for weeks or months. Often enough, too, they might be interred in a single grave, sometimes with Commonwealth war grave headstones side by side. Most often, where they were and are remembered by permanent headstone, it is in the classic form to 'An Unknown Soldier/Sailor of the 1939-45 War', as found, for example, in Rathfran Cemetery, Killala, and Dugort, Achill in Co. Mayo.

Canadians:
Among the personnel of the other Air Forces of Commonwealth and Allies to perish and be buried in Ireland, the Canadians were the most prominent.

NEAR RIGHT
Col Dan Bryan, Chief Staff Officer, G2, Irish Army Intelligence.

MIDDLE RIGHT
The grave of an Unknown Sailor of the 1939-1945 War.

FAR RIGHT
The war grave, in Belmullet, of Canadian, Thomas Elvin Mitchell, lost on Nerissa.

Many such, of course, were stationed in Northern Ireland and paid with their lives, either in combat or in ferrying combat-aircraft from Canada and the United States. Of forty war graves of members of Canadian Forces commemorated by the CWGC in the Republic, some twenty-eight were casualties of the First and twelve of the Second World War. It is not certain at this stage how many of the First War twenty-eight were Irish-born. Of their twelve Forces' personnel of the Second War, however, nine were almost certainly Canadian-born. There are only three doubtful ones: Lieutenant Hugh Massy Baker of the Royal Canadian Engineers, who died in July 1940, buried and commemorated in Bansha Church of Ireland Churchyard in County Tipperary in the Baker Family plot there, although his parents, Massy and Mildred Baker, had an address in Rockliffe, Ottawa;[3] the second was Private Michael Joseph McDermott of the South Saskatchewan Regiment, RCIC, who died in the last days of the war, on 5 August 1945, and is commemorated in Kilgobbin Old Church Cemetery, Stepaside, Co Dublin;[4] the third was the Royal Canadian Air Force pilot, Richard Irvine of Monkstown, referred to in a previous chapter.

The earliest deaths of Canadian Forces' personnel buried in the Republic of

Ireland were those of five Canadians killed on 30 April 1941: Corporal Duncan Bell, born in Scotland but living in Verdun, Quebec, a member of the Royal Canadian Army Medical Corps; Captain George Dixon Morrow of Winnipeg, a member of the Royal Canadian Artillery; twenty-one year old Corporal Francis Gordon Harrison of Victoria, British Columbia, attached to the Army Corps of Military Staff Clerks; twenty-year old Lieutenant Thomas Elvin Mitchell of New Brunswick, of the Carleton and York Regiment, RCIC; twenty-one year old Sub-Lieutenant Edward Gorton Robbins of Victoria, serving in the Royal Canadian Navy. A sixth casualty on that date was John Robert Townshend of London, Ontario, a captain in the Royal Canadian Artillery, who was buried in Bonamargy Cemetery in County Antrim. What, tragically, they had in common was that they were all journeying from Halifax, Nova Scotia, to Liverpool in the troopship S.S. *Nerissa* ,when, as described earlier, she was torpedoed and sunk with the loss of 207 of a complement of 287. Thereafter, their ways parted, being washed ashore in different places and buried in separate cemeteries.

Thomas Elvin Mitchell's body was discovered by local man Anthony Dixon, at 8 o'clock on the morning of 23 May at Aughadoon, Belmullet, and was

buried in Kilcommon Erris Cemetery.[5] George Morrow was found beached at Renvyle, four days later, by local man Padraig Flaherty, and next day was laid to rest in Ballinakill St. Thomas Church of Ireland Churchyard, Moyard:[6] here he is permanently remembered with the inscription:

> *Until the day break and*
> *the shadows fade away.*

Duncan Bell was located at 7pm on 6 July at Carntullagh Head, near Killybegs Harbour. Initially identified, mistakenly, as a Sergeant Wilson of Toronto, he was interred in Killybegs Catholic Cemetery, on its highest point overlooking the water.[7] Not too far away, Edward Gorton Robbins was cast up at Dunkineely on 5 July, and was laid to rest in secluded and historic Killaghtee. There was a sad sequel to this: his parents back home in Oak Bay, Victoria, had been supplied by the Canadian High Commission in Dublin, via Ottawa, with all available information as to his finding and burial; this notwithstanding, three years later, and out of the blue, they began inquiring whether religious services had been provided at his interment. As High Commission First Secretary, Garland, remarked: 'I suspect that some busybody has been telling the parents that Robbins was thrown into a pauper's grave'. As it transpired, the local rector, Canon Steele and the local

Catholic curate, Fr Joseph Kelly, had officiated together at the burial.[8]

Francis Harrison – 'Gordon' to his family – had been a talented pianist and an active participant in his community, a server in his local St. Peter's Anglican Church in Regina. He was only twenty when he left his work with the Canadian Colonization Association, to enlist. He had entrained at Regina on 17 April 1941 for overseas service; three days later, he embarked on the *Nerissa* for his first and its last voyage. His remains were washed ashore at Enniscrone on 26 May and buried in Easkey, Roslea Cemetery, County Sligo.[9] In all, eighty-three Canadian servicemen lost their lives in the sinking of the *Nerissa*, along with eleven American aircraft-ferry pilots and three RAF pilots of the British Commonwealth Air Training Programme: one of these was Navy Commander A.G. Weir, already mentioned in an earlier chapter, and, buried close by, the young Thomas Elvin Mitchell.[10] In addition, a further forty-three individuals, including crew members, perished.[11]

Later that year, on 24 October 1941, in an air crash off the Cork coast at Schull, Sergeant Douglas Woodman of Ontario was apparently the only survivor, but not for long: badly injured, he was removed to the military hospital at Mallow

RIGHT
The war grave of
Canadian Corporal,
Duncan Bell, Killybegs
Catholic Cemetery, Co.
Donegal, lost on Nerissa.

where he died four days later. Full military honours were accorded when his coffin, draped with the Union Jack and carried by Irish Army pall-bearers, led by the No.2 Army Band, was taken in procession for burial in Goold's Hill Cemetery, Mallow. He was laid to rest there in the presence, among others, of a UK Representative, acting for Sir John Maffey; Edward Garland representing the Canadian High Commission; Captain Richard St. John Colthurst representing the British Army, and Commandant Quigley representing the Chief of Staff of the Irish Army.[12]

In the following year, another Canadian airman came down, off the Cork coast: one of a crew of three, Pilot Sergeant Dudley Newlove of Islington, Ontario, was killed on 20 April 1942. He was found floating fifteen yards off shore, seven miles west of Bantry, over a month later, at 3 o'clock in the afternoon of 28 May. Months afterwards, enquiries came from Canada concerning some personal effects, specifically a wrist-watch or bracelet, apart from a ring which had been secured and sent home: as for the missing watch, the man who coffined the remains, Jeremiah Tisdell, confirmed to the authorities that one arm had been missing when the remains had been found.[13] Sergeant Newlove was laid to rest in Bantry Abbey, overlooking Bantry Bay and Whiddy Island, close

by the German graves. A maintenance agreement was signed as early as October 1942 and a standard, Canadian, temporary wooden cross was erected on 13 November. Inspections every year from 1944 to 1949 reported its being in good order, although a local woman in correspondence with Newlove's mother cast doubt on this at the end of the 1940s: in response, further inspections gave categoric assurances that the grave was still in good condition.[14] It probably got even more attention than most, since a local man, George Cooke, took a personal interest in it, maintaining the cross and surroundings: then, in 1953, it secured its permanent headstone.

Three years after Robbins's burial, another Canadian airman's burial gave rise to concerns over religion. On 11 March 1944, Air Gunner Ivor Smithson of the Royal Canadian Air Force was killed in a plane crash near the Irish coast. It was not until 9 July that his body was found at Derrygimbla, off the Galway coast, near Clifden. With local Catholic curate, Fr. Thomas Martin, officiating, his remains were laid to rest in the remote Ballyconneely Catholic Cemetery, his plot in a corner of the graveyard being within yards of the sea. Garland expressed concerns to William Warnock of External Affairs at this burial in a Catholic cemetery: *'the deceased might very well have been of non-Catholic*

faith', he remarked, adding that this *'might not be well-received by the late I. L. Smithson's bereaved relatives and friends in Canada'.*

Garland held off informing Ottawa of the burial until it could be ascertained 'as to whether a Protestant clergyman as well as a Catholic priest might have attended at the burial'. In a memorandum, Warnock commented: 'We shall have to watch the religious issue in any future Canadian cases'.[15] Not that there were many more such burials in the jurisdiction thereafter: no such problems appear to have arisen with the burial of Richard Irvine in Mount Jerome, following his death in February 1945, or of Michael Joseph McDermott in Kilgobbin, Co. Dublin, following his death on 5 August in the same year.

However, not all Canadian servicemen who died in or were washed ashore in the jurisdiction were actually buried there. Three instances suffice. Flight Lieutenant James Constabaris of Vancouver, a Royal Canadian Air Force Officer working with RAF Ferry Command, in Dorval, Quebec, was killed on 23 May 1942. He was discovered six days later at Drumanoo, Killybegs. He was a crew member of a plane that crashed into the sea off Lenadoon, County Sligo. On the day after the discovery, his remains were handed over to RAF officers at Pettigo;

he was brought across the border and buried in Irvinestown Church of Ireland Churchyard.[16] Similarly, Pilot Officer Frederick Greenwood of Vancouver was killed on 6 September 1944. Twenty days later, Henry Doherty of Carrickabraghey, near Clonmany, Inishowen, found the remains: after two days, these were handed over to the British authorities at Bridgend Frontier Post, by military escort; he, too, was laid to rest in Irvinestown.[17] Finally, Stanley Gaudin of Toronto, a Canadian Air Force pilot flying with 172 RAF Squadron, was killed on 5 October 1944 when his plane crashed in Galway Bay, five others surviving. His remains and personal effects, including cross, medal and Bible, were also handed over to the British authorities; he was buried in Drumachose Church of Ireland Churchyard, commemorated there with twenty-five others of the 1939-1945 War.[18]

What determined whether dead Canadian military personnel were handed over or buried locally is not clear. It cannot have been a matter of policy, since the majority were not handed over, nor a matter of proximity to, versus distance from, the border, given that Gaudin was found in Galway. It may have been at the wish of next of kin but, in some cases, the period between identification in Éire and transfer to

Northern Ireland would hardly have allowed for this. Whatever it may have been, it did not apply to the only known case of a Second World War Canadian, not a member of the fighting forces, who is buried here. James Sorley Craig was a Radio Officer of the Merchant Navy, serving on the Belgian-registered *Ville de Gand*. When the 7,500-ton steamship, en route from Liverpool to New York, was sunk on 18 August 1940 by *U-48*, 200 miles west of Ireland, he became the first Canadian casualty of the 1939-1945 War to be buried in Éire. Captain Raoul Carlier and fourteen crew out of fifty-three lost their lives. Of these, the only identified body to drift ashore was Craig's. The twenty-two year old from Ottawa was found at 2.30 on the morning of 24 September, almost two months later, at Ballyliffin, Clonmany: in one pocket, eleven snapshots of a young woman; in another, photographs and certificates of his own, and a letter from his girlfriend. Buried in Carndonagh Workhouse Graveyard on that same day, in a grave marked by an iron cross bearing his name, he was assumed to have been a member of the Canadian Merchant Navy. The Canadian authorities requested a photograph of his grave, whenever it would have its standard Canadian wooden cross erected – which actually replaced the iron cross on 13 June 1942 – exactly a month before Garland at the Canadian High

Commission requested Chettle at the IWGC to ensure the grave was marked.[19] A year after the war's end, although the cross was plumb and clean, the grave itself was overgrown with grass and weeds – a state of affairs that required redress, which came, but not for quite some time.[20]

Australians and New Zealanders:

When it came to the commemoration of Australian and New Zealand Forces' personnel, the situation was far different. Commonwealth War Grave Commission and OPW records together reveal the names of only nineteen Australian and five New Zealand military personnel of the First War buried in the jurisdiction, and for the Second World War, no serving Australian and only one serving member of a New Zealand unit.

There is one member of the Australian military buried here in the wake of the Second War, and it constitutes an unusual case. Gunner James Winters, a Charleville man and a veteran of the 1st Brigade Australian Field Artillery, died on 23 March 1956 and was laid to rest in Charleville (Holy Cross) Cemetery, County Cork. The IWGC asked the OPW to erect a standard headstone over his grave, even though his death occurred almost nine years after the terminal date of 31 December 1947. The Australian Government had

requested that his grave be so honoured, on the basis that its own Department of Repatriation accepted that Winters' death was attributable to his war service. In such cases, apparently, the Australian Government paid for the supply and erection of a Commission headstone and for the maintenance of the grave; in Winters' case the memorial was in place by May of 1958.[21]

The sole Second World War New Zealand Forces' member commemorated here is Air Gunner, Sergeant Edward McCord of the Royal New Zealand Air Force, who died, aged twenty-six, on 15 October 1942. A native of Longford, Edward was second in a family of eight who were born and grew up in Aughintemple House. In the late 1930s he and his older brother Charles had emigrated to New Zealand where they worked at farming near Dunedin. They both joined up there, Charles joining the New Zealand Army, and Edward entering its Air Force as a wireless operator. He was sent to Canada for training and thence to the UK, where he died in a plane crash over London on a night flight where he had substituted for the regular crew member. His remains were brought home to Edgeworthstown by train and laid to rest in Ardagh Cemetery.[22]

Americans:

Unlike the Canadians, the Americans, as a matter of policy and practice, exhumed their dead and generally repatriated them to the United States or, alternatively, to central cemeteries such as the US Military Cemetery, Cambridge, or to Brookwood, outside London. According to George W. Power of the American Graves Registration Command at Cambridge, England, the US War Department was empowered by Congress to remove remains of deceased US Forces' personnel and permission from next of kin was not required.[23] In the case of this jurisdiction, they appear to have been very few indeed. In May 1944, the American Minister in Dublin requested permission for the exhumation and removal to Northern Ireland of four American airmen killed in a plane crash in 1944 and buried in Killarney. Other than these, the only notable case was that of Robert Glenn Smith, another victim of the sinking of *Nerissa* in April 1941. He was one of a number of Air Transport Auxiliary pilots who perished in that calamity. It was 8 July before his remains were washed ashore at Kilronan, on Inishmore, in the Aran Islands. He was a commercial pilot from Warsaw, Indiana, attached to the Air Transport Auxiliary; when found, his sole possessions were a pilot's licence, driver's licence, a snapshot and two five-dollar bills; he was buried in Cill

RIGHT
Ahamlish Cemetery,
Co. Sligo, last resting place
of an unnamed Chinese
member of the S.S. Betty.

Éine graveyard on the next day. It was not until 1947 that arrangements were made for his exhumation and transfer to England, for burial in the American Military Cemetery, Cambridge.[24]

Asians:

Of the various cases of Asian and European casualties of the Second World War whose bodies came to be buried in Ireland, without known exception all were victims of shipping disasters. Among the Asians were the Chinese seamen, Chu Ning Lei and Lum Foey Chuen. The remains of Chu Ning Lei were washed ashore at Creevy, Ballyshannon, County Donegal, on 29 August 1940, but there was no evidence of the circumstances of his death and little of the circumstances of his life, apart from a gold ring, one coin and a character reference from William Noon, master of the S.S. *Yunan.*[25] He was laid to rest in Mullinashea Graveyard, Ballyshannon, on 29 August 1940. On the day after his discovery, another Chinese seafarer was washed up at Cliffoney, County Sligo, with nothing found to aid identification apart from a lifebelt bearing the name S.S. *Betty.* Presumably, the two men were among the thirty out of thirty-four crew of the British-registered *Betty,* torpedoed by *U-59* about thirty-five miles west of Tory Island a fortnight before, on 14 August.

She had made the long journey from Saigon, bound for Liverpool, when she was sunk. This second Merchant Navy man was buried in Ahamlish Cemetery, in the same burial ground as eight other commemorated war dead: but his grave is unmarked and unremembered.

Seaman Chuen was washed ashore at Ballinoulart near Cahore Point, Wexford, on 8 May 1941. The fifty-one year old native of Hong Kong had been in the Merchant Navy, serving in various ships as far back as 1916. The circumstances of his death were not clear and he was buried in Ardamine Cemetery, Courtown, on the day his remains were found. These apart, the north-western Atlantic also claimed the life of fifty-nine year old Arab, Messen Mohamed, who was born in Aden and came ashore at Portnablagh on 28 July 1940. Given the date of the discovery of his remains, he may well have been yet another victim of the fate of the *Arandora Star.* Whatever the circumstance, and although a British Colonial-registered Merchant Navy man, no Commonwealth headstone marks his burial place in the graveyard near Dunfanaghy.[26] Among other tragic cases was that of ship's cook C. Valu of Ceylon. He was one of four known victims of the loss of *Nailsea Lass,* on 24 February 1941. The 4,000-ton British freighter was homeward bound from Calcutta and Cape Town when

torpedoed by *U-48*, sixty miles west of Fastnet. Valu was still alive when found, but passed away in the local Garda Station. All four, J. Lee, J. Roberts, T. Bayley and Valu, were buried just outside the walls of Derrynane Catholic Cemetery.[27]

Europeans:

Like the Asians, the European casualties of the Second World War buried in Ireland were, and are, largely unremembered or certainly uncommemorated. Typical of the sinking of European trading vessels and their passengers was that of the 2,500-ton Dutch steamship, *Stolwyck*, with the loss of ten of its twenty-eight crew, off Inishdooey Island, North Donegal: in this case, however, not due to attack, but to the ship's running aground on 7 December 1940. Three of the lost crew were washed ashore at Falcarragh on 12 December and buried in Killult.[28] In these cases and in that of the death of Dutch seaman Nobel, found floating near the shore at Dundeady and buried in Rathberry Burial Ground, Castlefreke, on 12 April 1941, the Irish authorities decided that they were not war graves and were not marked as such. If the Dutch authorities had confirmed to the contrary, External Affairs and the OPW would have undertaken their marking and maintenance.[29]

Among known Belgians, the earliest identified victim was Florant Ceulemans, who was found at Bunaninver on the Donegal coast, on 14 September 1940. He was buried in the 'Strangers' Plot' of Magheragallon Catholic Cemetery.[30] Nothing is certain of his final circumstances and, given the length of time between death and coming ashore in many instances, he could have been a crewman lost from *Mohamed Ali El Kebir*, on 7 August, *Upwey Grange* on 8 August, or *Dunvegan Castle* on 28 August 1940. No such uncertainty as to origin, but anonymity as to names attaches to two Belgians found dead in a lifeboat at Moneypoint, County Clare, on 25-26 March 1941; never identified, they had been aboard the *Adolphe Urban* out of Bruges.[31] They were interred in Kilrush Shanakyle Cemetery, unmarked.

Among Europeans whose graves in Ireland were to be recognised as war graves and to be marked by Commonwealth War Grave headstones were those of one Spaniard, and separately, three Norwegians. The Spaniard was Alfonso Pimentil, bosun on the S.S. *Cortes*, in convoy en route from Lisbon to Liverpool when sunk, with unknown losses, in the Finisterre (now Fitzroy) sea area, by *U-203*, on 26 September 1941. Pimentil was found, two weeks later, on the west coast and

was laid to rest in Clifden (Ard Bear) Cemetery, Galway. This is its only Second World War grave; initially unmarked, it later became the subject of difficulty in the 1950s when there was disagreement as to its correct location.[32] As for the first of the Norwegians: on 19 October 1941, seven miles south-east of the Tuskar Rock, the Norwegian S.S. *Rask* was attacked by German aircraft and sunk. Of the eight aboard who were killed, three were recovered: twenty-two year old Englishman, John Stanley, the gunner; forty-five year old Norwegian sailor, Otto Lie, and eighteen-year old mess-boy from Cumberland, Patrick Tierney. The bodies of Tierney and Stanley were picked from the sea by the S.S. *Wallace* and landed at Rosslare on 21 October. According to information supplied by External Affairs to the Norwegian Consul, all three were buried together in St. Ibar's, Crosstown: commemorated there to this day, Otto Lie's grave is marked by the distinctive Norwegian war grave headstone.[33]

The second of the Norwegians was Captain Hans Gullestad of the motorship *Hidlefjord*. The vessel was in convoy, homeward bound from Bermuda, when attacked by German aircraft, ten miles from the Smalls Lighthouse, west of St. David's Head. Three German fighter planes were involved, the first killing the helmsman,

Steffen Hushovd. It then dropped two bombs, setting fire to the ship. Of two lifeboats, only one got away, the other catching fire. Only four survived from a crew of twenty-seven Norwegians, five South Africans, two Australians and one Briton. *The Hidlefjord* drifted west, ablaze, before disappearing off Tuskar Rock on the next day, along with another stricken vessel of that convoy, the British-registered *San Conrado*. It was two months before the remains of Hans Gullestad came ashore at Cullenstown Strand, on 25 June 1941.[34] He was laid to rest in the old graveyard at Craigue Little, Duncormick, a wooden cross bearing his name, until the question of permanent commemoration arose – not without its own mishaps.[35]

The third and final case was that of Norwegian Air Force Pilot, Nils Bjorn Rasmussen. He was working for RAF Ferry Command out of Dorval, Quebec, and was delivering a Boston Bomber aircraft from Newfoundland to Britain. He made a forced landing at Tulladoohy, five miles west of Crossmolina, at 6.30 on the evening of 25 October 1942. On landing, the plane capsized and Captain Rasmussen was trapped underneath: he was dead when extricated from the wreckage. From personal effects, he appeared to have been a Catholic; consequently, a requiem mass was held for him in Crossmolina on 27 October

NEAR LEFT
The S.S. Rask.

FAR LEFT
The war grave of Nor-
wegian RAF pilot, Nils
Rasmusssen, Kilmurray
Cemetery, Co. Mayo.

1942, before his remains were escorted, with full military honours, to his burial in Kilmurray Cemetery. Here the local undertaker erected a temporary wooden cross in 1943, at which time local caretaker, John Gallagher, entered into an agreement to maintain his grave.[36] It was not until 1961, however, that the Norwegians arranged with the OPW for the provision of the permanent headstone which still marks his grave to this day.[37]

Right
Renvyle Catholic Cemetery,
Co. Galway.

*And sleep at last
Among the fields of home*

*Thomas Shannon, Leading Signalman
H.M.S. "Drake"
17 May 1942*

Sligo Cemetery

Chapter 18

The Quest for a New Accord, 1941-1950

As the war casualties mounted and the grim succession of burials proceeded, the search for agreement on the issues of temporary and permanent marking, and on the protocols of communication, acquired an urgency from 1941, which had been missing from September 1939. The immediate, if less difficult, issue was that of the temporary marking of the graves of the recent dead. Local authorities might provide a reasonable temporary marking, but in most cases they did not, and resented the fact, in the first place, that the cost of burials fell on their straitened budgets. This issue of burial costs took External Affairs by surprise so that, in August 1941, it had to advise Finance:

It is in accordance with international custom for the State within whose territory members of belligerent forces are interred to assume responsibility for the cost of the burial of such persons, and accordingly…request that the sanction of the Minister for Finance may be conveyed for the defraying of such expenditure…from State funds.[1]

They could not yet estimate what the ultimate costs would be, but since September 1939, some 150 burials had taken place, at £4 per burial and approximately £5 per inquest. The local authority in Donegal, for one, was baulking at the cost of these burials, and indeed, of the preceding inquests,

so much so that, with frequency of bodies being washed ashore rising, and the resultant costs and burdens falling unequally on the coastal counties of the North West, the decision was taken to dispense with coroners' inquests, and to recognise instead the authority of a local doctor's examination as sufficient for proceeding with burials, in cases of bodies washed ashore.[2]

Temporary wooden crosses:
In January 1941 the Government decided that it would cover the cost of the temporary marking of these graves and their maintenance, and further decided that temporary wooden crosses for this purpose should be 'uniform' for all belligerents – a pious hope in one respect, as it transpired.[3] External Affairs' request for drawings of those then being used by the British was speedily responded to, Antrobus enclosing samples to Boland early in January.[4] The British design bore the monogram of the Imperial War Graves Commission, surmounted by the Crown. The prospect of crowns on crosses rekindling the ire of councillors in Clare on the one hand, or the spectacle of swastikas on crosses in country churchyards on the other, did not bear contemplation. Thinking back to 1941, from his position as Ambassador to the

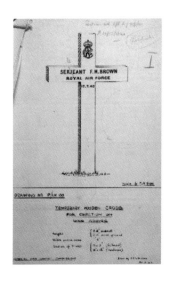

United Kingdom in 1950, Boland, in a telegram to External Affairs, put it thus:

As a matter of history it may interest you to know that when the decision about regimental badges was deferred in 1941, the reason was not so much the difficulties which had previously arisen in Sligo and Clare, as the fact that whatever we did for the British at that time would have had also to be done for the Germans, and possible difficulty was anticipated about putting the Swastika on German graves, particularly as most of them would have been in Protestant graveyards... The temporary wooden crosses used by the Imperial War Graves Commission elsewhere bear the appropriate regimental badges stencilled at the top. The British agreed that these should be omitted from the wooden crosses erected by our Board of Works, but whether we told them at the time our reason for wanting them omitted, I cannot remember.[5]

In the event, the OPW's Principal Architect, John Fairweather, came up with a design bearing the monogram 'OPW Éire' which deValera as Minister for External Affairs agreed would be preferable – appropriately Celtic, patriotic and proprietary, it could have been a triumph of trade-marking.[6] As against this, the Assistant Secretary in External Affairs complained 'couldn't we suggest something more inspiring than OPW?'[7] Despite this, even the UK Office in Dublin was content, Norman Archer

advising the Dominions Office that the addition of the OPW monogram 'will, no doubt, be a further safeguard against defacement and it is to be hoped that no one will raise political objections to the design'.[8]

The Germans:

In the mission to memorialise the war dead, it was the Germans who were quickest to provide the verifications required for the marking of the graves and the erection of temporary wooden crosses. By August 1941 there were over thirty graves of German airmen, in places as far apart as Kenmare and Kilmuckridge. Clearly pressed for progress by the German authorities, Boland in External Affairs impatiently inquired of the OPW Secretary, in December 1941, whether any of the crosses had yet been erected over these graves – 'the first of these lists was furnished to you about five months ago'.[9] In fact, by late January, all thirty-three of these crosses had been erected, painted in 'German field grey', with white lettering. Because the Germans had been quickest off the mark, theirs was the colour that went on the first sample crosses that the contractors were preparing for the OPW. The Canadians were next with the verifications for their six notified war dead to the end of 1941. However, when their crosses were inspected at the OPW by High Commissioner John Kearney, he was apoplectic that they were painted dark grey as for the Germans. After a very hasty visit to External Affairs, he came away placated at their quickly undertaking that all the British Commonwealth and Allied temporary crosses would be painted white with black lettering.[10]

The Canadians:

As with the Germans, the Canadian authorities were also pressing for the speedy marking of their war graves and were insistent on cross inscriptions that were in fact larger than those already provided for the Germans and those intended for the British.[11] While the process of erecting the Canadian crosses went smoothly, for the various authorities in Dublin, whether Canadian, External Affairs or OPW Head Office, it appeared to go slowly. Nolan in External Affairs had sent a list of six Canadian war dead to the OPW in late December 1941. These were Lieutenant Thomas E. Mitchell in Belmullet Church of Ireland Cemetery, Mayo; Corporal Francis G. Harrison in Easkey Cemetery, Sligo; Corporal Duncan Bell in Killybegs Catholic Cemetery, Donegal; Captain George D. Morrow in Ballinakill Protestant Cemetery, Letterfrack, Galway; Sub-Lieutenant Edward G.

Robbins in Baile na Gréine Cemetery, Dunkineely, Donegal; and Sergeant Douglas A. Woodman in Mallow, Cork. Nolan asked to be notified when the crosses had been erected.[12]

In the case of the grave of Thomas Elvin Mitchell in Belmullet, the OPW appeared to experience difficulties in getting the job completed. Their local officer, C. P. Kenna of Castlebar, visited the grave on 26 January. He got the consent of the local rector, Canon Rogers, on the same day, for the erection of a wooden cross,[13] and a maintenance agreement between Canon Rogers and the OPW was in place in February. The providers, Thomas Dockrell, despatched the six Canadian crosses by rail in early March and Brandon at OPW Head Office had, at that same time, instructed Kenna to locate suitable contractors for their erection.[14] Then came delays: several letters issued from an impatient Brandon to Kenna over March and April, culminating in a strident request to know why there had been no replies, not even to a telegram of 24 April – 'You were in Belmullet between 16 and 24 April, so did you inspect war graves then? Have all the crosses been erected? If not, what action are you taking to expedite?' Within ten days, Kenna reported that Mitchell's grave was in good order with the cross duly erected.[15] Having regard to the fact that Nolan in

BELOW
OPW 1929 drawing, template for Naval Badge.

External Affairs had not supplied the texts for the six inscriptions to the OPW until 14 February, and that the crosses had not arrived in Castlebar until early March, the delay was hardly culpable. At the mercy of contractors who, in turn, were at the mercy of petrol rationing and long distances, as was Kenna in Castlebar, the latter hardly warranted hectoring over a job completed in early May 1942.

Crosses for the British war dead:

As for the crosses on war graves of members of the British Forces, this was a larger challenge, their numbers far exceeding those of other Allied or German military. By March 1941 there had already been around 200 British war dead burials in Éire, apart from the burials of civilians washed ashore.[16] In August 1941 Boland had alerted Nolan to complaints he had received from Archer of the UK Office in Dublin, and indeed from the German Legation, about the poor state of maintenance of these comparatively recent war graves. He suggested that Nolan might send a note to the OPW. Nolan was not impressed:

I am afraid, so far as the British are concerned, the neglected condition of their war graves is entirely their own fault. They have not yet furnished us with the necessary details for the

Office of Public Works in regard to a single one of their graves, and until they do so, the Office of Public Works cannot undertake the maintenance of the graves for the simple reason that they don't know where the graves are until they receive official confirmation from us that it is a belligerent war grave, to which the Government decision applies, and we cannot give them the necessary particulars until we receive the lists from the Legations concerned.

As for the German graves, having queried the OPW, Veale assured Nolan on 26 August that the OPW 'are doing their best to get things moving', but Nolan himself confided to Boland, 'I seem to detect an undertone of "festina lente" in the OPW reply'.[17] By March 1942 this matter with the British was still at issue. Archer gingerly offered a tentative suggestion: the British Legation might arrange for temporary preliminary maintenance of their war graves, as he understood the Germans were apparently doing. Nolan's admission of being unaware that the Germans were so doing led him to a characteristic expostulation:

If Mr Archer was anxious to have the British war graves maintained, 'with as little delay as possible' the best way is for him to have pressure brought to bear on the Imperial War Graves Commission with a view to getting them to supply us with the necessary data more rapidly…Why the British cannot deal with

*BELOW
OPW 1930 drawing, template for Royal Regiment of Artillery Badge.*

*these matters with at least the same degree
of dispatch as the Germans passes my
comprehension; they are always raising this,
that, or the other point, wasting their time and
our own – and all over what is, in the main, a
perfectly straightforward routine job.*[18]

All of this, however, originating
in concern over the provision of
temporary crosses, was part of a
wider issue that bedevilled the Irish
and British authorities in the quest for
a new agreement – the old issue of
communication.

The OPW shows reluctance:

The Irish Government decision to
make an arrangement similar to that
of 1926, except that the British and
other belligerents would pay for any
permanent memorials, was conveyed to
the British on 1 February 1941. Their
own proposal to send an IWGC Officer
– Harry Chettle as it turned out – to
discuss details, was welcome in Dublin,
but the Dominions Office was warned by
Antrobus:

*there may be some question of not putting on
permanent headstones the badges of the regiment,
having regard to the possibility that some ill-
disposed persons might be encouraged to deface
the headstones. Colonel Chettle will, no doubt, be
fully briefed on this point, which will certainly
be raised.*[19]

As to why the Irish Government insisted
that the British (and other belligerents)
pay for permanent headstones, Boland
had explained that the country 'might
become a theatre of war and that the
expense would then be very large'. It
was a decision that appeared to cause no
dismay, with the IWGC expressing their
'great satisfaction' at the overall decision
of the Irish authorities, and were now
keen to send Colonel Chettle over to
Dublin 'at the earliest opportunity'. The
visit, and resulting conference at the
OPW on 18 March, dealt largely with
administrative minutiae, but there were
a few areas of disagreement. Chettle
informed his hosts that the functions
of the IWGC in relation to British
Merchant Navy men had been extended
to all British civilians who died as a result
of the war. While the IWGC had yet
made no decision whether or not such
victims were to be deemed entitled to
IWGC headstones, the Commission was
now responsible for the identification
and registration of their places of
burial. The OPW Secretary, Fagan,
made it clear, in response, that such war
casualties did not fall within the terms
of the Government's January 1941
decision, and the OPW, though willing to
supply the Commission with particulars
of such civilians, was not prepared to
accept responsibility for them, unless a
new decision in this regard was taken by
the Government. Chettle countered by

pointing out that the IWGC function in respect of civilians applied to the graves of Irish citizens in Britain, mentioning that of 700 deaths from air raids on Coventry, some 400 of the victims were Irish citizens. Despite this, Fagan of the OPW continued to take a relatively hard line. When Chettle suggested that, as in the past, Vesper might return to be seconded to the OPW, Fagan and Boland demurred and suggested instead that he be attached to the UK Office under the British Representative, Sir John Maffey. There was nothing personal about this: it was logical within the context of Irish neutrality, and Antrobus conceded that this was 'probably the correct view'. It also had the added advantage that the OPW could decline responsibility for collecting the details of the identities and burial locations of the war dead. Fagan was adamant that either External Affairs or the IWGC would marshal these particulars for transmission in lists to the OPW for the purpose of temporary marking and maintenance.

It was agreed, as in the past, that all communication about war graves with members of the public living in Éire would be conducted by the Irish Government, and for those living in the UK it would be conducted by the Commission. It was further agreed that the question of permanent headstones – and, by extension, therefore, the

question of regimental badges – would be left until the war had ended.

Finally, it was agreed between the Irish spokesmen present that there was a need for an interdepartmental conference of External Affairs, Justice, Local Government and the OPW to work out internal procedures.[20]

The interdepartmental conference took place in the Department of External Affairs, on 30 April 1941, eighteen months and more than 350 burials after the war had begun. It was called to work out the administrative arrangements consequent upon the Government decision of January, to enable the OPW 'to proceed with the erection of temporary wooden crosses'. In their very first decision Fagan got what the OPW wanted: that External Affairs would collect information on the deaths from the various foreign legations in Dublin, pass them on to Local Government and Justice for verification and locations, the completed lists to be forwarded to the OPW for the erection of crosses. Wherever there might be a doubt as to whether a grave was a war grave or not, the matter would be left to External Affairs to decide.[21]

Confusion abounding:

Following on this, the very next day Boland notified Antrobus of these arrangements and suggested that the IWGC 'might pass on direct to the Office of Public Works here the particulars of the graves that are to be maintained and temporarily marked by us'. This was a curious suggestion underlined by its recipients and annotated 'not direct – through External Affairs'[22] It was all the more curious in that, as early as 16 April, the Dominions Office had advised Antrobus in Dublin that they saw 'no objection to the Commission's communicating direct with the Éire Department of Public Works'.[23] On receipt of Boland's note, the Dominions Office prepared the text of a draft agreement with the Irish Government, along the lines discussed at the April conference:

1. *The Irish Government would supply the UK Representative with the precise details of burials – the names, the cemetery, the exact location within the cemetery – of British and Commonwealth Servicemen and Civilian war dead, for transmission to the IWGC.*

2. *The IWGC in turn would supply the OPW with the details for inscription on the crosses, including those for the graves of Merchant Navy men.*

3. *The OPW would periodically notify the IWGC of the erection of these crosses.*

4. *The Éire Government desires that communications between the OPW and the IWGC should pass through the Offices of External Affairs and the UK Representative.*

5. *The question of permanent marking is deferred for future consideration.*

6. *The Irish Government would secure perpetuity for British Service graves and maintain them in good order.*

An item about the Irish Government corresponding with residents in Éire and the British Government corresponding with those in Great Britain and Northern Ireland was carelessly composed, in that it made no reference to residents outside either jurisdiction.[24] Nolan's critique of the document, on 12 May 1941, picked up on this point, insisting that the Irish Government would correspond with all next-of-kin outside the United Kingdom and, on the question of communication between the IWGC and the OPW going through External Affairs and the UK Office in Dublin, 'it is Mr Antrobus and not me who desires this somewhat roundabout channel of communication'.[25] This must have been a misconception on Nolan's part: the co-operating parties were still at cross purposes when, in

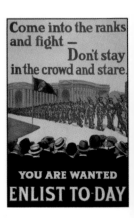

early June 1941, a Dominions Office official, Kimbar, informed the IWGC that the Irish Government preferred that communications between the IWGC and the Éire Department of Public Works should not be direct but should pass via the Éire Department of External Affairs and the UK Representative's Office.[26] The cross purposes grew in complexity in the course of June: Ware was naturally unhappy at this indirect method of communicating, but Stephenson, the Undersecretary of State, assured him that

it is, of course, part of a general policy of the Éire Authorities to centralise in the External Affairs Department all communications with outside Governmental Authorities. If, however, you feel it undesirable that this circuitous channel should be used, we are quite prepared to ask Archer, who has succeeded Antrobus, to endeavour to persuade the Éire authorities to modify their request.[27]

All of this is slightly bizarre in light of a note from Boland to Fagan on 19 June:

the British people here have suggested that correspondence between the IWGC and yourselves should pass through the British Representative's Office and this Department. Although this roundabout channel is a bit of a nuisance, we have told them that we will agree to its adoption.[28]

It would appear that the cross purposes had been caused on the Irish side: Fabian Ware had contacted Dulanty, the Irish Representative in London, to urge the desirability of direct communication between the IWGC and the OPW. On being apprised of this, Boland told Archer of the UK's Dublin Office, on 31 October 1941, that External Affairs was 'now ready to agree the direct contact desired by Sir Fabian', and re-iterated that, if the IWGC wanted one of their officers seconded to Dublin, it were better done by attachment to the UK Representative's Office and not to the OPW. However, on balance, both sides thought the best solution might well lie in the IWGC's sending their officer on occasional visits rather than by taking up residence in the UK Office.[29]

Boland, in November 1941, now clarified matters for Dulanty, regarding Ware's wish for direct communication. That wish was the result of a misapprehension:

There is no objection to the principle of direct correspondence between the two bodies on our part, the OPW's part or the British Legation's part. The difficulty is that the OPW's role is a very limited one and very different from when Captain Vesper was here some years ago.

He went on to explain that the OPW had nothing to do with any particular grave until notified by External Affairs and they were, as regards war graves, not in the business of seeking particulars, establishing identities or securing their recognition as war graves this time around. In practice, this burden now fell on External Affairs as 'the co-ordinators in the whole thing', and he concluded bluntly: 'The Office of Public Works are rigidly opposed to any extension of their present limited role'. External Affairs still would not object if the IWGC wanted to send a man over for a couple of months, and not even to such an officer's being then in direct contact with the various offices, 'but he would have to be attached to Sir John Maffey's Office and not to any Irish Government Department'.[30] This, however, as the UK Dublin Office confided to London, was exactly what Sir John Maffey did not want.[31]

On being presented with Boland's clarification and his rider that, of course, the Irish authorities wished to simplify procedures, the IWGC now sent Colonel Chettle to Dulanty in mid-November with some suggestions that, unintentionally, caused a further rising of hackles at Iveagh House. Fully accepting the central co-ordinating role of External Affairs, Chettle suggested by way of improved procedures, that External Affairs might in future specify the precise location of war graves when furnishing particulars to

the UK Representative's Office, and that if the War Graves Commission decided that a particular grave came within their ambit, they would 'like to communicate the necessary instructions in respect of the grave, direct to the OPW'. The suggestions, well meant, were unfortunate. As External Affairs informed Dulanty, for the past six months they had been already providing the precise locations to the UK Office. As for the IWGC deciding whether a particular grave in Ireland was a war grave of the present conflict or not,

First and foremost it is for us, not for the Imperial War Graves Commission, to decide whether a particular grave is covered by the Government's decision … the instructions to the Office of Public Works in the matter must, consequently, be given by us and not by the Imperial War Graves Commission.[32]

Chettle sought to repair the damage with a letter to 'Johnnie' Belton, Secretary of the Irish High Commission in London. The Colonel was glad to hear that External Affairs had been providing precise locations for war graves since 1941, and he went on to propose a simple way of communication that would recognise the central and deciding role of External Affairs.[33] The critical initiative, however, in trying to restore harmony was taken by Norman Archer, the First Secretary, British

Representative's Office in Dublin: on 7 January 1942 he advised the Dominions Office that the IWGC should send an official to try to 'iron things out'

Re-enter Vesper:

That task fell to the valiant Vesper, working at the time out of Belfast as the IWGC's Inspector for the Northern Ireland District. On instructions, he called on Archer, on Tuesday 20 January, for a briefing, and renewed acquaintance with Veale at the OPW that afternoon. As ever, Vesper was concerned at not exceeding his brief, believing that he was simply ordered by the IWGC to discuss some practical issues with the OPW. However, following a flurry of phone calls between Archer in Dublin, the Dominions Office, the IWGC headquarters in London and External Affairs, Boland invited Vesper, with Archer, for discussions at Iveagh House. He was authorised to go beyond his original brief and to assist 'in any question that arose'. Boland who was au fait with Vesper's earlier work in Dublin, told him that he felt 'we could settle any outstanding questions'. He confided to Vesper and Archer that, 'contrary to the views of his subordinates', he wanted to set up a small committee on war graves, a kind of 'clearing house' between the IWGC and the OPW and served by a secretary who would act as liaison. When Archer mentioned that Vesper was stationed in Northern Ireland and that he could be invited down from time to time to assist this committee, at its request, Boland 'jumped at the suggestion' to use Vesper in an advisory capacity, and asked him to meet Nolan for a discussion on outstanding questions.

When Vesper met Nolan he found indeed that, in regard to Boland's suggestion for a small working committee,

he seemed to take a peculiarly definite stand in opposition, said it might be an advantage if the UK Representative was 'cut out', and I knew that Mr Archer (unlike Mr Antrobus) was agreeable to this.

Archer was well pleased with the way the two meetings had gone and said he would ask Boland to put up a proposal that Nolan, the External Affairs working specialist on war graves, be the liaison, and that the committee idea be dispensed with and that Vesper might come down to advise and assist as required.[34]

Two days later, a clearly gratified Nolan, in a long letter to Chettle, agreed, as the most satisfactory working arrangement, that he, as the liaison, would now communicate directly with Chettle himself rather than Nolan going through the UK's Dublin Office and Chettle going through the Dominions Office. Between them they would exchange and finalise verification details: that when External Affairs confirmed that a given grave was a war grave within the Irish Government's terms, a list would be supplied to the OPW for temporary marking.[35]

With an almost audible sigh of relief, Norman Archer confessed to Boland that 'this would be a great step forward. I feel sure that the War Graves Commission should welcome this'.[36] How right he was: Chettle, in a letter to Nolan at the end of January, enclosing a list of twenty nine more war dead in Donegal, remarked that he had consulted Fabian Ware ,'and we agree the procedure now proposed. May I add my personal thanks for your readiness to meet our point of view'. Vesper, in turn, was gratified that the Commission considered 'his recent visit to Éire a success'.[37] Despite the euphoria, and meeting of minds, he was to find Nolan no easy touch. On Vesper's first Dublin visit to Nolan after this, on 15 April 1942, mainly on the gruesome subject of unidentified bodies washed ashore or found at sea – he told Nolan that in the UK they assumed they were British merchant seaman unless there was evidence to the contrary. Nolan would have none of this, and, without evidence,

the Irish would refuse to recognise their burial places as war graves.[38]

More was to follow. Nolan was equally exercised by the fact that the IWGC recognised for war grave status Irish members of the British and Commonwealth Forces who a) died outside of Ireland from wounds or illness contracted as a result of war service and were returned to Ireland for burial and b) such Irish members who, suffering from war-contracted wounds or illness, were sent home on leave to Ireland and died there. Indeed, a supplemental IWGC Charter of 5 March 1940 extended the categories of persons eligible for war grave status as a result of this new world conflict. He gave Vesper clearly to understand that, while the Government would, at its own cost, mark and temporarily maintain the war graves of military and merchant navy men, it would not pay the cost of similarly treating the graves of Irish members of the British and Commonwealth Forces of this war who died inside Ireland or who were brought home for burial. It was prepared to mark and maintain them but only if the IWGC paid for this.[39] Chettle accepted and this was formally agreed in September 1942.[40] At the time of this exchange there were about fifteen such cases of Irish members of the Commonwealth Forces dying and buried in Ireland, and, in his note of

RIGHT
William Warnock,
Department of External
Affairs.

advice to Finance and the OPW on the matter, Nolan was his usual trenchant self:

It was never the intention of the Minister for External Affairs that graves located in this country in the circumstances just indicated should be a charge on public funds...[the decision of the Government was to]... apply only to the graves of such members of the belligerent forces who die in this country while actually engaged in the course of their duties (e.g. airmen) or whose bodies are washed ashore on our coasts. The British Authorities want all British and Dominion war graves to be brought within the scope of our arrangement and it is proposed to inform them that this will be done so long as they cover all expenditure.[41]

At that point some fifty-one British, thirty-five German and six Canadian graves had their temporary crosses, bearing the monogram 'OPW Éire', erected over them. By June 1944 the number of new war graves with temporary crosses had risen to ninety British, forty German and seven Canadian.[42] It may well have been the case, thereafter, that the business ran smoothly enough between the IWGC, External Affairs and the OPW. As Vesper himself was to remark a decade later, very few remains were washed ashore after early 1942 and, as for routine visits to Dublin by him, there were none between April 1942 and 1 December 1943, when he was instructed to call on William Fay at External Affairs – Nolan in the meantime had been moved on to higher office in Iveagh House. His visit found the OPW carrying out the graves maintenance conscientiously and satisfactorily and, as regards the temporary crosses, 'the same excellent standard of work and finish is being maintained'. As for his visit to External Affairs, Fay advised him that 'there was nothing of an urgent nature, and that the arrangement generally was working smoothly'.[43] Vesper's very positive and comprehensive report on this visit found Ware very gratified and hoping that Vesper could make such visits at fixed intervals.[44] However, matters were running so smoothly that there was nothing untoward in 1944. Not until February 1945 – with the prospect of an Allied victory in the West, as the Russians captured Stettin on 2 February and the Americans broke through the Siegfried Line on the 4th, did a new phase begin, or rather, an old phase reassert itself.

'An unsolved, complicated business': In that same month of February 1945, on the question of arrangements for permanent war grave memorials for the fallen of the Second World War, Chettle contacted a new man at Iveagh House, William Warnock, back in

Dublin from his previous posting as Chargé d'Affaires in Berlin. He advised Warnock that the question of 'who should erect permanent headstones was left over in 1941, for future consideration, but it was not contested, so far as my memory of the discussion in Dublin goes, that headstones would be erected'. Apparently, not receiving any substantive reply to this, he announced to Warnock in April 1945 that Vesper hoped to visit Dublin in the early summer to call upon him.[45] Interestingly, upon Vesper's visit, on 27 June, Warnock asked him if the IWGC had as yet formulated any final plans for permanent marking, to which Vesper responded 'it was not yet possible'.[46]

After the War's final end with Japan's unconditional surrender on 14 August 1945, it was a year before the IWGC renewed its active concern for its war graves in Éire. By that stage, both it and the Irish Government were aware of some 420 graves of the War, but the status of the majority as regards responsibility for costs of upkeep was uncertain. There were 90 British Commonwealth War Graves falling within the terms of the Irish Government decision of January 1941. A further 88 fell outside these terms, being the remains of Irish service men and women brought back to Ireland for burial or dying in Ireland. This

left almost 250 – at that point – whose status had yet to be determined and Chettle was now becoming anxious to sound out External Affairs and the OPW as to permanent memorials and maintenance.[47] What followed, however, was a perplexing period of confusion, delays and cross purposes.

Chettle and Vesper visited Dublin in early September 1946. They met Tommy Woods, who was standing in for Nolan's successor, Cremin, at Iveagh House. Having agreed to exchange the most up-to-date lists on some 400 war graves, Chettle then raised the subject of permanent headstones. Chettle was either inadequately briefed, forgetful or disingenuous: when Woods mentioned the Irish understanding that the British authorities would bear the cost of permanent memorials, Chettle seemed taken aback and intimated that the understanding was that the procedure in this matter would be the same as that employed for the graves of the 1914-1918 War, that is, that the Irish Government would shoulder the responsibility for permanently marking these graves.[48]

Woods then produced for them a copy of the External Affairs' letter to Antrobus of 1 February 1941 and an extract from the report of the conference in the OPW of 18 March 1941 – in which

Chettle had participated – and from which report, Woods pointed out, 'it was quite clear that the British authorities were informed of our proposal that they should bear the cost of permanent marking'.

Having settled this point, Woods went on to indicate that External Affairs should like to have something to say on the question 'of the inscription which we would put on the permanent headstone'. Chettle countered by expressing the hope that 'we would find the Commission inscription acceptable in full', but Woods parried with the final remark that it would have 'to be left over for discussion when the question of the erection of the permanent headstones came up'. Chettle, it seems, agreed, but it begged the question why he was at the meeting at all if this main purpose of the meeting could not come up for progress then.[49] On 6 December 1946, he sent to External Affairs a note of his understanding following the early September meeting with Woods, namely, that the Irish Government was not prepared to pay for the 1939-1945 permanent memorials, but were prepared to instruct the OPW to carry out the work for the IWGC on an agency basis, and that 'the Éire Government will agree to the use of the standard Commission headstone'.[50] This was not exactly what Woods had agreed, since he had insisted that External Affairs wanted a say on the nature of the inscriptions.

In Chettle's six-point summary there were two other matters on which he appeared to have entertained premature or plainly incorrect assumptions: the one, that the Irish Government 'would wish to have the services of a Commission Officer to advise in the early stages of the work'; and the other, that while the Irish Government, as in the case of the previous conflict, would correspond with relatives in Éire, the IWGC would do so with relatives in Great Britain, Northern Ireland, 'Canada, Australia and the other Dominions'. The former assumption may have been premature, but the latter was factually erroneous for the First War, and at odds with what the Irish Government had insisted on doing during the course of the Second War. Strangely, despite these major misconceptions on Chettle's part, his memorandum received no response and provoked no reaction.[51]

As Vesper, now retired from his Northern Ireland duties, recollected four years later: 'When we had the matter nearly settled the whole subject seemed to get shelved but some time or other it may come forward again. The whole [sic] is rather an unsolved complicated business.'[52]

At this point an IWGC official, relatively new to war grave dealings with Ireland, entered the story. Edward J. King had Irish connections in Wexford and holidayed in Ireland after the War. In late January 1947, perhaps by way of a prompt to External Affairs for a reply to Chettle's memo, he sent Cruise O'Brien a drawing of the standard IWGC permanent headstone then being erected in various theatres of the recent war. O'Brien duly acknowledged it but without any reference to the Chettle memorandum.[53] Extensive correspondence developed between King and O'Brien over the next six months, but always on questions of specific war victims and their graves, and never once on the policy issues raised by Chettle in his September 1946 visit and his December 1946 memorandum.

In these circumstances, while King was on vacation with his family in Wexford in August 1947, he took the opportunity to write to O'Brien: he asked for an interview to make his acquaintance and to have 'a chat' over a few war grave matters. There is, to date, no detailed account of this meeting at Iveagh House on Wednesday 20 August, but according to King, O'Brien promised 'an early reply' to Chettle's memorandum. None came.[54] In its absence, King now contacted Vesper in October, asking him to visit Dublin to try to secure

confirmation from External Affairs of what Chettle asserted as having been agreed in September 1946. Vesper duly met O'Brien at Iveagh House on 2 and 3 December 1947 and put it directly that the IWGC had 'now reached the position where they wanted to go ahead with the erection of the permanent headstones', were preparing a draft contract, and wanted a decision from the Irish authorities on these distinct points:

a) maintenance of the graves:
   whatever about the cost of erecting permanent headstones, the IWGC had understood that, as in the case of the 1914-1921 war graves, the OPW would maintain and pay the costs thereof. The conference which Chettle and he had had with Woods 'left them in doubt on this point'. O'Brien told him that he too thought that the OPW would pay for the maintenance of the graves.

b) loan of an IWGC officer:
   whether the OPW was going to do the work of construction on an agency basis and, if so, would they need Vesper's services. On this, O'Brien consulted P.S. Carney, the OPW successor to George Fagan as Secretary, and informed Vesper that the OPW would do the work on an agency basis but that Vesper's services would not be needed;

THE QUEST FOR A NEW ACCORD, 1941-1950

c) regimental badges on permanent headstones:
   here, coming to the heart of the matter, Vesper was informed that, as the decision on this had been left to An Taoiseach, O'Brien could not give him an answer.

It appears, however, that Vesper was asked, unofficially, if the Commission would drop its insistence on the regimental badges, 'a suggestion which was thoroughly repugnant to Commission policy and practice'.[55] Vesper then requested a formal written note on the responses to the first two issues, which he was promised, 'without delay'. This time it was without delay, as O'Brien formally advised the IWGC on 9 December. For once, there was definite clarity on the issues of the OPW paying for maintenance and the IWGC paying the OPW for erection of the permanent stones on an agency basis. On the question of the regimental badges, however, there was silence.[56]

In reporting this conversation to Cremin, it is interesting that O'Brien took the trouble, in a further minute of 8 December, to observe that

as in our 1926 Agreement, it is clear in our Memo of 31 December 1940, paragraph 8, that we will make ourselves responsible for the cost of maintenance of these graves…. But the question of the inscription and badge presents some difficulties.[57]

Reporting to Archer at the UK Representative's Office, Vesper described his meeting with O'Brien as 'most friendly' and indicated that both OPW and External Affairs would be happy for a Commission representative to be available for consultation and for Vesper to visit Dublin in that capacity 'from time to time'. Archer was relieved that matters had gone well, not least because, with some of the war graves in bad condition, he was apprehensive of possible critical press publicity. It was an understandable anxiety since, the War being over, the relatives and friends of the war dead were more likely to be able to visit. It can, however, have been no consolation to him that the issue of the regimental badges remained as a stumbling block on the road to progress.

When, on 15 December, O'Brien requested some sample drawings of headstones from the IWGC, as the specimen in External Affairs seemed 'to have disappeared', he told Vesper that this matter was still being considered.[58] If this raised hope, it was a false one. When the IWGC considered Vesper's report on his visit with O'Brien, they were high in praise of their official's 'tact and discretion', and his report was 'warmly recommended'. This did not,

BELOW
Enlisting the Irish: 1914 War Recruitment Poster

however, offset their dismay on learning that the OPW was going to insist on a sixteen and a half per cent overhead charge, the normal overhead it charged the British and all other legations for work of any kind done on their behalf. Nor did it do anything to remove their anxiety about the insignia. The Commission did not mind submitting the text of proposed inscriptions for scrutiny by External Affairs, in order to satisfy them that 'no unfortunate wording, possibly of a political nature, appears in a personal inscription'. However, when it came to the regimental badges, King advised Vesper that the Commission

would be most reluctant to agree to any departure from tradition and it is hoped that your efforts to have the point dropped will be successful. Pressure to alter or to add to Regimental Badges would certainly raise adverse criticism and jeopardise Commission sanction of the whole arrangement...I am puzzled by the motive at the back of the suggestion.[59]

Vesper was not too happy about this stance, given all the trouble he had encountered a decade before, from the Clare and Sligo authorities on the one hand, and the British Legion on the other. Pointing out that the Irish general election campaign was then 'in full swing', he thought it best not to press the matter further or to visit Dublin again to that end until the election ferment

had subsided. 'Although', he observed, 'it would be impossible to ask for more friendly receptions than I had and all my interviews were in a most amicable manner', he nonetheless concluded

The OPW agrees with me that it is unfortunate that the question should be raised at all now. You will appreciate that, while the old prejudice has subsided, it still keenly exists and will do for many years to a degree, but never or seldom in the minds of officials.[60]

With the general election over and new coalition government, under John A. Costello, in power from 18 February 1948, the unfortunate and ever-faithful Vesper was ordered back to Dublin by the IWGC, to attempt to get the agency overhead fee waived and to try 'to get the (headstone) layout approved as it stands'. He was advised to hasten to Dublin: 'it would be unsafe to postpone your visit much longer in case another general election should be held in the near future'.[61] Vesper only appeared at Iveagh House on 2 March, where he met O'Brien's successor as regards war graves, J. G. Molloy, who promised that the new Minister for External Affairs, Sean McBride, would be approached about the layout of permanent headstones 'immediately'. As for overhead agency fees, Molloy insisted that this was a matter for the OPW and arranged for Vesper to see Veale's OPW

successor, Boyle, on the matter. Here he was told that a waiver was unlikely, but that the IWGC would have to make a formal case to External Affairs: they would send it on a journey to the OPW Commissioners and then on to the Minister for Finance.[62]

In the meantime, having heard nothing further from Molloy, Vesper, on 1 May 1948, sent him a personal note of reminder, inquiring 'approximately when will you be in a position to write to the Commission', to which a reply came, this time from O'Brien, regretting the delay and hoping to let him have a decision 'at an early date'.[63] May went and June came, but still no decision. King, who was about to holiday in Ireland again before retiring from the IWGC in mid-July, took this opportunity to ask O'Brien for an interview, to see if there was any movement on headstone layout. Agreeing to the meeting, O'Brien explained the delay: there was a new Minister who was very busy, and they had not yet had the opportunity to put the issue to him. Nevertheless, O'Brien hoped for news before King and he would meet. When the 'long and cordial' meeting took place on 5 July, King was 'astonished' when O'Brien asked him for the history of the row over regimental badges in the 1930s, wanting to learn which local authorities had objected, their reasons for objecting and whether

any of the 1939-1945 war graves were in these areas. He told King he needed this in order to prepare a briefing paper for the Minister, 'in case some similar objections were raised on this occasion'. King retorted that it was 'absurd to raise again old bitternesses' and asked for a direct interview with the Minister. O'Brien, however, declined, telling him that the matter had not yet been even put to the Minister. He added, interestingly, that the Department of External Affairs felt 'quite sure that neither the Cabinet nor anyone else in Éire would raise any objection to the regimental badges. If they did, the matter would have to be discussed formally with the Commission'. King concluded, not without optimism, that

The vexed question of regimental badges may be resolved satisfactorily to the Commission without any further demarche at this end.[64]

Nevertheless, events continued to move slowly, or not at all. It was already the end of November 1948 before one Iveagh House official, the 'dour Derry Counsellor', Brian Gallagher, could ask his colleague Leo McCauley whether the former Taoiseach, deValera, had ever taken the decision on the matter, only to be told that he had not.[65] A week later, McCauley advised the Secretary of External Affairs that the decision ought to be in favour of allowing the badges,

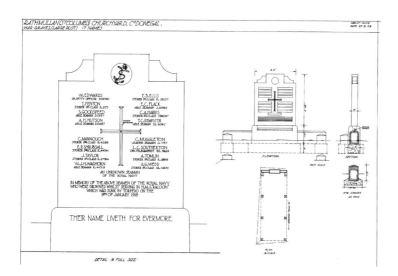

'though I do not suggest that a decision to this effect would override the wishes of a local authority'.[66] He rather hoped that the Clare Board of Health 'may not now make the same objection', even as Gallagher had advised him that the Clare authorities' objection had applied to the dead of the First World War: 'The circumstances of the Second World War are rather different and it may be that the Board would not take the same view in regard to the dead of that war. Would it be possible to ascertain this?', he wondered. For all this speculation, however, nothing happened for quite a while: indeed, in the whole course of 1949, as the country moved from Éire to become the Republic of Ireland, nothing at all happened in the matter of graves and badges.

Pleas for a definite decision:

It was, presumably, in some frustration, that an IWGC official, F.C. Sillar, contacted Dulanty in London, in April 1950, to rehearse summarily the history of negotiations on the matter. Referring to the last acknowledgement from External Affairs in November 1948, he mentioned that 'We have heard nothing further from Dublin since then'. Recognising that the Irish Government 'was fully occupied with major constitutional questions', the IWGC would nonetheless be grateful for a reply, 'as we sometimes find it difficult to answer relatives who enquire when the headstones over their graves will be erected'.[67] Once again a long delay ensued, but it appears that the recourse to Dulanty eventually brought some attention to the issue. An External Affairs official, D. W. Waldron, on 19 August 1950, prepared a draft letter to the Taoiseach, advising that there was no objection in External Affairs to the regimental badges being permitted and that it fell to the Taoiseach to decide in accordance with the Government decision of January 1941, or for him to take it back to Cabinet for decision. Remarkably, however, in drafting this, the Iveagh House officials had still not consulted their own Minister, and Gallagher advised McDonald that they should put the matter to him by way of a draft memorandum from the Minister to the Government.[68] It was late September 1950 before that draft was available but, by that stage, the IWGC was at the end of its tether. As Boland, now Irish Ambassador to the UK, put it, in exasperated tones, to External Affairs:

We are being plagued here by the Imperial War Graves Commission to know when they may expect our authority for the erection of headstones over British war graves in Ireland.... I am afraid that the delay is robbing us of the fruits of the gesture we made during the war when we agreed, as an act of humanity, to provide and

maintain graves of British personnel killed or washed ashore on our territory, free of charge. Having provided and maintained the graves at our own expense, I don't see why we should object to the Commission's erecting headstones at theirs.

On their side the Commission say they are getting many letters of complaint from relatives and find it extremely difficult to give them convincing replies. ...Try to give us a definite decision for transmission to the Imperial War Graves Commission as soon as possible.[69]

By this stage, not only was the London Embassy being plagued by the Commission, but the Commission was being plagued by the British Legion in Ireland, as was the OPW.[70] Telegrams then followed from the Irish Embassy to Iveagh House on 17 and 20 November, beseeching a response to Boland's October letter.[71] The New Zealand High Commissioner in London, Sir William Joseph Jordan, now joined the chorus, with a letter to Boland on 29 November, asking the latter 'to intimate to your Government that New Zealand is interested and that we hope a favourable answer may soon be received'.[72] Finally, on 8 December 1950, the Government took the decision, agreeing to the inscription of the regimental badges, subject to the consent of the next of kin.[73] The old year ended and the new began with the indefatigable Vesper accepting the IWGC offer to be, once again, their officer for war graves in Ireland.

RIGHT
Gable at Termon Old
Graveyard, Co. Donegal.

Remember me when hope is dead
I will give you faith to burn, instead,
Scottie.

John Alexander McDonald, Able Seaman,
H.M.S. "Patroclus"
3 November 1940

Renvyle Catholic Cemetery, Co. Galway

Chapter 19

New Construction, 1951-1955

If the Department of External Affairs and the OPW thought that the work of marking the graves of 1939-1947 would be comparatively easy compared with the work involved in the war graves of 1914-1921, it was understandable.[1] They were, after all, only one-fifth in number. However, the process proved far from as easy as they might have hoped, and the OPW's idea that they could dispense with the services of an attached Commission Officer was soon dispelled. There were, at times, almost intractable problems of identification, location and isolation. Although most graves had been located, identified and temporarily marked with wooden crosses, there were places which had never been visited or marked. Indeed, in March 1951, Boyle of the OPW notified External Affairs of a discrepancy in the total number of graves – the lists now coming from the IWGC contained more names and places than Dublin had reckoned upon. Boyle complained that either the IWGC had failed fully to notify External Affairs, or, that External Affairs had failed to notify the OPW.[2] Understandably too, the IWGC lost little time in trying to kick-start the process, with a letter to External Affairs in February 1951. Oliver Holt, now the Commission Officer liaising with External Affairs and the OPW, re-introduced Vesper – with a rather surprising misunderstanding of what had

transpired in the negotiated past. He stated that the latter 'should again be attached to the Department [the OPW] to advise on the placing of contracts for the marking, engraving and erection of headstones and so forth'.

His reference to Vesper's 'attachment to the OPW' elicited no comment from External Affairs when Horan replied at the end of March, nor indeed did Holt's reference to the desirability of the IWGC's being permitted to deal directly with the OPW, 'on matters of detail', precipitate any protest.[3] On the contrary, Horan assured him that there was no problem with this, and added that External Affairs 'will always be ready to assist you if you have any difficulties in the future'.

The great tour:

As Holt envisaged it, the veteran inspector 'will personally visit the great majority, if not all, of the graves, so that the Commission may have a complete survey before contracts are placed for the manufacture and erection of headstones'.[4] It may have been a considerable comfort to the unfortunate Vesper, suffering from ulcers and advancing in years, that, this time round, the IWGC provided him with the support of a clerk-driver and an Austin Saloon car. A.E.V. Shephard was 'an exceptionally able driver with a good mechanical knowledge':[5] a good job too, as, on this undertaking, they covered 8,000 miles in visiting over 500 new graves in over 250 burial places throughout the Republic.

On arriving in Dublin, Vesper met the First Secretary at the British Embassy and the Canadian Ambassador, encountered some friendly new faces in Boyle and Carney at the OPW, and renewed ties with his old assistant, Brandon, still dealing with war graves. Within days he was off on his first tour of some forty burial places, encountering blizzards on the way. By mid-May 1951, he and Shephard still had over a hundred burial places to visit and it was the end of June before his preliminary tour of investigation was completed.[6] He had to explain to his superiors in England, who wanted their car and driver back, that the numbers of burial places 'are nearly double the original estimate', and 'are more scattered than I had anticipated'.[7] Furthermore, there was the problem of the 'unknowns' and, in late July 1951, Shephard had compiled a list of twenty-seven cemeteries that would have to be revisited for verifications.[8]

Around that time, following a stomach haemorrhage, Vesper's duties changed from full to half-time. He was putting in around fifteen days a month, yet even then 'largely working here as an official of the Office of Public Works'. As late as late September he was up to his eyes working with officials at OPW head office and local Assistant Architects, with identification and verification concerns that stretched from Donegal to Wexford.[9] It was not until late December 1951 that he was ready to wrap up his regular duties at the OPW in St. Stephen's Green, and could finish his commitment in the Republic, apart from occasional visits if required by the IWGC, or requested by the OPW.[10] Always solicitous for the welfare of the Commission's work in Ireland, he gave long notice, as he had done in the 1930s, of the need to ensure there would be periodic visits by the IWGC into the future.[11]

Engaging the contractors:
Given the unexpectedly difficult task the Second World War graves presented, even the first schedules for the eventual contractors would not be ready for despatch to the OPW until December 1951 or January 1952. The IWGC was fretting about this, six months before then, with Oliver Holt wondering whether the OPW might be able to get any preparatory work done by way of initiating the quarrying of stone and the cutting of headstones prior to

inscription.[12] Vesper acted on this at once, proposing to the OPW in August that the time had come to start inviting tenders for 340 war graves known at that point, as distinct from the fifty that held the remains of 'Unknowns' and the seventy-five that were distinguished by private permanent memorials. In addition, there was the issue of how best to manage the thirty-six war graves in Glasnevin, over and above those of the 1914-1921 period that were already inscribed on its central Memorial.[13] All of this, however, fell to the lot of the OPW, after Vesper left Dublin and returned the North on 21 December 1951.[14]

If Holt and the IWGC wanted to get moving on the preliminary work in August, Carney, the OPW Secretary, would have none of this: he was not going to authorise the engaging of contractors and then keep them waiting for the work. For once, the delay was on the IWGC side, validating Carney's concern: the schedules were not ready and, indeed, would not be ready for despatch to Dublin until the end of the year.[15] The IWGC Chief Records Officer, the ever short-fused Carless, offered Vesper and the OPW no consolation when he retorted:

With the best will in the world, Records Department cannot cope with the Headstone Programme for seven Districts, six Agencies and all the countries outside these Districts simultaneously… the process of producing Headstone Schedules is far more complex than most people seem to realise. They don't just appear by the pressing of a button;

and, with an ominous parting shot, concluded:

The only assurance that I can give you is that you will have the majority of the Schedules by the end of April 1952; I express the hope, however, that you will have enough to keep your contractors busy within a month or so.[16]

At the end of the day, it was not until December 1951 that Vesper, on behalf of the OPW, could indicate to the IWGC that they were ready in Dublin to invite five or more contractors to bid for the first contract, that for Leinster, and requesting a supply of tender documents.[17]

Leinster:

The tenders for the then 126 headstones for 49 burial grounds did not close until June 1952, the bids ranging from £3,160 to £3,213. The monument masons and sculptors, C.W. Harrison and Sons, who had completed the previous Leinster contract in the 1930s, were the successful, lowest bidders and were engaged to complete the work by

the end of January 1953. It was a tight enough schedule, since their success was not notified to them in writing until mid-September 1952.[18] Holt, under pressure from understandably importunate relatives, already in November was anxiously inquiring of progress on this contract and wondering why 'would it not now be possible for tenders to be invited… for the other provinces'. Meanwhile, as late as 24 November, Harrison's were still waiting for the texts of the inscriptions and for the designs of the regimental insignia, two days before the OPW was asking them what progress they had made, and reminding them of the completion deadline of 26 January 1953.[19] It was 1 December before they got their inscriptions and badge designs. Consequently, William Brandon was not at all surprised that Harrison simply could not complete by the assigned date, and had to be given an extension to the end of April 1953.[20] Working in several different locations at once, they were confident of meeting this new deadline. By the beginning of April they had erected half of the required total of what were now 127 headstones. While not meeting their list by the April deadline, they had completed the entire contract by the end of June 1953, although it was April two years later before final payment to them was authorised.[21]

That list included a diverse cross section of Englishmen and Irishmen: Sergeants Beard and Rostern in a single grave in Arklow; Squadron Leader MacClancy in St. Fintan's, Sutton; Skipper J. C. Barber and his shipmate W. Coe, of the *Aberdeen*, buried side by side in Drogheda Calvary workhouse cemetery; Petty Officer Peter Harold of H.M.S. *Folkestone*, who came from Merrion Road, Dublin, died in 1943 aged thirty-seven, and ended in Dean's Grange Cemetery in County Dublin, leaving behind a seventy-seven year old mother.[22] By no means least was a significant cross section of young Irishwomen. These included Private Lorna Scott-Martin of the ATS who died, aged twenty-four, in 1943 and was buried in Clontarf Cemetery; Lance Corporal Annie Flynn, also of ATS, who died, aged twenty, in 1945 and was commemorated in Portlaoise; Leading Aircraftswoman Rosemary Cox, also aged twenty, died in April 1945 and was interred at St. Patrick's, Dundalk; Corporal Bridget White of the Women's Auxiliary Air Force, died, aged twenty-seven, in 1944 and remembered in stone in Clonmacnoise Old Abbey; Leading Aircraftswoman Kathleen Mollaghan, twenty-three years old when she died in 1943, and commemorated in Drumlish Catholic Churchyard, Longford — women whose stories have not yet been adequately told.

Munster:

The Munster contract was not as extensive in number, involving seventy-six war graves, but was more scattered, since these were to be found in fifty-eight separate burial grounds from Miltown Malbay in Clare, through Cahersiveen in Kerry and Skibbereen in Cork, to Dungarvan in Waterford. When the tenders arrived in December 1952 – in this case only two – the lower came from Thomas McCarthy & Sons of Cork, who had undertaken the headstone construction twenty years before, for the First World War contract.[23] With their tender accepted on 22 January 1953, they were instructed to complete by 7 September. Although the limestone slabs from the quarry did not reach McCarthy's works until the end of March 1953, it was nonetheless an understandable anxiety on Brandon's part when he asked Scully, the OPW Assistant Architect in Cork, for a progress report. As late as mid-August, Brandon understood that 'the Contractor has not yet erected a single headstone. Is that the position?': Brandon was labouring under a misapprehension, however, as, at that point, eleven had been erected in Cork and Tipperary and a further thirty-nine stood carved and ready for erection. In fairness to McCarthy, with one extension granted, by early October he had constructed all but four of the stones for which he had been supplied with details, and he was awaiting particulars from the OPW for sites in Waterford, West Cork and Kerry, for stones which had been 'ready for some time'.[24] One of the sources of delay, outside the control of IWGC, OPW or contractor, was the provision of consent by the next of kin. Typical in this was the case of the grave of Private Christina Mary O'Donoghue of the ATS: she died in January 1947, at the age of nineteen, and was buried in Glandore Old Cemetery, County Cork. It was not until late October 1953 that her mother provided location details and consent to the OPW to proceed with marking. In other cases, the delay could be occasioned by cemetery authorities who insisted on their own schedules and procedures for foundations before permitting the stones to be put up: so it was with the Cork City authorities in November 1953.[25] McCarthy had completed his contract within the year, three months after the original completion date, hardly a poor performance in the circumstances.[26]

Connaught:

The contract for Connaught included the two Ulster counties of Cavan and Monaghan but excluded Donegal which, because of its distance and the number of its war grave sites, became the subject of its own contract. The

Connaught, Cavan and Monaghan contract involved ninety-seven stones in forty-four cemeteries and was won by Robins of Portarlington and Harold's Cross, Dublin.[27] It was October 1954 before these had been masoned, carved, lettered, and passed after inspection by OPW officials. Such delay, though not explained, could prove a cause of grief to next of kin. Major W. M. Mair of the Sligo Branch of the Legion took up the cause of the memory of Private Eileen Mills of the ATS. She had enlisted in Omagh in October 1944 and died two years later in Lurgan Hospital at the age of nineteen. Her parents, James and Mary Mills of Sligo Town, at the time of her death had been promised a war grave memorial stone by the War Office. Apparently, after years of calling on the local OPW Office, her parents got the Legion to take up her case and their representations happened to reach the IWGC and OPW just before Robins was awarded the Connaught contract. Once again, it was the contractor, Robins, in January 1955, who ended up pressing Williamson at the OPW for 'the remainder of the plans as we would like to complete work and clear off our books'.[28] It was June 1955 before all that Robins had contracted to do had been signed off by the OPW as completed, involving, in the end, some ninethy-eight memorials in forty-four cemeteries. As elsewhere, delay was not always to be laid at the door of the Commission, the OPW or the contractor. Consider the case of the grave of one of two Irishmen, out of eight Second World War graves in Ahamlish Church of Ireland Churchyard, County Sligo. As the OPW district Officer, L. G. Coakham, reported in July 1955:

Ahamlish, Co Sligo: The map of this graveyard was delayed for a considerable time as the grave could not be located. The Grave Commissioners were approached and, after months' delay, gave the address of the next of kin. The grave was then located and the map completed but, when the stone, together with seven others, was being erected, an uncle who, I understand, was part-owner of the grave, refused to allow the stone to be erected. The stone was taken back to Cavan, the Contractor's distributing centre. However, the mother of the deceased prevailed, and permission was given for erection.[29]

In Sligo also there occurred the doleful case of Aircraftsman First Class, John Christopher Oates, of the RAF Volunteer Reserve. In October 1956, Holt of the IWGC contacted the OPW directly, concerning the cases of twenty members of the Commonwealth Forces who lost their lives as a result of the Second World War and the location of whose graves they were unable to trace. Oates was one of them: he had passed away at home in March 1946.

They had an address for his wife, at Harmony Hill, Sligo, but could find no trace of her. In November 1956, the OPW District Officer for Sligo Region managed to trace an eighty-year old aunt who informed him that, after John Christopher's death, his widow and two children had left Sligo for England; the aunt 'has never heard from them since. She has no idea of the widow's whereabouts'.[30] They were last heard about in Birmingham but with no known address. Nevertheless, through persistent local enquiries, they were able to uncover the precise location of his grave in Sligo Cemetery where he had been buried on 28 March 1946. As a consequence they were enabled to provide his plot with a permanent memorial.

Finally, in County Monaghan there arose the equally pathetic case of Private Edward Conlon of the Pioneer Corps. He had served in the First War and died in the Second, on 23 September 1942, at the age of forty-eight, leaving his widow, Mary Anne, in Cootehill. His was another case where the War Graves Commission was unable to locate his grave. Mary Anne had died in 1955 and his only son, Anthony, was living in Birmingham at an unknown address. Again, the OPW District Officer was able to locate Edward's two brothers, Joseph and John, both also former British soldiers. They took the OPW

officer, O'Rourke, to Edergole Old Graveyard in Monaghan and showed him the exact spot where Edward had been buried in September 1942: this old graveyard, dating from 1720, was disused and there were no markings of any kind on his grave.[31]

Donegal:

The work in Donegal involved a known fiffty-nine war graves in thirty burial places, with the contract going to Monaghan & Sons of Mountcharles, in April 1954.[32] For the most part, they were single graves in isolated cemeteries. Such was that of local man, William George Bradley, of the S.S. *Empire Taginia*, laid to rest in the beautiful setting of ancient Iskaheen, where Niall of the Nine Hostages was reputedly buried more than fifteen hundred years before; or the solitary war grave, in Ardara Holy Family Catholic Churchyard, of the Torquay man, St. John Clifford, of the Devonshires, who was washed ashore after the sinking of the *Arandora Star* on 2 July 1940; or the lone war grave of the Stranorlar-born Mary Jo Browne, of the Women's Auxiliary Air Force, who died aged twenty-two and was remembered by her parents, Michael and Agnes, in Stranorlar Catholic Cemetery. But, as in the aftermath of the First World War, so also for the Second: what was striking about Donegal was the

NEAR RIGHT
Cecil St. John Clifford of
Torquay, Arandora Star
victim, Holy Family
Catholic Cemetery,
Ardara, Co. Donegal.

MIDDLE RIGHT
Mary Jo Browne, WAAF,
in Stranorlar Catholic
Cemetery, Co. Donegal.

FAR RIGHT
The grave of Takeshi
Uyeda of the S.S.
Manchester Brigade, in
Magheragallon Cemetery,
Co. Donegal.

clustering of groups in some relatively small cemeteries: ten war graves of Cruit Island, in Rosses Bay, so beautifully maintained to this day; or the cluster of eight that includes the Japanese Takeshi Uyeda, of the S.S. *Manchester Brigade*, in the equally spotless yet remote Magheragallon Cemetery; or the group of six soldiers and seamen in the ancient, wild, and remote ruins at Termon Old Graveyard near Maghery – at rest there close by two unknown German airmen and the uncounted local dead.[33]

Once again there were the inevitable delays. The OPW explicitly absolved Monaghan of any responsibility for this and, with the weather working against him, extended his contract completion date to the end of March 1955.[34] In one instance, that of Kiltooris Old Graveyard at Rosbeg, the place was in such a state of neglect that Holt, who knew from copies of photographs taken by a visitor, wondered if they should consider removing the bodies of Lieutenant J. P. Thyne and Able Seaman R. B. McLeod to Upper Fahan.[35] With circumstances still operating against him, Monaghan was granted another extension to the end of August 1955, but it was December 1955 before the OPW declared the contract completed, with seventy-two headstones in thirty-one cemeteries – except for the problem posed by Kiltooris.[36]

While the north-west, west, and south-west coastal burial grounds created serious challenges in location, identification and commemoration, as shall be seen again shortly, Dublin, too, with its large public cemeteries of Glasnevin, Dean's Grange and Mount Jerome, posed its own challenges, as it had done for the war graves in the 1930s. Because of their extensive codes of regulations, and the heavy daily volume of their sensitive business, the authorities at these three large Dublin cemeteries were sticklers for procedure. This was clearly evident in their approach to the erection of temporary wooden crosses as it was to maintenance agreements and the provision of permanent headstones.

Dean's Grange:
In the south of Dublin County, at Dean's Grange, there were already seventy-five war graves. A further twenty-seven came to be added during the course of the Second World War : at least twenty-two of these were from Ireland, and the majority of these were from Dublin, mainly from the Dean's Grange neighbourhoods of Blackrock, Dun Laoghaire and Killiney. They ranged from Privates like Jack Eager of Sallynoggin, through Army Chaplains such as Holy Ghost Father, James Curran, to Ship's Masters such as Andrew Breslin, from Cabra in north

Dublin city, Master of the M.V. *Teasal*, out of Cardiff, and Stanley Hollinshead, Master of the S.S. *Alexandra*, out of Liverpool, who left a widow in Dun Laoghaire when he died in December 1943. The list included a Surgeon Rear-Admiral, Sir William Ireland de Courcy Wheeler of H.M.S. *Bacchante*, an armoured cruiser that had been involved in the Gallipoli landings in 1915. A past President of the Royal College of Surgeons in Ireland, he was the author of publications in medicine and surgery; twice mentioned in despatches during the First War, he died on active service during the Second, in September 1943, at the age of sixty-four.

The routine pattern of operations and procedures evolved here as it did elsewhere in Ireland. The maintenance agreement of 1936 with the OPW had to be extended, piecemeal, from 1946, to the new graves as they came to be occupied by the victims of the Second War.[37] From the early 1940s, the temporary wooden crosses arrived from Dockrell's in small batches, with John Cullen, the Dean's Grange Registrar, signing formal consents for the erection of every one.[38] An example, typical in most ways, that illustrates the detailed process entailed, is that relating to Stoker Petty Officer Peter Harold of Dublin. He was serving on H.M.S. *Folkestone*, which survived the war, although he

did not: dying in June 1943, aged thirty-seven, he was buried in Dean's Grange. In October 1943 William Fay of External Affairs advised the OPW of the existence of this war grave, after his parents, James and Sarah Harold of 278 Merrion Road, had asked the IWGC to arrange for the marking of his grave. Fay, supplying its exact location, requested the OPW 'to have the work put in hand as soon as possible'. On 23 November Dockrell's delivered the inscribed wooden cross to Dean's Grange and on 1 December the Cemetery Registrar, Cullen, authorised its erection. Eight days later, William Veale for the OPW co-signed the maintenance agreement form for Harold's grave and on 11 January 1944 Cullen informed the OPW that 'the grave of Stoker P.O. Peter Harold has been put in order'. Then, on 25 March 1944, the OPW duly notified External Affairs that all had been completed. Regular inspection reports from the OPW through to 1948 found his and the other graves being well maintained but, by that stage, the inscription lettering was fading. In over-optimistic expectation that permanent headstones might be erected there 'in the near future', the repainting of his and other wooden crosses was deferred. By early 1949, the annual maintenance fee of five shillings per war grave paid to Dean's Grange by the OPW was deemed inadequate by the Cemetery Authority

in the face of rising prices; their standard fee to the ordinary public had just been raised from ten to fifteen shillings per year. The Board considered the matter in relation to war graves and requested a raise to seven shillings and sixpence, 'being half of the new charge'. The OPW accepted, considering it 'appears to be reasonable'.[39] Then on his tour of inspection, as prelude to the provision of permanent headstones, Vesper visited Dean's Grange in April 1951 and verified Harold's and the other Second World War graves there.

Up to this point, this was the typical sequence for any standard war grave of the Second World War in Ireland. It then became slightly untypical, as Harrison's moved in to erect the Dean's Grange memorials. In December 1952, Boyle at the OPW requested Harrison to suspend action on a headstone for Harold, 'as we understand his grave is marked by a family memorial'. Perhaps the family grew tired waiting for the standard Commonwealth headstone to appear: his mother, Sarah, had died six years before, aged eighty. Three months later, the IWGC confirmed that it wanted the headstone order for Harold's grave cancelled, since it now had a private permanent memorial.[40]

Not all were as generally routine as this. Consider the case of William Breen, of Dublin, a forty-four year old private of the Pioneer Corps. He fell ill when on leave and died on 26 August 1941. His widow could not afford the costs of his interment and he was buried in what might, in other burial places, have been considered a pauper's grave: as far as this cemetery's authorities were concerned, there were no paupers' graves in Dean's Grange, and he was in fact buried in a burial plot where his family once had rights, but which rights had ceased with the passage of time.

A brother of his, J.P., then living in Slough, Bucks, asked the IWGC if they could assist by having him exhumed and reburied in a private, instead of a 'common', grave. The Commission informed Vesper in Dublin that they could not possibly pay for such a course 'and to do so might create a precedent affecting other cases of burial in "common graves"'. J.P. himself was a badly disabled victim of service in the First World War; their father had also served in that War, as had William, as well as serving in the Second. It was in response to the IWGC's normal initiative of contacting next-of-kin to advise of their hope to erect a permanent standard stone over William's grave that J.P. had written, thanking them for this kind initiative: he explained that he could not afford the £15 17s. Dean's Grange required to exhume and re-inter in

Fr. John Dempsey	2ND JAN.	1940	34	YRS.
Mr. Desmond Connay	5TH JULY	1940	20	"
Bro. Gall Walsh	1ST FEB.	1941	90	"
Fr. John J. Kearney	5TH APRIL	1941	75	"
Mr. William Hickey	19TH JUNE	1941	22	"
Fr. Hugh Evans	23RD DEC.	1943	83	"
Fr. James Gerard Curran	4TH MAY	1944	37	"
Fr. Richard Walsh (White Fathers)	9TH MARCH	1979	68	"
Fr. John Francis Horgan	1ST MAY	1979	63	"
Fr. John F. Roche	27TH JULY	1979	69	"
Fr. Sean Guina	6TH DEC.	1983	54	"
Fr. Joe Halpin	17TH JULY	1988	77	"
Fr. Joseph N. Corless	25TH SEPT.	1990	80	"
Fr. Robert Stanley	27TH JAN.	1996	81	

FAR LEFT
Jack Eager of Sallynoggin, in Dean's Grange Cemetery.

NEAR LEFT
Fr James Curran, Army Chaplain, in Dean's Grange Cemetery.

a new private plot, and so asked the Commission if they could arrange this.

Vesper was contacted by Holt in early June 1951 and, consulting the Dean's Grange authorities, was told that William's existing plot could be purchased for £5, and a standard IWGC headstone erected thereon. He concluded that:

As we can mark and maintain this grave, and further, as there is space for the wife to be buried in the grave, we cannot possibly entertain this application.[41]

So it was that Private Breen got his IWGC permanent headstone in Dean's Grange, in the plot where he had originally been laid to rest.

Unusual, too, was the hardship case of Dubliner Private Jack Eager of the 8th Battalion, Royal Sussex Regiment, who died in August 1940, aged thirty-eight. Doubtless, as in the case of William Breen, Eager's widow, Anne, was informed by the IWGC of the hope of permanently marking his burial place in Dean's Grange. She wrote to the Commission in September 1944 explaining that the Cemetery authority could 'hold' his grave for her for six months, and if she could find the required £4 10s.6d. during that time, the plot would be hers. As she explained:

I will not be able to pay it out as I have only me [sic] pension I have from the Government. I believe you will buy it out for me. Will you please let me know as soon as possible. I filled in all particulars on form and enclose same.[42]

In notifying the OPW in late October 1944, as advised by Chettle of the IWGC, Warnock of External Affairs explained to them that

The cost of acquiring this grave in perpetuity would be properly chargeable to the Commission and I am to request that the authorities of Dean's Grange Cemetery be informed to this effect.[43]

Mount Jerome:

In the south city, at Harold's Cross, was Mount Jerome Cemetery: it was unusual among large Dublin cemeteries, or indeed, among Irish cemeteries generally, in containing more war graves of 1939-1945 than of the 1914-1918 War. While it had thirty-five graves of the latter as registered by the IWGC, it contained thirty-nine graves of the Second World War. Of the latter, at least thirty-two of the dead had come from Dublin City and County, and many of these from the surrounding districts: four from Crumlin, three from Rathmines, two from Rathgar, and one each from Terenure and Kimmage. They ranged from RAF personnel such as Aircraftman

RIGHT
The Dean's Grange plot
of the Holy Ghost Fathers,
including British Army
Chaplain, Fr. James Cur-
ran.

1st Class, Edward J. Lynnott of Cabra, who died aged twenty-one in September 1945, through Private Patrick Power of Rathmines, a Pioneer Corps soldier, to Test Pilot and Second Lieutenant Thomas Derek Saul of 64 Squadron RAF, who died on 15 December 1947, aged twenty-eight.

Here again were histories of hardship and compassion. Private Patrick Power, for example, died in the South Dublin Union on 21 June 1946, aged thirty-five, leaving behind his widow, Dora. Arising from the precedent of Private Jack Eager in Dean's Grange, in February 1947 Cruise O'Brien at External Affairs was alerted to the not dissimilar case of Patrick Power. His widow had begun the process of purchasing his grave but was unable to find the full sum of £7 1s., due to straitened circumstances. O'Brien consulted the OPW who assured him it was indeed a case 'properly chargeable to IWGC'.[44]

In the meantime, the widow sought an interview with External Affairs and here learned that the IWGC did indeed propose to effect the purchase. Unfortunately, time was running out: the cemetery authorities were requiring the purchase to be completed by 21 June, and she had unresolved anxieties. She contacted the IWGC concerning their proposal to help, and wondered:

I would like to know if your conditions would bar me from any further burials in this grave, also I would like if possible be allowed to put flowers etc on it. After all, it's all we have left of a good husband and father.[45]

Edward King of the IWGC very quickly contacted her with assurances and then contacted External Affairs with a request, on the IWGC's behalf, to expedite the purchase, remarking to O'Brien, 'she has made a very human appeal for help with which I know you will sympathise'.[46] On foot of a note from O'Brien, the Mount Jerome authorities consented to extend the date for completion of purchase to 31 December 1947. The purchase was effected in time, the Grave Deed being secured by the OPW for transmission to the IWGC, via External Affairs, in the spring of 1949.[47]

Glasnevin:

To the 161 war graves of the 1914-1921 conflict, which Vesper verified when he went to Glasnevin again in July 1951, he now had to add a further thirty-six graves of the Second World War. Fourteen of these bore temporary wooden crosses, six had private permanent memorials, but a further sixteen were unmarked at the time. While no single military service predominated, the largest discrete cluster was that of nine RAF personnel,

followed by seven former members of the Pioneer Corps. There was only one Royal Navy man, Stoker A. J. Blake of H.M.S. *Ambrose*, who died in July 1944. As it had proven impossible to erect the 161 standard IWGC headstones in the 1930s, and a central cenotaph had to be erected instead, it was now initially thought that the IWGC and OPW would somehow add the thirty-six new names to this monument, if possible, or, failing that, to erect 'a miniature memorial' instead.[48]

By August 1951 Vesper had three options to put to the OPW architects: either, an inscription step at each end of the First World War Memorial, or, a miniature copy of it at a suitable distance from it, or a memorial seat bearing the thirty-six names, placed opposite the existing Memorial. He got OPW Assistant Principal Architect, McNicholl, to visit the site, and the latter concluded against the first option; he thought it best simply to produce plans of the area to send to the IWGC, and for the Commission to decide on the preferable format. While, by early October, McNicholl was going off the idea of a separate miniature, Holt at the IWGC felt that Vesper's third option, of a memorial seat, might be preferable in the context of the area. Very soon, however, the preferred option had become one for a separate Memorial and a seat.[49]

Whatever plan was decided upon, Vesper was aware that the Dublin Cemeteries Committee would have to give approval. Given that he knew Nowlan, the current Superintendent, who had been Assistant Superintendent when Vesper worked with the cemetery authorities in the 1930s, he was confident that whatever might be the proposal, it would at least get a fair hearing: however, he wanted some despatch in the matter as 'I would like the approach to be made while I am still attached to the Office of Public Works'.[50]

Initial formal overtures were made to the Glasnevin authorities in early September 1952. The latter responded quickly, in October. They baulked at the extent of ground implied in the draft plans, but they were prepared to allocate the chosen site at reduced dimensions, in consideration of a charge of £1,200.[51] The IWGC's reaction to this was one of surprise and dismay. Writing privately to Boyle of the OPW, in late January 1953, Oliver Holt confessed:

We are seriously perturbed at the suggestion that the Commission should make an offer for the site. As you will appreciate, the Commission have carried through numerous transactions of this nature with Cemetery Authorities in various parts of the world and I may say that it has been the general practice for the land to be provided free of cost…. If the suggestion that

NEAR RIGHT
RAF Aircraftman Edward Lynnott in Mount Jerome.

FAR RIGHT
Patrick Power, Pioneer Corps. in Mount Jerome.

the Commission should make a payment for the land is seriously pursued, I very much fear that it may jettison the proposal altogether. This would be a most unfortunate outcome, particularly as the next of kin have already been informed of the proposed Memorial.

Whatever about the practice of cemetery authorities elsewhere in the world, Glasnevin was a private charitable body and not State land. As Boyle explained to the IWGC, 'this site is not owned by a Local Authority but is a private company' and that they could not operate at a loss.[52] In view of the fact that the Irish State had had to purchase its own plots, at whatever reduced fee, after embarrassing haggling in the 1920s, the IWGC's comment surprises. Holt now wanted Boyle to get the OPW to approach the Glasnevin authorities to reconsider, before an official response issued from the Commission.[53]

Brandon was now sent to sound out the DCC Secretary, and was given to understand their difficulties: they were running short of land in that area; at the same time, they were operating at a financial loss, and had to ensure that all ground be 'revenue earning'. Though valuing the site at £1,200, however, they were prepared to grant it, in the circumstances, for half this price. The OPW concluded that 'we must therefore moderate our requirements if the War

Graves Commission is not prepared to pay for the site': either they would have to abandon the plan for a new cenotaph and memorial seat, and opt for a smaller memorial adjacent to the existing one, or else seek 'a small corner site of no grave value'.

This report led McNicholl to another site meeting with the Cemetery Superintendent. The latter helpfully suggested that if a new smaller cenotaph, within the path side of the existing Memorial, 'could be achieved on a more intimate scale', then the Cemetery authorities 'might be more sympathetic'. As such a site would be between the existing Memorial and the boundary wall of the Cemetery, the OPW thought it would have little value as 'grave space' and they were hopeful DCC might therefore grant it 'gratis'. As it transpired, the OPW was correct: on 10 April 1953, DCC Secretary, Maguire, informed them that Glasnevin 'will grant, free of charge, the alternative site'. Boyle therefore advised the IWGC that there was 'no possibility of obtaining free of charge any more elaborate site than the one now offered'.[54]

Uncharacteristically, there was no speedy reply from the IWGC. Indeed, five months later, OPW Secretary Carney wished to know from them 'if the proposal to erect an additional

War Graves Memorial… has been abandoned'. It took a full year from the OPW's April 1953 letter, conveying the good news of the free grant of the proposed site, before Holt responded to Carney. Apologising for the twelve months' silence, Holt explained that, given the nature of the site offered, 'the whole matter had to be looked at afresh and I can only plead abnormal pressure of work for my silence'. The formal Commission response, which he enclosed, was presented in almost contradictory tones of resigned acceptance and simultaneous gratitude: while they would 'naturally have preferred' an alternative, 'they much appreciate the co-operation of the Cemetery Authorities in offering this piece of land free of charge, and they gratefully accept that offer'.[55]

The actual design for the Second World War Memorial was drafted by the IWGC's architects, with OPW architects being requested to comment – a precise reversal of the procedure of the 1930s for the First World War Memorial designed by Harold Leask. The DCC approved the final design in October 1954 and then bettered this, by simultaneously granting the site of the two Memorials in perpetuity to the IWGC, in a combined plot of thirty-two feet by thirty-eight.[56] This deed of grant went to IWGC lawyers in December

1954 and, following amendments, was finally executed in May 1955. The thirty-six names to be commemorated were confirmed by the Commission in July 1955, and three tenders, ranging from £445 to £510, were received in October, the winning tender being submitted by Robins Brothers.[57]

Once again, the process of construction was beset by delays, as delivery of the raw material was slow; extensions had to be given, but Robins completed the construction in April 1956, and finished off the project with planting of shrubs that autumn. Finally, at the point where the IWGC's Chief Administrative Officer, E. A. Griffin, made arrangements to visit the new Memorial, the news came through to the OPW of the passing away of P. E. Vesper, just at the biblical three score years and ten.[58] While his own grave in South London knows no such grand memorial – just a simple stone[59] – it would have been a not inconsiderable comfort to him to have known, eight months before, the contents of the letter which Oliver Holt of the IWGC sent to Carney of the OPW, on 4 November 1955:

Dear Sir,
    Thank you for your letter of 2
November ...informing me of the virtual
completion of the work of placing headstones on
British Commonwealth War Graves in the Irish
Republic... I should like to express my thanks
for all the asistance given.[60]

Right
The Pieta,
German War Dead
Cemetery, Glencree,
Co. Wicklow.

Chun leaba I nGleann Crí
Tré pheannaidh is tré phéin
I gcéin, ar son mo thír,
Do thug mo chinnúint mé

verse by Stan O'Brien
German War Dead Cemetery
Glencree
Co. Wicklow

Chapter 20

The German War Dead Cemetery: Glencree, 1951-1964

In the years after the War the gradual return of even a limited extent of 'normality' led to a natural anxiety of the bereaved to visit the burial places of their lost ones. The Germans were no exception, even if the degree of post-war disorganisation for them was somewhat greater than for some others. The German Legation in Dublin in the late 1940s and early 1950s was certainly handling its share of enquiries from individuals and organisations like the Red Cross and the Volksbund Deutsche Kriegsgräberfürsorge, or German War Graves Commission. From the early 1950s the Legation in Dublin and the German War Graves Commission in Kassel shared concern at the condition of their graves in Ireland, with the latter expressing its readiness to accept responsibility for them, were that possible.[1] In February 1952 it requested External Affairs to provide a detailed list of known German war graves, the names of the interred and their exact locations. By late March the OPW had supplied a list of forty-eight individuals in thirty separate cemeteries; by June 1953 the list had grown to fifty-one war dead, and by July 1956 it had reached fifty-two.[2]

Seeking a site:

Ireland was a small country in the extent of its German war graves as much as in its geographical extent; nevertheless, for the few relatives who managed to reach Dublin during these years, it came as a frustration and unexpected burden that they might have to travel on and spend scarce money in finding burial places in parts of Cork, Kerry, Galway or Donegal. Dr Kolb, who was Cultural Attaché at the Legation in the early 1950s, raised this concern with Valentin Iremonger of External Affairs in 1953. He was anxious to explore the possibility of obtaining a site in or near to Dublin to which the remains of deceased German military personnel could be removed for re-interment. He thought that if this might be acceptable to the Irish authorities, then the OPW could look after the question of finding a site and arranging for the transfer. Iremonger consulted the OPW and came back to Kolb with the somewhat unhelpful observation that, even if the idea might be agreed in principle, then the Legation itself would have to obtain the site. He suggested that Kolb might approach cemetery authorities in and around Dublin to see if they could provide the necessary ground space.[3]

Sometime after he first raised the issue with Iremonger, Kolb came back to him to say he had made no

RIGHT
The commemoration
stone with verses
by Stan O'Brien,
German War Dead
Cemetery, Glencree.

Mein Los war der Tod
Unter irischem Himmel
Und ein Bett in Irlands
guter Erde + Was ich ge-
träumt, geplant/band
mich ans Vaterland +
Aber mich wies der Krieg
zum Schlaf in Glencree
+ Leid war und Schmerz,
was ich verlor und gewann
+ Wenn Du vorübergehst,
Sprich ein Gebet, daß
Verlust sich in Segen
verwandle.

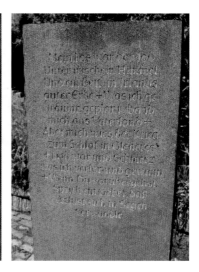

progress whatsoever and had become 'disheartened about the whole business'. In his innocence, he thought that the Irish Government might make a present of a site to the German authorities who would then take the matter to a conclusion. Kolb pointed out that in 'all other European countries' the Governments of these countries had done this and then had left it to the German War Graves Commission to look after the identification, transportation and re-interment of their war dead. Although Kolb did not make the point, it was hardly a huge area of land for which he hoped. So far as the German War Graves Commission, the OPW or External Affairs knew at that time, it was a matter of only fifty-two graves scattered in thirty cemeteries: forty-six relating to the 1939-1945 War; the six of the 1914-1918 War consisting of three prisoners of war and three civilian internees who had all died in Ireland during that war.

An extraordinary suggestion:
Iremonger raised the issue within External Affairs, in particular with T. V. Commins, subsequently Ireland's Ambassador to Italy. Commins was far from enthusiastic: he felt that to 'centralise' the war graves in the fashion suggested might 'create a sort of shrine'. Commins instead thought they should

suggest to the German Legation that they ask the German War Graves Commission to consider removing these remains 'back to Germany altogether'. Iremonger accepted that this might be appropriate in theory but he felt they had to ensure that the German authorities received exactly the same treatment from Ireland, in the matter of war graves, as the British had. This was, he pointed out, the principle at the heart of the External Affairs' memorandum to Government of 31 December 1940, which Government had adopted as its policy in regard to the treatment of the war graves of the two World Wars.

Having reflected further on the matter, Commins became even more resolutely opposed to the idea:

I am convinced that we, in this country, should in no circumstances support, morally or materially, this idea of centralised burying places for the dead of any of the big powers. These places become shrines, inevitably, and lead to occasions such as Poppy Days and the like which can readily give rise to breaches of the peace.

As for our actually buying and presenting a cemetery to the German Government, I think the suggestion is extraordinary.[4]

Having so forcefully put his position, he added, somewhat incongruously:

I would like to study the whole thing closer, however, before committing myself to a definite view.

He asked to be briefed precisely on the nature of the Irish relationship with the British in this regard.

There the matter rested – or stagnated – until early September 1953, when Baron von Richthofen of the Legation called to see Commins at Iveagh House. In the course of a discussion of the Irish Government's bomb damages claim against the Germans, the Baron reviewed the issue first raised by Kolb: Commins told him that External Affairs had not completed its consideration of the matter as a prelude to submitting a position paper to Government. He left von Richthofen, however, in little doubt what the position would be:

We in this Department who have examined it were satisfied that, for a number of reasons, the German request would, in the circumstances of this country, be a very difficult one for the Government to agree to.

In essence, for the Government to concede on this would create a precedent which in the future might prove 'highly embarrassing and undesirable'. Von Richthofen responded phlegmatically

that he appreciated their viewpoint, that his Government did not deem the matter 'important' and that the Irish authorities should consider the matter 'withdrawn'. Following this, the External Affairs officials were happy, in their own words, to 'let the hare sit'.[5]

Renewing the quest:

Whatever about von Richthofen's assurance that the matter was not important, the German Government did not let the hare sit. Less than a year later, their Legation sent a note to External Affairs asking the Irish authorities to give consideration to this question of a single graveyard for their war dead in Ireland. They called the Irish Government's attention to agreements made between the German Federal Government and the Governments of Belgium and Luxembourg, empowering the German War Graves' Commission to make arrangements for the establishment and care of suitable burial grounds. They requested the Irish Government to make a site available in or near Dublin, either part of an existing cemetery, or otherwise, for a permanent central burial ground. They concluded by suggesting that such a site might be given to the Germans as a free gift or on permanent loan. They tried to reassure the Irish Government that

'no elaborate monument or memorial park' was envisaged, but only, as in other countries, 'a simple cemetery'. To anticipate a counter-suggestion by the Irish Government that the remains of the German war dead be exhumed and repatriated, they pointed out that

the transference of the remains to Germany would be contrary to the tradition by which a soldier is buried in the soil of that country where he died or where his body was discovered.[6]

This was in July 1954. Receiving official acknowledgement, but no effective response, they sent a further two reminders over the next twelve months: by autumn 1955 they had still received no substantive reply.[7] However, the matter would not go away: Iveagh House had to address it. In briefing Tommy Woods on the issue at this time, Commins rehearsed Iveagh House's argument that a central cemetery had the potential to become a 'shrine' and 'give rise to remembrance days, demonstrations etc'. He now added a new dimension to this: that the Irish authorities feared that to yield to the German wish might create a troublesome precedent: 'a similar request might be received from the British authorities whom it would then be difficult to refuse'. Commins now admitted that there was nothing *per se* against the idea and that such centralised

war cemeteries were common in other countries; nevertheless, he still advised that they should tell the Germans that 'we would not be prepared at the present moment to accede to their request'.[8]

There was a little difficulty in the External Affairs' stance over 1953 to 1955: if equality of treatment were the principle used to justify their approach, then it was hardly equal that the British and Commonwealth Allies, through the agency of the OPW, were just then getting on with the business of replacing their temporary wooden crosses of 1939-1945 with permanent headstones. Furthermore, as will be shortly seen, although in Ireland they had no single central war dead burial ground, in Grangegorman Military Cemetery they had access to the next best thing. Already by 1950 there were 613 military dead of the First World War commemorated there by the IWGC and, eventually, there would be another 11 of the Second World War[9]. For the Germans, on the other hand, the OPW, in the mid-1950s, was still maintaining their graves and replacing their wooden crosses with further wooden crosses as need arose. Yet, whether by design or default, the British had never approached the Irish Government with an identical proposal for a single place of committal and commemoration.[10] As shall be seen in the next chapter, when

they did seek and succeed in getting even partial relocation of their war dead, it was simply from very isolated burial places to regional ones, like St. Mura's at Upper Fahan, for the west and north-west, or to Grangegorman for the rest of the country.

The German Legation did not give up. In March 1955 and again in September, it reminded External Affairs of the request for a decision on the July 1954 proposals. Their persistence paid: sometime between September 1955 and June 1956 the Government, or External Affairs, relented and conceded the principle of a central war dead cemetery for the Germans. How that about-turn happened is not clear: Government and Cabinet minutes make no mention of it, but by spring 1956 the OPW had been approached about finding a possible site for such a development.

Finding a site:

The OPW came up with the idea of the possible use of lands surrounding the old reformatory at Glencree in Co. Wicklow. This land they held on a yearly tenancy through the Land Commission, pending its formal vesting in the Minister for Finance. They were confident the Land Commission would not object to its subdivision in the event of the site's being viable and acceptable.[11] In March

or early April 1956, External Affairs and German Legation staff visited the Glencree site and Kolb thought it might have potential; it was agreed that the Minister for Finance be sounded out as to whether he would consent to have it assigned in some form or other for such a purpose. The consent was forthcoming and communicated on 27 August 1956, by Belton of External Affairs to a very appreciative Dr Klarenaar of the Legation.[12] This was not before time, perhaps: in December 1956 the Legation conveyed complaints by a visitor to the burial place of Anton Böhner in Cnoca'chairn Famine Graveyard, Dingle, where reportedly, the war grave was 'hardly recognisable, the wooden cross with its inscription almost rotten and that, before long, the grave would be impossible to identify'. External Affairs admitted the cross needed replacing but insisted the grave was being maintained in good order; within months, however, a new cross was in place.[13]

It was late the following summer when Herr Tischler and Herr Munarretto, the architects from the German War Graves Commission, arrived in Dublin to commence practical discussions and to view the possible site.[14] It was an apprehensive Assistant Principal Architect, J. P. Alcock of the OPW, who, on 23 August 1957, took the German Minister, his Attaché and the visitors

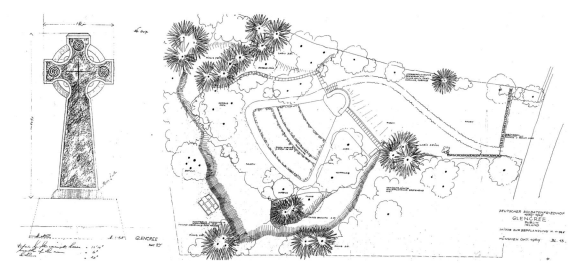

to view the Glencree site. What they found was not exactly prepossessing: the site identified by External Affairs and Dr Kolb on their original visit did not appeal, surrounded as it was by makeshift outbuildings attached to an adjoining cottage. The visiting party, however, became attracted by the potential of a disued quarry in the opposite direction, which offered the prospect of 'a very beautiful approach with a most dignified enclosure'. To the unexpected and intense relief of the OPW, the German architects and Minister became 'very enthusiastic': an extensive area, 'with room for a cross that could stand at the summit of the low cliff'. Furthermore, according to an Iveagh House official, it was 'an old quarry which I gather the OPW would be glad to be rid of'. The positive German reaction to the site surprised more than the OPW. As late as September 1958 the Minister for External Affairs, Frank Aiken, felt the site offered was not very suitable and thought 'it may give an impression of an attitude on our part which would, in all the circumstances, be unfortunate'.

Belton agreed. Discussing the matter with the German Minister, Felician Prill, he regretted that the choice of sites had been so limited. The latter reassured him that all the German officials who had seen the site were perfectly happy about its location and never entertained any doubt about its suitability. He explained that the German War Graves Commission had, in other countries, always sought sites of scenic beauty and that nowhere had they found such an ideal site as Glencree. Their selection of the Glencree site was unshakeable.[15]

By May 1958 Tischler's design for the cemetery had been approved by all the German authorities concerned: their War Graves Commission was only awaiting the final consent of the Irish authorities to commence the work of laying it out. It took no more than a week for the OPW to approve the design and boundaries of the plot and they awaited instructions as to whether ownership of the site was to be transferred to the Germans or merely a licence for the plot to be issued to them.[16] By September 1958 it had been decided that the transfer would take the form of a licence in perpetuity.[17] Inevitable technical and legal difficulties intervened over the coming months to ensure delay, including a German Legation objection to a clause in the draft licensing agreement that would have made them liable for the payment of rates: the eventual final agreement gave the site 'free of rates or other outgoings'. The Germans had argued, incorrectly, that Irish public cemeteries were exempt from rates: this was true only of such

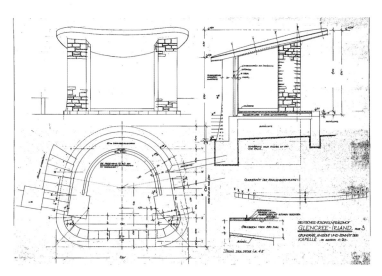

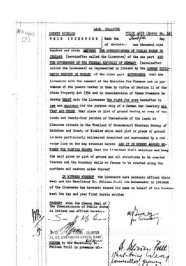

parish burial places where a right of free burial applied. Nevertheless, they would have to pay for its future maintenance.[18] For the Germans, the issue over rates was not a matter of financial cost: they wanted the grant of the licence to be 'an unqualified free gift' from the Irish Government. This was the basis on which all German cemeteries elsewhere had been created. In March 1959, Aiken, 'having regard to the close and friendly relations that exist between the two countries', advised that the German request be granted.[19] Not to be outflanked, the Valuation Commissioners insisted that the rates must be levied: they claimed that 'many cemetery authorities' had gone to court to secure exemption from rates and had failed; that, therefore, to allow the concession to the Germans would generate adverse reactions, especially from various Catholic Cemetery Authorities who, in recent years, had extended their grounds and incurred additional rates as a result. The Commissioners suggested, therefore, that the Irish Government assume responsibility for their payment, and, that given the location, the burden would not be great. They suggested, therefore, that Finance sanction the rate as a charge on the Government Property Vote, which Finance did – with unusual despatch.[20]

Beginning the work:
It was early in May 1959 that Herr Endler of the German War Graves Commission arrived, with car and tools, to begin the grim work of exhuming the German war dead, even as the Glencree site was being constructed. That construction was almost completed by September 1959,[21] and at that stage the retired Chancellor of the German Legation in Dublin, Bruno Achilles, was brought in, as liaison for the German War Graves Commission in Ireland, in the work of searching, exhuming and re-interring.[22] It was a month later that the Federal German and British authorities concluded their agreement concerning the future care of German war graves in the United Kingdom. The agreement provided for the transfer of all German war dead in the UK to a central cemetery: the German Military Cemetery at Cannock Chase in Staffordshire, which resulted from this agreement, was officially dedicated in June 1967. It was, of course, a huge operation by comparison, commemorating some 5,000 German and Austrian war dead.

Meanwhile, in Ireland, for once the delays appeared to be on the other side. The Irish authorities' draft letter of agreement and indenture had been sent to the German Foreign Office for approval in June 1959; in February

NEAR RIGHT
Hans Joachim Endler,
German War Graves
Commission.

FAR RIGHT
Walter Trepte, President
German War Graves
Commission and deValera
at the time of the Glencree
Cemetery inauguration.

1960 Iveagh House was still waiting for news, but the German reply, approving arrangements, came later that month, and in late July 1960 the licence agreement had been signed by both parties.[23] Interestingly, the Minister for External Affairs did not want any ceremony to mark the signing of this license agreement.[24]

Bizarrely, at this point, the ghost of the *Arandora Star* came back to haunt, though not to halt, proceedings. In the first part of 1960, Colonel Moran of the Legal Branch of the Irish Defence Forces came upon the grave of a German, Rudolf Heinz-Dellit, in County Sligo. He had written to the relatives to inform them of his discovery and they wrote back wondering about the possibility of a headstone for the grave. As it happened, Heinz-Dellit had been washed up on shore at Cloonagh near Lissadell, Sligo, on 20 August 1940, and had been buried in the nearby Carrigans Cemetery. Papers on his person indicated that he had been an employee of the Carl Zeiss optical firm in London. Enquiries by the Irish High Commission led to the Zeiss Company's confirmation that he had worked for them until he was interned at Seaton Camp, Devonshire, some months before. The firm, which was closing down its London branch, for understandable reasons, had not heard from him for several weeks and sought certainty as to the fact that the body was his. He had, of course, been put aboard the *Arandora Star*, bound for Canada, when it was sunk with its terrible losses in early July 1940.[25]

Now Colonel Moran wondered if it might be possible for the remains to be removed to Glencree. External Affairs understood, correctly, that Glencree was not exclusively for the use of German military personnel, but was for Germans, regardless of occupation, who perished in Ireland as a result of either of the two World Wars. At the same time, they held that it was not their concern whomsoever the German Federal authorities wished to bury there and it was for the latter to decide if Dellit should be interred and commemorated in Glencree.[26] In the end, the Germans did just that.

The Heinz-Dellit case proved only a beginning in the sad business of identification, recovery and new commemoration. The German Commission's work in the summer of 1959, in co-operation with the OPW and Garda Síochána, brought the official total to fifty-three identified remains for re-interment in Glencree. In the course of this work, they became aware, from conversations with local people, of the graves of unidentified casualties, some of whom may have been Germans. By September 1960 the German War

Graves Commission had discovered some 116 unidentified dead of the 1939-1945 conflict, a large percentage of whom they suspected to be German military or civilian internees, mainly from the *Arandora Star*. Their conviction that a significant number of those they located were Germans was based on the fact that the IWGC, through Vesper's investigations, had already identified most of the British Commonwealth war dead a decade before. An identification expert was brought from Germany in September 1960 to try to identify some of the unknowns:[27] His on-site investigations throughout the country brought the original 53 identified to 59, 6 of them from World War One. He located the remains of some 29 airmen and seamen and 46 German victims of the *Arandora Star*.[28] At his work's end, the Glencree German Cemetery had become the final resting place for the remains of 134 war dead, including one Belgian originally found dressed in German uniform.

Inauguration:

With this unhappy task completed, the issue of a formal inauguration of the Glencree German War Cemetery came to the fore. The inaugural ceremony was arranged for 9 July 1961. It was to be a non-religious ceremony arranged by the German War Graves Commission.

Its President, the German Ambassador, Embassy officials and some fifteen to twenty relatives of the German war dead were expected to constitute the core attendance. There were to be speeches by the Commission President and the Ambassador, and they hoped that some Irish representative might speak.[29] As to the Irish presence and contribution, an important role was to be played by national school teacher, Stan O'Brien, president of the Ireland-German Society. He had composed the three poems engraved in English, German and Irish at the cemetery. [30]

As inaugural occasions go it was a quiet and dignified affair, well-attended by German officials, naval officers and ratings, and eight relatives of the dead. The Irish Government was represented by Aiken as Minister for External Affairs, who laid a wreath. The principal speaker, Walter Trepte, President of the German War Graves Commission, spoke of the two nations, divided by the sea, meeting 'to honour the German soldiers who many years ago met their deaths in Ireland'. He and those who had travelled from Germany were

very moved to see how many of the leading personalities, representatives of the Ministries and public offices and, above all, the numerous people of this country themselves who are taking part in our hour of consecration.[31]

The German Ambassador, Dr Adolph Reifferscheidt, in thanking Aiken for his attendance, which 'was not only an act of diplomatic courtesy but was also an act of real friendship', spoke of these dead as 'victims of the criminal regime of National Socialism', and of the determination of the German people 'to see that such senseless wars would not occur again'. His speech did not go unremarked: commenting on the occasion, an *Irish Times* editorial observed, somewhat oddly:

Those who gathered in Glencree yesterday were there to honour the dead of a sovereign nation which had been at war. This was no place for political speeches. It may seem a little strange, therefore, that Dr Reifferscheidt, the Ambassador to Ireland of the Federal Republic of Germany, should have introduced a note of acrimony. By pointing out that the Germans were victims of 'the criminal regime of National Socialism', he may have been warranted in reminding people of Hitler's misdeeds, and thereby have done his country a political service. Nevertheless, his words were not merely unkind to the visiting relatives of the dead, but could be interpreted too clearly as casting a slur upon gallant men who died in the honourable faith and fear of soldiers.[32]

Ironically, if unintentionally so, the guard of honour on the occasion was provided by crew of the visiting German frigate, *Gneisenau*.

Completing the deal:

In advance of that occasion the Germans were hoping for an 'Exchange of Notes', formally outlining the agreement. The legal advisors to External Affairs indicated that such a move would constitute, in effect, an international agreement and, as such, would have to go to Government for decision whereas, up to this point, the business had been kept practically at interdepartmental level.[33] External Affairs felt a formal Exchange of Notes was unnecessary and decided to let the matter sit, unless the Germans returned to it, as indeed they did. On 26 January 1962, the German Cultural Attaché, Dr Rumeline, called into Iveagh House to say his Government wanted to finalise the matter. As intergovernmental agreements were the norm in such matters of war graves, Iveagh House was not altogether unsympathic to the Germans' wish.[34] However, under pressure on so many fronts, and seriously lacking in the staffing levels they needed, External Affairs took a long time in bringing this item close to the top of their list of matters to get done. Eighteen months after Rumeline's visit, the matter was still not advanced. Eventually, in April one year later again, External Affairs submitted the draft text to the Government. Finally, on 20 April 1964, the Government authorised the Minister for External Affairs to conclude

NEAR LEFT
Stan O'Brien (on right) and
Walter Trepte at the
Glencree Inauguration.

FAR LEFT
The Glencree German
Cemetery Cross in the
distance

an International Agreement with the
German Federal Republic on the war
graves at Glencree, which was duly
concluded on 13 May 1964.[35]

Resting where no shadows fall

Jack Rostern, Wireless Operator, RAF
24 February 1942

Arklow Cemetery
Co. Wicklow

Chapter 21

Isolation - Exhumation, 1930-1960

With the main work of construction on British Commonwealth headstones accomplished by the autumn of 1955, the OPW and IWGC could be forgiven if they had assumed that all that the future held would be quiet years of routine maintenance. The thirty years ahead, however, were to prove not so quiet and the matter of maintenance not as routine as either the OPW might have hoped or the IWGC expected.

Of caretakers and caretaking:

On as basic a matter as caretaking, securing the good will of competent caretakers proved to be more difficult as the years passed and payment levels stagnated. From their outset, the standard maintenance agreements always provided for a level of recompense that was never anything other than modest. To an extent, its modesty was founded on a strong element of good will, combined with economies of scale: if caretakers were already on site for the general maintenance of burial places, the few additional war grave headstones were a minor addition of labour and expense. While neither the OPW nor the IWGC ever argued this point publicly with the burial grounds' authorities, it was implicit in the proferred level of recompense. This was true even before the graves of the Second World War

became their responsibility, and was as evident in their dealings with major urban or suburban cemetery authorities, such as Dublin's Dean's Grange, as it was with small, secluded burial grounds like Donegal's Killaghtee.

As seen earlier, the original maintenance agreement with the Dean's Grange authorities, instituted in 1936, was for five shillings per war grave per year, half the charge to the public. This was still the rate in 1949 when the authorities raised the public charge from ten to fifteen shillings per grave, per year: even then, the OPW, and hence the IWGC, secured a bargain offer of half that sum from 1949.[1] As late as 1963, the rate there was still seven shillings and sixpence per grave, per year, for fifty-nine maintained graves. In the far north-west, near Glenties, County Donegal, a similar problem arose with the old burial ground at Kiltorris, Rosbeg: here the sole war dead occupant was Lieutenant J. P. Thyne of the Royal Army Medical Corps, drowned in the sinking of the *Mohamed Ali El-Kebir* on 7 August 1940. For that sole war grave, in 'this old country graveyard surrounded by sand', a maintenance agreement had been struck between the OPW and parish priest, Fr. John Byrne of Ardara, in April 1942. Six years later, an inspection by the OPW's local office revealed the grave was overgrown with grass and nettles.

A letter was dispatched to Fr. Byrne asking him to request the caretaker to remedy matters. Fr. Byrne, however, was dead. Early in the next year the OPW Assistant Architect, Caffrey, left a maintenance agreement form with local curate Fr. Finnegan of Kilcloney, to try to get someone to take over the cleaning of the grave. Fr. Finnegan's reply was not encouraging: the local caretaker had told him that he had got nothing 'for several years' doing the job and considered five shillings per year 'a pretty low figure'. A somewhat desperate Caffrey concurred:

If this man will not take on the cleaning I am afraid that no one will be found to do the work. The rate of five shillings per grave is completely outmoded by the decline in the value of money and is no longer attractive.[2]

Presumably with some reluctance, this local caretaker soldiered on with the five shillings, but four years later a replacement had to be found as he finally left Kiltooris to find work in Dublin.

Such payment and such problems were not new nor confined to remote coastal graveyards. As far back as 1932 the OPW entered into a caretaker saga in the matter of the war grave of RAF air mechanic, C. J. Sheridan of St.Ignatius Road, Drumcondra, Dublin. He had died in service, on 16 August 1921, at twenty-one years of age and had

been buried in Celbridge Church Lane Cemetery – the sole grave there of either major war. The cemetery was owned by Captain R. J. C. Maunsell, of the family occupying the stately Oakley Park Home, formerly Celbridge House, County Kildare, from 1840 until 1935. In 1929 Richard Maunsell had given permission – one of the first ever given – for a standard headstone on Sheridan's grave. When the OPW sought a maintenance agreement three years later, Captain Maunsell had been long gone to London, and his Celbridge home was beginning to fall into disrepair. However, although unable to help directly, he recommended his local cemetery caretaker, Michael Foley, for the job, at the five shilling fee. Foley took up the task, but soon left Tea Lane, Celbridge, for Dublin and, in July 1935, asked for back pay as, allegedly, he had, only been paid once. He, however, suggested Thomas Masterson, also of Tea Lane, who had taken over as the family cemetery caretaker. Masterson took over in June 1935 but in November was driven to write, (verbatim):

Dear Sir
Just a line too Let you know that i took over this Cemetery on the 9th June Last and I Done this graves up too the Preasant and i think that i am intickled too money for this year and if not i will Have Know more to Do with it.
Yours truly[3]

In fairness to Masterson, the OPW acknowledged internally that he had been doing a very good job with Sheridan's grave, and William Brandon admitted to Assistant Architect Geoghegan that

Unless we meet the caretaker …it would seem that the grave will not be maintained, since, as pointed out in your Memo of 1st instant, Mr. Masterson holds the keys of the cemetery Gate which is kept locked.

The patient Masterson, according to OPW reports, kept up the good work, but, as late as 1939 had to put in a claim for fifteen shillings, or three years' back pay.[4] The long-suffering caretaker was still doing an excellent job eleven years later, but, it seems, still having to wait unduly for his money:

> *Dear Sir,*
> *Would you kindly let me have the money for what work I done at above Cemetery. As I can't afford to wait any longer for payment. Also I would like you to know that I spent two days cleaning the stone. And I don't expect you shall find a man for seven shillings sixpence a day these times. Please send me on whatever you are going to pay for cleaning the stone. After all any man is entitled to what he earns. God know I am waiting long enough to be paid. I have nothing only what I earn myself. I would like if you got some one else to keep the graves clean as five shillings is too small.*

In response to the above, the OPW minuted 'This had better be attached to file as we are now, evidently, without a caretaker at this cemetery'. They then settled with him for ten shillings for maintenance and fifteen shillings for cleaning Sheridan's stone, but, at the same time, were trying, in vain, to secure a successor:

The finding of a successor to Masterson as a caretaker is proving difficult to date. It appears that the people contacted do not like to draw his tongue on them – enquiries being pursued.[5]

The local Garda Sergeant was endeavouring to help them find a replacement but ended up in hospital, following an accident, not, presumably, at Masterson's hands. Eventually, in late July 1950, another resident of Tea Lane, Peter Farrell, was signed up for the position, still at five shillings per year.[6] Two years later, Sheridan's grave was still being excellently cared for – by Masterson – and the OPW thought they had better cancel the agreement with Peter Farrell, who made no difficulty in this termination of contract. Finally, at the end of 1955, Thomas Masterson himself passed away, to be succeeded immediately by his son-in-law, ratified in April 1956. Right to the end of the 1950s and well beyond, this solitary war grave continued to be kept in good order. Either unflappable patience or irresistible

inflation brought recompense: in 1959 the OPW's payment was increased to ten shillings per year, almost thirty years after its introduction.

This was not exceptional. At Kilbarrack Cemetery, Sutton, County Dublin, where there were three graves of the First World War and one grave of the Second, the caretaking was in the hands of Margaret Harford at five shillings per annum, from 1936 to 1955, without known complaint. When her successor, Christopher Morgan, took over on 28 January 1956, however, it was at a princely six shillings per annum[7]. Even more striking was a case at Barna Old Graveyard, two miles west of Salthill, Galway, where lay the remains a twenty-one year old Gunner, Thomas Curran, Royal Field Artillery, who died on 17 December 1915. His then unmarked grave was verified and registered in October 1932, given its headstone and provided with a maintenance agreement with local man, Peter Faherty, in July 1936, at five shillings per annum. The years passed until one day, in June 1960, Faherty wrote to OPW Head Office,

Dear Sir
I am forwarding the form re War Grave (Barna) I would feel very grateful if you could allow me something more, five shillings isn't very much considering I have been doing it since 1915. I hope you will consider my application and oblige.

Not all were as patient or as polite as Peter Faherty. Consider finally, from a host of caretaker annals, the case of the grave of Waterford man, Private Arthur Hennessy, in Ballygunner, St. Mary's Catholic Churchyard. A member of the 15th Battalion Welch Regiment, he died aged twenty-two on 8 February 1941. His was the only Second World War Grave in a cemetery that contained two victims of the earlier conflict, Gunner J. Madigan of the Royal Garrison Artillery, and 3rd Battalion Connaught Rangers Sergeant, William Clarke. The cemetery administrator, Fr. Michael Barron, consented to the erection of a permanent headstone in October 1951, but when it came to effecting a maintenance agreement, he refused to sign the usual form: his reason was 'the caretaker who does other war graves in the Cemetery would not undertake the work involved for less than ten shillings per annum'. This caused a flurry of exchanges: the OPW in February 1953 pointed out that they had an agreement with Fr. Barron for the two First World War graves at five shillings per annum and requested him to accept this for Hennessy's grave. The reply was strongly worded:

I am perfectly well aware of an agreement (24/5/44) to maintain 2 graves for five shillings per annum. That was in continuance of an agreement made in 1937 with my

LEFT
Brookwood Memorial,
Surrey: in memory of war
dead with no known grave.

predecessor here. I should think it is fairly
obvious that it is impossible to get work done in
1953 at the same rate of pay as obtained in
1937. Even in 1944 the caretaker was not at
all anxious to continue at the five shilling rate.
Consequently I cannot agree to payment at the
five shilling rate for Private Hennessy's grave.
I cannot see any possibility of getting the work
done at less than ten shillings per annum.

Yours faithfully
Ml Barron,
Administrator.

Fr. Barron won the day, on 13 May 1953
extracting agreement from the OPW
at ten shillings per annum, while, seven
years on, others laboured at half the
rate.[8] Similar disputes arose all over the
country, with a particularly protracted
one over the Sligo Cemetery war grave
of Eileen Mills of the ATS, who died
in March 1946. This dispute with Sligo
Corporation ran for several years in the
1950s. Gradually, however, in place after
place, by 1960 the OPW had to concede
higher payments in face of a growing
number of caretakers who declined to
take on the work.[9] Such problems were
inimical to good order but proved minor
in contrast with those which arose over
isolated graves.

Isolation:

The tragic stories behind those lost at sea
whose remains were washed
ashore were exemplified in their most
extreme form in a case like that of
Sapper Wallace. John George Wallace
was yet another of the victims of the
sinking of the *Mohamad Ali El Kebir*. He
was washed ashore at Port, Rossan Point,
near Glencolumbcille, County Donegal,
on 8 September 1940. The unfortunate
man was buried at the bottom of a
200-foot cliff, at the edge of the sea,
above a shingle shelf, in a spot virtually
inaccessible by land. Nonetheless, those
who found and buried him managed to
mark his grave with a cross. The British
authorities at their UK Dublin Office
were duly informed of this in September
1940, and a standard war grave wooden
cross was fixed there in 1942.[10] With
the War's end, and the understandable
concern to have him laid to rest where
his burial place could be visited and
publicly commemorated, in January
1946 the OPW sought to remove his
remains to Glencolumbcille. The only
access to the spot at Port was a mere
grass track and it was impracticable,
if not impossible, to raise the coffin,
with heavy hauling tackle, up the cliff
face. It was therefore decided to move
the remains by sea, beaching a boat to
recover the coffin; that boat in turn to
be towed by another. Arrangements
were made with a local boat-owner to

NEAR RIGHT
The war grave in
St. Mura's of
Francis Palmer of the
Devonshires, Arandora Star
victim.

FAR RIGHT
The Church ruins at
Termon Old Graveyard.

effect this, but, having regard to the seas and winter weather, it was decided to implement this proposal at a more clement time. When Chettle of the IWGC made enquiries in June 1946, the news he heard was dire: the OPW were making arrangements for the transportation when a February storm washed away into the sea the bank in which the remains were buried. No trace was left of body, coffin or cross and, as Warnock at External Affairs put it, somewhat lugubriously, 'in the circumstances, I am afraid there is nothing we can do unless the body should be washed ashore again'.[11] When Chettle paid his visit to Dublin in September 1946 to discuss larger issues, it was nonetheless agreed that Sapper Wallace would be still remembered by a wooden cross, in some suitable cemetery immediately away from the coast. In the event, this Scottish soldier found alternative commemoration on the famous Brookwood Memorial in Surrey, built to remember the 3,500 men and women of the Commonwealth Land Forces who have no known grave.[12]

Few histories can have been as harrowing to the next of kin, but quite a number were not far removed. The Master of the vessel from which Wallace perished also lost his life in that disaster. John Pratt Thomson, the forty-nine year old skipper, drowned on 7 August 1940

and was washed up at remote Ugool, Killadoon, Louisburgh, County Mayo. He was laid to rest in a place known locally as Ugool Burial Ground, twenty yards from the north bank of Killary Harbour, his grave marked by a six- inch mound of clay, nothing more. The burial place itself lay in commonage, and, according to the Westport Gardaí, 'had not been used, before this, for the past one hundred years'.[13] The place was an old Famine burial place, reportedly inaccessible at certain times and seasons; so Vesper informed the IWGC as he made his 8,000-mile inspection tour of Ireland in 1951. At that stage, the IWGC was still uncertain as to its status as a war grave.

Not all isolated graves were necessarily remote, but still posed problems. Such was the case with that of Private Martin Maloney, of Castlemitchell, Athy, 7th Battlion Leinster Regiment, who died of wounds on 13 March 1917. He was buried in Geraldine (Tullagorey) Old Graveyard, in the civil parish of Kilberry, two miles north-east of Athy, County Kildare. When Vesper visited this in May 1929, the grave was located on the farm of a Mrs O'Neill, off the Athy-Curragh Road, in rough ground, overgrown with weeds. Although the grave itself was privately owned, this burial ground in the 1920s was administered by the Kildare Board of

Health and Public Assistance. They gave the permission for the headstone on 24 May 1929, and signed a maintenance agreement with the OPW on 29 January 1935. It was well-kept for a few years and then amnesia set in. When the grave's care became an issue for the OPW in 1949, the Kildare authorities could find no record of the grave and no record of its ever having had a caretaker.[14] A new caretaker, appointed in late 1949, died in March 1952 and his widow lived too far away to be able to take over. The only willing soul found in 1952 was a fourteen- year old boy and not until the following year, by paying seven shillings and sixpence instead of five shillings, could they get an adult to take on the duty. This man revolted in 1957 and a saga of discontent and mutual frustration between him and the OPW ensued.[15]

Most isolated graves, however, were remote and suffered the problems of that isolation. So it was with the case of the burial place of Private Francis Palmer of Plympton, Devon, 7th Battlion Devonshire Regiment: he perished with the *Arandora Star* on 3 July and came ashore on 14 August at Tullyillion, some miles north-west of Burtonport. The remains were in such a dreadful state that the Medical Officer of Health advised immediate burial in a field close to where they were washed ashore.

Private Palmer was, therefore, laid in the ground by the back wall of a field, in land belonging to Mr John Gallagher of Burtonport. The latter could not have been more accommodating to the OPW, consenting to the erection of a temporary wooden cross and permitting the fencing of the grave to protect it from grazing cattle; he himself personally erected the cross and made it clear the piece of ground was given by him rent-free. Although reports throughout the 1940s found the grave to be well kept, by 1950 the cross had become loose and stones were scattered on the grave. The sheer remoteness of the place made visitation difficult: on 28 April 1954 the remains had to be exhumed for reburial in St. Mura's, Upper Fahan.[16]

Termon:

Equally remote and difficult of access was the ancient burial ground of Termon, near Maghery, County Donegal. By the end of the Second World War it contained the graves of at least nine identified British, and two unidentified German military casualties. The Britons included the remains of fifty-two-year-old Captain Thomas William Clayton of Scarborough. Formerly of the North Lancashire Regiment, in August 1940 he had re-enlisted, as an officer of the Pioneer Corps; he was already a veteran,

mentioned in despatches during the First War, and now met his death on the 7-8 August 1940, as yet another casualty of the *Mohamed Ali El Kebir*. He was found washed ashore, at seven in the morning of 7 September 1940, his sole possessions a wrist-watch, cigarette case, three shillings and fourpence.[17] His body, and that of two of his Corps, Private Thomas Petch, also a First War veteran, and Private John Surley of Newcastle-on-Tyne, were laid to rest side by side. At the time, Termon Old Graveyard was difficult to access, and still is today. In the summer of 1947 his widow, Jenny, came to Dungloe to visit the grave and was shocked to find his, and the others, in an 'old, disused cemetery, completely overgrown': her son could not take photographs until he had cleared the lot away. Although she was wrong about its being disused at the time, since there was a burial there in 1969, it is now disused, with a new cemetery at Maghery. One need not doubt her that it was overgrown: it was still so in the autumn of 2005.[18] Jenny Clayton appealed to the authorities that her husband and comrades, as 'lost soldiers', should be exhumed and reburied in a more suitable cemetery. Commenting on this plea in March 1948, Vesper advised Brandon at the OPW that if they acceded to her request 'we should have to exhume the other 4 or 6. We can do nothing more about this, at present'.[19]

The case of Captain Clayton raised general issues of policy in regard to isolation, exhumation and reburial which need to be considered here. Repatriation to Britain, or elsewhere in the Commonwealth, was out of the question. As in the First World War, so in the Second, it was explicitly prohibited. On 4 October 1945, on behalf of the member Governments of the UK, Canada, Australia, New Zealand, India, Newfoundland and South Africa, the IWGC issued a statement that the return of their war dead could neither be undertaken nor allowed. It was made clear to External Affairs, when next of kin wished to repatriate a dead officer's remains from Ireland to Canada, that the prohibition applied to Éire as to anywhere else.[20] The radical solution of repatriation was out.

Vesper's unwillingness to act in regard to the Clayton grave, in March 1948, was understandable to the extent that the future, permanent treatment of all the Second World War graves had yet to be resolved, especially between the British and Irish Governments. Interestingly, in a discussion he had with J. G. Molloy of External Affairs that March, he raised the question of the possible exhumation of five or six bodies from isolated graves in Donegal and their possible reburial in some graveyard across the border in

HEADSTONE STANDARD ALPHABET &c.   Nº

LEFT
Headstone Standard
Alphabet, 1927.

Derry. According to his own account
of this discussion, Molloy assured him
that 'we would have no objection to this
course and that we would not consider it
a reflection on the OPW':

In fact it was the OPW who had
suggested this course owing to the
difficulty of proper maintenance arising
from the isolated position of the graves.
The OPW told Vesper in January that, in
some cases, exhumation and reburial in
Grangegorman Military Cemetery might
be advisable.[21]

When Edward King of the IWGC
visited External Affairs and the OPW in
July 1948, a significant discussion took
place on this question of exhumations
and reburials, but with a shift of attitude
on the Irish side. The Irish authorities
now stated their preference, that, as a
general rule, the bodies of war dead
should not be moved across the border,
lest it imply a slur on themselves, and
were glad that the IWGC appreciated
this point. Furthermore, they were not
anxious to encourage exhumations and
reburials elsewhere within the State,
as this implied they were unable to
maintain such graves *in situ*. At the same
time, they agreed with King and the
IWGC that graves in disused cemeteries
and churchyards presented 'very great
problems' and would not be averse to the
IWGC, in due course, putting forward

for exhumation 'a limited number of
the very worst cases', to be effected
whenever the permanent headstones'
process would commence.

Three years later, when that time had
come, and Vesper was effectively back to
Dublin, Oliver Holt at the IWGC took
up the question again. Interestingly, it
was over concern with the specific case
of Captain Clayton that he revived the
discussion. Following Jenny Clayton's
representations in the summer of 1947,
King had contacted Vesper in November
to ask him to explore the possibility of
the exhumation and relocation of the
Captain's remains. When Vesper then
raised it with the authorities in Dublin,

*apparently the Irish were sympathetic and it was
concluded that there would be no real difficulty
in moving this and other graves from Termon, in
addition to a few more from other places, subject
to the consent of the next of kin.*

Indeed, Iveagh House even sent the
IWGC a supply of Local Government
exhumation forms for the purpose,
but the matter was postponed until
the general programme of headstone
construction got underway.

In considering the matter at this time,
the IWGC had laid down a general
ruling that all such cases should be
dealt with *ad hoc*, on the basis that

WAR·GRAVES·
INSCRIPTION·ON·HEADSTONES·   FULL·SIZE.   NEG·N° 12289
DATE·2·10·29·

THEIR NAME LIVETH
FOR EVERMORE

· See·elevations·of·headstones·for·arrangement·of·words·

if reasonable maintenance was not possible or likely, exhumation and reburial, at IWGC expense, should be recommended. Such removal should be to the nearest accessible burial ground where adequate maintenance could be assured. Furthermore, 'long hauls' were to be deprecated, as was removal from Éire, except in cases where the nearest accessible burial place was immediately across the border, and where 'the formalities of taking the body across the frontier are not unduly formidable'.[22] Overall, Holt thought there might be upwards of twenty potential exhumation cases in question. As he had promised Mrs Clayton in August 1949 to raise this policy of 'concentration' with the Irish Government, he asked Vesper if it might now, in 1951, be timely to resurrect the issue with them. Somewhat surprisingly, in view of his generally accommodating attitude, Vesper took a different and determined line over Clayton's and the other British War Graves in Termon. Having visited the site, he found all nine known Commonwealth war dead buried in a line, in shelter, against the west wall of the ruin. Despite the repeated requests from the Clayton family for reburial elsewhere, Vesper insisted, as did the local farmer on whose land the ancient cemetery lay, and the local parish priest, and the OPW, that, although old 'and difficult of access', Termon was a recognised graveyard: consequently,

there was no need to exhume and rebury. Instead, what was proposed by Holt as a compromise and accepted by Vesper and all the other interests – apart from the Claytons – was the adoption of a practice the IWGC used in cases of isolated graves in France, namely, to lay a large concrete covering over the graves into which the headstones would be cemented.[23] There the matter rested, and nothing more was done over the next fifty-eight years other than the erection of standard headstones instead: except that the remains of the two German airmen were exhumed and reinterred in Glencree, while Captain Clayton's and his comrades' headstones lie within the ruins among the colt's foot vegetation.

Exhumation:
Despite the position he had taken on the Termon war graves, in the light of the general ruling on exhumation handed down by the IWGC in March 1951, Vesper prepared a short-list of eight cases to be recommended for exhumation and reburial. The places identified included Carndonagh Workhouse Graveyard. Here there were no memorials to permanently mark the graves of James Sorley Craig, the Canadian casualty of the Belgian *Ville de Gand;* none of Marine Archie Lovegrove of the *Cape St. Andrew;* nor

Left
Isolated war grave of
Joseph Conroy of
Roundstone, deckhand on
HMS Vivid, at Gurteen,
Co. Galway

of Ernest Winspear of the *Nerissa* – all
plots deemed 'very difficult to mark
and maintain'. Also on the list was
the Clondahorky (Strangers') Burial
Ground, containing the remains of
Engineer Sydney Perry of the *Manchester
Brigade*; the Tullyillion grave of Francis
Palmer from the *Arandora Star*; the
Milford Workhouse Cemetery with the
burial plot of Charles Walmsley of the
Corncrake; the Doaghmore isolated grave
of an unknown British seaman, washed
ashore on 14 September 1940, and
buried in a disused graveyard in a field
near Fanad Head; and the Ugool burial
plot of Master Mariner Thomson of
the *Mohamed Ali El Kebir*, in a field near
Killary Harbour.[24]

By July 1951, Vesper's list of potential
exhumation cases had risen to fifteen
and he wondered if, in the event of the
IWGC's deciding to proceed, they should
be relocated to Grangegorman Military
Cemetery in Dublin, something he had
discussed with the OPW Secretary, who
agreed with him in this.[25] Surprisingly,
Holt at IWGC Headquarters was not
keen on the choice of Grangegorman,
'unless we can make more satisfactory
arrangements for the maintenance of
this cemetery'.[26] Vesper remonstrated,
admitting 'I know how you feel about
Grangegorman Military Cemetery',
but pointing out that it was at least in
the charge of a permanent caretaker

and staff, employed by the Office of
Public Works: the alternative was
the difficult situation of trying to get
good maintenance for small country
churchyards. He insisted that one group
of fifteen to twenty graves relocated to
Grangegorman 'would be much better'.
He was overruled and had to set about
finding the idyllic alternative of Holt's
preference.[27] In all of this he consulted
closely with the OPW's Assistant
Architects, notably E. G. Caffrey in
Donegal, where most of the potential
cases lay. Caffrey and his staff were vital
in helping him to keep the list to a bare
minimum, based on their professional
judgement and experience as to whether
particular isolated graves were readily
maintainable or not.[28] As Vesper
ruminated on where he might rebury
these war dead, Carless and Holt at
headquarters in England now suggested
the adoption of the practice they were
then using in the case of war graves in
West Africa: leave the unmaintainable
where they lay, but commemorate them
on a simple, central memorial at a more
convenient site.[29]

Vesper himself responded warmly
enough to this idea and that a memorial
in a fairly central churchyard would be
'infinitely more desirable than exhuming
the remains'. It would be particularly
valuable in commemorating war dead
buried on some of the islands and other

areas difficult of access; but he wondered how relatives might react, especially those who had been told they were going to get individual standard headstones bearing their chosen inscriptions. But even though he, Holt and the OPW all favoured alternative central commemoration, in the end the matter was one for the IWGC at its highest level. They decided otherwise. Holt explained to Vesper, in late November 1951, how an IWGC conference on the subject decided that

the abandonment of the graves, particularly in a country situated so close to our own shores, was really out of the question and that there was no alternative but to concentrate them in some conveniently situated cemetery.[30]

Vesper had anticipated this outcome by two months: in late August he had thought that Letterkenny might prove a suitably central location if needed.[31] However, his special visit there in January 1952, after discussions with the Church of Ireland authorities in Dublin, led him and Dr Crooks, the local Church of Ireland man, to agree that no suitable site in or near to Letterkenny could be found. It was late January when he met Canon Dickson at St. Mura's, in Upper Fahan, where the large and well-tended First World War plot for the lost of H.M.S. *Laurentic* decided the matter for him. Hence it was, with the formal consent of the Canon and his Select Vestry, that St. Mura's became the place in which those war dead exhumed in Donegal and Mayo found their final resting place.[32]

Before the exhumations and reburials were organised, the OPW required to satisfy itself as to the identities and nationalities of the nine involved; that there were no religious or other objections from next of kin in respect of this burial ground; and no objections from External Affairs, Local Government in Donegal and Mayo, or from the local farmers in whose land some of the graves were situated. It was July 1953 before these permissions, including those of the relatives, had been finally and fully secured.[33] It was April 1954 before the contract for the undertaking had been placed. The exhumations were carried out on 27 and 28 April in Mayo and on 4 May 1954 in Donegal. In Upper Fahan Churchyard, at 4 p.m. on Thursday 6 May 1954, all nine were laid to rest again: J.S. Craig, A.L. Lovegrove and E.W. Winspear from Carndonagh; S.E. Perry from Dunfanaghy; F.P. Palmer from Tullyillion; J.P. Thomson from Ugool; C. Walmsley and an 'unknown' from Milford, and finally, another unknown, from Doaghmore. Lieutenant J.P. Thyne and Seaman R.B. McLeod, exhumed from Kiltooris, followed two years later,

NEAR LEFT
*The war grave of
Norwegian Captain
Hans Gullestad in Craigue
Little Cemetery,
Duncormick, Co. Wexford.*

FAR LEFT
*Craigue Little Cemetery,
Duncormick, Co. Wexford.*

on 7 May 1956.[34] For some relatives and friends, the sad story of such isolated war graves had come to an end. It was not so for all, however.

The Norwegian Captain:

The case of Hans Gullestad, Norwegian Master of the *Hidlefjord*, was to re-emerge years after his burial in St. Mogue's, Craigue Little, near Duncormick, County Wexford. Otto Lie, his fellow countryman and crew member of S.S. *Rask*, buried in St. Ibar's, had received his permanent memorial in 1958, not before some red tape over the duty free importation of the headstone.[35] For Gullestad's next of kin, however, matters became more complicated and his circumstances took on an aspect of miscommunication, if not of mystery. The Norwegian authorities understood, incorrectly, that his body had gone down with his ship: it had been washed ashore on 26 June 1941, found by local man, Philip Holmes, buried and marked with a temporary cross. This does not appear to have been known to them, to judge from enquiries made by their London Legation in April 1959. A Patrick Ffrench, then living in Newport, Monmouthshire, son-in-law of the local man who found Gullestad washed ashore, alerted the relatives, and so began the trail of further enquiries. It transpired that the mariner's

personal effects and the ship's papers had been forwarded by the Gardaí to the Norwegian Consulate in Dublin in September 1941, and were receipted as such. The *Hidlefjord's* owners, Kornelius Olsen of Stavanger, had never received the papers.

Since Gullstad's grave was relatively isolated, the Norwegian authorities, began, at the end of the 1950s, to make enquiries about the possibility of exhuming his remains for cremation. As permission for cremations was not granted in the Republic at that time, the Acting Consul in Dublin, J.R. Hollwey, assumed that Liverpool would be the nearest centre where this could be carried out, if the relatives wished to pursue this option to its conclusion. Wexford County Council gave permission for the exhumation in July 1959, but for reasons unclear, the exhumation was not pursued.[36] Instead, in 1960, the War Graves Commission became involved, as agents for the Norwegians, in arranging with the OPW for a permanent headstone.[37]

Twenty years after its original installation, Gullestad's grave was located, still with its wooden cross in place, and the OPW gave explicit directions to the Norwegians and the IWGC as to where the permanent stone was to be despatched. A stone duly

arrived and was erected in November 1961. Unfortunately, in December 1961, the OPW was informed that the wrong stone had been sent to Ireland: Gullestad's memorial had been sent to the Faeroe Islands, in error, and one for the Faeroe Islands had ended up on Gullestad's grave in Wexford. It was May 1962 before Gullestad's headstone arrived back from the Faeroes; duly erected, it was visited by his relatives from the mid-1960s. [38] For them, too, at last, the saga of this isolated war grave had come to an end. For the OPW and the IWGC, however, their burdens were only beginning, as recourse to exhumation continued and a new recourse to alternative commemoration commenced.

Far-called our navies melt away-
On dune and headland sinks the fire
Lo, all our pomp of yesterday
Is one with Nineveh and Tyre

Rudyard Kipling
Recessional

Chapter 22

Troubles And Neglect, 1955-1985

While the remains of Captain Clayton and his dead comrades were left in place at Termon after the Mayo and Donegal exhumations and removals to Upper Fahan over 1954-1956, the next exhumations were those of Italians and Germans. Two Italian *Arandora Star* victims were exhumed and repatriated to Italy: Annibale Finazzi, who had been buried in Frosses Catholic Churchyard on 14 August 1940, was returned to his homeland for reburial in April 1959; Francesco Rabaiotti, who had been interred in Slievemore Graveyard, at Keel, Achill Island, on 10 August 1940, was repatriated to Italy on 6 June 1959.[1] The exhumation and removals of the Germans to Glencree has already been described, but one case of German exhumation in particular was to generate controversy and attacks in the British press. Ironically, the attacks were not against the Germans, but against their own authorities in Britain and, in particular, against the Commonwealth War Graves Commission, as the IWGC had become in March 1960.[2]

A field where horses graze:

When the trawler *Aberdeen* was sunk on 12 March 1941, its skipper, John Barber, and second mate, William Coe, were its only dead to be found on the Irish coast. They were buried in Little Calvary Cemetery, Drogheda, also known as the Drogheda Workhouse Graveyard. In due course they were remembered by temporary wooden crosses and later by permanent CWGC headstones. Not far from them, in the same place, lay the remains of German airman, Walter Hoppmann. He was removed from this desolate field-cemetery in the course of the removals in 1960 to Glencree, where his remains now lay in more dignified surroundings. This proved too much for a columnist with the British Sunday newspaper, *People*. In February 1961 it published, side by side, contrasting photographs of the desolate place in which Barber and Coe were commemorated, in contrast to the impressive final resting-place of the Germans. As a photo caption put it: 'Horses trample on the graves of these British heroes. Beside them were buried two German pilots, but now see their present resting-place, in a splendid war cemetery'. A local Drogheda woman had alerted the *People* journalist by a letter in which she bitterly complained:

When I see two poor British seamen, who helped to feed you during the war, buried in a dump near my home, it makes my blood boil to think that nobody cares.[3]

While the CWGC rightly pointed out that Barber and Coe were not forgotten, that their graves were marked by the permanent standard war grave

headstones, the journalist pointed out that Drogheda Little Calvary was, in fact, a field, known as Bully's Acre – 'no cemetery at all, but a field where horses graze'. It galled him to note that the British 'should have to be taught the decencies towards our war dead from the nation that produced Adolf Eichmann'.

The CWGC lost little time in reacting to this criticism. On 1 March 1961, CWGC Northern Area Superintendent, W. A. Pettigrew, contacted the OPW, remarking that their present situation was not 'good'. He asked if, in view of local feeling, press comment and the German removals, the OPW would have any objection to the removal of Barber's and Coe's remains to Grangegorman Military Cemetery. The OPW responded quickly and positively that they could provide the required spaces free of charge and with the guarantee of non-disturbance in the future. While today Grangegorman is a splendid example of a well-kept military cemetery, Pettigrew's request was a true sign of desperation: Grangegorman had not been in the best of shape and for some years it had not been a source of any comfort to the CWGC. Oliver Holt's reluctance to contemplate its use for the Donegal and Mayo exhumations in the mid- 1950s has already been noted. In 1958 the Cemetery was reported as being 'in very poor order',

with a caretaker of advanced years trying to keep its acres in trim with a scythe. Various kerbs, rails and 'other encumbrances' were anathema to the CWGC. By dint of pressure and persuasion from the very end of the 1950s to the middle of the 1960s, they managed to get the OPW to experiment with converting one section of it to pure lawn, plain, simple and free of kerbs, glass and plastic globes. A new young caretaker was appointed, provided with an assistant and supplied with a mower. By the time Admiral Sir Guy Grantham, as Vice-Chairman of the CWGC, paid his first war graves' visit to Ireland in October and November 1964, he was gratified to learn of the great progress which had been made in converting the cemetery into a clean, simple, lawn-based garden of commemoration.[4]

Pettigrew's timing of his request had been fortunate, or perhaps the decision to exhume and relocate these war dead to Grangegorman precipitated the moves that led to improvements in the latter. Barber and Coe were exhumed from Drogheda, Little Calvary, at noon on Tuesday 5 September 1961 and re-interred in Grangegorman later that day.[5] Although perhaps not evident at the time, it was the beginning of a process whereby Grangegorman Military Cemetery became the refuge and recourse from abandoned or

neglected war graves elsewhere. In 1963 the remains of Private David Beary of the Royal Munster Fusiliers, who died in 1915, were removed from Tipperary County Home Cemetery where, by 1960, the graves were no longer being tended, and where there were no known relatives; he was re-buried in Grangegorman on 17 May 1963. Two days before this, the remains of an unidentified British airman, buried over twenty years before in Oranmore Old Graveyard in Galway, were laid to rest in the Blackhorse Avenue cemetery. On 17 May also, the 1916 Insurrection re-entered history-making, when five officers killed or dying of wounds from the fighting between 26 and 30 April, and who had been buried in the grounds of Dublin Castle, were exhumed. In the presence of the Military Attaché, Brigadier Thicknesse, members of the British Legion and with Archdeacon Jenkins and Fr. F. Quinn officiating, they were laid to rest in Grangegorman.[6]

In May of the following year, a case of exhumation and reburial as bad as that in Drogheda arose in respect of Peter Hopkins of the Royal Irish Regiment. He died in March 1919 and was buried in Cross Burial Ground, Mayo, in a common field where animals grazed. Children had been buried there from time to time. Because of his grave's location and neglect, his remains were exhumed on 21 May 1964 and reburied in Grangegorman next day.[7]

Quite the worst case of neglect, however, was found not in some remote place, but within the capital. Here, in St. James's Church of Ireland Churchyard, near Kilmainham, where new burials had ceased from 1954, and where the church saw its final service in April 1963, was a burial place neglected to an extreme extent. Eight CWGC headstones here marked nine of the known war graves. One, unmarked, that of RAF mechanic, Christopher Dolan, was never found, but it was almost impossible to locate the eight stones in the jungle-like conditions – so the CWGC Director General was informed in July 1964. A CWGC report of two years earlier had said of St. James's: 'this is quite definitely the worst Churchyard in the Irish Republic containing war graves'.[8] Regional Director Woodgate concluded, in 1964, that 'it is impossible to maintain the graves to the normal Commission standard' and recommended that, while the remains stayed in their graves, approval be given to remove the headstones to Grangegorman, by way of alternative commemoration. By the mid-1960s therefore, Grangegorman Military Cemetery, itself being improved, was beginning to become the preferred site for reburials and alternative commemoration. If this was by default

RIGHT
OPW drawing of stamdard
war gravestone layout.

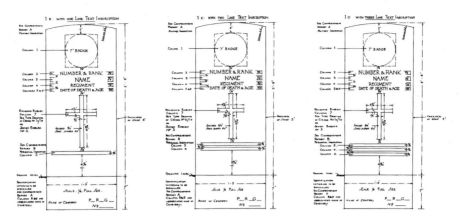

rather than by policy decision, it was nonetheless a timely development in the face of new troubles elsewhere.

The Curragh Military Cemetery:

The other major military cemetery in the region, that at the Curragh, in County Kildare, had as chequered a history as Grangegorman. In the middle of the 1950s there was a low-key inquiry from the British Embassy as to the state of affairs there. A woman visiting her brother's war grave in October 1953 was shocked at the Curragh Cemetery's condition: on her previous visit, some years before, she found it had been 'beautifully kept up', but 'now it looked altogether neglected and overgrown, the gates smashed open and indication of deliberate vandalism'. As a result of her complaint, the matter was investigated by the British Embassy's Military Attaché, Colonel Stewart, and in January 1954 he found many of the stones broken. As Stewart reported:

Incidentally, an Irish gentleman who accompanied me expressed himself as somewhat mystified at signs of apparent vandalism, as he had never heard of any of his countrymen interfering with British graves, and the priests would certainly not countenance it.[9]

Stewart found an old caretaker there who had been appointed by the Curragh Ranger, but who was clearly unable for the job.

Walsh-Atkins of the British Embassy reported the 'period of neglect' to the Commonwealth Relations Office in September 1954 and advised that 'somebody' should make 'a tactful suggestion' to the Irish authorities that the current care of the place was apparently not adequate. When Stewart's successor as Military Attaché, Colonel Lindsay, visited in late 1954 in the presence of Irish Army officers, he noted that they, too, were struck by the state of the place but, like him, did not seem to know who was responsible for its care and maintenance.[10] Whatever representations were made, the OPW took the place in hand during the winter of 1959-1960, using a contractor to remove old trees, shrubs, kerbs and railings and sealing it off from the ubiquitous sheep. Further visits in 1964 and 1969 found the place 'tremendously improved', with the grass cropped and following the natural contours of the place.[11] As elsewhere, however, the story was frequently one of cycles of improvement and deterioration. By 1972 the CWGC Deputy Regional Director, Cole, was lamenting the fact that at the Curragh Military Cemetery once again 'there was genuine cause

for complaint'. The OPW was taken aback also, and the blame was left fully at the doorstep of the Department of Defence, who now appointed the Bailiff for the property. By 1975 the OPW had had to step in, appoint a contractor who felled over eighty trees in the cemetery and restored the place to an acceptable standard.[12] Thirteen years later, in 1988, in view of one complainant visitor, the cemetery again displayed 'a disgraceful state of neglect and appears to have suffered from vandalism'. He wanted action, not least because he felt strongly that 'the Irish ex-soldiers and servicemen generally were wiped out of the national consciousness after 1922 and we want to restore them to honourable memory'.[13]

At the far end of the country another historic military cemetery, that at Ballincollig, was coming under a critical spotlight in the same decade. In 1983 the Cork Branch of the British Legion complained that this graveyard was 'completely overgrown' and, echoing a refrain from the 1920s and 1930s, asked the CWGC to reconsider their contractual commitment to the OPW and entrust the Ballincollig war graves' upkeep to the Legion itself. Five years later, in September 1988, the CWGC Director visited and came away distinctly unimpressed:

It presents a very depressing sight – and we just saw it to advantage for the vegetation had just had one of its bi-annual cuts'.[14]

The other Cork County Military Cemetery, at Fermoy, had been no different, ten years earlier. In March 1978 the *Irish Weekly Examiner* condemned 'the disgraceful state of the military cemetery at Fermoy' and an Irishman living in Harrow complained forcefully to the CWGC about this state of affairs at the time.[15] Sadly, the place had been well-tended until the untimely death of its caretaker in a fire, some years before, and after that, it fell derelict.

Vandalism:
Relative remoteness from centres of population was no guarantee against acts of vandalism, as was suspected more than once in respect of the Curragh Military Cemetery. Sadly, this fact was put beyond any doubt in 1973 when vandals attacked the German Cemetery at Glencree. On the afternoon of Friday 24 August an unidentified group, using black paint, defaced the gilded inscription on the Pieta with names and slogans; on an inside wall of the memorial they had sprayed offensive slogans and the name 'Ulrike Meinhof', while the threshold was defaced with the words 'First of May Group'.[16]

The culprits were never identified nor apprehended. It was symptomatic, too, of the carelessness with which diplomatic documents can be drafted, that responsibility for the costs of restoration was unclear. Paragraph two of their 1964 international agreement provided that 'the Government of Ireland guarantees the protection of the German War Graves', while paragraph five stipulated that 'the Government of Ireland is in no way responsible for the costs of maintenance'. While the Germans were advised by External Affairs to place a compensation claim with Wicklow County Council, when the affair came to its conclusion the OPW ended up doing the work and paying for it out of their own budget.[17]

It was, however, from the 1970s, in the major urban centres like Cork and Dublin that the main trouble with vandalism and delinquency arose. It is remarkable that, up to that point, malicious damage to individual war graves was almost unknown. Most notable in this regard was the absence of politically motivated damage to, or destruction of, war grave headstones. Public monuments to the military or the war dead were another matter, as the destruction of the war memorial in Limerick in 1957, the blowing-up of General Gough's equestrian statue in the Phoenix Park, Dublin, in the same year,

or that of Nelson's Pillar in O'Connell Street, Dublin, in 1966, exemplify.

However, when it came to individual memorials in the 500 plus cemeteries containing war graves, it seemed that peaceful co-existence was the universal norm. Typically, the First World War grave and headstone of Sergeant James O'Grady in Kilmeena Cemetery, County Mayo, who died in April 1919, could safely survive untouched beside the monument to the IRA killed in the Kilmeena Ambush of May 1921. This was a particularly emotive episode in the War of Independence, given the IRA defeat and the revulsion caused by the fact that the Black and Tans dumped the bodies of the dead and wounded outside Westport Police Barracks.[18] The one apparent exception proved the rule: the damage done to the standard war grave headstone of Canadian Forces engineer, Lieutenant Hugh Massy Baker, in Bansha Church of Ireland Churchyard, Tipperary, on 12 November 1954, turned out to be the result of a personal grudge by a dismissed employee of Baker's uncle.[19] But, as time passed, thirty years on, mindless vandalism became a new phenomenon.

The most serious cases arose in Cork in regard to the old Military Cemetery at Assumption Road. During the years from 1963, when Julia McSweeney

FAR LEFT
*The Gough Memorial,
Phoenix Park, blown up in
1957.*

NEAR LEFT
*The Memorial to the
IRA Volunteers killed at
Kilmeena in May 1921*

was resident caretaker, there were few problems, but this changed as soon as she retired early in 1972, leaving a vacancy. Sometime between 3 and 5 July 1972, a total of twenty-one of its eighty-three Commonwealth War Grave headstones and five permanent private memorials were damaged or destroyed. This was a considerable feat of malice, given that the convicted perpetrators were two local youths aged only thirteen and fourteen years. So great was the destruction, with costs amounting to over £1,180, that the identification of each headstone with its original grave was not possible. The popular press made much of the scandal, with the *Sunday World* proclaiming, 'Graveyard Ghouls Ruin Cemetery'.[20] Doubtless to its great embarrassment, the OPW had to request the CWGC to re-supply a layout plan of the Cemetery's war graves.[21] The destruction was all the more tragic, in that a mere two years before it, Percy Grieve, MP for Solihull, Birmingham, on a visit to the grave there of his uncle, Major Charles Grieve, was delighted at the first-class upkeep of the cemetery.[22] The OPW responded to the attack with a full programme of renovation, the repair of a damaged boundary wall and the restoration of a caretaker's lodge. It was, however, in vain. There were mounting problems with caretaking: repeated attacks by vandals in the course of the next decade destroyed

the buildings beyond repair. The OPW Regional Office in Cork confessed that the situation had got out of hand. By 1981, 'despite the best efforts of the OPW in a difficult situation', matters seemed beyond remedy and had reached a point of crisis: the CWGC deemed that any further expenditure of money and effort could hardly be justified.[23] Bernard Egan of Harrow, who had complained about the state of Fermoy Military Cemetery in 1978, had even more to deplore when he visited Cork Military Cemetery in the summer of 1982 and complained to the Taoiseach and local TDs;

In a disgraceful and wrecked state … caretaker's lodge has the slates from the roof all over the place. Grass, weeds and defaced headstones make it look a sorry sight.[24]

By 1985 the Commission was receiving complaints about the Cork situation from as far away as Greece, whence their local Supervisor, R. J. Kemp, sent them a hard-hitting report from the *Cork Evening Echo*, entitled 'The Crime of Cork's Old Soldiers' Graveyard'.[25] Yet, years later, during the CWGC Area Director's visit, a further forty of their eighty-three headstones were found to have been vandalised and required replacement, at the OPW's expense.[26] The situation reached its depths when a step, unprecedented in the history of

war graves administration in Ireland, was taken: in October 1983 all eighty-three CWGC headstones were removed from the cemetery and put into storage pending alternative developments.

Alternative commemoration:

The twenty years from 1970 constituted a problematic period in the story of war graves administration in Ireland. It was not just the problem of vandalism which, after all, was not peculiar to the Irish urban scene. CWGC memorials in the UK and France also suffered at the hands of hooligans from this time. In Ireland, however, the situation was compounded by the Northern troubles. Visitation of sites, so major a matter of concern for the Commission from the 1930s to the 1950s, for the first time became difficult in some places, impossible in others. War graves in cemeteries along the Border effectively became impracticable to inspect. Political tensions did not help matters, especially when in February 1972 the British Embassy was burned down. The war graves files, along with those relating to weightier contemporary political matters, went up in flames. At that point the CWGC suspended inspection visits, although Brigadier McMullen, the Military Attaché, offered to help them by liaising directly with the OPW. In that spirit he visited Glasnevin with an OPW

architect in August 1972 and sent to the CWGC a generally favourable report on its condition.[27] Despite the Brigadier's reassurances to them that 'there should be no risk in a resumption of your Inspectors' normal visits', the CWGC decided to suspend visits for that year.

These political problems were further compounded by economic difficulties and profound social change. The economic difficulties circumscribed the efforts of the OPW to maintain standards in war graves' maintenance: this responsibility was, after all, when put into perspective, but a minor part of its huge and ever growing range of responsibilities during a time of staffing cutbacks. Social change was another matter: apart from the impinging of housing estates on local environments that included graveyards, relative rural depopulation created further and unexpected difficulties. Old Catholic and Protestant rural parishes saw ageing and declining populations, so that local burial places became easy victims of unintended neglect. The churches themselves, with the best will in the world, increasingly lacked the financial resources to maintain their burial places to adequate standards. Even where the OPW and CWGC managed to keep up individual war graves, it was often within burial grounds that had themselves become jungles. This was by

LEFT
The Memorial to the IRA Volunteers killed at Kilmeena in May 1921.

no means an exclusively rural problem, as the appalling case of St. James's Church of Ireland burial ground, near Kilmainham, has already exemplified. The crisis over Cork Military Cemetery merely brought such concerns to a head and precipitated a policy rethink on the part of the Commonwealth War Graves Commission in Ireland.

Despite the political turmoil in the North and along the Border, the CWGC managed to visit all sites in the Republic over the period 1977-1981, including over one hundred near the Border which had been uninspected for ten years. Dismissing any suggestion of wilful neglect, the UK Area Director, R. G. Wall, and his team in 1981 identified 116 sites that were now utterly unmanageable, in cemeteries that were completely abandoned and, in some cases, totally inaccessible because of brambles and scrub. Some 174 affected graves were identified as definitely requiring some kind of alternative commemoration, and a further ten graves in nine sites were found not to have been permanently marked. All this was in addition to the general problem posed by the Cork Military Cemetery.[28]

The Assistant Director-General, P. R. Matthew, accepted the compelling evidence of the need for alternative commemoration, while leaving these unmanageable graves undisturbed. He supported a proposal that a suitable memorial should be erected in Grangegorman Military Cemetery on which could be commemorated the burials in Cork Military Cemetery, as well as the unmaintainable memorials in the abandoned or neglected graveyards.[29] While confident that the CWGC governing authorities would accept a properly prepared submission to this effect, there were doubts and misgivings as to actually pushing a Grangegorman proposal with the authorities in Dublin: As one official, A. S. Laing, put it:

Do we erect a memorial in alternative commemoration at Grangegorman now, or do we, because of the political difficulties and risk of damage, wait until later? If we decide to wait, do we make a temporary Book of Remembrance and, if so, where do we put it? Obviously, getting on for two hundred names cannot be allowed to drift without commemoration.[30]

Within the next twelve months Cork City Corporation had become involved and, following discussions with the OPW and CWGC, thought the best solution for the Military Cemetery problem was to transfer the property to the City, to develop the site as an amenity area, transferring the CWGC headstones for commemoration elsewhere and moving the older military headstones

to run along a perimeter wall. The last suggestion apparently was first mooted by local resident, Mrs Barbara de Foubert of Blackrock, Cork.[31] Her proposal, which had the support of the Cork City authorities, was taken up by the OPW and referred to the CWGC. At meetings with the OPW in Dublin, in April and again in September 1982, R. G. Wall of the CWGC expressed the Commission's support for this proposal.[32] This was indeed the solution ultimately arrived at, but it took a good while in being realised.[33] Following discussions between the CWGC and the OPW in Dublin in September 1982, by January 1983 the CWGC Director was pressing for a decision that would enable them to relocate their Cork headstones to Grangegorman and to get on with the erection of a new memorial there. Agreement in principle was reached in the course of 1983. That September the Commission Authorities approved funding in excess of £15,000 for the construction of the new Grangegorman Screen Wall Memorial, which was approved by the OPW in February 1983.[34] That construction proceeded smoothly, and was completed in April-May 1984. The whole exercise had been kept low profile, at the request of the Office of Public Works. Such shyness of publicity was something the CWGC fully shared with the OPW: the Commission deliberately refrained from responding

to newspaper press criticisms that were misinformed or uninformed on these developments. As its UK Area Director, Terry Penfold, observed in 1985: 'rebuttals would be unwise as we wish to maintain as low a profile as possible in the Republic of Ireland'.[35]

A Memorial Park forgotten?

No hallowed shrine sacred to the memory of the war dead was secure, it seems, from the depredation and deterioration that marked these decades. Of all the examples of decline and disintegration, perhaps the most lamentable was that which occurred at Islandbridge in Dublin. The Irish National War Memorial had been achieved there after such effort and expenditure that its growing plight threatened to become a national scandal. Ill luck in the form of disease may have plagued its trees, but indifference, indigence and vandalism played on even larger part in the decay of the country's only great national memorial to the dead of the two World Wars.

As originally designed, this great project included provision for a splendid bridge over the Liffey, linking the Memorial Park to the Phoenix Park proper. None of this had happened by the time it was first used in 1940. Neither were there public shelters or facilities. The Irish

National War Memorial Trustees, with £10,000 left in their fund by then, had approached the Government with a view to realising the full plans. In March 1939, the Minister for Finance had responded by indicating, in principle, a willingness to go 'fifty-fifty' on the basis of a total maximum cost of £20,000. Unfortunately, the bridge project was costed by Lutyens at £34,000-£43,000, depending on materials.[36] Abandoning the Bridge, the Trustees now suggested, as a more economical alternative, ornamental railings and entrance gates, for which Lutyens provided plans, at an estimate of £11,000. The Trustees were willing to contribute £7,000 if the Government would put up £4,000, but the Taoiseach decided 'that in view of war conditions he feels now that the question of State assistance for further works at the Memorial cannot be usefully pursued'. Indeed, the OPW memorandum on this account added: 'when the opening would take place it would be done quietly to avoid undue attention'. This attitude on the part of the OPW was well-established: when visiting Dublin in June 1939, Vesper had learned from inside the OPW that

It was the Board's intention to make the ceremony (if there be a ceremony at all) as quiet and informal as they possibly can, because

they are anxious to avoid any possible unpleasant incident or controversy.[37]

At the time, and for long after, the larger Park, of which the War Memorial plot is but a part, was never formally opened to the public and the plot was railed off in a fashion, remaining closed except on Armistice Days and the days from August 1946 into the late 1950s when the Old Contemptibles used it to remember their part in the First World War.[38] The INWM Committee and members, however, never gave up the hope for a formal opening ceremony and, in the years after the Second War, they pressed strongly at times for this. There were, however, attempts to blow up the War Memorial in 1956 and 1958. The Government, as a result, continued to defer the matter, partly because of the threat of damage and partly because the scheme and project had not been fully completed,[39] in particular the entrance from Inchicore Road. Although the INWM Trustees endeavoured to cover the estimated cost of this entrance, estimated at £13,000, from the funds which had accumulated since 1939, the OPW was conscious that the Memorial Park as a whole had never been finished. On the contrary, expanses of it in the meantime had been leased to various interests, including Dublin City Corporation who used its section for allotments and a rubbish dump.

The OPW itself in 1963 deplored the whole area's 'unkempt appearance which is out of keeping not only with the Lutyens-designed Memorial and Plot – which is its centrepiece, but also with the Phoenix Park of which it is purported to be an extension'. Assistant Principal Architect, McNicholl, and Parks Superintendent, Barry, wanted to see the whole park area reclaimed and developed. The proposal for the Lutyens Bridge was resurrected and the OPW wondered if the Trustees of the INWM might be willing to help with the cost of the Park and the Bridge. Now the OPW hoped that, with such a development, 'the opening of the park and Memorial Plot would follow as a matter of course'. In a new way of looking at the matter, they felt that once it was in use as an open park 'malicious damage to the memorial would appear less likely'.[40]

Four years passed before a meeting of the OPW and the INWM representatives in May 1967 agreed in principle to a scheme of work to provide public shelter and convenience, the construction of a warden's lodge, the provision of a new water supply and a proper boundary wall to the Memorial Plot.[41] For this the Trustees were now willing to put up £15,000 of their remaining £20,000. Representations made to the Minister for Finance eighteen months later led to the engaging of Fehilly, landscape

architects, to prepare plans on foot of a general appraisal of the whole area. Their report favoured a large-scale development, involving multiple recreational facilities for the Park area. However, as all this was likely to cost too much, the Parliamentary Secretary with responsibility for the OPW suggested an eighteen-hole public golf course instead. Given that the Corporation had just then finished using the western end as a dump, and were about to start landscaping it, the golf course, at £840,000, plus £30,000 for a clubhouse, appeared a possibility.[42] None of this materialised; instead, over the next fifteen years, the uncompleted Park and Memorial deteriorated, and badly so. Its monuments crumbling to decay, one of its granite pillars was demolished by a stolen car, the pergola's oak beams sagging as a result; the elms destroyed by disease; the rubbish-strewn fountains dry; the gates and fences broken to let in grazing animals; the flowers long gone, tree stumps and broken glass abounding. By 1985 it was reaching the point of an erupting public outcry, with journalist Helen Lucy Burke, among other commentators, producing a severe criticism of 'Dublin's Forgotten Park'. She wrote in April 1985: 'If the Danes had left such a monument behind them, would we have let it fall into decrepitude?'[43]

To live in the hearts
Of those we love
Is not to die

Owen Mitchell, Private, 7th Devonshire Regiment
2 July 1940

Easkey (Roslea) Cemetery
Co. Sligo

Chapter 23

A Future For The Past?

By the mid-1980s public neglect and political indifference, at the highest level, to the burial places of the war dead, and to the rituals of commemorating them, may have reached its extreme point. There were, even then, however, signs of emerging commitment to acts of improving change, no longer confined to the completely worthy but well-established concern for Ireland's ancient monuments. What is notable about these developments is the extent to which they were local in origin; but what is most striking about them is the extent to which they were due to the concern, commitment and drive of individual good citizens. It was, to a great degree, their initiatives that paved the way, in atonement for the past and recovery for the future.

Recoveries:

As noted earlier, the processes of rural parish decline on the one hand, and suburbanisation on the other, brought multiple problems for war graves, military cemeteries and burial places in general. Ironically, while the proximity of housing estates could constitute a major problem for some of the military cemeteries, as in Cork City, and indeed at times in Grangegorman itself from the 1980s, this was not always so. The case of Ballincollig Military Cemetery makes for an interesting exception. At

the time when Cork Military Cemetery was at its worst, Ballincollig was little better. In 1983 the Cork Branch of the British Legion complained to their headquarters in Pall Mall that it was 'completely overgrown ... a disservice'.[1] Five years later it still presented 'a very depressing sight', as the Commission's Director-General lamented in a report on a visit there in September 1988. He admitted that the ten World War graves were clearly identifiable and the stones with their inscriptions recently scrubbed clean, but, hidden behind a high wall, the cemetery was padlocked against vandals.[2] At the end of the following decade the situation was transformed for the better, largely due to local concern and initiative. At the turn of the millennium, under the auspices of the Ballincollig Enterprise Board, a community group led by Anne Donaldson and Eileen O'Sullivan devised a plan of action for the restoration of the Military Cemetery, and raised funds for its clean-up and for an archaeological survey conducted by Sheila Lane. Given Ballincollig's long and rich military history as the main artillery barracks in Munster, this was an important restoration initiative, giving a hopeful future to a significant past.[3] Support by the local rector, Rev. Francis Rutledge, and colleagues, and practical aid by the OPW, Heritage Council and Cork County Council, were all critical

for the project. The restoration was not only a remarkable success, but was, paradoxically, aided into the future by a housing development around its perimeter that actually seems to have helped reduce its exposure to vandals. Furthermore, the success of the project was capped by Anne Donaldson's production of the only published history of a military cemetery in Ireland to date.[4] The Ballincollig story was but one, if particularly fine, example of a physical and intellectual recovery of a forgotten and neglected past.

A second example came from the Curragh where, once again, by the late 1950s, there were complaints of neglect and vandalism. In 1988, however, in association with the Kildare Archaeological Society, the Kildare Heritage Project was launched as a FÁS Scheme. The participants worked with the Society and the CWGC in archiving the burials in the Curragh Military Cemetery, and, in the process, brought a new awareness of its historic interest and importance.[5] For all that, it was not unqualified progress and a recurrent cycle of restoration and decline continued to bedevil the place. As late as 1996, a Dublin-based ex-RAF man complained of its 'very poor condition ....generally run down, with fallen headstones'.[6] In some ways the upkeep here was almost an impossible task. It

was difficult to keep trim with mowers, given the nature of the terrain. Allowing sheep to graze was simultaneously a solution to long grass and a cause of damage – their fleeces and dyes badly stained the stones. Furthermore, efforts to keep them out were thwarted by individuals who opened gaps in the stone walls to get them access. Nothing short of twenty-four hour security duty, seven days a week, all year round, could prevent this. To a Commission inspection team in 1999, the place was again a mess, with dirt and sheep droppings at its entrance; yet even they conceded that 'the site is quite eerie and difficult to know how it could have its grass cut without sheep-grazing'.[7]

Other very positive developments, however, based on local initiatives in cooperation with central and local government bodies, have grown up since the mid-1990s to alter the situation profoundly for the better. Impressive among them is the restoration of St. John's Famine Graveyard outside Tipperary Town. In August 1847, St. John's Graveyard was opened to accept the remains of the unfortunate people who died in Tipperary Workhouse and Fever Hospital. The Commonwealth headstones of three First World War soldiers are to be found here, close by the graves of the area's Famine dead: they are located in a hillside

cemetery, beautifully restored in 1995 by an alliance of Friends of St. John's and the Government employment agency, FÁS. Tipperary Town itself, again through local initiative, aided by Government and the European Union, witnessed the construction, on the site of the old Military Barracks, of a superbly crafted monument, elegant yet unpretentious. Built from the remaining stones of the Officers' Mess at these Barracks, the initiative owed its life to the Tipperary Remembrance Trust, which brought together members of ex-military associations, including the Royal Munster Fusiliers' Association and citizens committed to peace and reconciliation. It is dedicated to the memory of all men and women from the Island of Ireland who gave their lives for the cause of peace and freedom worldwide, from the First World War to the present: it lists names of soldiers who served in the Defence Forces of Ireland, the United Kingdom, Australia and the United States. In the presence of Commonwealth and American Military Attachés, the monument was unveiled on 30 September 2005 by President McAleese.[8] It symbolises an inclusiveness and reconciliation of present with past that is profoundly expressive of the change from forgetting to remembering.

In Portlaoise, the memorial commemorating the seventeen officers and 160 local men of the 4th (Reserve) Battalion Leinster Regiment who died in the First World War was originally unveiled in 1928. It had fallen on hard times in the intervening years. Likewise, the Armistice Day commemorations there, which had lapsed for over forty years, were revived in 1990. A restoration committee renewed the monument, which was rededicated at a well-attended public ceremony that November. Then, in 2001, the structure was moved to a new Peace Park at Millview. This restoration and revival owed a great deal to the actions of individuals, notably Pat O'Brien, founding member of the town's Remembrance Committee, and Councillor Tom Keenan, chairman of the Restoration Committee.[9]

The memory of the Leinster Regiment was also of renewed concern and interest, at its original home in County Offaly. As far back as 1961, the local Legion was endeavouring to renovate the old Leinster Regiment Memorial, originally located in Crinkill Military Barracks there.[10] The memorial was eventually moved to Birr Military Cemetery at Crinkill. Here, over the years 2003-2004, a heritage project was organised by the local Tidy Towns Committee, led by Mr Pat Kelly. They involved the children of sixth class in Crinkill National School, led by their teacher, Mrs Teresa Kelly, to create an archive of the memorial inscriptions in

A FUTURE FOR THE PAST?

the graveyard. This project, supported by the Heritage Council, and involving a major renovation of the cemetery and provision of a fine map board, did much to rehabilitate this long-established and long-forgotten Military Cemetery. The ceremony marking the restoration of the cemetery and the creation of its archive was presided over by Minister of State, Tom Parlon.

A similar commitment to historical rehabilitation was evident in Bandon, County Cork. Here, in September 1995, a group of local people were concerned to commemorate the seventy-four soldiers from the area known to have died in the First World War, as likewise those from the area who had served in the Second War. They committed themselves to raising the funds to erect a memorial in their honour. It was with remarkable despatch that they achieved this, raising the required finance within three months. In January 1996 they secured permission to erect the memorial at the front of the local County Council Offices and, one month later, it was duly erected. The Bandon War Memorial Committee continued its work of commemoration by holding an annual ceremony there each November and by producing two original publications. The first, *Bandon District Soldiers Died in the Great War*, brought the known district World War dead from 74 to 200. It was

launched by the then Taoiseach, John Bruton, in April 1997, a symbolically significant act in itself. They produced their second work, *A Journey of Remembrance*, on 31 March 2005.[11] It was in County Cork also that 131 men of Fermoy who fell in the First World War were commemorated by a new memorial unveiled by An Taoiseach, Bertie Ahern, on Sunday 8 October 2006. As in so many other cases, this achievement in remembrance initially owes its greatest debt to the commitment and belief of one individual, in this case, Fermoy man and former soldier, Paudie McGrath.[12]

As with Tipperary Town, so too with Leighlinbridge in County Carlow, where an impressive peace park was opened by the banks of the River Barrow in September 2002. Its centrepiece was a monumental arch based on the design of the Menin Gate Memorial, elegant in its simplicity and scale, recovering, for the present and the future, the memory of those people of the area who gave their lives in the course of the two World Wars.[13] Upwards of 500 from the county perished in the 1914-1918 conflict. Once again, the initial passion and commitment of one individual, in this case John Kenna, was the inspiration for this community achievement of commemoration.[14] Individual initiative played the critical role also in the way in which County

Mayo came to recover the lost history of its own First World War dead. Here P.J. Clarke of Ballina and Michael Feeney of Castlebar carried out the remarkable work of putting together the history of the more than one thousand Mayo comrades who took part in that conflict.[15] From there, Michael Feeney went on in 2002 to convene the meeting that began the project for the Mayo Peace Park Garden of Remembrance in Castlebar. Likewise, in the centre of the island, the people of Moyvoughley in 2000 produced the history of their own district, quite explicitly devoting space in it to the memory of its own war dead. Subsequently, under Councillor Joe Flanagan and his committee colleagues, at their Community Centre in 2002 they unveiled the memorial plaque to the Moyvoughley fallen.[16]

In Limerick, also, the present made atonement for its past. The war memorial there, constructed in 1929, had been destroyed by an explosion in August 1957[17]; upon recconstruction, it was re-dedicated in 1992. Finally, among many other local community initiatives, there is the commemorative stone in Magheragallon, Derrybeg, County Donegal, which owes its existence to the mindfulness and commitment of Kitty and Veronica McBride in particular. They and their neighbours in Gweedore lived childhoods full of the memories of the young local people who enlisted for peace and freedom over 1939-1945; they were full, too, of the sad accounts of those of other nations who were washed upon their shores. In July 2005 their journey of remembering culminated in the unveiling of the memorial stone in Magheragallon, to the memory of the soldiers from Gweedore who were lost in wars far from home: a memorial unique in war grave commemoration as being the only one exclusively rendered in Irish.

I gCuimhne ar na
Saighdiúirí as Gaobh Dobhair
A cailleadh
I gcogaidh i bhfad ó bhaile

1914-1918
1939-1945

Cuir Paidir Leo

Marine memorials:

Among other examples of this community-based commitment to recovering the past was the construction of memorials to the country's merchant seamen who perished in war. From shortly after the Second War, many attempts to publicly commemorate them were made in vain. In 1977 an independent national memorial committee was established and, after thirteen years of travail, finally

succeeded in their efforts when the National Memorial at City Quay in Dublin was unveiled. Similarly, memorials to Irish seafarers and to victims of war at sea were unveiled elsewhere, including seamen's memorials in Waterford City, in Cork City at Penrose Quay, and in Cobh, where also is located the fine memorial to the victims of the *Lusitania*, while victims of the *Leinster* are commemorated in Dun Laoghaire, among other places. Another particularly fine example of a seafaring community in remembrance is that at Kilmore Quay in Wexford, where, on 31 December 1999, in memory of those lost at sea, the first sod was turned for a new Memorial Garden at Forlorn Point, looking out to an area known as 'The Graveyard of a Thousand Ships'. The Kilmore Quay Memorial Garden was completed, and officially opened by Minister of State, Hugh Byrne, on 17 June 2001 – a project initiated by the local community and seafarers, and aided by central and local government. One of the most interesting examples outside the country is the Irish Merchant Navy Memorial Plaque and Plinth in memory of its merchant men lost during the Second World War: sponsored by the Irish Seamen's Relatives' Association, it is located in the British Merchant Navy's section of the National Memorial Arboretum in St. Alrewas, Staffordshire, where it was unveiled on 24 September 2001.

Individually and collectively, these initiatives and developments coalesce into a significant movement of the Irish reconsideration of its past. In the context of the central concerns of this present study, however, there are two developments in particular that exemplify and confirm these acts of recovery, restoration and completion: one relates to the issue of the regimental badges, the other to the Irish National War Memorial at Islandbridge.

Regimental badges:

On 8 December 1950 the Irish Government at last took the decision which the Commonwealth War Graves Commission had long sought, consenting to the construction of permanent headstones over the graves of the dead of the Second World War. In doing so, the Government ignored the issue of regimental badges to this extent: it did not object to their being engraved on the stones wherever no one else objected; equally, it did not insist that they be engraved wherever they were to be erected. Consequently, the Inter-Party Government's position, and that of subsequent governments, was not unlike that of de Valera himself, in February 1941: they would not object to them and they would not object to any authority that did object to them. Consequently, alone among public

authorities in the whole country, Clare County Council continued to refuse, or, to be more exact, it would appear that there was a general presumption that, if asked about the matter, they would continue to refuse. For a long time, it appears, they were not formally or publicly asked.[18] Consequently, when the permanent headstones were erected in the 1950s, in the public authority cemeteries in County Clare they were constructed without their badges, while those in Clare's private burial places bore the regimental emblems. There were six cemeteries containing eleven memorials minus their badges: Ennis Drumcliff with two; Ennistymon with five; and one each at Ennis, Clare Abbey; Crusheen (Kylewince); Kilquane, which held the remains of P. F. McNamara of the Canadian Infantry; and Bunratty Old Graveyard, containing the memorial to Private Williams, killed on Bunratty Bridge in 1921. There were three cemeteries containing eleven memorials with badges: two were private burial grounds, Miltown Malbay Church of Ireland Churchyard, with four memorials and Kilrush Church of Ireland Churchyard with six. Ironically, the one public authority cemetery in the control of Clare County Council that contained a single memorial with badge was that of Drumcliff. The exception proved their rule: the headstone over Able Seaman Joseph Garvey's grave contained a memorial with badge – but, because it was a Merchant Navy emblem, despite his ship being H.M.S. *Victory* of the Royal Navy, the stone was not disallowed. This situation appears to have held true until the middle of the 1990s.

It was in 1996 that one individual, a Limerick man holidaying in Clare, was struck by the Clare anomaly. Tadhg Moloney, with a deep interest in the Irish involvement in the First World War, not least because his grandfather and granduncle had fought in the War, was, and is, a leading figure in the Royal Munster Fusiliers' Association. He took up the issue with the CWGC and Clare Council in 1996, asking if they would have any objection to the badges being added.[19] No positive reply was forthcoming: two years later, however, when he wrote to the Gay Byrne Show on RTE Radio to highlight the matter, the County Council took notice. On 14 December 1998 the Council considered various correspondence on the issue. Councillor Patricia McCarthy, seconded by Councillor Paul Bulger, proposed a motion that the regimental insignia be placed on the stones, regardless of the regiment concerned. This was opposed by Councillor Bridget Makowski, supported by Councillor P. J. Burke, who proposed an amendment 'That Clare County Council withhold recognition

of Regimental Badges on graves of British War Dead until the Good Friday Agreement be implemented in full'. A vigorous debate ensued, with Councillor McCarthy pointing out that

We can't rewrite history. We can only try to change the future. People fought for what they believed in; whether they fought in the Irish, English or American Army, let them rest in peace and honour.

The County Secretary, Tom Coughlan, added that the debate was taking place in a context in which the Council Vice-Chairman, Seán Hillery, had represented them at the opening of the Island of Ireland Peace Park at Messines, Belgium, a few months before.[20] In a meeting that began with thirty Councillors present, the Makowski-Burke amendment was lost by sixteen votes against, two for and with five abstentions: the original motion to allow the badges was carried by an identical number of votes.[21] On 11 January 1999 Clare County Council formally notified the CWGC that they no longer had any objection to the insignia being engraved. The OPW, who at no stage got involved in these deliberations, informed the CWGC that the matter was essentially one for the Council and, as for themselves, they had no objection. In this manner the long saga came to its end. It was striking testimony not only to changed times but to the significance

of the action of one individual and his commitment to preserving the memory of the war dead. In an act of symbolic and practical completion, it was followed in late 1999 by the unveiling of a plaque at Ennistymon Cemetery: erected by the North Clare War Memorial Committee, in memory of the area's men and women who fought and died in 'the great war for civilisation', it was also dedicated to all Irish men and women who died in war, at home and abroad, especially in the service of the United Nations. Erected 'in a spirit of peace and reconciliation', it was unveiled on 21 November by Paddy Harte, as joint co-executive chairman of the Journey of Reconciliation Trust. The choice of presiding figure was an appropriate one. Harte, more than any other single individual, was himself largely responsible for the achievement of the Island of Ireland Peace Park at Messines, inaugurated on 11 November 1998, and since then, among other initiatives, has gone on to promote the Journey of Remembering County Books of Honour project.

Restoration:

The most significant work of restoration to emerge in this time of renewal was that conducted at Islandbridge. Its decline had been a disgrace and its recovery proved costly. The OPW's decision to restore was effectively

taken in 1985, thus predating by some years the many local projects already described.[22] Financial constraints apart, the OPW's freedom to act had been delayed for long by uncertainty over Dublin Corporation's plans for a new by-pass road through the Inchicore North Estate. Until the exact route of the by-pass was certain, forward planning and actual work were precluded.[23] The laying of a major pipeline through the Park in 1984, as part of the Greater Dublin drainage scheme, was a further setback. Two years later, the August storm of 1986 severely damaged the avenues of golden poplars, nature completing the destruction already well-advanced by vandals. With the years of uncertainty and neglect, the complement of maintenance staff fell from twelve in 1969 to three by 1987, their own canteen and workshops being abandoned after being repeatedly set alight.

At the very time in 1985 that the OPW began to see its way to a programme of repair they were approached by the long-suffering INWM Trustees who, as before, in the 1960s, 1940s and 1930s, offered to provide supporting finance. It was directly due to the INWM's subvention that the critical initial work of railing off the Memorial Park at a cost of £60,000, completed in 1987, finally kept the stolen cars, stray horses and invading vandals at bay, enabling the real work

of restoration to proceed in earnest. In December 1986, a special OPW task force to identify the required works, and to secure the required staffing, had commenced its task. The extent of progress achieved by May 1987 was sufficient to convince the INWM of the seriousness of the OPW's programme: in consequence, they then agreed to co-fund additional expenditure of £48,000 each party, for the restoration of stone work and the infrastructure of the sunken gardens. By the end of 1987 over £460,000 had been spent on replanting trees and shrubs, architectural restoration and provision of machinery and facilities.[24] The programme for the following year included the restoration of the ponds and fountains. The latter had been powered originally by an ingenious hydrostat system, independent of the city water supply. Unfortunately the piping for this was unwittingly destroyed by Dublin Corporation during the Chapelizod bypass construction, and the stream supplying the water had been diverted by the Corporation. By the end of 1988 the fountains had been restored to full operation. Better things were to follow. Lutyens' Temple, which had never been built, was finally constructed, and opened by Bertie Ahern, then Minister for Finance, in 1994. One final project of the original Lutyens' plan, the pedestrian bridge over the Liffey, is now the sole piece absent from the complete

A FUTURE FOR THE PAST?

NEAR RIGHT
The Lusitania memorial,
Cobh.

MIDDLE RIGHT
Regimental Badge on
CWGC headstone in
Co. Clare.

FAR RIGHT
The 90th Anniversary of
the Battle of the Somme,
Islandbridge, 2006.

BELOW
Tipperary Town Memorial
Arch Plaque

mosaic, but, already in 1987, the Memorial Park, according to one expert, had been 'transformed from a wreck into a thing of timeless beauty'.[25] In the following September, a long-delayed, if semi-formal, opening was finally accomplished when church dignitaries gave their blessings in the absence of any Government representation.[26]

When Minister Ahern opened the Temple in June 1994 to mark the completion of the great programme of restoration, he described that programme in general, and the construction of the Temple in particular, as a tribute to the co-operation of the INWM Trustees and the OPW. Referring to their shared hope, and his own desire, to see the Lutyens' Bridge realised, he remarked, in words that were as much a confession concerning the past as an exhortation for the future:

> *it was our national duty to maintain this memorial which commemorates those who died tragically in the battlefield.*[27]

The times, indeed, were changing. A year later, in April 1995, John Bruton as Taoiseach, in the first government-led ceremony commemorating the Irish dead of the Second World War, fifty years after its ending, secured the official recognition of the Memorial at last.[28]

Eleven years later again, in 2006, on the ninetieth anniversary of the Battle of the Somme, that acknowledgement was complete when President McAleese and Taoiseach Ahern presided over the State's fullest recognition and commemoration of Ireland's World War dead, at the Irish National War Memorial Park.[29] That recognition went well beyond the State: members of political parties North and South, the head of the Northern Ireland Civil Service, Ambassadors from the Commonwealth participants in the First War, as well as those of France and Germany, laid wreaths, as did Major General David O'Morchoe for the Royal British Legion, on behalf of the Irish who died at the Somme. Such full-scale commemoration was long overdue, and in that context, perhaps, the pomp and circumstance were not inappropriate.

Yet, for all that, when the music fades and the speeches cease – 'the tumult and the shouting dies' – it is in quiet cemeteries across this land that the silent headstones ask if there may always be a future for this now remembered past.

Endnotes

Introduction

[1] Figures for enlistment and war deaths are a subject of varying estimates. For the First World War, see P. Callan, 'Recruiting for the British Army in Ireland during the First World War', *Irish Sword*, 17, 1987-88, pp.42-56; P. J. Casey, 'Irish casualties in the First World War', *Irish Sword*, 20, 81, 1997, pp. 193-206; D. Fitzpatrick, 'Militarism in Ireland, 1900-1922', in T. Bartlett and K. Jeffery,(eds.), *A Military History of Ireland*, Cambridge 1996, pp.379-406; K. Jeffery, *Ireland and the Great War*, Cambridge 2000, pp.5-6.

[2] T. Johnstone, *Orange, Green and Khaki: The Story of the Irish Regiments in the Great War, 1914-1918*, Dublin 1992; M. Dungan, *They Shall Not Grow Old: Irish Soldiers and the Great War*, Dublin 1997; K. Jeffery, *Ireland and the Great War*, Cambridge 2000.

[3] R. Doherty, *Irish Men and Women in the Second World War*, Dublin 1999, and *Irish Volunteers in the Second World War*, Dublin 2002; B. Girvin and G. Roberts (eds.), *Ireland and the Second World War: Politics, Society and Remembrance*, Dublin 2000; R. Fisk, *In time of War: Ireland, Ulster and the Price Of Neutrality, 1939-45*, London 1983. Other pioneering studies for the two World Wars include Callan, loc.cit., Casey, loc. cit., T. Denman, *Ireland's Unknown Soldiers: The 16th (Irish) Division in the Great War, 1914-1918*, Dublin 1992; M. Dungan, *Distant Drums: Irish Soldiers in Foreign Armies*, Belfast 1993; T. Dooley, *Irishmen or English Soldiers? The times and world of a southern Catholic Irish man (1876-1916) enlisting in the British army during the First World War*, Liverpool 1995; M. Staunton, *The Royal Munster Fusiliers in the Great War, 1914-1919*, unpublished MA thesis, University College Dublin, 1986.

[4] D. Fitzpatrick, *Politics and Irish Life, 1913-1921: Provincial Experience of War and Revolution*, Cork,1997; D. Fitzpatrick, (ed.), *Ireland and the First World War*, Dublin 1986; N. MacFhionnghaile, *Donegal, Ireland and the First World War*, Leitirceannain 1987; J. Durney, *Far from the Short Grass: the Story of Kildare Men in Two World Wars*, 1999; P. Maguire, *Follow them up from Carlow*, Carlow 2002; D. Hall, *World War One and Nationalist Politics in County Louth, 1914-1920*, Dublin

2005; P.J. Clarke & Michael Feeney, *Mayo Comrades of the Great War, 1914-1919*, Ballina, 2006.

[5] J. Winter, *Sites of Memory, sites of mourning: the Great War in European cultural history*, Cambridge 1995; J. Leonard, *The Culture of Commemoration, the culture of war commemoration*, Dublin 1996; J. Hill, *Irish Public Sculpture: A History*, Dublin 1998; A. Dolan, *Commemorating the Irish Civil War: History and Memory, 1923-2000*, Cambridge 2003; N. Johnson, *Ireland, the Great War and the Geography of Remembrance*, Cambridge 2003.

[6] The figures are discussed in Chapter One.

[7] There is a solitary two-page article on the general subject: M. Staunton, 'First world war graves in Ireland', *An Cosantóir*, 46, 1, 1986, pp. 13-14; and a few articles on local aspects: S. Fitzgerald, 'The Arklow war graves', *Journal, Arklow Historical Society*,1992-93, pp.22-23; P. Lecane, 'World War 1 Casualties commemorated: memorials in Co. Wicklow', *Wicklow Roots*, 4, 1999, pp.10-12; J. Mackey, 'A Small Graveyard in a Dublin Hospital', *Genealogical Society of Ireland Journal*, vol. 2, no. 4, winter 2001, pp. 231-233; see also, S. Taaffe, 'Commemorating the fallen: public memorials to the Irish dead of the Great War', *Archaeology Ireland*, 13, 3, 1999, pp.18-22.

Chapter 1

[1] S. Snelling, *VCs of the First World War: The Naval VCs*, Stroud 2002, pp. 64-72; CWGC, *Cemeteries, Churchyards and Memorials in the Republic of Ireland*, hereafter referred to as CWGC data base: the data base is unpaginated.

[2] M. Gilbert, *The Routledge Atlas of the First World War*, 2nd ed. reprint, 2002, p.135.

[3] F. Ware, *The Immortal Heritage: An Account of the Work and Policy of the Imperial War Graves Commission during the twenty years 1917-1937*, Cambridge 1937, pp. 23, 34; P. Longworth, *The Unending Vigil: the History of the Commonwealth War Graves Commission*, 3rd ed. Barnsley 2003, p.97.

[4] D. Preston, *Wilful Murder: The Sinking of the Lusitania*, London 2002; S. Molony, *Lusitania: An Irish Tragedy*, Cork 2004; P. O'Sullivan, *The Lusitania: Unravelling the Mysteries*, Cork 1998 are among the more recent accounts.

[5] Molony, op.cit. pp. 77-96.

[6] *Cork Free Press*, 8 May 1915, *The Cork Examiner*, 12 May 1915, Molony, op.cit pp. 86-87; Preston, op.cit., p.117.

[7] J. Hill, *Irish public sculpture, a history*, Dublin 1988, pp. 196-197; Molony op.cit., pp.156-159.

[8] See Chapter Fourteen.

[9] P. Lecane, *Torpedoed: The R.M.S. Leinster Disaster*, Penzance 2005, pp. 164-183, 194-195. While Lecane points out that it is not possible to say exactly how many perished, his statistical analysis is the most thorough to date; he gives a figure of 532 dead out of 778 who sailed. See also,R. Stokes, *Death in the Irish Sea: The Sinking of the R.M.S. Leinster*, Cork 1998.

[10] CWGC, CEM13944, Grangegorman Military Cemetery, Inspection Report, Tuesday 27 October 1964; see also V. Igoe, *Dublin Burial Grounds and Graveyards*, Dublin 2001, pp. 127-132.

[11] Whitefields Archive, Grangegorman Military Cemetery, Register of Burials, 13 Oct 1918-8 Sept 1960, pp.1-11.

[12] Grangegorman Military Cemetery, Register of Burials, 29 Aug 1904-11 July 1908, p.201, consecrated by Canon Bourke on 3 November 1918 for 'the burial of Imperial Forces from South Africa, New Zealand, Australia and Canada'.

[13] N. Furlong and J. Hayes, *County Wexford in the Rare Oul' Times*, vol IV, Wexford 2005, pp 94-103: Lecane, op.cit., pp. 239-255; P. Conran, 'Military and naval aviation in Ireland, 1913-1922', *An Cosantóir*, 32, 1972, pp. 158-162.

[14] Grangegorman Military Cemetery, Register of Burials, 13 Oct 1918-8 Sept 1960, p. 10; Lecane, op.cit., pp.209-210, 251.

[15] Grangegorman Military Cemetery, Register of Burials, 14 Aug 1918-26 May 1941 (Army Book 127), pp. 7, 31, 53 for the exhumations of Sergeant John Rose, Privates C.W. Tennant, M. Morris and Clarence Sussman: Morris on 28 September 1920, the others on 25 April 1922.

[16] J.M. Brown and W. Roger Louis, *The Oxford History of the British Empire*, vol. IV, *The Twentieth Century*, Oxford, 1999, p. 117. The enlistment and casualty figures for Canada, Australia and New Zealand which follow in the text are also from this source. The largest number of colonial combatants came from India which, by the time of the Armistice, had 943,000 serving in the theatres of war; they also had the largest number of colonial combatants killed,

at over 64,000.

[17] See Chapter Eight.

[18] Lecane, op.cit. p.234.

[19] See Chapter Nine.

[20] The figures in Tables 1-3 in this Chapter, and in Tables 5-7 in Chapter Sixteen, are based on the Commonwealth War Grave Commission Registers for the Republic of Ireland and Northern Ireland, as interpreted by the author: where the figures differ, as they may do, very marginally, from those held by the CWGC, as of October 2006, they do so on the basis of the author's own site visits.

[21] A similar disproportionate incidence is found in the case of war deaths of 1918 for the United Kingdom: 1914 – 7,487; 1915 – 15,541; 1916 – 22,654; 1917 25,616; 1918-34,463; 1919 – 15,434; 1920 – 6,156; 1921 – 2,579: figures courtesy of the CWGC.

[22] W. J. Bergin, 'Clonmel's Military Barracks', *An Cosantóir*, 43, 1983, pp. 268-270; 'Military Barracks, Tipperary Town', ibid., 44, 1984, pp.128-129; 'Military barracks, Cahir, and military barracks, Clogheen, Tipperary', ibid., 44, 1984, pp 243-247; P. O'Farrell, 'Athlone, a garrison town' in M. Keaney and G. O'Brien, eds., *Athlone bridging the centuries*, Mullingar 1991,pp.62- 78; P. Walsh, 'The barracks of Ireland: Templemore Military Barracks', *An Cosantóir*, 32, 1972, pp. 220-224.

[23] See Chapter Four.

[24] M Staunton, 'Kilrush, Co Clare and the Royal Munster Fusiliers: the experience of an Irish town in the First World War', *An Cosantóir*, 16, 65, 1986, pp. 268-272.

[25] Information supplied by Mr Gerard 'Guss' O'Halloran, Ennistymon, and Mr Tadhg Moloney, Limerick.

[26] P.J. Casey, 'Irish casualties in the First World War', *Irish Sword*, 20, 81, 1977, pp.193-206; P. Callan, 'Recruiting for the British Army in Ireland during the First World War', *Irish Sword*, 17, 1987-88, pp. 42-56; D. Fitzpatrick, *Politics and Irish Life, 1913-1921: Provincial Experience of War and Revolution*, 1998 ed., p.93.

Chapter 2

[1] OPW9/A22/1/21/38, *War Graves – Cemetery Registers*, William Brandon, OPW minute, 13 May 1938; W. J. Veale to OPW Commissioners, 30 September 1938.

[2] CO739/11, G.Walker, GHQ, Phoenix Park, to War Office, 21 April 1922. Walker listed the numbers of graves of 1914-21 in eight of the military cemeteries in figures at odds with those of the CWGC: his are as follows, with the corresponding CWGC numbers in brackets:

Grangegorman	644	(613);
Curragh	152	(103)
Cork	141	(83);
Limerick King's Island	38	(39)
Fermoy	24	(22)
Ballincollig	12	(10)
Birr	2	(3);
Tralee	1	(10).

It is not certain how this discrepancy can be explained, but, in other citations of war grave numbers, the War Office admitted at the time that their figures were unreliable.

[3] Grangegorman Military Cemetery, Register of Burials, 29 Aug 1904-11 July 1918.

[4] Grangegorman Military Cemetery, Register of Burials, 14 Aug 1918-26 May 1941 (Army Book 127), pp.88-90, entries for 21 October 1920. For the final exhumations and reburials of five British officers from the grounds of Dublin Castle in May 1963, see Chapter Twenty Two.

[5] NAI, FIN S004/12/24, J.J. Healy, Secretary, OPW, to A.D. Codling, Secretary, Finance, 6 November 1924. The OPW accepted responsibility for the maintenance of the grounds, not for the maintenance, repair or replacement of these cemeteries' memorials: see ibid., Healy to Finance, 12 November 1925.

[6] Grangegorman Military Cemetery, Register of Burials, 29 Aug 1904-11 July 1918, copy of letter from James Skinner, AQMG, War Office, 12 March 1898.

[7] Ibid., 109, 114, 201. Murphy was interred on 20 Jan 1917, Harpar on 13 June 1917.

[8] Ibid., George E Shanahan, OPW, to Finance, 15 March 1923.

[9] CO 783/4, Correspondence Register, Irish Free State, Mrs Brady to IWGC, 21 February 1924 on behalf of her mother, Mrs Gregory. The Colonial Office referred the request to the Irish Government; Whitefields Archive, Phoenix Park, Grangegorman Military Cemetery, Register of Burials, 14 Aug 1918-26 May 1941, (Army Book 127), p.117.

[10] Ibid., p.95.

[11] CWGC 1076/1089/2 Part 1, 'G.W.D.' for Elizabeth D'Arcy, Mountjoy Street, to Undersecretary of State, War Office, 25 November 1924; headstone inscription, Grangegorman Military Cemetery; Grangegorman Military Cemetery, Register of Burials, 13 Oct 1918-8 Sept 1960, p.30, interred on 22 June 1943.

[12] Fin S004/12/24, Codling, Finance, to Secretary, OPW, 9 December 1924.

[13] CWGC 1077/1089/2 Part 3, E. J. King for Secretary, IWGC, to General Secretary, British Legion, London, 23 April 1931: Grangegorman Military Cemetery, Register of Burials, 14 Aug 1918-26 May 1941 (Army Book 127), pp.111-124.

[14] CWGC CEM13944, Mrs G. E. Gilmore to CWGC, 3 December 1967; Director-General, CWGC, to Mrs Gilmore, 5 January 1968.

[15] Grangegorman Military Cemetery, Register of Burials from 1960, entry 7 Nov 2000.

[16] F. A. D'Arcy, *Horses, Lords and Racing Men: The Turf Club, 1790-1990*, Kildare 1991, pp. 28, 54, 137-38, 154-174; C. Costello, *A Most Delightful Station: the British Army on the Curragh of Kildare, Ireland, 1855-1922*, Cork 1996, pp.25-44.

[17] CWGC CEM14024; B.O.P. Eugster, War Office, to Undersecretary of State, Commonwealth Relations Office, 7 January 1955. On the evacuation, see A. Kinsella, 'The British military evacuation', *Irish Sword*, 20, 1997, pp.275-286; N.R. Brannigan, 'Changing of the guard. Curragh Evacuation 70 years on', *An Cosantóir*, 52, 12, 1992, pp.29-30.

[18] FIN S055/0011/27, George H. Burnett to Finance, 14 Feb 1927.

[19] CWGC, CEM14024, Lt. Col. G.J.P. Goodwin, CRE, Curragh District, to Headquarters, Irish Command, 21 November 1921.

[20] Whitefields Archive, Royal Hibernian Military School Cemetery Register, p.1: the first burial there was that of thirteen-year old Christopher French, who died from peritonitis on 30 March 1851 and was interred on 2 April. He had joined the School in 1848. For further details on the School see Chapter Three.

[21] Whitefields Archive, Royal Hibernian Military School Cemetery Register, p.54, 4 March 1919.

[22] FIN S004/12/24, B.B. Cubitt, War Office, to Army Finance Office, Department of Defence, Dublin, 24 September 1924; E. Brennan, Secretary, Defence, to Secretary, OPW, 22 April 1925; Royal Hibernian Military School Cemetery Register, p.65, entry for 1 October 1997.

[23] NAI, Royal Hospital Kilmainham Cemetery Register. I am grateful to Vivien Igoe and to Gregory O'Connor of the National Archives for help with this information.

[24] OPW9/A22/7/1/37, Cahir Kilcommon British Military Cemetery [sic.] Co Tipperary, Tenure Agreement, 11 September 1885; OPW minute, 24 June 1924; FIN S004/12/24, F.W. Taylor, OPW, to Secretary, Defence, 28 June 1923; J.J. Healy, OPW, to Finance, 7 May 1924.

[25] CO 739/11, G.Walker, GHQ, Phoenix Park, to War

Office, 21 April 1922; Healy, OPW, to Finance, 7 May 1924; OPW9/A22/7/1/37, List of Ex-British Military Cemeteries in the Irish Free State; Map Board, Crinkill Cemetery. Note: there is the alternative spelling, Crinkle, and the two spellings are a matter of divided opinion in the locality.

[26] CWGC 1077/1089/2 Part 3, Col. Chettle to Vice Chairman, IWGC, 16 September 1931; OPW 9/22/7/1/37, List of Ex-British Military Cemeteries in the Irish Free State, J.J. Healy to Shortall, OPW, Maryboro [sic], 17 June 1924. See also D. Harvey & G. White, *The Barracks: A History of Victoria/Collins Barracks*, Cork 1997, pp. 19, 28.

[27] CO739/11, G.H. Walker, GHQ, Phoenix Park, to War Office, 21 April 1922.

[28] CWGC 1076/1089/2 Part 3, Chettle to Vice Chairman, IWGC, 18 June 1931.

[29] CWGC 1976/1089/2 Part 1, Secretary to the Provisional Government of Ireland Cabinet Committee to Secretary, IWGC, 15 July 1922.

[30] FIN S004/12/24, J.J. Healy, OPW, to Finance, 7 May 1924; A. Donaldson, *British Military Graveyard, Ballincollig, Co Cork, Ireland, 1810-1922*, pp.53, 62-64.

[31] CWGC 1077/1059/2 Part 3, Director of Works to Enquiries Branch, IWGC, 6 April 1932; CWGC CEM13808, P.E. Vesper; from OPW, to Director of Works, IWGC, 22 April 1931; FIN S004/12/24, Healy, OPW, to Finance, 7 May 1924; N. Brunicardi, 'The Military Camp at Fermoy', *Irish Sword*, 16, 1986, pp. 328-331. See also Chapters Two, Five and Eight.

[32] D. Breen, *My Fight for Irish Freedom*, Dublin 1989, p.162; F. O'Donoghue, *No Other Law*, Dublin 1986, p.157; T. Sheehan, *Execute Hostage Compton-Smith*, Dripsey 1993, p. 110; C. Townshend, *The British Campaign in Ireland*, 1919-1921, Oxford 1975, p.150.

[33] Sheehan, op.cit., p. 108.

[34] *The Times*, 30 May, 2 June, 24 Aug 1921.

[35] UCDA, FitzGerald Papers, P 80/C, Private Secretary to Minister for Defence, to Desmond FitzGerald, FitzGerald to Lloyd Davies, 16-19 May 1925.

[36] *The Irish Times*, 5 March 1926; Sheehan, op.cit. p.148 incorrectly states the year of location and recovery as 1925.

[37] Sheehan, op.cit., pp. 145-149; *The Times*, 25 March 1926.

[38] OPW7/33/4, Limerick Military Cemetery, Commissioners of Woods and Forests to Principal Secretary of State for the War Department, 30 July 1856.

[39] Ibid., S.P. Skinner, 4 August 1928, Minister for Finance, Indenture, 6 December 1924.

[40] FIN S004/12/24, Healy, OPW, to Finance, 7 May 1924.

[41] OPW9/A121/2/8/54, Mrs E. Kinchington, Newcastle, New South Wales, to IWGC, 28 January 1948; E. J. King, IWGC, to P.E. Vesper, OPW, 28 January 1948; OPW9/ A22/1/12/36, War Graves: Maintenance of Cemeteries in Co Kerry: maintenance agreement signed by F. Cox, caretaker, Killarney New Cemetery, 17 January 1947 and by P.S. Ó Chearnaigh, OPW, 13 May 1948.

[42] See Chapter Ten.

Chapter 3

[1] National Archives, Kew, CAB27/154, no.31, Macready to Secretary, The War Office, 7 Jan 1922; N. Macready, *Annals of an Active Life*, 2 vols. London 1924, ii.649.

[2] NA, WO 32/3045, Royal Hospital Kilmainham, Closure of, in particular the correspondence between the War Office and the Commandant and Secretary of the Royal Hospital Kilmainham, John Steele, over 25 March 1926 to 17 March 1930; Kew, DO 35/9148, copy of William Fay, Department of External Affairs, to Archbishop Gregg of Armagh, 28 Apr 1954; G.P. Carr, War Office to A.R. Swinnerton, Commonwealth Relations Office, 27 March 1956.

[3] Ibid., R. Paterson, John Steele, Royal Hospital Kilmainham to B.R.T.Grindle, Assistant Secretary, War Office, 17 March 1930;

[4] NAI, G3/21, Government Minutes, 20 Dec 1955, Order signed by Costello on 20 Dec, coming into effect on 31 Dec 1955.

[5] G.H. O'Reilly, ed., *History of the Royal Hibernian Military School*, Dublin, Dublin 2001, p.22.

[6] NA, CO739/4, IFS Correspondence Book, War Office to Colonial Office, 30 January 1922.

[7] Website, A. W. Cockerill, www.achart.ca/hibernian; I am indebted to a private source for this information.

[8] M. Hopkinson, *The Irish War of Independence*, Dublin 2002, p.201. Hopkinson gives a figure of 624 members of the British security services, with deaths on the other side at about 752, of whom around 200 were civilians.

[9] CWGC Archives, Maidenhead, CWGC1076/1089/2 Pt 1, Macready to Secretary IWGC, 28 February 1922, Disposal of Military Cemeteries in Ireland.

[10] NA, CAB27/153: Cabinet, Ireland: Conclusions of a meeting held at the Colonial Office, Friday 10th

February 1922. This body was later renamed The Cabinet Committee on Irish Affairs.

[11] Longworth, op.cit., pp.1-5.

[12] Ware, op.cit.,p.25.

[13] Ware, op.cit., pp.11-12; Longworth, op.cit., pp.20-27.

[14] Ware, op.cit., pp.40-41.

[15] Longworth, op.cit., p.42.

[16] NA CO 739/24, Miscellaneous Offices:IFS, March-Dec 1923, G. G. Whiskard, Colonial Office, to Sir Fabian Ware, IWGC, 27 Dec 1923.

[17] CWGC Cem 14024, Lt.Col. G. P. Goodwin, Curragh District, to Headquarters Irish Command, 21 Nov 1921.

[18] CWGC 1076/1089/2 Pt 1, H. E. Cheeseman to the Secretary, The War Office, 18 Nov 1922.

[19] National Archives of Ireland (NAI), OPW9/A22/7, H.J. Creedy, War Office, to Secretary, OPW, 5 July 1924.

[20] CWGC Cem 14242, Birr Military Cemetery, R. Nixon to the Secretary, IWGC, 9 July 1923.

[21] CO783/1/1, 20 March 1922;CO739/B, G.B. Freeston to War Office, 27 July 1922.

[22] CO739/11, L. Curtis to Creedy, War Office, 3 March 1922; CO739/11, G. Walker, GHQ Ireland, to War Office, 21 April 1922..

[23] CO739/11, Antrobus to Browne, 28 Apr 1922; Browne to Antrobus, 2 May 1922.

[24] CO739/11, Freeston, Colonial Office, to the Secretary, IWGC, 15 July 1922.

[25] Ware, op.cit., pp.59-60.

[26] CWGC, Minutes of Meetings, WG 1712, 21 Feb 1922; Minutes of Meetings, 20 Apr 1922.

[27] CWGC 1076/1089/2 Pt 1, Curtis, Colonial Office, to Ware, 3 March 1922; CWGC, Minutes of Meetings, 21 March 1922.

[28] CWGC, Minutes of Meetings, WG 1729, 23 May 1922.

[29] CWGC 1076/1089/2 Pt 1, Faber to Browne, 25 May 1922; Browne to Faber, 27 May 1922.

[30] CO739/13, Arthur Browne to Secretary, The Provisional Government of Ireland Cabinet Committee, 22 July 1922.

[31] CWGC, 1076/1089/2 Pt 1, Browne to General Officer Commanding-in-Chief, The Forces in Ireland, 25 March 1922.

[32] CO739/22, Creedy to Secretary, The Treasury, 25 July 1922.

[33] CO739/22, and CWGC 1076/1089/2 Pt 1, Meiklejohn, Treasury Chambers, to Secretary, IWGC, 5 Sept 1922.

[34] CO739/22, G. L. Barstow, Treasury Chambers, to Secretary, War Office, 30 November 1922.

[35] CWGC 1076/1089/23 Pt 1, Arthur Browne's Summary of exchanges, dated IWGC 24 Jan 1923.

[36] Ibid., E F Dalton, 18 Jan 1923, Arthur Browne, 24 Jan 1923.

[37] CWGC 1076/1089/2 Pt 1, Arthur Browne to Vice-Chairman Ware, 5 March 1923.

[38] Ibid., Arthur Browne to Lord Stopford, 7 March 1923.

[39] Ibid., 1076/1089/2 Pt 1, Director of Works to P.A.S., 4 Apr 1923.

[40] CO732/22/25750, Niemeyer to Undersecretary of State for the Colonies (Irish Branch), 23 May 1923.

Chapter 4

[1] CO 739/19, Richard Mulcahy, Aire Cosanta, to N. G. Loughnane, Vice-Regal Lodge, 12 Oct 1923.

[2] Ibid., Mulcahy to Loughnane, 17 Oct 1923 for a list.

[3] NAI, OPW9/A121/2/8/54, T.Carless, IWGC, to P. E. Vesper, OPW, 20 June 1951; Vesper to Carless, 22 June 1951. The Registry of the CWGC records them on its data base for the Republic of Ireland, but has not assigned any names to them.

[4] M. Ryan, *Tom Barry, IRA Freedom Fighter,* Cork 2003, p.36.

[5] For various accounts of this now controversial encounter, see T. Barry, *Guerilla Days in Ireland,* Dublin 1949; E. Butler, *Barry's Flying Column: the story of the IRA's Cork No 3 Brigade, 1919-1921,* London 1971; P. Cottrell, *The Anglo-Irish War: The Troubles of 1913-1922,* Oxford 2006, pp.56-57; P. Hart, *The IRA and its Enemies: Violence and Community in Cork, 1916-1923,* Oxford 1998; Hopkinson, op.cit; Ryan, op.cit.; C. Townshend, *The British Campaign in Ireland, 1919-1921,* Oxford 1975; C. Townshend, 'The Irish Republican Army and the Development of Guerrilla Warfare, 1916-1921', *English Historical Review,* vol. 94, April 1979, pp. 318-345.

[6] CO 739/19, Mulcahy to Loughnane, 17 Oct 1923.

[7] Ibid.

[8] NAI, OPW9/A22/1/456/40, Bunratty Old Graveyard: Report by Vesper, dated 22 Oct 1935, of site visit, on 13 Apr 1932, to the grave of Pte R. W. Williams.

[9] CO 739/19, Mulcahy to Loughnane, 12 Oct 1923; Hart. op.cit., p.280.

[10] Sheehan, op.cit., pp.65-78.

[11] *The Times*, 13, 14, 15 Dec 1923.

[12] UCDA, Hugh Kennedy Papers, P4/572, Cosgrave to Kennedy, (?) Nov 1922, Cosgrave to Commander-in-Chief, 4 Nov 1922.

[13] CWGC 1076/1089/2 Pt 1, R. Carson to War Office, 22 Aug 1

[14] Ibid.

[15] CWGC 1076/1089/2 Pt 1, Army Council to Undersecretary of State for the Colonies, Irish Branch, 29 May 1923.

[16] Ibid.

[17] CO 739/19, Loughnane to General Mulcahy, 27 July 1923.

[18] NAI, OPW9/A22/1/456/40, Vesper to the Secretary, OPW, 15 Apr 1932.

[19] CWGC 1076/1089/2 Pt 1, Cubitt, War Office to Secretary, IWGC, 20 Aug 1925, Browne to Cubitt, 11 Sept 1925.

[20] CO 783/4, Register of Correspondence, Irish Free State, 12 Sept 1923.

[21] CO 739/18, Irish Free State 1923, Minutes of meeting between Colonial Office and War Office , n.d., Sept 1923.

[22] CO 739/19, Mulcahy to Loughnane, 12 Oct 1923.

[23] CO 739/19, Loughnane, Vice-Regal Lodge, to Freeston, Colonial Office, 17 Oct 1923.

[24] CO 739/19, Freeston to Loughnane, 27 Oct 1923.

[25] Ryan, op.cit., p.47; L. Whyte, *The Wild Heather Glen: the Kilmichael Story of Grief and Glory*, Cork 995, p.153. He is not commemorated by the CWGC on their register.

[26] *The Times*, 23 Dec 1923.

[27] FIN S004/0081/24, Army Finance Office to Finance, 21 March 1924, Finance to Army Finance Office, 31 March 1924; The Times, 15 December 1923.

[28] CO 739/19, Mark Sturgis, Colonial Office, to Secretary, War Office, n.d. but around 27 October 1923.

[29] CWGC 1076/1089/2 Pt 1, Cubitt, War Office, to Browne, 19 Oct 1923; Browne to Cubitt, 26 Oct 1923.

[30] CO 783/4, Register of Correspondence, Irish Free State, 20, 27 Oct 1923.

[31] *The Cork Examiner*, 6 Sept 1924.

[32] *Freeman's Journal*, Sat 6 Sept 1924, p.6; The Times, 6 Sept 1924.

[33] CWGC website, www.cwgc.org/search/casualty_details.

[34] UCDA, Blythe Papers, P24/117, FitzGerald Papers, P80/1064, Exhumations from Cork Jail: the thirteen were: Cornelius Murphy on 1 Feb; Sean Allen, John Lyons, Timothy McCarthy, Thomas O'Brien, Patrick O'Mahoney and Daniel O'Callaghan on 28 February, buried in one grave; Maurice Moore, Thomas Mulcahy, Patrick Ronayne and Patrick Sullivan on 28 April 1921, buried in one grave, Patrick Casey on 4 May 1921, and Daniel O'Brien on 16 May 1921.

[35] Ibid., Justice Memorandum to the Executive Council, 20 Dec 1924; and, Item for Agenda of Executive Council, undated but 23 Dec 1924.

[36] The site is now part of the campus of University College Cork. I am grateful to Kieran Burke, Executive Librarian, Local Studies, Cork City Library for this information.

[37] Townshend, op.cit., pp.203-206. See also Cottrell, op.cit. p.7.

Chaper 5

[1] CWGC 1076/1089/2 Part 1, Sturgis to Treasury Secretary, 8 June 1923.

[2] CO 739/22, Waterfield, Treasury, to Whiskard, Colonial Office, 11 June 1923.

[3] Ibid., Minute of 4 June 1923, Freeston to Whiskard.

[4] Ibid., Waterfield to Whiskard, 11 June 1923.

[5] CWGC 1076/1089/2 Part 1, undated internal IWGC memorandum to Browne, June 1923.

[6] Ibid., Browne to Secretary of State for the Colonies, 15 June 1923.

[7] Ibid., Minutes of Conference held in the War Office, IWGC attending, to discuss disposal of Military Cemeteries in the IFS, n.d. July 1923.

8 CO 739/22, Whiskard to Loughnane, 12 Sept 1923, summarising Curtis's letter of 23 July 1923.

9 NAI, Fin S004/12/24, G. E. Shanahan, Assistant Secretary, OPW, to the Secretary, Ministry of Finance [sic], 15 March 1923.

10 Ibid., Ryan to Shanahan, 21 March 1923.

11 Ibid., Thomas Gorman, Army Finance Office, to Ryan, Finance, 3 April 1923; J. P. McCurran, Local Government, to Finance, 29 May 1923; S. Brennan, Finance, to Waterfield, Treasury, 4 May 1923.

12 Ibid., Waterfield to Brennan, 19 June 1923.

13 DFA 239/89, James Boyd to Dominions Office, 8 Apr 1929.

14 CO 739/22, Waterfield to Whiskard, 28 Aug 1923.

15 Ibid., Whiskard to Loughnane, 12 September 1923.

16 Ibid., Irish Free State, vol.2, Loughnane to Whiskard, 18 Sept 1923.

17 Ibid., Colonial Office internal memo, Freeston to Whiskard, 26 Sept 1923; the Minutes of the meetings of the Commissioners of Public Works do not reveal any reference to the issue during this period.

18 CWGC 1076/1089/2 Part 1, War Office draft letter to Treasury, Oct 1923.

19 CO 739/20, Minute by Whiskard of conference with IWGC, dated 13 Dec 1923.

20 R. S. Hill, ' Sir James Allen,1855-1942',in *Oxford Dictionary of National Biography*, Oxford 2004; R. L. Weitzel, 'Pacifists and anti-militarists in New Zealand' in *New Zealand Journal of History*, 7, 1973, pp. 128-147.

21 Dáil Éireann, *Debates*, vol.5, 21 Nov 1923.

22 CWGC 1076/1089/2 Part 1, internal IWGC memo, Browne to Ware, 13 Dec 1923.

23 *Annual Report of the Imperial War Graves Commission*, 1921-1922, HMSO 1922, p.14.

24 CO 739/20, Whiskard to Ware, 14 Dec 1923.

25 Ibid., Whiskard to Waterfield, Treasury, 14 Dec 1923; Whiskard to Rowlands, War Office, 14 Dec 1924.
26 CWGC 1076/1089/2 Part 1, A Draft Despatch to the Irish Free State, Colonial Office, Dec 1923.

27 Ibid, Whiskard to Ware, 27 Dec 1923.

28 Ibid., Proposed Draft from Treasury to Colonial Office,

n.d., but enclosed as a copy in Waterfield to Ware, 31 Dec 1923.

29 CO739/24, Whiskard to Waterfield, 14 Jan 1924.

30 CWGC, 1076/1089/2 Part 1, Browne to C K P [Major C K Phillips, Land and Legal Advisor], 21 January 1924.

Chapter 6

1 The Supplemental Charter of 10 August 1921 empowered the IWGC to act on behalf of any government of any part of the Empire, in carrying out arrangements with the government of any foreign state in relation to the graves of officers and men of the Forces, of allies or of enemies who died in any part of the Empire during the 1914-1918 War. CWGC 1076/1089/2 Part 1, Despatch No 115: J. H. Thomas to Governor-General, Irish Free State, 21 Feb 1924.

2 NAI, DFA239/89, Secretary DEA to Secretary, Executive Council, 5 May 1924 summarises the contents of the memorandum of 25 January 1924.

3 NAI, PEC 1, G2/3, Minutes of the Executive Council, p.150, 9 Feb 1924, p.170, 26 Feb 1924; Dept of An Taoiseach (DT), S 3569, Imperial War Graves Commission, Breathnach, Secretary DEA, to Secretary, Executive Council, 25 Jan 1924.

4 DFA239/89, Thomas to Governor-General Healy, 10 March 1924.

5 Ibid., 239/89, MacDonnchadha, Secretary to the Executive Council, to Secretary, Ministry of External Affairs, 25 Apr 1924.

6 Ibid., 239/89, Secretary, DEA, to Secretary, Executive Council, 5 May 1924.

7 G2/3, Minutes of the Executive Council, p.279, 8 May 1924; DFA 238/89, MacDonnchadha to Secretary, DEA, 8 May 1924.

8 UCDA, Hugh Kennedy Papers, P 4/588, Cosgrave to Kennedy, Apr-May 1924.

9 Ibid., 239/89, Phelan to Secretary of State for War, 5 May 1924; NAI, Governor-General Papers, F 278, copy of Cubitt to Phelan, 20 May 1924.

10 Ibid., Governor-General Papers, F 278, Thomas to Healy, Despatch No 324, 27 May 1924; CWGC, 1076/1089/2 Part 1, Thomas to Healy, 27 May 1924, Thomas to Healy, Despatch No 291, 14 May 1924.

11 G2/3, Minutes of the Executive Council , p..338, 28 June 1924; DFA 239/89, Codling, Finance, to Secretary, Executive Council, 24 June 1924; MacDonnchadha to Secretary, DEA, 30 June 1924.

[12] Ibid., Healy to Secretary of State for the Colonies, 7 July 1924.

[13] See Chapter Eleven.

[14] CWGC 1076/1089/2 Part 1, Colonial Office to Ware, 4 Sept 1924.

[15] Ibid., Notes of a conference regarding War Graves in Ireland, held at the offices of the Imperial War Graves Commission on Friday 24 October 1924.

[16] Ibid.

[17] Ibid., Whiskard to Waterfield, 25 Oct 1924.

[18] DFA 239/89, Secretary, DEA to Secretary, Dept of Finance, 14 Nov 1924.

[19] CWGC 1076/1089/2 Part 1, Waterfield to Whiskard, 29 Nov 1924.

[20] DFA 239/89, Amery, Colonial Office, to Healy, Governor-General, 9 Feb 1925.

[21] CWGC 1076/1089/2 Part 1, Amery, Dominions Office, to Healy, 21 Sept 1925.

[22] Ibid., internal IWGC memo, Browne [almost certainly to H. F. Chettle, Director of Records], 20 July 1925.

[23] Ibid., Browne to Under Secretary of State, Colonial Office, 23 July 1925.

[24] DFA 239/89, Secretary, DEA, to Secretary, Finance, 26 May 1925.

[25] Ibid., Secretary, DEA, to Secretary, Finance, 5 Feb 1926.

[26] None of the papers consulted, whether those of Finance in the National Archives of Ireland, or the Blythe or FitzGerald Papers in UCDA, indicates this.

[27] M. Kennedy & J.M. Skelly, eds., *Irish Foreign Policy, 1919-66: From Independence to Internationalism*, Dublin 2000, p.22.

[28] CWGC 1076/1089/2 Part 1, Meredith, the Rectory, Buncrana, to the Secretary, IWGC, 20 July 1925.

[29] Ibid., Howard, Donagh Rectory, Glasslough, to IWGC, 9 Sept 1926. Robert Steenson's grave eventually, in the 1930s, got its standard war grave headstone.

[30] Ibid., Lord to Secretary, IWGC, 22 Sept 1926, Secretary, IWGC, to Lord, 28 Sept 1926, and Lord to Secretary, IWGC, 30 Sept 1926.

[31] Ibid., Tynan to Secretary, IWGC, 4 Aug 1925; B S C Greene, IWGC, to Tynan, 6 Aug 1925.

[32] Ibid., Scanlon, Tralee Branch, British Legion, to Tynan, Secretary, British Legion Irish Area, 23 Sept 1925; Tynan to Secretary, IWGC, 26 Sept 1925; Browne, IWGC, to Undersecretary of State, Dominions Office, 30 Sept 1925.

[33] Ibid., Peacocke to General Cobbe, 11 Oct 192; Cobbe, India Office, to Browne, IWGC, 13 Oct 1925; Browne to Cobbe, 17 Oct 1925.

[34] Ibid., Cross to Ware, 20 Nov 1925.

[35] Ibid., Browne to Director of Records, 22 March 1926; Cross to Ware, 23 Apr 1926.

[36] Ibid., Ware to O'Connor, 18 May 1926.

[37] NAI, DT, S.3569, Amery to Governor-General, 4 June 1926, Despatch No 188; DFA 239/89, Secretary, DEA to Secretary, Finance, 10 June 1926; Whiskard to O'Hegarty, 4 June 1926.

[38] DFA 239/89, O'Hegarty to Lester, 10 June 1926; Secretary, DEA, to Secretary, Executive Council, 11 June 1926; DT, S 3569, S.P. Breathnach (i.e. Joseph Walshe) to O'Hegarty, 11 June 1926.

[39] CWGC 1076/1089/2 Part 1, Browne to Undersecretary of State, Dominions Office, 25 June 1926.

[40] Ibid., Browne, internal IWGC memorandum, 25 June 1926.

[41] Ibid., Tooker, Tralee, to Secretary, IWGC, 15 June 926, Browne to Tooker, 19 June 1926.

[42] Ibid., Whiskard to Browne, 24 July 1926.

[43] Ibid., Heath to Ware, 19 July 1926.

[44] NAI, DT, S.3569, Whiskard to O'Hegarty, 11 Aug 1926.

[45] DFA 239/89, O'Hegarty to Secretary, DEA, 14 Aug 1926.

[46] Ibid., Secretary , DEA, to Secretary, Executive Council, 18 Aug 1926.

[47] DT, S.3569, Amery to Cosgrave, 7 Oct 1926.

[48] Ibid., Cosgrave to Amery, 14 Oct 1926.

[49] NAI, Governor-General Papers, F 278, Despatch No 240, Healy to Dominions Secretary, 1 Nov 1926.

[50] NAI, DT, S.3569, Stephenson, Dominions Office, to O'Hegarty, 20 Nov 1926; CWGC 1076/1089/2 Part 1, Ware to Undersecretary of State, Dominions Office, 9 Nov 1926; DFA 239/89, Secretary, DEA, to Arthur Codling, Finance, 7 Dec 1926.

51 Ibid., Lester to O'Hegarty, 7 Jan 1927.

52 Ibid., Codling to Lester, 24 Dec 1926.; Secretary, DEA, to O'Hegarty, 7 Jan 1927; Secretary, DEA, to Secretary, Finance, 8 Jan 1927; Codling, Finance, to Secretary, DEA, 28 Jan 1927; Secretary, DEA, to Secretary, Finance, 1 Feb 1927.

53 For 1916, see C. Townshend, *Easter1916: The Irish Rebellion*, London 2006 ed., pp. 270, 393; for 1919-1921, see Hopkinson, op.cit., pp.201-202.

54 Ibid., Secretary, Dept of the President, to Heath, 21 Jan 1927.

55 CWGC 1076/1089/2 Part 1, Widdows, War Office, to Undersecretary of State, Dominions Office, 4 Jan 1927; Walker, Admiralty, to Undersecretary of State, Dominions Office, 21 Jan 1927.

56 CWGC, 1076/1089/2 Part 1, and DFA 239/89, Governor-General to Secretary of State for the Dominions, 1 Nov 1926.

Chapter 7

1 CWGC 1076/1089/2 Part 1, Browne to Whiskard, 19 Feb 1927.

2 DFA 239/89, Whiskard to O'Hegarty, 24 Feb 1927; MacDonnchadha, Dept of the President, to Secretary , DEA, 25 Feb 1927.

3 Ibid., Secretary, DEA, to Secretary, OPW, 1 March 1927; Secretary, DEA, to Secretary, Dept of the President, 1 March 1927; CWGC 1076/1089/2 Part 1, M. M. Murphy, Office of the Secretary to the Executive Council, to Whiskard, Dominions Office, 3 March 1927; Whiskard to Browne, 11 March 1927.

4 CWGC, 1076/1089/2 Part 1, Cross to Ware, 4 Apr 1927.

5 Ibid., IWGC internal memorandum, 6 Apr 1927.

6 Ibid., Ware to Secretary, OPW, 13 Apr 1927; Cassedy to Secretary, IWGC, 13 Apr 1927.

7 Ibid., Chettle to Newham, 21 Apr 1927.

8 Ibid., Browne to Whiskard, 26 Apr 1927.

9 Of the twelve military cemeteries, only Fort Carlisle remained under British control, until 1938.

10 Ibid., Veale, OPW, to Newham, 27 Apr 1927.

11 Ibid., Newham to Veale, 26 Apr 1927; Ware to Cassedy, 4 May 1927.

12 Ibid., Ware to Secretary, OPW, 13 May 1927; Cassedy to Ware, 13 May 1927: their letters crossed in the post.

13 Ibid., Cross to Ware, 21 May 1927;Whiskard to Browne, 22 June 1927.

14 Ibid., IWGC internal memorandum dated 28 June 1927, unsigned but almost certainly by Browne; Browne to Whiskard, 1 July 1927.

15 Ibid., Noblett to IWGC, 25 July 1927; IWGC to Noblett, 27 July 1927.

16 Ibid., Pinsent to Ware, 15 Sept 1927.

17 Ibid., Ware to Pinsent, Treasury Chambers, 16 Sept 1927.

18 CWGC 1076/1089/2 Part 2, Ware to Secretary, OPW, 31 Oct 1927.

19 DFA 239/89, Codling to Secretary, DEA, 10 Jan 1928, enclosing copy of signed minute of 27 Oct 1927 from Codling to Walshe of Foreign Affairs.

20 CWGC 1076/1089/2 Part 2, Cassedy to Ware, 18 Nov 1927.

21 DFA 239/89, Andrew Donohoe, Arklow, to Secretary, IWGC, 24 Oct 1927; Lovat, Dominions Office, to Minister for External Affairs, 9 Nov 1927.

22 CWGC 1076/1089/2 Part 2, internal IWGC memorandum, Chettle to Browne, 22 Nov 1927.

23 Sir H. F. Batterbee (1880-1976), Assistant Secretary at the Dominions Office, subsequently was British High Commissioner to New Zealand, 1939-1945.

24 DFA 239/89, Batterbee to S. Murphy, DEA, 17 Jan 1928.

25 CWGC 1076/1089/2 Part 2, Ware to Batterbee, 25 Nov 1927.

26 DFA 239/89, Extract from Secretary's Memorandum to Minister, 30 Nov 1927.

27 CWGC 1076/1089/2 Part 2, IWGC unsigned internal memorandum, 11 Feb 1928

28 DFA 239/89, Batterbee to Walshe, 20 Dec 1927. There was no Minister for Public Works at that time, rather a Parliamentary Secretary with responsibility for Public Works, then James A. Burke.

29 Ibid., Tynan, Organising Secretary, British Legion (Ireland) Southern Area Headquarters, to the Undersecretary of State, Dominions Office, 24 Nov 1927.

[30] Ibid., DEA internal minute, Lester to Walshe, 24 Dec 1927.

[31] CWGC 1076/1089/2 Part 2, Cassedy to Ware, 7 Jan 1928; Ware to Batterbee, 12 Jan 1928.

[32] DFA 239/89, Batterbee to S. Murphy, 17 Jan 1928.

[33] CWGC 1076/1089/2 Part 2, IWGC internal memorandum, dated 11 Feb 1928, minuting a conversation between Harding and Ware of the same date.

[34] Ibid., Lester to Batterbee, 3 Apr 1928.

[35] Ibid., Harding to Ware, 25 Apr 1928.

[36] Ibid., Ware to Batterbee, 22 May 1928.

Chapter 8

[1] CWGC 1076/1089/2 Part 2, and DFA239/89, Lester to Ware, 26 May 1928.

[2] CWGC database, *Cemeteries, Churchyards and Memorials in the Republic of Ireland*. For Kildare men who served in the two World Wars see Durney, op.cit.

[3] NAI, OPW9/A22/1/35/38, Temple Hill (The Friends' Cemetery),Blackrock, Co Dublin, site visit report.

[4] Richard Croker was the first Irish racehorse owner to win both the English Derby and Irish Derby in the same year, 1907, with his horse Orby. He lived at Glencairn, near Kilgobbin, a house which subsequently became the official residence of the British ambassador in Ireland. See D'Arcy, op.cit., pp. 231-232.

[5] CWGC 1076/1089/2 Part 2, Chettle to Ware and Browne, 11 June 1928.

[6] Ibid., Chettle to Browne, 19 July 1928.

[7] Ibid., Ware to Batterbee, 9 July 1928

[8] Ibid., Batterbee to Ware, 17 July 1928.

[9] Ibid., Brown to Chettle, 18 July 1928, Chettle to Browne, 19 July 1928.

[10] Ibid., Chettle to Thorn, 5 July 1928.

[11] Ibid., Ware to Hanson, 13 July 1928, Hanson to Ware, 14 July 1928. The response of the Department of Finance is not evident but had it been positive, doubtless Hanson would have conveyed as much to the Commission.

[12] Ibid., Chettle to Ware, 31 July 1928.

[13] Ibid., Browne to Ware, 26 July 1928.

[14] Ibid., Ware to Hanson, 3 Oct 1928.

[15] CWGC personnel records, communication from archivist.

[16] CWGC 1076/1089/2 Part 2, Whiskard to Ware, 8 Oct 1928; Browne to Whiskard, circa 10 Oct 1928; Hanson to Ware, 11 Oct 1928.

[17] DO 130/20, Tynan to Antrobus, Office of the UK Representative, Dublin, 4 March 1951. See also, J. Mackey, 'A Small Graveyard in a Dublin Hospital', *Genealogical Society of Ireland*, 2, 4, winter 2001, pp.231-233. I am grateful to Ms Mary Mackey, National Archives, Ireland, for this reference.

[18] CWGC, UKC/CEM 13944, Grangegorman Military Cemetery. The five were: Lt. Godfrey J. Hunter (26), 5th Royal Irish Lancers, 26 April 1916; Lt. Algernon Lucas (37), 2nd King Edward's Horse, 29 April; Lt. Guy V. Pinfield (21), 8th Hussars, 24 April; Lt. Philip A. Purser, Army Service Corps, 30 April; Lt. Basil H. Worsley-Worswick (35), 2nd King Edward's Horse, 29 April.

[19] Ibid., Vesper to Secretary, IWGC, 30 Oct 1928; Vesper to Chettle, 3 Nov 1928; Vesper to Chettle, 23 Nov 1928.

[20] Ibid., R. W. Murphy, IWGC, to Vesper, 16 Nov 1928.

[21] Ibid., Vesper to Chettle, 22 Nov 1928; Chettle to Vesper, 30 Nov 1928.

[22] *Irish Times*, 31 Jan 1929; *Derry Journal*, 21 Nov 1928; *Gaelic American*, 15 Dec 1928; *Daily Mail*, Brisbane, 5 Jan 1929. For concern over the graves of the Irish patriot dead, see Chapter Eleven.

[23] *Díospóireachtaí Parlaiminte, Seanad Éireann*, vol 12, 17 July 1929 and, DFA 239/89, DEA minute to Private Secretary, Minister of Finance, 25 Nov 1929.

[24] See Chapters Nine and Ten.

[25] *Irish Independent*, 12 June 1929.

[26] DO117/152, Stamfordham to J. Edgcumbe, 10 June 1929.

[27] Ibid., Stamfordham, Windsor Castle, to E. J. Harding, Dominions Office, 12 June 1929.

[28] DFA, Early Series, EA 231/3, Reports Received from Professor T. A. Smiddy, High Commissioner in London, 1928-1929: confidential: interview with the Secretary of State for Dominion Affairs, 17 June 1929.

[29] DO 117/152, Stamfordham to Secretary of State, Dominions Office, 19 June 1929.

[30] Ibid., Cosgrave to Granard, 19 June 1929.

[31] See Chapter Twelve.

[32] OPW9/A22/1/83/38, Upper Fahan Cemetery, Donegal, Vesper's report on site visit, 20 Feb 1929; and, Veale to Rev. H. O'Donnell, 21 Oct 1932.

[33] Ibid., A121/4/49/43, signed agreement dated 6 and 20 February 1936.

[34] Ibid., A22/1/484/40, Kildeema Burial Ground, Co Clare, Vesper to Chettle 4 Sept 1933.

[35] Ibid., Chettle to Vesper, 16 Sept 1933; Vesper to Chettle, 18 Sept 1933.

[36] Ibid., Annie Mahony to Joseph O'Donoghue, 11 Feb 1935; Mahony to the Secretary, OPW, 18 Feb 1935.

[37] Ibid., Veale to Secretary, IWGC, 10 and 18 Dec 1936.

[38] OPW 9/A22/1/380/39, Ballylaneen, St. Anne's, Catholic Churchyard, Patrick Biggane, Fulham, to OPW, 22 Dec 1930. See also, Lecane, op.cit., pp.93, 197, 235.

[39] The family memorial also has the wrong date of death engraved, stating November, instead of October 1918.

[40] CWGC 1077/1089/2 Part 3, Vesper to Chettle, I Nov 1929.

[41] OPW9/A22/1/45/38, OPW Annual Reports, Report by Vesper to Commissioners of Works, 5 April 1930.

[42] CWGC 1077/1089/2 Part 3, Vesper to Secretary, OPW, 3 Apr 1930, enclosing his report for the year ending 31 March 1930.

[43] Ibid., Vesper's report on progress of work to 31 March 1931, dated 28 Apr 1931; Vesper's report for year ended 31 March 1933, dated 21 June 1933.

[44] Ibid., *Minutes of the Proceedings of the 168ᵗʰ Meeting of the Commission, 13 Dec 1933.* For later difficulties, see Chapter Ten.

[45] OPW9/A22/1/45/38, Vesper to Secretary, OPW, 5 July 1932.

[46] Ibid., OPW internal minute, Veale to Commissioners, 30 Oct 1935: see Chapter Ten.

[47] CWGC 1076/1089/2 Part 2, internal IWGC minute, Browne to Ware, 3 Apr 1929; CWGC 077/1089/2 Part 3, Vesper to Secretary, IWGC, 15 Apr 1929.

[48] Ibid., Vesper to Browne, 8 Aug 1930.

[49] DFA 239/89, Director of Records, IWGC, to Secretary, OPW, 7 Oct 1931; Cassedy to Secretary, DEA, 15 Oct 1931; O'Hegarty to Cosgrave, 24 Oct 1931; Cosgrave to O'Hegarty, 10 Nov 1931.

[50] Ibid., Walshe, Secretary, DEA, to Secretary, OPW, 17 Nov 1931.

[51] Ibid., Cassedy to Walshe, 25 July 1935.

Chapter 9

[1] NAI, OPW 7/33/2, Grangegorman Military Cemetery, files no.1 & 2; OPW 7/33/1, construction schedules for various Dublin burial grounds from Dean's Grange to Drumcondra.

[2] *Ninety Ninth Annual Report of the Commissioners of Public Works for the year ended 31ˢᵗ March 1931*, p.13.

[3] *One Hundredth Annual Report of the Commissioners of Public Works, Report for the year ended 31ˢᵗ March 1932*, p.14.

[4] OPW 9/A22/1/5/36, McCarthy & Sons to OPW, 7 Feb 1936; OPW 9/A22/1/50/38, K. Robins to Vesper, 26 July 1932.

[5] *One Hundred and Sixth Annual Report of the Commissioners of Public Works, Report for the year ended 31st March 1938*, p.36.

[6] See Chapter Ten.

[7] CWGC 1077/1089/2 Part 3, Vesper to Ware, 11 Aug 1933.

[8] Ibid., 1077/1089/2 Part 3, Chettle to Ware, 16 Sept 1931.

[9] Longworth, op.cit., pp.36-37, 68-69, 125.

[10] The six are located in the following cemeteries: Belfast City, Belfast Dundonald, Belfast Milltown, Carnmoney, Irvinestown and Derry City. It is not clear why no Stone of Remembrance was ever erected in any of these. Information courtesy of the Commonwealth War Graves Commission.

[11] CWGC 1076/1089/2 Part 2, IWGC internal memo, Ware to Assistant Secretary, Finance, 27 July 1929.

[12] Ibid., 1077/1089/2 Part 3, Ware to Hanson, 3 Nov 1931.

[13] Ibid., 1077/1089/2 Part 3, Chettle to Browne to Ware, 21 Oct 1931; the underlining is Chettle's.

[14] Ibid., Chettle to Ware, 20 Oct 1934.

[15] Here the Cross of Sacrifice is actually of Lutyens' design, not Blomfield's; see Jeffery, op.cit., pp. 119, 175, n.34. There is an unusual War Memorial Cross in the grounds of the old Royal Hibernian Military School in the Phoenix Park that vaguely resembles the Blomfield standard Cross of Sacrifice,

but not of the same dimensions or style, and without the facing bronze sword.

[16] OPW 9/A22/1/19/37, IWGC, Enquiries from Relatives re eligibility for standard headstones, Margaret Byrne to Secretary, OPW, 23 Feb 1933; Daniel Mulcahy to OPW, 3 July 1934.

[17] *Irish Press*, 20 Nov 1935.

[18] OPW 9/A22/18/1/40, Application for a headstone for a grave of a former member of the Irish Republican Army, Secretary, OPW, to Joseph A Purcell, n.d., but on or after 13 Dec 1935.

[19] OPW 9/A22/1/50/38, Paulstown (St.Paul's) Catholic Churchyard, Co Kilkenny, Robins to Vesper, 26 July 1932; Veale to Mrs Kate O'Neill, 10 August 1932.

[20] Ibid., O'Neill to Secretary, OPW, 11 August 1932.

[21] Ibid., Veale to Robins, 16 Aug ust 1932; Veale to O'Neill, 16 August 1932.

[22] Ibid., OPW internal memorandum by Veale, 2 Aug 1938.

[23] Ibid., M. Connolly to A.S.Rice, OPW, 2 July 1941.

[24] CWGC data base, Casualty Details, Grange-gorman Memorial, www.cwgc.org/search/casualty_details.

[25] OPW 9/A121/4/156/51, Ferrybank Catholic Churchyard, Co Kilkenny, E. Brennan, P.P., to Vesper, 5 Aug 1930.

[26] Ibid., Assistant Architect 'FG', to Division A, OPW, 15 August 1933.

[27] Ibid., site visit report by Assistant Architect, 14 June 1939.

[28] OPW9/A22/1/481/40, Rosscarbery (The Abbey) Graveyard, Co Cork.

[29] OPW 9/A22/1/538/40, Kilshannig Church of Ireland Churchyard, Co Cork, report by Vesper, 1 December 1932 on site visit, 25 November 1932; CWGC data base, Casualty Details, Grangegorman Memorial, (Panel 10), www.cwgc.org/search/casualty_details.

[30] OPW 9/A22/1/437/40, Skibbereen Chapelyard Graveyard.

[31] Ibid., Veale to Denis Herlihy, 16 April 1932; OPW internal minute, 13 June 1935; Brandon to Parnell Martin, 28 August 1935; Parnell Martin to Secretary, OPW, 21 October 1935; Veale to Herlihy, 14 December 1935; OPW internal minute, 7 April 1940; CWGC data base, Casualty Details Grangegorman Memorial.

[32] L. Ó Broin, *Protestant Nationalists in Revolutionary Ireland: The Stopford Connection*, Dublin 1985, p.177; P. Hart, *The IRA and its Enemies: Violence and Community in Cork, 1916-1923*, Oxford 1998, p.231; P.Cottrell, *The Anglo-Irish War: The Troubles of 1913-1922*, Oxford 2006, pp.70,77

[33] OPW 9/A22/1/453/40, South Kilmurry Graveyard, Co Cork, Mrs J. Kerr to OPW, n.d. but circa 19 September1932; Vesper site visit report, dated 18 November 1931; CWGC data base, Casualty Details, Grangegorman Memorial.

[34] OPW 9/A121/2/2/41, Brandon, OPW internal memo, 3 September 1941. The eight were: Cornamanagh, Athlone: St. Peter's, Kilscoran; St. Michael's New Cemetery, Tipperary; St. George's, Drumcondra; St. John the Baptist, Drumcondra; Castlegannon, Kilkenny; St. George's, Carrick-on-Shannon. The only authority, known to this writer, to insist on a fee for title was Sligo Corporation.

[35] OPW 9/A22/1/31/38, St. George's Burial Ground, Whitworth Road, George Freeman, Hon. Secretary, Select Vestry, to Vesper, n.d. but between 28 Jan 1929 and 22 Oct 1930.

[36] Ibid., Elizabeth Pobjoy to Secetary, OPW, 12 Dec 1930.

[37] CWGC 1076/1089/2 Part 2, Ware to Hanson, 7 May 1929; Hanson to Ware, 14 May 1929.

[38] P. Lecane, *Torpedoed! The RMS Leinster Disaster*, Penzance 2005, p.215; Igoe, op.cit., p.129. The number 145 is given in CWGC CEM 13944, Grangegorman Military Cemetery, internal memorandum of 1968, n.d.

[39] CWGC 1076/1089/2 Part 2, George Barraclough to IWGC, 30 March 1929.

[40] Ibid., Ware to Hanson, 15 July 1929.

[41] OPW 9/A22/1/530/40, Ballynacally (Kilchreest) Cemetery, Co Clare, Chettle to Vesper, 12 Jan 1933; Thomas Slattery to Secretary, OPW, 25 Apr 1933; Michael Slattery to Secretary, OPW, 19 Feb 1934.

[42] Ibid., McCarthy, report dated 1 Dec 1937 on site visit, 29 Nov 1937.

[43] *One Hundred and Fifth Annual Report of the Commissioners of Public Works, Report for the year ended 31st March 1937*, p.12.

[44] CWGC 1077/1089/2 Part 4, T. J. Raftery for Secretary, OPW, to Secretary, IWGC, 13 July 1935. For further requests for Vesper's advice, see Chapter Thirteen.

[45] Ibid., Vesper to Secretary, OPW, 2 July 1935.

Chapter 10

[1] OPW9/A22/1/451/40, Killiskey Church of Ireland Churchyard, Co Wicklow, Vesper's report dated 9 June 1931 of visit on 4 June 1931.

[2] Ibid., Canon Moore to Secretary, OPW, 19 and 31 August 1931.

[3] Ibid., J. C. Hehir, OPW, to W. Vandaleur, 30 January 1937.

[4] Ibid., annual OPW site visit inspection reports in NAI and OPWSTSG.

[5] E de Groot, 'Bel-Air Hotel', *Ashford and District Historical Journal*, No1, July 1991, pp. 30-32. I am grateful to Ken Hannigan of the National Archives for this information and reference.

[6] OPW9/A22/1/12/36, War Graves Maintenance in Cemeteries under the control of the Kerry Board of Health., Veale to Organising Secretary, British Legion, 12 June 1936, in response to the latter's of 17 May 1936.

[7] Ibid., P. S. O'Mahoney to Secretary, OPW, 2 May 1936.

[8] D. McMahon, 'Roger Casement: An account from the archives of his reinterment in Ireland', in *Irish Archives*, Spring 1996, pp.3-12; K.Grant, 'Bones of contention: the repatriation of the remains of Roger Casement', *Journal of British Studies*, 41, 3, 2002, pp.329-353.

[9] Dáil Debates, 5 December 1935, vol. 59, no. 6, col.1943.

[10] Ibid., 2 April 1936, vol.61, no. 2, col 865.

[11] McMahon, loc.cit., p.12.

[12] OPW 9/A22/1/12/36, OPW to Co Kerry Board of Health, 12 June 1936.

[13] Ibid., Co. Kerry Board of Health to OPW, 1 July 1936.

[14] Ibid., Ó hÉigeartaigh to Chairman & Parliamentary Secretary to OPW, 3 July 1936; OPW to Department of External Affairs, 11 July 1936.

[15] Ibid., G. P. O'Shea to Brandon, 19 July 1946.

[16] Ibid., Brandon to O'Shea, 31 Dec 1946.

[17] Ibid., Kerry County Manager to O'Shea, OPW, Killarney, 3 Jan 1947

[18] Ibid., as follows: Tralee (Ratass) Cemetery – caretaker N. C. Hanafin, 15 Jan 1947; Killarney New Cemetery – caretaker Frederick Cox, 17 Jan 1947; Keel Cemetery – caretaker James Breen, 25 Feb 1947; Killorglin Cemetery – caretaker Timothy O'Brien, 28 Feb 1947; Cahersiveen (Kilvarnogue) Cemetery – caretaker John Clifford, 28 Feb 1947. Curiously, the OPW's signatory, P. S. Ó Chearnaigh, did not sign until 13 May 1948, the delay unexplained.

[19] NAI, DT Private Office, TAOIS 97/9/279, Graveyards – condition of, 7 October 1935 to 7 July 1938.

[20] The OPW's quest for co-operation with local authorities almost came to grief in Longford also, where, in September 1936 members of the Board of Health took exception to the request to care for British Commonwealth war graves to the neglect and exclusion of the graves of 'the Men who fell in 1916'. The Board Chairman deplored the fact that there was no public department of state to care for these. The Board passed a resolution calling on the Government to set aside money for the maintenance of the 1916 graves, but agreed to carry out the OPW's request for maintenance of the Commonwealth war graves in the county. See *The Longford Leader*, 19 Sept 1936.

[21] *The Sligo Champion*, 5 November 1932.

[22] Sligo Corporation Minute Book, *Minutes of Proceedings of Special Meeting, 26 Oct 1932*; DFA 411/1A, OPW Memo, 9 July 1948, War Graves 1914-1918, Erection of Headstones, rehearses the history of the issue for the information of External Affairs.

[23] OPW 9/A22/1/527/40, Veale to Quin, 10 June 1933.

[24] CWGC 1077/1089/2 Part 3, H. F. Robinson, IWGC, to Secretary, OPW, undated but, from contextual evidence, clearly November 1934.

[25] CWGC 1077/1089/2 Part 4, Vesper to Chettle, 29 March 1935.

[26] Ibid., Vesper to Chettle, 3 Apr 1935, enclosing copy of Notes of My Opening Statement.

[27] Ibid., Vesper to Chettle, 11 Apr 1935.

[28] Ibid., *Minutes of the 182nd Meeting of the Imperial War Graves Commission,15 May 1935*: marking of graves in the Irish Free State.

[29] OPW 9/A22/1/527/40, *Querrin Templemeade Cemetery, Co Clare*, McCarthy to Veale, 19 May 1936.

[30] CWGC 1077/1089/2 Part 4, Tynan to Secretary, OPW, 7 May 1936.

[31] Ibid., Brandon to Vesper, 29 May 1936.

[32] DFA 411/1A, OPW Memo, 9 July 1948; OPW, STSG, A22/1/13/36, *War Graves, British; Erection of Headstones: Attitude of Sligo Corporation and Clare Board of Health in the matter*, W.J. Veale to Town Clerk, Sligo, 17 July 1936; Town Clerk Seán Ó hUigín to Secretary, OPW, 12 Aug 1936.

[33] Ibid., Cassedy to Secretary, IWGC, 19 Aug 1936.

[34] Ibid., Vesper to Chettle, 27 Aug 1936; also, Vesper to Chettle, 24 Aug 1936.

[35] Clare County Council, *General Minute Book, Minutes of Proceedings at monthly meeting*, 4 Oct 1937.

[36] OPW 9/A22/1/527/40, Ó hÉigeartaigh to Connolly and Kent, 4 January 1937.

[37] Ibid., P J Raftery, OPW, to Secretary, IWGC, 4 June 1937; Chettle to Secretary, OPW, 25 June 1937.

[38] *Irish Press*, 29 Sept 1937.

[39] Clare County Council Archives, *Minutes of Proceedings of Clare County Board of Health, 27 Sept 1937*, p.19.

[40] *Clare Champion*, 2 Oct 1937, *Cork Examiner*, 29 Sept 1937, *Cork Evening Echo*, 28 Sept 1937.

[41] CWGC 1077/1089/2 Part 4, Vesper to Chettle, 30 Sept 1937; Chettle to Vesper, 19 Oct 1937.

[42] See Chapters Eighteen and Twenty-Three.

Chapter 11

[1] Igoe, op.cit., p.104; R. Bateson, *Dead and Buried in Dublin*, Warrenstown 2002.

[2] Glasnevin Archives (hereafter GA), DCC, General Committee Minute Book, vol G 33, *minutes of meeting of General Committee, 12 July 1922*, Secretary's Report, pp.10-14.

[3] Ibid., Report by Superintendent, 12 July 1922.

[4] Ibid., Rotation Committee Minute Book, vol. R 32, *minutes of meetings on 18 and 28 July 1922*, pp.150, 158; see also,A. Dolan, *Commemorating the Irish Civil War, History and Memory, 1923-2000*, Cambridge 2003.

[5] GA, Rotation Committee Minute Book, vol. R 32, *minutes of meetings on 13 and 17 October 1922*; NAI, FIN S0044/0013/24, Heavey, internal memorandum, President Griffith's Grave, 17 Oct ober 1922.

[6] GA, Rotation Committee Minute Book, vol. R 32, *minutes of meeting on 17 October 1922*,; Nowlan, Acting Superintendent, to Chairman of Rotation Committee, 16 October 1922, p.215.

[7] NAI, FIN S0044/0013/24, Heavey, internal emorandum, President Griffith's Grave, 17 October1922.

[8] Ibid., G. McGrath, Accountant General, to Michael Hayes, 20 October 1922.

[9] Ibid., John O'Connell, Secretary, Dublin Cemeteries Committee, to Joseph McGrath, Minister for Labour, 20 October 1922.

[10] Ibid., George McGrath to President, 8 November 1922.

[11] Ibid., Coyle, Acting Secretary, DCC, to M. J. Heavey, 17 Nov 1922.

[12] GA, General Committee Minute Books, vol.G 33, minutes of meeting on 6 Dec 1922, p.24.

[13] Ibid., minutes of meeting on 3 January 1923, pp.29-30.

[14] NAI, Dept Finance, FIN S004/0013/24, Comptroller and Auditor General, to Professor T. A. Smiddy, 18 Jan 1923; John O'Connell, Secretary, DCC, to M. J. Heavey, 19 January 1923.

[15] Ibid., Heavey, internal memorandum, 26 Jan 1923.

[16] GA, General Committee Minute Book, vol. G 33, minutes of meeting on 7 February 1923, p.36; FIN S004/0013/24, Heavey, internal memorandum, 23 January 1923, and O'Connell to Heavey, 8 February 1923.

[17] FIN S004/0013/24, McGrath to Hayes, 12 February 1923; Heavey to O'Connell, 22 February 1923.

[18] Ibid., O'Connell to Heavey, 21 March 1923.

[19] Ibid., George McGrath to Smiddy, 18 January 1923, citing a note from Smiddy, dated 26 December 1922; see also A. Dolan, op.cit., pp.117, 127; D. Fitzpatrick, 'Commemoration in the Irish Free State: a chronicle of embarrassment' in I. McBride, ed., *History and Memory in Modern Ireland*, Cambridge 2001, pp. 184-203.

[20] Ibid., George McGrath to President, 9 January 1923.

[21] Ibid., Cosgrave to Commander-in-Chief, 18 February 1923; Mulcahy to Cosgrave, 3 March 1923; UCDA, Blythe Papers, P 24/152, D. Ó hÉigeartaigh to each member of the Executive Council, 12 December 1923.

[22] UCDA, Mulcahy Papers, P 7/B/178, Army Council decision, 2 March 1923.

[23] FIN S004/0013/24, Mulcahy to Cosgrave, 4 April 1923.

[24] UCDA, Mulcahy Papers, P 7/B/178, Army Council decision, Saturday 17 June 1923.

[25] GA, Rotation Committee Minute Book, vol. R 32, *minutes of meeting on 29 May 1923*.

[26] FIN S004/0013/24, Cosgrave to Kinkead, 8 May 1923.

[27] Ibid., Kinkead to Cosgrave, 7 June 1923.

[28] GA, Rotation Committee Minute Book, vol. R 32, *minutes of meeting on 29 June 1923*, pp. 398-399,407.

[29] Ibid., General Committee Minute Book, vol. G 33, *minutes of meeting on 4 July 1923*, p.53.

[30] Ibid., Rotation Committee Minute Book, vol. R 32, *minutes of meeting on 6 July 1923*.

[31] FIN S004/0013/24, Note for Executive Council Meeting, addressed to Minister for Finance, 5 October 1923.

[32] Ibid., Gorman to Secretary, Ministry of Finance, 11 January 1924, in reply to queries from Finance.

[33] Ibid., Kinkead to Smiddy, 31 January 1924.

[34] Ibid., McGrath to President, 11 March 1924; McGrath to Heavey, 11 March 1924.

[35] Ibid., McGrath to President, 30 April 1934, quoting a letter to Smiddy on 12 March 1924.

[36] Ibid., McGrath to Heavey, 30 April 1924.

[37] Ibid., McGrath to President, 30 Apr 1924, enclosing a letter from the DCC.

[38] GA, Visiting Committee Minute Book, vol. V 7, *minutes of meeting on 8 March 1924*, p.417; NAI, PEC 1, Executive Council Minutes, 28 June 1924.

[39] FIN S004/0013/24, S. Ó hÓgáin to Comptroller and Auditor General, 21 June 1924; Ó hÓgáin to Heavey, 30 June 1924; PEC 1, *Executive Council Minutes*, 5 July, 12 July 1924.

[40] GA, Rotation Committee Minute Book, vol. R 34, *minutes of meeting on 20 June 1924*, pp.139-140, containing M. Griffith to DCC, 19 June 1924.

[41] FIN S004/0013/24, Secretary, Executive Council to Army Finance Officer, 12 July 1924.

[42] GA, Rotation Committee Minute Book, vol. R 34, *minutes of meetings on 18 July and 15 August 1924*.

[43] Ibid., General Committee Minute Book, vol. G 33, *minutes of meeting on 6 Aug 1924*, p.83, incorporating copy of C. D. Coyle, Acting Secretary, DCC, to Thomas Gorman, Army Finance Office, 6 August 1924.

[44] FIN S004/0013/24, D. O'Sullivan, Army Finance Office, to Secretary, Dept of Finance, 18 August 1924.

[45] GA, Rotation Committee Minute Book, vol. R 34, *minutes of meeting on 22 August 1924*, p.165.

[46] Dolan, op. cit, p.128, citing FIN S004/0013/24, Dept of Finance memorandum, 10 December 1925.

[47] Dolan, op.cit., pp.119,128; T. P. Coogan, *Michael Collins, a biography*, Dublin 1991, pp. 428-432.

[48] FIN S004/0013/24, Dept of Finance internal memorandum, first draft, 24 April 1931.

[49] Ibid., J.J. McElligott to Lt. Gen. P. McMahon, 21 May 1931.

[50] FIN S 004/0098/25, Army Burial Plot:Mount Prospect Cemetery, Glasnevin: Sanction for Maintenance by Army, Secretary, Dept of Defence to Secretary, Minister for Finance, 1 May 1925.

[51] GA, Rotation Committee Minute Book, vol. R 34, *minutes of meeting on 1 May 1925*, p.286.

[52] FIN S 004/0098/25, Secretary, Dept of Defence, to Secretary, Minister of Finance, 1 May 1925.

[53] Ibid., internal Finance memorandum, 7 May 1925.

[54] Dolan, op.cit., p.129.

[55] GA, General Committee Minute Book, vol. 8, *minutes of meeting on 11 July 1925*, p.16.

[56] Ibid., Visiting Committee Minute Book, vol. V 8, *minutes of meeting on 15 Aug 1925*, p.19.

[57] FIN S004/0098/25, C. O'Connor, Secretary, Dept of Defence, to Secretary, Dept of Finance, 8 April 1926; J. Houlihan, Finance, to Secretary, Defence, 14 April 1926; Houlihan to Secretary, DCC, 14 April 1926; GA,Rotation Committee Minute Book, vol. R 34, *minutes of meeting on 16 April 1926*, p.424.

[58] Ibid., O'Connor to Secretary, Dept of Finance, 20 Aug 1928.

[59] Ibid., P. J. Raftery, OPW, to Secretary, Dept of Finance, 31 August 1928; O'Neill, Finance, to O'Connor, Defence, 5 September 1928.

[60] Ibid., M. Deegan for Secretary, Defence, to Secretary,DCC, 27 February 1929; Coyle, DCC, to Secretary, Defence, 6 March 1929.

[61] Ibid., MacMahon, Defence, to Doolin, Finance, 22 April 1929, reporting a conversation with Coyle of the DCC; Raftery, OPW, to Secretary, Finance, 27 March 1929; MacMahon to Doolin, Finance, 22 April 1929.

[62] GA, Rotation Committee Minute Book, vol. R 36, *minutes of meetings on 20 and 27 June, and 15 August 1930*, pp.171,173,199.

[63] Ibid., Rotation Committee Minute Book, vol. R 36, *minutes of meeting on 15 December 1931*, pp.385-387.

[64] FIN S 004/0098/25, Army Burial Plot, Doolin, Finance to Secretary, Defence, 15 Dec 1932, 18 Oct 1933, 22 Dec 1934 etc.,Warren, Defence to Secretary, Finance, 3 January 1949.

[65] CWGC, CEM 13942, Part 1, Glasnevin, Vesper to Secretary, IWGC, 17 Feb 1932.

[66] GA, DCC Letter Books, vol. 78, P. J. Quinn, Acting Secretary, to Mrs Fitzpatrick, 21 Oct 1931.

[67] CWGC, CEM 13942, Vesper to Secretary, OPW, 17 February 1932; see also *Extracts from the Bye-laws of the Dublin Cemeteries Committee*, Dublin 1906.

[68] GA, General Committee Minute Book, vol. G 33, 7 October 1931, p.271; DCC Letter Books, vol. 78, Acting Secretary, DCC, to Secretary, OPW, 7 October 1931.

[69] CWGC, CEM 13942, Vesper to Secretary, OPW, 17 February 1932; for Leask, see D. McCabe, *Major Figures in the History of the OPW: Celebrating 175 years*, Dublin 2006, pp. 41-47 and Dolan, op.cit., p.10.

[70] CWGC, CEM 13942, Chettle to Vesper, 20 Apr 1932.

[71] GA, Rotation Committee Minute Book, vol. R 36, *minutes of meeting on 19 April 1932*, p.442.

[72] CWGC, 1077/1089/2, Part 3, Chettle to Vice-Chairman, 23 October 1934.

[73] GA, Rotation Committee Minute Book, vol. R 37, *minutes of meetings on 11 and 22 Jan 1935*, pp.367, 370; Visiting Committee Minute Book, vol. V. 8, *minutes of meeting on 26 Jan 1935*, p.427.

[74] GA, Rotation Committee Minute Book, vol. R 37, *minutes of meeting on 1 March 1935*, p.383; vol. R 38, *minutes of meetings on 13 and 16 March 1936*

[75] *104th Annual Report of the Commissioners of Public Works for the year ended 31st March 1936*, p.4.

[76] CWGC 1077/1089/2 Part 4, Vesper to Assistant Secretary, Records Division, IWGC, 11 May 1937.

Chapter 12

[1] NAI, Department of An Taoiseach (henceforth DT) S4156A, *Proposed National War Memorial*, Memo MMD 30/10/29, Decision of the Cabinet, Cab.4/110/29/10/29, item No 1.

[2] *Irish Times*, 18 July 1919; Lt. Col. Boydell, 'The Irish National War Memorial: its meaning and purpose', in *British Legion Annual*, 1941, pp.15-51; N.C. Johnson, *Ireland, the Great War and the Geography of Remembrance*, Cambridge 2003, p.84.

[3] *Seanad Debates*, vol.8, 9 March 1927, speech of Andrew Jameson; Boydell, loc.cit.p.24.

[4] DT, S 4156A, Leon T. MacAmhlaoibh, Finance, to Secretary, Executive Council, 24 Nov 1924.

[5] DT, S 3370, Executive Council to General Sir Bryan Mahon, 30 Oct 1923, Mahon to Cosgrave, 2 Nov 1923, Glenavy to Cosgrave 1 Nov 1923.

[6] NAI, PEC 1, Taois G2/3, *Executive Council Minutes, Tues 15 May 1924*: the wording approved was 'In memory of Irish barristers who fell in the Great War, 1914-1918.... Their name liveth unto generation and generation'. See also UCDA, Hugh Kennedy Papers, P4, 1349, March-May 1924; This memorial was subsequently moved, in 1931, to the Law Library, Four Courts Dublin, following the restoration of the latter: see A.P. Quinn, *Wigs and Guns: Irish barristers in the Great War*, Dublin 2006, pp. 57-8,61.

[7] Ibid., C. Ó hUigínn, memorandum to members of the Executive Council, 29 October 1924.

[8] Ibid., Paul Banim, President's Office, to each member of the Executive Council, 6 November 1924;

[9] Ibid., W. P. Walker to Desmond Fitzgerald, Minister for External Affairs, 8 November 1924; for Moore's attack on Macready see DFA/Early Series – 2/139, Moore to Macready, 4 February 1921.

[10] DT, S 3370, Extract from minutes of the Executive Council, 10 November 1924, Cab. C.2/145.

[11] J. Leonard, 'The twinge of memory: Armistice Day and Remembrance Sunday in Dublin since 1919' in R. English and G. Walker, eds., *Unionism in Modern Ireland: new perspectives on politics and culture*, Dublin 1996, pp.105-106.

[12] DT, S 3370, Extract from minutes of the Executive Council, 4 November 1924, Report by Minister for Justice, C.2/143.

[13] Ibid., Secretary, Dept of the President, to Secretary, Dept of Finance, 26 October 1926; Amery to Cosgrave, 18 October 1926; Cosgrave to Amery, 30 October 1926.

[14] Ibid., Extracts from minutes of the Executive Council, 23 October 1925, C.2/222, and 10 November 1925, C.2/224.

[15] Ibid., Extract from minutes of the Executive Council, 1 December 1924, C.2/148.

[16] DT, S 4156A, John Sweetman to Cosgrave, 1 August 1925; The Leader, 1 August 1925.; Sweetman to Cosgrave, 10 August 1925; Secretary to the President to Secretary, Executive Council, 26 August 1925.

[17] Ibid., Ó hÉigeartaigh to James McNeill, 8 April 1926.

[18] Ibid., Copy of High Court Judgement, Thurs 18 March, 1926, Record No 1926-2421.

[19] *Dáil Debates*, vol. 19, 29 March 1927.

[20] *Seanad Debates*, vol. 8, 9 March 1927, 7 April 1927.

[21] DT, S4156A, undated memorandum, Irish National War Memorial: Proposed Gateway to the Phoenix Park; Denis P. Shanaghan, Finance, to Secretary, Executive Council, 6 June 1928; memorandum by Michael McDunphy re Cabinet decision of 10 July 1928, Cab.4/41, item no.2.

[22] Ibid., Jameson to Cosgrave, 19 Feb 1929.

[23] Ibid., M. McDunphy to Minister for Education, 2 March 1929; J. P. Clare, Private Secretary to the Minister for Justice; Secretary to the Minister for Local Government to Secretary , Executive Council, 7 May 1929; L. J. Kavanagh, Secretary, Dept of Lands & Fisheries to Secretary, Executive Council, 4 April 1929; Secretary, Dept of Defence to Secretary, Executive Council, 8 April 1929; these are the only extant responses located to-date. The twelve proposals were:
   1. A monument;
   2. A hall;
   3. A park;
   4. An industry for the unemployed;
   5. A ship to sail around Ireland with reduced fares for ex- Servicemen's families;
   6. A house with grounds;
   7. A relief fund for distressed relatives of ex-Servicemen;
   8. A gallery for the Hugh Lane pictures;
   9. An apprenticeship scheme;
   10. Playgrounds in new housing estates;
   11. A housing scheme;
   12. A children's education fund.

[24] Ibid., McDunphy to Banim, 12 June 1929.

[25] Ibid., Hanson to Ó hÉigeartaigh, Dept of the President, 23 October 1929, marked 'confidential'; Cosgrave to McDunphy, 28 Oct 1929.

[26] NAI, FIN 1/2301, Claim of Office of Woods, London, for rents due in respect of Inchicore North, Long Meadows Estate, Curragh etc., 11 Apr 1923 to 30 Sept 1926.

[27] DT, S 4156A, McDunphy memorandum, 30 October 1929 on Cabinet decision of 29 October 1929, Cab 4/110, item No 1, National War Memorial.

[28] DT, S 4156 B, Cosgrave to Jameson, 2 December 1929; Jameson to Cosgrave, 5 December 1929.

[29] Ibid., Cosgrave to Byrne, 12 December 1929.

[30] For Lutyens and Ireland see J. Brown, *Lutyens and the Edwardians: An English Architect and his Clients*, London 1996, pp. 99-103, 145-158, 214.

[31] Victoria & Albert Museum, Royal Institute of British Architects, Lutyens Letters, LUE 19/15/1-7, Sir Edwin to Lady Emily Lutyens, 24 July 1930.

[32] *The Sunday Times*, 31 August 1930.

[33] DT, S4156B, T. J. Byrne, Irish National War Memorial: proposed location on Longmeadows and Inchicore North Estates, 23 November 1930; Byrne to President, 13 November 1930; McDunphy Memorandum, 19 November 1930; Extract from minutes of meeting of Cabinet on 29 November 1930, CAB 5/26, item No.1.

[34] Ibid., Jameson to Cosgrave 24 April 1931; Cassedy to Private Secretary to the President, 20 June 1931; Cosgrave to Jameson, 15 July 1931.

[35] Ibid., National Memorial: Dept of Finance, Memorandum for Executive Council,15 September 1933; Mr T J Byrne's Report to INWM Committee, 14 December 1931; *Irish Times*, 15 December 1931.

[36] *Irish Press*, 31 December 1931.

[37] DT, S 4156B, Leyden to Ó hÉigeartaigh, 7 January 1932; Boydell, loc.cit., p.31.

[38] Leonard , loc.cit., p.106;

[39] DT, S 4156B, McDunphy to Private Secretary to the Minister for Finance, 23 September 1933; Boydell, loc.cit. p.31.

[40] Ibid., Extracts from minutes of Cabinet Meeting, 19 February 1935, Cab 7/288, item 4.

[41] V & A, RIBA, Lutyens Letters, LUE 20/7/1/i-iv, Sir Edwin to Lady Emily Lutyens, 6 August 1935.

[42] DFA, 246/1/343/E/23 Embassies, Brussels Mons Memorial, Count G. O'Kelly deGallagh to Secretary, External Affairs, 14 November 1923.

[43] DFA 247/1, Secretary, External Affairs to O'Kelly, 21 June 1924.

[44] Ibid., Secretary, External Affairs to O'Kelly, 28 June 1924.

[45] Ibid., Secretary, External Affairs to O'Kelly, 1 July 1924.

[46] Ibid., Secretary, External Affairs to O'Kelly , 17 July 1924.

[47] NAI, DFA/P 289, O'Kelly to Director of Publicity, External Affairs, 18 May 1924.

[48] DFA 249/1, 762/E/25, O'Kelly to Secretary, External Affairs, 1 May 1925.

[49] DFA251/950/E/26, O'Kelly to Secretary, External Affairs, 30 June 1926.

[50] Ibid., O'Kelly to Secretary, External Affairs, 30 July 1926.

[51] DFA 250/1, 224/130, Lester to O'Kelly, 15 July 1926.

[52] DFA 251, Secretary, External Affairs, to O'Kelly, 6 August 1926; O'Kelly to Secretary, 26 August 1926.

[53] 'Area Annual Report for the Year 1936', *British Legion Annual*, Irish Free State, 1937, p.18.

[54] DT, S4156B, Jameson to Cosgrave, 24 October 1931. The comment arose from an occasion when the Legion had asked the INWM Trustees for a grant of £400 to pay for the preparation of a Last Post evening ceremony at Loos Memorial.

[55] Ibid., S3370A, Extract from minutes of Cabinet meeting on 23 October 1925, C2/222 – the Cabinet upheld the Garda Commissioner's refusal of permission to use College Green.

[56] Ibid., S3370A, Extract from minutes of Cabinet meeting, 10 November 1024, C/2/145 for Maurice Moore's role in 1924; Banim to Hickie 2 November 1928 and Hickie to President 31 October 1928; Hickie to President, 24 October 1929; Extract from minutes of Cabinet meeting, 20 October 1931, Cab. 5/87, for Shaw's deputising role in 1931.

[57] *Irish Times*, 10 November 1936.

[58] DT, S3370B, Extract from minutes of Cabinet meeting, 28 October 1932, Cab. 6/84, item No.10.

[59] Ibid., Cabinet minutes, 24 October 1933 adopted these conditions, and they were repeated in 1934, 1935 and 1936: Cabinet minutes, 26 October 1934, then 4, Cab 7/180; MÓ M.(Maurice Moynihan) to Dagg, 2 November 1935; Cabinet minutes, 13 October 1936, Cab 7/360 item 2.

[60] Ibid., McDunphy minute of 12 November 1935. 'At the Church Parade which started from Eden Quay, 10 November at 10.30 a.m. I noticed that the four Legion flags which bore the Union Jack in the corner, were carried. I think this is contrary to the spirit of the permission for this parade'; see also *Irish Times*, 9 November 1936.

[61] Ibid., S4156C, Jameson to President, 9 March 1937.

[62] Ibid., W. A. Honohan, Finance, to Secretary, Dept of An Taoiseach, 22 March 1937.

[63] DT, S3370B, H. Wilson, INWM, to Secretary, OPW, 30 August 1937.

[64] DT, S4156B, Doolin, Finance, to Moynihan, Secretary, Dept of An Taoiseach, 2 September 1937.

[65] Ibid., Doolin, Finance, to Moynihan, Secretary, Dept of An Taoiseach, 2 September 1937.

[66] Ibid., Ó hÉigeartaigh to Doolin, 1 September 1937 and marginal note therein by Doolin referring to his discussion with Moynihan on 13 April 1937. Jameson had shown Ó hÉigeartaigh letters he had received from the Dublin Branch of the Legion.

[67] DT, S4156C, Extract from Cabinet Minutes, 3 September 1937, Cab 8/7 item 4.

[68] DT, S3370B, Extract from File S4156, P. S. O'Muireadaigh, Private Secretary, to the Taoiseach, 6 September 1937; Moynihan, minute, 9 September 1937.

[69] DT, S4156B, H. J. Wilson, Secretary INWM Committee, to Andrew Jameson, 5 October 1937.

[70] Ibid., Jameson to deValera, 6 October 1937.

[71] DT, S 3370B, McDunphy to Secretary, Dept of An Taoiseach, and Moynihan to Secretary, Finance, 21 October 1927.

[72] *Irish Press*, 18, 21 February 1938.

[73] DT, S4156, B. P. Kennedy, Assistant Secretary, Dept of An Taoiseach, to Major J J Tynan, 1 September 1938.

[74] DT, S4156 C. Kennedy, minute, 25 September 1938.

[75] Ibid., Tynan to Kennedy, 13 October 1935; Moynihan to Murray and Kennedy, 27 October 1938.

[76] Ibid., Moynihan, minute, 2 November 1938.

[77] Ibid., Kennedy, minute, 15 December 1938.

[78] Ibid., Walshe, Secretary, External Affairs, to Secretary, Dept of An Taoiseach, 20 January 1939.

[79] Ibid., H. Wilson to Private Secretary to the Premier [sic], 14 February 1939; Kennedy to Wilson, 13 February 1939; Wilson to Private Secretary to the Prime Minister [sic], 21 March 1939; Secretary to An Taoiseach to Wilson, 4 April 1939.

[80] Ibid., Moynihan to Wilson, 27 April 1939.

[81] Ibid., Dept An Taoiseach, internal memorandum, 28 April 1939, see also Jeffery, op.cit., pp 122,123; Hill op.cit. p.161.

[82] Ibid., Kennedy to Moynihan, 27 April 1939.

[83] J. T. Carroll, *Ireland in the War Years*, Newton Abbot 1975, pp.107-108.

84 Ibid., Tynan to the Secretary, Dept of An Taoiseach, 16 May 1939.

85 Ibid., Kennedy, internal memorandum, 16 May 1939.

86 Ibid., Irish National War Memorial Committee – Statement by British Legion, Ireland, (Southern Area) to Kennedy, internal minute, 16 May 1939; *Irish Press, Irish Independent, Irish Times,* all 17 May 1939.

87 *Irish Press,* 21 June 1939.

88 DT, S 4156B, Kennedy to Moynihan, 24 July 1939.

89 DT, S3370B, P. Breen, D/ Cigire, Detective Branch, Dublin Castle, to Ard Cheannphort, Special Section, 13 October 1941.

90 See Chapters Twenty-Two and Twenty-Three.

Chapter 13

1 CWGC 1077/1089/2 Part 3, Chettle to Vesper, 22 Nov 1934, quoting from copy of a letter from Lester to Batterbee, 3 April 1928.

2 DFA 239/89, George P. Fagan, OPW, to Secretary, Finance, 12 May 1937.

3 CWGC 1077/1089/2 Part 4, Vesper to Chettle, 27 May 1936.

4 Ibid., Vesper to Director of Records, 31 July 1936.

5 Ibid., Chettle to Vesper, 21 April 1937.

6 Ibid., Vesper to Chettle, 11 May 1937.

7 DFA 239/89, Fagan, OPW, to Secretary, Finance, 12 May 1937; Dagg, Finance to Secretary, External Affairs, 3 June 1937; Walshe to Secretary, Finance, 5 June 1937.

8 Ibid.

9 CWGC 1077/1089/2 Part 4, Veale to Vesper, 26 July 1937.

10 Ibid., Vesper to Chettle, 29 July 1937.

11 Ibid., Chettle to Secretary, OPW, 14 Jan 1938; Raftery, OPW, to Secretary, IWGC, 4 Feb 1938.

12 Ibid., Vesper to Assistant Secretary, Records, IWGC, 25 April 1938.

13 Ibid., Ware to Director of Records, 18 March 1938.

14 Ibid., Harding, Dominions Office, to Ware, 29 Dec 1937; Harding to IWGC, 18 May 1938.

15 NAI, CSORP, 6433 0f 1915, police report by G. Hurst, Castlebar, 27 March 1915.

16 CSORP, 1775 0f 1915, Mrs. N. Yung, 15 Nov 1914; A. D. Guiney, District Inspector, North Cork, 26 Jan 1915.

17 CSORP, 22618 of 21 Dec 1914.

18 P. Walsh, 'The Barracks and Posts of Ireland – 20: Templemore Military Barracks', An Cosantóir, 32, 1972, pp.220-224.

19 CSORP, 27218 0f 1918, Major General L. B. Friend to Undersecretary of State, Dublin Castle, 27 Jan 1916.

20 J. Smith, *The Oldcastle Centenary Book: A History of Oldcastle – commemorating St. Brigid's Church, 1904-2004*, Oldcastle 2004, pp.35-38.

21 CWGC 1076/1089/2 Part 1, Memorandum re St. Mary's Churchyard, Templemore, Co Tipperary, 5 May 1927; Vice-Chairman, IWGC, to Secretary, OPW, 13 May 1927.

22 DFA 239/89, Codling, Finance, to Secretary, External Affairs, 10 June 1928

23 OPW9/A121/1/14/36, Chettle to Vesper, 10 Oct 1930.

24 CWGC 1076/1089/2 Part 2, Chettle to Secretary, OPW, 2 Apr 1928.

25 Ibid., Browne, internal IWGC memorandum, 22 March 1928.

26 OPW 9/A22/1/344/39, Templemore Catholic Cemetery, Tipperary, Grave Registration Form and site visit report by Vesper, 30 Apr 1930; and OPW memorandum, 11 Jan 1937.

27 OPW 9/A22/1/14/36, Maintenance of War Graves in the Irish Free State (1914-1921), Secretary, German Legation, to Secretary, OPW, 15 Sept 1936.

28 Ibid., OPW internal memorandum, Brandon, 23 Sept 1936, with postscript by William Veale.

29 Ibid., Boyd-Barrett to Buildings Division, OPW, 18 Nov 1936; Veale to Secretary, German Legation, 19 Nov 1936; Veale to Secretary, External Affairs, 18 Feb 1937; see also Smith, op.cit., p. 36.

30 Ibid. Secretary, German Legation, to Secretary, OPW, 21 Dec 1936.

31 Ibid.

32 Ibid., Hempel to deValera, 27 July 1937, 15 Dec 1937.

[33] Ibid., Secretary, German Legation, to Secretary, OPW, 23 Feb 1937; Chettle to Secretary, OPW, 2 June 1938; Veale to Chettle, 8 June 1938; Veale to Chettle, 28 Oct 1938.

[34] CWGC, 1077/1089/2 Part 5, Chettle to Vesper, 17 Apr 1939

[35] Ibid., Chettle to Vesper, 25 May 1939.

[36] DO 35/1107/16, War Graves in Éire: Questions arising from the present war, Leisching to Stephenson, Dominions Office, 8 Feb 1940.

[37] Ibid., Stephenson minute, 9 Feb 1940.

[38] DFA 239/89, Imperial War Graves Commission: British Military Graves and Memorials in the Irish Free State; Burials up to 31 August 1921, External Affairs internal memorandum,16 May 1940.

[39] DO 35/1107/16, Ware to Undersecretary of State, Dominions Office, 16 Apr 1940.

[40] Ibid., Chettle to Dixon, Dominions Office, 22 May 1940; Chettle to Undersecretary of State, 9 Aug 1940; Stephenson to Maffey, 15 Aug 1940; Costar, Dominions Office internal minute, 31 Aug 1940.

[41] See Chapter Fourteen.

[42] DFA 239/92, British and Other Belligerent War Graves in Ireland: suggested arrangements re burials resulting from the War of 1939, External Affairs, internal memorandum, 27 May 1940.

[43] DO 35/1107/16, Antrobus to Costar, 14 Aug 1940.

[44] DFA 239/92, External Affairs, internal memorandum, 3 Sept 1940.

[45] OPW 9/A121/2/8/54, Mr P. E. Vesper's Semi-Official Correspondence re 1939/45 War Graves, Chettle to Vesper, 27 Aug 1940.

[46] Ibid., Chettle to Veale, 10 Sept 1940.

[47] DFA 239/92, Nolan to Burke, OPW, 30 Sept 1940. The full costs of the First World War graves were: (see table below)

[48] DFA 239/92, Nolan to Assistant Secretary, External Affairs, 28 Sept 1940.

[49] Ibid.

[50] OPW 9/A22/15/1/40, Nolan to Secretary, OPW, 23 Apr 1940; OPW memorandum, 29 Apr 1940.

[51] OPW 9/A121/2/8/54, Vesper to Chettle, 12 Oct 1940.

[52] C. Cruise O'Brien, Memoir: My Life and Themes, Dublin 1999, p.112.

[53] DO 35/1107/16, Ware to Stephenson, 23 Oct 1940; Stephenson to Antrobus, 7 Nov 1940; OPW 9/A22/15/1/40, Boland to Secretary, Finance, 15 Oct 1940.

[54] OPW 9/A22/15/1/40, Boland to Secretary, Finance, 15 Oct 1940; DFA 239/92, T. C. S. Dagg, Finance, to Secretary, External Affairs, 21 Dec 1940.

[55] DO 35/1107/16, Antrobus to Stephenson, 20 Nov 1940;

[56] Ibid., Ware to Stephenson, 2 Dec 1940.

[47] DFA 239/92, Nolan to Burke OPW, 30th September 1940. The full cost of the World War One graves was:			
Year	Headstone Erection £ - s - d	Maintenance £ - s - d	Total £ - s - d
1926-27	- - -	311 - 1 - 2	311 - 1 - 2
1927-28	- - -	373 - 1 - 5	373 - 1 - 5
1928-29	- - -	566 - 18 - 1	566 - 18 - 1
1929-30	351 - 13 - 6	657 - 17 - 2	1009 - 10 - 8
1930-31	2704 - 13 - 2	609 - 14 - 0	3314 - 7 - 2
1931-32	1494 - 2 - 4	702 - 8 - 0	2196 - 17 - 1
1932-33	1564 - 14 - 3	605 - 2 - 10	2169 - 17 - 1
1933-34	1087 - 4 - 1	624 - 10 - 5	1711 - 14 - 6
1934-35	1014 - 10 - 6	595 - 3 - 11	1609 - 14 - 5
1935-36	972 - 11 - 2	648 - 13 - 2	1625 - 4 - 4
1936-37	430 - 10 - 11	706 - 15 - 0	1137 - 5 - 11
1937-38	31 - 10 - 5	764 - 11 - 9	796 - 2 - 2
1938-39	146 - 7 - 6	752 - 8 - 10	898 - 16 - 4
1939-40	6 - 15 - 0	770 - 6 - 6	777 - 5 - 6
1940-to Sept	- - -	361 - 14 - 7	361 - 14 - 7
Total £:	£9808 - 12 - 10	£9050 - 6 - 10	£18858 - 19 - 8

57 DFA 239/92, Boland, External Affairs, to Secretary, Finance, 17 Dec 1940.

58 Ibid., External Affairs, Memorandum for Government, 31 Dec 1940.

59 OPW 9/A22/15/1/40, Kennedy, Assistant Secretary to the Government, to Secretary, External Affairs, 22 Jan 1941.

60 Ibid., Boland, External Affairs, to Secretary, Dept of An Taoiseach, 17 Feb 1941.

Chapter 14

1 Conversation with Mr. McClure, 24 Aug 2006. See also www.inishowenonline.com/arandora (courtesy of Mr. Mick Morgan).

2 Office of War Information, Washington, OW13789, Press Release, Tuesday 28 November 1944.

3 A. Williams, *The Battle of the Atlantic*, London 2002, pp.16,103-104, 113-115, 124-125; J. Slader, *The Fourth Service: Merchantmen at War, 1939-45*, Dorset 1995, pp. 68-92, 293,312.

4 T. Allen, *The Storm Passed By: Ireland and the Battle of the Atlantic, 1940-41*, Dublin 1996, pp 10-11.

5 D. Hickey & G. Smith, *Star of Shame: the Secret Voyage of the Arandora Star*, Dublin 1989, p. 240; the foregoing and what follows, until indicated otherwise, is based largely on this source and, in addition, on R. Woodman, *The Real Cruel Sea: The Merchant Navy in the Battle of the Atlantic, 1939-1943*, London 2004, pp.126-127; and on the following websites: http://perso.orange.fr/cdasm.56/dictionnaire/041.pdf; www.bluestarline.org/arandora.html; www.inishowenonline.com/arandora; www.thearandorastar.com/as-italian-list.htm; www.ubootwaffe.net/ops/sunk.cgi

6 L. Mosley, *Backs to the Wall: London under Fire, 1940-1945*, (1st ed. 1971), Newton Abbot 1972, p.58.

7 M. Kochan, *Britain's Internees in the Second World War*, London 1983, pp. 57-59; L. Sponza, *Divided Loyalties: Italians in Britain during the Second World War*, Bern 2000, p.120; L Sponza, 'The British Government and the Internment of Italians' in *Immigrants and Minorities*, 11, (3), Nov 1992, pp. 125-144.

8 M. Kochan, *Prisoners of England*, London 1980, p.125.

9 Mosley, op.cit., pp.57-59, 79-80, 82-86.

10 *Parliamentary Debates*, 5th series, vol. 362, 9 July 1940, cols.1074-1076.

11 Hickey & Smith, op.cit., p.214.

12 Ibid., op.cit., p.207.

13 Ibid., p.213.

14 Kochan, *Prisoners of England*, p. 3.

15 Ibid., p.218.

16 The estimate is by Sponza, *Divided Loyalties*., p.105.

17 DFA 411/184, Antrobus to Boland, 18 November 1940; Nolan to Secretary, Justice, 25 November 1940; DFA 411/184B, 'BO'R', Secretary to The (Irish) Representative, London, 21 October 1942.

18 DFA 241/184, Dead Bodies washed Ashore on the Coast of Ireland: Correspondence to November 30th, 1940, Boland, External Affairs, to V. Berardis, Italian Legation, 12 September 1940.

19 Ibid.

20 Ibid., see also www.inishowenonline.com/arandora/collar,html.

21 DFA 241/184, Boland to Edward Hempel, German Legation, 18 November 1940.

22 See also *Irish Independent*, 14 August 1940, for Sligo and Donegal inquests, including that on Kirste.

23 DFA 241/184, McDonald to Nolan, 19 December 1940; Nolan to McDonald, 19 December 1940; Nolan to McDonald, 6 January 1941. McDonald was subsequently Secretary to the Irish Legation in Rome: see M. Kennedy, *Ireland and the League of Nations, 1919-1946*, Dublin 1996, pp.223,245.

24 *Irish Independent*, 14 August 1940.

25 DFA239/92, Iseult Cochrane to Secretary, External Affairs, 31 August 1940.

26 Information from database, courtesy of Dr. Michael Kennedy, Royal Irish Academy.

27 Woodman, op.cit., pp154-155; www.uboatwaffe.net; http://perso.orange.fr/cdasm.56/dictionnaire/478.pdf; www.mohamed ali el- kebir.freewebspace.com/Personal%20Recollections.htm.

28 Database, Bodies Washed Ashore, courtesy of Dr. Michael Kennedy, Royal Irish Academy.

29 DFA 241/184, Nolan, External Affairs, to Secretary, Justice, 22 November 1940; S. Beppa, Japanese Consul to Walshe, Secretary, External Affairs, 20 November 1940.

[30] www.uboatwaffe.net/ops/ships.cgi?boat.

[31] H. H. Smith, *A Yellow Admiral Remembers*, London 1932; H.H. Smith, *An Admiral Never Forgets*, London 1936.

[32] DFA 241/184A, C. Ó Conbhraidh, Superintendent Templechrone, Donegal Division, to Commissioner 'C', 5 December 1940; OPW9/A22/15/1/40, Brandon to Veale, 26 February 1942; Veale to Brandon, 26 February 1942.

[33] Williams, op.cit, pp.122-123; Woodman, op.cit., pp. 209-210, 265; www://homepage.ntlworld.com/annemariepurnall/patroclus,html. 25/10/2005.

[34] DFA 241/184A, Boland to Antrobus, 30 December 1940.

[35] DFA 239/92A, Nolan to Chettle, 20 June 1942.

[36] DFA 241/184A, Nolan to Secretary, Justice, 26 April 1941.

[37] DFA 241/184A, Constable James Groundwater, Orkney Constabulary, to Chief Constable, Police HQ, Kirkwall, 1 January 1941; Chief Constable W. Colin Campbell, Orkney Constabulary, to Garda Siochána, Mulranny, Co Mayo, 27 January 1941.

[38] Woodman, op.cit., p.283; http://ssnerissa.com. For the pre-war and wartime history of the S.S. *Nerissa*, see *The Encyclopedia of Newfoundland and Labrador*, St. John's Newfoundland, vol. 4, 1993, p.37; Anon., 'The New Red Cross Line Steamer, 'Nerissa', *The Newfoundland Quarterly*, vol. 26, No 1, summer 1926, pp. 12-13; H. Wells, 'Newfoundlanders carried to a watery grave on the troopship Nerissa', *The RB Weekender*, 5-11 March 1989, pp.75-76. I am grateful to Carl White, Centre for Newfoundland Studies, Memorial University, Newfoundland, for these references.

[39] For the Canadians and Americans, see Chapter Seventeen.

[40] DO 130/19, War Graves: Bodies washed ashore (British) [Year 1941], Nolan, External Affairs, to J. D. Craig, Office of the British Representative, Dublin, 28 October 1941.

[41] DFA 241/184A, Nolan to Garland, 29 October 1941.

[42] OPW9/A121/3/8/42, Canadian War Graves: Carndonagh Workhouse Graveyard, Ó Chearnaigh, OPW, to Secretary, Donegal Council, 20 August 1954.

[43] DO 130/18, Part 1, War Graves: Bodies Washed Ashore (British), Nolan to Craig, 29 July 1941; Craig to Nolan 29 September 1941.

[44] DO 130/19, Mary Weir to Rector of Belmullet, 26 September 1941.

[45] OPW9/A121/2/11/57, Maintenance Agreement, William T. Mussell, 15 April 1946, Ó Chearnaigh, OPW, 8 May 1946.

[46] DFA 241/184A, Tomás de Burca, Superintendent, Clifden, to Commissioner 'C', 5 July 1941.

[47] OPW9/A121/3/5/41, Canadian War Graves: Ballinakill Protestant Cemetery, Vesper, site visit report, 7 May 1951.

[48] DFA 241/184B, Inspector P. J. McNamara, Superintendent's Office, Westport District, Mayo Division, Garda Síochána, Report, 22 January 1942; OPW9/A121/4/263/53, Ó Chearnaigh, OPW to Secretary, IWGC, 20 September 1955.

[49] DFA 241/184A, William O'Brien, Superintendent, Mayo Division, Westport, 30 June 1941; W. Warnock, External Affairs to M. E. Allen, Office of the British Representative, 20 October 1945; Allen to Warnock, 21 January 1946; DFA 239/92A, Nolan to Chettle, 6 August 1942.

[50] OPW9/A121/2/8/54, Vesper to Carless, 20 September 1951.

Chapter 15

[1] The nationalities of the dead of the wars of 1914-1918 and 1939-1945 who were buried in Ireland included individuals from Aden, Australia, Austria, Belgium, Canada, Ceylon, China, Czechoslovakia, England, Estonia, Finland, Germany, Ireland, Italy, Japan, Netherlands, New Zealand, Norway, Poland, Russia, Scotland, Spain, Sweden, USA and Wales.

[2] T. Allen, *The Storm Passed By: Ireland and the Battle of the Atlantic, 1940-1941*, Dublin 1996, p.19.

[3] *The People* [Wexford], Wed 23 Oct 1940.

[4] DFA 241/184, Dead Bodies Washed Ashore on the Coast of Ireland: Correspondence to November 30th 1940; *The People*, 23 Oct 1940.

[5] DFA 241/184, G.A. Flynn to Commissioner C2 Division, 20 November 1940; The Wicklow People, 23 Nov 1940.

[6] *The People*, 23 Oct 1940.

[7] DFA 241/184, reports of bodies washed ashore, 19-26 October 1940; OPW 9/A121/1/1/41, Tomás MacChudghaire, Local Government and Public Health, to Secretary, OPW, 3 July 1941.

[8] Ibid.

[9] DFA 241/184, Boland to Hempel, 2 Dec 1940.

[10] *The Drogheda Independent*, Sat 2 Nov 1940.

[11] Ibid., DFA 411/30, Iremonger, External Affairs, to German Legation, 17 May 1952.

[12] DFA 241/184, Boland to Antrobus, 2 Dec 1940.

[13] Allen, op.cit. pp. 80-82.

[14] *The Cork Examiner*, 6, 10 Feb 1941.

[15] OPW 9/A121/1/1/41.

[16] DFA 241/184A, B. Hart, Superintendent, Killarney, to Commissioner 'C', 26 March 1941.

[17] OPW9/A121/1/1/41, External Affairs to Secretary, OPW, 20 August 1941; DFA 411/30, External Affairs to German Legation, 15 May 1957.

[18] DFA 241/184A, M. Higgins, Ceannphort, Cork Division, Gardaí, Clonakilty, to Commissioner 'C', 21 May 1941.

[19] *The Cork Examiner*, 6 May 1941.

[20] DFA241/184A. L. Maher, Inspector, Clonakilty, to Commissioner 'C', 6 June 1941; P. Doyle, Superintendent, Bandon, to Commissioner 'C', 22 May 1941, and 16 May 1941; Boland to Hempel, 20 May 1941.

[21] OPW9/A121/1/1/41, Tomás MacChudghaire, Local Government and Public Health, to Secretary, OPW, 3 July 1941.

[22] Ibid., DFA 411/30, External Affairs to German Legation 18 June 1953, enclosing letter from German Red Cross to Irish Red Cross.

[23] OPW 9/A121/1/2/1/41, Nolan to Secretary, OPW, 17 Nov 1941.

[24] DFA 411/30, External Affairs to German Legation, 18 June 1953. The German War Graves Commission has no record of Falk's death on the given date in Wexford, but his name is on a List 'B' in External Affairs file DFA/411/30.

[25] DFA 241/184/3, DWF Bonnefeld.

[26] OPW9/A121/1/1/41, Nolan to Secretary, OPW, 23 Apr 1942; DFA 411/30, External Affairs to German Legation, 18 June 1953.

[27] *The Cork Examiner*, 5 March 1942.

[28] OPW9/A121/1/1/41, Warnock to Secretary OPW, 12 September 1944.

[29] F. Forde, *The Long Watch: the History of the Irish Mercantile Marine in the Second World War*, Dublin 1983, pp.122, 142-143; C. Molohan, *Germany and Ireland, 1945-1955: Two Nations' Friendship*, Dublin 1999, pp.13-14, 35-36; DFA 411/30, External Affairs to German Legation, 4 Apr 1952.

[30] DFA 411/30, German War Graves in Ireland, (1941-1960), Boland, External Affairs, to Fagan, OPW, 8 April 1941, enclosing a first list of fourteen German war dead.

[31] DFA 411/30, H. Thomsen to Belton, 31 Jan 1941; Belton to Thomsen, 27 Feb 1941.

[32] DFA 411/30, Nolan to Secretary OPW, 30 July 1941; DFA 239/92, Boland to Nolan, 11 Aug 1941, Thomsen, German Legation, to External Affairs, 4 July 1941.

[33] DFA 40/30, Boland to Secretary, OPW, 9 Dec 1941.

[34] OPW 9/A121/2/1/141, Brandon to Assistant Architects, 18 Dec 1941.

[35] Ibid., Fagan to Secretary, External Affairs, 19 Dec 1941.

[36] Ibid., Boland to Fagan, OPW, 31 Dec 1941.

[37] OPW9/A121/2/41, Boland to Fagan, OPW, 2 Jan 1942, and minute from Veale.

[38] OPW9/A121/3/8/42, Canadian War Graves: Carndonagh Workhouse Graveyard, Veale, OPW, to Secretary, External Affairs, 12 Sept 1942; despite the file title's referring to Carndonagh, many of these OPW war grave files which relate to a specific, named cemetery contain information relating to other cemeteries and burial places, sometimes far removed from the one in the title.

[39] OPW9/A121/1/1/41, Nolan to Secretary, OPW, 20 Aug 1941; J. Boyle, OPW, to Assistant Architects, 11 Dec 1941.

[40] DFA 411/30, Hempel to deValera, 8 Apr 1942.

[41] Ibid., Nolan, External Affairs, to Veale, OPW, 21 Apr 1942, reporting on Hempel's visit to Iveagh House on 18 April.

[42] OPW9/A121/1/1/41, and DFA 411/30, Veale to Nolan, 22 April 1942.

[43] DFA 411/30, Nolan to Secretary, OPW, 6 June 1942.

[44] DFA 411/1, British and their Imperial War Graves in Ireland: Arrangements etc re Burials, External Affairs memorandum to Nolan, 6 Nov 1943.

[45] See Chapter Twenty.

Chapter 16

[1] Woodman, op.cit., pp. 154, 694; Slader,op.cit, p.65; Slader states the figure at nine AMC;s, but Woodman names them as *Carinthia, Scotstown, Andania, Laurentic, Forfar* and *Patroclus*.

[2] DFA 241184A, Boland to Antrobus, 7 April 1941.

3 OPW9/A121/4/49/43, William Fay, External Affairs, to Secretary, OPW, 9 October 1943; J. W. Nolan, OPW, to Secretary, External Affairs, 25 March 1944; OPW9/A121/4/50/43, Ballynakill Church of Ireland Churchyard, Women Soldier Wren M.M. Clarke, A.S. Rice, site visit report, 5 November 1943.

4 OPW9/A121/4/64/45, British War Graves, Glasnevin Cemetery, OPW internal memorandum, 2 May 1945, P. J. Quinn, DCC, to Secretary OPW 13 June 1945, T. Brennan to OPW, 28 June 1945; Brennan to Bradshaw, OPW, 4 February 1954.

5 CWGC data base.

6 Woodman, op.cit., pp. 11-20; Williams, op.cit., p. 16; Slader, op.cit., p. 21.

7 DFA 239/92A, Nolan to Chettle, 20 June 1942; www.theshiplist.com/ships/lines/houlder.html OPW9/A121/4/2/45, War Graves, 1939: Kilcommon Erris – Belmullet, Rev. Albert Scott, Rector, to OPW, 23 November 1954.

8 Bodies Washed Ashore, database, courtesy of Dr Michael Kennedy, Royal Irish Academy.

9 DFA 241/184, Nancy N. Cotton to Garda authorities, Belmullet, 30 September 1940; Inspector Ryan, Belmullet to Commissioner 'C', Kilmainham, 8 October 1940.

10 DFA 241/184A, Boland to Antrobus, 20 January 1941; www.ubootwaffe.net/ops/ships.cgi ? Boat = 37; DFA 241/184A, Nolan to Secretary, Justice, 26 April 1941. Lovegrove's, as with other war grave remains in Carndonagh Workhouse Cemetery, were exhumed and reburied in Upper Fahan, St. Mura's, a decade later: see Chapter Twenty-One.

11 Woodman, op.cit., p.226; http://perso.orange.fr/cdasm/dictionnaire/275.pdf; www.uboatwaffe.net/ops/ships.cgi? boat =103; DFA 241/184A, Mrs L. A. Creed, Eastbourne, to British Representative, [sic], Dublin, 11 November 1941; UK Office to Boland, 22 November 1941.

12 DFA 241/184A, Nolan, External Affairs, to Secretary, Justice, 26 April 1941.

13 DO 130/18, Part 1: War Graves: Bodies Washed Ashore (British), Craig, UK Office, Dublin to V. Waldron, Merchant Marine Office, Milford Haven, 29 September 1941; DFA 241/184, B. M. Fitzgerald, Drogheda Gardaí, to Commissioner '2C', 20 January 1942.

14 See Chapter Twenty-One.

15 DO 130/19, Nolan to Craig, 29 December 1941.

16 TCD, Boland Papers, Ms 10470/73, Return of casualties caused by attacks on Irish ships.

17 Forde, F., *The Long Watch*; D. Brunicardi, 'The Mercantile Marine in the Second World War', *An Cosantóir*, 52, 4, 1992, pp.34-36; Brunicardi gives a figure of 136 Irish mercantile marine deaths but it is not clear if this refers to Irish nationals or to all deaths of merchant men serving in the Irish mercantile marine in the course of the Second World War; the Irish Seamen's Relatives Association states the figure at 128 Irish out of 149 Irish merchant navy deaths: see www.irishseamen'srelativesassociation.org/History. For Irish merchant seamen's memorials and commemorations, see Chapter Twenty Three. Irish seamen serving in the British, Commonwealth and United States merchant navies had their graves marked or their names memorialised by the official bodies of these states when their own merchant navy dead were being commemorated.

18 CWGC database.

19 DFA 241/184.

20 DFA 241/184B, Garda Report, 9 April 1942.

21 DFA 241/184A, External Affairs to British Embassy, 25 September 1953; DFA 239/92A, Nolan to Chettle, 20 June 1942.

22 Ibid., E. G. LeTocq, British Embassy, Dublin, Iremonger, External Affairs, 7 August 1953; www.cwgc.org/search/casualty_details.aspx?casualty=1532353.

23 *The Cork Examiner*, 21 January 1942; DFA 241/184B, Nolan to Craig, 24 March 1942.

24 DO130/19, Nolan to Craig, 18 December 1941; DFA 241/184B, Nolan to Craig, 24 March 1942.

25 S. Fitzgerald, 'The Arklow War Graves', *Journal, Arklow Historical Society*, 1992-1993, pp.22-23.

26 OPW9/A121/4/64/45, British War Graves: Glasnevin Cemetery, OPW memorandum, 13 September 1945; www.cwgc.org/search/casualty_details.aspx?casualty=2701502.

27 DFA 411/1/1, Warnock, Secretary, External Affairs, to Secretary, Irish Red Cross, 28 February 1945.

28 DFA 411/1A, McDonald, External Affairs, to Secretary, OPW, 10 September 1949; *The Cork Examiner*, 29 July 1943.

29 Information supplied by Mrs Maureen Easby, sister of Nancy, and by Ms Susan Easby, her niece.

30 A sense of this history, nonetheless, is well-conveyed in R. Doherty, *Irish Volunteers in the Second World War*, Dublin 2002 and in Mary Muldowney, *The Second World War and Irish Women: An Oral History*, Dublin 2007.

Chapter 17

1 OPW9/A121/2/6/39, *War Graves 1939-45: Verification of Records for Imperial War Graves' Commission*, Vesper, site visit report and Graves Registration Report Form, 17 May 1951.

2 UCDA, P 71, Colonel Dan Bryan Papers, doc. 144, record of exchanges between Oscar Metzke and Herr Thomsen of the Legation, the Legation and Berlin, 12 Dec 1942 to 15 Jan 1943. The case of Metzke is not mentioned in S. Enno, *Spies in Ireland*, 1st ed. Hamburg, 1961, translated ed. London 1963.

3 CWGC data base.

4 His mother is named as Mary Shepherd of Saulte Ste Marie, Ontario, and it may be that they emigrated to Canada following the death of his father: see www.cwgc.org/casualty_details.

5 DFA 241/184A, Dan Bryan, Defence, to Secretary, External Affairs, 10 July 1941.

6 Ibid., Bryan to Secretary, External Affairs, 16 July 1941.

7 Ibid., Garland to Nolan, 3 November 1941.

8 DFA 241/184/15, Warnock, External Affairs, memorandum 23 June 1944; Warnock to Garland, 21 July 1944.

9 Bodies Washed Ashore database, courtesy of Dr Michael Kennedy. www.ssnerissa.com/default.asp?q=remembering_harrison;
10 See Chapter Fourteen.

11 www.ssnerissa.com/default.asp?q=stories_tragedy.

12 *The Cork Examiner*, 29 October 1941; OPW9, A121/3/1/41.

13 DFA 241/184/6, Pilot Sergeant Dudley Newlove, Walshe, External Affairs, to J. D. Kearney, High Commissioner for Canada, 9 November 1942.

14 OPW 121/3/9/42, maintenance agreement, Joseph Cremin, 7 November, Ó Chearnaigh, OPW, 24 October 1842; Assistant Architect T. J. McCarthy to Division 'A', 14 November 1942; McDonald, External Affairs, to Secretary, OPW 23 November 1949; D. Conway, for Assistant Architect, to O'Shea, OPW, 20 February 1950; Ó Chearnaigh, OPW, to Secretary IWGC, 30 December 1953.

15 DFA 241/184/16, S. Ó Ceallóig, Galway Public Assistance Authority, to Secretary, Department of Local Government, 16 November 1944; Garland to Warnock, 14 August 1940; Warnock, internal memorandum, 18 April 1944.

16 DFA 241/184/7, Garland to Nolan, 25 June 1942.

17 DFA 241/181/17, Warnock, phone call to Garland, 28 September 1944.

18 DFA 241/184/18, Warnock to Garland, 26 October 1944.

19 DFA 241/184, Report by Garda Superintendent T. Herphy, 26 September 1940; OPW9, A121/3/1/41, Nolan, External Affairs, to OPW, 18 May 1942 and 15 July 1942; A121/3/8/42; Assistant Architect R. A. Guise Brown, G.R.R. Form, 17 April 1942; DFA 239/92A, Garland to Chettle, 13 July 1942.

20 See Chapter Twenty-One.

21 OPW9, A121/4/234/52, Regional Director, IWGC to Secretary, OPW, 21 May – 18 September 1957, Mrs Elizabeth Winters, Charleville, to OPW, 24 February 1958; Assistant Architect to Division 'A', 6 May 1958.

22 Their sisters, Frances and Phyllis Mc Cord, also served in the war, Phyllis in the RAF where she saw service in Algiers and Cairo. I am grateful to Mrs Phyllis Clarke (nee McCord) of Rosses Point, Co Sligo, for this information.

23 DFA 411/4/2, George W. Power to External Affairs, 10 Feb 1947.

24 DO 130/19, Craig, UK Office, Dublin, to Chief Establishment Officer, Air Transport Auxiliary, White Waltham, 15 October 1941; P.L. Kiek, Chief Establishment Officer to 'British Consul' [sic], Dublin, 29 September 1941; DFA 411/4/2, George Power to External Affairs, 10 February 1947.

25 DFA 241/184A, correspondence between the Chinese Consulate and the Irish High Commission, both in London, 20 & 21 February 1941; DFA 241/184, Boland to Irish High Commissioner, 14 November 1940; External Affairs internal memo to Nolan, undated, but late October to mid-November 1940.

26 DFA 241/184, Boland to Antrobus, 9 September 1940.

27 DO 130/18, Boland to Antrobus, 3 May 1941; DO 130/20, Archer to Nolan, External Affairs, 28 August 1941; Archer to Chettle, 28 August 1941, Archer to Boland, 23 August 1941.

28 DFA 241/184A, J. R. Weenink, Netherlands Consul-General, to Minister, External Affairs, 6 November 1941; Nolan to Weenink, 29 October 1941;

29 DFA 239/92, Nolan to Assistant Secretary, External Affairs, 30 March 1942.

30 DFA 241/184, Belgian Counsellor to Minister for External Affairs, 26 October 1940; DFA 241/184B,

Secretary, External Affairs to Chief Registrar, Custom House, Dublin, 20 August 1942.

[31] DFA 241/184A, Nolan to Maurice Coor, Belgian Legation, 29 June 1941; James Dawson, Kilrush Gardaí, to Commissioner 'C2', n.d.; Nolan to Secretary, Justice, 17 June 1941.

[32] www.uboatwaffe.net/ops/ships.cgi@boat=203; OPW9/A121/4/247/52, Clifden (Ard Bear) Catholic Cemetery.

[33] DFA 241/184A, Nolan to Craig, UK Dublin Office, 8 November 1941; J. E. Betson, Norwegian Consul, to Secretary, External Affairs, 8 November 1941; Nolan to Betson, 6 November 1941; DFA 241/184B, Betson to Secretary, External Affairs 3 December 1941.

[34] DFA 241/184A, W. Fay, External Affairs, to Betson, Norwegian Consul, 18 September 1941; www.warsailors.com/singleships/hidlefjord.html.

[35] DFA 241/184A, Nolan to Betson, 2 August 1941; for later developments, or misadventures, see Chapter Twenty-One.

[36] OPW 9/A121/5/2/42, site visit report by Assistant Architect, L. W. Manning, 19 April 1943; maintenance agreement signed by John Gallagher, 5 Feb 1943, and by Ó Chearnaigh, OPW, 11 March 1943.

[37] DFA 239/92A, Captain P. Kilroy to Commissioner 'C', Kilmainham, n.d. but c.25 October 1942; DFA 241/184/10; Kilroy, Ballina Gardaí, to Commissioner 'C', 23 December 1942; Nolan to Chettle, 7 November 1942; OPW 9/A121/5/2/42 & 43, Kilmurray Cemetery: Norwegian War Grave, correspondence from 30 Jan 1943 to 12 Oct 1961.

Chapter 18

[1] OPW 9/A121/2/2/41, *War Graves: Responsibility for the Cost of Burials*, Secretary, External Affairs to Secretary, Finance, 5 Aug 1941.

[2] *Derry People*, 24 Aug 1940.

[3] OPW 9/A22/15/1/40, Design of Temporary Wooden Crosses, Boland, External Affairs, to Secretary, OPW, 31 Jan 1941.

[4] DO130/20/1/12, and DO35/1107/16/14, Ware to Stephenson, 3 January 1941, Antrobus to Boland, 10 January 1941.

[5] DFA 411/1B, Boland to Secretary, External Affairs, 5 Dec 1950.

[6] DFA239/92, Veale to Secretary, External Affairs, 17 April 1941, Boland to Secretary, OPW, 5 May 1941; OPW9/

A22/15/1/40, Boland to Commissioners OPW 5 May 1941.

[7] DFA239/92, Assistant Secretary to Nolan, 20 April 1941.

[8] DO130/20, Archer to Costar, 6 June 1941.

[9] OPW9, A22/1/15/40, Boland, External Affairs, to Secretary, OPW, 9 December 1941.

[10] OPW9/A121/2/8/54, Vesper to Chettle, 28 January 1942.

[11] OPW9/A121/2/3-4, War Graves 1939 – Canadian – Temporary Wooden Crosses Contract, Nolan, External Affairs, to Secretary, OPW, 31 January 1942.

[12] OPW9/A121/2/11/57, Canadian War Graves in Belmullet, 1937, Nolan to Secretary, OPW, 23 December 1941.

[13] Ibid., Kenna to OPW, 28 January 1942; J. Rogers to Secretary, OPW, 26 January 1942.

[14] Ibid., Brandon to Kenna, 13 March 1942.

[15] OPW9/A121/2/3-41, Temporary Wooden Crosses for Canadian War Graves, Brandon to Kenna, 29 April 1942; OPW9/A121/2/11/57, Brandon to Kenna, 2 January 1942, Kenna to Brandon, 28 January 1942, OPW9/A121/4/2/42, Kenna to OPW, 9 May 1942.

[16] DFA239/92, George Fagan, OPW, to Boland, External Affairs, 26 March 1941, recording the joint estimate by Boland and Antrobus.

[17] DFA239/92, Boland to Nolan 11 Aug 1941, Nolan to Assistant Secretary, External Affairs, 13 August 1941.

[18] DFA239/92, Nolan to Assistant Secretary, OPW, 30 March 1942.

[19] DO130/20, Boland to Antrobus, 1 February 1941; Antrobus to Stephenson, 5 February 1941; Stephenson to Antrobus, 3 March 1941; J. D. Craig, UK Representative to Éire, to Boland, 5 March 1941.

[20] DFA239/92 External Affairs minute, 21 March 1921; Walshe, Secretary, External Affairs, to Secretary, Department of An Taoiseach, 28 March 1941; DO 130/20, Chettle to Undersecretary of State, Dominions Office, 10 April 1941.

[21] OPW9/A121/1/1/41, Belligerent War Graves 1939-1945, Notes on conference held in Department of External Affairs, 30 April 1941; DFA239/92.

[22] DFA239/92, and DO130/20, Boland to Antrobus, 1 May 1941.

23 DFA239/92, copy of Costar to Antrobus, 16 April 1941.

24 DO130/20, Antrobus to Boland, 8 May 1941, enclosing this undated, unsigned draft document.

25 DFA239/92, Nolan to Assistant Secretary, External Affairs, 12 May 1941.

26 DO139/20, G. Kimbar, Dominions Office, to Secretary, IWGC, 4 June 1941.

27 DO130/20, J. E. Stephenson to Ware 24 June 1941.

28 OPW A22/15/1/40 and DFA239/92, Boland to Fagan, 19 June 1941.

29 DO130/20, Archer to Costar, 31 October 1941.

30 DFA239/92, Boland to Dulanty, 3 November 1941.

31 DO 130/20, Archer to Costar, 31 October 1941.

32 OPW9/A22/1/15/40, External Affairs to Dulanty, High Commissioner, London, draft reply to Dulanty's communication of 24 November 1941.

33 DFA239/92, Belton to Boland, 19 January 1942, citing a note from Chettle between 16 and 19 January 1942.

34 OPW9/A121/2/8/54, Vesper to Chettle 28 January 1942.

35 Ibid., Nolan to Chettle, 23 January 1942.

36 Ibid., Archer to Boland, 21 January 1942.

37 Ibid., Chettle to Nolan, 29 January 1942; OPW9/A121/2/8/54, Vesper to Chettle, 11 February 1942.

38 OPW9/A121/2/8/54, Vesper to Chettle, 20 April 1942.

39 DFA239/92A, Chettle to Nolan 7 May 1942, recapitulating the main points raised at Nolan's meeting with Vesper on 15 April 1942.

40 DFA239/92A, Nolan to Chettle, 5 August 1942,;Chettle to Nolan, 4 September 1942.

41 Ibid., Nolan to Secretary, Finance, and to Secretary, OPW, 12 May 1942.

42 Ibid., Nolan memo, 20 June 1942; DFA 411/1, External Affairs document, B: War Graves, 15 June 1944.

43 DFA 411/1. British and other Imperial War Graves in Ireland: Arrangements re Burials resulting from War, 1939, Vesper to Fay, External Affairs, 23 November 1943; OPW9/A121/2/8/54, Vesper to Inspector of Records, IWGC, 7 December 1943.

44 CWGC, 1077/1089/2 Part 5, Vesper to Director of Records, 6 December 1943; Chettle to Vesper, 24 January 1944.

45 DFA 411/1, Chettle to Warnock, 28 February 1945; Chettle to Warnock 11 April 1945.

46 Ibid., Warnock, internal memo, 27 June 1945.

47 OPW9/A121/2/8/54, Chettle to Vesper, 10 July 1946; OPW9/A121/2/5/46, Veale, OPW, to Secretary and Commissioners, OPW, 3 September 1946.

48 DFA 239/89, Woods to Cremin, 5 September 1946.

49 Ibid., Woods to Cremin, 5 September 1946.

50 DFA 411/1, Chettle to Warnock, 6 December 1946; OPW9/A121/2/8/54, King to Vesper, 17 October 1947, citing Chettle's memo of 6 December 1946.

51 OPW9/A121/2/8/54, King to Vesper, 17 October 1947.

52 Ibid., Vesper to Regional Officer, Northern Ireland [sic], 6 January 1950.

53 DFA 411/1, O'Brien to King, 25 January 1948.

54 DFA 411/1, Edward King, Courtown Hotel, to O'Brien, 15 August 1947; OPW9 A121/2/8/54, King to Vesper, 17 October 1947.

55 OPW9/A121/2/8/54, King to Secretary, IWGC, 13 July 1948.
56 CWGC, CEM14024, O'Brien to Secretary, IWGC, 9 December 1947.
57 DFA 411/1A, O'Brien to Cremin, 8 December 1947.

58 OPW9/A121/2/8/54, O'Brien to Vesper, 15 December 1947.

59 OPW9/A121/2/8/54, King to Vesper, 22 January 1948.

60 OPW9/A121/2/8/54, Vesper to King, 28 January 1948.

61 Ibid., King to Vesper, 20 February 1948.

62 Ibid., Vesper to Secretary, IWGC, 6 March 1948.

63 Ibid., Vesper to Molloy, 1 May 1948; O'Brien to Vesper, no date but before 18 June 1948.

64 DFA 411/1A, King to O'Brien, 18 June 1948; O'Brien to King, 23 June 1948. King to Secretary, IWGC, 13 July 1948.

65 DFA, 411/1A, 'BÓ'G' (Brian Gallagher) to McCauley, 30 November 1948.

[66] Ibid., McCauley to Secretary, External Affairs, 9 December 1948.

[67] CWGC, CEM 14024, Sillar to Dulanty, 12 April 1950; OPW9/A121/2/5/46, Boland to D. O'Hegarty, Chairman, OPW, 24 May 1950.

[68] DFA 411/18, 'DPW' to McDonald, 19 August 1950; Gallagher to McDonald, 22 August 1950.

[69] Ibid., Boland to Nunan, Secretary, External Affairs, 11 October 1950.

[70] Ibid., Boyle, OPW, to B.P.McLoughlin, Hon Secretary, British Legion, Clonmel Branch; McDonald to Oliver Holt, IWGC, 15 November 1950.

[71] Ibid., Irish Embassy London, Telegrams 3775 & 3797, 17 November and 20 November 1950 respectively, to Secretary, External Affairs.

[72] Ibid., Jordan to Boland, 29 November 1950: Jordan (1879-1959), New Zealand High Commissioner in London from 1936 to 1951, had fought in France in the New Zealand Expeditionary Force from 1914, became President of the New Zealand Labour Party in 1933, and President of the Council of the League of Nations in 1938, in the same year as deValera was President of the Assembly: for Jordan, see B. J. Foster, 'Jordan, Sir William Joseph, P.C., K.C.M.G., in A.H. McLintock, ed., *An Encyclopaedia of New Zealand*, 1966.

[73] NAI, CAB 2/12, Minutes of the Cabinet, 8 Dec 1950: the full text of the decision reads: 'Following consideration of a memorandum dated the 2nd December, 1950, submitted by the Minister for External Affairs relative to the graves, situated in the State, of personnel of the British armed forces who died in World War, 1939-1945, it was agreed that British regimental badges could be inscribed on the headstones to the graves, on the understanding that the relatives of the deceased personnel concerned would, where possible, be consulted in the matter in each case'. See also, DFA 411/18, Nolan to Private Secretary to Minister for External Affairs, 8 December 1950. Surprisingly, however, the decision of Friday 8 December, formally conveyed that day by Nolan, now the Government Secretary , had not reached Boland when, on Monday 11 December, he wrote to Nunan in External Affairs to let him know 'as soon as ever the Government have reached a decision'. This renewed urgency was occasioned by the New Zealand High Commissioner's intervention in the matter. See ibid., Boland to Nunan, 11 December 1950. It was not until after 4 p.m. that afternoon that External Affairs wired Boland with the decision.

Chapter 19

[1] Eligibility for war grave status applied to Forces' personnel and merchant seamen dying between 3 Sept 1939 and 31 Dec 1947 as a result of war service: see OPW 9/121/4/234/52, Regional Director, IWGC, to Secretary, OPW, 18 Sept 1957.

[2] DFA 411/1B, Boyle, OPW to Secretary, External Affairs, 16 March 1951.

[3] OPW9/A121/2/8/54, T. J. Horan, External Affairs, to Holt, 31 March 1951, cited in ibid., Holt to Vesper, 4 April 1951.

[4] DFA 411/1B, O.D. Holt to Horan, External Affairs, 23 February 1951.

[5] OPW9/A121/2/8/54, Vesper to Commander A. K Pallot, IWGC, 24 July 1951.

[6] Ibid., Vester to J. H. Day, Transport Officer, IWGC, 10 May 1951; Vesper to Caffrey, OPW Letterkenny, 2 August 1951.

[7] Ibid., Vesper to Pallot, 15 June 1951.

[8] Ibid., Shephard to Vesper, 21 July 1951.

[9] Ibid., Vesper to Shephard, 25 September 1951; Vesper to E. Michelmore, IWGC, 25 September 1951.

[10] Ibid., Vesper to Establishment Officer, IWGC. 20 December 1951.

[11] Ibid., Vesper to Holt, 2 May 1951.

[12] Ibid., Holt to Vesper, 19 August 1951.

[13] Ibid., Vesper to Superintending Clerk, Division A, OPW, n.d., August 1951.

[14] Ibid., Vesper to Shephard, 17 December 1951.

[15] Ibid., Vesper to Holt, 24 August 1951.

[16] Ibid., Carless to Vesper, 1 September 1951.

[17] CWGC Box 4002, File A11/73, Headstones: Republic of Ireland, Vesper to Superintendent, Headstone Branch, IWGC, 10 December 1951.

[18] OPW9, A121/4/202/52, Imperial War Graves: Contract for Headstones: Leinster, J. Boyle to Secretary, IWGC, 30 June 1952; T. J. Morris, OPW, to Harrison & Sons, 17 September 1952.

[19] Ibid., Holt to Boyle, 15 November 1952; Harrison and Sons to Secretary, OPW, 24 November 1952, Boyle to Harrison, 26 November 1952.

[20] Ibid., Boyle to Harrison, 30 December 1952; Brandon to McNicholl, 19 January 1953, McNicholl to Brandon, 20 January 1953; Boyle to Harrison, 22 January 1953.

21 Ibid., T. F. Williamson, OPW, 5 April 1955.

22 OPW9/A121/4/49/43, Imperial War Graves, 1939-1945, Deansgrange, Boyle, OPW to Harrison, 18 December 1952.

23 OPW9/A121/4/203/52, Boyle to Secretary, IWGC, 29 December 1952.

24 Ibid., Brandon, OPW, to B. Scully, Assistant Architect, OPW, Cork, 15 August 1953; Scully to Brandon, 20 August 1953; McCarthy to Secretary, OPW, 8 October 1953.

25 Ibid., OPW 'Division A' to Scally, 26 November 1953; Scally to 'Division A', 18 November 1953.

26 Ibid., McCarthy to OPW, 28 November 1953, Williamson, 13 January 1954.

27 OPW9/A121/4/263/53, Imperial War Graves: Contract for Headstones (Connaught, Ulster Group excluding Co Donegal), Division 'A' to Williamson, 30 April 1952.

28 Ibid., J. O'Brien, Area Secretary, British Legion, Ireland (Southern Area) to Secretary IWGC., 15 December 1953, O. D. Holt to Secretary OPW, 6 January 1954, Ó Chearnaigh to Secretary, IWGC, 15 January 1954; M. E. Robins to Williamson, OPW, 15 January 1955.

29 Ibid., L. G. Coakham, memorandum, 6 July 1955.

30 OPW9/A121/2/11/51, Imperial War Graves: Request from IWGC to trace graves, Holt to Secretary, OPW, 10 October 1956; C. J Walsh, Sligo District Office, OPW to Fairweather, Assistant Architect, OPW, Dublin, 14 November 1956.

31 Ibid., A O'Rourke to Division A, OPW, 27 November 1956; Assistant Architect B. P. Hayden, minute, 16 October 1957; Ó Chearnaigh, OPW, to Regional Director, UK Region, IWGC, 25 November 1957.

32 OPW9/A121/4/264/54, Headstone Contract: Donegal, Division 'A' to Williamson, 30 April 1954.

33 Ibid., OPW list, 29 February 1953, document No.1. Note that while the IWGC schedule as given to the OPW at this time lists ten war graves for Cruit and seven for Magheragallon, today the CWGC list only five for Cruit and five for Magheragallon. For the two nameless German airmen, see OPW 9/121/2/8/54, Vesper to Holt, 3 May 1951.

34 Ibid., Ó Chearnaigh, minute, 4 November 1954,; Caffrey to Williamson, 23 February 1955.

35 Ibid., Holt to Secretary, OPW, 5 October 1954. See Chapter Twenty-One for the policy and practice on exhumations.

36 Ibid., Ó Chearnaigh to Secretary, IWGC, 11 December 1956.

37 OPW9/A121/4/49/43, Imperial War Graves, 1939-45, Dean's Grange, J. Cullen, Registrar and Secretary, Dean's Grange Joint Burial Board, to Secretary, OPW, 30 September 1942, acknowledging a list of seven additional war graves for which the OPW requested maintenance as per the 1936 Maintenance Agreement.

38 Ibid., Cullen, authorisation signed 1 December 1943 for the grave of Petty Officer Peter Harold of Merrion Road; Thomas Dockrell to Secretary, OPW, 23 November 1943.

39 Ibid., Fay, External Affairs, to Secretary, OPW, 9 October 1943; Dockrell to Secretary, OPW, 23 November 1943; Cullen, Authorisation Form 'D', 1 December 1943; Veale, OPW, to Cullen, 9 December 1943; Cullen to Secretary, OPW, 11 January 1944; Nolan, OPW, to Secretary, External Affairs, 25 March 1944; P. McBradaigh, OPW, to Walsh, OPW, 30 July1948 and 5 October 1948; Cullen to Secretary, OPW, 4 February 1949; OPW internal minute, 3 March 1949.

40 Ibid., Boyle, OPW, to Harrison, 18 December 1952; Holt to Secretary ,OPW, 6 March 1953.

41 OPW9/A121/2/8/54, J.P. Breen to Holt, IWGC, 6 May 1951; Holt to Vesper, 18 May 1951; Campbell, IWGC, to Vesper, 25 May 1951; Vesper to Holt, 4 June 1951

42 OPW9/A121/2/2/41, War Graves, 1939: Responsibility for Cost of Burials, Mrs Anne Eager to IWGC, 20 September 1944.

43 OPW9/A121/4/49/43, and DFA411/1, Warnock, External Affairs, to Secretary, OPW, 28 October 1944, citing Chettle to Warnock, 12 October 1944

44 OPW9/A121/2/2/41, Brandon, memorandum, 30 October 1944; O'Brien, External Affairs, to Secretary, OPW, 18 February 1947; Secretary, OPW to Secretary, External Affairs, n.d.

45 DFA 411/1, Dora Power to IWGC, 4 June 1947.

46 Ibid., King to O'Brien, 19 June 1947.

47 Ibid., R. Robertson, Secretary, Mount Jerome, to O'Brien, External Affairs, 11 June 1947; Secretary ,OPW to Secretary, External Affairs, 25 April 1949; L. A. Richards, IWGC, to Butler, External Affairs, 16 May 1949.

48 OPW9/A121/4/218/52, *British War Graves: Glasnevin: Additional Memorial Contract*, Vesper, site visit report on 15 June 1951, dated 20 June 1951.

49 To judge from a minute by Brandon to McNicholl: See ibid., internal OPW minute, 10 October 1952.

50 Ibid., Vesper to Superintendent Clerk, Division 'A', and to Assistant Principal Architect, G. McNicholl, 29 August 1951; McNicholl, to Division 'A', OPW, 20 September 1951; McNicholl to Division 'A', 4 October 1951; Vesper to Holt, 12 October 1951.

51 Ibid., Secretary, Dublin Cemeteries Committee to OPW Commissioners, 8 October 1952.

52 Ibid., Boyle to Holt, 16 April 1953.

53 Ibid., Holt to Boyle, 20 January 1953.

54 Ibid., Brandon, internal OPW minute, 4 February 1953; McNicholl, internal OPW minute, 25 February 1953; Maguire, Secretary, Dublin Cemeteries Committee to Secretary OPW., 10 April 1953; Boyle to Holt, 16 April 1953.

55 Ibid., Holt to Carney, 1 April 1954.

56 Ibid., Maguire, Secretary, DCC, to Secretary, OPW, 15 October 1954.

57 Ibid., Holt to Secretary OPW, 29 December 1954, 17 May 1955, 22 July 1955; Williamson minute, 12 October 1955.

58 Ibid., Holt to Carney, 14 June 1956, 19 June 1956: Vesper, born on 10 June 1886, died on 15 June 1956.

59 He is buried and commemorated in Merton & Sutton Joint Cemetery, at Morden, London. The assistance and advice of Ms Jenny Tapping of Merton Environment Department and of her colleague, Mr Mark Waldron, Cemetery Superintendent, in locating the grave and supplying photographs, is gratefully acknowledged.

60 CWGC, Box 4002, File A11/73, *Headstones: Republic of Ireland*, Holt, Secretary, IWGC to Secretary, OPW, 4 November 1955.

Chapter 20

1 German Foreign Office, Political Archives, German Legation, Dublin, to Auswart.Amt. Bonn, 4 Dec 1951, von Trützschler, Bonn, to German Legation, Dublin, 1 March 1952, vonRichthofen, Dublin to German Foreign Office, Bonn, 12 July 1952, Volksbund Deutsche kriegsgräberfürsorge, Kassel to German Foreign Office, 23 Oct 1952. I am grateful to Dr Elke von Boeselager of the German Foreign Office and Dr Wolfgang Weithoff, German Embassy, Dublin, for these references.

2 DFA 411/30, External Affairs to German Legation, 29 February 1952; OPW to External Affairs, 25 March 1952; External Affairs to German Legation, 4 April 1952 and 18 June 1953; German Red Cross to Irish Red Cross, 8 February 1952, inquiring about the grave of Horst Felber, buried in Mornington Catholic Cemetery near Drogheda; German Red Cross to Irish Red Cross, 10 October 1952, requesting information on a list of German War Dead in Ireland; Belton, External Affairs, to Dr F. R. Klarenaar, German Legation, 31 July 1956.

3 DFA 411/30, German War Graves in Ireland, 1941-1960, Iremonger to Commins, External Affairs memorandum, 13 May 1953.

4 Ibid., Commins to Iremonger, 13 May 1953.

5 Ibid., Internal memorandum, Commins to 'E.K.' [Kennan], 29 September 1953.

6 Ibid., German Legation to External Affairs, 29 July 1954.

7 Ibid., External Affairs to German Legation, 12 August 1954, stating that a note in response to their July proposal 'will be sent to the Legation as soon as possible'.

8 Ibid., Commins to Woods, internal memorandum, 4 October 1955.

9 Of these 101, 7 were direct burials, 83 were alternative commemorations of graves in the former Cork Military Cemetery, and 11 were alternative commemorations of war graves elsewhere in the country. See Chapters Twenty One and Twenty Two.

10 DFA 411/30, External Affairs ms memorandum, 31 August 1953.

11 Ibid., Tyrrell, Secretary, OPW, to Secretary, Finance, 28 June 1956.

12 Ibid.,Belton to Klarenaar, 27 August 1956; Klarenaar to Belton, 31 August 1956.

13 Ibid., Secretary, External Affairs, to Secretary, OPW, 31 December 1956; External Affairs to German Legation, 15 May 1957; German Legation to External

14 Ibid., Dr E. Briest, German Legation, to E. McWhite, External Affairs, 16 August 1957.

15 Ibid., Alcock, OPW, memorandum to OPW Division 'D', 27 August 1957; External Affairs memo to Belton, 30 August 1957; 'C.C.C.' to Belton, 15 September 1958; Belton to Secretary, External Affairs, 16 September 1958.

16 Ibid., Belton to Alcock, OPW, 13 May 1958; OPW to Secretary, External Affairs, 24 May 1958.

17 Ibid., F. Aiken, Minister for External Affairs, to Felician Prill, Minister, German Legation, 16 September 1958.

18 Ibid., Briest, German Legation, to J Belton, External Affairs, 7 November 1958; P. J. Murphy, Solicitor, Finance, draft agreement, 30 December 1958.

[19] Ibid., Belton to Valuation Commissioners, 23 March 1959.

[20] Ibid., Secretary, Valuation Office, to Secretary, External Affairs, 7 April 1959; M. Bhreathnach, Finance, to Secretary, External Affairs, 29 April 1959.

[21] Ibid., D. C. Ó Gríofa, OPW, to Secretary, External Affairs, 30 September 1959.

[22] DFA 411/30II, Otto Margraf, VDK, Kassel, to External Affairs, 7 September 1959.

[23] DFA 411/30II B. Ó Riordan, External Affairs, to German Legation, 29 July 1960. For text of license agreement see ibid., 12 October 1060.

[24] Ibid., External Affairs minute, 26 July 1960.

[25] DFA 241/184, Irish High Commissioner, London, to Secretary, External Affairs, 22 October 1940.

[26] DFA 411/30, External Affairs, internal memo, 12 June 1960.

[27] DFA 411/30II, German Embassy to External Affairs, 23 September 1960.

[28] DFA 411/30III, Information leaflet, undated, by Bruno Achilles, Care for the War Graves: a service towards man.

[29] DFA 411/30/II External Affairs, minute of meeting on 12 June 1961 between M. L. Skentelbery and Herr Rumeline of the German Embassy.

[30] I am grateful to Conall O'Brien of Wexford, son of Stan O'Brien, and to Mide Gerrard of Nenagh, his daughter, for information pertaining to Stan, in particular in relation to the engraved poems on the triangular memorial stone in Glencree. A schoolteacher in Dublin, Stan had been active for the charity, Caritas, as an Inspector of Displaced Persons' Camps in Germany in the 1950s. It is understood that it was at the invitation of the German Ambassador that Stan had undertaken to compose the poems.

[31] *The Irish Times*, 10 July 1961.

[32] Ibid.

[33] DFA 241/30/II External Affairs internal memo, 22 June 1961.

[34] Ibid., Waldron, External Affairs, 6 February 1962.

[35] DFA 411/30/III, Treaty Series 1964, No.9, Exchange of Notes between the Government of Ireland and the Government of the Federal Republic of Germany concerning German War Graves in Ireland, Dublin 13th May 1964.

Chapter 21

[1] Dean's Grange Joint Burial Board, Minute Book, Vol.8, 6 February 1936, OPW9/A121/4/49/43, J. Cullen, Dean's Grange, to Secretary, OPW, 4 February 1949; Dean's Grange, *War Graves Folder*, No.14, Maintenance Agreement signed. J. Cullen, 20 November 1962, & OPW, 7 January 1963.

[2] OPW 9/A121/4/15/42, Kiltorris Old Graveyard, Rosbeg, Boyle, OPW to Fr. John Byrne, 28 May 1948; J. Finnegan, C.C., to Caffrey 28 January 1949; Caffrey to Division 'A', 15 February 1949.

[3] OPW9/A22/1/100/38, Celbridge Church Lane Cemetery, Veale, OPW to Capt. R. J. C. Maunsell, 25 April 1929; Maunsell to Secretary, OPW, 27 October 1932; Veale to Michael Foley, Celbridge, 4 November 1932; T. Masterson to OPW, 22 November 1935.

[4] Ibid., Masterson to OPW, 21 February 1939.

[5] Ibid., Masterson to OPW, n.d., but very late 1949 to early 1950; OPW minute, commenting on the above, is dated 23 February 1950; Morgan, OPW, to Masterson, 15 February 1950; OPW internal minute, 5 May 1950.

[6] Ibid., OPW Maintenance Agreement, 9 September 1950.

[7] OPW9/A22/1/37/38, Kilbarrack Cemetery, Sutton, maintenance agreements dated 1 September 1936 and 26 January 1956.

[8] OPW9/A121/4/157/51, Ballygunner St. Mary's Catholic Churchyard, Co Waterford, Assistant Architect M. Connolly, to Division 'A', OPW, 6 November 1951; Boyle, OPW to Fr. Michael Barron, 13 February 1953; Barron to Boyle, 16 February 1953.

[9] OPW 9/A121/4/36/42, Sligo Cemetery, various letters and documents from 10 August 1948 to 31 December 1959.

[10] DFA 411/1/1, Warnock, External Affairs, to Chettle, 9 July 1945; Nolan, External Affairs, to IWGC, 10 June 1942.

[11] DFA 411/1/1, W. J. Nolan, OPW, to Secretary, External Affairs, 11 January 1946; Warnock, External Affairs, to Chettle, IWGC, 22 July 1946; DFA 239/89, External Affairs memorandum from T. Woods to C. Cremin, 5 September 1946..

[12] Brookwood Memorial, Surrey, Panel 7, Column 2.

[13] DFA 241/184B, Inspector P. J. McNamara, Westport, 22 January 1942.

[14] OPW9/A22/1/141/8, Secretary, Kildare County Council, to Secretary, OPW, 1 July 1949.

[15] OPW 9/A22/1/141/38, Geraldine, Tullagorey, Old Graveyard, Kildare, various letters to and from OPW over 10 May 1929 to 24 July 1957.

[16] OPW9/A121/4/6/42 War Graves 1939, Tullyillion, Burtonport, Assistant Architect R. A. Guise Brown, report, 20 April 1942; John Gallagher and OPW, maintenance agreement, 4 and 18 March1942; Guise Brown minute for OPW, 12 March 1942; Gallagher to Guise Brown, 24 May 1942; Ó Chearnaigh, OPW, to Gallagher, 20 August 1954.

[17] DFA 241/184, Garda Síochána, Donegal Division, Dungloe District, Report, 11 September 1940.

[18] OPW9/A121/2/8/54, Mrs J. Clayton, Scarborough, to IWGC, c.1 July 1947.

[19] Ibid., Vesper to Brandon, 18 March 1948.

[20] DFA 411/1, Chettle to Warnock, 13 November 1945, copying the official announcement as published in the press on 4 October 1945.

[21] DFA 411/1A, External Affairs minute, 'J. C. M'., 12 March 1948;

[22] OPW9/A121/2/8/54, Holt to Vesper, 27 March 1951.

[23] Ibid., Vesper to Holt, 3 May 1951; Holt to Vesper, 21 May 1951.

[24] Ibid., Vesper to Holt, 28 August 1951.

[25] Ibid., Vesper to Holt, 3 July 1951.

[26] Ibid., Holt to Vesper 5 July 1951.

[27] Ibid., Vesper to Holt, 10 July 1951.

[28] Ibid., see for example, Vesper to Caffrey, 22 August 1951.

[29] Ibid., Holt to Vesper 9 October 1951.

[30] OPW9/A1221/4/175/51, Exhumations, Vesper to Holt, 17 October 1951; Vesper to Holt, 19 October 1951; Holt to Vesper 29 November 1951.

[31] OPW9/A121/2/8/54, Vesper to Secretary IWGC, 28 August 1951.

[32] OPW9/A121/4/175/51, Vesper to Secretary IWGC, 25 January 1952; Canon G W Dickson to Vesper, 8 March 1952.

[33] Ibid., Holt to Secretary, OPW, 28 July 1953.

[34] Ibid., Dickson, Fahan Rectory, to OPW, 10 May 1954; Assistant Architect Loftus, inspection report, 24 May 1956; DFA 411/1, Ó Chearnaigh, OPW, to Secretary, External Affairs, 19 November 1954; S. Kennan, External Affairs, to

Secretary, OPW 23 December 1954; Assistant Architect W. D. Roger, 29 June 1956.

[35] OPW 9/A121/5/2/43, Redmond, OPW, to Secretary, Industry & Commerce, 25 Feb 1961.

[36] DFA 411/61, Hans Gullestad file, Hollwey to Secretary, External Affairs, 10 Apr 1959; Superintendent J. Crotty, Wexford Division, to Commissioner 'A', 20 July 1959; Secretary, External Affairs, to Hollwey, 28 July 1959.

[37] OPW, STSG, A121/5/3, War Graves: Norwegian – Craigue Little Cemetery, Duncormick, Regional Works Officer, IWGC, to P.G. Furlong, OPW, 12 Oct 1960.

[38] Ibid., M.Yates, Regional Director IWGC, to OPW 4 Dec 1961; ibid., internal OPW memo, Thomas J. Clifford to Assistant Architect C.W. Higginbotham, 14 Feb 1966.

Chapter 22

[1] Italian Embassy to External Affairs, 19 January 1960, External Affairs to Italian Embassy, 7 December 1959; DFA 411/60, Francesco Rabaiotti, Italian: identification of his grave in Achill for the Italian Legation, Italian Embassy to External Affairs, 27 May 1958, External Affairs to Italian Embassy, 17 February 1959.

[2] The Imperial War Graves Commission became the Commonwealth War Graves Commission by way of Supplemental Charter of 28 March 1960; see OPW9/A22/15/1/40, British Embassy to External Affairs, 12 May 1960.

[3] *People*, 26 February 1961.

[4] CWGC, Cem 13944, Grantham to J. Cullinane, Commissioner, OPW, 6 Nov 1964.

[5] OPW StSG, A121/4/175/51 W. A. Pettigrew, CWGC, to Secretary, OPW, 24 July 1961; G.D. Stapleton, Assistant Architect, to Division 'A', 7 September 1961; Grangegorman Military Cemetery Register, Burials from October 1960, entries for 5 Sept 1961.

[6] CWGC, CEM 13944, Report by CWGC Northern Area Superintendent, Pettigrew, 27 May 1963; Grangegorman Military Cemetery Register, Burials from October 1960, entries for 15, 16 & 17 May 1963.

[7] Grangegorman Military Cemetery Register, Burials from October 1960, entry for 22 May 1964.

[8] CWGC CEM13944, J. A. Woodgate, Regional Director, UK Area, to Director-General, CWGC, 27 July 1964; Igoe, op.cit., pp241-249.

[9] DO 35/6144, DS [Stewart] to Walsh-Atkins, n.d. but after January 1954.

[10] Ibid., Walsh-Atkins, British Embassy, to J. Gordon, Commonwealth Relations Office,13 September 1954; Dominions Office minute, 12 January 1955.

[11] CWGC, CEM 14024, W. F. Cole, Deputy Regional Director, to Director General, CWGC, 16 May 1960; CWGC site visit report, 27 October 1964; Cole, site visit report, 11 September 1969.

[12] Ibid., Cole to Regional Director, 30 July 1971; John McMahon, OPW to W. A. Rattigan, CWGC, 5 November 1975.

[13] Ibid., J. O'Connell to CWGC, 29 August 1988.

[14] CWGC CEM13755, Cork Branch British Legion to Royal British Legion, London, 11 April 1983; CWGC Director General, site visit report, September 1988.

[15] *Irish Weekly Examiner*, 30 March 1978; CWGC CEM13808, B.D. Egan to Secretary CWGC, 5 April 1978; M. Sweeney to Secretary, CWGC, 21 July 1986.

[16] DFA 411/30B/III, German Embassy to External Affairs, 10 October 1973.

[17] Ibid., Department Finance to Secretary, External Affairs, 16 April 1975; G. Maher, OPW to Secretary, External Affairs, 16 June 1975; External Affairs to German Embassy, 19 June 1975.

[18] For the Kilmeena Ambush see M. Hopkinson, *The Irish War of Independence*, Dublin 2002, pp.134-135.

[19] DFA 411/1B, Garda Superintendent Carroll to Commissioner, Crime Branch, 25 November 1954. Carroll's report was explicit in insisting that 'the damage caused has no political significance'. The twenty-one year old Lieutenant Baker's parents lived in Ottawa; he died while on leave, as a result of a fall from a horse, while visiting his uncle Allen Baker, in March 1942. It may well be that a more comprehensive knowledge of local cemetery histories may contest this general point, but the OPW and CWGC cemetery records have so far yielded no evidence to the contrary.

[20] *The Sunday World*, 21 March 1972.

[21] OPW9/A22/1/20, M. Ní Oistín, OPW to Mrs J. McSweeney, Military Cemetery Lodge, Cork, 19 June 1963; OPW minute, 5 July 1972; CWGC, CEM13790, T. J. Miskelly, OPW to Pettigrew, CWGC, 20 July 1972; C. E .Allen, CWGC, to C. E. Gent, Department of the Environment, Croydon, 7 March 1974.

[22] OPW9/A22/1/263, Cork Military Cemetery, OPW minute by T. J. Miskelly, 14 September 1970; CWGC to OPW, 23 September 1970.

[23] Ibid., W. J. Symons, Chief Financial Officer CWGC, to K. Sherman, Directorate of Defence Services, Croydon, 30 December 1981.

[24] Ibid., Egan to CWGC, 24 June 1982; S.G. Campbell, Director and Information Services, CWGC, to Egan, 7 July 1982.

[25] *Cork Evening Echo*, 25 August 1984; CWGC CEM13790, Information Officer to UK Director, CWGC, 17 January 1985.

[26] Ibid., U. G. Machin, UK Area, to Information Services, CWGC, 21 September 1983.

[27] CWGC CEM 13942, F. McMullen to Secretary, CWGC, 26 April 1972; McMullen to Cole, CWGC, 7 Aug 1972.

[28] Ibid., Director, UK Area, to CWGC, 6 November 1981.

[29] Ibid., P.R. Matthew, CWGC minute, 9 November 1981.

[30] Ibid., A. S. Laing to Matthew, ADG, CWGC, 10 November 1981.

[31] OPW9/A22/1/263, B. de Foubert to Peter Barry, n.d. but late December 1981 or early January 1982: referred to by J. Higgins, Assistant City Manager to OPW, 11 January 1982.

[32] Ibid., U. Cluxton, OPW, to Wall, 3 March 1982; OPW minute, 14 September 1982; minutes of meeting in City Hall, Cork 27 September 1982, between Corporation, OPW and CWGC representatives.

[33] Ibid., Higgins, Cork Corporation, to R.G. Wall, CWGC, 18 October 1982; OPW minute, 11 May 1983.

[34] OPW9/A121/4/56/3, Grangegorman Memorial D. Twomey, OPW minute, 13 May 1982; Grangegorman Memorial, Twomey, OPW minute, 13 May 1982; Wall, CWGC, to Ms Sheehan, OPW, 14 January 1983, and 22 September 1983; Cluxton, OPW, to Wall, CWGC, 1 March 1983.

[35] Ibid., Penfold to Director, Information Services, CWGC, 10 January 1985.

[36] OPW Archives, P 17/2/4: Phoenix Park Irish National War Memorial: Final Taking Over, 'C' Division 22 October 1940.

[37] CWGC 1077/1089/2 Part 5, Vesper to Assistant Secretary for Records, IWGC, 14 June 1939.

[38] Taoiseach, S 3370 E, internal DT minute, Nolan, 1 August 1947, S 3370 E. Nolan to Secretary, Finance, 25 July 1958.

[39] OPW Archives, F96; 5/35, Irish National War Memorial and Park, 27 June 1963.

[40] OPW Archives P 17/2/4, Minutes of meeting between OPW and INWM Trustees, 17 May 1967; K. Fagan, Secretary, INWM Trustees, to Secretary OPW, 8 June 1967.

[41] Ibid., P 17/4/1. OPW to Secretary, Dept of Finance, 10 November 1971.

[42] Ibid.

[43] *Sunday Tribune*, 14 April 1985, 'Dublin's Forgotten Park'. See also, *Evening Herald*, 5 April 1986.

Chapter 23

[1] CWGC CEM13755, *Ballincollig Military Cemetery, Co Cork*, R.Frost , Royal British Legion, Pall Mall, to CWGC, 15 April 1983.

[2] Ibid., Extract for inspection visit report, September 1988.

[3] Ibid., D. Symons, UK Area Director, to N.Harris, Records Officer, CWGC., 2 November 1999.

[4] A. Donaldson, *British Military Graveyard, Ballincollig, Co Cork, Ireland, 1810 to 1912*, Ballincollig 2003. This work apart from being a history of the Military Cemetery, is a valuable record of a contemporary community restoration project.

[5] CWGC, CEM14024, *Curragh Military Cemetery*, B. McGee, Information Officer, CWGC, to O. Martin, Kildare Heritage Project, 10 October 1988; also information kindly supplied by Mr. Mario Corrigan of Kildare Public Libraries.

[6] Ibid., letter of 1 July 1996.

[7] Ibid., CWGC inspection tour report, 10-20 May 1999.

[8] *Royal Munster Fusiliers' Association Journal*, Autumn 2005, p.4.

[9] *Laois Nationalist*, 18 November 2002, 17 November 2000, 10 November 2005; T. Denman, 'Portlaoise War Memorial', *Irish Sword*, 18, 72, 1991, pp.239-240.

[10] CWGC CEM14242, *Birr Military Cemetery*, Pettigrew to Regional Director, CWGC, 30 September 1970; MacKae report, 25 May 1961; Cole to Area Superintendent, 7 October 1970; Pettigrew to Regional Director, 31 March 1971.

[11] B. Ellis and W. Good, eds., *A Journey of Remembrance: Walks in the Footsteps of Bandon Soldiers*, Bandon 2005.

[12] *Irish Examiner*, 5, 9 Oct 2006.

[13] P. Maguire, *Follow them up from Carlow*, Naas 2002.

[14] *Carlow Nationalist*, 30 Sept 2002; Michael Conry, speech at the unveiling of the War Memorial in Leighlin, in *Carloviana*, year 2002, pp4-5; Maguire, op.cit., p.178. I am grateful to Dermot Mulligan, Curator, Carlow County Museum for information and assistance on this matter.

[15] P.J. Clarke & M. Feeney, *Mayo Comrades of the Great War*, 1914-1919, Ballina 2006. I am grateful to Mrs Bea O'Grady of Castlebar for this reference.

[16] Moyvoughley Historical Committee, *Moyvoughley and its Hinterland*, Moyvoughley, Co Westmeath, 2000, pp. 247-251.

[17] *The Limerick Chronicle*, 12 Nov 1929, 8, 10 Aug 1957; *Limerick Leader, Cork Examiner, Irish Times*, 8, 10, 11 Nov 1929; I am grateful to Tadhg Moloney, Limerick, for these references.

[18] The records of the Clare County Council, OPW and CWGC from 1950 to 1990, examined by this author, have not yielded evidence of requests to the Council to reconsider its position.

[19] *Clare Champion*, 18 December 1998.

[20] Ibid.

[21] Clare County Council Archives, *Minutes of Council Meetings 1998*, CC/MIN/41, meeting of 14 December 1998, item 7; further information supplied by private individuals and the CWGC.

[22] *Irish Times*, 27 March 1985.

[23] OPW STSG, *Irish National War Memorial Park, Restoration Report*, paragraphs 2.2 and 2.3.

[24] Ibid.,

[25] OPW STSG, Dr. M. Miller, Lutyens Trust, to OPW, 2 November 1987.

[26] Hill, op.cit., n.52, p.269.
[27] OPWSTSG, P5/106, *Irish National War Memorial: Official Opening of the Temple*, 30 June 1994; *Irish Times* 28 April 1995; Hill, op.cit., p.161.

[28] Hill, op.cit., p.161.

[29] *Irish Times*, Monday 3 July 2006.

Bibliography

Primary Sources

Dublin

Department of Defence,
Military Archives:

  Central Registry Files (Ordinary):
  Cemeteries: Army Burial Plot,
  Glasnevin, 2/40658 Ms 442 - Three
  Band Boys, remains of

Dublin Cemeteries Committee,
Glasnevin Archives:

  General Committee Minutes
  Rotation Committee Minutes
  Visiting Committee Minutes
  Letter Books

Dún Laoghaire-Rathdown Council:

  Dean's Grange Cemetery Registers
  and Correspondence

Irish Architectural Archive:

  Photograph Collections

National Archives:

  Chief Secretary's Office Registered
  Papers
  Department of An Taoiseach
  Department of Finance
  Department of Foreign Affairs
  Government and Cabinet Minutes
  Governor General
  Office of Public Works

National Library of Ireland:

  Piaras Beaslaí

Office of Public Works
(St. Stephen's Green):

  Registry Cemetery Files
  Irish National War Memorial File
  Minutes of Commissioners
  Annual Reports of Commissioners

Office of Public Works
(Whitefields, Phoenix Park):

  Grangegorman Military Cemetery
  Registers
  Royal Hibernian Military School
  Cemetery Register

Trinity College Dublin:

  Frederick Boland
  Harold Leask

University College Dublin Archives:

  Ernest Blythe
  Daniel Bryan
  Eamon de Valera
  Desmond FitzGerald
  Michael Hayes

T.M. Healy
Sighle Humphreys
Hugh Kennedy
Seán MacEntee
Patrick McGilligan
Seán & Maurice Moynihan
Richard Mulcahy
Diarmuid O'Hegarty

Clare

Clare County Archives:

Clare County Council Minutes
Clare Board of Health and Public
Assistance Minutes

Sligo

Sligo County Library:

Sligo Corporation Minutes

London

Imperial War Museum:

Photograph Collections

National Archives, Kew:

Cabinet: Provisional Government of
Ireland Cabinet Committee
Colonial Office
Commonwealth Relations Office
Dominions Office
Treasury
War Office

National Maritime Museum, Greenwich:

Photograph Collections

National Portrait Gallery:

Photograph Collections

Victoria and Albert Museum/
Royal Institute of British Architects:

Edwin Lutyens

Royal British Legion, Pall Mall:

Miscellaneous documents

Maidenhead and Leamington

Commonwealth War Graves
Commission Archives:

Correspondence Files
Cemetery Files (Republic of Ireland)
Commission Meeting Minutes

Berlin

Auswärtiges Amt Archives:

Correspondence with Dublin Legation

Kassel

Volksbund Deutsche
Kriegsgräberfürsorge:

Correspondence Files
Photographic Collections
Annual Reports

Official Publications

Dáil Éireann: Minutes
Seanad Éireann: Minutes
Parliamentary Debates, House of
Commons
Parliamentary Debates, House of Lords
Annual Reports of the Commissioners
of Public Works
Annual Reports of the Imperial/
Commonwealth War Graves
Commission

Newspapers and Periodicals

British Legion Annual
Carlow Nationalist
Clare Champion
Cork Evening Echo
Cork Examiner
Cork Free Press
Daily Mail
Derry People
Evening Herald
Freeman's Journal
Gaelic American
Irish Independent
Irish Press
Irish Times
Irish Weekly Examiner
Laois Nationalist
Limerick Leader
Longford Leader
Sligo Champion
The Drogheda Independent
The Limerick Chronicle
The People [Wexford]
The Sunday Times
The Sunday Tribune
The Sunday World
The Times
The Wicklow People

Secondary Sources

Allen, T., *The Storm Passed By: Ireland and the Battle of the Atlantic, 1940-41*, Dublin 1996.

Atkinson, E., 'Canada's Irish regiments', *Irish Sword*, 21, 84 1988, pp. 133-136.

Bartlett, T. & Jeffery, K., eds., *A Military History of Ireland*, Cambridge 1996.

Barry, T., *Guerrilla Days in Ireland*, Dublin 1949.

Bateson, R., *Dead and Buried in Dublin*, Warrenstown 2002.

Bergin, W. J., 'Clonmel's military barracks', *An Cosantóir*, 43, 1983, pp. 268-270.

------------- ,'Military barracks, Tipperary town', *An Cosantóir*, 44, 1984 pp. 128-129.

--------------, 'Military barracks, Cahir, and military barracks, Clogheen, Tipperary', *An Cosantóir*, 44, 1984, pp.243-247.

Boydell, Lt. Col., 'The Irish National War Memorial: its meaning and purpose', *British Legion Annual*, 1941, pp. 15-51.

Brannigan, N. R., 'Changing of the guard: Curragh evacuation 70 years on', *An Cosantóir*, 55, 12 1992, pp. 29-30.

Brown, J., *Lutyens and the Edwardians: An English Architect and his Clients*, London 1996.

Brown, J.M. & Louis, W. R., *The Oxford History of the British Empire*, vol. IV, *The Twentieth Century*, Oxford 1999.

Brunicardi, D., 'The Mercantile Marine in the Second World War', *An Cosantóir*, 52, 4, 1992, pp.34-36.

Butler, E., *Barry's Flying Column: the story of the IRA's Cork No.3 Brigade, 1919-1921*, London 1971.

Buttimer, J., 'The great withdrawal', *An Cosantóir*, 39, 1979, pp. 365-369.

Callan, P., 'Recruiting for the British army in Ireland during the First World War', *Irish Sword*, 17, 1987-88, pp.42-56.

Cantwell, B. J., 'Memorials to military and naval personnel in county Wicklow', *Irish Sword*, 15, 1982, pp.45-56.

Carroll, J.T., *Ireland in the War Years*, Newton Abbot 1975.

Casey, C. & Ward, C. ,'A window on history', *History Ireland*, 5, 1, 1997, pp. 5-6

Casey, P. J., 'Irish casualties in the First World War, *Irish Sword*, 20, 81, 1997, pp. 193-206.

Clarke, P.J. & Feeney, M., *Mayo Comrades of the Great War, 1914-1919*, Ballina 2006.

Cockerill, A.W. www.achart.ca/ hibernian

Conran, P., 'Military and naval aviation in Ireland, 1913 to 1922', *An Cosantóir*, 32, 1972, pp. 158-162.

Coogan, T.P., *Michael Collins, a biography*, Dublin 1991.

Costello, C., *A Most Delightful Station: the British Army on the Curragh of Kildare, Ireland, 1855-1922*, Cork 1996.

Cottrell, P., *The Anglo-Irish War: The Troubles of 1913-1922*, Oxford 2006.

Cummins, P.J., 'Aerial combat over neutral Ireland August 1942', *An Cosantóir*, 50, 11, 1990, pp. 17-20.

D'Arcy, F.A., *Horses, Lords and Racing Men: The Turf Club, 1790-1990*, Kildare 1991.

Davidson, N., 'I Praise the Coastwatcher', *An Cosantóir*, 56, 2, 1996, pp. 24-25.

deGroot, E., 'Bel-Air Hotel', *Ashford and District Historical Journal*, no.1, July 1991, pp.30-32.

Dempsey, P., 'The gardening distiller… Andrew Jameson of Howth and his connection with the Irish National War Memorial Gardens', *Irish Garden*, 9, 7, 2000, pp. 46-48.

Denman, T., 'Sir Laurence Parsons and the raising of the 16th (Irish) Division, 1914-15', *Irish Sword*, 17, 1987-88, pp. 90-104.

------------, *Ireland's Unknown Soldiers: The 16th (Irish) Division in the Great War, 1914-1918*, Dublin 1992.

Doherty, R., *Irish Men and Women in the Second World War*, Dublin 1999.

------------, *Irish Volunteers in the Second World War*, Dublin 2002.

Dolan, A., *Commemorating the Irish Civil War, History and Memory, 1923-2000*, Cambridge 2003.

Donaldson, A., *British Military Graveyard, Ballincollig, Co Cork, Ireland, 1810-1922*, Ballincollig 2003.

Dooley, T., *Irishmen or English Soldiers? The times and world of a southern Catholic Irish man (1876-1`919) enlisting in the British Army during the First World War*, Liverpool 1995.

Dublin Public Libraries, *Directory of Graveyards in the Dublin Area: an index and guide to burial records*, Dublin 1990.

Dungan, M., *Distant Drums: Irish Soldiers in Foreign Armies*, Belfast 1993.

------------, *They Shall Not Grow Old: Irish Soldiers and the Great War*, Dublin 1997.

Durney, J., *Far from the Short Grass: the story of Kildare Men in Two World Wars*, Naas 1999.

Ellis, B. & Good, W., *A Journey of Remembrance: Walks in the Footsteps of Bandon Soldiers*, Bandon 2005.

English, R. & Walker, G. eds., *Unionism in Modern Ireland: new perspectives on politics and culture*, Dublin 1996.

Fanning, R., 'Neutral Ireland?' *An Cosantóir*, 49, 9, 1989, pp. 45-48.

Ferguson, K., 'The Royal Hospital and the Battle of the Boyne', *Irish Sword*, 28, 1990, pp. 80-81.

Fisk, R., *In Time of War: Ireland, Ulster and the Price of Neutrality, 1939-45*, London 1983.

Fitzgerald, S., 'The Arklow war graves', *Journal, Arklow Historical Society*, 1992-93, pp.22-23.

Fitzpatrick, D., *Ireland and the First World War*, Dublin 1986.

-----------------, 'Militarism in Ireland, 1900-1922', in T. Bartlett & K. Jeffery, eds., *A Military History of Ireland*, Cambridge 1996, pp.379-406.

-----------------, *Politics and Irish Life, 1913-1921: Provincial Experience of War and Revolution*, Cork 1997.

----------------, 'Commemoration in the Irish Free State, a chronicle of embarrassment', in I. McBride, ed., *History and Memory in Modern Ireland*, Cambridge 2001, pp.184-203.

Forde, F., 'The New South Wales Irish rifle regiment of the Australian army', *An Cosantóir*, 30, 1970, pp. 69-74.

------------, *The Long Watch: The History of the Irish Mercantile Marine in the Second World War*, Dublin 1983.

Foster, B.J., 'Jordan, Sir William Joseph, P.C., K.C.M.G.', in A.H. McLintock, ed., *An Encyclopaedia of New Zealand, 1966*.

Furlong, N. & Hayes, J., *County Wexford in the Rare Oul' Times*, vol. iii, Wexford 1996, and vol. iv, Wexford 2005.

Gibson, T.A. Edwin & Ward, G. Kingsley, *Courage Remembered: the story behind the Construction and maintenance of the Commonwealth's Military Cemeteries and Memorials to the Wars of 1914-1918 and 1939-1945*, London 1989.

Gilbert, M., *The Routledge Atlas of the First World War*, London 2002.

Girvin, B. & Roberts, G., eds., *Ireland and the Second World War: Politics, Society and Remembrance*, Dublin 2000.

Grant, K., 'Bones of contention: the repatriation of the remains of Roger Casement', *Journal of British Studies* 41, 3, 2002, pp. 329-353.

Hall, D., 'A journey of remembering: book of honour', *Journal of the County Louth Archaeological & Historical Society*, 24, 4, 2000, pp. 566-567.

----------, *World War One and Nationalist Politics in County Louth, 1914-1920*, Dublin 2005.

Hanley, B., 'Poppy Day in the '20s and 30s', *History Ireland*, 7, 1, 1999, pp. 5-6.

Hart, P., *The IRA and its Enemies: Violence and Community in Cork, 1916-1923*, Oxford 1998.

Harvey, D. & White, G., *The Barracks: A History of Victoria/Collins Barracks*, Cork 1997.

Hefferon, M., 'Royal Hospital, Kilmainham', *An Cosantóir*, 30, 1970, pp.1-4.

Helferty, S. & Refaussé, R., *Directory of Irish Archives*, 4th ed., Dublin 2003.

Hickey, D. & Smith, G., *Star of Shame: the Secret Voyage of the Arandora Star*, Dublin 1989.

Hill, J., *Irish Public Sculpture: A History*, Dublin 1998.

Hill, R.S., 'Sir James Allen, 1855-1942', *Oxford Dictionary of National Biography*, Oxford 2004.

Hopkinson, M., *The Irish War of Independence*, Dublin 2002.

Horgan, B., 'The Second World War and the saga of the Irish Regiment of Canada', *Irish Sword*, 21, 84, 1998, pp. 121-132.

Igoe, V., *Dublin Burial Grounds and Graveyards*, Dublin 2001.

Jeffery, K., *Ireland and the Great War*, Cambridge 2000.

Johnson, N.C., *Ireland, the Great War and the Geography of Remembrance*, Cambridge 2003.

Johnstone, T., *Orange, Green and Khaki: The Story of the Irish Regiments in the Great War, 1914-1918*, Dublin 1992.

Kearns, A.P. 'Luftwaffe operations and neutral Ireland, Autumn, 1940', *An Cosantóir*, 44, 1984, pp. 408-412.

Kennedy, M., *Ireland and the League of Nations, 1919-1946*, Dublin 1996.

Kennedy, M. & Skelly, J.M., *Irish Foreign Policy, 1919-66: From Independence to Internationalism*, Dublin 2000.

Kinsella, A., 'The British military evacuation [1922]', *Irish Sword*, 20, 1997, pp. 275-286.

Kochan, M., *Prisoners of England*, London 1980.

--------------, *Britain's Internees in the Second World War*, London 1983.

Lécane, P., 'Loose threads and sharp edges: Kingstown's World War I dead', Parts 1-3', *Dún Laoghaire Genealogical Society Journal*, 4, 1995, pp. 145-148; 5, 1996, pp. 61-66, 127-131.

--------------, 'World War I casualities commemorated: memorials in county Wicklow', *Wicklow Roots*, 4, 1999, pp. 10-12.

--------------, *Torpedoed! The RMS Leinster Disaster*, Penzance, 2005.

Leonard, J., 'The culture of commemoration: the culture of war commemoration', *Cultures of Ireland*, 1996.

Leonard, J., 'The twinge of memory: Armistice Day and Remembrance Sunday in Dublin since 1919' in English, R. & Walker, G. eds., *Unionism in Modern Ireland*, Dublin 1996, pp. 99-104.

Lohan, R., *Guide to the Archives of the Office of Public Works*, Dublin 1994.

Longworth, P., *The Unending Vigil: the History of the Commonwealth War Graves Commission*, 3rd ed. Barnsley, 2003.

Lynch, J. P., 'Lest we forget', Oughterany, *Journal of the Dunadea Local History Group*', 1, 2, 1995, pp. 72-76.

McBride, I., ed., *History and Memory in Modern Ireland*, Cambridge 2001, pp. 184-203.

McCabe, D., *Major Figures in the History of the OPW: celebrating 175 years*, Dublin 2006.

McCarthy, P., 'The R.A.F. and Ireland, 1920-22', *Irish Sword*, 17, 1989, pp. 174-188.

MacCauley, J.A., 'The Dublin Fusiliers', *Irish Sword*, 6, 25, 1964, pp. 257-70.

------------------, 'The Dublin Fusiliers: part 2', *Irish Sword*, 10, 1971, pp. 56-67.

McCullagh, G., 'The South African Irish regiment', *Irish Sword*, 15, 1983, pp. 145-148.

McEvoy, D., 'Some World War I veterans in Kilkenny', *Journal of the Kilkenny Archaeological Society*', 50, 1998, pp. 3-9.

MacFhionnghaile, N., *Donegal, Ireland and the First World War*, Leiterceannain 1987.

Mackey, J., 'A Small Graveyard in a Dublin Hospital', *Genealogical Society of Ireland Journal*, 2,4, winter 2001, pp.231-233.

McLintock, A.H., ed., *An Encyclopaedia of New Zealand*, 1966.

McMahon, D., 'Roger Casement: an account from the archives of his reinterment in Ireland', *Irish Archives*, spring 1996, pp. 3-12.

MacNamara, P.J., *The Widow's Penny: the memorial record of the Limerick men and women who gave their lives in the Great War*, Limerick 2000.

Maguire, P., 'Carlovians in the Great War', *Carloviana*, 45, 1997, pp. 74-75, 93.

-----------, *Follow them up from Carlow*, Carlow 2002.

Molohan, C., *Germany and Ireland, 1945-1955: Two Nations' Friendship*, Dublin 1999.

Molony, S., *Lusitania: An Irish Tragedy*, Cork 2004.

Mosley, L., *Backs to the Wall: London under Fire, 1940-1945*, London 1971.

Moyvoughley Historical Committee, *Moyvoughley and its Hinterland*, Moyvoughley, Co Westmeath 2000.

Muldowney, M, *The Second World War and Irish Women*: An Oral History, Dublin 2007.

Mullagh, M. & Condon, L. *History of James Stephens Barracks*, Kilkenny, Kilkenny 1987.

Myers, K., 'The Irish and the Great War: a case of amnesia' in English, R. & Skelly, J. eds., *Ideas matter: essays in honour of Conor Cruise O'Brien*, Dublin 1998, pp. 103-108.

Nelson, J., 'Irish soldiers in the great war: some personal experiences' *Irish Sword*, 11, 1974, pp. 163-179.

O'Brien, C. Cruise, *Memoir: My Life and Themes*, Dublin 1999.

Ó Broin, L., 'Maurice Moore and the National Volunteers', *Irish Sword*, 13, 1979, pp. 317-322.

----------, *Protestant Nationalists in Revolutionary Ireland: The Stopford Connection*, Dublin 1985.

O'Farrell, P., 'Remembering the war', *An Cosantóir*, 39, 1979, pp. 346-347.

--------------, 'Athlone, a garrison town' in Keaney, M. & O'Brien, G., eds., *Athlone bridging the centuries*, Mullingar 1991, pp.62-78.

O'Reilly, G.H., *History of the Royal Hibernian Military School Dublin*, Dublin 2001.

O'Sullivan, P., *The Lusitania: Unravelling the Mysteries*, Cork 1998.

Preston, D., *Wilful Murder: the sinking of the Lusitania*, London 2002.

Quinn, A.P., *Wigs and Guns: Irish Barristers in the Great War*, Dublin 2006.

Ryan, M., *Tom Barry, IRA Freedom Fighter*, Cork 2003.

Slader, J., *The Fourth Service: Merchantmen at War, 1939-45*, Dorset 1995.

Smith, H. H., *A Yellow Admiral Remembers*, London 1932.

--------------, *An Admiral Never Forgets*, London 1936.

Smith, J., *The Oldcastle Centenary Book: A History of Oldcastle – commemorating St. Brigid's Church, 1904-2004*, Oldcastle 2004.

Snelling, S., *VCs of the First World War: The Naval VCs*, Stroud 2002.

Sponza, L., 'The British Government and the Internment of Italians', *Immigrants and Minorities*, 11, 3, Nov 1992, pp.125-144.

-------------, *Divided Loyalties: Italians in Britain during the Second World War*, Bern 2000.

Staunton, M., 'First World War graves in Ireland', *An Cosantóir*, 46, 1, 1986, pp. 13-14.

Staunton, M., *The Royal Munster Fusiliers in the Great War, 1914-1919*, MA thesis, University College Dublin, 1986.

-----------, 'Kilrush, Co Clare and the Royal Munster Fusiliers: the experience of an Irish town in the First World War', *An Cosantóir*, 16, 65, 1986, pp.268-272.

----------, 'Boer war memorials in Ireland' in McCracken, D. P. ed., *Ireland and South Africa in Modern Times*, Durban 1996, pp. 290-304.

Stokes, R., *Dead in the Irish Sea: The Sinking of the R.M.S. Leinster*, Cork 1998.

------------, *U-Boat Alley: the U-boat war in the Irish Channel during World War I*, Gorey 2004.

Taaffe, S., 'Commemorating the fallen: public memorials to the Irish dead of the Great War', *Archaeology Ireland*, 13, 3, 1999, pp. 18-22.

Townshend, C., *The British Campaign in Ireland, 1919-1921*, Oxford 1975.

-------------, 'The Irish Republican Army and the Development of Guerrilla Warfare, 1916-1921', *English Historical Review*, vol. 94, April 1979, pp.318-345.

-----------------, *Easter 1916: The Irish Rebellion*, London 2005.

Walsh, P. ,'The Barracks of Ireland, 20: Templemore military barracks', *An Cosantóir*, 32, 1972, pp. 220-224.

Ward, M., 'Memorials of the dead in Julianstown church', *Ríocht na Mídhe, Journal of the County Meath Historical Society*, 9, 2, 1996, pp. 133-141.

Ware, F., *The Immortal Heritage: An Account of the Work and Policy of the Imperial War Graves Commission during the twenty years 1917-1937*, Cambridge 1937.

Weitzel, R.L.,'Pacifists and anti-militarists in New Zealand', *New Zealand Journal of History*, 7, 1973, pp.128-147.

Williams, A., *The Battle of the Atlantic*, London 2002.

Winter, J., *Sites of memory: sites of mourning: the Great War in European cultural history*, Cambridge 1995.

Whyte, L., *The Wild Heather Glen: the Kilmichael Story of Grief and Glory*, Cork 1995.

Woodman, R., *The Real Cruel Sea: The Merchant Navy in the Battle of the Atlantic, 1939-1943*, London 2004.

Young, P., 'Military archives in the Defence Forces', *An Cosantóir*, 37, 1977, pp. 274-75.

Websites:

www.achart.ca/hibernian

www.bluestarline.org/arandora.html

www.cwgc.org/search/casualty_details

www.homepage.ntlworld.com/ annemariepurnall/patroclus

www.inishowenonline.com/arandora

www.mohamed ali el-kebir.freespace.com

www.ssnerissa.com/default. asp?=remembering_harrison

www.thearandorastar.com/as-italian-list. html

www.theshiplist.com/ships/lines/ houlder.html

www.ubootwaffe.net/ops/sunk.cgi

www.warsailors.com/singleships/ hidlefjord.html

List of Illustration Acknowledgements

Except where acknowledged below, all photographs in this volume are copyright of either the OPW or the author, those supplied by the OPW being through the agency of Padraig and Mary O'Reilly of Shannon Images.

Key :
A = *Above*;
B = *Below*;
L = *Left*;
M = *Middle*;
R = *Right*

FL = *Far Left*;
ML = *Middle Left*;
NL = *Near Left*;
FR = *Far Right*;
MR = *Middle Right*;
NR = *Near Right*;

Bundesarchiv, Koblenz: 216 FL, 229 FR;

Commonwealth War Graves Commission, Maidenhead: 104 L, 129 M, 182 FL & NL, 334 L, 355 R;

Coxhaven (ASK): 13 A;

Department of the Environment, Heritage & Local Government: 171, 356 B, 357 B, 368 ML;

Imperial War Museum: 4-5, 8 B, 16 B, 17 B, 20-21, 31 B, 216 NL, 231 FR & R, 217 R;

Irish Architectural Archive: 36 NL, 173 FR, 352 FL;

John Smith & Oldcastle Historical Committee: 201 R, 202 L;

Ken Finlay, Dublin: 177 R;

Kevin McLaughlin, photo of Glasnevin Cemetery: 153;

Lefevre Fine Art, London, on behalf of the Edward Burra Estate: 192-3 ;

Manchester Liners' Old Shipmates Association: 227 R;

Memorial University, Newfoundland: 228 L;

Merton Council, London: 313 R;

Michael Kennedy, Royal Irish Academy: 287 R, 288 FL & NL, 293 R, 318 L;

Michael Pocock: 218 L;

National Archives of Ireland: 122 L, 123 R, 127 R & FR, 175 R, 178 L, 198 L, 199 R, 200 NL & FL, 202 lower L, 203 R, 277 NR & FR, 287 R, 288 NL& FL, 293 R, 318 L, 322 NL, 347 R;

National Library of Ireland: 35 FR, 47 B, 70 B, 168 B, 174 NL, 180 L, 190 B, 210 B, 312 B, 343 R;

National Maritime Museum, Greenwich:
9 R, 39 NR, 87 R, 215R, 230 L, 231
NR, 246 NL, 249 NR, 250 L , 253 R,
255 R, 258 L, 272; 314;

National Museum of Ireland: 146 FL,
ML & NL;

National Photographic Archive (National
Library), Dublin: 53 FR, 157 R;

National Portrait Gallery, London: 35
NR, 38 FL, ML & NL, 40 FL & NL, 46
L, 53 NR & MR, 67 R, 75 R, 76 L, 84
L, 85 R, 97 NR, 98 L, 115 R & FR,
121 R, 145 R, 147 R, 173 MR, 174 ML,
181 R, 204 L, 205 R, 220 FL, ML & NL,
221 R, 283 R, 295 R;

Nicholas Furlong, Wexford: 19 R, 237 R,
239 R, 242 NL;

O'Grady family, London, P.J. Clarke &
M. Feeney: 353 MR;

Parslow family, Channel Islands and
Steve Snelling: 7 NR & FR;

Pauric Dempsey, Royal Irish Academy:
173 NR;

Rector and Vestry, Tullow Church of
Ireland, Foxrock, Dublin: 49;

Royal Air Force Museum, London: 217
R;

Royal Dublin Fusiliers' Association: 183
R;

© Siegfried Sassoon, by kind permission
of the Estate of George Sassoon:
inside back flap of cover/dust jacket.

The Board of Trinity College, Dublin:
138 B, 228 B, 253 B, 282 B, 291 B;

University College Dublin Archives
Department: 77 R, 78 L, 86 FL & NL,
99 R, 158 L, 263 NR, 281 R, 290 L, 292
L;

Volksbund Deutsche
Kriegsgräberfürsorge, Kassel: 233, 315,
320 FL, 321 R, 322 FL, 323 NR & FR,
324 L, 326 NL & FL, 351 R.

Index

Arbour Hill, 22, 40

Ardagh Cemetery, Longford, 260, 268

Ardamine Cemetery, Courtown, Wexford, 269

Ardara Holy Family Catholic Churchyard,
Donegal, 304, 305, 330

Ardcath Graveyard, Meath, 13

Ardcavan, Wexford, 234

Archer, Norman, 277, 279, 283-6, 291

Ardent, 216

Ardill, H, Captain, 248-9

Arklow, 13, 16, 97, 224, 235, 257

Arklow Cemetery, 97, 102, 255-6, 301, 328

Armagh, war graves in, 16, 247

Armistice Day, 136, 185, 362
 in Dublin, 173-4, 176, 178, 185-6, 191, 356
 in London, 173-4
 Irish Government absence from, 181, 184,
 185-6

Arnott, Lady, 172

Ashton-under-Lyne (Hurst) Cemetery, 58

Aspin, Ernest, Marine, 224

Asylinn Cemetery, Roscommon, 64, 69

Athenia, S.S., 249, 251

Aughadoon, Belmullet, Mayo, 263

Aught Point, Donegal, 11

Auschner, Hans, Unteroffizier, 239

Australia, 3, 11, 12, 16-18, 31, 68, 219, 234, 289,
337, 362

Australian Navy, 10

Australian war dead, 3, 10, 12, 30-31, 104, 113,
142, 149, 267, 268

Austria, 203

Austrian internees, 203, 222, 322
 war dead, 3, 198-99, 201, 203

Auxiliaries, 51, 52

Avonmouth, 6, 223

Azores, 6, 249

B

Bacchante, H.M.S., 306

Baker, Hugh Massy, Lieutenant, 263-4, 351

Baldwin, Stanley, 143, 145

Ballinacarriga Hill, Dursey Head, Cork, 239

Ballinakill (St. Thomas) , Church of Ireland
Churchyard, Moyard, 192, 229, 264, 278

Ballaughbee Burial Ground, Allihies, Cork, 239

Ballincollig Barracks, Cork, 50, 52, 360

Ballincollig Enterprise Board, 360

Ballincollig Military Cemetery, 16, 22, 28, 40,
350, 360, 361

Ballybogan Cemetery, Donegal, 257

Ballycastle New Cemetery, Mayo, 222

Ballyconneely Catholic Cemetery, Galway, 265,
266

Ballyconneely Protestant Cemetery, Galway, 236

Ballygunner Churchyard, *see* St. Mary Catholic
Churchyard, Ballygunner, Waterford

Ballyliffin Bay, Donegal, 237, 267

Ballymacoda (The Hill) Old Graveyard, Cork,
249

Ballynacally (Kilchreest) Old Cemetery, 136

Ballyness Strand, Falcarragh, Donegal, 248

Ballyvaldon, Wexford, 235

Ballyvourney, Cork, 51

Bandon, Cork, 53, 55, 81, 133-5, 363, 366

Bandon District Soldiers, 363

Bandon War Memorial, 134, 366

Bockmeyer, August, 202

bodies washed ashore, 118, 204-6, 219-224, 226, 229-30, 235-9, 248, 252-55, 263, 265, 267, 269, 271, 276, 286-7, 323, 335, 337, 342

Boer War, 30

Bohermore Cemetery, Galway, 13

Böhner, Anton, Leutnant, 238, 320

Boland, Frederick, 208-9, 236, 240-1, 276-7, 279-83, 285-6, 294-5

Bollengo, Italy, 220

Bonamargy Cemetery, Antrim, 263

Bonnefeld, Werner, Oberfeldwebel, 239

Boothby, Robert, MP, 217

Boundary Commission, 75, 81

Bourke, Parliamentary Secretary, Finance, 113

Boyd, James, 64

Boyd-Barrett, Richard, OPW Officer, 201

Boyle Cemetery, Roscommon, *see* St. Coman's

Boyle, J., OPW Secretary, 293, 298, 299, 307, 310, 311

Boyle, Roscommon, 64

Braatz, Adolf, 239

Bradfield, Elizabeth, 134

Bradfield, Tom, 134

Bradley, William G., 304

Brandon, William, OPW Officer, 130-1, 137, 144-5, 148-9, 194-5, 225, 240, 278, 299, 301-2, 311, 332, 337

Breen, J.P., 307

Breen, William, Private, 307-8

Bremen, 221

Brennan, Edward, Fr., 131

Breslin, Andrew, Master, 305, 310

Brew-Mulhallen, Vivian, 172, 189

British Army, 27-8, 34-5, 39, 51, 55, 58, 147, 176, 184, 204, 265
    Army Chaplains, 56, 112, 305, 308, 309
    Army Council, 39-45, 54, 66, 88, 92

British Columbia Regiment, 254

British Commonwealth, *see* Commonwealth

British Compensation (Ireland) Commission, 52, 53

British Embassy , 183, 299, 349, 353
    see also, United Kingdom Office,
    United Kingdom Representative

British Empire, 16, 37-8, 42, 67, 77, 114, 204

British Expeditionary Force, 36

British Legion, vii, 24, 68, 75, 82, 85, 88, 100, 112, 142, 147-50, 174, 178, 182-91, 292, 295, 303, 348, 350, 360, 362, 369

British Military Attaché, 112, 182-4, 348-9, 353, 362

British Red Cross, 36, 256

Brooks, J., Private, 52

Brookwood Military Cemetery, Surrey, 268, 334-5

Browne, Lord Arthur, IWGC Officer, 40, 43-6, 57, 63, 67-8, 71, 75-77, 80, 83-5, 92-3, 95, 98, 110-112, 121, 200-01

Browne, Mary Jo, Aircraftwoman, WAAF, 304, 305

Bruger, Joseph, Fr., 199

Bruton, John, 363, 369

Bryan, Dan, Colonel, 262-3

Buchanan, Alieda, 199

Buckley, James, Seaman, 248

Bullen's Bay, Kinsale, Cork, 238

Bunaninver, Bunbeg, Donegal, 220, 226, 239, 270

Bunbeg Church of Ireland Cemetery, 39, 225

Carter, Frank, S., Trooper, 222

Casanare, S.S., 225-6

Casement, Catherine I.T., widow of Lt Col
  Casement, 142

Casement, Roger, Lieutenant Colonel, 142, 143

Casement, Sir Roger, 142-44, 154, 155

Cashelfean, Cork, 237

Cassedy, Thomas, OPW Secretary, 93-4, 97,
  102-3, 108-9, 122-23, 149

Castlefreke Burial Ground, 238, 270

Castlebar, Mayo, 199, 230, 278-9, 364

Castle Forbes, 115

Castlemitchell, Athy, Kildare, 335

Castletown, Easkey, Sligo, 221

Castletownroche, Cork, 262

Castletown Conyers Old Graveyard, Limerick,
  257

Caswell, William, Engineer, 250

Cavan, 302, 303
  war graves in, 15, 247

Cavan, Earl of, 190

Cavasso, Italy, 221

Cavina, S.S., 9

Celbridge Church Lane Cemetery, Kildare, 331,
  332

Celbridge House (Oakley Park), 331, 332

Cemetery Registers, 122

Cenotaph,
  College Green, Dublin, 174
  Glasnevin Cemetery, 310, 311
  Leinster Lawn, 167, 175, 177
  Whitehall, London, 173, 174, 179, 182

Ceulemans, Florant, Seaman, 270

Ceylon, 234

Chamberlain, Neville, 219, 221

Chamberlain, Richard, Seaman, 8

Channel Islands, 214

Chapel Strand Cemetery, Arranmore, Donegal,
  224, 248

Chapman, C.A., 50

Charleville, Cork, 50, 267

Charleville Holy Cross Cemetery, 51, 267

Cheeseman, H.E., Major, 39

Chettle, Harry, F., Colonel, IWGC Officer, 93,
  98, 104, 108-112, 117, 127-8, 136, 146-7,
  149-51, 165-7, 191, 194, 196-7, 200-01, 203,
  207-8, 230, 267, 280-1, 284-90, 308, 335

Chick, William, F.G., Private, 222,226

Chinese war dead, 3, 204, 236, 269

Chuen, Lum Foey, Seaman, 269

Churchill, Winston, 40, 43, 190, 218

Cill Éine Graveyard, Inishmore, 268-9

Civic Guards, *see* Gardaí

Civil War, 29, 43, 57, 62, 95, 115, 130, 154, 172

Clare, 29, 43, 57, 62, 95, 115, 130, 154, 172
  Clare Abbey Cemetery, 366
  Board of Health, 146-7, 150, 151, 210, 294
  County Council, 150, 366, 367
  war graves in, 15, 150, 247, 254, 257, 270,
    302, 366; *see also* North Clare War Memorial
    Committee

Clare Island Burial Ground, Mayo, 229

Clarke, Joseph H., Lieutenant Commander, 249

Clarke, Kathleen, Senator, 114

Clarke, Margaret, WRNS, 249, 257

Clarke, P.J., 1, 364

Clarke, Peter, Private, 222, 223

Clarke, Tom, 114

Clarke, William, 154

Clarke, William, Sergeant, 333

Dominions Office, iv, 3, 55, 62, 64, 81, 83-88, 92-100, 102-04, 110, 112, 114, 194, 201, 204-5, 208, 277, 282-3, 285-6

Dominions Secretary, 115

Doncaster, Arthur, Leading Aircraftman, 254

Donaldson, Anne, 360-1

Donegal, vi, 10-12, 39, 43, 115-16, 120, 205, 212, 214-15, 219, 222-5, 248-9, 254, 260, 269-70, 276, 278, 286, 294, 296, 299, 302, 304,316, 330-01, 334, 336, 340-01, 346-7, 364,368
    war graves in, 10, 14-16, 43, 85, 88, 113, 128, 219-20, 223, 226, 237, 239, 247-8, 251, 257, 265-66, 304-05, 307, 337, 341

Doneraile (St. Mary Church of Ireland Churchyard), 256

Donohoe, Andrew, father of John, 97, 98

Donohoe, John James, Private, 97

Donohue, Tom, Captain, 239

Donoughmore, Cork, 29

Doolin, Walter, 187

Doran, Luke, caretaker, 135

Dose, Willi, 237

Dove, G.R.A., Lieutenant, 52, 57

Down, 8, 10, 16
    war graves in, 16, 24

Doyle, Henry, Lieutenant, 12

Drake, H.M.S., 24809, 274

Drogheda Calvary Graveyard, 236, 252, 301, 346, 347

Drumachose (Christ Church) Church of Ireland Churchyard, 266

Drumanoo, Killybegs, Donegal, 266

Drumcliff Cemetery, Ennis, Clare, 150, 366

Drumlish Catholic Churchyard, Longford, 258, 301

Dublin, 2, 11, 13, 23-24, 27, 29, 35, 40, 52, 54, 56, 58, 68, 74, 77, 79-80, 85, 92-5, 97, 103-04, 108, 110-12, 115-16, 120, 122-3, 126, 131, 137, 148, 150, 166, 168, 172, 175, 1`94, 196, 200, 204-05, 208, 278, 280-01, 288, 294, 298, 306, 307, 316, 318, 320, 331, 335, 338, 351, 354
    Armistice Day Commemorations in, 174-5, 178, 180-01, 185
    British Legion and ex-servicemen in, 173, 185, 188
    City Quay Memorial, 365
    Easter Rising in, 122
    Imperial War Grave Commission visits to, 93-4, 100, 103-4, 108-10, 112, 114, 121, 127-8, 146, 194, 204, 207-8, 280, 286-88, 290-02, 299-300, 335, 356
    war graves in, 14-17, 112-13, 247, 305, 308, 330, 333

Dublin Castle, 23, 53, 57, 112, 173, 348

Dublin Cemeteries Committee (DCC), iv, 154-67, 311-12

Dublin City Commissioners, 175-76

Dublin Corporation, 180, 356, 368

Duckmore Strand, Clare, 254

Dugort Church of Ireland Churchyard, Achill, Mayo, 140, 262

Dulanty, John, 283-4, 294

Dümmler, Gerhard, Gefreiter, 239

Dundalk (St. Patrick's), Cemetery, 257, 301

Dunera, S.S., 219

Dungan, Myles, 1

Dunkirk, 214

Dun Laoghaire, vi, 11, 13, 305-6, 365

Dunmanus Bay, Cork, 237

Dunvegan Castle, S.S., 246, 248-9, 270

Durney, James, 1

Durrus, Cork, 237

Dursey Head, 239

Dursey Island Cemetery, Cork, 239, 241

Dutch war dead, 3, 204, 234, 270

Dynish Island, Galway, 236

Granard, Earl, 115

Grangegorman Military Cemetery, 11-18, 22-6, 40, 56-7, 63, 106, 108-9, 112, 120, 122, 126, 128, 131-7, 140, 152, 164, 257-8, 319-20, 338, 340, 347-9, 354-55, 357, 360

Grantham, Sir Guy, CWGC Vice-Chairman, 347

Greece, 37, 151, 352

Green Howards, 52

Greenock, 216, 218

Greenwood, Frederick, Pilot Officer, 266

Gregory, James, Gunner, 24, 25

Gregory, Lady, 13

Gregory, Mrs., 24

Grieve, Charles, Major, 352

H

Harpar, T., Crimean veteran, 23

Harrick, M.K., QMAAC, 28

Harrison, C.W., 126-7, 300-01, 307

Harrison, Francis G., Corporal, 263-4, 266, 278

Harte, Paddy, 367

Haverford, S.S, 14

Hayes, Seán, 151

Hayes, D.J., 132

Hayes, John, S., 132

Hayes, Michael, 95, 156-7, 161

Healy, Tim, 74, 76, 87

Heath, E.C., Colonel, 85, 88

Heavey, M.J., 155-7, 160-01

Hegemann, Hans, Gefreiter, 236, 238

Heinz-Delitt, Rudolf, 323

Hempel, Edward, 203, 235, 240-2

Henderson, caretaker, 135

Henderson, R.K, Lieutenant, 52

Hill, Judith, 1

Hill, John K., Pilot, 253

Hillery, Seán, 367

Hitler, Adolph, 215, 218

Hohaus, Feldwebel, 237

Hollinshead, Stanley, Master, 306

Hollwey, J.R., 342

Hollywood Cemetery, Down, 10

Holmes, Philip, 342

Holt, Oliver, IWGC Officer, 298-301, 303, 305, 308, 310-12, 338-41

Holy Trinity Burial Ground, Achill, 226-7, 251

Hood., H.M.S., 229

Hooper, Henry, Fireman, 9

Hooper, Samuel, Seaman, 10

Hopkins, Peter, Private, 348

Hoppman, Walter, Gefreiter, 236, 240, 346, 348

Horan, T.J., 298

Houlihan, J., 164

Howard, G.W.A., Rev., 81

Howth Castle, 179

Hugh Lane Gallery, 177

Hughes, P., 163

Hull, 224

Hushovd, Stefan, Seaman, 271

Hyndford, S.S., 9

I

Imperial Conference (1917), 37, (1918) 37, (1923), 66, (1926) 86-7, 174

Imperial War Graves Commission, i, iv, 2, 7-9, 14-15, 24, 26-8, 31, 34-47, 50, 54-5, 57-8, 62-3, 65-71, 74-84, 86-87, 92-104, 109-111, 113, 116-17, 120-3, 127-9, 131, 136-7, 146-51, 162, 166-7, 185, 194-8, 200-01, 203-5, 207-9, 229-30, 255-6, 267, 276-77, 279-89, 290-300, 303-4, 306-12, 319, 324, 330, 335, 337-40, 342, 346
   Charters of, 8, 37, 40, 43, 66-7, 69, 71, 74, 93, 101, 204, 207, 286
   Irish Free State and membership of, *see* Irish Free State; *see also*
   Commonwealth War Graves Commission

Immortal Heritage, 2, 198

Inchageela Old Graveyard, Cork, 56

Ingard Point, Wexford, 235

Inishdooey Island, Donegal, 270

inquest, 52, 55, 222, 235, 237, 276

Insurrection of 1916, *see* Easter Rising

INWM, *see* Irish National War Memorial

IRA *see* Volunteers

Ireland-German Society, 324

Ireland's Memorial Records, 172

Iremonger, Valentin, 316-7

Irish Army, 46, 54, 57-8, 71, 167, 254, 262, 265, 349
   Army Council, 158
   Army Mutiny, 75
   Army Plot, Glasnevin, 76, 155-6, 158-9, 161-5

Irish Citizen Army, 122

Irish Embassy, London, 295

Irish Guards, 13, 27, 97, 109

Irish Free State
   Cabinet, 26, 58, 74-6, 86-8, 159-60, 172-5, 177-8, 180-81, 186-8, 209, 218-9, 293-4, 320
   Executive Council, 52, 74-5, 84, 87, 175-6
   membership of Imperial War Graves Commission. 68, 71, 75-9, 83, 86-7, 100-01, 113
   High Commission, London, 68, 78, 84, 115, 283-4, 323

offer to care for World War One graves, 75-6, 78-9, 83, 94, 98, 100, 103
responsibility for cost of war graves, 47, 62, 64, 69-70, 75, 88
World War Two graves arrangements with British, 205-10, 276, 279-80, 282, 287, 290-5

Irish Merchant Navy, 253 *see also* Merchant Navy

Irish Merchant Navy Memorial, 365

Irish National War Memorial , iv, 128, 172-91, 195, 355-7, 365, 367-9
   Committee, 115, 172-3, 175, 177-90, 356
   Trustees, 173, 176-9, 186-7, 189-91, 356-7, 368-9

Irish Press, 129, 188

Irish Seamen's Relatives Association, 365

Irish Times, 113, 175, 183, 190, 325

Irish Weekly Examiner, 350

Ironside, George, Sapper, 227

Irvine, Richard, Air Bomber, 256, 263

Irvinestown Church of Ireland Churchyard, Fermanagh, 266

Iseo, Italy, 214, 220

Iskaheen Catholic Cemetery, Donegal, 304

Island of Ireland Peace Park, Belgium, 367

Islandbridge, Dublin, ii, 128-9, 163, 172-91, 195-6, 355, 365-9; *see also* Irish National War Memorial

Isle of Man, 118, 217

Italy, 11, 37, 207, 214, 317, 346

Italian
   exhumations, 346
   internees, 200, 215, 217-8, 222
   war dead in Ireland, 3, 204, 214, 219, 222, 236, 246

Italian League for the Rights of Man, 218

Iveagh House, 284-5, 287-88, 290, 292-5, 318-9, 321, 323, 325, 338; *see also* External Affairs, Department of

IWGC, *see* Imperial War Graves Commission

Lambay Island, 179

Lamentani, Umberto, 218

Land Commission, 160, 320

Laois,
    war graves in, 15, 247

Lane, Edward, Private, 222

Lane, Sheila, 360

Laracy, Francis, Lieutenant, 12

Laumen, Franz, 218

Laurentic, H.M.S. (World War One), 9-10, 12, 116, 225, 341

Laurentic H.M.S. (World War Two), 225-6, 230, 249

Lavery, Vincent, Stoker, 249

Lea, Frederick, Leading Aircraftman, 254, 257

League of Nations, 188

Leask, Harold, OPW Architect, 150, 167, 312

Lee, J., Seaman, 270

Lehane, Jim, 51

Lei, Chu Ning, Seaman, 269

Leighlinbridge, Carlow, 363, 367

Leinster headstone contract, 126, 300

Leinster Lawn Cenotaph, *see* Cenotaph, Leinster Lawn

Leinster Regiment, 16, 26-8, 39, 60, 83, 96, 335, 362

Leinster, R.M.S., 10-17, 23, 26, 116-18, 122, 136, 365

Leisching, Percivale, 204-5

Leitrim
    war graves in, 15, 247

Lemass, Seán, 9

Lenadoon, Sligo, 266

Lenox-Conyngham, Hubert M., Major, 109, 112

Leonard, Jane, 1

Lester, Seán, 84, 86-7, 99, 101, 104, 108, 194-5

Letterkenny, Donegal, 341

Licho, F., Horseman, 7

Lie, Otto, Seaman, 270-1, 342

Liebe, Heinrich, Korvettenkapitän, 223

Lilley, John, Private, 26

Limerick, 16, 28, 30, 40, 51, 117, 126, 129, 364, 366
    war graves in, 15, 28, 30, 126, 128-9, 247, 257
    War Memorial, 351, 364; *see also* King's Island Military Cemetery, Mount St.Laurence Cemetery

Lindsay, Colonel, 349

Linnett, Stanley, Wireless Operator, 9

Linton, Isaac, Fireman, 8

Liverpool, 7, 8, 181, 215, 217, 219, 226-7, 252, 254, 263, 267, 269-70, 306, 342

Lloyd Davies, George, MP, 29

Local Government, Department of, 64, 177, 281, 338, 341

London, 9, 98, 101-03, 108, 121, 180, 220-1, 226, 250, 268, 312, 323, 331; *see also,* Armistice Day, Colonial Office, *Daily Mail,* Dominions Office, Imperial Conference, Imperial War Graves Commission, Irish High Commission, Irish Embassy, *The Times,* War Office

London Metropolitan Police, 219

Londonderry,
    war graves in, 15, 247; *see also,* Derry

Longford, vi, 115, 258, 260, 268, 301
    war graves in, 15, 247

Longworth, Philip, 2

Long Meadows Estate, Inchicore, Dublin, 172, 178

Lord, J.C., Rev., 82

Lorenz, Wilhelm, Gefreiter, 234-5

Lough Foyle, 16, 237

Loughnane, N.G., 54, 56, 63, 65

Louth, 8, 236, 252
   war graves in, 15, 236, 247, 252

Lovat, Lord., 97-100, 102, 109-10

Lovegrove, Archie, Marine, 251, 339, 341

Lucas, Dora E., 221

Luftwaffe, 229, 231, 236-7, 239, 241

Lusitania, R.M.S., 7-10, 18, 28, 365

Lusitania Memorial, Cobh, 11, 369

Lutyens, Sir Edwin, 127, 179-82, 356-7, 368

Luxembourg, 200, 318

Lynch, Michael, Seaman, 10

Lynch, Garda Sergeant, 117

Lynnott, Edward J., Aircraftman, 309, 311

M
MacClancy, Michael R., Squadron Leader, RAF, 301

MacFhionnghaile, Niall, 1

Machine Gun Corps, 50, 100, 112, 145

MacIntyre, Donald, Captain, 225-6, 231

Mackrow, Clifford, Engineer, 250

MacNamara, P.F., Private, 366

Macready, Sir Nevil, General, 34-8, 44, 50-1, 174, 182

Macroom, Cork, 52, 56, 199

Macroom Castle, Cork, 51-2

Macroom Four, 52, 54, 56

Maddocks, Sir Henry, MP, 41

Madigan, J., Gunner, 333

Maffey, Sir John, 204-8, 265, 281, 284

Magheragallon Catholic Cemetery, Donegal, 220, 222, 224, 226, 239, 248, 252, 254, 270, 305, 307, 364, 368

Maghery, Donegal, 221, 305, 336-7

Magri, A.F., 218

Maguire, Paul, 1

Maguire, Mr, DCC Secretary, 311

Mahon, Sir Bryan, 173, 176

Mahony, Annie, widow of Michael Mahony, 117

Mahony, Michael, Coastguard, 117

Mair, W.M., Major, 303

Makowski, Bridget, 366-7

Malin Head, 10, 215, 223, 227, 251

Mallow, Cork, 132, 264-5, 278

Maloney, Martin, Private, 335

Maloney, Michael., Private, 28

Manchester, 50, 53, 214, 220, 224, 257

Manchester Band Boys, 53, 55-6

Manchester Brigade, S.S., 224-5, 227, 249, 305, 340

Manchester Regiment, 50, 53, 55-7

Marchesi, Charles, Domenico, 218

Mars, H.M.S., 39, 88

Martin, Bernard L., Lance Corporal, 26, 29

Martin, J. Parnell, OPW Officer, 133

Martin, Thomas, Fr., 263

Mashona, H.M.S., ii, 214, 229-31

Masterson, Sergeant, 254

Masterson, Thomas, 331-2

Matthew, P.R., CWGC Officer, 354

Matthews, Robert, Lieutenant, 28

Maunsell, R.C.J., Captain, 331-2

Maurice, Sir Frederick, Major General, 188

Mayerhoefler, Karl, 218

Miranda, H.M.S., 6

Mitchell, Owen, Private, 223, 358

Mitchell, R.R., Lieutenant, 10

Mitchell, Thomas Elvin, Lieutenant, 228, 263-4, 278

Mittermaier, Alois, Unteroffizier, 238, 241

Modrzejewski, Hubert Obergefreiter, 238, 241

Mogeely Catholic Cemetery, Cork, 240

Mohamed, Messen, 269

Mohamed Ali El-Kebir, 223-4, 226-7, 249, 270, 330, 337, 340

Mollaghan, Kathleen, Leading Aircraftwoman, 258, 301

Mollenhauer, Kurt, Oberleutnant, 234

Möller, Hans, 221

Molloy, J.G., 292-3, 337-8

Moloney, Tadhg, 366

Molony, Senan, 8

Monaghan , 81, 302-04
  war graves in, 15, 247

Monaghan & Sons, masons, 126, 304-05

Mons, 182

Montreal, 6-8, 224

Moore, Canon, Killiskey, 142

Moore, Maurice, Volunteer, 29

Moore, Maurice, Colonel, 174,176

Moorfowl, 57-8

Moran, Colonel, 323

Morgan, Christopher, caretaker, 333

Mornington Catholic Cemetery, Louth, 236

Morris Castle, Wexford, 235

Morrow, George Dixon, Captain, 192, 229, 264, 278

Moruzzi, Ernesto, 219

Moruzzi, Maria, 219

Moruzzi, Peter, 219

Moruzzi, Pietro, 219

Moulton, Edwin, Captain, 215-16

Mount Brandon, 234, 256

Mount Gabriel, Schull, Cork, 239

Mount Jerome Cemetery, Dublin, 12, 249-50, 256, 266, 305, 308-09

Mount St. Lawrence Cemetery, Limerick, 16, 128

Moynihan, Maurice, 187, 189-91

Moyvoughley, Westmeath,364, 366

Mulcahy, Daniel, 129

Mulcahy, Michael, 129

Mulcahy, Richard, 51-2, 54-7, 65, 157-8, 163

Mulcahy, Thomas, 29

Mullinashee Church of Ireland Burial Ground, Ballyshannon, Donegal, 226

Mullinger, Isabella, Private, ATS, 257-8

Mulranny, Mayo, 226-7

Munarretto, Herr, 320

Munster, 28, 30, 122, 133, 360
  headstone contract, 126, 302
  Memorial Cross, Ypres, 183; *see also*, Royal
  Munster Fusiliers

Murphy, Donal, Sculptor, 9

Murphy, James, Crimean veteran, 23

Murphy, John, Boatswain, 227

Murphy, Lombard, 172

Murphy, Matthew, Captain, 13

Murphy, S., External Affairs, 102-03

Mussolini, Benito, 218

N

Naas Catholic Cemetery, 108

Nailsea Lass, 269

Naniwa, 250

Narvik, 214, 216
National Anthem, 114-15

National Army, *see* Irish Army

National Seaman's Memorial, City Quay, Dublin, 365

National Memorial Arboretum (UK), 365

National Socialism, 325

Nazis, 214, 217-18, 221-22, 235

Nelson's Pillar, Dublin, 150, 351

Nerissa, S.S., 227-9, 249, 263-6, 268, 339

Nevin, Michael, 146

New Barracks, *see* Victoria Barracks

Newcastle, Wicklow, 253

Newcastle-on-Tyne, 337

Newfoundland, 7, 10, 215, 217, 228, 271, 337
Navy, 9-10
war graves, 9-10, 19, 113

Newham, T.W., Captain, IWGC Officer, 93-4

Newlove, Dudley, Pilot Sergeant , 265, 267

News Chronicle, 251

New York, 7, 113, 158-60, 216, 267

New Zealand, 41-2, 67-8, 260, 268, 295, 337
High Commission, 38, 295
war dead, 3, 11-12, 31, 113, 234, 267
war graves, 12, 16, 18, 31, 113, 268

Netherlands, 205, 214

Nicator, H.M.S., 14

Niebauer, Josef, Unteroffizier, 238

Niemeyer, Otto, 46-7, 71

Nixon, R., 39

Nobel, M., Seaman, 270

Noblett, Andrew, Rev., 96

Nohoval Catholic Cemetery, Cork, 238

Nolan, Edward, 234

Nolan, N.G., 207-8, 222, 225, 228, 240-2, 278-9, 282, 285-88

Noon, William, Captain, 269

North Clare War Memorial Committee, 367

North Dublin Union, 23

Northampton, 251

Northern Ireland, 14, 16-18, 46, 99-101, 103-4, 111-12, 116, 127, 148, 189, 194-5, 197-8, 200, 207, 262, 282, 285, 289, 365
Prime Minister of, 189
removal of war dead to, 266-8
war graves in, 14-17, 31, 200, 246-7, 262

Norton, James, TD., 143

Norway, 214, 216, 342
Norwegian Consul, 271, 342
war dead, 3, 8, 204, 234, 248, 270-1, 342
war graves, 8, 270-2, 342

Nowlan, J.W., 155, 166-7, 310

Nugent, Mary, 237

Nyhan, Charles, Dr., 237

O

Oakley Park, *see* Celbridge House

Oates, John Christopher., Aircraftman, RAF, 303-4

O'Brien, Conor Cruise, 281, 290-3, 309

O'Brien, Daniel, Private, 30-1,

O'Brien, Pat, Portlaoise, 362

O'Brien, Patrick, Stoker, 249

O'Brien, Stan, 232, 314, 317, 324, 326

Ó'Chearnaigh, P.S., OPW Secretary, *see* Carney

ÓCinnéide, P, *see* Kennedy, Paul

Skinner, S.P., 30

Slattery, Francis, Captain, 136-7

Slattery, Michael, brother of Francis, 137

Slattery, Thomas, father of Francis Slattery, 136-7

Slievemore Graveyard, Keel, Mayo, 346

Sligo, 134, 138, 145-9, 219, 221-2, 224, 266, 277, 303-4, 323, 357
  British Legion Branch, 303
  Cemetery, 145, 148, 244, 274, 304, 334
  Corporation, 145-6, 148, 151, 210, 249, 292, 334
  war graves in, 15, 17, 145, 148, 151, 221, 223-4, 247-9, 257, 269, 278, 303, 304, 323, 334

Smedley, Denis, Sub-Lieutenant, 248

Smiddy, T.A., 115, 158, 160

Smith, Humphrey Hugh, Vice-Admiral, 224-5

Smith, Jean, widow of H.H. Smith, 225

Smith, John, 200

Smith, Leonard, Radio Officer, 252

Smith, M.E., Private, 12

Smith, Robert Glenn, Pilot , 268

Smithson, Ivor, Air Gunner, 265-6

Snell, Harry, MP, 218

Soames, G., caretaker, 42

Söchtig, Rudolf, 234-5

Society of Friends, *see* Friends

Solf, Herman, 218

Somme War Memorial, 179

Somme, 90th anniversary commemoration, 190, 369

Sorensen, Reginald, Baron, MP, 218

South Africa, 36, 45, 337
  war dead, 18

South Dublin Union, 34, 309

South Irish Horse, 13, 146

South Kilmurry Graveyard, Cork, 133

Spaniard, war grave of, 248, 270; *see* Pimentil

Spellerberg, Ludwig, 200, 202

Spike Island, Cork, 30, 42

Srelane Cross, Ovens, Cork, 50

Stamfordham, Lord, 114

Stanley, John, Gunner, 271

Stannard, David S., Group Captain, 256

Stradbally Catholic Churchyard, Waterford, 257

Steele, John Curtis, Canon of Raphoe, 264

Steele, Thomas, Lieutenant, 10

Steenson, Robert, Private, 81

Steevens' Hospital, Dr., Dublin, 34, 36, 112, 119

Stephenson, J.E., 88, 204-5, 208, 209, 283

Stettin, 287

Stewart, A.D.G., Lieutenant Colonel, 349

Stirling, Winifred, Nurse, 12

Stolwyck, S.S., 270

Stone of Remembrance, 127-8, 130, 179

Stopford, Lord, IWGC Officer, 46

Stranorlar, Donegal, 223, 304

Stranorlar Catholic Cemetery, 304-5

Stratton, E.C.J., Private, 28

Strauss, George, MP, 217-8, 220

Strickland, Sir Peter, General, 29

Sturgis, Mark, 53, 57

Sturm, Johannes, Dr., 236

Submarine *A5*, 88

Sultan, S.S., 227

Sunday World, 352

War grave sites in the Republic of
Ireland, within the remit of the OPW, as
mentioned in the text:

*(Note: while there are world war grave sites in
every county, those in counties Carlow, Cavan
and Leitrim do not feature in the text)*

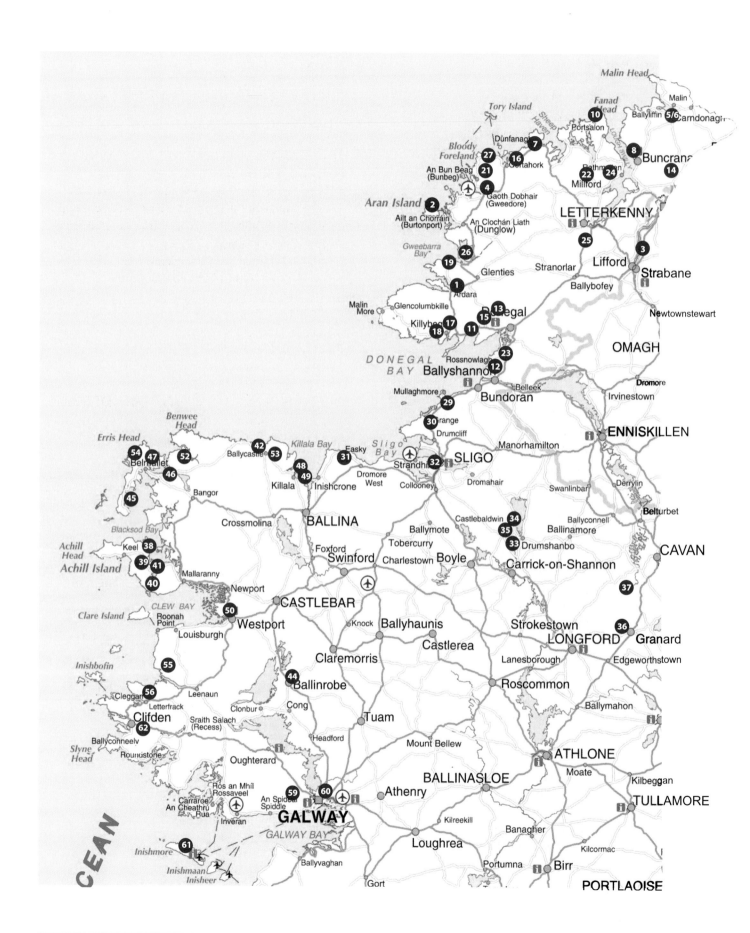

MAP 1

Map 1
Northwest, West, Midlands (West)

Donegal
1. Ardara Holy Family Catholic Churchyard
2. Arranmore, Chapel Strand Cemetery
3. Ballybogan Cemetery
4. Bunbeg Church of Ireland Cemetery
5. Carndonagh Catholic Cemetery
6. Carndonagh Workhouse Cemetery
7. Clondahorky Strangers' Burial Ground
8. Cockhill Catholic Cemetery
9. Cruit Island Catholic Cemetery
10. Doaghmore
11. Dunkineely, Baile na Gréine Cemetery
12. Finner Cemetery
13. Frosses Catholic Churchyard
14. Iskaheen Catholic Cemetery
15. Killaghtee Old Graveyard
16. Killult Cemetery
17. Killybegs Catholic Cemetery
18. Killybegs Old Graveyard
19. Kiltooris Old Graveyard
20. Maghery, Donegal,
21. Magheragallon Catholic Cemetery
22. Milford Workhouse Cemetery
23. Mullinashee Church of Ireland Burial Ground, Ballyshannon
24. Rathmullan, St.Columb's Church of Ireland Churchyard
25. Stranorlar Catholic Cemetery
26. Termon Old Graveyard
27. Tullaghobegley Church of Ireland Churchyard
28. Tullyillion Graveyard

Sligo
29. Ahamlish Cemetery
30. Carrigans Cemetery
31. Easkey (Roslea) Cemetery
32. Sligo Cemetery

Roscommon
33. Ardcarne (St Beaidh) Church of Ireland Churchyard
34. Asylinn Cemetery
35. Boyle, St. Coman's Cemetery

Longford
36. Ardagh Cemetery
37. Drumlish Catholic Churchyard

Mayo
38. Achill, Dugort Church of Ireland Churchyard
39. Achill, Keel, Slievemore Graveyard
40. Achill, Kildavnet Catholic Graveyard
41. Achill, Holy Trinity Church of Ireland Churchyard
42. Ballycastle New Cemetery
43. Clare Island Burial Ground
44. Cross Burial Ground
45. Fallmore Graveyard
46. Gweesalia Graveyard
47. Kilcommon Erris Church of Ireland Churchyard
48. Killala, Crosspatrick
49. Killala, St. Patrick's Church Of Ireland Churchyard
50. Kilmeena Cemetery
51. Kilmurray Cemetery
52. Pulatomish Graveyard, Mayo
53. Rathfran Catholic Graveyard
54. Termoncarragh Gr aveyard
55. Ugool Burial Ground

Galway
56. Ballinakill (St. Thomas) , Church of Ireland, Moyard
57. Ballyconneely Catholic Cemetery
58. Ballyconneely Protestant Cemetery
59. Barna Old Graveyard
60. Bohermore Cemetery
61. Cill Éine Graveyard, Inishmore
62. Clifden , Ard Bear, Cemetery

MAP 1

451

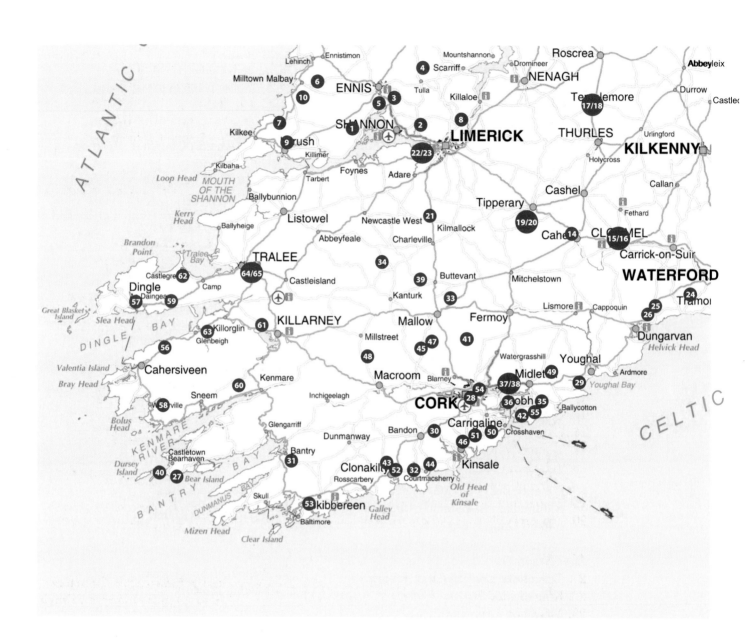

Map 2:
Southwest, Midlands (South) & South

Clare
1. Ballynacally (Kilchreest) Old Cemetery
2. Bunratty Old Graveyard
3. Clare Abbey, Ennis
4. Crusheen (Kylwince) Cemetery
5. Drumcliff Cemetery, Ennis
6. Kildeema Burial Ground
7. Killard Church of Ireland Churchyard
8. Kilquane Cemetery
9. Kilrush , Shanakyle Cemetery
10. Milltown Malbay Church of Ireland Churchyard

Offaly
11. Birr Military Cemetery, Crinkill
12. Birr Old Graveyard
13. Clonmacnoise (Old Abbey) Graveyard

Tipperary
14. Bansha Church of Ireland Churchyard
15. Cahir, St. Mary's Cemetery, Tipperary
16. Cahir Military Cemetery Plot
17. Templemore Catholic Cemetery
18. Templemore St. Mary's Church of Ireland Churchyard
19. Tipperary County Home Cemetery
20. Tipperary, St. John's (Famine) Graveyard

Limerick
21. Castletown Conyers Old Graveyard
22. King's Island Military Cemetery
23. Mount St. Laurence Cemetery

Waterford (West)
24. Ballylaneen , St. Anne's Catholic Churchyard
25. Stradbally Catholic Churchyard
26. Stradbally, St James's Church of Ireland Churchyard

Cork
27. Ballaughbee Burial Ground, Allihies
28. Ballincollig Military Cemetery
29. Ballymacoda (The Hill) Old Graveyard
30. Bandon, Kilbrogan Catholic Graveyard
31. Bantry Abbey Burial Ground
32. Castlefreke Burial Ground
33. Castletownroche Cemetery
34. Charleville Holy Cross Cemetery
35. Cloyne Cathedral Churchyard
36. Cobh Old Church Cemetery
37. Cork Military Cemetery
38. Cork , St. Finbarr's Cemetery
39. Doneraile (St. Mary) Church of Ireland Churchyard
40. Dursey Island Cemetery
41. Fermoy Military Cemetery
42. Fort Carlisle Military Cemetery
43. Glandore Old Graveyard
44. Gullanes St. Joseph's County Home Burial Ground
45. Kilshannig Church of Ireland Churchyard, Mallow
46. Kinsale, St. Multose Churchyard
47. Mallow, Goold's Hill Cemetery
48. Inchageela Old Graveyard
49. Mogeely Catholic Cemetery
50. Nohoval Catholic Cemetery
51. Ringrone Graveyard
52. Roscarbery (The Abbey) Graveyard
53. Skibereen Graveyard
54. South Kilmurry Graveyard
55. Upper Aghada Cemetery

Kerry
56. Cahirsiveen (Killavarnogue) Cemetery
57. Cnoca'chairn Famine Graveyard, Dingle
58. Derrynane Cemetery
59. Keel Cemetery, Castlemaine
60. Kenmare Old Catholic Cemetery
61. Killarney New Cemetery
62. Killiney Churchyard
63. Killorglin Cemetery
64. Tralee Military Cemetery
65. Tralee Rathass Graveyard

MAP 2   453

Newbribde

Kildare

Portarlington

NAAS

1

2 4

7

Enn kerry

9

Blessington

BRAY

Greystones

8

5

Stradbally

Athy

3

Ashford

10 Wicklow

Glendalough

Wicklow
Head

eyleix

Baltinglass

Rathdrum

Avoca

CARLOW

Castlecomer

Tullow

Arklow

6

Gorey

12

Bagenalstown

Bunclody

14

Courtown

13

Ferns

Graiguenamanagh

Thomastown

Enniscorthy

18

20

17

New Ross

11

16 WEXFORD

23

19 Rosslare

WATERFORD

Ballyhack

Wellingtonbridge

22 ge
East

21 Fethard

15

SAINT GEORGE'S CHANNEL

ore

24

Dunmore East

Hook Head

Kilmore Quay

Saltee
Islands

Carnsore Point

Map 3

Map 3:
East & Southeast

Kildare
1. Celbridge Church Lane Cemetery
2. Curragh Military Cemetery
3. Geraldine (Tullagorey) Old Graveyard
4. Naas Catholic Cemetery

Laois
5. Portlaoise Cemetery

Wicklow
6. Arklow Cemetery
7. Blessington, St. Mary Church of Ireland Churchyard
8. Killiskey Church of Ireland Churchyard
9. Glencree, German War Dead Cemetery
10. Rathnew Cemetery

Kilkenny
11. Ferrybank Catholic Churchyard
12. Paulstown Cemetery

Wexford
13. Ardamine Cemetery, Courtown
14. Clonattin Old Cemetery
15. Craigue Little, St. Mogue's Cemetery, Duncormick
16. Crosstown , St. Ibar's Cemetery
17. Killila Burial Ground
18. Kilmuckridge Burial Ground
19. Kilscoran, St Peter's Church of Ireland Churchyard
20. Rathnure Cemetery
21. Templetown Graveyard

Waterford (East)
22. Ballynakill Church of Ireland Churchyard
23. Ballygunner, St Mary's Catholic Churchyard
24. Drumcannon

MAP 3   455

MAP 4

Map 4:
East, Northeast & Midlands (East)

Dublin
1. Clontarf Cemetery
2. Dean's Grange Cemetery
3. Drumcondra, St. George's Burial Ground
4. Glasnevin (Prospect) Cemetery
5. Grangegorman Military Cemetery
6. Kilbarrack Cemetery, Sutton
7. Kilgobbin Old Church Cemetery
8. Kilmainham, Royal Hospital Cemetery
9. Kilmainham St. James's Church of Ireland Churchyard
10. Mount Jerome Cemetery
11. Phoenix Park, Royal Hibernian Military School Churchyard

Meath
12. Ardcath Graveyard
13. Oldcastle Catholic Cemetery
14. Oldcastle Workhouse Cemetery

Louth
15. Mornington Catholic Cemetery
16. Drogheda, Calvary Old Graveyard,
17. Dundalk St. Patrick's Cemetery,

Westmeath
18. Mullingar, The Asylum Burial Ground

Monaghan
19. Edergole Old Graveyard
20. Glasslough Church of Ireland New Cemetery

MAP 4

457

OPW
The Office of Public Works
Oifig na nOibreacha Poiblí

ISBN 0-7557-7589-9

9 780755 775897

The Office of Public Works
Oifig na nOibreacha Poiblí